WOMEN LETTER-WRITERS IN

Women Letter-Writers in Tudor England represents one of the most comprehensive studies of women's letters and letter-writing during the early modern period to be undertaken, and acts as an important corrective to traditional ways of reading and discussing letters as private, elite, male, and non-political. Based on over 3,000 manuscript letters, it shows that letter-writing was a larger and more socially diversified area of female activity than has been hitherto assumed. In that letters constitute the largest body of extant sixteenth-century women's writing, the book initiates a reassessment of women's education and literacy in the period. As indicators of literacy, letters yield physical evidence of rudimentary writing activity and abilities, document 'higher' forms of female literacy, and highlight women's mastery of formal rhetorical and epistolary conventions.

Women Letter-Writers in Tudor England also stresses that letters are unparalleled as intimate and immediate records of family relationships, and as media for personal and self-reflective forms of female expression. Read as documents that inscribe social and gender relations, letters shed light on the complex range of women's personal relationships, as female power and authority fluctuated, negotiated on an individual basis. Furthermore, correspondence highlights the important political roles played by early modern women. Female letter-writers were integral in cultivating and maintaining patronage and kinship networks; they were active as suitors for crown favour, and operated as political intermediaries and patrons in their own right, using letters to elicit influence. Letters thus help to locate differing forms of female power within the family, locality and occasionally on the wider political stage, and offer invaluable primary evidence from which to reconstruct the lives of early modern women.

James Daybell is Professor of Early Modern British History at University of Plymouth, and Fellow of the Royal Historical Society. He has authored and acted as editor for a number of books including: *The Material Letter in Early Modern England: Manuscript Letters and the Culture and Practices of Letter-Writing, 1512–1635* (2012), *Women Letter-Writers in Tudor England* (2006), and *Early Modern Women's Letter-Writing, 1450–1700* (2001). He is currently Co-Director (with Kim McLean-Fiander, University of Victoria, Canada) of the British Academy and Leverhulme funded project 'Women's Early Modern Letters Online, Co-Director (with Svante Norrhem, Lund University) of the AHRC-funded network, 'Gender, Politics and Materiality in Early Modern Europe'. He is also co-presenter and writer of the Histories of the Unexpected Podcast (with Dr Sam Willis), which is hosted on Dan Snow's History Hit Network. His co-authored work, *Histories of the Unexpected*, will publish later this year.

Women Letter-Writers in Tudor England

JAMES DAYBELL

For Sophie

Best wishes

James

OXFORD
UNIVERSITY PRESS

OXFORD
UNIVERSITY PRESS

Great Clarendon Street, Oxford, OX2 6DP,
United Kingdom

Oxford University Press is a department of the University of Oxford.
It furthers the University's objective of excellence in research, scholarship,
and education by publishing worldwide. Oxford is a registered trade mark of
Oxford University Press in the UK and in certain other countries

© James Daybell 2006

The moral rights of the authors have been asserted

First published 2006
First published in paperback 2018

Published in the United States of America by Oxford University Press
198 Madison Avenue, New York, NY 10016, United States of America

British Library Cataloguing in Publication Data
Data available

Library of Congress Cataloging in Publication Data
Data available

ISBN 978–0–19–925991–5 (Hbk.)
ISBN 978–0–19–883097–9 (Pbk.)

For Julia

Preface to paperback edition of *Women Letter-Writers in Tudor England*

It has been some 12 years since *Women Letter-Writers in Tudor England* was first published by Oxford University Press, and the occasion of its appearance in paperback prompts me to consider how the field of early modern women's letter-writing has developed over the intervening decade. Above all there has been an enormous amount of new and innovative interdisciplinary scholarship on women's letters and letter-writing, which encompasses socio-linguistic, rhetorical and material analyses alongside more straight-forwardly historical and literary studies, and this work is captured in important new collections, such as James Daybell and Andrew Gordon, eds, *Women and Epistolary Agency in Early Modern Culture, 1450–1690* (London: Routledge, 2016). There have been a substantial number of PhDs—many of which I have been fortunate enough to examine—produced over the last 10 years by scholars working in this area, which have yielded important monographic studies, notably Gemma Allen, *The Cooke Sisters: Education, Piety and Politics in Early Modern England* (Manchester: Manchester UP, 2013), Graham Williams, *Women's Epistolary Utterance: A Study of the Letters of Joan and Maria Thynne, 1575–1611* (Amsterdam and Philadelphia: John Benjamins, 2013), Melanie Evans, *The Language of Queen Elizabeth I: A Sociolinguistic Perspective on Royal Style and Identity* (Transactions of the Philological Society Monograph Series 45) (Oxford: Wiley-Blackwell, 2013); Diana Barnes, *Epistolary Community in Print, 1580–1664* (Farnham: Ashgate, 2013).

One of the most significant developments in the field has been the attention given to materiality, and the question of how far the physical form of texts was shaped by considerations of gender. These were issues discussed in *Women Letter-Writers in Tudor England*, but have been developed much further in James Daybell, *The Material Letter in Early Modern England: Manuscript Letters and the Culture and Practices of Letter-Writing, 1512–1635* (Basingstoke: Palgrave Macmillan, 2012), and James Daybell, 'The Materiality of Early Modern Women's Letters', in *Women and Epistolary Agency in Early Modern Culture, 1450–1690*, ed. By James Daybell and Andrew Gordon (London: Routledge, 2016), pp. 55–77. Questions of materiality also extend to the scribal circulation of letters and the politics of archives, which are explored in James Daybell, 'Gendered Archival Practices and the Future Lives of Letters' in *Cultures of Correspondence in Early Modern Britain, 1550–1642*, ed. by James Daybell and Andrew Gordon (Philadelphia: University of Pennsylvania Press, 2016), pp. 211–236; James Daybell, 'Gender, Politics and Archives in Early Modern

Britain' in *Gender and Political Culture in Early Modern Europe, 1400–1800*, ed. by James Daybell and Svante Norrhem (London: Routledge, 2016), pp. 25–46; and James Daybell, 'Women, Politics and Domesticity: The Scribal Publication of Lady Rich's Letter to Elizabeth I', in *Women and Writing, c.1340–c.1650: The Domestication of Print Culture*, ed. by Anne Lawrence-Mathers and Phillipa Hardman (Woodbridge: Boydell and Brewer, 2010), pp. 111–30.

Finally, in 2006, this book broke new ground in establishing the range and extent of women's epistolary activities, and scope of archival material that has survived for the early modern period more broadly. As a result of recent scholarly editions, as well as pioneering digital humanities projects, we now have much easier access to a vast corpus of early modern letters. Among the most important new printed editions of women's letters are: *The Letters Lady Anne Bacon*, ed. by Gemma Allen (Camden Society Publications/Cambridge UP, 2014); Elizabeth I, *Elizabeth I: Autograph Compositions and Foreign Language Originals*, ed. by Leah S. Marcus and Janel Mueller (Chicago London: U of Chicago P, 2003); Carlo M. Bajetta, Guillaume Coatalen and Jonathan Gibson (eds), *Elizabeth I's Foreign Correspondence: Letters, Rhetoric and Politics* (Basingstoke: Palgrave Macmillan, 2014); and *The Letters of Elizabeth Stuart, Queen of Bohemia*, ed. by Nadine Akkerman, 3 vols (Oxford: Oxford UP, 2011–). Among digital editions, one of the best is A. Wiggins with A. Bryson, D. Smith, A. Timmermann and G. Williams, (eds) *Bess of Hardwick's Letters: The Complete Correspondence, c.1550–1608* [On-line resource], (2012). www.bessofhardwick.org [accessed 12 May 2018]. My own work with Kim McLean-Fiander as co-Director of the 'Women's Early Modern Letters Online' project (WEMLO) http://emlo-portal.bodleian.ox.ac.uk/collections/?page_id=2595 has produced a union catalogue of early modern women's letters as part of the University of Oxford's 'Early Modern Letters Online' project. Scholarly editions and digital finding tools have in turn invigorated scholarship on manuscript texts that are now so readily available, and have meant that the field of women's letters continues to flourish.

May 2018
St Leonards
JRTD

Acknowledgements

First and foremost I owe a huge debt of gratitude to my supervisor and mentor (and latterly colleague and friend) Ralph Houlbrooke for his encouragement and guidance over many years. His enthusiasm for this project and his scholarly example are beyond compare. I am also grateful to my Ph.D. examiners Anne Curry and Anthony Fletcher, and to Sir Keith Thomas and the anonymous readers for Oxford University Press, whose useful and rigorous comments helped so much in developing the ideas in this book. Others to whom I am grateful for reading and commenting on chapters or parts of this book include Roger Dalrymple, Adam Smyth, and Alan Stewart, who read the whole manuscript in its entirety. All mistakes are alas undoubtedly my own.

I also take this opportunity for reflection to thank those people who have taught me history over the years: in particular John Philip, who more than any teacher inspired me, first firing my historical imagination at an early age; and at Hertford College, Oxford, my tutors Geoffrey Ellis, Christopher Tyerman, Andrzej Olechnowicz, and especially Toby Barnard, who developed my interest in early modern social, cultural, and political history. As an undergraduate my curiosity in matters early modern was further sparked by exposure to the teaching and ideas of among others: Ian Archer, the late Gerald Aylmer, Susan Brigden, Robin Briggs, C.S.L. Davies, J. H. Elliott, Steven Gunn, Christopher Haigh, Felicity Heal, Clive Holmes, the late Jennifer Loach, Scott Mandelbrote, Lucy Wooding, Blair Worden, and Jenny Wormald. The Early Modern Research Centre at the University of Reading also provided a stimulating interdisciplinary environment in which to study and work, and I would like to thank my many friends and colleagues there: Cedric Brown, Alan Cromartie, Andrew Gurr, Christopher Hardman, Elizabeth Heale, Richard Hoyle, Mark Hutchings, Helen Parish, Diane Purkiss, Adam Smyth, and Andy Stewart.

Several institutions have supported my research over the past few years, without whose help this book could not have been written. First, I am grateful to the University of Reading for its generous support of my research over a substantial period of time, including a three-year doctoral research studentship and a postdoctoral research fellowship; and I would also like to thank the University of Reading Research Board and the School of History for their very generous travel and research grants. Secondly, I am grateful to the Faculty of Humanities and Social and Behavioral Sciences at Central Michigan University for generously awarding me an alternative assignment in my second semester and a summer scholars award in my second year, and to the university's Faculty Research and Creative Endeavors Committee for a major research grant which enabled me to spend the summer of 2004 in London completing the final manuscript. I am also grateful to the Folger Shakespeare Library and the Huntington Library for awarding me research fellowships to consult their rich archives. The staff of the countless archives and libraries that I used during the course of research also merit thanks, and especially those at the Bodleian, British Library, Cambridge University Library, the Centre of Kentish Studies, the Folger, the Greater London Record Office, Kendal Record Office, Lambeth Palace Library, the National Archives at Kew, and Warwick County Record Office.

All scholarship is to some extent a product of sociability. This book is no exception, having profited from innumerable conversations. I thank Steve Gunn, Diarmaid Maculloch, and the late Jeremy Maule for generous archival references. For palaeographical advice I am indebted to Diane Greenway, Professor M. B. Parkes, and Laetitia Yeandle. Many others have discussed issues of an epistolary nature, and offered useful advice and suggestions: Tim Amos, Leeds Barroll, Patricia Brewerton, Chris Chapman, Stanley Chojnacki, Elizabeth Clarke, David Como, Jane Couchman, Ann Crabbe, Pauline Croft, Richard Cust, Richard Dutton, Jerome de Groot, Jacqueline Eales, Susan Frye, Jonathan Gibson, Andy Gordon, Germaine Greer, Barbara Harris Dan Hedley, Ann Hughes, Martin Ingram, Marika Keblusek, James Knowles, Vivienne Larminie, Anne Laurence (the medievalist), Anne Laurence (the early modernist), Arthur Marotti, Lynne Magnusson, Steven May, Michelle McDonough, Clare McManus, Natalie Mears, David Norbrook, Helen Ostovich, Helen Payne, John Platt, Mary Prior, Sasha Roberts, Beth Robertson, Karen Robertson, the late Conrad Russell, The Lord John Russell, Elizabeth Sauer, Gary Schneider, Bill Sherman, Hilda Smith, Graeme Smyth, Goran Stanivukovic, Sara Jayne Steen, Ted Vallance, Alison Wall, Claire Walker, Jennifer Ward, Valerie Wayne, Susan Whyman, and Sue Wiseman. I am also grateful for the comments on papers delivered at conferences and seminars: in particular I would like to acknowledge the audiences of the IHR Early Modern Britain Seminar, Kent University Early Modern Studies Seminar, Oxford Early Modern Seminar, Sixteenth Century Studies Conference, North American Conference of British Studies, Renaissance Society of America Conference, University of Maryland Early Modern Research Seminar, University of Reading Early Modern and History Department Seminars, and the conferences on Women's Letter-Writing in England, 1450–1700, and Women and Politics in Early Modern England that I organized at the University of Reading. I am further indebted to the editorial team of Anne Gelling, Jeff New, and Eva Nyika at Oxford University Press for their expert guidance throughout the publication process.

Finally, the writing of this book has been made all the more bearable by the support of family and friends. I am grateful to my parents and my sister Elizabeth for their constant support; now that I am in distant lands, the significance of letter-writing and more modern forms of communication is brought home all the more sharply. Cumulatively these acknowledgements attest to the many coteries and communities of which I have been fortunate enough to be a part throughout my academic life; none, however, is more valuable than that of Ari Berk (a Tudor historian at heart) and Kristen McDermott, whose company over the last few years of writing this book has provided an oasis of conviviality and discussion on matters Tudor and Stuart. Above all, however, I owe more than words can say to Julia Fox, who in addition to being my wife is also *my* 'best friend'. She has read, commented on, and lived with this book more than anyone with the exception of myself; more importantly, she has brought so much shared happiness and meaning to my life, and taught me the true eternal nature of companionship, love, and marriage. It is to her that this book is lovingly dedicated.

J.R.T.D.

Mount Pleasant, Michigan

Contents

Abbreviations

Berks.RO	Berkshire Record Office
BIHR	*Bulletin of the Institute of Historical Research*
BL	British Library
BL, Addit.	British Library, Additional MS
BL, Cott.	British Library, Cottonian MS
BL, Eg.	British Library, Egerton MS
BL, Harl.	British Library, Harleian MS
BL, Lansd.	British Library, Lansdowne MS
BL, Ro.	British Library, Royal MS
BLJ	*British Library Journal*
Bodl.	Bodleian Library, Oxford
Cecil	Hatfield House, Herts., Cecil Papers
CKS	Centre for Kentish Studies, Maidstone
CUL	Cambridge University Library
DNB	*Dictionary of National Biography*
EETS	Early English Text Society
EHR	*English Historical Review*
ELH	*English Literary History*
ELR	*English Literary Renaissance*
EMS	*English Manuscript Studies*
Folger	Folger Shakespeare Library, Washington, DC
GEC	George E. Cokayne *et al.*, *The Complete Peerage of England, Scotland, Ireland, Great Britain and the United Kingdom, Extant, Extinct or Dormant*, 13 vols. in 14 (London: St Catherine's Press, 1910–59; repr. Gloucester: Alan Sutton, 1982–98)
GLRO	Greater London Record Office
HJ	*Historical Journal*
HLQ	*Huntington Library Quarterly*
HMC	Historical Manuscripts Commission
HT	*History Today*
HWJ	*History Workshop Journal*
JBS	*Journal of British Studies*
Kendal RO	Kendal Record Office, Cumbria

L&P	*Letters and Papers, Foreign and Domestic, of the Reign of Henry VIII*, ed. J. S. Brewer, J. Gairdner, R. H. Rodie, *et al.*, 21 vols. and *Addenda* (London, 1862–1932)
Lisle Letters	Muriel St Clare Byrne (ed.), *The Lisle Letters*, 6 vols. (Chicago: University of Chicago Press, 1981)
LPL	Lambeth Palace Library
MSS	Manuscripts
NA	National Archives, Kew
NA, S 10	National Archieves, Kew State Papers, Domestic, Edward VI
NA, S 11	National Archieves, Kew State Papers, Domestic, Mary I
NA, S 12	National Archieves, Kew State Papers, Domestic, Elizabeth
NA, S 15	National Archieves, Kew State Papers, Domestic, Addenda
NA, S 46	National Archieves, Kew State Papers, Domestic, Supplementary
NA, Ward	National Archieves, Kew Court of Wards Records
NRA	National Register of Archives
NRO	Norfolk Record Office, Norwich
OED	*Oxford English Dictionary*
P&P	*Past and Present*
PMLA	*Publications of the Modern Language Association*
RQ	*Renaissance Quarterly*
RES	*Review of English Studies*
RO	Record Office
SCJ	*Sixteenth Century Journal*
SQ	*Shakespeare Quarterly*
Staffs. RO	Staffordshire Record Office
STC	*A Short-Title Catalogue of Books Printed in England, Scotland, and Ireland and of English Books Printed Abroad, 1475–1640*, ed. A.W. Polland and G. R. Redgrave, *et al.*, 3 vols. (Second edition, London: Bibliographical Society, 1976–91)
TRHS	*Transactions of the Royal Historical Society*
WCRO	Warwickshire County Record Office

Note on Conventions

Original spelling and punctuation have been retained. I/j and u/v have been distinguished, and 'th' substituted for 'γ'. Abbreviations and contractions have been extended by the use of square [ ] brackets; insertions are indicated by upward arrows ^^, and deletions by a strikethrough line. Modern translations of eccentric spellings have been provided in brackets. Dates are given in Old Style, but the year is taken to begin on 1 January. In the footnotes dates are presented in a shorthand day/month/year format. Place of publication is London unless otherwise stated.

1

Introduction

The letter-writing activities of the indomitable Elizabethan matriarch and ambitious dynast, Elizabeth Talbot, countess of Shrewsbury (*c.*1527–1608), better known as 'Bess of Hardwick', are the best-documented of any sixteenth-century English woman with the possible exception of Elizabeth I.[1] More than 200 of her letters, to and from over sixty correspondents, are extant, many preserved among her own papers.[2] Her voluminous correspondence represents in microcosm the range of letters and letter-writing activities of other Tudor women letter-writers of the aristocracy, gentry, and mercantile groups. Throughout her long life—a life largely documented by her correspondences—letters and letter-writing performed important functions for Elizabeth Hardwick. Conducting correspondence allowed her to maintain close communication with immediate family and household members; to keep abreast of family, local, national, and European news. As a secondary patronage function, the writing of letters worked to oil the wheels of kinship and patronage networks. It enabled her to maintain a firm grip on estate and household management, and to direct her vast building programmes, to transact business and expedite legal disputes, and to intervene as an intermediary or patron in suits for favour and patronage. Viewed as a whole, the countess's correspondence is also emblematic of many of the central themes of this socio-cultural study of Tudor women's letters and letter-writing—female education and literacy; family, gender, and other social relations; and the role of early modern women in patronage and politics—and acts as a useful corrective to traditional ways of reading and discussing letters as private, elite and non-political.

In common with most Tudor women, little is known about Elizabeth Hardwick's early upbringing and education. The indirect evidence of her letters, however, indicates that she was at least taught to write (as well as to read): her large, untidy, and rather angular italic handwriting features throughout much of

---

[1] The best biographical study of Bess of Hardwick is Durant, *Bess of Hardwick*. See also Williams, *Bess of Hardwick*; Rawson, *Bess of Hardwick and Her Circle*. (For full references to works cited, see the Selected Bibliography.)

[2] Bess of Hardwick's papers are held mainly at the Folger Shakespeare Library (X.d.428), and are distinct from the Shrewsbury/Talbot manuscripts relating to the family of her last husband, George Talbot, seventh earl of Shrewsbury, now kept at Lambeth Palace Library and Longleat. Her outgoing correspondence is scattered throughout numerous collections.

her correspondence.[3] Bess's initial training and instruction in writing, reading, casting accounts, and religion in all likelihood took place during the 1530s, and was typical of that of a daughter of the lesser gentry. Scrutiny of her handwriting, spelling, grammar, and punctuation, however, indicates a woman practised in the art of writing and a level of scribal activity and competence in stark contrast to earlier generations of women.[4] The uses to which she put her writing skills— conducting correspondence and keeping accounts—suggests that writing literacy was essentially considered as a functional skill, one that was deemed useful for women involved in household and estate management and which increasingly formed part of the education of upper-class English women over the course of the sixteenth century.[5]

The countess of Shrewsbury's letters also highlight the public and private reading and writing practices associated with early modern women's correspondence. While the majority of her letters were penned in her own distinctive hand, over a third were written by a secretary, or bear the signs of collaborative authorship. The complexity of the letter-writing process likewise extends to the dispatch and reading of letters. Many of her letters were intimate in the sense of being intended for a singular readership; others were written for more communal perusal, conveyed unsealed to be passed around family members, or intended for wider 'unintended' audiences. Analysis of the countess's correspondence in terms of the mechanics of composition, delivery, and receipt thus exposes a variety of archetypal epistolary practices that in combination work to erode, but not completely erase, notions of early modern epistolary exchange as a private, purely personal and singular activity.

In its entirety, the countess's correspondence illustrates the breadth of social contacts that numerous women enjoyed, which were at times geographically far flung and often extended well beyond household and family. Bess cultivated an array of correspondents from a wide range of groups beyond immediate family, kin, household members, and other dependants; these include John Lenton who predicted a 'violent death' for Elizabeth I, and Dorothy Lady Stafford, a close friend from early in Bess's court career.[6] The countess's letters also document the range of activities in which she engaged; her famed interest in building, for example, can be glimpsed in letters to her servants as she oversaw the repair and rebuilding of Chatsworth, and in correspondence with Sir John Thynne about

---

[3] Evidence of Bess's ability to read is provided in her household inventory, which details the contents of 'Lady Shrewsbury's Bed Chamber', including 'my Ladies bookes viz: Calvin uppon Jobe, Covered with russet velvet, the resolution, Salomans proverbes, a booke of meditations, too other bookes Covered with black velvet', as well as 'a lyttle deske to write on guilded': *The Hardwick Inventories*, ed. Boynton, 31–2.

[4] Her writing skills compare favourably with the atrocious hand of her last husband, George Talbot: see e.g., Folger, X.d.428 (85, 86, 87, 88, 93): *c.*1568, *c.*1569, *c.*1570.

[5] Folger, X.d.486: 'Account Book of Sir William and Lady Elizabeth Cavendish, 1548–1550', contains extensive entries in Bess of Hardwick's own hand.

[6] Folger, X.d.428 (52, 120): 12/08/1571, 13/01/1601.

the development of Longleat.[7] Interestingly Bess's letters reveal little about her ideologically or about her religious views, a trait shared by sixteenth-century women's correspondence more generally, although something of her confessional credentials can be gleaned from her choice of correspondents. Indeed, correspondence with the infamous recusant-hunter Richard Topcliffe, and the obvious confessional bias of the news of persecutions of 'preests and recusants' she received from James Montagu, dean of the Royal Chapel, hint at a zealous Protestant agenda, despite the countess's supposed 'conservative' religious inclinations.[8]

While not necessarily inward-looking or reflective of an inner self, Bess of Hardwick's correspondence reflects the ways in which early modern women's letters textualize family and other relationships, mirroring the social and gender hierarchies of their social worlds through modes of address, language, style, and tone. The spectrum of epistolary styles deployed in Bess's letters are displayed, on the one hand, by her deferential letters to the queen, written in presentation hand, and obeying the rules of manuscript spacing with the signature placed in the bottom right-hand corner of the page; and in contrast, by her curt and authoritative letters to servants. The quality and nature of family relations can likewise be elicited from her letters: correspondence survives with three of her four husbands, Sir William Cavendish, Sir William St Loe, and George Talbot, earl of Shrewsbury. In her own letters to these men she resembles not at all the submissive wife of Tudor precept; what emerge from the exchange of marital letters instead are three complex relationships that altered over time, inflected by character, circumstance, and age. Importantly, her letters show little of the codes of female deference (whether real or feigned) that marked some women's writing in the sixteenth century. Moreover, letters addressed to her from social subordinates are couched in a language of deference, familial obedience, and service which allowed the writer and addressee to uphold social decorum. Thus, Frances Pierrepont wrote 'humbly craving' her mother's 'moste honorab[le] and continuall bo[u]nty'; while her son, Charles Cavendish, 'humbly beseeched' her ladyship's 'dayly blessinge'.[9]

In examining the nature and purpose of women's correspondence, Bess of Hardwick's letters highlight the often overtly political intent of female letter-writers which counters traditional understanding of women's letters as domestic, parochial, and non-political. A substantial proportion of her correspondence was highly pragmatic, written to conduct business or cultivate patronage relations. She corresponded regularly in support of her own suits, involved as she was in countless legal disputes over property and inheritance. She sought assistance, for example, from Sir Julius Caesar in an action brought against her and her son William Cavendish by Robert Allyn, Hugh Needham, and John Wright 'in behalf of themselves and inhabitants in and near the forrest of the high peake, wherein they alledge that they should have common pasture for their cattle'.[10]

---

[7] X.d.428 (82): 14/11/[1552]; Durant, *Bess of Hardwick*, 47, 108.
[8] X.d.428 (125, 59): 09/07/1577, 20/02/1606.
[9] X.d.428 (68, 6): [1603], [1600].   [10] BL, Addit., 12506, fo. 209: 1603.

Likewise, the countess's acrimonious separation from the earl of Shrewsbury led to numerous epistolary efforts to solicit support for her cause. She petitioned Lord Burghley to help conclude her 'longe delayed mattars', because, she argued, 'tyll then my enemys wyll take great advantage to sture up my lorde ageanst me and myne and styll devide us'.[11] In addition to petitioning on her own behalf, she actively promoted her family, servants, and wider circles of friends and acquaintances in various patronage suits for land, office, and justice, procuring for them more nebulously 'friendship' and advice. Well connected at court and of high status socially through her successive advantageous matches, she was superbly placed to exert influence as an intermediary. In a series of letters to John Manners, the countess of Shrewsbury put before him numerous suits: she asked Manners to aid Edward Slater in his case against Lady Bowes, and to assist Sir Edward Dyer to the office of executor to Mr Beresford.[12] Her cousin Henry Foljambe was approached to 'deal well' with the recently widowed Elizabeth Flint, sister of her servant Rolland.[13] Similarly, the countess wrote to Thomas Lord Paget to act justly towards her servant Robinson, who had been accused of murder, and was to come before him at the Stafford assizes, and also to intercede on behalf of her servant Mr Duport, whom she informed Paget had been 'molested by some tenants, of your manor of Winisell'.[14] Her activities in Staffordshire also occasioned letters to Richard Bagot, the local sheriff, whom she requested to deal favourably with her in a matter concerning a 'lewd workman, Cust', and to support her in a case against the widow Bagshawe of Wotton.[15]

Letter-writing as a *political* activity can also be glimpsed in the important communicative and news-related functions that it performed for Bess of Hardwick, allowing her to keep abreast of current events. Indeed, detailed analysis of her correspondence reveals her as a woman at the centre of an extensive correspondence, news and intelligence network.[16] When absent from London, Bess received letters from family, servants, friends, wider social contacts, and semi-professional newsletter writers keeping her up to date with court and national events and news from the capital. Conversely, when at court or absent from one of her residences, she received regular reports from her servants, estate stewards, and legal advisors on various matters: household and estate management, children and other family members, the numerous legal cases in which she was involved, the progress of her building works, and events within the locality. The countess was also regularly kept up to date with the latest religious and political developments in Europe by correspondents who recycled for her the contents of continental newsletters.

[11] NA, SP12/206/17: 06/10/1586.   [12] HMC, *Rutland* (1888), i. 337, 386: 1597, 1602.
[13] SP46/24/35: [temp. Eliz.]
[14] Staffs. RO, Paget Papers, D603K/1/4/9, D603K1/7/47: 29/03/1576, 28/11/1581.
[15] Folger, L.a.843, 844: 19/09/1594, 14/04/[1600/1604].
[16] For detailed discussion see Daybell, 'News Networks of Elizabeth Talbot', 114–31.

Thus, as a case study the diverse correspondence of Bess of Hardwick reflects many of the varied and nuanced aspects of Tudor women's letters and letter-writing. It challenges traditional understandings of letters as private documents, highlighting the often collaborative nature of the composition process; and the ways in which letters were dispatched and read further complicates a model of epistolarity as an exchange of letters between two individuals. The range of correspondents documented by her letters indicates not only the breadth of social contacts that she enjoyed, but also, more importantly, that early modern letter-writing was not solely an elite and male activity: many of those with whom she corresponded were below the ranks of the nobility and gentry, and almost a third were women. Finally, the range of uses for which she utilized letters—to acquire and circulate news and to mediate in patronage suits—provides a useful corrective to scholarly perceptions of women's letters as non-political.

Letters represent by far the most copious body of sixteenth-century English women's surviving writing, viewed in the broadest terms. This socio-cultural historical study indicates that letter-writing in England constituted a much larger and more socially and geographically diversified area of female activity than has hitherto been assumed; it was an activity that extended beyond the narrow confines of the court, royal women, and the aristocracy to include female members of the gentry and middling classes. This book is based on a significant archival base—well over 3,000 manuscript letters by more than 650 individual women for the period 1540 to 1603—found within family collections, in legal and institutional archives, and among the State Papers and papers of government officials. It studies 'real' rather than 'fictional' correspondence, focusing in particular on the vernacular prose letter, which can be divided by function and sub-genre (for example, letter of petition, love letter, letter of condolence, and 'familiar' letters), and excludes the treatment of letters in literature, and other epistolary forms, such as the verse epistle, dedicatory epistle, and epistolary novel.[17] Taken as a whole, this book reassesses the extent of women's writing and reading literacy during the sixteenth century; explores the impact of shifts in letter-writing practices and conventions; and highlights the increased importance attached to women's ability to write. It asserts that letters are valuable primary evidence for the reconstruction of the often obscured lives and experiences of early modern women, offering a unique way into a female realm. Letters represent complex documents requiring layered interpretations, and they provide a privy source, unrivalled both as immediate records of family, social, and gender relations and as examples of women's writing that is often personal and self-reflective in expression. The study also highlights the

[17] Guillén, 'Notes Toward the Study of the Renaissance Letter', 70–101, distinguishes at least seven kinds of writing associated with the letter form: the neo-Latin prose letter, the vernacular prose letter, the neo-Latin verse epistle, the vernacular verse epistle, the tradition of the theory of the letter, practical manuals for letter-writing, and letters inserted within other genres. See also Cormican, 'Letter as a Genre', 23–5; Patterson, 'Letters to Friends', 203–32; Trimpi, 'Epistolary Tradition', 60–75.

extensive range of women's interests and the degree to which women exerted power and influence in political and patronage arenas, and were able to operate traversing the fluid boundaries between the 'public' and the 'private', the 'political' and the 'domestic'. Furthermore, letters display the degrees of proficiency and sophistication with which certain women utilized the epistolary genre as a means of articulation and self-presentation, and they demonstrate female mastery of language and rhetorical strategies.

Increasing female literacy during the sixteenth century promoted greater epistolary privacy, which led to more intimate and individual types of correspondence, in the sense that women were distanced from the mechanics of scribal composition. By the end of the sixteenth century it was more common for women to sit down with a pen than with an amanuensis, unlike their late-medieval counterparts; however, business missives were still regularly composed through the medium of a secretary, as indeed they still are today, and it was possible for a completely illiterate (in the modern sense) woman to be part of an epistolary culture, albeit via an amanuensis or reader.[18] The ability to write correspondence with their own hands (and the act of corresponding), however, enhanced women's personal control over their own writing. Although it is important not to exaggerate the impact of literacy, women who could endite their own letters had obvious advantages over women who were writing illiterate: they were able to conduct personalized correspondence in maintaining social and business relationships; to write more-intimate letters to family members; and to achieve greater degrees of personal control over language and self-expression, as well as to maintain a tighter grip on household and business affairs. In addition to increasingly private methods of letter-writing, epistolary conventions changed during the late fifteenth and sixteenth centuries. Renaissance letter-writing manuals further encouraged freer and more relaxed styles of communication, gradually supplanting the medieval *ars dictaminis* which rigidly accentuated distinctions between superiors and subordinates. There is, therefore, a clear prima facie case for arguing that no single medium is as potentially illuminating as letters, which appear on the surface to yield the most intimate and immediate forms of women's writing; yet as with diaries, wills, or court depositions, they too are subject to their own generic and rhetorical conventions and methodological problems. As a source, correspondence manifests the variety of women's experiences and mentalities, often detailing the minutiae of daily life. By their very nature and purpose, letters represent immediate records of the early modern family, in that they document relationships between individuals. Surviving correspondence from women exhibits differing degrees of deference, closeness, emotional dependency, and affection within marital, familial, and wider social relationships.

The period as a whole is marked by women's growing familiarity and inventiveness with letters and letter-writing practices and methods, and by the

---

[18] Dalrymple, 'Reaction, Consolation and Redress', 16–28; O' Mara, 'Female Scribal Ability', 92.

expanding range of functional and more individual or singular uses for which letters were employed. At a basic level, correspondence acted simply as a method of communication, allowing women to conduct business concerns; muster practical, financial, and emotional support; keep in touch with immediate family members; and undertake important roles in maintaining kinship and patronage networks. Over the course of the century, however, letters were increasingly utilized by women as literary, creative, and religious outlets. As texts they were used to express various emotional states. It is these 'autobiographical' aspects of letters that afford the most interesting insights into women's selves, whether constructed or reflected, an issue discussed in Chapter 6. How far letters can be considered 'autobiographical' is an important question, especially in light of recent theoretical and critical approaches to the 'self' and 'selfhood' which challenge received notions of the 'self' or 'selves' as linguistic, cultural, or social constructs subject to historical relativity. In one sense letters represent a 'technology of the self', a vehicle through which female letter-writers composed a self or selves through writing; the very process of writing a letter prompted women to view themselves in relation to others, for example, a daughter writing to a parent, a wife corresponding with a husband, a female suitor petitioning a government official.[19] Female letter-writers were further prompted to categorize themselves by social status, gender, nationality, and religion, as well as by more identifiable traits such as character, temperament, health, age, appearance, and education. Letters actioned by dispute or conflict convey among the most vivid expressions of self in terms of individual rights. In addition to this presentation of an outer self, however, letters are also arguably reflective of interiority, a woman's 'inner self' (or more precisely how this was represented). During the period letter-writing performed an increasing range of functions that led to a degree of inwardness. In some ways letter-writing appears to have provided a form of cathartic or psychological release through which women formulated and worked out issues and concerns. Letters written to confessors or preachers on matters of spiritual development encouraged confessional self-examination; the experience of illness or dying prompted similar inward reflection.

Scholars have long viewed women's letters as documents ripe for historical inquiry. In the nineteenth century M. A. E. Wood published her magisterial *Letters of Royal and Illustrious Ladies* (1846), a three-volume work that printed the texts, with commentaries, of several hundred women's letters from the period 1103 to 1558. However, the Rankean focus of the time on diplomacy and politics relegated women's history to no more than the biography of exceptional or 'worthy' women, a genre that can be traced back to classical authors.[20] With the possible exception of Macaulay, who looked at the treatment of women as

---

[19] Foucault, 'Technologies of the Self', 16–49; Webster, 'Writing to Redundancy', 40–1.

[20] e.g. Ballard, *Memoirs of Several Ladies of Great Britain*; Strickland, *Lives of the Queens of England*; Wood, *Lives of the Princesses of England*. Davis ' "Women's History" in Transition', 83–103; Eales, *Women in Early Modern England*, 7–9.

an important indicator of seventeenth-century morality, mainstream historical inquiry generally excluded women, as it did the lower classes; potential source materials were either overlooked or considered irrelevant.[21] Thus, in the 1860s a British Museum archivist cataloguing a volume of 'letters and papers concerning the disputes between Anthony Bourne and his wife' described the collection as being 'of no importance', although it included numerous letters by Elizabeth Bourne depicting the experiences of an Elizabethan gentlewoman separated from her husband.[22] The long-term prejudice against women's letters that this book is designed to combat is further illustrated by Virginia Woolf, who argued that 'letters did not count' as literature, a view influential among many literary critics until relatively recently.[23] The 'demasculinization of history' in the twentieth century, however, brought about by the women's suffragist movement, the rise of social history, and above all by the fusion of feminist political agendas and New Left history in America during the 1960s, saw women's history emerge as a vital and vibrant field of study.[24] More recent generations of women's and social historians working on early modern women and the family have trawled the archives for 'autobiographical' sources written by women—diaries, journals, household accounts, and commonplace books as well as letters—in order to provide a corrective to male-voiced prescriptive sources, such as conduct books, sermons, and religious and political tracts, and to shed new light on women's lives and experiences during the sixteenth and seventeenth centuries.[25]

Although letters have previously been recognized as a valuable and illuminating source for social history, studies have tended either to concentrate on individual families or individual letter-writers: exemplary are Alison Wall's seminal study of the women of the Thynne family; Jacqueline Eales's work on Brilliana Harley and the Harley family; and Vivienne Larminie on the seventeenth-century Newdigates and the redoubtable Lady Anne Newdigate.[26] This focus on individuals and families, perhaps an institutional feature of social and family history, has precluded the study of letters as a single source, in the way that diaries have been approached as a genre, and prevented the mapping of the social prevalence of letter-writing abilities more generally among women of the period. In that it concentrates solely on letters as a source, this book thus represents the first comprehensive study of early modern women's letter-writing

---

[21] Harrison and McMillan, 'Some Feminist Betrayals', 376.   [22] BL, Addit., 23212, fo. 2.
[23] Woolf, *A Room of One's Own*, 63. Ezell 'Myth of Judith Shakespeare', 579–92.
[24] Stoianovich, *French Historical Method*, 158; Hufton, 'Women in History', 127; Breisach, *Historiography*, 391–94; Scott, 'Problem of Invisibility', 5–29.
[25] Recent general studies include, Mendelson and Crawford, *Women in Early Modern England*; Laurence, *Women in England, 1500–1700*; Peters, *Women in Early Modern Britain*; Houlbrooke, *English Family*; Fletcher, *Gender, Sex and Subordination*; Crawford, *Bodies, Blood and Families*. See also Velz, 'Giving Voices to the Silent', 263–72.
[26] Wall, 'Elizabethan Precept', 23–38; ead., 'Deference and Defiance', 77–93; Eales, *Puritans and Roundheads*; ead., 'Patriarchy, Puritanism and Politics', 143–58; Larminie, *Wealth, Kinship and Culture*; ead., 'Fighting for Family', 94–108. See also 'Letters and Will of Lady Dorothy Bacon', ed. Key, 77–112; Stuchen, 'Letters of Lydia Dugard', 32–8.

so far undertaken. As such it participates in an important process of recovery of sixteenth-century women's manuscript writing, and contributes to the tireless work of generations of feminist scholars who, provoked by an absence of female-authored texts and a desire to uncover women's experiences, attitudes, and opinions as distinct from men's, have sought to establish a corpus of women writers as a counterbalance to the male canon.[27] Furthermore, manuscript letters represented an acceptable form of writing for women, and survive in far greater numbers than conventional published works, which were produced by a small minority of highly educated women and which formed the focus of initial surveys of women's writing.[28]

Viewed from the perspective of women's writing, this study's concentration on letters is at least partly framed in response to Margaret Ezell's call for greater attention to be paid to women's manuscript writings, an area of research that has witnessed considerable growth in recent years.[29] Outside of the discipline of history, new approaches to literary criticism have broken down the barriers of formal genres to incorporate a range of forms, and have made increasing use of manuscript sources, a mode of production that bypassed the need for literary patronage, editors, and publishers. Attention has also focused more appropriately on different arenas of female activity, for example, the court, the law courts, and more especially the household, with references to the various types of writing produced within these contexts.[30] Furthermore, the impact of post-structuralist theory in collapsing the boundaries of what constitutes a 'literary' text has led to consideration of more material and personal forms of writing, which have required the development of new reading techniques and methods of interpretation.[31] Such texts include household accounts, recipe books, religious meditations, letters, diaries, autobiographies, depositions, petitions, and even needlework, each bringing its own idiosyncrasies of textual production and its own methodological problems for interpretation.[32]

Interest in letters and letter-writing has led to a range of truly interdisciplinary inquiries, including literary, lexical, historical, social, cultural, paleographical, manuscript, and gender-based. While historians have long utilized letters as

[27] Ezell, 'Myth of Judith Shakespeare', 579–92.

[28] e.g. Hageman, 'Recent Studies in Women Writers of the English Renaissance', 228–75; and subsequent 'Recent Studies in Women Writers' by Ziegler, *ELR* 24/1 (1994), 229–42, Steen, *ELR* 24/1 (1994), 243–74, and White, *ELR* 30 (2000), 457–93.

[29] Ezell, *Writing Women's Literary History*; ead., *Social Authorship*. See also Beal and Ezell, *Writing by Early Modern Women* (2000); Burke and Gibson, *Early Modern Women's Manuscript Writing*; Justice and Tinker, *Women's Writing and the Circulation of Ideas*. On scribal publication see Love, *Scribal Publication*; Marotti, *Manuscript, Print and the English Renaissance Lyric*; Hobbs, *Early Seventeenth-Century Verse*.

[30] Ezell, *Patriarch's Wife*; Hackett, 'Courtly Writing by Women', 169–89.

[31] de Grazia, 'What Is A Work? What Is A Document?', 199–207; Mendelson and Crawford, *Women in Early Modern England*, 6–11. Cf. Thomas, *History and Literature*.

[32] e.g. Pennell, 'Perfecting Practice? Women, Manuscript Recipes', 237–58; Jones and Stally-brass, *Renaissance Clothing*, 134–71; Graham *et al., Her Own Life*; Wilcox, 'Private Writing and Public Function', 47–62; Mendelson, 'Stuart Women's Diaries', 181–210.

historical sources, recent critical work has challenged the ways in which we read and understand early modern letters and letter-writing practices. Amanda Gilroy and W. M. Verhoeven have questioned traditional approaches to what they describe as 'non-fictional' letters, which 'were regarded as an unproblematic historical source, giving us unmediated access to a writer's thoughts', arguing instead that they be subjected to a range of theoretical and critical literary analyses.[33] The work of various scholars has registered the interpretative complications of early modern correspondence. Fay Bound, for example, has interrogated the idea of letters as social documents capable of shedding light on emotions such as love, arguing that love-letters followed literary conventions, and questioning their ability to express any subjective emotional experience.[34] In her work on Erasmus, Lisa Jardine has discussed the ways in which familiar epistles were used in the construction of charisma in print; the effective transmission of feeling in familiar letters was considered a 'humanistic text skill'.[35] Similarly, Gary Schneider has persuasively argued that the language of affect is pervasive in letters both to intimate relations and to political officials, and that the manoeuvring of the language of the familiar was a frequently employed rhetorical strategy used in a variety of social situations.[36] The nature of epistolary conventions has been further examined by Lynne Magnusson, who explores the ways in which the textbook letters of Erasmus and Angel Day might have 'scripted' social interaction.[37] Finally, work on material culture has taught the importance of treating letters as more than merely 'documents' or 'texts'. Indeed, the work of Jonathan Gibson and others on the materiality of the Renaissance letter is a reminder that letters generate meaning through material forms: manuscript space, handwriting, folding, and seals.[38] This body of recent critical work on early modern letters poses numerous important issues relating to the very nature of letters as a historical source which this book seeks to address: the extent to which letters can be considered as 'personal', 'private', or 'autobiographical' forms of writing; how far letter-writing was a collaborative or mediated activity; the degree to which language, whether conventional or normative, is reflective of genuine emotional states, and thus can be utilized to study the nature and quality of interpersonal relationships; whether letters and the process of letter-writing encouraged an interiority and inner self-awareness. At the heart of these questions are the purposes for which letters were written: pragmatic, business-related, familial, religious, literary, cathartic—categories not hermetically sealed, but that bleed into one another.

Finally, having examined historical, literary, and critical approaches to early modern letters, a further theoretical approach is provided by the lens of gender.

---

[33] Gilroy and Verhoeven, 'Introduction', *Prose Studies: Correspondences*, 121–6. See also Bergeron, *King James and Letters of Homoerotic Desire*; Schneider, *The Culture Of Epistolarity*; Earle, 'Introduction: Letter Writers and the Historian', 1–12; Van Houdt, *Self-Presentation and Social Identification*; Daybell, 'Recent Studies in Sixteenth-Century Letters', 331–62; id., 'Recent Studies in Seventeenth-Century Letters', 135–70.   [34] Bound, 'Writing the Self?', 1–19.
[35] Jardine, *Erasmus, Man of Letters*.   [36] Schneider, 'Affecting Correspondences', 31–62.
[37] Magnusson, *Shakespeare and Social Dialogue*, ch. 3.   [38] Gibson, 'Significant Space', 1–9.

In tandem with women's and queer studies, theorists have promoted gender as a category of analysis and motor of change, identifying the socially constructed distinctions between men and women, and how gender affected the experiences of individuals in the past in terms of work, legal rights, status, life choices, and education.[39] This has fostered more comparative approaches through which women's lives are depicted and measured in relation to men's. While it is important to stress that 'woman' by no means represents a universal historical category, and that women's experiences were inflected by factors other than gender (such as social status, religion, education, and geography), it is central to this study that the theories and practices of letter-writing in the early modern period were radically gendered. This means, as we shall see, that the gender of senders and recipients affected composition and modes of address, and that writers of both sexes were required to negotiate these gender assumptions; that levels of female and male confidence and educational ability were assumed and challenged; and that differences in the nature and subject-matter of men and women's letters were anticipated. Women letter-writers operated within a set of assumptions—many of which they followed, some of which they challenged. Did women only write in the hands prescribed for them? Did they only deal with the matters permitted to them? Did women have access to and consume the same kinds of news as their male counterparts? While many of these issues are dealt with throughout subsequent pages, they are addressed more directly in Chapter 8, which explicitly compares the letters of married couples.

Importantly, what emerges from this study are the similarities between men's and women's letters in terms of content, method of composition and reading, and the materiality of letters. This book is, therefore, more than an examination of women's letters; it has much to say about letters in general in the absence of a full-scale study of the manuscript letter and cultural practices of letter-writing. Furthermore, although comparison is important to define 'women's' letters, concentration on mainly female letter-writers is justified by the fact that it redresses the balance of neglect for women's history, facilitates an important recovery of primary materials, and usefully contributes to our understanding of female education and literacy, female social relations, and women's involvement in politics.

FEMALE EDUCATION AND LITERACY

Attempts to write the history of female education are hampered by the relative informality of teaching provision for women in early modern England. Since most women were excluded from male centres of learning—the grammar

---

[39] Scott, 'Gender: A Useful Category of Historical Analysis', 1053–75; ead., *Gender and the Politics of History*; Bock, 'Women's History and Gender History', 7–30; Parr, 'Gender History and Historical Practice', 354–76; Shoemaker and Vincent, *Gender and History in Western Europe*; Alberti, *Gender and the Historian*.

schools, universities, and Inns of Court—historians are deprived of institutional records which so well elucidate the education of boys and young men.[40] By contrast, the majority of women were taught either within the household, a practice that has left comparatively few documentary sources beyond a small number of educational texts, occasional details of educational provision in household accounts, and passing references in autobiographical writings and correspondence, or in the Church, where they received religious education. Likewise, universal estimates of female literacy—at its most basic definition, the ability to read and write—based on sampling signatures are quantitative, offering limited (if any) analysis of the nature and extent of women's reading and writing abilities. The ability to perform a rudimentary signature rather than making a mark, an act that could be learnt as a trick, does not provide a qualitative indication of the extent of individuals' literacy skills. It cannot reflect the fluency and frequency with which women wrote or indicate whether they could pen letters, maintain accounts, keep a diary, or write poetry and plays; nor does it register complex comprehension and reading practices. The study of Tudor women's letters, however, provides a more complex and nuanced picture of the range and hierarchies of female writing and reading abilities in England during this period. Letters represent unique sources not only as physical evidence of rudimentary writing activity and abilities—for example, the quality of women's handwriting, the nature of their spelling and composition—but also in that they document the range of literary and cultural uses for which women utilized their literacy skills. Moreover, read as texts as well as, rather than merely as, historical documents, letters highlight female mastery of the literary and formal conventions of the epistolary genre.

Historians have shown that girls' education in Tudor England was differentiated along gender lines from that of boys in terms of educational setting, the nature and range of subjects taught, and the social purpose of instruction.[41] Although there is some evidence that girls below the ranks of the gentry attended schools, many specifically forbade female entry; in those that accepted female pupils it appears doubtful whether instruction for girls extended beyond basic reading.[42] For the majority of the upper classes the locus of female education was the 'domestic sphere' or household; the quality of educational provision was uneven and largely dependent on favourable parental attitudes. Teaching was provided informally and formally by mothers, governesses, or tutors: Lady Grace Mildmay, for example, received lessons from a governess, while Lady Anne

---

[40] On the education of boys see Simon, *Education and Society*; Charlton, *Education in Renaissance England*; O'Day, *Education and Society*; Moran, *The Growth of English Schooling*; Jewell, *Education in Early Modern England*; Orme, *Education and Society*.

[41] Charlton, *Women, Religion and Education*; Friedman, 'Influence of Humanism', 57–70; Pollock, 'Teach Her to Live', 231–58; McMullen, 'Education of English Gentlewomen', 87–101; Whitehead, *Women's Education in Early Modern Europe*; Kelso, *Doctrine for the Lady*; Gardiner, *English Girlhood At School*.

[42] McMullen, 'Education of English Gentlewomen', 91; Adamson, 'Extent of Literacy', 192–3.

Clifford was tutored by the poet Samuel Daniel.[43] Girls were also commonly placed in the households of kinsfolk or influential noblewomen to finish their education and extend their network of social contacts. Lady Margaret Hoby was trained in the household of the countess of Huntingdon, and Lady Lisle's daughters were placed with local French aristocracy while they were in Calais.[44] A select group of exceptional women, which included Princesses Elizabeth and Mary, Lady Jane Grey, and the daughters of Thomas More, Anthony Cooke, and Henry Fitzalan, had access to a male world of classical learning, although recent scholars have downplayed the radical impact of humanistic thought on female education, highlighting instead the conservative assumptions that underpinned aspects of programmes of study.[45] Indeed, Margaret Sommerville has shown that 'classical, scriptural, patristic and medieval authorities' upon which Renaissance thought was based shared a basic assumption of women's intellectual inferiority to men; and certain writers questioned whether women were in fact rational beings.[46] For most women, though, education ordinarily consisted of a diet of religious instruction, learning the skills of housewifery (which could include needlework, dressing meat, and keeping accounts), music, and reading. A further component of education and upbringing was the socialization of young girls, and the inculcation of gendered codes of female behaviour. The nature of women's education was further restricted by the different purposes for which male and female learning was intended. Whereas men were educated for public roles, in order that they might serve the State as able administrators, proponents of female education sought to instruct women for the domestic sphere, to be 'good' wives and mothers.[47]

In the absence of institutional records and curricula, collections of family letters can be mined for what they reveal about parental attitudes and the nature of girls' education. Parental ambition for girls is glimpsed in a letter from Jane Tutoft to the Norfolk gentleman Nathaniel Bacon concerning the education of her daughter in his household: 'let her lern to wryt & to rede & to cast acount & to wash & to bru & to backe & to dres meat & drink & so I trust she shal prove a great good huswyf.'[48] Sir Edward Molineux placed his daughters with a cousin in 1551, in order that they would be brought up in 'vertue, good manners and larning to playe the gentlewomen and good huswyffes, to dress meat and oversee their households'.[49] Susanna Darnell wrote to her daughter Elizabeth Vernon requesting that she take good 'sisterly care' of her sister Mary, 'for now she is yn

---

[43] Pollock, *With Faith and Physic*, 6; *The Diaries of Lady Anne Clifford*, ed. Clifford, 2.

[44] Moody, *Diary of Lady Margaret Hoby*, p. xvii; *Lisle Letters*, iii. 217.

[45] O'Day, *Education and Society*, 184; Friedman, 'Influence of Humanism', 57–70; McMullen, 'Education of English Gentlewomen', 94–7; Kaufman, 'Juan Luis Vives on the Education of Women', 891–6; Grafton and Jardine, *From Humanism to the Humanities*, 55–7.

[46] Sommerville, *Sex and Subjection*, 10–11. See also Maclean, *Renaissance Notion of Woman*.

[47] Jardine, 'Isotta Nogarola: Woman Humanists: Education for What?', 231–44; Watson, *Vives and the Renascence Education of Women*, 54; Dowling, *Humanism in the Age of Henry VIII*, ch. 7; Sowards, 'Erasmus and the Education of Women', 77–89.

[48] Folger, L.d.603: *c.*1572.   [49] Gardiner, *English Girlhood*, 119.

makeng on mariag', adding that she was to 'make her [sister] goe clenly & nete in her clothes and call on her for reding and writing'.[50] Parental prescriptions of this nature indicate that basic reading and writing skills, along with other practical accomplishments, were increasingly deemed to be important for gentlewomen in their capacity as wives and mistresses of households. The benefits of literacy witnessed here are thus largely viewed as functional. For some parents, however, there was also a spiritual impetus to female acquisition of literacy skills: the Puritan John Penry, for example, corresponded with his wife Helen from prison, enjoining her to bring up their daughters to read and write: 'when they are capable of any hardye labor I knowe that yow will not let them be Idle if possible yow can let them learne both to reade and also to write.'[51] Correspondence can also be used to observe the gendered demarcation of educational responsibilities among parents. Sir Robert Sidney, in a letter to his wife Barbara, discussed the education of their children: 'I left it to yourself as I do still since I see you wil not bee other wise pleased for the girls I kan not mislike the care you take of them but for the boies you must resolve to let me have my wil for I know better what belongs to a man than you do indeed I wil haue him from his nurse for it is time and now no more to bee in the nurcary among wemen.'[52] While Lady Sidney could oversee the education of daughters, she was forbidden to interfere in the education of her sons. Sir Robert's directives echo those of Sir Thomas Elyot in *The Boke Named The Governor* (1531), which repeated Quintilian stipulating that at the age of 7 boys should be placed in the care of a male tutor: 'after that a child is come to seven years of age I hold it expedient that he be taken from the company of women.'[53] References of this nature, fleeting and sporadic though they are, nevertheless help to paint a much fuller picture of the varied nature and provision of women's education; to document parental attitudes as forces of pedagogical change, and the extent to which these deviated from or followed prescriptive educational texts; and to highlight the impact of religion in the gradual extension of reading and writing skills to women.

Focusing more specifically on the teaching of writing, scholars have demonstrated beyond doubt that women were taught to write less frequently than their male counterparts. Estimates of female writing ability for the sixteenth century have been almost universally low. Indeed, David Cressy in his ground-breaking study of literacy and the social order in early modern England concluded that 'most women did not need to be able to write', adding that 'the domestic routine of cooking, sewing and child-rearing had little need for reading . . . even among those social and economic groups where the men had regular dealings with paper and ink, the women were usually illiterate'.[54] Calculations of female literacy using signatures are

---

[50] SP46/24/224: n.d.   [51] BL, Addit., 48064, fo. 20: 1593

[52] CKS, De L'Isle, U1475, C81/97: 20/04/1597.

[53] Elyot, *The Boke Named The Governor* (1531), ed. Lehmberg (1962), 19.

[54] Cressy, *Literacy and the Social Order*, 128. Cressy estimates that only 1% of women could sign their names in 1500, compared with 10% of men. By the beginning of Elizabeth's reign some 5%

imperfect, however, and present numerous methodological and interpretational problems.[55] Indeed, women are severely under-represented in the sources utilized to measure signing literacy, such as probated wills and ecclesiastical court depositions. The social composition of female deponents is also not proportional with their numbers within society as a whole; wives of gentlemen, clergymen and yeoman, for example, are poorly represented in court materials. Furthermore, estimates of female literacy are undifferentiated by social status, and collective totals of female signatories, therefore, probably underestimate literacy levels among women of upper and middling groups.[56]

A more optimistic assessment of levels of female writing literacy, especially among elite, mercantile, and professional groups, is provided by the evidence of early modern women's letters, which are extant in much greater numbers than hitherto has been assumed. The use of letters as evidence of female literacy clearly privileges 'literate' groups, and does not represent a 'universal' measurement of literacy in the way that signatures are capable of population-wide comparison of literacy rates differentiated by social status, gender, chronological period, and geographical location; though it does permit a more qualitative examination of hierarchies of literacy. Letters themselves represent material sites of female literary production, yielding direct evidence of female scribal abilities. A close study of letters provides detailed knowledge about aspects of women's writing skills, among them the quality of their handwriting, spelling, grammar, and punctuation. Exemplary in this area is the work of Caroline Bowden, who has submitted the texts of Elizabethan and early seventeenth-century women's letters to rigorous scrutiny, grading levels of literacy on a scale of 1 to 5.[57] Studied in this manner, letters reveal much about the competency and proficiency with which women wrote, and how easily and frequently they put pen to paper; whether letter-writing was an everyday activity for women or one in which they seldom engaged. Above all, what emerges is the range of women's writing abilities encountered in the source material surveyed. At one level there are those women unfamiliar with the practice of writing, who could possibly scratch a signature or make a rudimentary mark; at the other end of the spectrum, however, are highly literate women, who achieved fluency in penmanship and were capable of writing in a variety of hands, styles, and genres, and a small number of exceptional

---

of women and 20% of men are thought to have been able to sign, which rose to 8% of women and 27% of men by 1600. Figures increased to 10% female literacy by 1640, compared to 30% male literacy: ibid. 176–77. Remoter areas of northern England and Cornwall exhibit greater degrees of illiteracy than southern counties: Cressy, 'Social Status and Literacy', 19–23; Stephens, 'Male and Female Adult Illiteracy', 1–7. It is not until the nineteenth century, however, that this gendered pattern of literacy breaks down: Vincent, *Literacy and Popular Culture*, 24–25; id., *The Rise of Mass Literacy*, 12. Cf. Charlton, 'Women and Education', 4.

[55] On signatures see Thomas, 'Meaning of Literacy', 102–3; Ford, 'Problem of Literacy', 31; Spufford, 'First Steps in Literacy', 410–12.

[56] Cressy, *Literacy and the Social Order*, 105, 115.

[57] Bowden, 'Female Education in the Late Sixteenth and Early Seventeenth Centuries', appendix. See also Winkelmann, 'A Case Study of Women's Literacy', 16–17.

women who corresponded in Latin. At a basic level then, letters are indicators of levels of female literacy and illiteracy. Only a small proportion of women for whom correspondence survives were unable to write for themselves; whether they did so or not, however, is another matter: secretaries were frequently employed by both men and women during this period to conduct correspondence. As argued in Chapter 3, the ability to write remained for many women a reserve skill, one that could be called upon when required. By the end of the sixteenth century, though, writing appears to have been more closely associated with everyday use, and greater importance was attached to personally written correspondence. Indeed, it is highly likely that by 1600 most women from landed and mercantile groups could achieve functional reading and writing literacy.

Evidence of women's reading ability, beyond the mention of books, is harder to discern from their correspondence. The physical activity of reading leaves very little trace, except where accompanied by writing. Fragmentary references highlight the need for more complex definitions of literacy that account for variations in reading (as with writing) ability. Keith Thomas has demonstrated that an ability to read black-letter print did not mean that an individual was equally proficient at reading roman type. Likewise, fluency in reading print does not indicate a woman's ability to decipher handwritten documents.[58] References in women's letters to the activity of reading correspondence are occasional and indirect; however, as Chapter 5 demonstrates, what emerges is not only a hierarchy of reading abilities, including those women who were fluent readers of script as well as those who need to have their letters read to them, but also the range of epistolary reading practices. Letters were read silently and aloud; perused closely and skimmed for details; preserved for reference and rereading; or intercepted, remaining unread by the intended recipient. They were read in withdrawn solitude in closets and chambers, read out by servants or bearers, passed around family and friends, and occasionally they entered the domain of scribal and print publication. Letters thus document more than mere reading ability; they help to unlock the complex process by which information was transmitted. Indeed, an analysis of the social practices relating to reading women's letters helps further to delineate early modern social boundaries of what constituted 'public' and 'private', 'intimate' and 'communal'.

Letters are unique sources for studying female education and literacy, not only as a site of women's basic literacy skills, in that they register rudimentary writing activity and abilities, but also in that they document different and occasionally 'higher' forms of female literacy beyond the actual penning of correspondence: book-ownership and women's reading practices; female involvement in the writing and circulation of manuscript poetry; interest in areas as diverse as music, architecture, medicine, theology, and playgoing; and female participation in the public 'male' world of the Republic of Letters. In this sense, letters represent

---

[58] Thomas, 'The Meaning of Literacy', 99–100.

a systematically untapped source for studying women's participation in broader cultural and literary activities; they provide evidence of female involvement in the kinds of activities usually associated with men and educated elites. In the absence of abundant source materials delineating the curricula for female education, correspondence offers indirect evidence of the kinds of skills learned by sixteenth-century girls, and attests to some of the uses—practical, religious, political, and leisure-related—to which as women they put their education. Early modern letters, therefore, document the nature and purpose of women's education. Yet letters are more than mere repositories of facts to be picked clean by the assiduous scholar. Viewed from the perspective of genre, women's letters reveal female mastery of the conventions of the form: they were conversant with the correct use of modes of address and closing salutations, as well as the formal structure of letters. In particular, women's letters of petition, written to government officials and the monarch to press suits and secure favour, most acutely reveal women's knowledge of and adherence to the rhetorical structure of epistolary writing.

EPISTOLARY MODELS AND SOCIAL RELATIONS

Historians working on Renaissance literature have long been alert to the need to read the writings of the period with attention to form as well as content, though this attention to rhetoric and structure rarely extends to documents such as letters, which themselves conform to generic conventions, following epistolary and rhetorical exemplars.[59] The question of how far Tudor women's letters were scripted by Renaissance epistolographies such as Erasmus's *De conscribendis epistolis* (1522) and Day's *English Secretorie* (1586) is integral to discussions of letters as an accurate index of the nature and quality of female social relations, discussions that have concerned social historians interested in the strength of family bonds and other social ties. To what extent, for example, are women's letters merely conventional, the social relations that they inscribe—whether deferential, affectionate, authoritative, familial, or submissive—modelled on standard epistolary forms, and reflective of wider societal behavioural and gender codes? If letters are standard and formulaic, in what sense are they capable of reflecting or representing genuine feelings and emotion? By the end of the period women's letters on the whole betray a more relaxed and open style and tone; however, it is unclear the degree to which this relates to shifts in letter-writing conventions from the medieval to the early modern period, which encouraged more individualistic epistolary forms, rather than reflecting other factors such as greater levels of female literacy, epistolary privacy, and a rise in women's status. The relationship between linguistic and generic conventions and social behaviour is complex, and has important bearings on the nature of early modern

---

[59] Sharpe and Zwicker, *Politics of Discourse*; Sharpe and Lake, *Culture and Politics*.

correspondence, the process of letter-writing, and the interplay between epistolary models and conventions and letters and letter-writers.

In turning to consider letter-writing guides themselves, numerous printed manuals were produced during the sixteenth century offering instructions and models that laid out the rules governing letter-writing. Writers and publishers were responding partly to an increasingly receptive audience among upper and middling-status groups. The medieval *ars dictaminis* and early sixteenth-century Latin formularies such as Erasmus's *Conficiendarum epistolarum formula* (1521) and his influential *De conscribendis epistolis* (1522), aimed largely at students of rhetoric, were modified for an increasingly receptive gentry and mercantile audience.[60] William Fulwood dedicated *The Enemie of Idlenesse* (1568) to the Merchant Taylors of London: 'I meane not I the cunning clerks to teach But rather the unlearned sort a few precepts to preach.'[61] Similarly, Angel Day's *The English Secretorie* (1586), Abraham Fleming's *A Panoplie of Epistles* (1576), and John Browne's *The Merchants' Avizo* (1589) were written for wider public readership.[62] Writers like Nicholas Breton, in *A Poste With a Madde Packet of Letters* (1602), utilized letters as a framework for social satire and semi-fictional writing intended for entertainment rather than instruction.[63] More specialized manuscript formularies also survive.[64]

Epistolographies of this kind outlined the art of letter-writing, mapping the generic boundaries of the Renaissance letter.[65] In his epistolary manual *De conscribendis epistolis*, Erasmus, following classical oratorical lines, adopted a tripartite division of epistles into deliberative, demonstrative, and judicial writing; letters of petition (the subject of Chapter 9) were classed as a sub-genre of letter, grouped in the deliberative or persuasive class. To the three main classical rhetorical types of epistle Erasmus added a new fourth category—the familiar letter. The latter, according to Erasmus, included letters which narrated events, provided news, both 'public' and 'private', contained congratulations and complaints, proffered advice or help, gave praise, or were written merely to amuse.[66] This fourfold Erasmian method of epistolary classification was adopted by other authors, including Day in his first edition of the *English Secretorie*.[67] A third edition of this book in 1595 contained new material, including additional examples of familiar epistles.[68] Day wrote that familiar letters were for 'ordinary causes and matters'.[69] William Fulwood, in *The Enemie of Idlenesse*, referred

[60] Gerlo, 'The *Opus de conscribendis epistolis*', 103–14; Henderson, 'Erasmus on the Art of Letter-Writing', 331–55; ead., 'On Reading the Rhetoric of the Renaissance Letter', 143–62; ead., 'Defining the Genre of the Letter', 89–105; Witt, 'Medieval "Ars Dictaminis" and the Beginnings of Humanism', 1–35.   [61] Fulwood, *Enemie of Idlenesse*, sig. Aiii^v.

[62] Robertson, *The Art of Letter-Writing*, 7; Hornbeak, *The Complete Letter-Writer*, 1. See also Mitchell and Poster, *Letter-Writing Manuals from Antiquity to the Present*.

[63] See also Anon., *The Prompters Packet of Private and Familiar Letters* (1612); Anon., *Cupids Messenger* (1629); Gent, *A Speedie Post With Certaine New Letters* (1625).

[64] BL, Addit., 48150, Yelverton, 161 (2). See also Folger, V.b.36, 8, fo. 1^r: 'Greetinges Subscritpions & farewelles of letters' [c.1610].   [65] Guillén, 'Notes Toward the Study'.

[66] Erasmus, *De conscribendis epistolis*, 71.   [67] Day, *The English Secretorie* (1586), 41–2.

[68] Sig. A2^v.   [69] Ibid. ii, 58.

alternately to 'domestical' and 'familiar' letters, attesting the mutuality of these categories. Fulwood argued that such correspondence was: 'more in use than any other for so much as their nature they are very necessary, to let our frendes understande of our estate, and of our businesse be it of helth, prosperitie, sicknesse, aduersitie, or any other domesticall and familiar thyngs.'[70] Familiar epistles by this definition encompassed a wide range of subjects and purposes; distinctions between sub-genres of letters, therefore, tended to be fluid. Indeed, the word 'familiari' according to Judith Rice Henderson is in many ways a catch-all term that 'can mean almost anything'.[71] The flexibility of generic boundaries likewise extended to other forms of letters: petitionary language—a language of deference and supplication—is found throughout a range of early modern correspondences, and not simply confined to formal letters of petition. Thus, categorizations of letters as 'familiar', 'domestic', or 'familial' in contrast to 'business', 'state', or 'political' correspondence are uneasy, muddying the degrees of overlap between these epistolary forms.[72] More neutral terms might be pragmatic or practical correspondence.

As Jonathan Gibson has persuasively argued, composite early modern epistolary theory was comprised of three interrelated traditions—the medieval *ars dictaminis*, early modern rhetorical theory, and the revived classical theory of the familiar letter—which were available in printed English letter-writing manuals and formularies.[73] The introduction during the Renaissance of familiar epistles as a category of letter emphasized more personal and intimate topics. This heralded a shift away from medieval letter-writing styles which were markedly utilitarian—used either to convey information or to make practical requests—and characteristically mechanical in methods of composition.[74] The emphasis in Renaissance letter-writing was not on adherence to strictly imposed rules, but on the adaptability and flexibility of epistles to any given subject, situation or task.[75] Vives and Macropedius both encouraged freedom in terms of the content and the arrangement of the body of the letter.[76] Erasmus advised improvisation in writing, since, in his view, reliance too heavily upon models invented by others encouraged laziness.[77] Similarly, Angel Day counselled letter-writers not to copy examples, but to 'become far more pithie in the matters you haue to write of'.[78]

---

[70] Sig. 69ᵛ.   [71] Henderson, 'On Reading the Rhetoric', 149; 151.
[72] On familiar letters see Thompson, 'Familiar Letters', 91–126; Stevens, 'Erasmus's "Tigress"', 124–40; Najemy, *Between Friends*, 30–3; Fitzmaurice, *The Familiar Letter in Early Modern English*; Dickson, 'Humanistic Influences on the Art of the Familiar Epistle', 11–22.
[73] Gibson, 'Letters', 615–19.
[74] Bolgar, 'Teaching of Letter-Writing', 246–47; Davis, '*Litera Troili* and English Letters', 235–37; Robertson, *Art of Letter-Writing*, 7–9.
[75] Erasmus, *De conscribendis epistolis*, 22; Bolgar, 'The Teaching of Letter-Writing', 253.
[76] Vives, *De conscribendis epsitolis* (1534), ed. Fantazzi (1989); Macropedius, *Methodus de conscribendis epistolis* (1543). Cf. Lipsius, *Epistolica institutio* (1587); Celtis, *Methodus conficiendarum epistolarum* (1537); Hegendorph, *Methodus epistolis conscribendi* (1526); Bradolino, *De ratione scribendi libri tres* (1498).   [77] Erasmus, *Conficiendarum epistolarum formula* (1521), 260.
[78] Day, *The English Secretorie* (1595), 54

Whereas the *ars dictaminis* accentuated differences between superiors and subordinates, humanists sought to revive the simpler epistolary forms of antiquity, encouraging the adoption of an easy, intimate style and expressions of individual feelings of affection.[79] Erasmus wrote: 'I approve the simplicity of the ancients . . . so that we might greet one another by the mere mention of names . . . what could be truer or simpler?'.[80] Elsewhere he considered that 'the wording of a letter should resemble a conversation between friends'.[81] Day, greatly influenced by the Dutch humanist, advised letter-writers to write 'louingly' to friends; and Fulwood cautioned against using 'superlatiue' language, recommending instead a 'certaine familiar reuerence' in correspondence with equals.[82]

In England, letter-writing manuals were not specifically addressed to women until the seventeenth century. The first book to cater for a purely female audience was Jacques Du Bosque's *The Secretary of Ladies* (1638), which was translated from the French.[83] By the late seventeenth century several other guides for women appeared, including Henry Care's *The Female Secretary* (1671) and Hannah Wolley's *The Gentlewoman's Companion* (1675).[84] In contrast, numerous collections of women's letters were published on the continent during the sixteenth century. The Italian humanist Ortensio Lando produced *Lettere di molte valorose donne* (Venice, 1548) and *Lettere della . . . Donna L.G. in Gazuolo con gran diligentia raccolte, & à gloria del sesso feminile nuovamente in luce poste* (Venice, 1552).[85] In 1586 the Parisian printer Abel L'Angelier published the *Missives de Mesdames des Roches de Poitiers, mère et fille*.[86] Furthermore, Christine de Pisan's *The Treasure of the City of Ladies*, last published in 1536 in French, included a section entitled 'an example of the sort of letter the wise lady may send to her mistress'.[87]

Earlier attempts were, however, made to cater for an English female audience. Dorothy Gardiner argued that in the early fourteenth century letter-writing guides in French provided models of letters by women, with rules and instructions given in Latin.[88] A manuscript letter-writing treatise written in French was also dedicated to Anne Boleyn in 1530.[89] Moreover, the vernacular letter-writing guides that emerged during the sixteenth century also appear to have been aimed at female readers who were untrained in classical languages and,

---

[79] Houlbrooke, *English Family*, 32–3; Grund, 'From Formulary to Fiction', 380.
[80] Erasmus, *De conscribendis epistolis*, 51.   [81] Ibid. 20.
[82] Fulwood, *Enemie of Idlenesse*, 3ᵛ; Day, *The English Secretorie*, 4.
[83] Du Bosque, *The Secretary of Ladies* (1638).
[84] Humiliata, 'Standards of Taste', 261–77; Mitchell, 'Entertainment and Instruction', 331–47.
[85] Burke, *Fortunes of the Courtier*, 49.
[86] Chartier, 'Secrétaires for the People?', 66. See also Altman, 'Political Ideology in the Letter Manual', 105–22; Tanskanen, 'No Lesse Plesaunt'; Dierks, 'Letter Manuals', 541–5.
[87] de Pisan, *The Treasure of the City of Ladies* (1405), trans. Lawson (1985), 98.
[88] Gardiner, *English Girlhood*, 63.
[89] BL, Ro., 20 BXVII, 'French Letter-Writing Treatise (1530) by Loye de Brun'.

unlike men, were not taught letter-writing skills at school.[90] These manuals provided instructions for female correspondents, outlining the manner and style in which to write, and afforded sundry examples for imitation. Book Two of Angel Day's *The English Secretorie* contains collections of various familiar letters, which the preface claims were, 'to satisfie the expectation of a number whom I haue been enformed to haue earnestly looked for and required it'.[91] The specimen epistles include 'a letter remuneratory from a gentlewomen of good sort to a nobleman her kinsman', and 'a letter gratulatorie from a wife to her husband'.[92] Fulwood's *The Enemie of Idlenesse* presents a wider range of family letters from a wife, a sister, a mother, and a daughter, as well as an epistle from a Lady to her lover.[93] These texts also provided women with access to a range of formal and business letters, while Breton's *A Poste With a Madde Packet of Letters* furnished amusing examples of letters from various female stereotypes, including a 'cunning' wife, a 'coy dame', and 'a fowle dowde'.[94] Female epistolary models were clearly also aimed at men, indicating the interchangeability of male and female epistolary styles: Erasmus, for example, advised male pupils to practise writing letters from women in the manner of Helen restraining Paris from an illicit love affair, or Penelope's letter to Ulysses. 'Similarly,' he wrote 'one may compose a letter from a wife to her husband who is tarrying abroad, telling him to hasten home.'[95] Although it is unlikely that Erasmus's manual was in fact read by many women, it offers exemplars which male amanuenses could have appropriated in writing for women in order to script or 'ventriloquize' 'female voices'.[96]

Female ownership of letter-writing manuals can be glimpsed through library lists and probate inventories. The inventory of Alice Edwards, the widow of David Edwards, fellow of Corpus Christi, Cambridge, drawn up on 18 July 1546 included Erasmus's 'Erasmus de constrybendis epistolis'.[97] A British Library copy of Nicholas Breton's *Poste With a Packet of Madde Letters, Newly Imprinted* [c.1650] (BL 10920.d.9) contains the ownership mark of Frances Wolfreston.[98] In addition, the countess of Bridgewater's library contained several epistolary works, including Day's 'The English Secretary (1607)', and in French, 'D'Ossats letters (1627)' and 'Le Secretaire des Secretaires (1610)'.[99] In addition to these prescriptive manuals, women as well as men collected, copied, and preserved in manuscript miscellanies and 'letter-books' letters they received and sent, form letters, and copies of exemplary letters of famous persons worth

---

[90] Hull, *Chaste, Silent and Obedient*, 25–6.   [91] Day, *The English Secretorie* (1595), sig. A3ᵛ.
[92] Ibid. ii, 64, 67.   [93] Fulwood, *Enemie of Idlenesse*, 110–14ᵛ, 134ᵛ–5.
[94] Breton, *A Poste With a Madde Packet of Letters*, sigs B3, C–C2.
[95] Erasmus, *De conscribendis epistolis*, 24.   [96] Harvey, *Ventriloquized Voices*.
[97] Leedham-Green, *Books in Cambridge Inventories*, i. 77–8. While the book was indeed in Alice's possession, it likely belonged to her husband (along with copies of Ovid, Horace, and Cicero), or may have been the property of the family at large.
[98] Morgan, 'Frances Wolfreston and "Her Bouks"', 197–219.
[99] Hackel, 'Countess of Bridgewater's London Library', 149, 152.

preserving and perhaps imitating. Peter Mack has argued that letters of petition, request, or recommendation were frequently copied into notebooks and manuscript miscellanies, for personal record, as stylistic exercises, and as models.[100] It is here that one finds the most examples of letters by women. Folger MS V.a.321, for instance, contains several letters to and from women, including petitionary epistles: 'a letter from Penelope Rich to Elizabeth I', 'a petition from Mary Cavendish to James I', 'a letter from Mary Lady Wingfield to Elizabeth I', and two anonymous petitions attributed to Elizabeth Brooke.[101] Anne Newdigate's letters, which were praised as examples of 'fayre wryting and most excellent inditing', were copied and circulated: Francis Beaumont 'bestowed' one such copy upon his niece.[102] The circulation of these letters attests the range of materials available for emulation by female letter-writers. Women were also the compilers of their own collections of letters in letter-books and commonplace books. Lady Margaret Hoby recorded in her diary: 'after dinner I Coppied out a letter which Mr Hoby had wretten to the Busshopp of Limbricke touching his agreement to peace.'[103] Several seventeenth-century examples survive: Lady Anne Southwell's (1573–1636) commonplace book includes two copies of letters written by her, a letter to her friend Cecily MacWilliam and one addressed to Henry Cary, Viscount Falkland; and Mary Evelyn (*c*.1635–1709), as well as preserving letters she received, entered select copies of her own letters into notebooks.[104] While it is hard to establish (beyond a handful of individuals) the extent to which women read Renaissance letter-writing manuals, or manuscript miscellanies containing exemplary epistles, and borrowed from them rhetorical models, there is evidence that women were formally taught to write letters. Young girls were tutored from the examples of classical letter-writers: Lady Jane Seymour was familiar with Cicero's letters, and both Elizabeth Cary and Brilliana Harley read and copied out Senecan epistles.[105]

The relationship between model and 'real' letters has been pointed out by a number of scholars. Indeed, Malcolm Richardson, while arguing for 'little significant influence of continental or English dictaminal theory' in the letters of middle-class English citizens from the fifteenth and early sixteenth centuries, maintains that they were instead influenced by business formats.[106] The rhetorician Peter Mack, in his study of the influence on 'everyday' correspondence of Renaissance rhetoric found in letter-writing manuals, likewise argues that

---

[100] Mack, *Elizabethan Rhetoric*, 109–10.
[101] Folger, V.a 321 6ᵛ–7ᵛ (Penelope Lady Rich), 15ᵛ (Mary Cavendish), 20ᵛ–21ʳ (Mary Lady Wingfield), 43ᵛ–44ʳ ([Elizabeth Brooke?]). In his discussion of Folger, V.a. 321, and the case of documents grouped as evidence to support a petition, Peter Mack argues that 'they would have been useful to the petitioner as a record and to anyone else seeking similar benefits as a model': *Elizabethan Rhetoric*, 109–10.   [102] Newdigate-Newdegate, *Gossip From the Muniment Room*, 102.
[103] *Diary of Lady Margaret Hoby*, ed. Moody, 162.
[104] Klene, *Southwell-Sibthorpe Commonplace Book*; Harris, 'Letterbooks of Mary Evelyn', 202–15.
[105] Lewalski, *Writing Women in Jacobean England*, 180; Eales, 'Patriarchy, Puritanism and Politics', 148.   [106] Richardson, 'Fading Influence of the Medieval *Ars Dictaminis*', 225–47.

'practical letters devoted to the conduct of business tend to convey expected content in a standard form'.[107] Indeed, in analysing how far women conformed to epistolary conventions in their correspondence, business or practical letter-writing forms most closely adhere to the formalities of Renaissance letters (see Chapter 9). By contrast, 'familiar' letters to family and friends, beyond the use of conventional opening, closing, and salutary forms, display a greater degree of freedom in terms of subject-matter and organization of the body of the letter than is found in petitionary epistles. Perhaps what is most interesting is where letters deviate from standard forms or display more individual modes of expression. Elizabeth Russell, for persuasive effect, signed herself in an epistle to her nephew Robert Cecil: 'By yo[u]r awnt that hath not above 600 L *de claro*[108] in the world to live on left. Elizabeth Russell. th[a]t liveth in skorn of Disdayne, mallice and rancor, fearing, serving and Depending only upon God and my soveraigne, Dowager.'[109] While female conversance with epistolary forms can be established in some cases through the direct evidence of letters themselves, it is hard, however, to determine the precise ways in which letter-writing conventions were disseminated among women. Evidence of female ownership and readership of epistolary manuals is slight, though Brilliana Harley cited Senecan epistles in her commonplace book.[110] Far more likely is that women's familiarity with epistolary conventions—in terms of opening, closing, and salutary forms, and structure—stemmed less from bookish example than from contact with the form, through receiving letters.

In general, letter-writing manuals such as those of Day, Fulwood, and Fleming upheld social and gender hierarchies. Daughters were enjoined to display filial obedience in writing to parents; wives to be obedient to husbands.[111] How far women in practice adhered to authoritarian codes of female behaviour has been hotly debated over the past few decades by historians adopting what can loosely be termed a 'sentiments approach' to the history of the family, an approach often relying largely on collections of family correspondence and analysis of modes of address and deferential language.[112] As a result of these debates, interpretations of the nature and quality of early modern social and familial relationships have greatly differed. Lawrence Stone's controversial yet influential *The Family, Sex and Marriage in England 1500–1800*, with its schematic outline of successive family types—the open lineage family, the restricted patriarchal nuclear family, and the closed domesticated nuclear family—depicted an absence of conjugal and maternal love and affection during the first half of the period, and presented women (and men) as cold and 'emotional cripples'. Indeed, Stone argued that 'social relations from the fifteenth to the seventeenth centuries tended to be cool, even unfriendly'.[113] Operating very

---

[107] Mack, *Elizabethan Rhetoric*, 114. [108] Clear or spare. [109] SP12/255/29: *c.*12/1595.
[110] Eales, 'Patriarchy, Puritanism and Politics', 148.
[111] Fulwood, *Enemie of Idlenesse*, 114–114ᵛ.
[112] Anderson, *Approaches to the History of the Western Family*, 39–64.
[113] Stone, *Family, Sex and Marriage*, 93.

much within the Stone school of thought, Miriam Slater, in her study of the seventeenth-century Verney family, sought to analyse the nature of family obligations and patterns of interaction by positing an anthropological model of patriarchy. Slater argued that role differentiation was determined by gender, birth order, and generation, portraying the family during this period as patriarchal, authoritarian, and primogenital, and ultimately as an instrument of control.[114]

By contrast, other historians, such as Margaret Sommerville, have shown the elasticity of restrictions on the functions performed by women, dependent on social status and position, and have outlined overlapping areas of female influence. Thus, in theory, while women in their capacities as wives owed dutiful respect to husbands, as mothers they commanded filial obedience from sons, and acting as mistresses of households they were empowered to instruct male servants.[115] Moreover, scholars studying documents produced by women themselves, such as correspondence and diaries, alongside prescriptive texts like conduct books and sermons, have drawn essential distinctions between precept and actual practice, assessing the degree to which women internalized restrictive female gender codes, and the ways in which these structured thought and behaviour.[116] Alison Wall has revealed the striking degree to which the women of the Thynne family displayed signs of independence and affection, while working within the confines of male authority, and simultaneously transgressing ideals of female submission.[117] Linda Pollock has also argued that the apparent divergence between ideals and reality arose from the conflicting demands of female education: on the one hand, girls internalized principles of female modesty, chastity, submissiveness, obedience to authority, and were conditioned to suppress wilful personalities; on the other, they were instilled with abilities to command, manage households, and assume various responsibilities in the absence of husbands.[118] Furthermore, scholars have stressed greater frequency of less unequal marital partnerships than previously assumed and highlighted women's participation in estate management and business interests.[119] Some historians, including Ralph Houlbrooke and Alan Macfarlane, have argued for a higher incidence of affective and emotional bonds during the late fifteenth and sixteenth centuries than has been previously acknowledged by some scholars.[120] Professor Houlbrooke maintains that family relationships were marked by

[114] Slater, *Family Life*, 25–31; ead., 'The Weightiest Business', 25–54. Cf. Mendelson, 'Debate: The Weightiest Business', 126–35.

[115] Sommerville, *Sex and Subjection*, 66–70. Recent research on women and the law, presents a more detailed understanding of the flexibility of patriarchal systems: Erickson, *Women and Property*; Gowing, *Domestic Dangers*; Stretton, *Women Waging Law*; Kermode and Walker, *Women, Crime and the Courts*.

[116] Houlbrooke, *English Family*, 101; Fletcher, *Gender, Sex and Subordination*, ch. 8.

[117] Wall, 'Elizabethan Precept', 28–31, 35–6.   [118] Pollock, 'Teach Her to Live'.

[119] Wrightson, *English Society*, 94; Houlbrooke, *English Family*, 106–7, 119.

[120] Houlbrooke, *English Family* 21, 103–4, 134–6; Macfarlane, *Marriage and Love in England*, 190–8, 301–3. Wrightson, *English Society*, 101–2; Sharpe, *Early Modern England: A Social History*.

gradual change over the period, and that apparent differences in sentiment and attitude are partly related to the changing nature and character of sources studied.[121] In particular, increased female literacy levels and the attendant rise in epistolary privacy promoted greater intimacy and openness in women's correspondence. Epistolary modes of address also changed during the late fifteenth and sixteenth centuries, with the introduction of more egalitarian and intimate forms, perhaps reflecting the more relaxed and open style of letter-writing extolled by Renaissance humanists.[122]

Textual affect arising from this relaxation of epistolary forms of address has wider implications relating to the nature of sixteenth-century family and social relationships. Given the potential for strategic use of affectionate, familiar, and emotional language in early modern correspondence—both in letters to family and petitions for patronage—traditional approaches of social historians who have read letters as standard 'autobiographical' forms have been challenged by scholars increasingly wary of viewing letters as transparent carriers of historical fact, capable of laying bare emotion and feeling.[123] This presents several challenges for historians studying letters for what they reveal about social and gender relations, the nature and quality of family ties, and the incidence of intimacy and affection present within individual relationships. How far, for example, does intimacy in letters merely reflect changing epistolary conventions, a change in the nature of letters as a source, rather than a fundamental shift in the way in which people lived and felt? To what extent can the textualization of emotion or friendship be regarded as in any way reflective of 'genuine' feelings? How far are women's letters mannered or sincere? Do they reflect true feelings or merely imitate appropriate styles? Is there a sense in which there was a formality in being informal, an affectation of being affectionate? How should one interpret the commonplace voices of maternal counsel and command, daughterly obedience and wifely duty? More essentially, is language (in the sense of writing a letter) in fact capable of capturing emotional states, feelings which in themselves are not material things, tangible to the touch, but are often inaccessible, eluding individual consciousness? These and other questions are explored more fully in later chapters.

The complex relationship between language and social phenomena is further highlighted by married women's correspondence to husbands, which over the course of the sixteenth century increasingly utilized a language of love and affect. Such a linguistic shift, as argued in Chapter 8, is less likely representative of a change in emotional bonds between husbands and wives than of changing cultural conventions—that is, use of loving words—which in itself strongly suggests that affection between spouses was becoming normative. Moreover, the evidence of sixteenth-century women's letters themselves expose the complexity

---

[121] Houlbrooke, *English Family*, 15.
[122] Ibid. 15; Constable, *Letters and Letter Collections*, 40; Bolgar, 'Teaching of Letter-Writing', 246–47. [123] Jardine, 'Reading and the Technology of Textual Affect', 78–97.

of women's emotional lives and the range in quality of relationships they experienced, which span from passionate to hostile, familiar to distant. Likewise, letters display an array of feelings and emotions. Focusing on a variety of letters produced in different contexts—daughters writing to parents, mothers to sons, sisters to siblings, women to male kin, mistresses to servants, and women to other women—Chapter 7 examines the status and position of women within society. As indicators of the differing intensities of individual relationships, letters yield confident, deferential, privy, and powerful forms of expression, indicating the interlocking spheres of female subordination and authority, as women's power and influence was under constant negotiation as it continually expanded and contracted.

THE POLITICS OF LETTER-WRITING

The early modern letter represents the dominant written form by which women exerted power and influence. Nowhere is this more explicit than in the study of letters of petition—suitors' letters, or letters of request—in other words, requests for favour made to monarchs and government officials. This form of correspondence documents the nature and scope of female petitioning activity, shedding light on women's involvement in patronage and politics. Female suitors made a broad range of patronage suits, both for themselves and on behalf of family, dependants, and other groups: 'friends', neighbours, and clients. For themselves, women wrote to procure grants of land, wardship, pensions, and annuities, and to settle disputes over jointure and inheritance; they also wrote seeking favour and advice, to influence local officials, and to secure justice and release from imprisonment. Acting as patrons and intermediaries, women wrote concerning the preferment of suitors to secular and religious offices, and the bestowing of land, titles, and honours, thus performing many of the same patronage functions as men. Letters of petition delineate the peculiarities of the early modern patronage system—a system that was fluid, plural, and shifting. Rarely did individuals operate through a single individual or patron; rather, they worked through numerous channels simultaneously and at different levels, both at court and within the provinces. As suitors, women commonly petitioned several individuals at once, often soliciting help through family and court networks; while as intermediaries women were approached as part of a larger process to mobilize as many connections as possible among officials, courtiers, and other persons of influence. In a suit for the position of under-sheriff of Norfolk, Nicholas Fermor, a client of the earl of Leicester, sought the intervention on his behalf of three female courtiers among a range of other well-placed individuals.[124] Furthermore, during Elizabeth I's reign gentlewomen of the

---

[124] Bodl., Tanner, 241, fos.1b–2: 31/10–03/11/1576.

Bedchamber enjoying intimate access to the queen were sought out by suitors to deliver letters by hand and expedite suits in person with kind words.

Read for language and rhetoric, women's letters of intercession display a rich vocabulary of patronage, favour, and 'political friendship'. Female letter-writers employed a Senecan language of mutual benefits: they promised repayment of favours in kind, assured the friendship of themselves and husbands, and mobilized alliances of family and 'friends'. Such usage probably derived less from knowledge of classical texts than the fact that Senecan language saturated the very social and cultural world in which they operated.[125] Although highly ritualized, women's easy familiarity with and utilization of a language of favour and reciprocity—a language typically seen as predominantly male—is suggestive of the high degree of confidence and authority with which many women wrote and intervened in areas traditionally viewed as male; their actions were not unusual or extraordinary, but a normal and necessary part of the social duties incumbent upon upper-class women as family members, mistresses of households, landowners and patrons in their own right. In this analysis, women's letters of intercession differ very little from the letters of male writers, which followed similar social hierarchies based on rank and social position. However, what is distinct to women suitors' letters (which they penned on their own behalves) as opposed to male suitors' letters is the calculated use of negative female gender assumptions in letters of deference: female 'weakness' or 'frailty' was a standard deferential trope. That it was culturally understood that women were able to manipulate male assumptions of female incapacity exposes the ways in which women could work within the limitations and constraints imposed by early modern society.

Beyond direct intervention in specific patronage suits, 'networking' letters to kin and court contacts more generally illustrate women's involvement in patronage and politics. Letters, among other sources of sociability—such as wills and household accounts—represent key materials for unlocking the complex political roles that women played both at local and national levels. The conducting of correspondence was central to oiling the wheels of kinship and patronage networks, and in cultivating useful contacts that could be called upon for future assistance. It was Lady Anne Newdigate rather than her husband who kept up regular correspondence with kin and court contacts; likewise, Lady Lisle's vast network of correspondents was indispensable to her in her distant business operations from Calais, especially in placing her daughters at court.[126] Here, letter-writing takes on a political significance as a secondary patronage activity. This fits in with the work of feminist scholars who have sought to reconceptualize various seemingly 'female' or 'domestic' and 'household' activities as political. Barbara Harris, for example, has argued for the importance of

---

[125] Salmon, 'Seneca and Tacitus', 169–88; Peck, *Court Patronage and Corruption*, ch. 1.

[126] Larminie, *Wealth, Kinship and Culture*, 10–17; Hanawalt, 'Lady Honor Lisle's Networks of Influence', 188.

gift-giving, hospitality, marriage arrangement, and the placing of children as important subsidiary patronage activities; Tricia Bracher has read as diplomatic the calligraphy of Esther Inglis; and Susan Frye, Ann Rosalind Jones, and Peter Stallybrass have highlighted the significance of needlework and embroidery—one of the tasks most clearly associated as 'feminine' and 'domestic'—as a site for female political action.[127]

Central to this study of Tudor women's letters is a rethinking of what constitutes political history, and a reconceptualizing of *politics* in order better to integrate women into traditional narratives. Such an agenda moves away from politics viewed purely in terms of male-dominated institutions—parliament, the Council, the Exchequer—towards a wider definition that acknowledges the primacy of interpersonal relationships and informal channels of power, which is characteristic of new Tudor political history.[128] Traditional models of patronage relations rest upon patriarchal conceptualizations of power which understand that significant *formal* and *direct* power was only conferred by institutional position and office—official posts from which women were excluded—and that women (where they were viewed to achieve influence) were forced to work through powerful men. Approached from this perspective which privileges direct and tangible rewards of patronage, it is easy to emphasize the restrictions on female agency. More recently, however, the work of several historians on women and patronage, including Sharon Kettering and Barbara Harris, has emphasized the plurality, fluidity, and non-institutional nature of early modern patronage relations, where influence was exerted indirectly through personal connections.[129] Such an approach, stressing the importance of marital alliances, kinship, and wider social contacts, is more akin to the socio-political studies of patronage undertaken by historians of early modern Europe, most notably Roland Mousnier, who emphasizes the complexity of patron–client bonds, distinguishing between different types of relationships based on kinship, service, landholding, clientage, and factional association.[130] Within this world of highly personalized relations it has been shown that women were intimately involved in matters of patronage: sustaining and strengthening patronage and kinship networks; operating as intermediaries and brokers, often in conjunction with coordinated family patronage strategies; and acting as

---

[127] Harris, 'Women and Politics', 259–81; Bracher, 'Esther Inglis and the English Succession Crisis', 132–46; Frye, 'Sewing Connections', 165–82; Jones and Stallybrass, *Renaissance Clothing*, 134–71.

[128] Daybell (ed.), *Women and Politics*; Gunn, 'Structures of Politics', 59–90; Alford, *Kingship and Politics*; Mears, *Queenship and Political Discourse*.

[129] Harris, 'Women and Politics'; ead., *English Aristocratic Women*; Kettering, 'Patronage Power', 817–41; ead., *Patrons, Brokers, and Clients*. See also Clarke, 'Patronage and Literature'; Munns and Richards (eds.), *Gender, Power and Privilege*; Sánchez, *The Empress, The Queen and the Nun*; Ago, 'Marie Spada Veralli, la buona mogli'.

[130] Mousnier, *Les Institutions de la France*. See also Eisenstadt and Lemarchand, *Political Clientelism, Patronage and Development*; Giry-Deloison and Mettam, *Patronages et Clientelismes*.

patrons in their own right.[131] Indeed, the early modern period marked an epoch of women's political influence, when, as Barbara Harris has argued, aristocratic women 'benefited from the evolution of the late medieval, and early modern English monarchy...when the growth of the crown occurred in a context in which the king lacked the financial resources to create a royal army or bureaucracy [and] depended on the unpaid service of the aristocracy whom he rewarded with the limited patronage at his disposal, and developed the court as the political and symbolic center of the monarchy'. The circumstances that allowed women significant political influence were relatively short-lived: by the late seventeenth century the growth of parliament and new bureaucratic institutions and the emergence of political parties 'drained power and resources from king, court, and patronage networks, the institutions that facilitated aristocratic women's political activity'.[132]

Part of this reconfiguration of women's letter-writing as political rests upon the fact that the boundaries between 'political' and 'domestic', 'public' and 'private', 'state' and 'family' are hard to separate during the early modern period. The blurredness of these categories works to undermine the binary opposition between male public and business arenas and restricted female domestic spheres, in which the household represented the sole locus of women's lives.[133] Indeed, the family functioned as a basic 'political unit' through which women operated; as Barbara Harris has argued, female roles of wives and mothers were 'careers' imbued with political significance.[134] Furthermore, the political goals and aspirations of the landed elite extended beyond influence over government, office, and policy, to include dynastic and family concerns: accumulation of land and wealth, maintenance of status and reputation, and advancement of family members' interests in careers and marriage.

In spatial terms too, the interconnectedness of 'public' and 'private' spheres is also apparent. Architectural studies indicate that houses designed to incorporate numerous communal chambers also offered private refuge: passages, walkways, closets, windows, and gardens.[135] Great noble households were themselves political institutions, which performed many of the functions—administrative, judicial, patronage, and military—later assumed by the State; women as members of aristocratic households were able to achieve political influence.[136] Furthermore, the responsibilities for household management and estate

---

[131] Larminie, *Wealth, Kinship and Culture*; Eales, *Puritans and Roundheads*; Payne, 'Aristocratic Women, Power, Patronage', 164–81; ead., 'Aristocratic Women and the Jacobean Court'; Hufton, 'Reflections on the Role of Women', 1–13; Harris, 'View From My Lady's Chamber', 215–47.

[132] Harris, *English Aristocratic Women*, 13.

[133] Crawford, 'Public Duty, Conscience', 58, 60. Warnicke, 'Private and Public', 123–40.

[134] Harris, *English Aristocratic Women*; ead., 'Women and Politics', 260, 281. Laslett, 'Family as a Public and Private Institution', 480–92.

[135] Girouard, *Life in the English Country House*, ch. 4; Ranum, 'Refuges of Intimacy', 207–63.

[136] Kelly, 'Did Women Have a Renaissance?', 35; Erler and Kowaleski, *Women and Power*, 1–13; Rose, *Women in the Middle Ages and the Renaissance*, pp. xvi–xvii.

administration required women to operate in other public spaces, such as law courts, often necessitating travel to London. And yet, despite the convergence of spheres during this period, contemporaries readily distinguished between 'public' and 'private' concerns, supporting the work of several historians who have recognized an emerging concept of privacy in early modern England.[137] Lucy Paulet, marchioness of Winchester, writing to her kinsman George Paulet separated his 'private busines' from the 'publique imployments' relating to his office; and Lady Hungerford wrote of Sir Robert Cecil's 'occupacion in publicke and serious affaires'.[138] Letters requesting favours in business matters were also sometimes termed 'private letters'. Katherine, duchess of Suffolk, in a missive to William Cecil concerning the purchase of Spilsby Chantry, mentioned the writing of 'p[ri]vate l[ett]res to belabour my frends'.[139] The word 'private' employed in this sense refers to the use of informal channels of power: writing personally to political allies regarding a particular suit, rather than operating through official routes and following formal procedures to have the correct bills drawn up. In reality, however, the two practices often worked in tandem; women both wrote informally and instructed bills to be framed. This indicates the importance of historicizing the terminology of 'public' and 'private' within its proper historical context.

Furthermore, women's letter-writing activities extended beyond the domestic sphere of the household, defined in either a pejorative or practical sense. Through letter-writing activities women were also engaged in the public sphere, defined in the Habermasian sense of informed public opinion. While Habermas argues that the public sphere did not emerge until the eighteenth century, the work of historians such as F. J. Levy, Richard Cust, and Joad Raymond on news has pushed the development of the concept back into the seventeenth century.[140] Analysis of sixteenth-century manuscript newsletters, however, enables one to locate the emerging development of a public sphere even further back still in the Tudor period, and indicates that women were very much involved in the formation of public opinion. Acting as gatherers, purveyors, readers, and writers of news, women participated in manuscript news networks that were local, national, and trans-national. The case study of Bess of Hardwick—a woman at the centre of a dense network of correspondents trafficking news—illustrates that women were recipients of newsletters, and the letters they wrote themselves frequently contained court, national, European, and transatlantic news, in

---

[137] Houlbrooke, *English Family*, 23; Pollock, 'Living on the Stage', 79–80; Ingram, *Church Courts*, 30, 244–45; Shaw, 'Construction of the Private'; Sauer, 'Maternity, Prophecy and the Cultivation of the Private Sphere', 119–48; Huebert, 'Gendering of Privacy', 37–67.

[138] BL, Harl., 4713, fo. 258: n.d.; Hatfield House, Cecil, 52, fo. 41: 22/06/1597.

[139] SP10/10/8: 18/05/1550.

[140] Cust, 'News and Politics', 60–90; Levy, 'How Information Spread', 11–34; Raymond, *The Invention of the Newspaper*; id., 'Newspaper, Public Opinion', 109–40. Halasz, *Marketplace of Print*; Backscheider and Dykstal, *Intersections of the Public and Private Spheres*; Harris, 'Historians, Public Opinion', 369–77. Cf. Mears, *Queenship and Political Discourse*, ch. 5.

addition to items about family, household, and locality. Female courtiers were conduits for news at court and purveyors of intelligence more generally, intelligence that found its way into the counties through correspondence and by word-of-mouth, and abroad through ambassadorial dispatch.[141] Furthermore, a few women were involved in the public male world of the Republic of Letters, engaging in correspondence with leading continental intellectuals via the medium of formal Latin epistles.[142]

An important strand of this book, therefore, is the politicization of early modern women's correspondence: female letter-writing as a social activity should not be understood merely as domestic, parochial and non-political in a traditional sense. The categories commonly used to delineate male and female arenas—'political' and 'domestic', 'public' and 'private'—were exceedingly porous during the sixteenth-century. Letter-writing activities associated with family and household assumed political resonance as secondary patronage activities. Women wrote letters to persuade and influence; to maintain and extend kinship and patronage networks; to gather and disseminate news; to further the careers and marriages of children; to broker and dispense patronage; to acquire favour and intervene in suits normally viewed as a strictly male domain. Moreover, women's letters in general display an awareness of the intricacies of the politics of language; female letter-writers were well equipped to marshal the weapons of codes of deference and social courtesy in their wide-ranging and diverse correspondences.

This book falls into two parts: the first deals with the writing, sending, and reading of letters; the second focuses on forms or types of correspondence, such as letters of petition and marital correspondence, examining the functions of letters and the social and gender relations they expose. The next chapter delineates more fully the scope of women's letters and letter-writing, discussing the composition of female letter-writers in terms of social and marital status, the frequency with which women dispatched letters, and the range of recipients with whom women corresponded. It also considers more fully the nature and contents of letters, posing several important questions. What did women write about? Were women's letters different from men's in terms of content? Do women's letters offer an alternative perspective on social issues from men's letters? Finally, the chapter looks at the materiality of letters and letter-writing: the physical characteristics of letters, and the material reconstruction of the letter-writing process. It examines when, how, and where women wrote their letters, as a way of elucidating more fully the nature and experience of early modern women's letter-writing, and drawing connections between traditionally defined domestic and household spheres, and political and business worlds.

---

[141] Wright, 'Change in Direction', 153.
[142] Robinueau *et al.*, 'Correspondance entre Erasme et Margaret Roper', 29–46, 121; O'Donnell, 'Contemporary Women in the Letters of Erasmus', 34–72.

2

Letters and Letter-Writers

The historical significance of sixteenth-century women's letters and letter-writing lies partly in the remarkable scope, variety, freshness, and sheer quantity of extant material. The intimate details of women's lives and experiences, together with the self-expression that letters promoted, contrast sharply with prescriptive texts such as conduct manuals, sermons, and religious tracts. This chapter, then, attempts to survey a relatively unexplored body of women's letters and to outline some of the source-related and methodological problems encountered. It also considers the physical characteristics of letters as a source, and the material reconstruction of the letter-writing process. What emerges is that early modern women's letter-writing was a much more extensive area of female activity than scholars have hitherto assumed. Letters themselves cannot adequately be categorized as 'private documents', but rather are immensely complex sources that generate meaning both textually and materially, lending themselves to a range of analyses: historical, literary, lexical, palaeographic, and gender-based.

The book focuses on the sixteenth century in particular because it represents a transitional stage both in terms of female literacy and epistolary writing, although several well-known medieval letter collections do contain letters by women.[1] First, the period is marked by the increased laicization of literacy and the acquisition of writing skills by growing numbers of people beyond professional scriveners and groups like merchants and lawyers, for whom writing formed a necessary occupational skill, and also displays greater levels of female writing ability and familiarity with letters.[2] Indeed, the years 1540 to 1603 witness a steady rise in both numbers of English female letter-writers and epistles written.[3] Secondly, over the sixteenth century emphasis was increasingly placed upon personal literacy, especially by the upper classes. Individuals were expected to pen correspondence themselves, rather than relying on amanuenses for scribal

---

[1] *Paston Letters and Papers*, ed. Davis; *Stonor Letters and Papers*, and 'Supplementary Stonor Letters and Papers', ed., Kingsford, pp. i–viii, 1–26; Truelove, 'An Edition of the Stonor Letters and Papers'; *Cely Letters*, ed. Hanham; *Plumpton Letters and Papers*, ed. Kirby; Payne and Barron, 'The Letters and Life of Elizabeth Despenser, Lady Zouche', 126–56; Swabey, 'Letter Book of Alice de Bryene', 121–45; Ward, 'Letter-Writing by English Noblewomen', 29–41; O'Mara, 'Female Scribal Ability', 109–10.   [2] Parkes, 'Literacy of the Laity', 275–97.
[3] Significant numbers of letters also survive for the early Tudor period, especially for the 1530s: *Lisle Letters*; Daybell, 'Political Role of Upper-Class Women'.

activity, which consequently promoted a rise in epistolary privacy. Furthermore, pioneering scholars working on individual women letter-writers during Elizabeth's reign often regarded their subjects as unique, unaware of other contemporaneous examples.[4] This book, therefore, seeks to locate such women within a wider framework of female letter-writing, transcending courtly milieux, and to contribute to an important re-examination of the sixteenth century as a period of significant female literary production and comparative advances in women's education and literacy.

The selection of 1603 as the terminal boundary for the study is shaped by the amount of primary sources. A preliminary survey of repositories in England, Scotland, Wales, and Ireland yielded in excess of 10,000 manuscript letters sent by women during the period to 1642, a much higher rate of survival than had previously been thought. Placing the onus on breadth and comprehensiveness of inquiry resulted in the imposition of narrower chronological constraints on the material and the restriction of focus to England, rather than concentrating on certain types of letters or specific collections, or undertaking a detailed study of individual letter-writers, families, or counties. For the Tudor period alone, a comprehensive search of available archival materials produced over 650 individual women who conducted correspondence between 1540 and 1603, and a largely untapped corpus of more than 3,000 manuscript letters.[5] Social and cultural history, however, of course does not fit the neat periodization of political narrative, with its clearly defined regnal years; thus, the cut-off point of Elizabeth's reign is not rigidly enforced, and examples are sometimes drawn from later decades to suggest the continuity and change of social structures and cultural trends, and to look forward to later early modern developments.

SURVIVAL OF DOCUMENTS

Research for this book is based on investigations of the manuscript holdings of most major repositories in the British Isles and the United States, including libraries, county records offices, and private collections. The aim here was a comprehensive study of women's letters. The book, however, does not attempt to offer an exhaustive catalogue of women's extant letters, and doubtless many items remain undiscovered, quietly decaying in private muniments rooms. In terms of how representative this material is, it is perhaps significant that almost all the

---

[4] Wall, 'Elizabethan Precept', 27; Klene, 'Recreating the Letters of Lady Anne Southwell', 246; Key, 'Letters and Will of Lady Dorothy Bacon', 77.

[5] The letters of Mary I and Elizabeth I are excluded from these figures, since most are official documents. For Mary's correspondence see Knighton, *CSP, Domestic, Mary I*. On Elizabeth's letters see Doran, 'Elizabeth's Religion', 699–720; Mueller, 'To My Very Good Brother', 1063–71; Harrison, *Letters of Queen Elizabeth*; May, *Queen Elizabeth: Selected Works*; Marcus, Mueller and Rose, *Elizabeth I: Collected Works*; Marcus and Mueller, *Elizabeth I: Autograph Compositions*. See also Crawford, *Letters of the Queens of England*.

collections consulted where there were records of male letter-writers supplied at least several examples of women's letters. Manuscript letters survive in several main types of archive: government state papers, legal and other institutional records, and in the papers of families and individuals.[6] Examination of these diverse archives presents a broader range of material than would otherwise have been produced by a study concentrating on a limited number of family collections. The repositories containing women's letters are geographically widespread, representing a large proportion of England, including the remoter Northern and Western counties, the Marches, and the Isle of Wight.[7] The survival of large numbers of women's letters in the State Papers, such as the records of the Privy Council and papers of government officials, including the lord treasurer and principal secretary and other political figures, is partly explained by administrative procedure and the bureaucratic impulse to maintain records. During this period distinctions between 'private' and 'official' papers were not clearly drawn; office-holders such as Burghley and Robert Cecil received both formal and informal secretarial support. Indeed, men like the earl of Essex and Anthony Bacon were also served by private secretariats, which systematically collected and processed paperwork, including correspondence, often producing copies of letters for permanent record.[8] Institutional archives such as Charterhouse Hospital similarly contain women's letters; indeed, many women wrote to the founder, Thomas Sutton, for financial assistance and loans of money.[9] In this manner, the missives dispatched by women to government and institutional bodies and individuals on a range of political, patronage, and business matters have been preserved.

Correspondence also entered the State Papers through interception by government intelligence networks because of its potentially seditious or incriminating nature: several letters from Frances Devereux to her husband the earl of Essex survive among the Cecil Papers at Hatfield House, seized by Robert Cecil's agents prior to the Essex Revolt.[10] Likewise, Anne, countess of Northumberland's

---

[6] While most women's letters survive in manuscript only, numerous are printed, scattered among record society volumes or printed as collections: Wall (ed.), *Two Elizabethan Women*; *Letters of Lady Arbella Stuart*, ed. Steen; *Correspondence of Lady Katherine Paston*, ed. Hughey; *Private Correspondence of Jane Lady Cornwallis*, ed. Braybrooke, and a new edition edited by Moody; 'Letters and Will of Lady Dorothy Bacon', ed. Key; McDonough, 'Life and Letters of Lady Anne Glemham'; *Letters of Dorothy Wadham*, ed. Gardiner; *Letters of Lydia Dugard*, ed. Taylor; *Letters of the Lady Brilliana Harley*, ed. Lewis; *Letters of Dorothy Moore*, ed. Hunter; *Elizabeth Cary, Lady Falkland: Life and Letters*, ed. Wolfe; *Conway Letters*, ed. Nicolson.

[7] On early modern Scottish women's letters see: Trill, 'Early Modern Women's Writing in the Edinburgh Archives', 201–25. The Brogyntyn and Clenennau MSS held at the National Library of Wales contain over 70 letters written by women between 1584 and 1700, and numerous undated letters; the Wynn Family of Gwydir papers are a rich source of seventeenth-century Welsh women's correspondence. Several sixteenth-century female letter-writers feature in the Erdigg MSS at Flintshire Record Office (D/E/2398, 2401). For Irish women's letters see O'Dowd, *History of Women In Ireland*, 226–27; *CSP Relating to Ireland in the Reigns of Henry VIII, Edward VI, Mary, and Elizabeth*.   [8] Hammer, 'The Uses of Scholarship', 39.

[9] GLRO, ACC1876/F/3/1–8: 1589–1611.

[10] Hatfield House, Cecil, 63, fo. 84: 11/8/1599.

letters to her husband and several Scottish lords dispatched in the aftermath of the rising of the Northern earls were confiscated and found their way into Burghley's possession.[11] Indeed, the State Papers Foreign and Domestic consist almost entirely of official papers or letters confiscated by the government, which promotes an event-based, crisis-ridden form of historical narrative. The volume of documents surviving for particular decades often relates to political circumstance; the relatively large numbers of women's letters for the 1530s and 1590s reflect the increased necessity for women to correspond during periods of crisis. The survival of documents for the 1530s, largely among Thomas Cromwell's papers, may also be related to Cromwell's administrative skill.[12] Espionage and intrigue aside, letters of a more intimate nature were among papers confiscated as evidence by officials engaged in legal inquiries. The letters of the mercantile Johnson family, which cover the period 1542–52, were gathered by the Privy Council in 1553 to be used as proof in bankruptcy suits in the Admiralty Court;[13] and the Lisle Letters of the 1530s were seized by the crown during Lord Lisle's trial for treason.[14] Usually recorded miscellaneously as exhibits, letters are also buried among court records, including those of the Courts of Wards and Liveries, Requests, Exchequer, and Chancery, where they were often introduced as evidence.[15]

Women's letters also survive among family papers deposited in the muniments rooms of country houses, though their existence is largely dependent on the propensities of individuals or families to hoard written materials: while certain families patently preserved everything, others kept little or nothing. Large numbers of letters were kept as records for legal or business purposes.[16] Several women, including Lucy Paulet, Margaret Clifford, and Elizabeth Manners, had copies made of important letters that had been sent to government officials.[17] Women's letters were also preserved in contemporary family histories. John Smyth included a letter he received from Lady Katherine Berkeley in his *Lives of the Berkeleys* (1618), on the grounds that it 'demonstrated her wit and intelligence'.[18] Cassandra Willoughby copied out and preserved for posterity many sixteenth-century women's letters in her *History of the Willoughby Family* (1702), letters otherwise lost to historians.[19] Copies of letters by exceptional women were also sometimes printed in early modern histories. Lady Margaret Bryan's letter to Cromwell concerning the education of Princess Elizabeth, and Anne Cecil's letter of complaint to her husband the earl of Oxford, for example, were both incorporated into the historical narratives of John Strype.[20]

[11] HMC, *Salisbury*, ii. 6–9.   [12] Elton, *Tudor Revolution*, 298–9.
[13] Winchester, *Tudor Family Portrait*, 13–14.
[14] *Lisle Letters*, i. p. 5. 'P.' is subsequently used to distinguish page from letter numbers.
[15] e.g. NA, SP46/27–42 (Exchequer Papers); NA, REQ2/157/478; NA, WARD10/22/1/10, 10/2/2/4.   [16] Watt, 'No Writing For Writing's Sake', 123.
[17] BL, Harl., 4713, fo. 260, n.d.; Kendal RO, WD/Hoth, Box 44, n.d; HMC, *Rutland*, i. 245, 3/04/1588.   [18] Broadway, 'John Smyth of Nibley', 83–4.
[19] Nottingham University Library, Middleton MSS; HMC, *Middleton*.
[20] Strype, *Ecclesiastical Memorials*, ii. 255; id., *Annals of the Reformation*, ii. 70.

Occasionally letters also survive in commonplace books or are incidental to other manuscript collections. For example, an original letter from Mary, countess of Pembroke, to the wife of Robert Sidney is contained within a sixteenth-century manuscript volume of poetry in the British Library.[21] Epistles preserved in this manner, separate from large bundles of miscellaneous papers, may conceivably have been retained for sentimental reasons. Furthermore, women as well as men collected, copied, and preserved in manuscript miscellanies and 'letter-books' letters they received and sent, form letters, and copies of exemplary letters of famous persons worth preserving and perhaps imitating.[22] From the seventeenth century onwards collections of women's letters, such as those of Katherine Philips, appeared in printed form.[23]

The survival of some letters, however, was a matter of chance: an early seventeenth-century letter from Lady Gower to her son Thomas, then an undergraduate at Wadham College, Oxford, was discovered serendipitously in 1836 hidden under a floorboard in a college room.[24] Concomitantly, the numbers of women's letters now extant represent only a fraction of those written during the sixteenth century. Large numbers of letters did not survive, having been discarded or lost to disintegration and decay. Although both Barbara Sidney and Mary Baskerville were evidently active letter-writers, only one letter composed by Lady Sidney has been uncovered. In both instances, these women wrote to husbands who were abroad on military service; their side of the correspondence is, therefore, unlikely to have survived due to the difficulties of preserving letters on board ship or on a battlefield. By contrast, the husbands' letters were dispatched to wives at home, where there was clearly greater likelihood of the correspondence's safe-keeping.[25] Alternatively, letters may have been destroyed, and writers often asked addressees to burn confidential or incriminating epistles. Although family collections contain letters of a more 'personal' and intimate nature, the surviving material may well be unrepresentative of the range of letters written during the period. The paucity of missives of a more transient, sexual or overtly emotional nature may be explained by their destruction, their recipients being eager to expunge them from the censure of posterity. Correspondence of particular individuals also commonly survives unequally for different periods of their lifetime; years of marriage or widowhood are usually more fully represented than childhood or adolescence.

The number of surviving women's letters is far outweighed by the number of men's letters remaining, perhaps indicating higher levels of male literacy and

---

[21] BL, Addit., 15232, fo. 1: 9/09/1590.   [22] Braunmuller, *Seventeenth-Century Letter-Book.*

[23] *Collected Works of Katherine Philips*, ii., ed. Thomas; Hageman, 'Making a Good Impression', 39–65.

[24] Davies and Garnett, *Wadham College*, 21, 145. *A Catalogue of the Muniments of Wadham College*, 4/27.

[25] Cecil, 87, fo. 138: to Robert Cecil, 24/08/1601. For Sidney's letters to his wife at Penshurst see CKS, De L'Isle, U1475/C/81; *The Correspondence of Robert Sidney*, ed. Hannay *et al.*; Baskerville's letters to his wife are in BL, Harl, 4762, *passim.*

familiarity with letter-writing, but also likely illustrating the greater range of opportunities that male writers had to employ letters, especially in official or business capacities. Moreover, men's correspondence is more likely to have been intentionally preserved, often as papers relating to their office. Nevertheless, the relative paucity of sixteenth-century correspondence in general, by both men and women, relates to the fact that most business was still conducted face-to-face; letter-writing was often only occasioned by the impossibility or impracticability of meeting in person. Thus, Katherine, countess of Northumberland, in a missive to Burghley wrote, 'I was twise to waite uppon your Lordship at yo[u]r howse but could not finde yo[u]r lo[rdship] at home whereby I am enforced to complaine unto you in wrytinge my great disquiett and discomfort'.[26] Furthermore, many considered letters unsuitable for their requirements, preferring oral methods of communication which they deemed more intimate: Elizabeth Nunne reported to her sister, the wife of Sir Bassingbourne Gawdy, that 'I had thought to haue sene you before this tyme and nowe I had rather speake then write but I ame otherwise letted'.[27] Over the course of the sixteenth century, however, women increasingly relied on the epistolary medium to discharge functions traditionally performed in person or orally by messenger.

LETTERS AND LETTER-WRITERS

Analysis of the social status of female letter-writers indicates that letter-writing during the sixteenth century represents a much larger area of female activity and one that was more socially and geographically diversified than has hitherto been assumed; letter-writing skills extended below the ranks of the aristocracy, court elites, and the wives and daughters of humanists. The majority of known female letter-writers were upper class. Some 60 per cent of women were members of the gentry; 30 per cent of writers were from the nobility. However, a significant proportion of women, almost 10 per cent, were from professional classes and the upper echelons of what can broadly be termed 'middling' groups, the wives or widows of lawyers, clergymen, merchants, and wealthier tradesmen.[28] Jane Yetsweirt, for example, was the wife of a printer; Joan Alleyn was married to the actor Edward Alleyn; Sabine Johnson's husband was the Staple merchant John Johnson. The literary evidence that survives, however, privileges elite and 'literate' women, and may not in fact fully reflect the actual social spread of letter-writing during the 1500s. Indeed, as Ralph Houlbrooke has argued in

---

[26] SP12/206/9: 5/12/1587. See also, Cecil, 183, fo. 76: 6/12/1601.

[27] BL, Eg., 2722, fo. 158: 3/2/n.y.

[28] The social status of sixteenth-century female letter-writers is similar to that recorded by Whyman in the Verney papers for the seventeenth and early eighteenth century: *Sociability and Power*, 6. Barry and Wilson Brooks, *The Middling Sort of People*; Cressy, 'Describing the Social Order', 29–44.

relation to early modern diaries, 'the chances of survival were much higher in muniments rooms of country houses than in towns, where dynastic continuity was far rarer, and residential mobility much greater'.[29]

There is, however, some evidence of women lower down the social scale being involved in letter-writing activities, which acts as a useful corrective to discussions of letters as an elite form. In a few cases actual examples of letters survive.[30] Thomas Sutton, as the founder of Charterhouse Hospital, received correspondence from unfortunate female kinswomen and numerous lower-class women, beseeching him to assist them financially.[31] A few letters also survive from female servants: the wetnurse Jane Baker, close to death, corresponded with Margaret, countess of Bath; Elizabeth Skynner wrote to her mistress Lady Muriel Knyvett; and a letter survives from Lady Grace Mildmay to her housekeeper.[32] For most ordinary women, however, no correspondence survives, yet familiarity or at least contact with epistolary cultures can be inferred from indirect evidence. Women who were only partially literate or unable to write could resort to scriveners or informal scribes to pen their letters for them; epistolary transactions of this sort by women well below elite or mercantile ranks are often recorded in scriveners' accounts or diaries.[33] Likewise, court records indicate that letters may have had a wider social currency than is suggested by actual survival rates of correspondence. In particular, studies of the peculiarities of courtship cases reveal that the exchange of love-letters, tokens, mottoes, fragments of romantic verse, or valentines formed a central part of early modern courtship practices; the literary communication of love in this manner, it was argued, was proof of marital intent.[34] Incidental references to letter-writing activity by lower-class women also exist in John Foxe's *Acts and Monuments*: the wife of Robert Glover corresponded with her husband on spiritual matters during his imprisonment, and Cicely Ormes wrote to the chancellor of the diocese of Norfolk recanting her Catholicism.[35] Finally, Renaissance literature, while it offers abundant examples of fully literate women conversant with epistolary forms, also often evokes a world in which ordinary women, who were partially literate or illiterate, inhabited the intersecting margins of oral and literate cultures in which letters played a pivotal role (see Chapter 5).[36]

---

[29] Houlbrooke, *English Family Life*, 7.

[30] A few letters by ordinary women survive from the seventeenth century, including one by a wetnurse: Mendelson and Crawford, *Women in Early Modern England*, 10.

[31] GLRO, ACC1876/F/3/1–3.

[32] CUL, Hengrave, 88/1, fo. 86; BL, Eg. 2713, fo. 300; Northampton RO, Westmoreland and Apethorpe MSS, W/A, misc., 55, fo. 1.   [33] *Diary of Robert Lowe*, ed. Sachse, 24, 28.

[34] Gowing, *Domestic Dangers*, 160; O'Hara, *Courtship and Constraint*, 70–1.

[35] Penny, 'Family Matters and Foxe's *Acts and Monuments*', 605; Macek, 'Emergence of a Feminine Spirituality', 75.

[36] e.g. Robertson, 'Revenging Feminine Hand', 116–30; Jardine, 'Reading and the Technology of Textual Affect', 78–97.

Looking at marital status, approximately 50 per cent of writers were married, while almost 40 per cent were widows.[37] This perhaps reflects the greater uses for which married women and widows employed correspondence, in order to maintain contact with diverse and far flung networks of family and kin, or to transact business for husbands, family, and themselves. The experiences of single women, however, are less well represented in family letter collections; unmarried women constitute only 10 per cent of writers.[38] Although there is some evidence of young girls writing love-letters, the majority of unmarried women's letters are from daughters to parents.[39] Indeed, several highly calligraphic epistles penned as examples of filial deference survive, presumably preserved for sentimental reasons or as examples of female learning. Survival or non-survival of letters may also reflect male policies of document preservation; correspondence from single women may have been considered less important or less worth keeping than letters from wives and married daughters. Numerous individual writers' letters span several years or decades and different stages of the female life-cycle, including childhood, adolescence, marriage, widowhood, and old age. Indeed, thirty-eight of the women studied wrote both as wives and widows, and for five women their correspondence covers the period before and during marriage, permitting examinations of individual letter-writers at different life stages, witnessing the development over time in female authority, personal confidence, and maturity.

Viewed by decade, the number of women letter-writers increases over the course of the sixteenth century. Approximately thirty women dispatched more than eighty letters during the 1540s, while over 230 female letter-writers are recorded for the 1590s sending well over 800 letters. In particular, the years 1570 to 1603 mark the real explosion in numbers of women writers: over 280 letters by some ninety female letter-writers were discovered for the period 1570 to 1579, and some 150 women sent over 450 items of correspondence during the 1580s. These statistics, although partly related to documentary survival, also reflect greater levels of female literacy and the social extension of letter-writing skills. Moreover, analysing the social and marital status of women chronologically indicates that letter-writing skills became diffused among an expanding range of groups over the course of the century. At the beginning of the period the nobility represent the largest category of female letter-writers, suggesting that the elite were broadly the first and most enthusiastic group to embrace ideas of women's education and literacy, and to utilize letters. However, by the end of the

---

[37] The rank of fathers was used to calculate women's social status, under the assumption that women learned to write as girls; where paternity could not be established, the status of husbands or women's own socio-economic circumstances were used.

[38] O'Day notes that the Bagot correspondence includes very few letters from single women, in contrast with the Ferrar family where unmarried women were involved in household decisions: 'Tudor and Stuart Women', 130. Whyman, 'Gentle Companions', 177–93; Peters, 'Single Women in Early Modern England', 325–45; Froide, *Singlewomen in Early Modern England*.

[39] *Autobiography of Thomas Whythorne*, ed. Osborn, 30–3.

century gentlewomen form the most sizeable group of letter-writers, accounting for almost two-thirds of writers. This reflects a number of factors, including: greater familiarity with letter-writing practices; increased survival of gentry papers, which itself may be partly related to rising literacy levels; and the greater numbers of the gentry class compared to the aristocracy. Additionally, increasing numbers of single women and women of professional and middling status are recorded by the 1590s, revealing the filtering of letter-writing and writing skills further down the social scale to a wider cross-section of women, and the expanding number of ways in which letters were utilized.

The corpus of surviving documents reveals the extensive range of correspondents to whom women dispatched letters. For most women only one or two examples of their correspondence survive; single letters or pairs are often of less scholarly use than larger collections of correspondence, in that they document single uncontextualized snapshots in time of the lives of individual women. However, such small numbers of letters are less an indication of the limited extent of female epistolary activity than of the chance survival of evidence. More than a quarter of female correspondents wrote significant numbers of letters: approximately 130 women wrote between three and ten letters; some thirty-five women composed between eleven and forty-nine missives; and several women, including Elizabeth Bourne, Anne Lady Bacon, Arbella Stuart, and Elizabeth Talbot, countess of Shrewsbury, wrote in excess of seventy letters each. Furthermore, some 25 per cent of women corresponded with more than one person: over 100 women wrote to three or more people; ten dispatched epistles to over ten addressees; and approximately 15 per cent wrote to both men and women. These larger clusters of letters written to various recipients facilitate a more analytical approach to the study of women's letters and letter-writing, allowing examination of individual authors' styles and personal relationships while illuminating the different ways in which women wrote to diverse family members or addressees of varying social status or gender, and delineating the nature and scope of women's epistolary activities. The evidence also enables analysis of several correspondents writing to the same person: in particular, male heads of families received letters from different female family members.

Analysis of letters by recipients reveals that over 50 per cent of correspondence was dispatched to family members. Of these, over half were to members of the 'nuclear' or 'elementary' family group of parents and children.[40] Over 200 letters

---

[40] Analysis of women's letters by recipient reveals that husbands represent 8.5% of the total number of people to whom letters were sent; fathers 2.5%, mothers 1.5%, parents (as a couple) 0.4%, sons 7%, daughters 1%, brothers 7%, sisters 2%, uncles 3%, aunts 0.5%, aunts and uncles (as a couple) 0.2%, nephews 2.5%, nieces 0.3%, male servants 2%, female servants 0.1%, masters 0.3%, mistresses of households 0.3%, monarchs 1%, and tradesmen 0.1%. Other male kin, including grandparents and those referred to as 'cousin', 'kin', or 'kinsman' constitute 12% of recipients; other female kin 2%; male neighbours and friends represent 7.5% of recipients; female neighbours and friends 3.3%. 'Neighbours' are often identified by the fact that letter-writers signed themselves 'your friend and neighbour'. The term 'friend' denotes those whom letter-writers

are from wives to husbands (see Chapter 8); some 110 letters are from daughters to parents, over 200 from mothers to children, and more than 190 from sisters to other siblings. While survival of letters is a factor here, women nonetheless appear to have written more frequently to close family members than to other groups. This supports the view that women's primary loyalties focused on their elementary family from whom they derived greatest emotional and material support.[41] It also suggests a desire or 'duty' among female letter-writers to keep in touch with their nuclear family of origin, as well as the patrilineages of their marital families, a social obligation often registered in familial correspondence.

Beyond immediate family members, women corresponded with various other social groups. More than a quarter of correspondence was sent to kinsfolk: uncles, aunts, grandparents, and wider kinship groups. Evidently literate women sought to foster and maintain kinship links which might later prove profitable emotionally and practically.[42] A small proportion of women's letters were written to servants, masters, and mistresses, largely dealing with the running of estates or households, which permit glimpses of women in positions of authority and command. Letters addressed to 'friends' or 'neighbours' reveal women's roles in establishing social contacts with extra-familial groups, and in the formation of wider epistolary networks and communities. Women also corresponded with, among others, tradesmen, tutors, printers, legal counsel, ecclesiastics, and physicians. Moreover, the most significant group of recipients (in that they account for more than one-third of correspondence) are government officials, to whom women dispatched letters of petition concerning legal and business matters and patronage. These letters, which form the basis of Chapter 9, challenge widely held misconceptions that women's letters, in contrast to men's, are parochial in character, chiefly dealing with 'family life and household matters'.[43] Finally, women also wrote over 100 letters of an 'informal' nature to government officials, either offering thanks and gifts or conveying news. Although seemingly 'familiar' in content, many of these letters were in fact written to oil the wheels of patronage and, therefore, assume an added political importance in the context of the petitioning activity. Indeed, 'networking' letters of thanks and gifts often followed, and sometimes preceded, requests for favour. This acts to blur the boundaries of 'public' and 'private' and the epistolary categories of 'domestic' and 'political' correspondence.

While women's letter-writing activities evidently did extend beyond the family, a woman writer's gender and social status appear to have restricted with whom it was appropriate for her to correspond. Although Amy Dudley, the wife of Lord Robert Dudley, could legitimately write to William Edney, a London

---

addressed as friends and are not identified as kin members or government officials. Finally, government officials constitute 35% of addressees.

[41] Houlbrooke, *English Family*, 18–19; Harris, 'Sisterhood, Friendship', 43.
[42] Cressy, 'Kinship and Kin Interaction', 44–6.
[43] 'Letters and Will of Lady Dorothy Bacon', 77.

tailor well below her in social status with whom she transacted business, other women seemingly experienced difficulty in writing to men of superior status with whom they were poorly acquainted and not related.[44] Martin Bucer's widow expressed anxiety in writing to Thomas Cranmer, then archbishop of Canterbury, whose 'rank and dignity' she claimed 'greatly deter[red]' her 'from writing'.[45] Although Wibrandis Bucer's caution might have been honorific, her situation may also have been complicated by her refugee status. Furthermore, a female writer's marital status could also limit the range of people to whom she could write. Indeed, Lady Elizabeth Russell felt unable as an unmarried woman, albeit a widow, to correspond directly with Henry Grey, earl of Kent, 'bicawse', she maintained, 'He is a widower and I a widdow'.[46] Lady Elizabeth Darcy, who had been recently separated from her husband, in 1595 rebuked Sir George Carew for writing amorous epistles to her. In reply to one of Carew's letters Lady Darcy stated, 'as you are a gentleman so regard my honor and neither write, nor send no more to me, for by the living god, if you doo, I will make it known where it shall be small to y[ou]r credit'.[47] In both cases the writers were concerned to protect their own reputation and sexual honour. Thus, while women maintained and established family and other social relationships through letter-writing, few appear to have cultivated entirely new connections by post; communication by letter was chiefly a way of consolidating existing relationships created through family, county, and court networks. The obvious exception here is letters written cold to government officials relating to patronage suits. And yet the unease of writing to someone unknown is reflected in Jane Roper's letter to Sir Charles Blount in which she described herself as a 'straunger in acquaytaunce vnknowne'.[48]

In terms of the gender of recipients, a substantial proportion of epistles, well over 250, were in fact written to other women.[49] Of these over 120 were to women of the nuclear family; over seventy were to other kinsfolk; and approximately one-quarter were addressed either to friends or neighbours. Indeed, some fifty-five individual women directed letters to other women, indicating female social networks both within and extending outside of the family. Having said this, the number of extant letters written to women is considerably lower than those sent to men. Given that many letters were in fact written to secure material support and advice, women were perhaps more likely to approach men concerning such matters rather than other women, since in a primogeniture society land and resources were most often concentrated in male hands. Indeed, the great majority of women's letters were sent to men, and in

---

[44] BL, Harl., 4712, fo. 277a: 24/08/n.y.
[45] Robinson, *Original Letters*, i. 363: [before 20/04/1552].
[46] Cecil, 30, fo. 26: 27/01/1596.   [47] Hengrave, 88/2 fo. 92: 1595.
[48] BL, Harl., 7002, fo. 16: n.d.
[49] Men account for almost 87% of recipients of letters; women for approximately 13%; and less than 1% of letters were addressed to married couples.

particular to husbands, fathers, sons, and brothers who account for over half of the male recipients. The high proportion of missives directed to these groups is explained by their social and economic importance. As heads of families such men were approached for help and assistance; women also conveyed humble epistles to them as a sign of obedience and respect. In the case of correspondence with husbands the relationship was often more one of partnership, while in that of letters to sons it was often (but far from uniformly) mothers who offered advice or were asked for help, and thus occupied the 'senior' position. Some letters were also addressed to both men and women, especially in the case of married couples. Daughters, for example, wrote to mothers and fathers jointly; nieces to aunts and uncles. Margaret Kitson and her sister Mary each wrote letters addressed to both parents.[50] Likewise, Katherine Everard directed a single letter to her uncle Sir Bassingbourne Gawdy and his wife.[51]

Read for their contents, women's letters outline the breadth of activities in which women engaged: marriage arrangement, the household economy and estate management, domestic and religious patronage, medicine and education, local, national, and European politics. Well over half of the letters relate to business concerns defined in the broadest sense, including legal, land, and rental disputes, discussions of jointures, annuities, and inheritance, and personal suits, suggesting that many women wrote letters for pragmatic reasons, seeking advice and information in their dealings. Yet while practical reasons might spur women in the first place to correspond, a wealth of topics are mentioned in passing in letters that are useful as records to those seeking to reconstruct the everyday lives and experiences of early modern women and the society in which they lived. Women's letters touch on topics as diverse as health, illness, disease and medicine, books and book-ownership, travel and transport, clothes and clothing, gifts and gift-giving, food and drink, jewels and jewellery, houses and gardens, birds and animals, leisure and pastimes, music and instruments, insults and physical violence, hospitality and entertainment, court and parliament news. They tell much about early modern social practices, and the activities that spanned the female life-cycle, including pregnancy, childbirth, breast-feeding, and the selection of godparents; attitudes to the education and upbringing of children; the customs of courtship and marriage arrangement, death and dying, bereavement, funerals, and burials. The recovery of letters in this sense is invaluable in that it helps to incorporate women traditionally 'hidden from history', or marginalized in everyday historical inquiry, into mainstream kinds of social, cultural, economic, political, and religious history. Furthermore, while broad similarities exist between men's and women's letters in terms of content, there are also marked differences. As expected, women might discuss women's affairs; indeed, Barbara Harris, using early Tudor women's correspondence, argues for a

---

[50] Hengrave, 88/2, fo. 58: 27/05/n.y.; ibid., 88/2, fo. 61: 01/04/n.y.
[51] BL, Eg., 2722, fo. 32: n.d.

distinctly 'female point of view' about pregnancy and childbirth.[52] Furthermore, female letter-writers, as Anne Laurence and Rosemary O'Day have argued, bring an alternative viewpoint to those of men on social affairs.[53] Anne Bacon's correspondence, for example, illustrates the ability of widows to intervene in ecclesiastical affairs.[54] Moreover, letters offer a unique perspective on early modern women, different from male-voiced prescriptive literature and sources such as diaries, which generally conform to strict religious interpretative models.

The concept of the 'everyday' in relation to early modern letters, however, is not unproblematic.[55] While letters often contain incidental information that provides useful insights into the continuities of life, correspondence was often occasioned by practical concerns, crises, and events. As O'Day has importantly reminded us, letters often 'focus upon events which individuals considered of great import-ance—for example, being in dire need, in serious debt, in pursuit of a suitor, in search of preferment, in a state of grief, or in need of a service'.[56] The danger is for historians to privilege too highly these events, to overplay the significance that they played in women's lives, to prefer crisis, change, and peculiarity to what is mundane, humdrum, and usual. In actual fact, letters represent a mere snapshot in time, a view of women's lives as static rather than evolving, and the relationships that correspondence documents as constant and unchanging, rather than fluctu-ating and changing. It is thus difficult to reconcile the juxtaposition between what is extraordinary and ordinary, and what is continuous and changing. Furthermore, in no way do letters reflect everyday practices in any universal sense: although letter-writing was not exclusively an elite activity, the women whose letters survive are largely members of the nobility and gentry, and mercantile and professional groups. Indeed, the sixteenth century was an age when to be literate was to be in a minority, and where the propensity to preserve correspondence and chance archival survival ensured historical posterity.

In practice, individual letters are rarely limited to single issues but instead tend to discuss a range of subjects. Indeed, the spontaneity of women's familiar letter-writing often provides a haphazard, almost 'stream-of-consciousness' or conversational quality to the correspondence, writers seemingly indiscriminately setting down topics as and when they entered their heads. For example, in 1572 Lady Audrey Aleyn wrote at some length to her brother Thomas Lord Paget concerning both domestic and political matters. She thanked him for his letters and wished his wife well in childbirth, discussing the provision of a wet-nurse and plans for the forthcoming christening, telling him that astrology had indi-cated that the child would be a girl: 'I could make you somewhat affeard

[52] Harris, 'Property, Power and Personal Relations', 606–32.
[53] Laurence, 'Begging Pardon for all Mistakes', 203–4; O'Day, 'Tudor and Stuart Women', 128.
[54] e.g. BL, Lansd., 43, fos. 119–20: 26/02/1585.
[55] On the 'Renaissance everyday' see Fumerton, *Cultural Aesthetics*; ead. and Hunt, *Renaissance Culture and the Everyday*; Braudel, *Civilization and Capitalism I: The Structures of Everyday Life*.
[56] O'Day, 'Tudor and Stuart Women', 129.

of a gyrle, for that Femynine signes rule much this yere.' Lady Aleyn's letter continues by detailing the progress of her brother's and her own suits at court, requesting a hawk for Lord Cobham, and outlining money matters in a postscript.[57] Likewise, in a letter to her daughter Elizabeth, Susannah Darnell interwove commendations to various family members with discussions of food, money, tokens, servants, her purchases of clothing and gifts, and Christmas preparations. Furthermore, the main body of the letter is followed by a series of random postscripts continuing on the margins of the paper and filling the entire page. These include details of further gifts and food items sent, snippets of news, and prescriptions for her daughter Margaret's education.[58] In general, this protean character of women's domestic epistolary writing lends an immediacy and richness uncharacteristic of other literary forms.

Women's letters survive in far greater numbers than any other form of women's writing for the sixteenth century. By comparison, the number of diaries, personal memoirs, and other 'autobiographical' types of writing prior to 1600 is very small. Extant diaries are also often more descriptive than analytical, conforming to conventional—usually religious—patterns and models.[59] In particular, diaries and memoirs such as those of Lady Margaret Hoby and Lady Grace Mildmay record events within a strict spiritual—or more precisely Protestant—explanatory framework, an account of one's daily actions or life before the eyes of God.[60] Correspondence, on the other hand, is generally unconstrained by such religious interpretative straitjackets, though letters to confessors or preachers performed a similar function of introspective religious scrutiny. On the whole, sixteenth-century women's letters reveal little ideologically about their writers' religious views, contrasting with other forms of women's manuscript writing.[61] While confessional identities emerge in the guise of female religious patrons preferring candidates to ecclesiastical office; in pious maternal counsel, such as the Puritan Anne Bacon's deep concern for the welfare of her son Anthony's soul; or forged (or suppressed in the case of recusants) in conflict with the authorities, the manuscript letter was usually not a forum for religious discussion or controversial doctrinal views. During a period of religious upheaval, correspondence was perhaps considered too insecure a medium for confessional matters. Although female letter-writers often made

---

[57] Staffs RO, Paget Papers, D603/K/1/3/40: 25/10/1572.

[58] SP46/24/224: [temp. James I].

[59] On early modern diaries see Houlbrooke, *English Family Life*; Macfarlane, *Family Life of Ralph Josselin*, esp. ch. 1; Foisil, 'Literature of Intimacy', 327–61. On female diarists see Mendelson, 'Stuart Women's Diaries', 181–210; Botonaki, 'Seventeenth-Century Englishwomen's Spiritual Diaries', 3–21.

[60] *Diary of Lady Margaret Hoby*, ed. Moody; Pollock, *With Faith and Physic*. Dowling and Shakespeare, 'Religion and Politics in Mid Tudor England', 94–102. Cf. *Diaries of Lady Anne Clifford*, ed. Clifford.

[61] Trill, 'Religion and the Construction of Femininity', 30–55; Hobby, *Virtue of Necessity*, 26–75; Hannay, *Silent But For the Word*.

sense of actions and daily episodes and ordeals in religious terms, familiar epistles reveal a broader range of modes of thought, both Catholic and secular. As 'ego-documents' emanating from and concerned with an individual female writer, such letters more commonly than diaries exhibit women's judgements and comments concerning people, events, and things; they express opinions and decisions, and convey feelings and emotional states. In short, letters shed light on the ways in which women understood, interpreted, and articulated their thoughts and experiences. Often viewed as a literary site where women could uninhibitedly lay bare their inner most feelings, such letters may be studied for what they reveal about the self and selfhood. Yet they are not transparent historical sources, windows into women's souls, capable of reflecting unmediated women's true 'inner selves', but rather complex documents subject to generic and linguistic conventions; texts that were socially and culturally coded, and the products of specific historical moments produced during separation.

Characteristically read as private, individual, intimate, and spontaneous, the early modern letter-writing process was in actual practice often a much more collaborative, communal, and strategic form, even among those women capable of writing for themselves. The nature of correspondence is also closely linked to the mechanics of letter-writing: the manner of composition and dispatch. Letters were dictated to or penned by secretaries; drafted, revised, and sometimes even ghosted by third parties; composed from notes and modelled on epistolary exemplars or formulaic templates. Chapter 3 outlines the nuanced collaborative textual methods by which letters were constructed, thus challenging scholarly notions of *personal* correspondence as private and singular, and complicating our understanding of early modern subjectivity and authorship, and the elusive 'female voice'. In some instances women's texts were ghosted or manipulated by men, which problematizes the very concept of *women's* writing as a uniquely female preserve. Likewise, the ways in which letters were delivered and read further unpicks perceptions of correspondence as intimate communication between two parties. Letters were sometimes dispatched unsealed to be read communally; passed around family and friends, forwarded to third parties, and sometimes read aloud; while occasionally they reached a wider public audience through circulation in manuscript by 'scribal publication' or in printed form. In a period prior to the establishment of the post office, the bearer was intrinsically bound up with the epistolary exchange, as the conveyor of reciprocal oral report, and in many cases as the physical representative of the letter-writer.

The generic complexities of sixteenth-century women's letters further emerge when one attempts to impose on them definitions of 'public' and 'private' forms of writing, meanings which inadequately describe the ways in which letters functioned. Traditionally distinctions have been drawn between published printed works aimed at a 'public' audience, on the one hand, which—with the exception of religious writings and translations—are viewed largely as a male concern during the Tudor period; and manuscripts, such as autobiographies, diaries, and letters intended for 'private', informal use and limited circulation, on the other hand, which are deemed to have been more acceptable modes of writing for women denied access to publication. These differences stem from modern concepts of authorship, readership, and literary forms based upon the commercialization of print. Such schematic divisions oversimplify the varied sophistication of epistolary writing, and obscure the diversity and often the formality of women's letter-writing activities. Indeed, Margaret Ezell notably argues that letters were in fact 'an established literary form in the Renaissance and the seventeenth century', and 'highly conventional public forms of address'.[62] Following her trail-blazing lead, scholars such as Elizabeth Clarke, Jonathan Gibson, and Victoria Burke have interrogated the categorization of women's manuscript writings (letters, diaries, spiritual journals, commonplace books, manuscript miscellanies, and receipt books) as essentially private, inward-looking forms, arguing that women often wrote manuscripts for public circulation with a wider political significance than that of recording personal thoughts or spiritual progress.[63] In much the same way, seemingly 'private' letters in several instances were copied and circulated as texts within manuscript communities, and functioned in ways both intended and unintended by the original letter-writer.[64]

THE MATERIALITY OF LETTERS AND LETTER-WRITING

Manuscript letters, as A. R. Braunmuller, Jonathan Gibson, and others have importantly shown, should not merely be viewed as texts or documents, but as complex forms that registered meaning both textually and materially.[65] The placing on the page of subscriptions, addresses, signatures, and superscriptions or salutations attribute significant meaning as important signifiers of social status and deference, as is indicated in letter-writing guides from the period. The first English epistolary manual to be published, William Fulwood's *The Enemie of Idlenesse* (1568), outlines rules for the positioning and wording of the superscription in a letter:

which must be doone according to the estate of the writer, and the qualitie of the person to whom wee write: For to our superiors wee must write at the right side in the neither end of the paper, saying: By your most humble and obedient sonne, or seruaunt, &c. Or,

[62] Ezell, *Writing Women's Literary History*, 34. Guillén, 'Notes Toward the Study of the Renaissance Letter', 70–101.

[63] Clarke, 'Elizabeth Jekyll's Spiritual Diary', 218–37; Burke and Gibson, *Early Modern Women's Manuscript Writing*.   [64] Daybell, 'I wold wyshe my doings', 137–8.

[65] Braunmuller, 'Accounting for Absence', 47–56; Gibson, 'Significant Space', 1–9; Steen, 'Reading Beyond the Words', 55–69; Walker, 'Manners on the Page', 307–29.

yours to commaund, &c. And to our equals we must write towards the middest of the paper, saying: By your faithfull friend for euer, &c. Or, yours assured, &c. To our inferiours wee may write on high at the left hand, saying: By yours, &c.[66]

Angel Day similarly connects the size of gap left between the body of the letter and the signature with the relative social standing of writer and addressee, but does not follow Fulwood in correlating social status with the left and right placing of the signature:

writing to anye personne of accompt, by how much the more excellent hee is in calling from him in whose behalfe the Letter is framed, by so muche the lower, shall the subscription therevnto belonging, in any wise be placed.

And if the state of honour of him to whome the Letter shall be directed doe require so much, the verye lowest margent of paper shall doe no more but beare it, so be it the space be seemelye for the name, and the roome fayre inough to comprehende it, which subscriptions in all sorts to be handled shall passe this order or substaunce to be framed.[67]

The spacing between different parts of the letter—between the main body of the letter, the subscription, salutation, and signature—was also important. The size of paper used for the letter, too, could show social deference. Antoine de Courtin's *The Rules of Civility*, which was translated into English in 1671, prescribed the use of 'large' sheets of paper, even for short letters, as a mark of respect.[68] In sum, these prescriptions concerning the physical layout and spacing of letters indicate that the more socially esteemed the addressee, the more blank paper with which they should be honoured. Conversely, given the expense of paper, the leaving of large gaps of blank space, itself an act of conspicuous consumption, registered the letter-writer's own social worth.[69] Use of deferential material forms is particularly pronounced in letters of petition, and also when writing to senior family members, when it was useful to inculcate a sense of reverence and social inferiority. Only when proper attention is paid to the material aspects of manuscript letters—which in addition includes the type of paper used, the way that it was folded, the use of wax, seals, and ribbon or string, the form and placing of the address—is it possible fully to decode the meanings of early modern letters, which presents distinct problems for those relying on modern printed editions of correspondence.[70]

[66] Sig. B2ᵛ. Fulwood's rules largely follow those outlined in the major source for his work, [Le Moyne], *Le stile de manière de composer, dicter, et escrire toute sorte d'espistres* (Lyons, 1566). Gibson, 'Significant Space', 2, 8 n. 10.

[67] Day, *The English Secretorie* (1586), sig. C2ʳ.   [68] de Courtin, *Rules of Civility*, sig. 11ᵛ.

[69] The way that a letter was folded equally signified the sender's status: Braunmuller, 'Accounting for Absence', 55.

[70] Hunter, 'How to Edit a Seventeenth-Century Manuscript', 277–310; Braunmuller, 'Editing Elizabethan Letters', 185–99; Klene, 'Recreating the Letters of Lady Anne Southwell', 239–52; Steen, 'Behind the Arras', 229–38. Several recent editions have sought to represent in print the material aspects of early modern letters: *Collected Works of Mary Sidney*, i, ed. Hannay, Kinnamon, and Brennan; Braunmuller, *Seventeenth-Century Letter-Book*.

The extent to which sixteenth-century female letter-writers followed the rules of spacing is uneven, as is true for men.[71] That women were aware of these conventions is borne out by analysis of the layout of their letters, which yields many examples where 'significant space' was used according to the status of the addressee and the purpose and occasion of writing. Lady Mary Keys's letters to William Cecil after her dismissal from court indicate her use of space as a unified part of her petitioning strategy. A letter of 6 September 1566, lamenting that she had been 'a greatte whill in the quenese maiestes desplessur', left a large gap between the last line of the letter and the closing subscription and signature ('your pore frynde to comande duringe my lyffe Mary Graye'), which was placed in the right-hand bottom corner of the letter, a visual representation of her penitent submission.[72] This manner of deferential signing, emphasizing as it did the letter-writer's inferior social status, need, and dependency on the addressee, was common practice among female petitioners in dire straits.[73]

The correspondence of Mary Herbert (née Sidney), countess of Pembroke, perhaps best illustrates a woman's understanding and use of the conventions of space for persuasive or honorific effect. In letters to Sir Robert Cecil, then secretary of state, the countess habitually left a small deferential horizontal gap on the first line between the mode of address, 'Sir', and the start of the letter.[74] On occasion she exaggerated the deployment of space where circumstances demanded greater deference, even though in terms of social hierarchy the countess could consider herself Cecil's superior. In a letter of 3 August 1602, which appealed to Cecil to help with administrative problems relating to the Castle and Borough of Cardiff, Mary Herbert left a horizontal gap between the opening address and the first line. The significance of this 'blanke' space she expressed at the outset of the letter:

Sir

Not that I can make any retorne vnto yow worthey of yow; but that this blanke may wittness what I woold had I powre to expres more then words can. A mynd more then thankefull, & a thankefullness answerable to that mynd w[hi]ch thus in paper forme (since otherwise it can not present the willing desire to pay the debtt it owes) doth onely apeere before yow.[75]

In a letter beseeching the queen to take her son, William, Lord Herbert, into her service at court, she left roughly an inch-and-a-half gap between the salutation 'Most sacred Soueraigne' and the body of the letter. A similar-sized gap was left in the concluding salutations between 'yor hyghnes most bownd' and 'the humblest of y[ou]r creturs', with the signature appearing in the bottom right-hand corner of the page, a sign of complete submission.[76] This form of

[71] Braunmuller, 'Accounting for Absence', 47–56; Gibson, 'Significant Space', 1–9.

[72] SP12/40/61: 06/09/1566. Cf. SP12/41/37, 02/12/1566. Interestingly, in none of her letters to Cecil does Lady Mary sign her surname as 'Keys', an act of defiance unlikely to have done her any favours. [73] Cecil, 53, fo. 87: 07/1597.

[74] Cecil, 53, fo. 6: 08/1597; 55 fo. 81: 29/09/1597.

[75] Cecil, 94, fo. 106. See also Cecil, 55, fo. 81: 29/09/1597. [76] Cecil, 90, fo. 147: 1601.

deferential signing was entirely conventional when writing to the monarch.[77] Male suitors writing to high-ranking women also observed the conventions of deferential signature placement. A letter from Laurence Cockson to Lady Burghley requesting her to intreat her husband in his behalf concerning his oil-making is signed in the bottom right-hand corner.[78]

Alternatively, the absence of respectful gaps in women's letters was used to indicate social superiority or equality. While the countess of Pembroke deployed space for tactical purposes in letters to Cecil and the queen, in writing to John Thynne, a man well below her in social standing, her letters left large areas of blank space after the signature to register her higher social standing.[79] A six-line letter thanking Thynne for his 'favour' to the 'wronged' Alice Blage filled merely a quarter of the page, including the closing salutation and signature, which were written immediately after the date, '1 of October. 1595'.[80] In a similar way, the incredibly status-conscious Lady Elizabeth Russell used the layout in her letters as a way of reinforcing the social hierarchy, particularly in writing to her nephew Robert Cecil. Where the prolixity of her letters permitted room, and did not force her to cram initials 'ER' into the bottom corner or along the margin, Lady Russell squashed her signature as close as she could to the last line of the letter.[81] She was in this sense trying to assert her own superior social standing in relation to her nephew, which was perhaps a calculated insult.

Handwriting—the kinds of hands or scripts used for letters—similarly obtains significant meaning.[82] Sara Jayne Steen has shown that Arbella Stuart wrote two different hands, an informal italic hand for familiar letters and rough drafts of court letters, and an 'elegant and fashionable formal italic hand' for presentation copies of her letters.[83] In letters of petition too, different kinds of handwriting could signify deference. Great care was often therefore taken in writing letters that were to be presented: Mary Herbert's holograph letter to Elizabeth I was penned in a neat hand, with none of the deletions and ink-blots characteristic of much of her other holograph correspondence.[84] Scribes were often used to make presentation copies of letters. Margaret Hawkin's autograph letter to the queen was written in an immaculate secretary hand, while for her 29 January 1603 letter to the queen, Elizabeth, countess of Shrewsbury, used the same scribe as for a letter written four days later to Robert Cecil.[85] The majority of surviving women's letters to the queen are in fact scribal. While a holograph hand connoted a certain intimacy between writer and addressee, it may be that

---

[77] e.g. Cecil, 42, fo. 48 (Margaret Hawkins), Cecil, 135, fos. 112, 127 (countess of Shrewsbury). Men also followed this convention in letters to Elizabeth: Cecil, 121, fo. 44 (George Carew); Cecil, 55, fo. 4 (Thomas Lord Howard).   [78] BL, Lansd., 28, fo. 52: 23/07/1579.

[79] May, 'Two Unpublished Letters', 88–97.

[80] Longleat House, Thynne, VI, fo. 311ʳ: 01/10/1595. See also, Thynne, VII, fo. 280ʳ: 27/09/1603.   [81] Cecil, 43, fo. 34: 01/08/1596.

[82] Daybell, 'Ples acsep thes my skrybled lynes', 207–23; Gibson, 'Letters', 615–19.

[83] *Letters of Lady Arbella Stuart*, 107, 111–13.   [84] Cecil, 90, fo. 147.

[85] Cecil, 42, fo. 48: 16/07/1596, Cecil, 135 fo. 127, 29/01/1603, Cecil, 135 fo. 129: 02/02/1603.

such an intimacy was inappropriate when writing to the monarch; to use a secretary was more formal, distancing oneself from the act of writing. Equally, the high proportion of scribal and holograph neat presentation letters to government officials may indicate something of the formality of the occasion of writing.

During the sixteenth century letters were generally written on paper rather than parchment or velum. The pieces of paper used for letters were cut from sheets measuring 35 centimetres by $47\frac{1}{2}$ centimetres.[86] The actual size of letters varied according to length of message and personal practice.[87] Numerous women utilized a full sheet of paper for only half a page of writing, signifying due deference to their recipient or their own high social standing; others sought to fill the entire space, cramming the margins with information, and turning over the page to continue on the reverse; certain women wrote on minute scraps of paper, trimming off any excess; others were impelled by urgency to write on what came easily to hand. In terms of paper, size was important: Mary, countess of Pembroke's brief correspondence with John Thynne extended to no more than a few lines, yet she asserted her superior status by utilizing an entire sheet of paper, an act that could also demonstrate humility.[88] Conversely, Thomas Compton felt obliged to apologize to his mistress Lady Mary Powell for the 'poore peece of paper' on which his letter was written.[89] Size of paper was also a matter of household economy; many of Elizabeth Bourne's missives after her separation from her husband were penned on small pieces of paper.[90] Likewise, Margaret Trew's missives to her brother Walter Bagot were written on a cropped half-sheet of paper,[91] while Susannah Darnell filled entirely the pages of her letters, turning the paper on its side to append a cramped series of postscripts.[92] Letters commonly ran to more than one side, which is in itself telling, indicating the prolixity of a given letter-writer, and suggesting sentimental or emotional reasons for writing. Anne Hungerford wrote a letter of more than six sides in length to her female confidante Dorothy Essex.[93] Meryell Littleton's letters to her aunt Lady Muriel Knyvett sometimes ran to more than one sheet of paper.[94]

Women's requests for writing paper are occasionally glimpsed in letters: Dorothy Gamage, for example, wrote to her husband asking him to 'send us some paper to write letters'.[95] Household accounts also reveal purchases of paper,

[86] Hunter, *Papermaking*, 229. Vellum was expensive, and rarely used for letter-writing; it was reserved for presentation copies of literary works, title deeds, and other legal documents where preservation was important.

[87] St Clare Byrne argues that uniform sheets of paper were usually $12\frac{1}{2} \times 16\frac{1}{2}$ or 17 inches, which folded in half made a four-page letter, or cut in half provided a single sheet of $12\frac{1}{2} \times 8\frac{1}{4}$ inches: *Lisle Letters*, ii. 103. [88] Thynne, VI, fos. 280^r, 311^r: 27/09/1603, 1/10/1595.

[89] Folger, X.c.51 (39): 14/03/1633. Compton's letter was approximately 'one-quarter of a standard-size letter': Stewart and Wolfe, *Letterwriting in Renaissance England*, 51.

[90] BL, Addit., 23212, *passim*. [91] Folger, L.a.900: 30/04/[1614?].

[92] SP46/24/224: [temp. James I]. [93] SP15/18/19: 25/03/1570.

[94] BL, Eg., 2715, fos. 93, 96, 101, 114, 129, 194, 300–1. [95] SP46/60/31: 11/05/1580.

which was a relatively expensive item.[96] The sheets used, however, differ greatly in quality, as did the quality of paper available at the time: the best paper was creamy coloured, while inferior grades were brown or grey.[97] A large proportion of the letters examined also feature watermarks, which can help in dating letters and in identifying where the paper was purchased.[98] In exceptional circumstances, in urgency, haste, under pressure, or imprisoned, letters were penned on other materials at hand. Elizabeth Wetherton wrote to her mother on a fragment of printed breviary with plainsong notation, presumably because paper was in short supply.[99] The paper used was sometimes specially decorated for purposes of presentation: Anne Clifford and Alathea Talbot both wrote on paper painted with a colourful floral border design.[100] The material sites used for letter-writing are thus suggestive of the circumstances under which they were composed.

As well as paper, a range of other materials was employed in the task of writing letters: pens and penknives for cutting and recutting quills; feathers of varying types to turn into quills (goose feathers were the most popular, but others were also used, including raven, crow, duck, peacock, turkey, and swan, which were the favoured quills of Elizabeth I); ink and its accoutrements, an inkpot or inkhorn, as well as a dust box, sand box, or pounce pot for sprinkling sand onto a manuscript in order to blot wet ink; wax, string, ribbons, seals, and signets used for sealing correspondence.[101] Writing in early modern England was quite a performance; Keith Thomas has remarked on the laborious nature of the technologies associated with writing.[102] The lessons of the writing arts, however, were taught from a young age. Writing manuals of the time aimed at a male and female audience provided basic guidance in penmanship. John deBeau Chesne and John Baildon's *A Booke Containing Divers Sortes of Hands* (1569), a Bodleian copy of which contains the ownership mark of Theophila Hackett, includes rules for children to write by, and instructions of 'how to make ink', 'how to make a pen', 'how to hold a pen', 'how to sit when writing', and 'how to write faire'.[103] Likewise, Martin Billingsley's *The Pen's Excellencie* (1618) contains 'rules for making a pen' and 'observations for holding a pen'.[104] Francis Clement's *The Petie Schole* (1587) outlined the materials needed for writing, and how to choose paper and quills.[105]

The purchase of ink and seals, and payment of letter-bearers, are recorded in household accounts, further suggesting that letter-writing for women was

---

[96] The earl of Leicester's accounts show several purchases of paper: 'Item for i quire browne paper and one white vjd' 'Item to Mr Bewe for paper by him bought at sundry times ijs iiijd': *Household Accounts and Disbursement Books of Robert Dudley*, ed. Adams, 43, 47. Hunter, *Papermaking*, 241.   [97] Hunter, *Papermaking*, 224.
[98] Briquet, *Les Filigranes*; Heawood, *Watermarks*.   [99] SP46/24/91: [temp. Mary I/Eliz I].
[100] *Proud Northern Lady*, 43; Durant, *Bess of Hardwick*, 217, 245 n. 2.
[101] 'Pounce', a fine sand was also used in the preparation of paper for writing. Finlay, *Western Writing Implements*.   [102] Thomas, 'Meaning of Literacy', 97–131.
[103] Bodl. Douce B675 (sig. G2).   [104] Sigs. 39ᵛ–40ᵛ.   [105] pp. 52–62.

an activity intimately connected with household duties. The second earl of Salisbury's Housebook of Gorhambury recorded payment of 5*d.* for purchase of 'Red inke and bottle' for the week ending 26 November 1637.[106] Recipes for making ink are frequently recorded in household manuals. *A Booke of Secrets* (1596) contained several different methods including recipes 'To make Inke to write vpon paper', 'To make Inke for parchment', 'To make inke vpon a suddaine, to serue in an extremitie', as well as instructions for making invisible ink, and suggested that 'a little wormewood water' should be added to the ink in order to deter mice and moths from eating the paper.[107] Thomas Lupton's *A Thousand Notable Things of Sundrie Sorts* (1579) deals with the preservation of letters, detailing how to prevent mice from eating them and how to treat paper to prevent it from burning; while *The Arte of Limming* (1573) explains how to make different-coloured ink and powder to apply to parchment so that it will receive writing.[108] Manuscript commonplace books and household receipt books contained similar instructions, either copied from printed works or passed on orally, and noted down for remembrance. The Dering Family Remembrance Book contained 'A receipt to make good Inke';[109] Elizabeth Bourne transcribed a recipe for making ink into her manuscript receipt book.[110]

Turning from writing materials to consider how letters were sent, the preparation of letters for dispatch involved its own attendant material idiosyncrasies. Envelopes were not used with English letters until the nineteenth century; instead letters were folded into a rectangular packet approximately 8 by 10 centimetres. The standard 'tuck and seal' format of folding involved creasing the letter twice horizontally, then folding it twice vertically, before tucking the left portion inside the right one, and sealing the seam with wax.[111] In most instances letters were sealed for purposes of security, to avoid prying eyes. Wax seals, where they remain intact, often bear armorial or family crests, or in the case of government officials a badge of office; but more often what remains are the fragments, faint traces, indents, or impressions of seals.[112] Remnants of string or floss used in combination with seals have also been preserved in numerous cases. Jane Skipwith's romantic correspondence with her cousin Lewis Bagot, for example, was sealed with two red seals and blue-and-red floss as a sign of intimacy.[113] Of particular note is a letter from Maria Thynne to her mother-in-law Joan Thynne, in which a lock of the sender's red hair remains attached to

[106] Munby, *Early Stuart Household Accounts.*
[107] W[illiam] P[hillip], *A Booke of Secrets* (1596), sigs. A3ʳ–B2ʳ.
[108] Stewart and Wolfe, *Letterwriting in Renaissance England*, 182; Anon, *The Arte of Limming* (1573), fo. viii.
[109] Folger, V.b.296: 'Dering Family Remembrance Book *c.*1580–1644', fo. 23.
[110] Daybell, 'Elizabeth Bourne', 24.
[111] Preston and Yeandle, *English Handwriting*, 60; *Lisle Letters*, i. p. 103.
[112] Ellis, *Catalogue of Seals in the Public Record Office.*
[113] Folger, L.a.852, L.a.853: 14, 17/04/[1610].

the seal, which was presumably intended as a sign of amity.[114] While sealing letters indicates concern with privacy, the seals themselves could also convey emotional sentiments; black seals were used in mourning.[115] A seal also acted as a personal mark of authentication (literally, a seal of approval), a guarantee along with a signature that a letter was genuine. Frances Dayrell sent to Mary Bagot an acquittance for £30, to which she added, '[I] have put to my seale and sett to my hande'; Lady Cooke signed and sealed an acquittance for one John Brewer as proof that she had received from him £100.[116] If a letter were fastened with another's seal it was uncertain whether or not the supposed signatory had read and approved the letter as sent. Furthermore, when a seal was broken on arrival, recipients feared for the contents of their letters. Thus, John Husee informed his master Lord Lisle that a letter containing a certificate from the Friars of Calais would need to be sent again, because 'the seal by carriage was melt and marred' and thus he feared it 'will scant be allowed'.[117] Records survive of women having their own personal seals, rather than using a family or household seals: a letter from Anthony Bacon mentions sending his mother a 'seale', and elsewhere Anne Bacon refers to her 'seale ring'; and Richard Petre paid 4 shillings for a seal for his wife in December 1597.[118] Finally, recipes for sealing wax of different colours also appear in household manuals: John Partridge's *The Treasurie of Commodious Conceits* (1591) includes instructions 'to make red sealing wax', and *The Arte of Limming* explains how to make red and green sealing wax.[119]

In addition to folding and sealing, letters were superscribed on the folded outside sheet (the address leaf), either by women themselves or by secretaries. In cases of secretarially written letters, it was common for secretaries to pen as well as address correspondence; letters that were personally written were also usually addressed by women with their own hand, though this was not always the case. A holograph letter from Jane Ashley, for example, was addressed in the hand of a secretary 'to the right wor[shipfu]ll and my especiall good freind Walter Bagott Esq: at his house at Blythfeld bee d[elivere]d'.[120] Addresses usually gave the name of both the recipient and the place where the letter should be delivered; the latter, where included, usually mentioned a house, or town and in some cases a hostelry where the recipient was staying. Other directions for delivery were rather more vague: Jane Barlow wrote on the back of a letter: 'Give this to my father in Lancashire.'[121] Formulas of address, however, vary greatly, depending largely

---

[114] *Two Elizabethan Women*, 21 Wall, 'Deference and Defiance', 77–93. Fletcher, *Gender, Sex and Subordination*, pl. 40.   [115] Folger, X.d.375, n.d. See also, Folger, X.d.490 (3).
[116] Folger, L.a.407: 26/11/1570; Joseph P. Regenstein Library, University of Chicago, Bacon Manuscripts of Redgrave Hall, 4222: 13/10/1615.   [117] *Lisle Letters*, iv. p. 282.
[118] LPL, Bacon, 656, fo. 7: 24/03/1596; Bacon, 656, fo. 47: Anne Bacon to Anthony Bacon, n.d. Lady Bacon's reference to her 'seale ring', refers to a signet, a small seal fixed into a finger-ring. Seals also came in the form of small metal moulds or seal matrices. Folger, MS V.a.334, fo. 23ᵛ.
[119] *Treasurie of Commodious Conceits*, ch. 7. Bodl. 8° F 8 (6) Linc. contains the name Catherine Haydell. Anon, *Arte of Limming* (1573), fo. xᵛ.   [120] Folger, L.a.17: c.1605.
[121] SP/12/158/6: 10/01/1583.

upon the rank of the recipient and their relationship to the writer. In some letters the address appears in the most extravagant and respectful form, others exhibit semi-formal titles, and a number of letters are addressed more informally. A letter from Lady Anne Lee to her brother Thomas Lord Paget was directed, 'To the ryght honorable and my very good lord and brother my lord paget of beawdesert at Burton gyve thess'; while Margaret Yaxley addressed a letter to Nicholas Bacon, 'To the Right Honorable and her singler goode Lorde Sir Nicolas Bacon knight Lord Keper of the Grete Seale of England'.[122] The variety of forms of address can be seen in the correspondence of Bess of Hardwick: Grace Cavendish dispatched a letter to her addressed simply 'to my Lady', while a letter from Frances Cobham was addressed 'to mi good cosyn the ladi seantelo'; James Crompe directed a letter 'to my singuler good ladye & mestres the Lady Elsabeth Seyntlo delyu[er] thes', while Sir William Cavendish addressed his letter 'to Besse cauendysh my wyff'.[123] In addition to instructions of where and to whom a letter should be delivered, writers frequently urged 'haste' upon carriers.

On arrival letters were opened and read (see Chapter 5), and then commonly endorsed on receipt by either the addressee or a secretary or clerk. Endorsements generally specify the date of arrival, name of sender, and the letter's contents, in order to facilitate filing and easy retrieval. Both personal and business letters were dealt with in this way, though different parties display varying degrees of assiduity in such referencing. Among the most likely letters to have been endorsed, however, are those dispatched to officials who were served by secretariats. One of Robert Cecil's secretaries endorsed a letter from his niece, 'Lady Susan Vere to my master'; a letter from Anne White to Richard Bagot contains the by-note, 'Mrs whites l[ett]res for Jo[hn] godwyn'.[124] Furthermore, letters endorsed with a date provide a useful method of establishing the time-lag between the writing and receipt of letters, and thus length of delivery time; endorsements may also be used for dating where documents are undated or partly dated.[125]

Returning to consider the inside of letters for a moment, a large proportion of letters are in fact dated, usually indicating the day, month, year, and place the letter was written. In practice, the dating of women's letters was far from uniform.[126] A letter from Eleanor, countess of Cumberland, was dated 'Att my lodge of Carlton the xiiiith day of february'; Dorothy Seymour dated a letter '18 Jan.'; while Joan Herrick merely dated a letter to her husband, 'this wensdaye nite'.[127] Letters written by secretaries are far more likely to have been dated fully than those written by women themselves. At the beginning of the period dates

---

[122] Paget Papers, D603/K/1/4/6: 09/10/n.y.; Bacon Manuscripts of Redgrave Hall, 4069: [20/11/1565].

[123] Folger, X.d.428 (8, 16, 13), 27/06/1589, 21/10/1560, 13/04/1550.

[124] Cecil, 183, fo. 123: 1601; Folger, L.a.960, 30/01/[1594?].

[125] e.g. Folger, MS X.d.494, fos. 1ʳ–2ᵛ.

[126] By studying where letters were written from and sent to, it is possible to reconstruct the distances over which women maintained social contacts by letter.

[127] WD/Hoth/Box 44, 14/02/1543; Berkshire RO, D/EN F6/2/7, 18/01/[c.1600]; Bodl., Herrick, Eng. Hist. c.484, fo. 18: n.d.

sometimes appear at the head of letters. Sabine Johnson's letters are dated in this manner; typical is a letter dated, 'Jesus a[nn]° 1551 the 31 of maie at glapthorne'.[128] This method of dating using the Latin prefix 'Jesus anno' seemingly as an invocation, conforms with certain (though not all) medieval dating practices, but is relatively rare in the sixteenth-century letters surveyed.[129] Usual practice appears to have been to date letters at the bottom, prior to signing. Less conventionally, in an example of a letter from Blanche Parry to Thomas Lord Paget written in 1577 the date appears at the foot of the letter before the signature, and the word 'Jesus' is written at the head of the page, again acting as an invocation.[130] This form of invocation may in some cases indicate the Catholicism of the letter-writer. Indeed, a number of examples of letters written by recusant women employ this method of letter-heading. A letter by Mary Wilford to her mother in the papers of the recusant Throckmorton family is headed with the phrase 'Jesus matia'.[131]

Letters have an afterlife by the very fact that they are extant today. Upon receipt and once endorsed and read, correspondence was then often preserved for purposes of record-keeping. Women were active in conserving their own correspondence: the countess of Essex, for example, kept letters from her husband in a casket under her bed; and in her own closet Sir William More's wife had a 'borded capcas' or small trunk for holding letters.[132] Eleanor Wheathill, Elizabeth Bourne, and Lucy, marchioness of Winchester, all referred in their letters to their 'papers and writings', which suggests a common practice of hoarding paperwork other that letters, such as deeds, wills, and other financial papers.[133] Lady Hoby described a morning spent in her closet 'sorting out papers'.[134] Lady Jane Bacon bound her incoming correspondence in bundles, which she labelled in her own hand.[135] In addition to preserving incoming correspondence, numerous outgoing letters survive as drafts or copies, kept as personal records of letters dispatched. Addressees also sometimes annotated the missives that they received, either underlining key words and phrases, or adding marginalia. Office-holders, for example, passed women's letters to other functionaries or government departments endorsed with instructions: a letter from Lady Elizabeth Radcliffe to Sir Walter Mildmay in which she 'craved' his letter as proof of payment of debts owed to the crown, included a note at the foot of it penned by Mildmay to Thomas Fanshaw, stating: 'I pray you Mr Fanshaw help this pore lady w[i]th the letter she writeth for.'[136] Additionally, letters themselves

---

[128] SP46/6/152.
[129] On medieval dating see *Cely Letters*, ed. Hanham (224, 225); Carpenter, *Kingsford's Stonor Letters* (250, 251).   [130] Paget Papers, D603/K/1/4/25: 19/01/1578.
[131] WCRO, Throckmorton, CR 1998/Box 60/Folder 4: 19/09/n.y.
[132] *Egerton Papers*, ed. Collier, 322; Evans, 'Extracts from the Private Account Book of Sir William More', 292.
[133] BL, Harl., 4762, fo. 59, 1590; BL, Addit., 23212, fos. 129–30, n.d.; BL, Harl., 4713, fo. 258, n.d.   [134] *Diary of Lady Margaret Hoby*, 95.
[135] Heal and Holmes, '*Prudentia ultra sexum*', 111. [136] SP46/18/126: n.d.

were used by recipients to make notes, perform financial calculations, and draft replies: scrawled on the bottom of a letter from Amy Beddingfield to Nathaniel Bacon were monetary calculations;[137] a letter from Anne Williamson to her husband contained notes of payments, suggesting that letters were a wider part of household business.[138] The letters of Anne Bacon, wife of Nathaniel Bacon, often contain pen-trails, where she practised writing her signature.[139] Occasionally senders' letters were returned with replies added at the bottom. Anne Lady Bacon, for example, wrote to her son Anthony on a letter that he had sent to her.[140] Women's letters, too, occasionally contain answers either at the foot of the page or on the reverse side. A letter from Dorothy Pakyngton to her brother Sir Thomas Kitson, written in 1571 on the death of her husband, concerning her jointure bears Kitson's reply and his readiness to 'performe the dutye of a frend and naturall love of a brother'.[141] Once dispatched, letters thus performed a range of functions ancillary to the letter-writer's initial purpose, almost acting as scrap paper.

In addition to technologies of writing associated with letters, it is also possible to reconstruct the letter-writing process, identifying where and when women wrote their letters and elucidating more fully the nature and experience of early modern women's letter-writing. Such reconstruction sheds light on a range of questions related to epistolary composition. Were letters penned in private chambers or closets, in secluded settings inside and outdoors, in communal rooms within the household, alone and in company, among family, friends, servants, and messengers? Was letter-writing associated with business and the household? To what extent can letter-writing be regarded as a leisure activity? Were there certain times of the day that were set aside for women to conduct their correspondence? What emerges is the varied nature of epistolary composition, an activity that could be both solitary and communal, which further collapses traditional understandings of letters as essentially 'private' forms, in the sense of being enclosed, secret, and individual. Furthermore, letter-writing viewed from the perspective of location draws connections between traditionally defined domestic and household spheres, and political and business worlds.

Letter-writers very rarely mention in their letters precisely from where they are writing, although much evidence survives of collaborative epistolary practices, indicating that letters were often not penned alone but composed in the presence of others (see Chapter 3). Sabine Johnson, for example, informed her husband, 'as I was closing this letter along came Preston with the money', indicating that her letter was written in the presence of a servant.[142] In the absence of direct references to the locations in which letters were written, the use of probate inventories allows one to recreate the domestic architecture of the sixteenth-century household, and to highlight the areas where writing

---

[137] BL, Addit., 41306, fo. 9: 29/12/1581.   [138] SP46/49/55: 09/12/1590.
[139] Folger, L.d.18, 19, 20, 21.
[140] Bacon, 651, fo. 207: 06/06/1595. See also, *Lisle Letters*, iii. 592, 592a.
[141] Hengrave, 88/2, fo. 31: 17/06/1571.   [142] SP46/6/152: 31/05/1551.

activities most commonly took place.[143] The household, as scholars have pointed out, allowed for interconnecting solitary and communal spaces, and should not be associated solely with privacy; such an approach, Sasha Roberts argues, masks 'the many distinctions of communal and personal, open and secret, public and private space within the elite home'.[144] However, the rise of private spaces such as bedchambers, studies, and closets in the houses of the nobility and gentry allowed for greater access to personal solitude; such spaces, usually well furnished for comfort, warmth, and storage, are frequently connected with reading, writing, contemplation, and prayer.[145] Sir William More's wife's closet included a desk for writing; the closet and chamber of Sir George Shirley's wife contained various items of furniture connected with writing: 'A chest of walnut tree, a great cabbonett, ii little cabbonetts, one ebony boxe, a spruce chest, a deske to write upon of crimson velvet, ii dozen of ffruite pursslen dishes and tunn dishes.'[146] The inventory of Hardwick compiled in 1601 indicates a distinction between the functions for which Elizabeth Shrewsbury used her withdrawing chamber and her bedchamber. Indeed, Peter Thornton argues that the withdrawing chamber, which adjoined her bedchamber, 'seems to have been more in the nature of a large private closet into which she could withdraw', while the bedchamber, furnished with desks and chairs for writing, was probably where she carried out her extensive correspondence.[147] A survey of Oxfordshire household and farm inventories in the second half of the sixteenth century reveals that among 'middling groups', where private or solitary rooms were rare, writing probably took place in the hall, a communal space within the household: the inventories of the widows Elizabeth Gibbs and Agnes Kinton record pens kept in the hall; the inventory of Joanna Robins is more detailed, recording, 'In the hall . . . a table, a backe benche, a paire of tressells, 3 formes, 3 stowells, an old chaire and a pen', while Joyce Edgellffyld had in her possession 'a pene & a forme & 2 tables'.[148]

The varied loci of letter-writing can also be inferred from a range of other media. The evidence of early modern paintings, for example, evokes the different places in which letters were written and read. Peter Sutton's study of mid-seventeenth-century Dutch genre paintings highlights the depiction of letters in scenes of everyday life, attesting the social currency of letters, which were composed and read in closets and taverns, alone in private, and in the company of bearers, secretaries or servants.[149] Renaissance plays likewise dramatize the

---

[143] Garrard, 'English Probate Inventories', 55–82. Cf. Spufford, 'Limitations of Probate Inventory', 139–74.

[144] Roberts, 'Shakespeare "creepes" ', 31; Knowles, ' "Infinite Riches in a Little Room" ', 3–29.

[145] On his and hers closets see, Stewart, *Close Readers*, 163–70. Cf. Orlin, 'Gertrude's Closet', 44–67; Ziegler, 'My Lady's Chamber', 73–90.

[146] Evans, 'Extracts from the Private Account Book', 292; 'Extracts from "An Inventory of the Goods at Astwell at Sir George Shirley's Death" ', in *Stemmata Shirliana*, 95.

[147] Thornton, 'Short Commentary on the Hardwick Inventory', 15–20, 31–2.

[148] Havinden, 'Household and Farm Inventories in Oxfordshire', 32, 58, 196.

[149] Sutton *et al.*, *Love Letters*.

spatiality of female letter-writing, an activity that could involve secretarial assistance, but more often than not was associated with the intimate architectural space of the early modern closet.[150] The nocturnal activities of the sleepwalking Lady Macbeth, for example, are witnessed by her gentlewoman, who describes her rising from bed, unlocking her closet, taking paper, and writing and reading before returning to bed.[151] While the male closet, as Alan Stewart has shown, was the site for the close relationship between a master and his male secretary based upon the transaction of knowledge, it is unlikely that mistresses interacted with male servants in their own closets.[152] Indeed, women's closets were a strictly female domain; the presence of a non-related male servant carried troubling overtones, threatening to female sexuality.[153] The dictation of letters, therefore, presumably took place in communal spaces within the household.

In looking at when women wrote their correspondence, the clearest picture comes from incidental references in letters themselves. Occasionally letters mention the precise time of day they were composed: writing to John Johnson during a plague year, the widow Margaret Baynham noted the time of her writing by relating it to the death of her niece: 'this being written in the mornyng John Crant and Margery my sesters daughter departed this worlde about xi of the clock before dynner.'[154] While individuals may have had different patterns or habits for when during the day they conducted correspondence, letter-writing was also a reactive activity; at a time before a regularized national post office, correspondence was occasioned by receipt of letters and the arrival and departure of bearers. The haste of bearers was a common apology among sixteenth-century letter-writers. In a letter reporting the safe landing of her husband at Plymouth, Elizabeth Ralegh apologized to Robert Cecil for her haste in writing, urged by the departure of a bearer; Frances Withipole informed her cousin John Hobart, 'I ame in hast for mr wyborne has [to] a way'.[155] Despite the often haphazard nature of dispatch, patterns do emerge indicating distinct times set aside for letter-writing. Married couples in several cases conducted correspondence when apart at the end of the day. Joan Thynne, for example, finished a letter to her husband John with, 'I end with sleepy eyes'.[156] Similarly, John Johnson, while in Calais, habitually wrote to his wife at the end of each day when undistracted by the pressures of commerce; he ended one of his letters, 'in hast going to bed at x of the clocke at nyght and wold ye were in my bed to tary me. I byd you good nyght good wyf'; another exclaimed, 'fare well and good night wife'.[157] This practice of regular correspondence may have been partly to report on household business transacted during the course of the day, but also writing before retiring to bed appears for some couples to have acted as a form of comfort during periods of absence.

[150] Roberts, 'Shakespeare "creepes"', 30–63; Orlin, 'Gertrude's Closet', 44–67; Ziegler, 'My Lady's Chamber', 73–90.   [151] Shakespeare, *Macbeth*, v. i. 4–8.
[152] Stewart, *Close Readers*, 163–70.   [153] Stewart, 'Gelding Gascoigne', 147–69.
[154] SP46/5/80: 01/04/1545.   [155] Cecil, 172, fo. 71: 08/1596; BL, Harl. 4713, fo. 296: n.d.
[156] *Two Elizabethan Women*, 27.   [157] SP46/5/139, 141: 08/11/1545, 15/11/1545.

A fuller picture of the letter-writing habits peculiar to an individual woman can be gleaned from the dairy of Margaret Hoby, who in measuring out her life in spiritual terms was assiduous in recording everything she did. The pages of her diary are filled with daily entries describing her everyday activities punctuated by meals, visitations, chores, prayers, and meditations. Usefully she records in some detail the writing of letters: 'Comminge home, I found Lettres that gaue me occasion to writ diuers waies', 'I wrett a litle and answered a letter from my Lady Ewrie', 'After praiers I wrett to my Mother', 'I wrett Letters to London'.[158] An entry for 15 June 1601 gives the impression of how correspondence fitted into a gentlewoman's daily regime: 'After I was readie, and had dispatched Hilari with letters to london, I talked with Mr Genkins tell he went away: after, I praied and dined: after diner my Cosine Robert Dakins Came, by whom I receiued letters from London: and so I wrett againe to mr Hoby, and kept him Companie tell his departure: and after I went about the house, and so went to priuatt praier and meditation.'[159] While correspondence was clearly occasioned by the exigencies of dispatch, often meaning that letter-writing was a reactive activity, a more detailed study of Lady Hoby's diary highlights the development of certain habits of letter-writing, influencing when she would correspond. She commonly conducted her correspondence early in the morning after private prayers and either before or just after breakfast, and then again in the evening after supper, before going to bed; the reading and writing of letters was also fitted around mealtimes: 'In the morning I praied and then I wrett a Letter to Doctor Brewer and so to breakfast'; 'After priuat prairs, I did writ a Letter: after, I did breake my fast'; 'I wret a letter to my mother, and so to bed'; 'I wret a Letter to my Cossine Isons, and praied priuately and so went to bed'.[160] The evening before she retired to bed was often the time that she wrote to her husband when he was absent from the household: '[I] wrett to Mr Hoby and dispatched a messhinger to him: after, I returned to priuat praier and examenation, and then went to bed.'[161]

Letter-writing for Lady Hoby was thus an important way of keeping in touch with family and friends, and conducting business, and her diary relates the frequency with which she wrote to different parties. While she corresponded on a regular basis to immediate family and kin, among her other recurrent correspondents were her physician, Mr Lister, and her personal chaplain, Richard Rhodes.[162] What emerges above all from reading her diary, however, is the degree to which reading and conducting correspondence formed a regular feature of her everyday life. Her experience, while unusual in that it was committed to diary form, is nonetheless representative of many women of noble, gentle, and mercantile birth, who as a group had regular dealings with ink and pen.

[158] *Diary of Lady Margaret Hoby*, 35, 98, 159, 179.   [159] Ibid. 151.
[160] Ibid. 9, 28, 30, 39, 52.   [161] Ibid. 53, 11, 12.
[162] Ibid. 79, 80, 127 (letters to Lister); 118, 119, 121, 125, 126, 127 128, 136, 139, 162 (letters to Rhodes).

3

The Composition of Letters

Analysis of the different methods by which women's letters were composed during the sixteenth century represents an important and central aspect of this study, in that it probes the very nature of women's letter-writing. Letters have traditionally been read as mirrors of early modern individuals, reflective of the true expressions and feelings of their authors and their inner as well as outer selves; they have also often been used by historians as straightforward depositories of historical fact. Looking at how letters were written, and by whom, disrupts comfortable notions of letter-writing as a solitary and private activity, and letters as examples of *women's* writing, documents or texts capable of echoing early modern women's 'voices' down the centuries. While many women during this period did indeed write letters for themselves, a significant proportion of women's letters were in fact either written by amanuenses, or bear the signs of having been written or composed by more than one person. Letters were dictated to scribes; written from notes by secretaries; passed to family members and friends for comments and amendments; drafted and reworked by legal counsel and government officials. This chapter, therefore, aims to outline the complex and varied textual methods by which letters were constructed, to elucidate the often collaborative nature of the letter-writing process, and thus to challenge scholarly notions of *personal* correspondence as identified with the private and the singular.

The issue of collective or 'mediated' writing, questioning as it does modern definitions of authorship and textual production, is one that has naturally concerned literary scholars of the late medieval and Renaissance periods, rather than historians, over the past couple of decades or so; and the very concept of 'authorship' has itself received strong rebuttal by critical theorists and postmodernists.[1] Recent literary scholarship has emphasized the 'collaborative', fluid, unfixed nature of Renaissance authorship. Arthur Marotti, for example, has highlighted the 'instability' and 'malleability' of the English Renaissance lyric within a 'system of manuscript transmission': 'texts', he argues, 'were part of an ongoing social discourse . . . inherently malleable, escaping

---

[1] Hirshfield, 'Early Modern Collaboration', 609–22; Love, *Scribal Publication*; Beal, *In Praise of Scribes*.

authorial control.'[2] Collaboration among early modern dramatists was also commonplace, and textual scholars have long debated the merits of distinguishing parts of plays that are authored by one particular author from those authored by others. Transcending the intricate arguments over precisely which lines to attribute to a particular author, scholars such as Jeffrey Masten, have importantly shown the collective and truly collaborative nature of dramatic production, which has greatly reshaped our understanding of the nature of early modern subjectivity and individuality (and in Masten's case sexuality), as well as definitions of authorship and the literary 'canon'.[3] The communal and social nature of extra-literary forms of the writing arts is depicted by Juliet Fleming in her study of early modern graffiti, which rethinks authorship as 'collective, aphoristic, and inscriptive, rather than individualist, lyric, and voice-centred'.[4] It is within this framework that I seek to situate my discussion of the composition of women's letters, arguing that even letter-writing must be recognized as a collaborative enterprise. Refiguring letters and the processes of letter-writing as potentially communal and collective, rather than simply as individual and exclusive, uncovers a different understanding of early modern epistolary authorship and individuality.

The methodological and conceptual problems of defining what constitutes a *woman* writer have recently concerned feminist literary scholars. Medievalists interested in the works of Julian of Norwich and Margery Kempe have discussed the 'literary authority' of supposedly female-authored texts that were in fact penned by male scribes.[5] Indeed, Julia Boffey has shown the difficulty of reconstructing the processes involved in writing, especially when intermediaries, normally male, were crucial in translating and disseminating women's writings: 'it is difficult', she argues, 'to assess the amount of first-hand contact with any of the texts which English women readers and would-be writers can have enjoyed.'[6] Renaissance scholars too have asked similar questions of supposedly female-authored texts. In an invaluable study, Margaret Ferguson illuminates 'the variety and complexity of concepts of "the woman writer"'.[7] She argues for a much wider definition of women's writing and authorship, one that encompasses various modes of composition, such as dictation and use of amanuenses, which distance women from technologies of writing.

Problems related to the retrieval of women's words have also been encountered by social historians in their use of depositional evidence, where the voice of a female deponent is muffled by legal and bureaucratic procedure, clerical

    [2] Marotti, *Manuscript, Print and the English Renaissance Lyric*, 135. Ezell, *Social Authorship*; Thomas, 'Reading and Writing the Renaissance Commonplace Book', 402–15.
    [3] Masten, *Textual Intercourse*.   [4] Fleming, *Graffiti and the Writing Arts*, 41.
    [5] Johnson, 'Trope of the Scribe', 820–38; Hirsh, 'Author and Scribe', 145–50.
    [6] Boffey, 'Women Authors and Women's Literacy', 159–82.
    [7] Ferguson, 'Renaissance Concepts of the "Woman Writer"', 149. Wright, 'Name and the Signature', 239–57.

manipulation, and scribal distortion.[8] Laura Gowing remarks that church court depositions do not permit 'unproblematic unmediated access to a recognizable "women's voice" '; yet at the same time, she detects the remarkable oral narrative skills of women, whose verbal utterances were transposed to text.[9] The legal oral testimony of female litigants, therefore, needs to be read in the institutional context in which it was produced; the layers of court protocol and record-keeping once constructed need to be carefully peeled away to reveal what is left that is attributable verbally to the female deponent.

When analysing women's letters the central problem remains to recover female participation in the writing process. In light of the complex production processes involved in corresponding, how does one conceptualize the role of women in writing letters separate from impact that other parties had on com-position? For letters composed collaboratively, the voice of a female signatory needs to be pared away from the secretarial and formulaic aspects of the com-position process; letters composed with an amanuensis rather than a pen expose the intersection of oral and literate modes in early modern methods of corres-ponding, and demonstrate women's extra-literary skills associated with author-ship, such as storytelling and the construction of coherent narratives. The full implications of the ways in which letters were composed, the input that an amanuensis might have had, the constraints imposed by a lack of epistolary privacy, and the self-censorship this would have led to are issues central to this study. The mechanics of letter-writing are of fundamental importance when looking at a range of interesting issues relating to women's writing, their lives, and letters. These include women's persuasive and rhetorical skills; the degree of confidence and authority that they displayed; self-fashioning and the creation of personas; empowerment and female agency; the intimacy and emotional content of letters; and the nature of family, social, and gender relations inscribed in correspondence.

WOMEN'S HANDS

Identifying whether a letter is actually written by a woman's own hand or whether it exhibits signs of scribal intervention is far from being an exact science, even for the most seasoned and expert palaeographers; the task of establishing a holograph hand is often a matter of some subjectivity. Yet these palaeographical questions relating to women's handwriting, and establishing who physically wrote the letters, are at the very heart of an analysis of epistolary composition and women's relation to the processes of letter-writing. The first task is to decide the scribal status of a letter, whether it was written in a woman's own hand or in that

---

[8] Stretton *Women Waging Law*, 9, 13–19. Holmes, 'Drainers and Fenmen', 166–95.
[9] Gowing, *Domestic Dangers*, 9, 232–62.

of an amanuensis; that is, whether the main body of the letter was actually written by a woman, or whether she merely signed a letter penned by a secretary or scribe. The former are referred to throughout this book as holograph or autograph letters; the latter as scribal or secretarial letters.[10]

At the outset, it is important to note that there is no such thing as an identifiably female hand for the sixteenth century.[11] However, some time before 1600, italic—a hand that was introduced into England at the beginning of the sixteenth century among university scholars—appears to have been established as the preferred hand for women.[12] The educationalist Richard Mulcaster, in his *Positions . . . For the Training up Of Children* (1581), prescribed italic for young gentlewomen, who he considered should be 'furnished' with the ability to write 'faire and swiftly'.[13] In a similar vein, the professional penman Martin Billingsley, in *The Pens Excellencie* (1618), recommended that women be taught to write in italic. For Billingsley, italic was the natural choice of hand for women because of the inadequacy of female memory, and their supposed intellectual inferiority: '[italic] is conceived to be the easiest hand that is written with *Pen*, and to be taught in the shortest time: Therefore it is usually taught to women, for as much as they (having not the patience to take any great paines, besides phantasticall and humorsome) must be taught that which they may instantly learne: otherwise they are uncertaine of their proceedings, because their minds are (upon light occasion) easily drawne from the first resolution.'[14] By contrast, continental opinion was divided over what scripts were deemed suitable for women to write. Similar to English prescripts, Lucas Materot's copybook published in 1608 and dedicated to Queen Marguerite de Valois advocated *lettres Italiennes bastardes*, a type of italic, which he claimed was 'facile à imiter pour les femmes'.[15] Alternatively, Lodovico Curione in *La Notomia delle Cancellaresche corsiue* (Rome, 1588) regarded secretarial script to be a hand used by women; his example of French secretary hand is labelled 'lettre qui escrivent les dames de France'.[16] Jodocus Hondius's anthology of hands of famous European writing masters, *Theatrum artis scribendi* (Amsterdam, 1594), included examples of the hands of two different women: Maria Strick, the Dutch calligrapher (who was formally recognized for her rendition of an italic script); and two pages of writing by Hondius's own daughter, Jacquemyne, in French secretarial hand.[17] By the end of the sixteenth century in England, however, italic was widely

---

[10] The *OED* defines 'holograph' as 'a deed, letter or document: wholly written by the person in whose name it appears', and autograph as 'to write with one's own hand', 'to copy or reproduce by autography', and 'to write one's autograph on or in; to sign'.

[11] For work investigating the differences between male and female handwriting see Davis, 'Analysis of Handwriting', 67–68.

[12] Dawson and Kennedy-Skipton, *Elizabethan Handwriting*, 12; Byrne, 'Elizabethan Handwriting', 199.

[13] Goldberg, *Writing Matter*, 138; Ferguson, 'Renaissance Concepts of the "Woman Writer"', 154; Mulcaster, *Positions . . .* (1581), 177, 180, 181.   [14] p. 37.

[15] Heal, *English Writing-Masters*, p. xxix.   [16] Goldberg, *Writing Matter*, 138.

[17] Van Uchelen, 'Dutch Writing-Masters', 319–46; Williams, 'A Moon to their Sun', 89, 96–8.

considered as a woman's hand, so much so that in *Twelfth Night* (1602) Maria is able to trick Malvolio into thinking that a 'sweet Romane hand' must be Olivia's.[18]

In practice too, italic was the hand used by the majority of English women by the end of the sixteenth century, and it was adopted by a number of court women and the daughters of humanists from as early as the 1530s.[19] Yet, the adoption of italic hand by women was at first gradual, uneven, and by no means uniform. For the first half of the century the popularity of italic among women was limited: it was not the hand learned by Lady Lisle's daughter Mary, nor that practised by Anne Boleyn.[20] Princess Elizabeth's childhood italic hand, learned under the guidance of the French tutor Jean Bellemain, was distinct from the hands of the older women with whom she was intimate, such as Margaret Bryan, Katherine Ashley, and Katherine Parr, 'all of whose scripts heavily employ secretary and other older letter forms'.[21] During this earlier period, women commonly practised later gothic or cursive hands: Katherine, duchess of Suffolk, wrote a fairly bold cursive hand, while the mid-Tudor letters of the mercantile woman Sabine Jonson reveal her cramped and angular hand.[22] In the fifteenth century Lady Margaret Hungerford wrote what M. A. Hicks describes as a 'large sprawling hand'; and the hand of Margaret Beaufort in a letter to the earl of Ormond written in 1497 exhibits an intermingling of secretary and anglicana forms.[23] Until the 1570s at least, italic was largely a fashionable social and cultural accomplishment for a learned minority. Moreover, by 1590 it was becoming increasingly popular amongst men of the nobility and gentry. The writing master Robert Wright, for example, taught the young earl of Essex a 'formal and flourished, if slightly stilted and laboured—almost drawn—italic hand'; in later years this developed into a type of free italic hand favoured in court circles.[24] Interestingly, Margaret Willoughby was taught to write a hand different from that of her brother Francis, who learned to write the Italianate humanist script.[25] Until the end of the sixteenth century use of italic was,

[18] Shakespeare, *Twelfe Night or What You Will*, III. iv. 28–9. During this period 'Italian' and 'Roman' are synonymous with italic: Schulz, 'Teaching of Handwriting', 415–16. I use 'italic' throughout for ease of reference.

[19] Heale, 'Women and the Courtly Love Lyric', 296–313; Baron, 'Mary (Howard) Fitzroy's Hand', 314–35. For examples of the italic hands of Katherine Parr, Lady Jane Grey, Princess Elizabeth, and Lady Lucy St John (née Cecil) see Fairbank and Wolpe, *Renaissance Handwriting*, pl. 29, 33, 28, 54. The daughters of Sir Anthony Cooke (*c*.1505–76), tutor of Edward VI, all learned italic hands: Bacon, 650, fo. 69 (Anne Bacon); NA, SP15/13/10 (Elizabeth Hoby), NA, SP12/155/97 (Katherine Killigrew), NA, SP10/15/79 (Mildred Cecil).

[20] *Lisle Letters*, ii. pp. 619–26; Anne Boleyn's childhood hand contains definite secretarial forms: Cambridge, Corpus Christi College, MS 119, fo. 21, [*c*.1514] (*L&P*, IV(i) 1).

[21] Marcus and Mueller, *Elizabeth I: Autograph Compositions*, p. xiv.

[22] SP10/8/35, SP10/9/58; SP46/5–7, *passim*.

[23] Hicks, 'Piety of Margaret, Lady Hungerford', 23.

[24] Davids, 'Handwriting of Robert Devereux', 354, 359. He suggests that Essex's signature reveals features derived from his mother Lettice Dudley's signature.

[25] Friedman, 'Influence of Humanism', 65; ead., *House and Household*, 17–20. Born into the upper gentry, Margaret Willoughby (b. 1544) had her education provided for by her uncle Henry Medley of Tilty, Essex from around April 1550.

therefore, less a marker of a writer's gender (and implicitly of female intellectual inferiority), than of his or her social status and educational background. Hilary Jenkinson asserts that such handwriting was 'the special property of the learned or travelled'; it was also predominant for those, such as Anthony Bacon, who engaged in continental correspondence.[26] In the case of Francis Willoughby, his clearer and more modern Italianate hand distinguished him from his sister and those of lower social status. Indeed, it is interesting that italic hand—a marker of social status and intellectual attainment—despite the claim that it was easy to write, should be extended from its use at the universities by men, as the hand deemed appropriate for women.

During the second half of the sixteenth century, however, a change in the type of scripts taught to girls and boys is discernible: in many families girls were instructed to write italic, while their brothers learned more businesslike secretarial scripts. An examination of the surviving letters of the sons and daughters of the gentleman Richard Bagot (d. 1597) of Blithfield, Staffordshire, further reveals gendered differences in the kinds of handwriting taught to boys and girls in the mid- to late-Tudor period. The holograph letters of Anne Broughton (née Bagot) (1555–1619), Lettice Kinnersley (née Bagot) (b. 1573) and Margaret Trew (née Bagot) (b. 1553), which largely survive from the period of their married lives, display the italic hands they learned during childhood; those of their brothers Anthony (1558–1622) and Walter (1557–1623), on the other hand, were penned in practised secretary scripts.[27] Comparison of wives' hands with those of their husbands similarly reveals differences. An account book kept by Lady Elizabeth Cavendish (1520–1608) and her then husband Sir William Cavendish (1505–57) for the period 1548–50, records both their hands: Lady Cavendish's a bold italic hand; Sir William's a clear secretary script.[28] The apparent differences in handwriting are only partly explained by sixteenth-century pedagogies and assumptions about female intellectual capacities. Girls and boys were taught to write in separate locations, which helped to perpetuate gendered handwriting; different scripts were also identified with specific tasks, functions, and environments—italic was synonymous with the world of learning and came to be identified as a feminine hand, secretary and court hands were associated with the worlds of business, government, and law.

Though italic was the hand most commonly used by women for correspondence, various scripts were in fact written by female letter-writers throughout the period taken as a whole, including later gothic, anglicana, cursive, secretary,

---

[26] Jenkinron, *Later Court Hands*, 63. See also Dawson and Kennedy-Skipton, *Elizabethan Handwriting*, 8–9, 12; Fairbank and Dickins, *Italic Hand in Tudor Cambridge*; Fairbank and Wolpe, *Renaissance Handwriting*, 28–34; Preston and Yeandle, *English Handwriting*, p. viii; Denholm-Young, *Handwriting in England and Wales*, 73; Hector, *Handwriting of English Documents*, 59–60; Wardrop, *Script of Humanism*.

[27] Folger: L.a.222–33 (Anne Broughton); L.a.594–605, 607–8 (Lettice Kinnersley); L.a.899–902 (Margaret Trew); L.a.36–45 (Anthony Bagot); L.a.94–7 (Walter Bagot).

[28] Folger, MS X.d.486.

and mixed hands. The copybooks, which begin to be published from about 1570 onwards, provided numerous hands that women would have had the opportunity of mastering.[29] Indeed, Jonathan Goldberg has argued that in England copybooks were specifically aimed at women, as well as other groups, including children prior to institutionalized schooling, and adults of middle age who were unschooled.[30] John deBeau Chesne dedicated his manual *La Clef de L'Escriture* (1593) to Ladies Mary, Elizabeth, and Alathea Talbot.[31] There is also evidence that women actually learnt to write using such manuals: the daughters of Thomas and Henry Percy, earls of Northumberland, were taught to write using a sixteenth-century French copybook given to the family by James, earl of Bothwell, in the 1550s.[32]

Scripts used by women during the sixteenth century also varied geographically. Several women in the Norfolk-based Bacon family, including Jane Bowes, Dorothy Bacon and Elizabeth Bacon, wrote large, bold secretary hands, a practice conceivably reflecting local practices of teaching writing.[33] However, more research needs to be undertaken in this area in order to explain why this difference occurred, and to establish more clearly the patterns of how different types of handwriting used by women varied geographically. The dissemination of different hands for women was also affected by generational, educational, and other social factors. Joan Thynne (1558–1612), the daughter of a London merchant, and thus a woman below the ranks of court elites and the aristocracy, wrote a hand 'unformed and straight in letter forms'; while a generation later her daughter-in-law, Maria Thynne (*c.*1578–1611), daughter of Lord Audley and a maid-of-honour at court, was taught to write a 'modified form of italic'.[34] The differences perceived between these two women are generational, but also related to social status and locus of educational experience.

By no means did all women write italic hands by the beginning of the seventeenth century. Elizabeth Cary wrote a mixed hand composed of both italic and secretary forms in her letters, and a generation later her daughters, whose scribal hands appear in *Lady Falkland, Her Life*, wrote a mixed script.[35] Indeed, over the course of the sixteenth century traditional classifications of hands, such as secretary and italic, begin to break down with the development of mixed hands. With the proliferation of printed books, and more people able to read and write, it was more difficult to 'maintain the purity of a particular script', and handwriting became 'more individualistic'.[36] This can be discerned in a letter

---

[29] Heal, *English Writing-Masters.*   [30] Goldberg, *Writing Matter*, 134.
[31] Ibid. 137.   [32] HMC, *Third Report, Appendix*, 114.
[33] Folger, L.d.186 (Jane Bowes), 267, 269, 441–3, 467–9 (Elizabeth Bacon, ?1541–1621). Jane Key notes that Dorothy Bacon's letters were penned in a 'bold secretary hand': 'Letters and Will of Lady Dorothy Bacon', 83.   [34] Wall (ed.), *Two Elizabethan Women*, p. xxxii.
[35] *Elizabeth Cary, Lady Falkland: Life and Letters*, ed. Wolfe, 227; Wolfe, 'Scribal Hands and Dating', 192–8.   [36] Preston and Yeandle, *English Handwriting*, p. viii.

from Queen Elizabeth written to James VI of Scotland in 1593, in which her hand, written at speed, mixes both secretarial and italic forms.[37]

While the development of more personally identifiable forms of handwriting aids in the detection of holographs, inconsistent hands are more problematic. Differences in an individual's hand were caused by numerous factors, including the speed of writing and the cut and quality of the quill used; equally, a writer's handwriting may have been affected by old age, illness, and emotional distress.[38] Variations in style may also have occurred over a period of time as hands and letter forms developed or 'matured': Elizabeth Russell's handwriting changed with age, 'from the schoolgirl copybook style of her twenties to the large and shaky script of her last years'.[39] Furthermore, different scripts were used for different purposes throughout the early modern period.[40] Certain women could write several hands, which they used on different occasions and for different types of document.[41] Arbella Stuart in her letters used two separate hands for different kinds of letters. Her familiar letters and the rough drafts of her court letters were written in an informal or free italic hand, whilst in the presentation copies of her court letters she used an elegant, formal italic hand.[42] Similarly, Frances Burgh wrote several types of italic: a formal almost copperplate hand, and a free-flowing more informal hand.[43] A few women, including Queen Elizabeth I and the calligrapher Esther Inglis, could write both secretary and italic hands.[44] The early Tudor writing mistress Elizabeth Lucar (1510–37), according to George Ballard, could write three different hands all of them 'faire'; and the French émigré Marie Presot mastered both the French and Italian hands.[45] This ability to write several different types of hand (a sign of a high level of literacy) illustrates further the palaeographical problems associated with women's letters.

Although some women, such as those of the Bacon family, wrote rather large and shaky secretarial scripts, it was nevertheless highly unusual for women—with the exception of women like the calligrapher Esther Inglis, Margaret Spitlehouse, the professional female scrivener, and perhaps Elizabeth Lucar—to write the kinds of accomplished and professional secretarial scripts routinely rendered by male secretaries.[46] This makes it relatively easier to establish a scribal from a holograph letter. In this context, it is generally (but not always) fair to assume

---

[37] Ibid. 64–7, pl. 21.

[38] Foisil, 'Literature of Intimacy', 332, 348; Steen, 'Manuscript Matters', 24–38; Davis, 'Analysis of Handwriting', 68.   [39] Farber, 'Letters of Lady Elizabeth Russell', 70.

[40] Thomas, 'Meaning of Literacy', 97–131.

[41] Goldberg, *Desiring Women Writing*, 151; id., *Writing Matter*, 240–1.

[42] *Letters of Lady Arbella Stuart*, ed. Steen, 107, 112–13.

[43] BL, Addit., 12506, fos. 371, 375, 381: 19/06/1604, 06/1604, 02/02/1604.

[44] Johnson, *Elizabeth*, 19–20; Scott-Elliot and Yeo, 'Calligraphic Manuscripts of Esther Inglis', 11–63.

[45] Ballard, *Memoirs of Several Ladies of Great Britain*, 36–7; Williams, 'A Moon', 89.

[46] Generally, the women who used a secretary hand wrote a rather large, bold script easily distinguishable from the hand of a professional writer. Craig, 'Margaret Spitlehouse, Female Scrivener', 54; Williams, 'A Moon', 89.

that if the signature contained in a letter is in a different hand from that of the main body of the letter then an amanuensis wrote it. Commonly one finds letters written in highly practised and proficient secretary hands bearing signatures in a different (often italic) hand.[47] There are, however, several complicating factors here. First, some women used a different hand for purposes of signing: Jonathan Goldberg has noted that Mary Shelton reserved a neat italic hand for signatures.[48] Hilary Jenkinson notes that in the Elizabethan period men who preferred secretary script often signed in italic as a sign of refinement.[49] Numerous women, especially among court circles, developed highly elaborate and personalized signatures; Queen Elizabeth employed a flourishing signature partly for purposes of authentication.[50] A further complication is that it was not unknown for secretaries to sign letters.[51] The clerk who penned a letter for Elizabeth, countess of Shrewsbury, second wife of George, fourth earl of Shrewsbury, to Protector Somerset signed it in the same hand that he used in the main body of the letter.[52] Similarly, six extant letters of Jane Basset, daughter of Lady Lisle, are written in four different hands, and in each case the signature is penned by the writer.[53] The attribution of female penmanship in these letters is doubtful. Taken together, these cases demonstrate that handwriting during the sixteenth century was not a singular possession or the identity of an individual person.

Since it is not always possible to establish a female scribe from handwriting alone, it is useful to look at circumstantial evidence. It is sometimes possible to rely on internal evidence contained within the letter. Women often mentioned whether they had written themselves or used an amanuensis; female letter-writers also frequently apologized for the deficiency of their hands. Comments of this nature, however, should not be accepted at face value or detached from palaeographical evidence. Jane Basset in one of her letters used the phrase, 'I pray you to pardon me of my rude writing', which if taken literally would suggest that the writing was her own; a later reference in the same letter to 'my writer', however, indicates her use of an amanuensis.[54] In this context the meaning of the word 'writing' is again ambiguous. As Muriel St Clare Byrne has argued in her detailed analysis of the Jane Basset's letters, the meaning can be read in several different ways: 'she could mean that she does not write as fully as she would like to because the scrivener had no time to write for her, and the business of writing for herself is difficult; but equally she could mean that the letter-carrier departed so hastily that she had no time to compose and dictate a long letter.'[55] Alternatively, studying a woman's letters from the perspective of a family collection might help to determine whether she was capable of writing or not, as women were often

---

[47] Hector, *Handwriting of English Documents*, 59; Goldberg, *Writing Matter*, 234–5.
[48] Goldberg, *Desiring Women Writing*, 145.   [49] Jenkinson, 'Elizabethan Handwriting', 23.
[50] Goldberg, *Writing Matter*, 247.
[51] Jenkinson, 'Notes on the Study of English Punctuation', 156.
[52] HMC, *Bath*, iv. 105: 22/12/*c*.1547–8.
[53] This led St Clare Byrne to ask 'could Jane Basset write?': *Lisle Letters*, iii. pp. 66–7.
[54] Ibid. 522.   [55] Ibid. iv. p. 67.

taught to write by their brothers' tutors or by writing masters. John Davies, the writing master, poet, and fellow tutor with Peter Bales to Prince Henry, numbered several women among his pupils, including Elizabeth Cary, Elizabeth Dutton, Anne Tracy, and Elizabeth Baskerville.[56] Numerous letters have also been established as holograph.[57] It is thus possible to build up a realistic expectation of the types of script women were able to write during this period. For many women one can examine extensive numbers of their letters—including holograph postscripts within secretarial letters—and in certain instances other writings, such as accounts, diaries, and manuscript miscellanies, and therefore be able to recognize their hand, or hands, with greater confidence. The same hand, for example, was used in the letters of Sabine Johnson as in the accounts that she kept in the absence of her husband, the Staple merchant John Johnson.[58]

Contemporaries readily considered it possible to identify individual writers' hands. Anne, countess of Warwick, differentiated between letters written by Sir Robert Cecil personally and correspondence conducted by one of his secretaries; Joan Thynne recognized with ease her husband's hand, and that of a scribe.[59] Furthermore, literature of the period in some cases reflects the assumption that an individual's handwriting could be distinguished from that of another. In George Gascoigne's *The Adventures of Master F.J.*, the fictional narrator GT was depicted on one occasion differentiating between letters written in Mistress Elinor's own hand and those written by her secretary: 'This letter I haue seene, of hir own hand writing: and as therin the Reader may finde great difference of style, from hir former letter, so may you nowe vnderstand the cause. Shee had in the same house a friend, a seruaunt, a secretary.'[60]

Elsewhere, the difficulties of distinguishing an individual's handwriting are used for comic or dramatic effect. In *As You Like It* Rosalind pretends that a letter actually written by Phoebe was not in fact in her own hand:

> I saw her hand. She has a leathern hand,
> A free-stone coloured hand. I verily did think
> That her old gloves were on; but 'twas her hands.
> She has a housewife's hand—but that's no matter.
> I say she never did invent this letter.
> This is a man's invention, and his hand.[61]

While Rosalind obviously recognizes Phoebe's hand herself, she seeks to convince Silvius that it is not hers.

---

[56] Woudhuysen, *Sir Philip Sidney*, 38.

[57] e.g. *A Select Collection of Interesting Autograph Letters*; Rawlins, *Four Hundred Years of British Autographs*. Manuscript catalogues and record society volumes commonly indicate a letter's holograph status, though this usually only indicates that the signature and hand used for the letter are consistent.   [58] SP46/5/3: fo. 2^r.

[59] Hatfield House, Cecil, 40, fo. 5, 13/04/1596; *Two Elizabethan Women*, 4, 07/03/1577.

[60] Gascoigne, *A Hundreth sundrie Flowres* (1573), sig. Biiij^r.

[61] Shakespeare, *As You Like It*, IV. iii. 25–30.

This in turn opens up the possibility of the forgery of letters. Several letters were apparently written in the name of Frances, countess of Essex, without her prior knowledge or consent. Writing to Sir John Puckering, the lord keeper, in 1594, the countess referred to a letter that Thomas Parker, a servant of her husband's, claimed she had written in favour of one Mr Dutton, Parker's adversary in the courts of Chancery and Star Chamber. The countess maintained that she could not 'call to minde anie such letter', fearing that her 'name hath been by some devise abused to the prejudice of the poore gentleman'.[62] Concern that people might surreptitiously add forged words to the end of letters encouraged some female letter-writers to fill the remaining blank manuscript space with diagonal lines in order to prevent tampering. The recto side of Princess Elizabeth's 'tide letter' to Mary I uses diagonal hatchings to fill the space between the main body of the letter and the salutation and signature.[63] Forgery of letters is also a standard device in plays of the period. In *Twelfth Night*, for example, Maria impersonates her mistress's handwriting, thus duping Malvolio, whose belief in the individuality of handwriting leads to his downfall. Here again, handwriting is not necessarily a singular possession or identity of a person, but rather a commodity that can be faked, an identity assumed. Fear of such treachery contributed to the insecurity associated with letters; many distrusted the post as a medium to communicate matters they wished to keep secret.

Forming an opinion of whether a signatory actually wrote a letter is more problematic in instances where only one extant letter may be studied for an individual woman. Equally, where a letter survives only in the form of a sec-retarial draft or copy, or in printed format, it is hard to determine whether the version that was sent was holograph or not. Despite these problems, it is possible to make judgements about the vast majority of the several thousand letters surveyed. While a large proportion of letters survive as drafts, copies or in print, over half the letters studied were actually penned by women in their own hands and approximately one-quarter of the letters examined were written by amanuenses.[64] Although a large number of women's letters can be established, at least by analysis of handwriting, as indeed having been personally written, a study of the different methods of epistolary composition presents a more complex and nuanced picture of female authorship of letters.

---

[62] BL, Harl., 6996, fo. 164: 05/06/1594.   [63] SP11/4/2, fo. 3.

[64] Over 1,800 holograph letters exist for the period 1540–1603. Holograph status is established only where more than one example of a woman's hand can be examined, or where internal evidence indicates a woman used her own hand. Scribal letters, of which over 800 examples survive for the same period, represent manuscripts written in a professional secretary script, where signatures or postscripts are in a different hand, and instances where letters state use of an amanuensis. In 143 cases only one letter survives for a given letter-writer, with no internal reference indicating by whom the letter was written; these letters are, therefore, excluded from the above calculations. Finally, over 450 letters either survive only in print or can only be viewed in print because access to original documents is denied by private owners. In most cases, except where the writing process is mentioned, little can be inferred about the letter's scribal status.

SECRETARIES, SCRIVENERS, AND AMANUENSES

The evidence of non-holograph letters reveals several categories of people employed by women to write letters. Most commonly used were secretaries, servants, or clerks, usually employed by members of the nobility and gentry, specifically for the purpose of writing.[65] The exact identities of these secretaries is often difficult to pin down, except in the case of certain well-known individuals who served famous women: Roger Ascham, for example, was famed for his services as Latin secretary to Mary I and Elizabeth I; Sir John Wolley, Charles Yetsweirt, and Thomas Edmondes served the latter; and the Italian-born David Rizzio was infamous as the French secretary of Mary, queen of Scots.[66] Secretarial careers were often pursued by literary writers, whose distinctive hands have been detected by manuscript experts: John Donne performed the services of a secretary for Sir Robert and Lady Anne Drury, with whom he travelled to the continent in 1611 to 1612; he composed a letter of thanks in French from Lady Drury to the duchesse de Bouillon.[67] Occasionally secretaries are mentioned by name in letters. Mary Throckmorton wrote to her father Thomas Throckmorton telling him, 'I desired Ridley to wryte me a letter to my uncle'.[68] An incidental reference to her use of a secretary is recorded by Lady Margaret Hoby in her diary: 'I wret a Letter by John Dousone to Richard Hodgsone'.[69] Alternatively, it is possible to establish the identity of an amanuensis by studying a whole collection, where the hand used in a letter can be compared with various other holograph hands. Muriel St Clare Byrne has identified in Lady Lisle's letters the scribal hands of John Husee and Thomas Larke, both of whom were Lisle servants.[70] Likewise, Norman Davis has described the range of different hands used in Margaret Paston's letters, including the hands of servants and family members, such as her husband and sons, as well as several 'unidentified' hands.[71] A petition to Cromwell from Lady Anne Skeffington asking for her safe passage home from Ireland after the death of her husband, Sir William, the lord deputy, has been identified as in the hand of Anthony Colly.[72] In the majority of cases, however, the scribe remains frustratingly anonymous, and even where a name

---

[65] On secretaries see Hammer, 'Use of Scholarship', 26–51; Smith, 'Secretariats of the Cecils', 481–504; *Correspondence of Reginald Pole*, ed. Mayer, 24–9, 36–7. For earlier periods see *Lisle Letters*, i. 59; Bennett, *Pastons and Their England*, 116–17.

[66] Owen, 'Sir John Wolley's Letter-Book', 16–18; May, *Queen Elizabeth I*, pp. xlii–xliii; Wormald, *Mary Queen of Scots*, 160–3.

[67] Joseph P. Regenstein Library, University of Chicago, Bacon Manuscripts of Redgrave Hall 4202: 1611–12. See also Bennett, 'Donne's Letters from the Continent', 66–78; Rambuss, *Spenser's Secret Career*; Höltgen, 'Sir Robert Dallington', 147–77.

[68] Throckmorton, CR1998/Box 60/11: n.d.

[69] *Diary of Lady Margaret Hoby*, ed. Moody, 34.   [70] *Lisle Letters*, iv. p. 229.

[71] *Paston Letters and Papers*, ed. Davis, i. p. lxxix; id., 'A Paston Hand', 209–21; id., 'A Scribal Problem', 31–64.

[72] *L&P*, XI 208; Wood, *Letters of Royal and Illustrious Ladies*, ii. 239–41: 01/08/1536.

can be traced there is often little in the way of biographical material to be found. In general terms, widows appear to have been more likely to have used their own personal servants to conduct correspondence than married women, who presumably employed household servants retained by their husbands. That wives could be involved in the hiring of secretaries, however, is indicated by a letter from Thomas Warley to Honor Lisle, in which he offered her the services of a priest whom, he claimed, could 'write a very fair secretary hand and text hand and Roman'.[73]

Through their intimate involvement with their mistresses' correspondence, secretaries were made privy to their most secret affairs. This access to secret knowledge often meant that secretaries were at the heart of political intrigues. In the aftermath of the hasty marriage of Lord Darnley and Elizabeth Cavendish, the countess of Lennox's secretary Thomas Fowler underwent close interrogation while his mistress was in the Tower in order to ascertain the extent of her involvement in the match, and that of the countess of Shrewsbury and Mary, queen of Scots.[74] Likewise, at Mary, queen of Scots' own state trial, her secretaries Gilbert Curle and Claud Nau were examined and gave evidence against her. Detailed records of their depositions survive, elucidating their roles as political confidants.[75]

Significantly, most secretaries were male, which may have had an effect upon the way in which women's letters were written. In popular literature at least, there is unease about the necessary closeness of the relationship between a male secretary and female mistress, a closeness with clear sexual overtones that impinged upon female chastity and threatened women's sexual honour.[76] There are, however, a few examples of early modern women acting in a secretarial capacity. Katherine Ashley, who was governess to Princess Elizabeth and later a woman of the Bedchamber when Elizabeth became queen, wrote letters on her mistress's behalf. Exactly how often Ashley acted as Elizabeth's secretary is unclear, but at least two instances of her secretarial activity survive. A letter from Princess Elizabeth to Protector Somerset informed him that rather than writing to Lord Admiral Seymour herself, 'I bade her [Ashley] write as she thought best, and bade her show it me when she had done'.[77] Ashley was also asked by Elizabeth to write a letter to William Cecil on behalf of a Scottish prisoner. It is noticeable that in her letter she felt it necessary to explain why she had been asked to write, where it would have been customary for the princess's secretary to do so: 'My ladys graces secretary beyng besy w[i]t[h] my lady about hyr lernyng, hyr grace was lothe to let hym to wrete thes letter, wharefore hyr grace commanded me to wrette hauyng no respecte to the rudenes of my wretyng.'[78] Later

---

[73] *Lisle Letters*, ii. 245. [74] Durant, *Bess of Hardwick*, 86.
[75] Steuart, *Trial of Mary Queen of Scots*, 132, 150–91.
[76] Stewart, 'Gelding Gascoigne', 147–69; Jardine, 'Reading and the Technology of Textual Affect', 91. [77] Cecil, 133, fo. 4/2: 28/01/1549.
[78] BL, Lansd., 1236, fo. 41: 02/08/1549.

examples of women's secretarial functions also survive. During the mid-seventeenth century Elizabeth Dallison (1610–65) wrote letters for her mother, Margaret Oxinden; and on occasion Katherine Oxinden (b. 1644) used her schoolmistress Margaret Jackson to write letters for her.[79] Hannah Wolley, in *The Gentlewoman's Companion* (1675), describes her own activities as her mistress's 'scribe or secretary': 'by inditing all her Letters; in the framing and well-fashioning of which (that I might increase my Ladies esteem) I took indefatigable pains.'[80]

In addition to secretaries, scriveners also wrote letters for women. These were professional scribes who were generally not employed directly by a family, but who operated on a freelance basis hiring out their writing skills.[81] A receipted scrivener's bill dated 7 November 1590 survives for Lady Jane Townshend.[82] There is also some evidence that such scribes wrote letters for people lower down the social scale who were only partially literate. H. R. Woudhuysen has identified the hand of the writing master Peter Bales in a petition to Burghley from Joan Pitt of Weymouth.[83] Ann Carter, the leader of the grain riots in Essex in 1629, similarly had her letters written for her.[84] Semi-professional letter-writers appear to have been widespread during the early modern period.[85] The fullest and most vivid account of the activities of a scrivener is the diary of Roger Lowe, an apprentice to a south Lancashire mercer during the 1660s, which records his informal scribal functions, including the writing of letters. Women frequently number among those who approached him to write letters: 'I was sent for to Bainfor longe to Anne Greinsworth to write letters to London and Preston'; 'Ellin Ashton came to me to write a letter for her, which I did'.[86] The women named in the diary and who used Lowe's letter-writing services are well below the social status of the kinds of women whose letters survive for the sixteenth century. Informal practices of this nature, although less well-documented for earlier periods, gave semi- or partially-literate women access to the world of letter-writing. Indeed, a late fifteenth-century letter in French sent from a woman to George Cely bears strong signs of having been penned by a professional letter-writer.[87]

Beyond these professional and semi-professional scribes, women also turned to family members to write letters for them. There are numerous cases of husbands who penned letters for their wives. A letter from Edith Lady Darcy to

[79] *Oxinden Letters, 1607–1642*, ed. Gardiner, pp. xxix, 233; *Oxinden and Peyton Letters, 1642–1670*, ead. 204.   [80] Wolley, *The Gentlewoman's Companion* (1675), 74.
[81] On scriveners see Woudhuysen, *Sir Philip Sidney*, 52–66. The household of Anne Clifford and the earl of Dorset was large enough to have its own scrivener, one Edward Lane, who is listed in the Catalogue of the Knole Household along with the secretary Mr Edwards: ibid. 57–8.
[82] Folger, MS L.d.795.
[83] Woudhuysen, *Sir Philip Sidney*, 62; BL, Lansd., 161, fos. 207ʳ–208ᵛ.
[84] Thomas, 'Meaning of Literacy', 105.
[85] Ibid. 106. Cressy, *Literacy and the Social Order*, 16; Owen, 'A Scrivener's Notebook', 17.
[86] *Diary of Robert Lowe*, ed. Sachse, 24, 28.
[87] *Cely Letters*, ed. Hanham, 49–50, 262: before 26/05/1479.

her son the earl of Westmoreland was drafted in her husband's hand.[88] Richard
Bertie, second husband of Katherine, duchess of Suffolk, wrote a letter for his
wife to the earl of Leicester.[89] Similarly, many of Muriel Tresham's letters survive
as drafts in her husband's hand, as do many of those of Anne Bacon, the wife of
Nathaniel Bacon of Stiffkey.[90] Alternatively, other relations could be used.
William Cavendish wrote to Burghley for his mother Elizabeth Talbot, countess
of Shrewsbury.[91] Elizabeth Clinton, countess of Lincoln, asked her nephew to
write for her to Sir Richard Marten, alderman of London, and Sir Julius Caesar,
judge of the Admiralty.[92] One of the commonplace books of Sir Stephen Powle,
a Six Clerk at the Court of Chancery, contains a letter 'ghost-written' by him on
behalf of Katherine Smyth, the granddaughter of Powle's second wife Margaret.
The letter, addressed to Samuel Harsnett, bishop of Norwich, beseeched him to
persuade her master, Thomas Lucas, to acquiesce to her love match with his son
Thomas Lucas, junior.[93] Obviously, it is useful to be able to establish precisely
who wrote a woman's letters. Where a husband can be shown to have written
letters for his wife, this throws up interesting questions regarding the influence
and affect he had over what was written, as well as the constraints that lack of
privacy might have imposed on the writing of a letter.

METHODS OF COMPOSITION

There are numerous methods by which letters were composed, each of which
would have affected the degree of control or level of input a woman could
achieve over her correspondence. It is essential, however, to point out here that
many women did in fact write their own letters, in most cases without help from
others. A large proportion of letters are in fact holograph. Where this was the
case, there is evidence to show that some women drafted their own letters. This
can be observed in numerous examples where a woman wrote the main body of
the letter herself and where subsequent changes to the initial text were made in
her own hand. Indeed, this appears to have been the case with Anne Newdigate's
correspondence; several letters written by her contain amendments or corrections
in her same hand.[94] A holograph draft of a letter in the British Library from Lady
Conway written to the Privy Council defending her husband exhibits similar
authorial amendments: Lady Conway crossed out in her letter the phrase 'I ame
[a] woman and have smale or no power to determine of any thing that is my

[88] *L&P*, 12(ii) 186/39: 26/03/[1528–30?].   [89] HMC, *Pepys*, 71–2: 28/12/1565.
[90] BL, Addit., 39828, fos. 75, 84, 85, 87, 90, 136, 136ᵛ, 137, 147, BL, Addit., 39829, fos.
35–35ᵛ; Folger, L.d.15, 16, 17, 18, 19, 20, 21, 23, 51, 476.
[91] BL, Lansd., 71, fo. 2: 21/09/1592.
[92] BL, Addit., 12506, fo. 81: 20/03/1588.
[93] Scott-Warren, 'Reconstructing Manuscript Networks', 31. Bodl. Tanner, 169, fos. 195ᵛ–96ʳ.
[94] WCRO, Newdigate Papers, CR136, B305, B306, B310, B311a. Arbella Stuart also drafted
her own letters: Steen 'Fashioning an Acceptable Self', 86–7.

husbands'.[95] Furthermore, several women—including, Anne Lady Bacon, Lady Elizabeth Russell, Margaret Clifford, countess of Cumberland, and Katherine, duchess of Suffolk—expressed themselves in very distinct and individual styles, easily identifiable throughout their letters, which argues strongly for the fact that they wrote them. Anne Bacon's letters of pious maternal counsel to her son Anthony are highly distinctive, and charged with her personality, as are the strident letters to Robert Cecil from his matronly aunt Elizabeth Russell. In both cases these groups of letters are unmistakeably the women's own work. Examples such as these of letters drafted or written by women suggest a high degree of personal female control over the texts they authored.

Having said this, one cannot always rely on a letter's holograph status, safe in the belief that a woman wrote it unaided, or that it represents the unimpaired 'voice' of a female signatory (if in fact this actually existed, since forms of societal, cultural, and religious mediation are built into modes of expression). Indeed, certain letters ostensibly written by women prove in fact to have been more collaborative than one might at first imagine. At the most basic level, there are examples of letters written by someone else that a woman merely copied out in her own hand. Frances, duchess of Suffolk, asked her then husband, her former equerry Adrian Stokes, to write a letter for her addressed to the queen. She wrote to him asking that he 'devise a letter, and rough draw it for me to copy, so that I may write to the Queen's Majesty for her goodwill and consent to the marriage'.[96] The letter was to deal with the delicate matter of seeking the sovereign's permission for the marriage of Lady Katherine Grey and Edward Seymour, earl of Hertford. Clearly, the duchess trusted Stokes to produce a letter that matched her requirements. Similarly, Sir Robert Sidney requested his wife Barbara to write to his 'frends' to secure leave for him from his military duties, outlining what she should write in her letter to Charles Howard, the lord admiral. Sidney informed his wife that, 'I would have you in any case write very earnestly to my lo[rd] Admiral. I wil write . . . & set down what you shall say to him'.[97] Thomas Morgan, a cipher clerk, spy, and a former secretary of the earl of Shrewsbury, forwarded a draft letter to Mary, queen of Scots, which he wished her to write to the countess of Arundel, and which he suggested might be delivered by means of the French ambassador.[98] Secretaries or government officials were also responsible for writing many of Queen Elizabeth's letters, especially in the case of her official correspondence, which presents problems in attributing to her the authorship of them. The queen's so-called 'autograph' compositions also present problems: a draft of the letter she sent to George Talbot, earl of Shrewsbury, dated 21 October 1572 survives with corrections in Burghley's hand.[99]

[95] BL, Addit., 23212, fo. 191: n.d.   [96] BL, Harl., 6286, fo. 33.
[97] CKS, De L'Isle, U1475, C81/65: 25/08/1595.
[98] Cecil, 164, fos. 30–40: 31/03/1586.
[99] May, *Queen Elizabeth I*, 143; SP12/89, fo. 128.

It was common practice for women to write a first draft of a letter and then seek help and advice in correcting and refining it. Frances Lady Burgh wrote to Thomas Windebank, clerk of the Signet, regarding a dispute between herself and the lord justices of Ireland and the earl of Ormond, arising over the lease of some corn. She sent Windebank a draft of a letter which she intended to be dispatched to Robert Cecil, asking him to, 'correct or make stronger if [there is] cause'.[100] Lady Anne Nevill, who hoped that her husband might be reinstated as *custos rotulorum*[101] in his locality, also approached Windebank to help in the phrasing of a letter that she wished to send in support of her husband's cause. 'Good frende and kinde neighbour', she wrote, 'polish my rough hewen speach proceading from a minde that never knew how to dissemble.'[102] In such cases, where a third party was involved in the writing of a letter, the language used was not entirely that of the signatory; and those changes made by a third party may have slightly altered the presentation or effect of certain phrases. Equally, those giving such assistance may have bolstered the letter with inventions of their own, perhaps advocating a different approach or argument for pleading a case, or the use of a specific rhetorical strategy.

In connection with this cooperative production, two letters are worth analysing in greater detail, in that they both illustrate a prominent male influence— of a brother in the first instance and a servant in the second—attempting to refashion the self-image of a woman sending the letter. In both cases the letters were from wives to their husbands during periods of marital dispute. The first example is a letter drafted by Robert Devereux, earl of Essex, for his sister Dorothy Percy, countess of Northumberland. In drafting the letter for the countess to send to her estranged husband, Essex hoped to achieve reconciliation between the couple. He wrote to his sister stating, 'you have writen to him [her husband] l[ett]res of contrary stiles, some that heale, & others agayne that rankle the wound that you have made in his hart, w[hi]ch makes him think you unconstant and commanded by your passions'.[103] Essex counselled his sister to employ a more submissive tone in her letters and drafted an example for her to send, writing, 'I do infinitly wisshe that you wold write unto him one l[ett]re more to this effect'. The drafted letter is quoted in full to illustrate the style that Essex wished his sister to adopt:

My lo[rd] I haue expected yo[u]r resolucion, w[hi]ch I am willing to hasten out of no ill respect to yo[u]r self. And therefore once again will desire that the cawses of these discontentments may not be revived nor disputed, for they are troublesom to me to think of & enemyes to a reconcilement w[hi]ch I offre with a resolved mind to deserve yo[u]r love seconded by hope of better reward thoughe of late myne ears have receaued terrifyng tales I will believe [*sic*] tyll your honor, wisdom & discretion will hold you from wronging both yo[u]r self & me & then I will promise my self a more happye life &

---

[100] Cecil, 64, fo. 88: 06/10/1598.   [101] The principal Justice of the Peace.
[102] SP12/279/20: 06/03/1601.   [103] Cecil, 179, fo. 157 (2): *c.*03/1600.

approve my desert both to you & the world, w[hi]ch doth constantly bynd me to be yo[u]r faithful wife.[104]

There is no evidence that the countess of Northumberland actually followed her brother's advice and sent the letter. It is important, however, not to mistake the letter as an example of her own writing or as representative of the way she felt toward her husband. It does not reflect the countess's own words, but rather speaks with a voice constructed by her brother; the relative submission and obedience revealed in the letter are not her own. The fact that Essex felt the need to advise her suggests that the tone of her former letters had been far from submissive. Moreover, it is interesting to note that, although the letter is generally polite and acquiescent, it is not as self-effacing as it might have been. A veiled yet firm resolve is still evident. This must, at least in part, be explained by the fact that if his sister's attempts failed to achieve the desired rapprochement with her husband, it was important in Essex's mind 'that it might appear to the worlde it was his fault [the earl of Northumberland's] & not yours that you live a sunder'.[105] On the one hand, there was a need for the countess to be seen publicly to have been a dutiful wife; on the other hand, total submission and personal admission of sole responsibility for the separation were not compatible with the maintenance of Devereux family honour. The letter, therefore, represents a carefully calculated response to these two considerations.

A useful complement to this letter is an epistle in the British Library from Elizabeth Willoughby to her husband, Sir Francis.[106] The letter is one of only three original letters of this writer that survive—all of which, incidentally, were penned by an amanuensis.[107] Interestingly, the letter appears to have been dictated and shows signs of modification by a secretary. At the bottom of the letter the secretary wrote, 'Madame as I haue altred this l[ett]re yow may w[i]th good warrant send it to S[i]r F[rancis] but in any wise remember the condicions how they stand w[i]th yow that yow be not overtaken w[i]th them'. The draft is full of crossings-out and other amendments in the same hand as this note. In part the alterations were made to correct grammatical errors; in addition, certain non-essential information seems to have been excluded. The main effect, however, was the toning down of certain passages. While the overall tone of the first draft appears to have been largely conciliatory, there are points in the text where Lady Willoughby's obsequious style displays an almost desperate desire

---

[104] Cecil, 179, fo. 157 (1): *c.*03/1600. Both the surviving letters are themselves copies in the hand of Edward Reynolds, one of Essex's secretaries: HMC, *Salisbury*, xiv. 127–8. On Dorothy Percy see Bracher, 'The Abuse(s) of Intimacy: Dorothy Percy and Male Relations', in 'Representations of Intimacy and the Historiography of Early Modern Private Life', 185–237.

[105] Cecil, 179, fo. 157 (2).

[106] Friedman, *House and Household*; ead., 'Portrait of a Marriage', 542–55.

[107] The remaining letters survive as copies made by Cassandra Willoughby in the late seventeenth century (University of Nottingham Library). Partial transcriptions of these are printed in HMC, *Middleton*, 504–610.

for reconciliation with her husband, revealing simultaneously extreme submissiveness and the frustration she felt towards him over his maltreatment of her. It is this more emotional, less controlled side of the letter that the secretary filtered out. This can be seen in the following passage; the parts of the text that have been struck through represent secretarial alterations:

I require no one iote of favor at yo[u]r handes ~~So I pray god to dele w[i]th me further as w[i]th a most faithles & periured parson both towardes him and yow~~ So againe if yo[u]r meaning be to have me acknowleg of my former forgettfullnes of my dutie ~~many wayes~~ towardes yow for & concerninge howshold matters only Then my answere is that that hath bene donne many times & long synce both by my l[ette]rs and by my self apon my knees ~~And for your further & full satisfaction herin I do here once agayne confesse to yow under my hand & seale that I have behaved my self towardes yow both unadvisedly & undutifully both in worde & deede many wayes & many tymes for the w[hi]ch I have bene & am very hartely sory humbly requiring yow both to forgive me & forgett it.~~[108]

This is a clear example of a secretary helping to construct a female persona—but the result is not the distortion of the writing to conform to inherently male ideas of female behaviour. Rather, it seems implicit that Elizabeth Willoughby was fully aware of the effectiveness of presenting a submissive self-image, but that this sometimes ran to excess; the secretary was merely colluding with her in the writing of the letter, to develop and shape it. Significantly, his alterations seem to have been designed to moderate Lady Willoughby's excessive submissiveness and to prevent her from taking the full blame for the rift in relations between herself and her husband.

Both of the letters discussed serve to qualify common-sense conceptions about the idea of single authorship, illustrating how 'female' postures could be manipulated by men or women, and the ways in which what appears 'personal' or intimate is in fact mediated. Indeed, Danielle Clarke argues that interest should not focus on identifying the female voice, but rather in 'understanding . . . its constructedness within early modern culture'.[109] Similarly, Elizabeth Heale has importantly cautioned that female-voiced poems were not necessarily written by women. These and other examples illustrate the way in which standard female voices—the dutiful and submissive wife, the obedient daughter, the rebuking mother—could be constructed by men as well as by women.[110] Standard gender stereotypes and models of this nature could be exploited for epistolary purposes when occasion required. Indeed, writing female-voiced letters was schoolboy practice: Erasmus directed pupils towards Ovid's *Heroides*, a storehouse of female epistolary examples, enjoining them to practice writing letters from women in the manner of Helen restraining Paris

[108] BL, Lansd., 46, fos. 65–66ᵛ: *c*.1586.
[109] Clarke, 'Women, Rhetoric and the Ovidian Tradition', 62.
[110] Heale, *Wyatt, Surrey and Early Tudor Poetry*, 45, 65 n. 23. Stewart, 'Voices of Anne Cooke', 88–102; Harvey, *Ventriloquized Voices*.

from an illicit love affair, or Penelope's letter to Ulysses. 'Similarly', he wrote, 'one may compose a letter from a wife to her husband who is tarrying abroad, telling him to hasten home.'[111]

Where the draft survives, as in the case of Elizabeth Willoughby's letter, there are several levels on which it might be read, each of them revealing. The first draft often reveals more of a woman's initial response to a situation, a response often lost as a result of rewriting. A study of successive drafts, however, discloses passages lost by subsequent amendments, and the toning-down of phrases considered inappropriate to commit to paper. In contrast with initial writings, the final product can be less spontaneous, showing how a woman wished to project herself rather than her spontaneous reactions. Letter-writing as an activity, therefore, is frequently more self-conscious and more calculated than might at first appear. This issue of the immediacy and spontaneity of women's letters has been explored by Sara Jayne Steen. In analysing the recurrent theme of illness in Arbella Stuart's correspondence, and the ways in which she drafted and redrafted her letters, Steen shows that women's letters are texts capable of complex or multiple readings. The essay, which investigates the competing balance between impulsiveness and calculation in Arbella Stuart's writing, alerts scholars to the fact that what outwardly appear to be genuine complaints of ill-health may in actual fact represent political strategy in her dealings with King James and the court.[112] Considerations of this nature regarding calculation, artifice, and strategy further complicate the process of recovering what might be described as the 'true' voice of a female letter-writer, and of reading beyond what is convention to what is personal.

A major problem arising where only a holograph final draft survives is evaluating how much help the female signatory received in writing the letter. In the case of correspondence that is established as having been written by an amanuensis, there are several different methods by which letters were composed. For example, letters could have been either dictated orally, or written from notes that a woman provided. Alternatively, secretaries might have used model or form letters, which they tailored for specific situations according to a woman's requirements.

Dictation was one of the principal ways in which writers communicated their letters to a secretary in order for him to write them. Indeed, it has been argued that the majority of men and women's letters composed during the late medieval period were dictated, a practice which seemingly continued throughout the sixteenth and seventeenth centuries, and indeed still continues today.[113] The task

---

[111] Erasmus, *De conscribendis epistolis* (1522), 24. Writing in a 'feminine voice' was common rhetorical training for schoolboys. Aphthonius's *Progymnasmata* recommended the examples of Hecuba and Niobe as models of highly charged, intense emotional forms of self-presentation: Jardine, 'Unpicking the Tapestry', 145. Jenson, 'Male Models of Feminine Epistolarity', 25–45.
[112] Steen, 'How Subject to Interpretation', 109–26.
[113] Constable, *Letters and Letter Collections*, 42–4.

of letter-writing in this instance should therefore be seen as merely mechanical and distant from the technologies of writing. Roger Chartier has also suggested that the ongoing practice of composing letters orally may have been related to the importance of rhetoric in letter-writing, which formed a major component of epistolary manuals produced during the Renaissance, as well as the relationship between letters and speech, with many letters in fact intended for reading aloud by the addressee.[114] In practice, however, assessing whether or not a letter was dictated is less straightforward. In several cases this can be achieved by examining the consistency of a particular writer's style over a range of letters. Correspondence is thought to have been dictated in circumstances where different letters by the same woman yield a similar style, irrespective of whether they were written in her hand or not. Muriel St Clare Byrne used this methodology in her work on the letters of Honor Lady Lisle. She argued that none of Lady Lisle's surviving letters were actually written in her own hand, but that they had been written by three different secretaries and that this, therefore, allowed for some degree of comparison. Indeed, what St Clare Byrne noted was the remarkable consistency in the style of Lady Lisle's letters, regardless of which of the three secretaries she used to write for her. She concluded that this evidence strongly suggested that the letters were dictated.[115]

This type of analysis will work only where a number of conditions apply. Above all, one must be able to detect a unique and personal style for a given epistolary author; in other words, that she wrote in a way that is distinctive enough for one to tell it apart from someone else's writing, which to some extent runs counter to the earlier comments about the construction of different female personas. This is further complicated where the phrasing used in letters is conventional. Certainly, some sixteenth-century letters are stylized and many writers adopted formulaic phrases with which to open and close their letters.[116] However, beyond polite observance of convention many letters display highly personal elements, often employing vivid and emotive language. Albrecht Classen has argued that the letters of many female writers 'show very surprising directness'.[117] A woman's writing may, for example, have been made distinct by the use of certain common words or phrases, or by the fact that she displayed a particular confidence and self-assurance in her letters, or that she showed a discernible personal intimacy with an addressee.

Additionally, only where there is a sufficient selection of correspondence for analysis is one able to detect whether a letter has been dictated or not. It is also essential that there are different types of business and family letters, which are both holograph and autograph to enable comparison. Furthermore, to ensure consistency one must compare only letters of the same type or letters written to

---

[114] Chartier, 'Secrétaires *for the People?*', 64.   [115] *Lisle Letters*, iv. pp. 229–31.
[116] Davis, '*Litera Troili* and English Letters', 237.
[117] Classen, 'Female Epistolary Literature', 3.

the same person: the tone of business letters may differ significantly from more intimate letters to family. Further problems arise, in that a woman's style may have changed between her dictating a letter and writing one herself. There are, as well, numerous formal and stylistic constraints that dictation imposed. Beyond this, there were variations in the way that dictation was carried out. Whilst some letters were dictated verbatim, for others the majority of the letter was dictated, leaving the secretary merely to add introductory and closing formulae, and perhaps the place and date of writing.

Of the several thousand letters examined for this study, there are approximately twenty individual women for whom a sufficient variety of correspondence survives to allow an assessment of their letters for the possibility of dictation. In the case of most of these women at least some letters show signs of having been dictated. For Katherine, duchess of Suffolk, there remains a correspondence to William Cecil, almost all of which she wrote herself. The countess's letters reveal a considerable degree of intimacy with Cecil. Writing to him, she was open, confident, authoritative, and often playful. On one of the few occasions she used a secretary to write to Cecil she stated, 'I wrote not this w[i]th myne owne hand vnto yow'. The letter bears all the hallmarks of dictation, rather than composition by secretary, similar in both tone and language to those letters that the duchess penned herself. 'What a weary begger I am', she familiarly described herself to her close acquaintance.[118] The style is instanly discernible as her own, redolent as it is of her usual determination and frankness of comment. This suggests that when the duchess of Suffolk used a secretary for her correspondence, he took down her dictation word for word. Where this was the case, women could maintain a high degree of epistolary control.

An alternative method of composition, other than dictation, was for an amanuensis to work from notes detailing what a woman wished to have included in the letter. Honor Lisle had notes made for a letter she wished to have written and sent to Madame de Riou, the aristocratic lady with whom her daughter was lodging at the time in France.[119] Similarly, Lady Bridget Norris produced minutes for a letter she wished Sir Robert Cecil to write to the lord deputy of Ireland; the notes were enclosed in a letter to Lady Ralegh. The letter to Lady Ralegh also sought to enrol Sir Walter Ralegh's help in composition: 'I haue framed the effect of a letter that I desire to Haue derected to the Deputy [of Ireland] from Mr secretarie. I trust yf S[i]r Walter Raleighe will take the paines to polishe them he shall also preuaile in the subscribing therin.'[120] The notes for the suggested letter from Cecil to the lord deputy of Ireland that were enclosed for Ralegh read as follows:

I haue deliuered unto your lo[rdship] the Queens pleasure concerning a companie to be leade by the constable of the Lady Noracyes castell desiring yow also ^at that tyme^ to

---

[118] BL, Lansd., 2, fo. 46: n.d.   [119] *Lisle Letters*, iii. p. 155.
[120] Cecil, 83, fo. 28: *c.*1600.

signifie unto the president [of Munster] that the same companie should be lodged on her lands the w[hi]ch shee complaineth not to be obserued by hym but other bands plased their greatlie to Her preiudice by the spoyle he maketh of her woods and other comodities I am therfore to desire yo[u]r lo[rdship] to graunte the La[dy] yo[u]r per-emtorie warrant to remove anie captaine that lodgeth on her land and to place theire, that in the leadinge of her overseer. But because yt is to be hoped that in shorte tyme the commission maie be lessened yo[u]r lo[rdship] maie make the warrant so that yf yt be not thought needfull to continewe the whole hundreth and fiftie or that there be more necessarie ocassion for the service to drawe them else wheare that then theire be onely so manie lefte in the castell as to yo[u]r lo[rdship] shall seem fytt to secure yt from anie sodaine violence being a place of verie great importance in the tyme of warre.[121]

Lady Norris clearly spelt out exactly what she wished to have included in the letter and suggested reasons to support her case. However, the letter's final form, its language and eventual content, would have been influenced to some extent by the recommendations made by Ralegh and Cecil.

In addition to dictation and working from notes, secretaries employed model or standard letters, the forms of which could be adapted to the individual circumstances of a woman's particular requirements. The use of such models was already widespread for both men and women well before 1500.[122] During the sixteenth century itself a large number of letter-writing manuals were printed, providing a range of sample letters for a variety of occasions, and secretaries also compiled manuscript formularies for their own personal use.[123] Exemplary letters by women also circulated in manuscript form, which gave women access to model letters.[124] Moreover, in practice secretaries did sometimes employ model letters when writing on a woman's behalf. This is well illustrated by three letters written by Elizabeth, countess of Lincoln, Lady Dorothy Stafford, and Lady Mary Scudamore to Sir Bassingbourne Gawdy, at a time when he was rumoured to be in the running for the post of sheriff of Norfolk. These three court ladies wrote to Gawdy on behalf of Mr Nicholas Fermor, a client of the earl of Leicester, whom they sought to place as his under-sheriff for the county if he himself was appointed to the post.[125] Strikingly, all three letters are almost identical in style, language, and content. Lady Scudamore's and Lady Stafford's letters are nearly exactly the same, word for word, including the mode of address, differing only slightly in the last two lines. The similarity of these letters reflects the use of standard forms in writing letters of recommendation, and perhaps

[121] Cecil, 83, fo. 27.
[122] Griffiths, 'Public and Private Bureaucracies', 120–1; Pantin, 'Medieval Treatise on Letter Writing', 326–82.
[123] Robertson, *Art of Letter-Writing*; Hornbeak, *Complete Letter-Writer*; Bolgar, 'Teaching of Letter-Writing', 245–53. For an example of a manuscript formulary see BL, Addit., 48150, Yelverton, CLXI (2): 'Robert Beale's Formulary Book'.
[124] Folger, V.a.321, fos. 20ᵛ–21, X.d.178.
[125] The letters survive as copies in Sir Bassingbourne Gawdy's letter-book. Tanner, 241, fos. 1b–2, 31/10–3/11/1576. Lady Stafford's original letter also survives: BL, Eg., 2713, fo. 54: 31/10/1576.

even the possibility that Fermor provided copies of or indeed penned the letter he wished to have sent on his behalf. The practice of appending signatures to form letters appears to have been quite typical. Anne Clifford recorded in her diary signing thirty-three letters 'with my own Hand', which were sent to the tenants of Westmoreland.[126] Such letters echo Falstaff's 'letters, writ with blank space' in Shakespeare's *The Merry Wives of Windsor*, where multiple copies were made of the same letter, with gaps into which the names of different people could be placed.[127] In either event, in the case of the letters dispatched on behalf of Fermor, the role a woman had to play in the actual writing of the letter was minimal. More significant was her position and influence at court, as well as the authority that a letter bearing her signature carried.

In each of the various methods of construction that I have outlined, the language used was not entirely that of the women who sent the letters, and the level of influence that a third party may have exerted varies from letter to letter. An epistle that was first drafted by a woman will have had a far greater level of input from a female signatory than one written specifically for her, the actual wording of which she would have had very little to do with. Likewise, a letter dictated verbatim is more likely to represent a woman's wording than those letters that were written from notes, where the secretary had greater freedom to shape the letter according to his own liking. In particular, when a woman drafted or dictated a letter the greater part of the text can be attributed to her. In relation to this, and to Margaret Ferguson's question, 'if a woman dictates her words to a male scribe, is she still to be considered a "woman writer"?' (a question rarely asked of male writers), it is important to remember that the rudimentary act of putting ink on a page was only one of a range of skills associated with authorship, including composition, communication, memory, imagination, legal and business acumen, and attention to detail.[128] Indeed, a woman who dictated a letter would still have used many of these skills, the only difference being that she would not have worked on paper herself, but rather orally. The fact that she did not pen her own words does not mean that she was not responsible for them; however, it does suggest that one must accept a relatively broad definition of women's writing to incorporate a range of methods of composition.

Nevertheless, it is sometimes hard to gauge exactly how closely a final letter matched a woman's initial intentions, as well as the level of control that she had over the contents of a letter.[129] The issue of how much influence a secretary might have exerted is one that concerned contemporary writers of the period. In theory, at least, the role of an amanuensis was thought to be to reproduce his

---

[126] *Diaries of Lady Anne Clifford*, ed. Clifford, 54, 233, *passim*.

[127] Shakespeare, *The Merry Wives of Windsor*, II. i. 72–73. See also BL, Lansd., 107, fo.156: 'John Gerard. A l[ett]re of his owne drawing for ye L[ord] Tres[urer] to signe to ye vniversity of cambridg for planting of gardens.'

[128] Ferguson 'Renaissance Concepts of the "Woman Writer" ', 151.

[129] *Letters of Henry VIII*, ed. St Clare Byrne, 200–1.

master's (or mistress's) words and not to add inventions of his own. Angel Day in *The English Secretorie* wrote that a secretary should: 'giue heed to obserue the Order, Method and Forme to him from his Lord or master deliuered: forasmuch as in discharge hereof he is utterly to relinquish any affectation to his owne doings, or leaning herein to any priuat iudgment or fantasie. His pen in this action is not his own, but anothers, and for this cause the matters to him committed, are to depend upon the humor of his commander, and upon none others.'[130] Broadly speaking, the degree of control a woman had over a letter depended entirely upon whether she was able to read it, and indeed whether she did so before it was sent. It is widely assumed that more women were able to read than write during this period, suggesting that those women who themselves could not write, but could read manuscript, were nevertheless able to achieve some degree of control over their correspondence.[131] In this sense, the input of female signatories into letters may in certain circumstances have been more a function of a woman's ability to read a letter than her ability to write one.

Moreover, there is widespread evidence to indicate that women did in fact look at and review the letters that were written and amended for them. John Drury, a servant of the countess of Bath, sent his mistress a copy of a letter that he had written for her and wished her to sign: '[I] umbely desyer your honor to put your hand to a letter that I have sent by this bearer, w[hi]ch is acordyng to a copy w[hi]ch I haue sent also not w[i]th standyng if ther be any thyng not greabell to your plesure & kindnes then to awltar yt as yt shall please you.'[132] It is clear from this that Drury expected the countess to read the letter and check whether it was acceptable for dispatch. Similarly, Elizabeth Bourne, who sometimes sought help in composition from others, thanked John Conway for correcting a draft of a business letter that she had sent to him, writing 'I wyll wryt the leter a newe and I lyke the altering of hit well'.[133] In this case, Elizabeth Bourne not only read the corrections that had been made for her, but also she implemented them, rewriting the letter herself.

Where such direct signs of the checking of letters are lacking, autograph signatures (which most letters contain) attest to women's review and reading of their letters. A signature is usually understood to connote the ability to read as well as at least a rudimentary level of writing ability.[134] Furthermore, in order to sign a letter a woman would need to have seen it before it was sent and presumably would have read it before signing. Additionally, many letters contain holograph postscripts, further evidence that women had contact with their letters before they were sent and that they were satisfied with the contents of correspondence that went out in their name. The final draft of a letter then would have incorporated suggestions made by a third party, to a greater or lesser

[130] (1595), ii. 132.
[131] Schofield, 'Measurement of Literacy', 316; Cressy, *Literacy and the Social Order*, 20; Spufford 'First Steps in Literacy', 410.   [132] CUL, Hengrave, 88/I, fo. 130: n.d.
[133] BL, Addit., 23212, fo. 153: n.d.   [134] Cressy, *Literacy and the Social Order*, 53–61.

extent; but in the final analysis, it was the woman alone who decided what was to be included and what to be excluded. Where a woman was highly literate and could read and write with great fluency she would have been able to exert a strong degree of control over the writing process, possibly even redrafting the letter herself in light of advice from others. In other cases, undoubtedly, control over correspondence would depend very much upon the level of a woman's literacy, that is, the competency with which she could write or read script.

EPISTOLARY PRIVACY

More nebulous than the issues of women's textual input and female authorship is the self-censorship that arose from an absence of epistolary privacy, caused by collaborative practices of letter-writing. Put more simply, there is a sense in which a woman would perhaps have been less inclined either to be as intimate, or as personal, in a letter written by someone else than she would in a letter written herself. Erasmus was concerned about the negative effects the use of secretaries had on correspondence, in that it impaired openness and freedom of expression, and prevented secrecy between signatory and addressee: 'If you dictate verbatim, then it is goodbye to your privacy; and so you disguise some things and suppress others in order to avoid having an unwanted confidant. Hence, quite apart from the problem of the genuineness of the text, no open conversation with a friend is possible here.'[135] The desire for confidentiality is also apparent in an epistle written from Lady Catherine Daubeney to Thomas Cromwell, in which she stated that she preferred to write in her own hand than to 'trust any so far as to know my mind'.[136] This suggests that there were certain matters of too sensitive a nature to be made privy to a third party and about which some women may have felt uneasy in sharing with a secretary. Angel Day in the section of *The English Secretorie* titled 'Of the partes, place and office of a Secretorie', wrote of the 'secresie, trust, and assurance, required at the handes of him who serueth in such place'.[137] When Elizabeth Talbot, countess of Shrewsbury, was unable to write to Burghley in her own hand, concerning her guardianship of Arbella Stuart, she asked her son to write for her rather than a secretary. She wrote to Burghley informing him that: 'I am inforced to vse the hand of my sonn W[illia]m Cavendysshe, not beinge able to wryte so much my self for feare of bringing great payne to my he[a]d, he only is pryvy to your lo[rdshi]ps letter, & neyther Arbell nor any other lyuinge, nor shalbe.'[138] Some business matters were shared with amanuenses, but there were others for which this would have been unsuitable. Therefore, where an amanuensis was used details may have been

---

[135] Osley, *Scribes and Sources*, 30.
[136] Wood, *Letters of Royal and Illustrious Ladies*, ii. 122: 1534.
[137] Day, *The English Secretorie* (1595), ii. 102.   [138] BL, Lansd., 71, fo.2: 21/09/1592.

either omitted or modified. The fact that most secretaries were male may also have made women more self-conscious about what they said to them, and thus about what they wished to be included, especially where letters were of an intimate or romantic nature. However, the extent of this modification would of course have depended on numerous factors, such as the woman's intimacy with and trust of the amanuensis, her own personal confidence and authority, and perhaps more important, the type of letter being written, as well as the woman's relationship with the recipient. Clearly, women who wrote their own letters might overcome the problems of epistolary privacy.

Nowhere is the potential effect of a lack of epistolary privacy more significant than in the study of the family, where letters have frequently been drawn upon to examine change over time in the intimacy and emotional content of relationships. In part, differences in sentiment are related to the nature of the sources studied. Those letters written using an amanuensis are less likely to read as personally or as spontaneously as holograph letters. Just as there were matters that one might not have shared with a third party, so too were there emotions and intimacies one would have been ill at ease in sharing with those outside the family, or even outside a particular relationship. In turn this necessitates scholarly sensitivity to different methods of epistolary construction. Ralph Houlbrooke has argued that correspondence conducted between husband and wife 'became a more personal and private matter' in the second half of the sixteenth century.[139] He sees this as stemming less from a changing view of a woman's place within society, or a marked shift in spousal affections, than from the increasing female literacy of the sixteenth century and the resultant rise in epistolary privacy that this promoted, as greater numbers of women wrote their own letters.[140] In this analysis, marital and other family relationships remain relatively constant over the late medieval and early modern periods, marked by slower and more gradual change than has been depicted by certain historians. Instead, what alters is the nature of letters, which are more likely to have been personally written during the second half of the sixteenth century, which encouraged individual and privy expression.

The effect that use of an amanuensis had upon the style and content of letters is particularly well illustrated by two letters from Lettice Dudley, countess of Leicester, to her son Robert Devereux, earl of Essex. One of the letters she wrote herself, whereas for the other she used a secretary. The majority of the countess's letters to her son were holograph, and it appears that she valued letters that were personally written. Indeed, she wrote to Essex of her joy in receiving a letter from him in his own hand.[141] The letter to her son for which she employed an amanuensis differs greatly from those to him written in her own hand.

---

[139] Houlbrooke, *English Family*, 101.   [140] Ibid. 101.
[141] WCRO, 'Essex Letter Book *c.*1595–1600', MI 229.

Full transcripts of both letters are provided in order that the difference between them may be clearly observed.

The first letter, dated 11 December 1598, was written in a small neat secretary hand and was only signed by Lettice Dudley. It requested Essex to intervene with the Council of the Marches in Wales on behalf of the dean of Lichfield over a disputed parsonage:

My good Sonn my Cozen Mr docter Bulleyn deane of Lichefielde hath bene an earneste suter to mee to entreate yow in his behalfe to put yo[u]r hande to a l[ett]re w[hi]ch I sende yow heareinclosed directed to the councell of the marches of Walles and also that yow woulde so mutch fauoure him as to procure the Lo[rd] Chamberlayne ^&^ the Lo[rd] Admyrall to joyne w[i]th yow and put theare hands also to the same l[ett]re his requeste to the Councell of the Marches is as yow ^may^ more at large perceiue by the l[ett]re directed by yo[u]r selfe to them That wheareas theare is now depending a matter in question before them touching the force of a lease graunted by one Charleton late parson of the parsonage of Banger in Wales to one Gerrarde for the sum of fortie marks yearely being woorthe at the leaste by the yeare (as the Deane Saythe) an Hundreth pounds w[hi]ch parsonage hir ma[jes]tie for his better mayntenance hath lately bestowed on him And fynding the beste parte of it so incombred by his prediccessor feareth unles hee may bee soom what countenanced by his good freends by writing to the said Councell to desire them that the matter may haue (and the rather at yo[u]r requests) sutch speedie hearing and determinacon as in equitie and conscience shalbee thoughte fitt ~~Otherwyse~~ hee shalbee longe delayed in his sute to the greate losse and hinderance of his present fortune I shoulde thearefore bee gladd the (poore Deane) mighte haue what fauoure in this case ~~mi~~ coulde conveniently bee afforded him and the rather in regarde that hee is our kynesman and my good neighboure and also keepeth a verie good howse for the releefe of his poore neighboures aboute him And so prayinge god to blesse and prosper yow in all yo[u]r proceedings I ende

From Drayton Bassett this xith of December 1598
your mother that derlye loueth you
L Leycester[142]

The second letter is holograph and undated, probably written sometime after Essex's return from Ireland in September 1599, but before his ill-fated revolt in February 1601. Written in a relatively large italic hand, it is representative of the familiar and flowing style the countess used when writing to her son. In it she offered him help and advice:

Swet Ro[bert] your self hath geuen me such a tast[e] of sume strang[e] matter to be loked for as I cannot be quiet tyll I know the trew caus[e] of your abcence and dyscontentment if it be but for Ierland I dought not but you ar[e] wyse and polytyke enufe to counter myne with your enemys whos deuelysh practyces can noe way hurt you but on wherfore my dere sonne geue me leue to be a lytle ielious ouer you for your good and intret you to haue euer god and your oune honore before your ey[e]s so shall you be sure that he will dyspos inded all as you say for the best in dyspyght of all enemyse my frend[143] and

---

[142] The closing mode of address and signature are in the countess's own hand.
[143] 'My frend' refers to her third husband, Sir Christopher Blount, whom she married in 1589.

I cannot but be trobled with thys news and doe wish our selues with you as he would sone be if we thought hys sarues nedfull or that you would haue it so w[h]ich let us know and he will leue all other ocasyons what so euer and will presentlye be with you well if it be but mens matters I know you have corage enufe if womens you haue metlye well paſſed the pyks [pikes] allredy and therein you shuld be skyllfull so praynge you not to be to secret from your best frends. I end beseching the allmyghtye to bles you euer in hys hyghest fauoure whill I am your mother derlyest. L Leycester

The first letter is notably more formal in tone than the second, which is fluid and expressive in its manner. The former is also appreciably less intimate and affectionate in style. Whereas the secretary conventionally addressed the letter to 'my good sonn', when writing herself the countess adopted the more informal and caring form 'swet Ro[bert]'. More significant are the letters' actual contents, the topics they deal with, and their level of candour. The first is a routine business letter dealing with patronage and giving a standard description of circumstances, with little in the way of a personal flavour to it. The second, on the other hand, concerns a highly sensitive political matter. In it, the countess shows obvious concern for her son's predicament, expressing herself, 'to be a lytle ielious ouer you for your good', and is critical of his enemies whom, however, she does not name. She also offers him both her help and that of her husband, Sir Christopher Blount, if needed. Blount was among those executed for their part in the Essex Revolt of 1601, and it may be his possible involvement in the revolt to which the countess referred. It is, thus, unlikely that Lettice Dudley would have entrusted to an amanuensis the writing of a letter of such high political import. There is an obvious freedom of expression in the countess's holograph letters, which is also found in other letters that women wrote themselves. What perhaps is harder to uncover is the extent to which within their letters women internalized societal values. In this sense, even when the layers of secretarial intervention, the epistolary conventions, the processes of drafting, and the different methods of construction have been peeled away, one is still left in search of the elusive voice of a female signatory, a voice itself shaped and conditioned by society and experience, and which was constructed differently according to the addressee and the very purpose of writing.

The sixteenth century thus exhibits widely differing degrees of female autonomy in the sphere of epistolary activity. At one end of the spectrum women read, signed, or even merely accepted unread what men had written for them, while at the other, they either wrote their own letters, or were able to make more independent use of suggestions that they had been given. Importantly, handwriting was not always a singular possession or the identity of an individual person; the function of writing was sometimes merely mechanical, and also, as in the case of dictated letters, distanced from the technologies of writing. As this chapter has argued, however, many women were able to exert a high degree of control over the final texts of their letters. Therefore, any attempt to define women's writing, for both the late medieval and early modern periods, must incorporate letters of a collaborative nature. In short, for a woman to be considered an author it is not necessary for her to have possessed the ability to write or actually herself to have written a text. What mattered instead was that she could communicate orally what she wished to have set down, or that she was able to participate in the process of revision. Although such a claim does not square with modern conceptions of authorship or textual production, it is one that would have been entirely acceptable during the sixteenth century for both women and men.

4

Female Literacy and the Social
Conventions of Letter-Writing

Sixteenth-century women's letters, as detailed in the previous chapter, exhibit widely diverging levels of scribal activity: at one extreme, women wrote entire letters themselves, at the other, secretaries both wrote and signed women's letters for them. These differences of the extent of scribal input reflect in part different letter-writing habits and conventions, the differing propensities of individuals to correspond in their own hands, material and bodily factors, and varying degrees of illiteracy and inequalities in the extent of women's literary abilities. As such, letters as a source are unparalleled as both indicators of ability levels of female literacy and illiteracy, and for what they reveal about the social conventions of literacy, that is, when and how literacy skills were utilized. Untangling the complex relationship between the skills of penmanship and customary epistolary practice is central to an understanding of the ways in which letters were composed. The fact that a woman did not write a letter herself, however, as V. M. O'Mara has argued for the late medieval period, is not necessarily an indication of her inability to write: it is likely that medieval tradition at least dictated the use of an amanuensis rather than a pen, and that personal literacy was reserved for other tasks and other occasions.[1] For the sixteenth century, many women who employed secretaries to compose letters could also themselves write, and indeed did so, depending on the type of letter, circumstance, and the nature of their relationship with the addressee. By approaching the letter-writing process from the perspective of the mechanics of composition, this chapter attempts to offer a more sophisticated picture of the habits and manners associated with early modern literacy practices. The chapter is therefore interested as much in attitudes to female literacy and writing in general as it is in actual levels of female literacy.

In the first instance, the chapter explores the nature and range of female writing proficiency, analysing the physical evidence of female scribal skills documented by letters. It also looks at shifts in letter-writing practices and conventions over the period, the circumstances in which secretaries were employed, and the increased importance attached to women's ability to write.

---

[1] O'Mara, 'Female Scribal Ability', 87–130.

Looking at when women actually wrote their own letters and when they relin-
quished the task to a secretary sheds light on the public and private uses of
literacy: the kinds of written subject-matters that required personal attention, as
opposed to those that one could safely communicate via a third party. Finally,
the chapter examines the extent to which letters document 'higher' forms of
female literacy, beyond orthography and penmanship, including ownership and
reading of books, and interest in poetry, music, medicine, theology, and plays.

LEVELS OF FEMALE WRITING ABILITY:
THE SCRIBAL EVIDENCE

Two contrasting female correspondents aptly demonstrate variations in levels of
women's ability to write during the sixteenth century and its impact on letter-
writing practices. Both women are from similar gentry backgrounds and wrote
between the late 1570s and early 1590s. The first is Mary Harding, the court
maid of Lady Bridget Manners, herself the daughter of Elizabeth, countess of
Rutland. Only four of Mary Harding's letters have survived, all of which were
sent to her mistress's mother keeping her abreast of court news, her daughter's
progress, and potential suitors.[2] Of particular interest is the fact that although
the letters bear her signature, Mary was apparently unable to write them herself,
relying instead on an amanuensis. Indeed, she wrote on one occasion, 'I write
noe oftner to your honour, thee caues is that I cannot write myselfe and I am
louthe to make any bodye acquainted withe my leaters'.[3] The second example is
Elizabeth Bourne, wife of Anthony, the son of John Bourne, Mary I's principal
secretary of state. Approximately seventy of her letters survive, largely from the
period when she was separated from her husband. In contrast to Mary Harding,
Elizabeth Bourne could write her own letters. Moreover, her letters display
'higher' forms of writing literacy than merely putting pen to paper: she was able
to write several different hands, composed original poetry, and wrote under the
pseudonyms Frances Wesley and Anne Hayes.[4] These pseudonymous letters she
referred to as her 'secrete syphers'.[5] Elizabeth Bourne was clearly a highly literate
woman who wrote most of her own correspondence, but she too on occasion
sought help from others to draft business letters.[6]

These two examples open up several interesting issues. First, they bring into
focus the range of women's writing abilities encountered in the material surveyed. At one extreme there are women unfamiliar with the practice of writing,
who were unable to pen their own letters and could at most possibly scrawl a
signature or make a rudimentary mark; at the other, however, are highly literate

---

[2] HMC, *Rutland*, i. 278, 18/11/1589; 300 [*c.*06/1592]; 301, 24/07/[1592]; 321, 24/07[1592].
[3] Ibid. i. 301.   [4] BL, Addit., 23212, fos. 193ʳ–193ᵛ, n.d.; 199, n.d.   [5] Ibid. fo. 193ᵛ.
[6] Ibid. fos. 118, 153: n.d.

women, who achieved fluency in penmanship and were capable of writing in various hands, styles, and genres. Most Englishwomen's letters were written in the vernacular, although several French and Latin epistles survive. A few classically educated women, such as Margaret Roper, Jane Grey, Dorothy Stafford, and Elizabeth Sandys, wrote Latin epistles and engaged in the public world of the Republic of Letters.[7] A Latin epistle also survives from Lady Cecil to William Cecil complaining about her negligent stable-man John Sturtenn, who stole some silver horse-buckles made as ornaments for horse-trappings.[8] As part of her upbringing and education in France, Anne Boleyn was taught to correspond in French, the language of the English court; a letter survives in French from a young Anne to her father, George Boleyn.[9] Lady Lisle's daughter Anne Basset, educated among the French aristocracy, corresponded to her mother in French.[10] It is also clear that many women employed secretaries to write for them out of choice, at other times writing for themselves. A fundamental distinction, therefore, needs to be drawn between a woman's ability to write and her propensity to do so based on convention, habit, circumstance, and inclination.

Central here is the question of how to discern whether or not a woman was herself capable of writing a letter. Assessment of female literacy and illiteracy in this manner relies largely on palaeographic analysis of letters. Of over 650 female letter-writers studied for the period 1540–1603, only secretarial letters survive for some 23 per cent. What proportion of these women were constrained to use an amanuensis because they were insufficiently skilled at writing personally to conduct correspondence is hard to gauge. In rare instances textual references register a sender's inability to write, as in the case of Mary Harding's apology, 'I cannot write myself'.[11] References of this sort to writing, however, present their own interpretive problems. Mary Harding's use of the verb 'to write' attains dual meaning: it refers, as in the first usage, to the act of sending letters and to letters that were dictated to or composed by an amanuensis, as well as to the actual penning of letters as in the second use of the word. 'Writing' in this sense becomes a passive activity, disconnected from the physical process of personally setting pen to paper. Another possible interpretation of 'I cannot write myself',

---

[7] Chavasse, 'Humanism in Exile', 165–85; Robinson, *Original Letters*, i. 2, 4–11. Cf. Sir Ralph Verney's warning to a friend in 1652: 'let not your girl learn Latin, nor shorthand: the difficulty of the first may keep her from vice . . . but the easiness of the other may be a prejudice to her, the pride of taking sermons notes hath made multitudes of women unfortunate', Verney, *Memoirs of the Verney Family*, i. 500.

[8] NA, SP12/39/58. Several women's letters contain Latin tags: Anne Lady Bacon (LPL, Bacon MS, *passim*), Lady Elizabeth Russell (e.g. Hatfield House, Cecil, 170, fo. 54), Maria Thynne (Longleat House, Thynne, VIII, fo. 6), and Audre Aleyn (Staffs RO, Paget Papers, D603, K1/10/2). See also *Official Papers of Sir Nathaniel Bacon of Stiffkey*, 220: Anne Townshend refers to her daughter's 'Latten verses', 27/12/1601.

[9] Paget, 'Youth of Anne Boleyn', 163–4. Female mastery of French was more widespread than knowledge of Latin, which was the preserve of only a select minority of women: Ong, 'Latin Language Study', 106–8, 110, 121. *Correspondance de François Hotman*, ed. Blok, 256: Penelope Rich to Jean Hotman, *c.*1590.   [10] *Lisle Letters*, iii. 578, 17/08/1535; v. 1126, 15/03/1538.

[11] HMC, *Rutland*, i. 301.

quite common indeed, is that a writer is temporarily incapacitated, for example by ill health, especially gout in the hand.

More widely reliable is a qualitative examination of secretarial letters for proficiency or fluency of autograph signatures.[12] This furnishes some indication of the true extent of a woman's writing skills. The majority of examples inspected are signed with italic hands different from the scripts used in the main body of letters. In numerous cases the signatures performed are elaborate and flourishing, suggesting familiarity with quill and ink. Indeed, Jonathan Goldberg has argued that an elaborate italic signature is often evidence of 'an extremely literate person'.[13] Alternatively, laboured or scratchy signatures may signify female correspondents unaccustomed to writing who found great difficulty even in signing their own names. The letters from Elizabeth Sutton to her husband Sir Thomas Sutton, founder of Charterhouse Hospital, are tortuously subscribed, suggesting that she was unused to writing.[14] Muriel St Clare Byrne concludes from Honor Lisle's awkward attempts at signatures that she was unable herself to write letters.[15] For both women producing a signature probably represented the limits of their writing abilities. More problematic are cases where only a single non-holograph letter survives for a particular woman, which accounts for over 143 female correspondents sampled. In such instances it is difficult to evaluate letter-writing habits and to assess competency at writing, beyond signing ability. In fact establishing conclusively an individual's inability to write letters from extant secretarial examples alone creates uncertainties: it may be that a woman for various reasons simply chose not to write herself. It is, therefore, highly likely that a greater proportion of women were in fact capable of writing letters than the number for whom there is direct literary evidence of their so doing.

A letter-writer who inscribed her correspondence with a mark instead of a signature is unlikely to have been able to sign her name, let alone write a letter.[16] Such appears to have been the case for Elizabeth Lambert who closed a letter to Thomas Stockwell with a mark.[17] It is doubtful that Joan Alleyn personally wrote her own letters to her husband, the actor Edward Alleyn, since elsewhere in the documents relating to him she witnessed a deed with a mark.[18] Many of her letters addressed to Alleyn were written by her stepfather, the theatrical manager Philip Henslowe.[19] Alternatively, use of initials to sign letters is less clear-cut. The fact that one signed initials rather than one's full name was more a matter of personal preference than indicative of poor writing ability. Numerous women perfectly capable of writing their own letters sometimes signed with their initials; these include Mary Sidney, Magdalen Montagu, and Arbella Stuart, all of whom

---

[12] Houston, *Literacy*, 144.   [13] Goldberg, *Desiring Women Writing*, 145.
[14] GLRO, ACC1876/F3/7/1–3, 5, 6, 1876/F3/7/2/68, 70, *c*.1600–2.
[15] *Lisle Letters*, i. p. 32, pl. 8j; ii. p. 700.
[16] Rylands, 'Merchants' Marks', 2; Sisson, 'Marks as Signatures', 21–2.
[17] *Miscellaneous Papers of Captain Thomas Stockwell*, ed. Rutherford, i. 15–16: 30/12/1603.
[18] *Catalogue of the Manuscripts and Muniments of Alleyn's College*, 24, n. 5.
[19] Ibid. 6, 8–11: *c*.07–09/1593.

were active writers.[20] In the case of Arbella Stuart, she possibly signed some of her letters post June 1610 to King James I and Queen Anne, with the initials 'AS', rather than 'Arbella Seymour', in order not to draw attention to her clandestine marriage to William Seymour.[21] Several letters of Anne, dowager countess of Northumberland, to Sir William Cotton written from the continent in 1576 were signed with a coded symbol, presumably to disguise her identity in the event that they were ever intercepted.[22] Far from indicating illiteracy, use of initials and symbols in these examples betray a sophisticated level of literacy.

For an individual woman, where examples of holograph correspondence, postscripts, or other types of writing such as accounts or diaries survive in addition to secretarial letters, one can reliably conclude that she was capable herself of writing letters, but chose not to do so. Well over a third of female letter-writers both wrote their own letters and used amanuenses as occasion required. Over the period as a whole, between 12 and 19 per cent wrote all their own letters. In real terms, therefore, the number of women for whom there is evidence of their actually writing letters rose from 50 per cent in the 1540s to some 79 per cent by the end of the sixteenth century. Additionally, the proportion of women for whom no holograph letters survive fell from 28 per cent in the first decade of the period to an estimated 17 per cent by the years 1600 to 1609. Taken together these changes point to an increase in levels of female literacy over the course of the century; they also mark a shift in the conventions governing letter-writing, whereby greater emphasis was placed on personally written letters.

Beyond answering the basic question of whether or not a woman was capable of writing her own correspondence, a close study of letters as sites of literary production provides detailed information about other aspects of women's writing skills, such as handwriting, spelling, grammar, and punctuation. Studied in this manner, letters reveal much about the competency and proficiency with which women wrote, and how easily and frequently they put pen to paper; whether letter-writing was an everyday activity for women or one in which they seldom engaged. Large numbers of women used abbreviations and contractions in their letters—the most common include, 'lo:' for Lord, 'la:' for Lady, 'matie' for majesty, and 'wch' for which—which indicates familiarity with the mechanics of writing. Presumably, women would have been taught as girls to use various standard abbreviations as part of learning to write. Increased use of abbreviations by the late sixteenth century suggests women's greater linguistic expertise.

Handwriting, however, is more difficult to interpret. While a scrawling, erratic hand may indeed indicate a woman unpractised in the art of writing, this is clearly not always the case. The letters of the classically educated Anne Bacon

[20] CKS, De L'Isle, U1500, C1/5, 6/05/c.1575; BL, Addit., 12506, fos. 73, 115, 161, 29/12/1587, 20/03/1603, 04/1604.   [21] *Letters of Lady Arbella Stuart*, ed. Steen, 79, 100.
[22] SP12/108/77: 8/08/1576; SP12/108/80: 16/08/1576.

are written in one of the most indecipherable sixteenth-century hands: a rough
and irregular hand that defies accurate description. It is possible that Lady
Bacon's hand deteriorated as she got older (most of her letters date from when she
was in her sixties), but it could also indicate speed of writing, or a cultivated
personal disdain for neat handwriting. Conversely, with the exception of presentation manuscripts where neatness was a prime concern, letters written in large,
bold italic scripts, with the words and lines regularly spaced out, may in actual fact
represent women unused to writing frequently. Such hands resemble the first
practice attempts by young girls such as Anne Clifford to handwrite letters, where
time and effort was taken to work on making correct letter–forms.[23] A letter home
to her mother from the seventeenth-century schoolgirl Katherine Oxinden reveals
her use of faint pencil lines to guide her writing of upper- and lower-case letters.[24]
Furthermore, comparisons of the handwriting of men and women of the same
social status (especially among the aristocracy for the first half of the sixteenth
century) often reveal that men's hands were as tortuous as women's, due in part to
their regular reliance on scribes. Educational accomplishment at handwriting was
dependent on several factors beyond gender: social status, level of schooling, frequency of writing, and aptitude. Taking a broad view of different examples of
handwriting, it is fair to say that women's ability to write improved over the course
of the sixteenth century. In general terms, the hands of women who were taught to
write towards the end of the period demonstrate a greater mastery of the pen in
terms of fluidity and competency of pen-strokes than women were capable of a
generation or so earlier. Improvement in the quality of handwriting perhaps
indicates that the teaching of writing skills to women became more widespread
towards the end of Elizabeth's reign.

Likewise, the spelling exhibited in women's letters generally improved over the
period, becoming to some extent more consistent and regular. An example of a
holograph postscript in a letter from Elizabeth, duchess of Norfolk, to her
brother Henry Lord Stafford illustrates the erratic spelling of a noblewoman
writing late in Henry VIII's reign. Indeed, M. A. E. Wood wrote that the hand
'baffles all attempts to decipher it satisfactorily . . . and it would be difficult to find
any writing, even of the period of Henry VIII, that so completely sets all rules of
orthography and penmanship at defiance'.[25] The postscript reads: 'Brorder I pra
you to ssand me my ness dorety by kass I kno har kon dessess se sal not lake hass
long hass I leffe and he wold be hord by me at hor haless I kyng he be hone kyne
tha ffaless drab and kouk and nat ben I hade hadehar to my couffert.'[26]

[23] *Proud Northern Lady*, 43.   [24] Fletcher, *Gender, Sex and Subordination*, pl. 25.
[25] Wood, *Letters of Royal and Illustrious Ladies*, iii. 189.
[26] Ibid. 191. Wood's translation reads: 'Brother, I pray you to send me my niece Dorothy,
because I know her conditions—she shall not lack as long as I live, an you would be heard by me at
(all), or else I think you be own kin to false drab and cook; *an not been* (had it not been) I had had
her to my comfort.' BL, Cott., Titus, B.I., fo. 162.

The duchess's atrocious spelling may in fact explain her use of a secretary for the main body of the letter. Elsewhere she wrote to Cromwell, 'I fear me that you cannot read my hand, it is so ill English. I pray you to send me word in writing if you can read my hand or not.'[27] Other female letter writers at the beginning of the period, however, did not deviate so drastically from more conventional spelling practices.

Despite greater orthographic regularity by the end of the sixteenth century, many women's letters still display eccentric spellings, which lend them a protean, oral, and almost conversational quality.[28] Removed from the kind of learned, contrived, easy informality of style extolled by Erasmus, women's letters exhibit many of the features associated with the spoken as opposed to the written word: colloquialisms, non-standard forms, and erratic or phonetic spellings. A short letter from Mary Hobart to her brother John is replete with phonetically spelled words, such as 'commendashenes' for 'commendations', 'youwar' for 'your', 'oggest' for 'august':

> Good bruther i Am not sortin of youwor be in at lunden
> but if i had you had harde from me before this tim
> but now hafeing good a messenger i Thout it good to
> wreyt unto you thincke kin ueri long to see you and
> longer to her from you the on i mite sum tim if you
> wold but good bruther ther for frindes soone forgot tim but my
> Thinckes it showld not be so with you and ei thus hopping
> you be in good helth and my bruther ed worde thous
> with my commendashenes to youwor swete selfe good
> bruther ihon and my bruther edword thus I cumit you
> to god from thorpe the xx of oggest
>
> > youwor ueri luffing
> > sister to her poywor
> > Mari hobarte[29]

In certain letters one can view the running together of words, which reflects the way they might have been elided in pronunciation: Lady Bacon wrote 'a nowld', for 'an old', 'tooutnot' for 'doubt not', while Elizabeth Cavendish wrote 'weonhores backe' for 'way on horseback'.[30] Elsewhere one can detect the influence on spellings of variations in regional dialect, especially in the rendition of names and places. Mary Herrick spelt her surname 'Erycke' leaving the 'h' silent; the countess of Warwick spelled Windebank as 'Wynnibayncke'.[31] Unusual words that women would not come across everyday were also

---

[27] *Letters of Royal and Illustrious Ladies*, ii. 222: 03/03/[1536].
[28] Scragg, *History of English Spelling*.   [29] BL, Eg., 2713, fo. 481: 20/08/n.y.
[30] BL, Addit., 41140, fos. 123–4, [24/10?–20/11/1597]; BL, Addit., 63109, fo. 10, 20/11/[1597]; Folger, X.d.428 (50), before 10/1574.
[31] Bodl., Herrick, Eng. Hist., 474, fo. 68, 1578; Kendal RO, WD/Hoth, Box 44, 10/08/n.y.

spelt more erratically or phonetically: Mary Herrick, for example, spelled 'pomegranate' as 'pounde garnyte'.[32]

The oral quality of women's letters is further indicated by the proverbial sayings contained in correspondence. Female usage of proverbs is evident in a letter from Katherine Wallop to Francis Walsingham, in which she preferred to his 'good consideration' her suit to transport some grain agreeable to a licence granted to her husband, Sir Henry Wallop: '... being a woman, lefte here at this tyme alone ... [I] ... must refer the same to yo[u]ʳ honors good consideration, vnto whom as vnto my onlie refuge I am enforced in my distres to fly being thervnto emboldened, by yo[u]ʳ honors accustomed frendshipp heretofore to my housbande, and to me shewed, yt is an ould saying, beggers must be no chusers.'[33] The last phrase 'beggers must be no chusers' is obviously proverbial; yet more broadly, many of the other phrases and images that Katherine Wallop selects in her letter of petition (her 'being a woman', his 'good consideration', her 'onlie refuge', being forced to 'fly', his accustomed 'friendship') are all traditional commonplaces, adages, or maxims. The proverbial forms are used here to persuade, a practice exhorted by William Fulwood: 'it is to be noted that divers Epistles may begin with a perfect sentence, authoritie, or common proverbe: prouided that it be altogether agreeable to the purpose that we entend to pers- wade or disswade.'[34] Indeed, Adam Fox has argued that sixteenth- and early seventeenth-century prose style contains 'a heavy "oral residue", a rhapsodic structure and a high degree of colloquiality which reflects the close association between the spoken and the written realms at this time'. More specifically, he argues that this is true of early modern letters, which attain a 'proverbial quality'; that 'the transferral of rhetoric' to written letters relies on adages used in oral delivery.[35] While male letter-writers did indeed employ oral forms in their correspondence, it is more likely that everyday speech provided an invaluable reservoir of persuasive maxims for women unversed in formal rhetoric.

In general, linguistic and orthographic variants may be more pronounced in women's than in men's letters, reflecting men's superior education and greater familiarity with the written word, though given that rules of orthography were far from fixed during this period, men's letters also exhibit eccentric spellings. In this sense women might, as Alison Truelove has argued, be considered as 'innovators of linguistic forms', in that they were more likely than men to adopt new and unusual modes of expression apparently found in everyday speech in their letters.[36] In fact, verbal traits in letters may be as much a function of social status and circumstance as of gender. Truelove, in her study of the late medieval Stonor letters, has argued that given scribal influence and formal stylistic con- straints, the letters of gentlewomen are less influenced by spoken colloquialisms than those of mercantile women.[37] An examination of spellings in sixteenth-century

---

[32] Herrick, Eng. Hist., 474, fo. 68: 1578.   [33] BL, Lansd., 28, fos. 147–8: 4/12/1579.
[34] *Enemie of Idleness* (1568), 15.   [35] Fox, *Oral and Literate Culture*, 131–2, 133.
[36] Truelove, 'Commanding Communications', 53.   [37] Ibid. 49–54.

women's letters supports her preliminary conclusions. Indeed, during this period the letters of women from the lowest social groups represented by this study—the daughters and wives of merchants—are most likely to exhibit oral traits. Among these individuals are the women of the Herrick family of Leicestershire, and Sabine Johnson, the wife of the Staple merchant John Johnson. Representative of Sabine Johnson's spelling is the postscript of a letter to her husband dated 1545; in it she wrote that her 'hataly desyer' [hearty desire] was that he 'com soong whom aghan' [come soon home again].[38] The issue of social status here works to complicate a simple male–female binary opposition of literacy levels, delineating differences of ability between social groups. Indeed, the kinds of differences detected in women's writing, such as irregular handwriting and phonetic spellings are evident in lesser-educated male writers too. The sixteenth-century musician and diarist Thomas Whythorne, for example, invented his own orthographic system.[39] Differences in levels of literacy are, therefore, not entirely gender-based, but rather nuanced by other variables such as social status and geographical region.

Individual female letter-writers appear to have been somewhat self-conscious of poor spelling, which on occasion may have deterred them from writing personally. This can sometimes be discerned from the letters themselves. Elizabeth Kitson wrote to Sir John Hobart that 'in this letter much false Incgliche I am suer you shall red but let tru meanynge connterfayl that falte', though this may have been an empty excuse.[40] An attempt to instil embarrassment at irregular spelling is glimpsed in Edmund Coote's *The English Schoole Maister* (1596). The manual, aiming to teach the rules of correct English spelling, was addressed to an audience 'that now for want' of 'true orthography...are ashamed to write unto their best friends: for which I haue heard many gentlewomen offer much'.[41] Robert Cawdrey's *A Table Alphabetical* (1604) was also, at least in part, 'gathered for the benefit & helpe of Ladies, Gentlewomen, or any other unskilfull persons'. It is notable, as Juliet Fleming argues, that attempts to regularize vernacular English spelling during the early modern period were often associated with women, and the perception that they were among those 'unskilful persons' requiring guidance by such manuals as Coote's and Cawdrey's.[42] In response to these negative associations, pride and self-esteem may well have encouraged women to acquire and improve literacy skills for purposes of correspondence.[43]

The reluctance of some women to write also may have been caused by the ridicule with which poor education and an inability to spell was sometimes met both within the family and outside it. Criticisms of the quality of female epistolary output are quite common: Philip Gawdy teased his sister-in-law for

---

[38] *L&P*, XX (i) 572: 25/04/1545.   [39] *Autobiography of Thomas Whythorne*, ed. Osborn.
[40] BL, Harl., 4712, fos. 412–13: 03/10/1597.   [41] Sig. A2.
[42] Fleming, 'Dictionary English and the Female Tongue', 175–6.
[43] Houston, *Literacy*, 104–5.

her 'fals[e] orthographye'.[44] More spiteful than this example of fraternal mocking is a letter from Elizabeth Bourne, written under the pseudonym Frances Wesley, which harshly reproved Lady Conway for what she described as her 'late learned eloquence':

you must sett aparte more of your idell exercyses, by larger tyme and more industrie of your scole M[aster]s to become a deaper student in rethoricke then yet you arr. a good wyll you showe such as yll wordes may sett forthe, but your scole M[aste]r . . . he maks you use many sentences and lytell substance and you tell straynge tales and no trothe, the faulte ys greate and I wyshe you to mende yt. though wee well some tymes take lyberty to speak barborously, yett owght yt not to be untrewly when the wyttness of our hand maks yt a recorde, but happelie you apply to the exercyse to become a plesyng scoler to your m[aste]r.[45]

With similar malevolence Maria Thynne scorned Joan Thynne, whom she had recently replaced as mistress of Longleat, for her penmanship: 'if you gave a fee to any counsellor to indite your letter, it was bestowed to little purpose.'[46] The effect of Maria Thynne's insults is heightened by the fact that they exposed social and generational differences in standards of literacy: eloquence and learning as well as noble birth enabled Maria to treat contemptuously her widowed mother-in-law Joan, the daughter of a London merchant.[47] Disparaging comments of this nature by other women—far from displaying stereotypical virtues of female humility and submissiveness on the part of the women issuing the insults—undercut conceptions of an imagined female community, and indicate an increasing unacceptability and intolerance of poor writing skills and illiteracy among upper-class women.

'SCRIBBLED LINES'

Female correspondents' unease in their own letter-writing abilities may be reflected in the considerable numbers of letters that apologize for 'scribbled lines' or 'rude writing'. Apologies of this nature are a striking feature of women's letters during this period: Mary Fitzroy, duchess of Richmond, referred to her 'evil hand'; Jane Neville, countess of Westmoreland, craved pardon from Burghley for what she described as her 'disordered and scribled lynes'; Elizabeth Mansell described herself to be 'as ill a clarke . . . as euer writt'.[48] Writers expressed regret for the poverty of eloquence and invention of their letters. Anne Glemham beseeched Julius Caesar to 'excuse' her 'scribled letter', explaining 'want of tyme, with the barrennes of my inuention enforceth me, thus to discouer my

[44] BL, Eg., 2804, fo. 84.   [45] BL, Addit., 23212, fos. 193–193ᵛ: n.d.
[46] Wall (ed.), *Two Elizabethan Women*, 34, c.1605.   [47] Ibid. pp. xv, xvii–xix, xxvi, xxx.
[48] SP10/7/1: 4/05/1549; BL, Addit., 46367, fos. 34ᵛ–35ʳ, 17/09/1575; BL, Addit., 41140, fo. 144: c.1593–4. See also SP12/171/25, 15/06/1584; Cecil, 157, fos. 48–9, 29/07/1570.

imperfections which is to be ouer shadowed with a vaile of good will by you'.[49] Lady Susan Bourchier informed Sir Thomas Kitson of her inability 'to delyuer my meaninge in suche wordes or foorme as maye be faltless to men of understandinge'.[50]

This trait of women's letters, however, was not confined to the sixteenth century: Linda Pollock has highlighted the extent to which seventeenth-century female letter-writers apologized for bad script and the trivial content of correspondence; and Patricia Crawford has shown that such self-deprecating comments were also characteristic of women's published writings.[51] While such self-criticism may represent for some women absence of self-assurance or embarrassment at lack of proficiency in writing, such comments can also mask a complex range of motives and customs, and should not be accepted at face value. Within learned circles at least it was an epistolary convention for both women and men to uphold a demeanour of false modesty: Lucy St John wrote to her father, Lord Burghley, in an elegant hand, yet courteously excused her 'bade writynge'; Bartholomew Kemp, clerk of the Great Seal, implored Anne Lady Bacon to pardon his 'rude l[ett]res'; Philip Gawdy wrote to his father expressing that 'I am to desire you that this rude scribled letter maye suffyse for this present with a remembrance of my duty to your good self'; and Edward Lord Zouche implored the countess of Warwick's 'pardon for my defectes by these rude lines'.[52] This manner of self-criticism, which was governed less by gender than by social status or position, allowed subordinates to demonstrate respect or defer-ence to superiors. While Lucy St John and Philip Gawdy's letters should be interpreted as marks of filial respect, Kemp's and Zouche's signify their deference towards women of higher social rank, obeying the social codes of letter-writing.

While men could register social inferiority in their letters, women in particular could exploit assumptions of female intellectual inferiority in order to project an aura of vulnerability and humility to male recipients—a strategy employed to good effect in business relations. Vivienne Larminie has argued that Anne Newdigate's criticism of her lack of skill in writing was symptomatic of nothing more than mere politeness.[53] This kind of mannered epistolary decorum is apparent in the letters of numerous other women. Lady Margaret Hoby, the famed diarist, wrote to her cousin Lady Anne Newdigate declaring that, 'tell now my head and hand hath been unperfit deliuerers of my mind'.[54] Many learned women were equally self-effacing in their letters regarding their literary talents. Lady Jane Seymour, in a letter to the theologians Bucer and Fagius, wrote that

[49] BL, Lansd., 158, fo. 92^v: 26/03/1598.

[50] CUL, Hengrave, 88/2, fo. 12: 18/02/1569. See also Hengrave, 88/2, fo. 26: 09/05/1570; Herrick, Eng. Hist., 475, fo. 156: 16/05/1582; Bodl., Tanner, 241, fo. 43b.

[51] Pollock, 'Teach Her to Live', 249; Crawford, 'Women's Published Writings', 215.

[52] BL, Lansd., 104, fo. 175: 1588; Bacon, 649, fo. 63: 13/03/1594; *Letters of Philip Gawdy*, ed. Jeayes, 36: 09/05/1588; BL, Eg., 2812, fo. 26: 31/07/1600.

[53] Larminie, *Wealth, Kinship and Culture*, 88.

[54] WCRO, Newdigate Papers, CR136/B 222: 01/06/1597.

she did not 'dare' to discuss the books they had sent her, for fear 'lest my ineloquent commendation of them may appear impertinent'.[55] Jane Grey wrote to Henry Bullinger: 'I entertain the hope that you will excuse the more than feminine boldness of me, who, girlish and unlearned as I am, presume to write to a man who is the father of learning; and that you will pardon that rudeness which has made me not hesitate to interrupt your more important occupations with my vain trifles and puerile correspondence . . . '[56] The relative youth of these writers as well as the stature of the men with whom they corresponded may in part have given rise to expressions of humility. However, it also suggests that among well-educated women a bearing of false modesty was considered to be a refinement, a matter of etiquette. This fine balance of decorum, modesty, and confidence is evident in a letter from Dorothy Osborne to William Temple, which she ends: 'You will never read half this letter, tis soe scribled, but noe matter, tis much worth it.'[57]

THE SOCIAL CONVENTIONS OF WRITING LETTERS

For significant numbers of sixteenth-century female letter-writers literacy was not an obstacle to conducting personal correspondence: a high proportion in fact wrote all their own letters, and for over a third of women examples of both holograph and secretarial letters survive. The latter group of women were obviously capable of writing letters themselves, but often chose to delegate the task to scribes. Given that a woman could write herself, the decision of whether or not to do so was dependent upon various factors unrelated to writing literacy: custom, the type and context of a letter, the relationship between writer and addressee, and circumstances. Accordingly, the present section attempts to map the broad patterns of letter-writing in order to identify the different contexts in which secretaries and amanuenses were employed by 'literate' individuals and those where women were more likely personally to engage in writing letters. The sixteenth century also witnessed increasing expectations that women be able to write their own correspondence, and greater value placed on correspondence written in one's own hand. By the end of Elizabeth's reign women were more likely to write letters themselves than use an amanuensis. While this reflects changes in epistolary conventions, it also indicates heightened female proficiency at letter-writing, brought about by pedagogical change and other social, cultural, and religious factors.

The choice for a normally 'literate' woman to use an amanuensis to conduct correspondence for her was influenced by a large number of factors. First, in numerous cases use of amanuenses was necessary for women rendered physically

---

[55] *Original Letters*, i. 2: 12/06/1549.   [56] Ibid. 10: [before 06/1553].
[57] *Dorothy Osborne: Letters to William Temple*, ed. Parker, 100.

incapable of writing by old age, ill-health, or emotional distress; letter-writing in these cases was less a function of literacy than related to the body or material conditions. On receiving letters from her mother that were not in her own handwriting, Anne Clifford feared the countess of Cumberland's imminent death: 'I perceived how very sick and full of grievous pains my dear Mother was, as she was not able herself to write to me.'[58] Anne Glemham apologized to Julius Caesar for not having written herself, 'by reason of the weaknes in myne eyes'.[59] Susan Grey, countess of Kent, claimed that an 'evil' pain in her finger rendered her unable 'to howld a penn'.[60] Corresponding with Sir Robert Cecil concerning the estate of her late husband, Robert, earl of Essex, following his execution for treason in 1601, Frances Devereux explained that she was too distressed herself to write: 'Good M[aste]r Sec[retary] beare w[i]th me that I write not all in mine owne hand, I beegann it but my weak sinnewes would not suffer me to proceed to the third line, but inforced me to use an others help in writinge what my distemperd brayne did confusedly digest.'[61] In this missive, material expression of the countess of Essex's mental suffering, whether sincere or affected, may have strengthened the petition by presenting her as a pitiable widow, an image with strong religious associations. The need here to apologize for using a secretary suggests that women were expected to write their own letters and wanted to do so.

An examination of groups of holograph and non-holograph letters within specific archives highlights the situations where it was appropriate or conventional to engage secretarial assistance and those where correspondents were expected to write in their own hands. In broadly discriminating formal or business letters, where the addressee was unknown to the writer, from family letters, the former were more commonly written by secretaries than by women themselves. Of eighteen letters discovered among the Exchequer papers at the National Archives, each of which dealing with financial matters, secretaries wrote all but two.[62] Additional letters survive for over half of the women, at least one of which is holograph, which attests that they could in fact write but had chosen not to correspond personally with Exchequer officials. Letters from other government and legal archives exhibit equally high numbers of secretarial correspondence. For example, of ninety-nine letters sent by women to Sir Julius Caesar between 1582 and 1603, during his time as a judge of the Admiralty Courts and as master of the Court of Requests, secretaries wrote two-thirds. In addition, almost all of the women who used a secretary to correspond with Caesar, on other occasions wrote letters with their own hands.[63] By contrast the proportion of holograph letters is usually much larger in collections of family papers: of forty-one women's letters in the Paget Papers, over thirty were penned

[58] Williamson, *Lady Anne Clifford*, 94. See also, SP12/190/36: 16/06/1586.
[59] BL, Lansd., 158, fo. 88: 14/03/1599.   [60] Folger, X.d.428 (38): 26/01/1593.
[61] Cecil, 85, fo. 139: 03/04/1601.   [62] SP46/27/39.
[63] For Caesar's papers see BL, Addit., 12503, 12506, 12507; BL, Lansd., 158, 162; SP12/283, 285.

by the female signatory.[64] Similarly, out of a group of thirty-five letters to the earl of Essex from his mother, sisters, and wife, only one was written by a secretary.[65] This high incidence of personally penned letters is representative of other collections of family papers surveyed.

Conventions governing the writing of letters become more pronounced when one examines an individual woman's entire correspondence, and compares methods of composition used for different types of letters: business or formal, domestic or familiar. The example of Anne, countess of Warwick, for whom there is a range of approximately thirty letters still extant, well illustrates this. Among the countess's letters, eight can be categorized as personal letters written to relatives conveying news and greetings; the remainder are more formulaic business letters to officials, dealing with administrative and patronage matters. All but two items of her personal correspondence are holograph, including three epistles addressed to her sister Margaret Clifford, and one to Sir George More, in which Lady Warwick assured him that she had 'imparted' to her majesty the matter concerning 'the office of yo[u]^r fathers'.[66] By comparison, only four business letters are in the countess's own hand, the others being produced by amanuenses. In sum, the more personal and intimate the relationship between sender and recipient, the more likely it was for a letter to be personally written. Conversely, the more formal the letter and the less personal the relationship, the more common it was for a sender to distance herself from the task of writing.

While customary to employ secretaries throughout the medieval and early modern periods, there is a discernible change during the sixteenth century, by the end of which increasing numbers of women wrote letters themselves. By contrast, in the fourteenth and fifteenth centuries most letters were the work of scribes.[67] In part this reliance on amanuenses may indicate low levels of late medieval lay literacy, especially among women. Alison Truelove argues that women of the Stonor family were more likely than men to dictate their letters than to write with their own hands; it is unclear, though, whether this reflects a gendered convention or inferior female literacy ability.[68] Certainly Barbara Harris's statistic that 12 per cent of aristocratic women who wrote wills for the period 1450–1550 either signed them or wrote the whole document themselves attests to some level of practical female literacy during this period.[69] Furthermore, during the late medieval period it was entirely conventional to employ scribes for the drudgery of writing, an activity separated from the intellectual effort of composition.[70]

[64] Paget Papers, D603, D1734.   [65] WCRO, 'Essex Letter Book *c.*1595–1600', MI 229.
[66] WD/Hoth, Box 44; Folger, Loseley, 3/75: 04/08/1600.
[67] Taylor, 'Letters and Letter Collections', 69.
[68] Truelove, 'Commanding Communications', 42–58.
[69] Harris, *English Aristocratic Women*, 34.
[70] Constable, *Letters and Letter Collections*, 42; O'Mara, 'Female Scribal Ability', 96–7.

During the sixteenth century too, use of a scribe spared correspondents this drudgery, considered by some to be demeaning and incompatible with nobility. The Spanish humanist Juan Luis Vives, for example, bemoaned the 'multitude of nobles who hope that they are going to be esteemed as better born in proportion as they are ignorant of the art of writing'.[71] The writing of business letters retained a sense of stigma during the sixteenth century, even though the ability to write became more widespread among the upper classes. The task of writing, involving the preparing of ink and paper and the cutting of quills, was deemed a tedious and messy one best left to servants.[72] In a letter to Sir Thomas Smith, Mary Fitzroy complained of the 'travail' of writing.[73] Clearly, a proficient secretary could alleviate the more arduous aspects of epistolary composition. Thus, a crucial distinction lay in the purpose of writing between formal and business writing on the one hand, which was considered menial, routine, and technical, and private and personal writing on the other, which was intimate, spontaneous, and creative. The former was normally undertaken by an amanuensis; the latter was increasingly (though importantly not always) conducted in women's own hands. The ability to write, therefore, was treated as a reserve skill by some women of the nobility and gentry, one that could be called upon when occasion required.

By the end of the sixteenth century, however, the act of writing appears for many women to have been regarded as an everyday skill. Margaret Hoby's diary richly documents the various uses for which she used writing; she was a regular correspondent and note-taker; she kept accounts and a commonplace book; writing was also central to her spiritual exercises of self-analysis; and her books were marginally annotated. Likewise, the various manuscript papers that survive for Lady Grace Mildmay evidence a highly literate Tudor gentlewoman, distanced from the court in rural Northamptonshire, who engaged in spiritual meditations, medical experiments, correspondence, and autobiographical writing.[74] While the uses to which these women put their literacy argues for the functional importance of writing, both clearly had a confessional impetus to write.[75] Concomitantly, the increased variety of uses for which early modern women utilized their writing abilities in everyday life, both practical and spiritual, stimulated acquisition of literacy skills.

In the context of the exigencies of women's everyday lives, delegation to a secretary can also be viewed as an efficient way to dispatch correspondence. Engulfed by business and legal affairs arising from estate and household management, women were responsible for large amounts of outgoing correspondence—petitions for favour to government officials, letters negotiating financial interests, intercessions on behalf of family members, suits on behalf of dependants and

[71] Goldberg, *Writing Matter*, 113.   [72] Thomas, 'Meaning of Literacy', 100.
[73] SP10/7/1: 04/05/1549.
[74] *Diary of Lady Margaret Hoby*, ed. Moody, p. xl; Pollock, *With Faith and Physic*.
[75] Houston, *Literacy*, 8, 147–50; Collinson, *Birthpangs of Protestant England*, 74–5.

clients—as recent work on women's letters testifies.[76] It was therefore only administrative good sense to employ a scribe to deal with what potentially could be an overwhelming amount of paperwork. This may well explain the reason why Anne Newdigate, a prolific correspondent on behalf of her family, sometimes employed a secretary for her formal letters.[77] Other women complained that the pressure imposed on them by business matters left little time to write letters themselves: Audrey Aleyn, in correspondence with her brother Thomas Lord Paget, stated, 'having diverse matters to move to you, I am driven to use a strang[e] hand'.[78] Lucy Paulet, marchioness of Winchester, requested Sir John Hobart to remember her to Lady Withipole, apologizing that 'had I had tyme amongest many of my busines at this instant I would have writen unto my La[dyship]'.[79] Again, these apologies are symptomatic of an expectation of personally written correspondence. At a pragmatic level secretaries were utilized for the speed and proficiency with which they could expedite the task. Indeed, a 'swift' hand was considered by Sir Michael Hickes, patronage secretary to Burghley, to be an essential secretarial skill.[80] When pressed for time women may have preferred to use a secretary. Alice, countess of Derby, hurried by a bearer's urgent departure, informed Robert Cecil: 'But that the jentleman was in hast, I had my selfe w[i]th my owne hande writt to you.'[81] In this sense, the sporadic nature by which letters were dispatched could determine whether a woman or her secretary wrote a letter.

Formal business writing, because of its technical precision, is more likely than familiar correspondence to exhibit signs of secretarial intervention or collaboration with a third party cognisant of legal, political, or financial practices. Letters of this sort needed careful wording, and although some women displayed impressive knowledge of law and administration many clearly felt it wise to procure expert advice in these areas. Elizabeth Hatton wrote to Sir John Hobart for his help to convey a tract of land, requesting that he inform her 'to what porpos & in what forme I shall wryte to thos that shall conuay the land . . . I know you will drawe out my meanyng beetor then I can seet it doune'.[82] Elizabeth Bourne, having first drafted a petition to the queen, then sought the assistance of Sir John Conway in honing it: 'acordyng to my sympell skyll I haue set doune my petycyon to her ma[jes]ty wych I have sent you to amend for I can doo it no beter and I thinke hit far from that hit should be I ther for pray you to correct hit & sende hit me and I wyll wryte hit neu.'[83] Although it is tempting to interpret such comments as indicative of female inexperience and insecurity in business matters, they more likely represent deferential codes of politeness, ploys to secure assistance and guidance. Both these women were in reality accomplished letter-writers who frequently penned their own missives.

[76] Daybell (ed.), *Early Modern Women's Letter Writing*, 11–13.
[77] WCRO, CR136, B307, B308, B309a. Larminie, 'Fighting for Family', 94–108.
[78] Paget Papers, D603 K1/3/40, 25/10/1572.   [79] BL, Harl., 4713, fo. 278ᵛ: n.d.
[80] Smith, *Servant of the Cecils*, 37.   [81] Cecil, 182, fo. 66: 25/06/1601.
[82] Tanner, 286, fo. 5: n.d.   [83] BL, Addit., 23212, fo. 118: n.d.

Moreover, innumerable correspondents, regardless of gender, sought technical advice in drafting letters. When Robert Bacon sought favour from his aunt Lady Elizabeth Russell to intervene with Lord Burghley for him in a disputed wardship case, he first wrote to his cousin Anthony Bacon, sending him a draft copy of the letter for his inspection. The letter was accompanied by the explanation: 'I have herew[i]th sent you a l[ett]re by me written to the la[dy] Russell w[hi]ch as you shal lyke you may use either in altering the same as you shal thinke best or in returning it unto me as yt is th[a]t I may wryght it agayn & then to sende th[a]t unto you.'[84] Anthony Bacon was approached because he was considered to be closer to the situation and, therefore, possessed of greater expertise in how to word the letter in a way that would appeal to his aunt.[85] More importantly, it was not uncommon for women to assist men in letter-writing, which stands as clear testimony of male confidence in female epistolary competence. John, earl of Bath, clearly considered his third wife Margaret to be a proficient letter-writer and regularly relied on her counsel. On one occasion he asked her opinion on a letter he had written to Lord Stourton, inviting her to make any amendments she felt necessary: 'I haue sent you a copy of the same, yf you shall so like it, if no I haue sent you a blanke & my name therunto, prayenge you and if any thinge be amysse therin to reforme the same accordinglye as you did the laste wiche I did very well like.'[86] George Talbot similarly valued his wife Elizabeth's judgement of his correspondence. The countess once informed her husband, 'my deare harte I haue sende your letter agene and thanke you for them they requyre no ansore, but when you wryte remember to thanke hym for them'.[87] Elsewhere the earl expressed his satisfaction at one of his wife's letters: 'your letter cam very well & I lyk them so well they could nott be amended.'[88] Husbands also entrusted wives to correspond on their behalves. Thomas Baskerville, the military commander, requested his wife Mary to send '2 or 3 lin[e]s from your self' to Lord Willoughby excusing that he himself had not written,[89] while Sir Robert Sidney charged his wife Barbara with replying to a correspondent's letter: 'I pray you write a letter of thanks to Mr Sanford and let him know that hee shall heare shortly from you.'[90] That women acted in such advisory and delegated capacities indicates high levels of female competence. Certainly Lady Grace Mildmay believed that her governess 'could apprehend and contrive any matter whatsoever propounded unto her most judiciously and set her mind down in writing either by letters indited or otherwise as well as most men could have done', and Sidney's mother Lady Mary's letter-writing skills were eulogized in Holinshed's *Chronicles*.[91]

---

[84] Bacon, 659, fo. 42: 20/09/1596. Robert Bacon's letter to Lady Russell survives in two drafts: Bacon, 659, fos. 41, 43.

[85] Bacon's letter failed to win Lady Russell's favour: Bacon, 659, fo. 148: 22/09/1596.

[86] Hengrave, 88/1, fo. 141: n.d.   [87] LPL, Talbot, 3205, fo. 66: n.d.

[88] Folger, X.d.428 (89): 1570.   [89] BL, Harl., 4762, fo. 25: n.d.

[90] CKS, De L'Isle, U1475, C81/108: 16/07/1604.

[91] Pollock, *With Faith and Physic*, 26; Magnusson, *Shakespeare and Social Dialogue*, 47.

Although it was customary to employ amanuenses for formal correspondence, many female letter-writers judged it important to correspond personally with officials where there existed bonds of political 'friendship' between sender and recipient. This in turn clouds distinctions between personal or private and business correspondence. The significance attached to holograph letters as a sign of respect for the addressee also explains women's frequent apologies for not using their own hands. In a letter to Burghley, petitioning for the wardship of Nicholas Halswell, Mary Sidney added a holograph postscript excusing her use of an amanuensis: 'I besyche your l[ordshi]pe pardon me I wryght no lardglier nor w[i]th my own hande, for I am so very syke as I canot indure to wryghte altho I must confes hit wer my part not to truble your good l[ordshi]pe in this or enny other suet w[i]thout further respect of your great coortesis and noble dealings w[i]th me.'[92] As Lady Sidney's note indicates, secretarial letters were judged less personal than holograph correspondence. Margaret Clifford expressed regret at the impersonal nature of a letter she dispatched to the duke of Lennox: 'excuse I pray your lo[rdship] an other bodies hand th[a]t hath expressed my hearte.'[93] In a personal political system, where individual relationships were paramount, privy communications lent a degree of confidentiality to exchanges between correspondents, which was central to cultivating and maintaining social and political contacts.

Correspondents also personally wrote letters to officials that contained politically sensitive material, prejudicial to family reputation and honour, which was best kept secret from servants or clerks. The process of using an amanuensis, which was far from private, inhibited openness and often led to self-censorship on the part of the sender. Anxious to assure William Cecil of the secrecy of her interventions with the queen for a renewal of his lease of the farm of Combe Nevell in Surrey, Anne Seymour ended her letter with the phrase 'w[i]t[h] myne owne hand I wret thys'.[94] The adverse effects of dictation are described in an Erasmian dialogue: 'If you dictate verbatim, then it is goodbye to your privacy; and so you disguise some things and suppress others in order to avoid having an unwanted confidant. Hence, quite apart from the problem of the genuineness of the text, no open conversation with a friend is possible here.'[95] Reflecting the Dutch humanist's remarks, Lady Catherine Daubeney, anxious to maintain confidentiality, informed Thomas Cromwell that she preferred to correspond with him in her own hand rather than to 'trust any so far as to know my mind'.[96] Writing oneself was thus one way of ensuring greater protection of business secrets. A letter's intimate nature alone, however, did not demand that the letter be written without a secretary or scribe. Elizabeth Wolley's letters to her father and brother, which discussed sensitive matters of family business, were almost all written by a secretary.[97] This is uncommon in an obviously literate woman, who signed and appended postscripts to her letters in italic, and whose father, Sir

---

[92] BL, Lansd., 17, fo. 41: 12/09/1573.   [93] WD/Hoth, Box 44: n.d.
[94] BL, Lansd., 13, fo. 90: 13/09/1571.   [95] Osley, *Scribes and Sources*, 30.
[96] *Letters of Royal and Illustrious Ladies*, ii. 122: 1534.   [97] Folger, Loseley, L.b.

William More, was a great book collector, and contained within his library 'a boke to lerne to wryte by' and 'the instruccion of a woman'.[98] Her choice not to correspond herself reflects perhaps both the degree of trust attained by secretaries as keepers of secrets, and the continuation throughout the sixteenth century of the convention that secretaries be employed for intimate and privy correspondence.

In circumstances where female letter-writers were forced to use an amanuensis, holograph postscripts offered women a way of personalizing secretarial letters. Postscripts written in one's own hand performed numerous functions. First, they were often used for personal greetings. Philadelphia, Lady Scrope, in a letter to Robert Cecil added in her own hand, 'let my most kind comendacions be remembred to your wiffe'.[99] Thus, at a high political level, women sought to cultivate contacts and relationships through postscripts to correspondence. Women also added greetings to letters written by their husbands. A letter from William Cecil, second earl of Exeter, to Sir John Hobart bears a postscript from his wife Elizabeth, in which she stated, 'I must remember my self sence he will not and with my best affecktion I dow it'.[100] Moreover, postscripts often included matters of a more intimate or private nature. Anne Bacon, at the end of a letter to her stepson Nathaniel Bacon, added personal sentiments to his wife Anne who had been recently delivered of a child: 'God be thanked for my dawghteres saff delyveraunce. Desyre her from me not to be to bowld of her selff in childbed for all she is so yowng & strong.'[101] In formulaic and routine business correspondence, holograph postscripts enabled women to add personal emphasis: Frances, countess of Hertford, in a letter to Dr Hale wrote, 'I pray you good Mr Hale showe my servaunt what plasure you may and I wyll thynk it done as to my selfe.'[102] Women also added postscripts to others' letters, to forward or underscore a case or suit. Thomas Lowe, for example, wrote to his master Thomas Sutton on behalf of Margaret Clifford regarding Sir Thomas's promise to lend her money. Sutton's reluctance to honour his promise caused the countess to add her own rather forceful postscript to the letter: 'if it hade be[e]n a lady that hade broking promies in time though not in truith yo[u] would have sayet we women ar[e] carlies but I assuer my self of you and of youer mony which you loue so much this your frinde that expikes your promies.'[103] Due to the nature of the countess's message it is surprising that the servant allowed his letter to reach Sutton. Holograph postscripts thus exhibit spontaneous and intimate forms of expression, uninhibited by secretarial constraints.

[98] Evans, 'Extracts from the Private Account Book of Sir William More', 290–1.
[99] SP15/33/24: 4/06/1594. See also Talbot, 3205, fo. 46: 23/06/1592.
[100] BL, Harl., 4712, fo. 225: 12/03/n.y.
[101] *Papers of Nathaniel Bacon*, ed., Hassell Smith *et al.*, i. 82: 06/08/1573.
[102] SP15/29/121: 06/1586. See also BL, Lansd., 158, fo. 80: 11/12/1599.
[103] GLRO, ACC1876 F/3/5/2/17: 02/09/1602.

The large proportion of holograph women's letters among family papers is in part due to the high expectations that correspondence between relatives should be personally conducted. Many looked upon writing letters oneself as a means of keeping in touch, as a duty or obligation, demonstrating obedience and respect. Lady Eleanor Zouche wrote to her cousin Thomas Randolph explaining that, despite her illness, the regard she had for him compelled her to write in her own hand: 'I haue bene very sicke, & not yet so well recouered th[a]t I can, & not in duer to wryt or to read but w[i]t[h] great payne, yet when I remember to whom it is, I can not in any wyse yeld to any excuse.' [104] Symptomatic of daughterly respect, Elizabeth Grey, wife of Henry Grey, wrote to her mother the countess of Shrewsbury stating, 'I nowe haue no other ocation to drawe me to trobell yo[u]r la[dyship] with my ill hande butt only to perfome my duty in humblye presentinge my seruice by euery messenger'.[105] Maternal complaints were commonly directed at sons for neglecting their duty and failing to write in person: Anne Bacon and Gertrude, marchioness of Exeter, both chided their sons for employing amanuenses when corresponding with them.[106]

Recipients clearly placed great value on letters from relatives where the services of a scribe had been dispensed with. Erasmus expressed this most clearly in a Latin dialogue: 'how warmly we respond whenever we receive from friends or scholars letters written in their own hands! We feel as if we were listening to them and seeing them face to face.'[107] In practice also, recipients of personally written letters registered their 'warm responses'. In appreciation of an epistle penned by her brother-in-law Burghley, Elizabeth Russell wrote thanking him for troubling to correspond in his own hand: 'I kiss the hand th[a]t tooke so muche payne w[i]t[h] penn.'[108] Alexander Colles reported to his mistress Lady Margaret Long that her future husband, the earl of Bath, 'dyd receive with much gentleness' her letter, adding that he 'gave you great thanks that it now pleased you to take the pains to write yourself'.[109] Sir Thomas Barrington, writing in the early seventeenth century, heaped thanks on his mother Lady Joan Barrington for not employing the services of an amanuensis: 'If your scribe had pen of steele and a hand of brass he could not write words enough to me to equall or counterbalance the last, which (though only two) yet coming from your owne hand they are more to me then a volume from your amanuensis, which yet are beyond all other expressions because penned from your comaundes.'[110] While an amanuensis writing at his mother's 'command' might have been preferable to other forms of expression, it was not preferable to a letter in her own hand. Time and effort taken to correspond oneself, rather than delegating the task to a clerk, demonstrated the attention given to a letter by a writer.

[104] BL, Harl., 6994, fo: 4, 28/04/1586.   [105] Talbot, 3205, fo. 104: 1604.
[106] Bacon, 651, fo. 328: 07/08/1595; SP11/5/35: 08/06/1555.
[107] Cited in Osley, *Scribes and Sources*, 29.   [108] BL, Lansd., 10, fo. 136: 25/08/1584.
[109] Hengrave, 88/I, fo. 10: 27/12/1547. Gage, *History and Antiquities of Hengrave*, 121.
[110] *Barrington Family Letters*, ed. Searle, 190: 13/05/1631.

The desire for letters to be written personally is perhaps strongest among married couples during the sixteenth century. While the number of women composing marital letters increased over the century, the proportion of wives writing their own epistles was consistently high throughout the period. Over 80 per cent of letters to husbands were personally written, based on the fact that they are holograph. This indicates the high degree of epistolary privacy between married couples. Of those women employing secretaries to write for them, only two appear to have done so because they were unable to write: Joan Alleyn, wife of the actor Edward Alleyn, and Elizabeth Sutton, both of whom corresponded between 1600 and 1603.[111] Most letters composed using an amanuensis were sent by women who would normally have written themselves but were prevented from so doing by illness or fatigue. Joan Thynne apologized to her husband for not writing in her own hand: 'I came to London this present Sunday at three of the clock. I did endure my journey very well but I was very weary at night, wherefore I hope you will pardon me because I did not write myself.'[112] Alternatively, third parties occasionally helped wives to construct letters to husbands where conflict within the marriage necessitated more carefully worded epistles. On the whole, however, letters to husbands were more likely than other types of women's correspondence to be written personally.

During a period of limited privacy, in which upper-class and mercantile married couples living in large households were surrounded by servants and were rarely alone together, it became increasingly expected that marital correspondence should be more personal. To some extent epistles represent one manifestation of the few fleeting and occasional private spaces possible within sixteenth-century marriage. Indeed, Martin Billingsley extolled the virtues of writing for women so that 'the secrets that are and ought to be, betweene a Man and Wife . . . in either of their absences may be confined to their owne privacy'.[113] This desire for epistolary privacy is also apparent among letter-writers: John Gamage wrote to his wife, 'I wold wyshe that my doings myght be a secret'.[114] Joan Thynne wished to keep confidential news of her son's disobedience in marrying without parental consent secret: 'for the keeping of it secret here, doubt you not of it, for here is no mistrust of this matter.'[115] Forced to correspond by secretary due to a pain in his hand, George, earl of Shrewsbury, informed his wife that he wished to 'defer' the answering of her letters until such time as he could write himself.[116] These and other examples support Linda Pollock's argument that spouses were concerned in their correspondence to keep secret matters relating to business, reputation, and honour.[117] This sense of shared confidences between couples reinforces the idea of marriage as a social and economic partnership.

---

[111] *Catalogue of the Manuscripts and Muniments of Alleyn's College*, 24, n. 5; GLRO, ACC1876/F3/7/1–3, 5, 6, 1876/F3/7/2/68, 70: *c.*1600–2.   [112] *Two Elizabethan Women*, 5: 06/03/1580.
[113] *The Pen's Excellencie* . . . (1618), 35.   [114] SP46/60/2: 02/1576.
[115] *Two Elizabethan Women*, 10: 08/05/1595.
[116] Folger, X.d.428 (104): 10/10/1580.   [117] Pollock, 'Living On the Stage', 85, 87, 89–90.

Moreover, there is a real sense in which greater personalization of letter-writing was encouraged by an increased desire of married couples to be more intimate, endearing, and affectionate in expression. As early as the 1530s Lady Lisle, writing from Calais, asked her husband to write to her himself of 'secret things', saying that two lines in his hand were better than a hundred from another.[118] While Lady Lisle trusted a secretary to write to her on her husband's behalf regarding 'business or necessary affairs', she wished Lisle to put pen to paper himself to 'signify' his 'gentle hart'. Importantly though, Lady Lisle's intimate letters to her husband were dictated verbatim, in contrast to her business letters where secretaries were left to add conventional introductory and closing formulae.[119] Several other wives showed dissatisfaction when they received letters from their husband not written in their own hands. Joan Thynne, in an epistle to her husband John, remarked that: 'I do not a little marvel that I hear from you but not by your own [hand], which surely giveth me occasion to think that you are not in good health. Wherefore sir, to put away such doubts I humbly desire you that you would take so much pains as to write to me yourself which shall not a little engladden me, whereas now I stand in great doubt.'[120] The fact that her husband had not written himself led Joan Thynne to worry that he had been ill. Likewise, Maria Thynne explained to her husband her dislike of his using a servant to write to her: 'I like not his writing in your name for it is as though thou were angry.'[121] These comments expressing women's surprise at receiving secretarial letters, further suggest that it was normal for husbands to correspond personally with their wives. Additionally, many wives who were themselves able to write attached importance to penning their own letters; the act of personally writing a letter imbued it with emotional significance absent from correspondence dictated to a third party. Elizabeth, countess of Shrewsbury, wrote tenderly to her husband the earl, explaining that 'of late I haue youssed to wryte letyll w[i]t[h] my owne hande but coulde nott now forbayre'.[122] At the root of these demands for holograph letters and gestures of intimacy lies the need or desire for married couples to communicate with one another in a more personal and private manner, unmolested by prying eyes.

While the desire to conduct more personal forms of correspondence with family may have encouraged some women to acquire enhanced literacy skills, women were also motivated by other practical considerations: writing and the ability to conduct correspondence allowed women greater command over their own affairs. Several early modern writers recognized the functional aspects of women being able to write. Richard Mulcaster, in his book *Positions* (1581), argued that women should be taught to write: 'many good occasions are oftentimes offered, where it were better for them to haue vse of their pen, for the

---

[118] *Lisle Letters*, v. 1544: 21/09/1539.   [119] Ibid. i. p. 32; iv. pp. 229–30.
[120] *Two Elizabethan Women*, 4: 07/03/1577.   [121] Ibid. 33: [after 08/1604].
[122] Talbot, 3205, fo. 73: n.d.

good that comes by it, then to wish they had it, when the default is felt.'[123] Arguing in favour of female education, the English writing master Martin Billingsley stated that writing was an essential skill for widows who wished to manage their estate: 'the practise of this art [writing] is so necessary for women, and consequently so excellent, that no woman surviving her husband, and who had an estate left her, ought to be without the use thereof.'[124] Despite his obvious self-interest, Billingsley extends the arguments of the practical benefits of writing literacy to include women. In practice too, the ability to write oneself led to greater epistolary control and presented opportunities for independent personal expression, for women to defend themselves and to set down their own words on paper. Anne Glemham wrote to Julius Caesar stating, 'I had expressed my mind in words'; Frances Withipole declared to John Hobart that she was 'resolued to wright my opinion'.[125]

A further reason for the importance of personally written letters lies in the fact that a woman's own handwriting (given concerns of forgery) conferred a particular authority on her correspondence and acted as proof or guarantee of a letter's contents. To Erasmus it was 'very easy to forge a signature but very difficult to forge a complete letter. A man's handwriting like his voice has a special individual quality.'[126] Lady Elizabeth Willoughby promised her son Percival that if he helped to discharge his father's debts she would strive to pass on her husband's estates to him, stating that he could 'lay her own handwriting to her charge'.[127] Lady Anne Hungerford in correspondence with William Darrell promised to marry him, stating 'I have swarne and wytnes of thys my hande that I wyll t[a]ke yow to my husbande'.[128] Documents produced in a person's own hand were considered more binding than those that were merely signed; they were also regarded as better witness of an individual's intentions. Thus, Mary Holcroft, disputing the will of her mistress Lady Hastings, wrote to Sir John Puckering, the lord keeper, requesting that he force her mistress's husband Francis Hastings, whom she alleged had falsely excluded her from the inheritance, to produce 'that draught of the will w[hi]ch he gave to his man strasmore to keepe w[hi]ch was of her owne hande writing'.[129]

When looking for explanations for the spread of literacy and why increasing numbers of women learned to write during the sixteenth century, historians of women's education have also looked at the role of parents as agents of pedagogical change.[130] Over the course of the sixteenth century the skills and practices associated with letter-writing increasingly formed an integral part of the education of an upper-class woman, one that would equip her with the necessary societal skills for her roles as mother, wife and, mistress of a household. Thus,

---

[123] pp. 177–8.   [124] Billingsley, *The Pen's Excellencie* (1618), sigs. 35–35ᵛ.
[125] BL, Lansd., 158, fo. 92, 26/03/1598; Tanner, 283, fo. 71: n.d.
[126] Osley, *Scribes and Sources*, 29.   [127] HMC, *Middleton*, 570: n.d.
[128] SP46/44/188: n.d.   [129] BL, Harl., 6996, fo. 95: 08/04/1594.
[130] Charlton, 'Mothers and Familial Education', 1–20; id., 'Mothers as Educative Agents', 129–56.

Lady Grace Mildmay in her autobiographical journal described how during the 1560s her governess had made her practise the writing of letters to various individuals, in much the same way that Renaissance schoolboys were drilled in epistolary exercises. She wrote that, 'and when she did see me idly disposed, she would set me to cipher with my pen... and sometimes set me to write a supposed letter to this or that body concerning such and such things'.[131] Elizabeth, countess of Shrewsbury, encouraged her granddaughter Arbella Stuart to practice letter-writing by copying examples of her own letters. A letter from the countess to Sir Thomas Cornwallis contains the instructions to the 6-year-old Arbella, her 'jewel': 'Good Juyll I pray you take payns to wryt out thes with your owne hand.'[132] Parents also were keen to encourage daughters to use letter-writing skills: Honor Lisle urged her daughter Anne, then at court, to practice her own hand in letters sent home.[133] At the age of 11 Lady Jane Grey was prompted to write to Lord Admiral Seymour.[134] A carefully written and dutiful letter also survives from Lady Mary Talbot to her parents, the earl and countess of Shrewsbury.[135] Elizabeth Cary honed her letter-writing skills at an early age by translating Senecan epistles; the notebooks of Rachel Fane (1620–80) likewise record her practice of translating 'epistles choisen out of' Seneca.[136] Robert Sidney's pleasure in his daughter Mary's progress in letter-writing is attested by his offer to reward her with a dress as a present. In a letter to his wife Barbara, Sidney wrote, 'I thank Mall for her letter and am ecseeding glad she writes so wel. tel her for me I will give her a new gown for her letter.'[137] Moreover, the writing of letters to family members could be part of the educative process, as part of childhood socialization to enforce deferential codes of filial respect: John and Mun Verney 'were forced to write regularly to family members, who sternly evaluated their progress'.[138] Changes in parental attitudes regarding the types of skills deemed necessary for daughters to acquire both affected the nature of female education and were influential in the spread and use of writing skills among women.

A crucial question is how far literacy or letter-writing ability had a positive effect on women's lives. Did an ability to write change the ways in which women could operate, the tasks they could undertake or the roles they could perform? While the transition from oral to literate societies is often assumed to represent a crucial stage in the development towards 'modernity', promoting abstract and rational thought, and complex bureaucratic organization, the early modern period was marked by the intersection of illiterate and written cultures.[139]

---

[131] Pollock, *With Faith and Physic*, 26.   [132] Talbot, 3198, fo. 172: 15/07/1582.
[133] *Lisle Letters*, v. 1126: 15/03/1538.
[134] SP10/5/5: 01/10/1548.   [135] Talbot, 3203, fo. 399: 25/05/n.y.
[136] Lewalski, *Writing Women in Jacobean England*, 180; Bowden, 'Female Education', 177–8.
[137] De L'Isle, U1475, C81/68, 06/10/1595.   [138] Whyman, 'Paper Visits', 18–19.
[139] Thomas, 'Meaning of Literacy', 97–131; Ong, *Orality and Literacy*; id., 'Writing is a Technology', 23–50; Fox, *Oral and Literate Culture*.

Seemingly illiterate women appear to have been highly active in areas of household and estate management, and political and religious patronage, whether operating face-to-face or through the intermediary of a messenger.[140] Furthermore, unlettered individuals had access to scriveners, or at a higher level to secretaries, who performed various scribal functions. Educational barriers therefore did not inevitably preclude women from epistolary activity. Thus, Elizabeth Shelton, herself unable to write, in 1603 sent a letter to her father complaining of the treatment that she was experiencing from her uncle, in whose household she had been placed. Despite her inability to write, not only was she able to persuade someone within her uncle's household to write a letter for her, but also she seems to have had it secretly conveyed to her father. 'I desire you in any wayes', she begged her father, 'let not my uncle knowe th[a]t I have writte unto you, for I gett one to write unawares to him by cause I hard him in such a rage.'[141] Women were able to conduct correspondence within difficult and restricted circumstances, despite their illiteracy. It is thus important to stress that the impact of literacy should not be overplayed as an emancipating force for women, however alluring this notion might be. Viewed within the context of late medieval and early Tudor evidence, female roles attain a degree of continuity: the ability to write did not usher in a period of increased female activity as patrons and intermediaries, as certain scholars have misleadingly argued. What survives is greater written evidence of these activities during the sixteenth century. If anything, the centralizing processes that increasingly moved government functions away from the periphery and great households towards court-based centres of power may in fact in some ways have reduced women's activities and influences.[142]

In the final analysis, however, acquisition of full literacy (the ability to read and write) conferred significant benefits that were denied to women whose partial or total illiteracy prevented them from writing their own letters. On one level, the ability to write letters allowed female members of the literate elite to keep better in touch with immediate family, kin, and wider social contacts. Women further down the social scale, where literacy levels were much lower and access to amanuenses more difficult, would have found the opportunities of communicating with geographically distant family more limited.[143] Obviously the availability of a trustworthy scribe was not always guaranteed. Beyond being able to conduct more personalized correspondence in maintaining social and business relationships, women who were able to write letters could also send more intimate correspondence to family members, achieve greater degrees of personal control over language and self-expression, and greater confidentiality in business, and could maintain a tighter grip on household and business affairs. An ability to write letters personally was clearly very useful.

---

[140] Ward, *English Noblewomen*, 129–42.   [141] SP46/57/204b: 18/12/1603.
[142] Erler and Kowaleski, *Women and Power*, 1–13; Rose, *Women in the Middle Ages and the Renaissance*, pp. xvi–xvii.   [143] Laslett, *World We Have Lost*, 234.

HIGHER FORMS OF LITERACY

Letters are also useful for the light they shed on a range of wider literary-related activities beyond the actual penning of correspondence. In this sense letters are not only a site of women's basic literacy skills, in that they register rudimentary writing activity and abilities—for example, the quality of women's handwriting, the nature of their spelling and composition—but also in that they document different and occasionally 'higher' forms of female literacy, such as the ownership and reading of books, familiarity with classical literature and history, involvement in the circulation of manuscript poetry, interest in areas as diverse as music, architecture, medicine, theology, playgoing, and female participation in the public world of the Republic of Letters. In this sense, letters represent a systematically untapped source for studying women's participation in broader cultural and literary activities; they provide evidence of female involvement in the kinds of activities usually associated with men and educated elites. In the absence of abundant source materials delineating the curricula for female education, correspondence offers indirect evidence of the kinds of skills learned by sixteenth-century girls, and attests to some of the uses—practical, religious, political, and leisure-related—to which as women they put their education. Moreover, read as texts rather than merely as historical documents or reliable depositories of fact, letters highlight female mastery of the literary and formal conventions of the epistolary genre.

Books receive occasional passing mention in sixteenth-century women's letters. The recusant Mary Wilford asked her mother whether she could 'spare the booke of the life of St Catherine', assuring her, 'you shall haue it againe uery safe';[144] Anthony Bacon conveyed to his mother a book from Théodore Bèze, which was written by 'mr Caster one of the frenche ministers'.[145] Alice Norton, wife of the Elizabethan Puritan Thomas Norton, was sent by her husband a copy of Foxe's *Book of Martyrs*: 'it is one of the faire good books', he wrote, 'that I have vowed my good daughter nan.'[146] In a postscript of Elizabeth Poley's letter to her brother Simonds D'Ewes, her husband asked his brother-in-law to purchase for his wife 'a Bible great . . . that has a black couer, w[i]th ye fayrest print for the weake eyes', together with copies of 'Withers of surrey his *Prophesyes*' and 'Perkins his *Cases of Conscience*'.[147] More revealing of women's reading practices—actually when and how women read—is the correspondence of Lady Catherine Gell which she regularly maintained with the Puritan divine Richard Baxter: in one letter she described how 'many a time I goe about my house

---

[144] WCRO, Throckmorton Papers, CR1998/Box 60/folder 1/4: 17/11/n.y.
[145] Bacon, 649, fo. 190: 02/06/1593.
[146] BL, Addit., 48023, fo. 32: 29/12/1581. On female readers of Foxe see Freeman, 'The Good Ministrye', 31–2.
[147] BL, Harl., 382, fo. 180ʳ. Charlton, *Women, Religion and Education*, 183.

among my servants when I had rather locke myself in a roome alone amongst my books'.[148] Katherine Seymour thanked her husband for sending her a book, informing him she had 'read with her heart as well as her eyes'.[149] Overwhelmingly, the kinds of books mentioned by women in their letters are religious in nature, which fits with current scholarly understanding of the books that early modern women read; there are few references in sixteenth-century letters to other types of texts that scholars have associated with a female reading public, such as household and technical manuals, and romances. Referring to books by title in this manner, however, is rare; letters should therefore be read alongside other types of sources, such as lists of books, inventories of women's libraries, book-bills, portraits, marks of book-ownership, book dedications, and wills and probate inventories which provide a much fuller picture of the kinds of books that women read.[150] Having said this, women were avid consumers of news. During the early seventeenth century the staunchly Puritan widow, Lady Joan Barrington, regularly received copies of corantos or newsbooks with letters from family and friends.[151] This female interest in news represents more than merely a superficial acquaintance with current affairs, but rather a well-informed, detailed understanding of British and European political events. It also suggests that in practice women read a broader, less restricted range of texts than was prescribed in educational texts.[152]

More common in women's correspondence than actual names of books are references to book-related transactions: the sending, giving and borrowing of books. In 1549 Lady Jane Seymour thanked Martin Bucer and Fagius for the books they sent.[153] Jane Cartwright wrote to Thomas Lord Paget asking him to try to recall the name of a book which, she stated, 'I think it be in italion';[154] Lady Frances Egerton, countess of Bridgewater, thanked Anne Newdigate for the gift of a book, 'w[hi]ch I hope will make [me] so skillfull against I see you, that I shall haue cause to acknowledge myself yo[u]r scholar';[155] and Anne Bacon sent to her son Anthony at Essex House 'a litle psalme boke of meeter', to which she fastened her 'seale ring'.[156]

Letters also make it clear that some wives had contact with husbands' books and libraries. Lady Dorothy Bacon arranged to have forwarded to her husband Nathaniel Bacon the book that he 'wryt for'.[157] Other wives were involved in the

---

[148] *Calendar of Correspondence of Richard Baxter*, ed. Keeble and Nuttall, i. 249; Charlton, 'Women and Education', 14–15.   [149] HMC, *Bath*, ii. 17: 1565.
[150] On women's reading of printed books see Pearson, 'Women Reading, Reading Women', 80–99; Hull, *Chaste, Silent and Obedient*; Wright, 'Reading of Renaissance English Women', 671–88; McKitterick, 'Women and their Books', 359–80; Meale and Boffey, 'Gentlewomen's Reading', 526–40.   [151] *Barrington Family Letters*, 201, 215, 223, 206–7.
[152] Vives, *Instructio[n] of a Christen Woma[n]* (1529), ch. 5: 'What bokes be to be redde and what nat.' Cf. Bruto, *Necessarie, Fit, and Convenient Education*, sigs. D4–D4ᵛ.
[153] *Original Letters*, i. 2: 12/06/1549. See also Hengrave, 88/1, fo. 37: 03/03/n.y.
[154] Paget Papers, D603, K/1/5/14: n.d.   [155] WCRO, CR136, B105: 04/05/1613.
[156] Bacon, 656, fo. 47: 18/03/1597.
[157] BL, Addit., 41140, fos. 121–2, 123–4: [24/10–20/11/1597].

sale and purchase of books. In a letter to Peter Martyr dated 15 July 1557, Maria
Ponet (née Hammond), the second wife of John Ponet, bishop of Winchester
under Edward VI, described how on her husband's death she inherited his
library, which, being 'left . . . a wretched widow', she later sold: 'he [John Ponet]
left . . . I know not how many or what kind of books, all of which, as I thought
they belonged to me, I sold them to that excellent person, and my very good
friend, master Cook.' On learning from John Jewell that among these volumes
she had in fact sold some of Martyr's own books, Maria Ponet at first tried to buy
them back, but failing to do that instead 'purchased new ones at the booksellers',
which she 'forwarded' to Martyr by the merchant John Abell.[158] Epistolary
evidence of this nature further reinforces the image of women's familiarity with
printed books beyond their role as readers. More broadly, women possessed
knowledge of where books could be bought and sold, and how they were kept.

Occasionally in their letters women discussed books in a more sustained way
than merely as either gifts or objects, referring to the actual contents of the books
they read. Most common are comments or opinions expressed about religious
books; this is particularly the case where the letter-writers themselves held strong
religious principles. Lady Elizabeth Russell, for example, well known for her
reformist attitudes in religious matters, sent the countess of Shrewsbury a religiously edifying 'litle booke', 'wherby', she wrote, 'your most Noble Lady may
know what my religion is'. The letter accompanying the book pressed the
countess to 'rede it', and not to be 'like the Deafe Adder that stoppeth her eares
and refuseth the voice of the charmer'.[159] Lady Isabel Bowes, wife of Sir William
Bowes the moderate Puritan Member of Parliament for Westmoreland, held
similarly strong opinions regarding the publication of the 'Oxford Book' put out
by the universities in 1603.[160] Sir William, in a letter to Gilbert, earl of
Shrewsbury, reported that his wife felt 'it carryeth sedition to Parliament and
King'. In a postscript to the same letter Lady Bowes urged the earl to condemn
the book.[161]

More broadly, women in their own letters employed a language and
vocabulary suggestive of a familiarity with a vast range of texts. At one extreme,
women made references to or cited from classical, biblical, or patristic texts. Lady
Russell's letters, for example, are littered with Latin tags culled from classical
authors and biblical verse. Textual analysis of her voluminous correspondence
indicates that she quoted from Horace's *Epistles* and *Satires*, Virgil's *Aeneid*, and
Juvenal's *Satires*; alluded to Herculean legend and to Castiglione's *Boke of the
Courtier*, which was translated by her first husband, Sir Thomas Hoby; and
referred to the Psalms, Ecclesiastes, Ezekiel, and Deuteronomy, the Gospels of
Luke and Matthew, and the Epistles of Peter, often quoting from the Vulgate.[162]

---

[158] *Original Letters*, i. 118–19: 15/07/1557.   [159] Talbot, 3203, fo. 410: n.d.
[160] Hasler, *Commons*, i. 467–9.   [161] Talbot, 3203, fo. 166: 17/12/1603.
[162] SP12/255/29; Cecil, 68, fo. 11; 30, fo. 26; 175, fo. 92; 53, fo. 88; 74, fo. 1; 179, fo. 92; 90,
fo. 152; 197, fo. 53: 1595–1605.

This is hardly surprising from the pen of the woman who translated *A Way of Reconciliation Touching the True Nature and Substance of the Body and Blood of Christ in the Sacrament*, and who was praised by John Harington for her Latin and Greek epitaphs for both of her husbands.[163] The letters of her sister Anne Bacon, who was also classically educated, are likewise littered with Latin, Greek, and Hebrew tags, which appear to have flowed from her pen almost as second nature; some of the Greek is actually a transcription of English words she wanted to keep secret. Lady Jane Grey too quoted the Bible in Hebrew in her correspondence.[164] The regularity with which these exceptionally well-educated women deployed their classical training in everyday correspondence, though far from typical of elite women in general, indicates the way in which it had almost become second nature for them, simultaneously functioning as a badge or marker of erudition and learning.

The letters of women less schooled in classical erudition also sometimes display knowledge of classical texts or authors. Anne Newdigate, in a letter suing for the wardship of her son, alluded to 'the romane Emperores' in her condemnation of men and remarriage, and the assertion of her desire to be 'master of my selfe'.[165] Vivienne Larminie has argued convincingly that Lady Newdigate's reference to the emperors of Rome arose less from a bookish knowledge of classical authors in the original, than from her awareness both of vernacular literature and drama that was classically inspired and of classical translations, or from imbibing such references orally: indeed, her husband made detailed studies of classical and continental authors, usually in translation, which he then used in writing his speeches.[166] Certainly some of Anne Newdigate's male correspondents by their use of literary references in their letters assumed a certain familiarity on her part with a range of writers and texts. The correspondence Lady Anne received from Francis Beaumont of Bedworth, for example, was resplendent with literary allusions and quotations that he obviously expected her to understand.[167] In one letter he quoted lines from Spenser's 'The Ruines of Time', while another reproduces for her a full stanza from Book Four of *The Faerie Queene*, 'bicause', as he writes 'I know how much you delight in all good learning, and in such honest verses, and to adde also some better tincture to my loath to departe, I wil set them downe as he wrytt them'.[168] Elsewhere, he makes reference to Chaucer's 'little Lady Emilie', and quotes, 'like as Troylus once sayed so I say "All this I did, and I can doe noe more; She cruel is and woe is me therefore"'.[169] There are also allusions to the Greek painter Timanthes,

---

[163] Lamb, 'Cooke Sisters', 108, 119; Schleiner, *Tudor and Stuart Women Writers*, 41–51.
[164] *Original Letters*, i. 4–7, 5, n. 2: 12/07/1551.   [165] WCRO, CR136, B311, n.d.
[166] Larminie, *Wealth, Kinship and Culture*, 121. Fox, *Oral and Literate Culture*, ch. 4, shows the ways in which history could be spread through oral tradition. Woolf, 'History, Folklore and the Oral Tradition', 32–3.   [167] Larminie, *Wealth, Kinship and Culture*, 96, 131.
[168] Newdigate-Newdegate, *Gossip From the Muniment Room*, 115, 127–8.
[169] Ibid. 130, 132.

'Pigmalions Image', Palamon, Cynthia, and Philodas, as well as to Orlando, 'not Furioso but di lassus'.[170] Similar literary and classical allusions are found in the letters of Peregrine Lord Willoughby de Eresby (1555–1601) to Margaret Clifford, whom he addressed as 'noble phylosophying lady'. In an undated letter Willoughby refers to Hermes and several female figures from classical antiquity: Philomela, Octavia, and Cleopatra.[171] Likewise, Richard Brabon swapped snippets of Latin with Lady Anne Drury in his letters.[172]

The correspondence of Elizabeth Bourne with Sir John Conway reveals more clearly the activities of a bookish sixteenth-century gentlewoman, who engaged in a wide range of literary interests.[173] In addition to receiving books from Conway— in one letter she asked him for the 'work' she had mentioned in her last letter[174]— he also sent her translations of Latin histories. 'This muche' he wrote to her, 'I have translated owt of the laten hystory I redd to you of late w[hi]ch you lyked so well[.] yf the englyshe plesse you, and that you can rede my yll hand I wyll translate the whole and sen[d] hyt to you.'[175] In another letter, Elizabeth Bourne discussed in detail another book that she had been sent and had read:

I dyd red of yor boke you sent me where in I fynd there is nothing to be compared to the love of to faythful frendes. thay parte on to a nother both welth and want; joye and grefe but never shale parte on a nother for any fortune this is that hath byn in ould tymes but is rare nowe in these dayes to be founde whye should not I joye that I haue such a frynde so perfect as euer was any and is reqyted wyth so perfect a frynde as thinckes not her selfe in feryour to any in ould tyme nor that shalbe her after . . .[176]

The phrase 'ould tymes' suggests that the book was again a history or perhaps an epic romance. In the context of her own life, as a woman separated from her violent husband, this passage of the letter is most revealing. Throughout her correspondence to Conway, Elizabeth Bourne reiterates her constant need of 'frends' to provide material, emotional, and above all legal support during a period of hardship and anxiety. Her reading of and commentary on the book was therefore a very personal one, one that was intimately entwined with her own situation. Her reflection upon the book's theme of friendship ('the love of two faithful frends') 'in ould tymes' leads to a lamentation of the present: friendship is 'rare now in these days'. At the start of this letter too she acknowledges her gratitude to Conway for sending her 'comfort': receipt of his letter next to seeing him 'gladdened' her. Elizabeth Bourne's very personal self-identification with her reading matter is striking, and her discussion of literature with her 'epistolary companion' enabled her further to praise him for his friendship. He was to her 'a frynde so perfect as ever was'.

---

[170] Ibid. 96, 118, 126, 130, 131.   [171] WD/Hoth, Box 44: 23/03/n.y.
[172] Joseph P. Regenstein Library, University of Chicago, Bacon Manuscripts of Redgrave Hall, 4227, 4224: 25/04/1615, n.d.
[173] Conway's own learned interests are testified by his publication of *Meditations and Praiers Gathered out of the Sacred Letters and Vertuous Writers* (1571).
[174] BL, Addit., 23212, fo. 152: n.d.   [175] Ibid., fo. 135, n.d.   [176] Ibid., fo. 152, n.d.

While Elizabeth Bourne and Conway, both of whom were married, clearly shared a mutual passion for books, their mutual passion apparently went beyond this. A later letter written by Elizabeth reveals unequivocally the clandestine romantic nature of her relationship with Conway.[177] Her choice of language and the imagery of romance in this letter—styling Conway as her own 'good knyght'; her description of the immeasurable 'joye' that his letters ('the lynes of my delyte') brought her, and his loyal service to her to triumph over her enemies ('he lyves to do nothing but love me and cares and devyses for me')—is again perhaps reflective of her reading.[178] Both letters suggest that the books she read shaped the way in which she perceived or constructed her own situation or identity. Her reading in this case conforms to one of the models of women's reading of romances outlined by Danielle Clarke, where 'the text is read in terms of its relevance to private concerns'. There is no sense from her letters that Elizabeth Bourne engaged in the kinds of 'complex interpretational manoeuvres', with an awareness or sensitivity to wider political allegory, that can be observed in Clarke's other female (often court-based) readers of early modern romances.[179]

In addition to reading histories and romances, Elizabeth Bourne's interest also extended to poetry.[180] Her letters contain several fragments of doggerel verse. On the back of one undated letter appears the cryptic rhyme, 'from whens hit cam hit, hath no name & whither, hit wyll hyt tellethe, the same'.[181] Another fragment is written on an address leaf: 'whyther this gothe hyt hath, no name from whence, hyt cometh hytt seythe, the same'.[182] Again the playful purpose of the verse is the obfuscation of the identity of the sender; this fits in with the repeated concern with detection evident throughout her letters: 'I wyshe you to kepe yo' letters safe o' burne them for you have spyes', she advised Sir John Conway in another letter.[183] These ephemeral and jocular poetic fragments aside, Elizabeth also appears to have exchanged poems with Conway. In one of her letters she self-effacingly lamented the quality of her own verse when compared with his: 'I would I could atayne to macke such fyne versys as you do that be so properly convayed.'[184] Another letter to Conway (probably dating from the early 1580s) contains an original Elizabethan poem in Elizabeth's own hand, which strongly points to her being its author:

> I hope, what happe?   thy happie states retyre
> I wyshe, what wealth?   thy constant hartes desyre
> I feale, what force?   the fyttes of thy dyspleass
> I pynne, wherein?   thy gryfe ys my dyseass
> I lyve, howe longe?   whylest you delight my lyfe

---

[177] On the romantic nature of this relationship, see Bradford, *Hugh Morgan*, 15–16.

[178] BL, Addit., 23212, fo. 158: n.d.

[179] Clarke, *Politics of Early Modern Women's Writing*, 232–64.

[180] On women's involvement with poetry see: Heale, 'Women and the Courtly Love Lyric', 296–313; Stevenson and Davidson, *Early Modern Women Poets*.

[181] BL, Addit., 23212, fo. 150ᵛ: n.d.   [182] Ibid., fo. 171, n.d.

[183] Ibid., fo. 177, n.d.   [184] Ibid., fos. 143–4, n.d.

I toyle, wherefore?   to free yo[r] state from stryfe
I crave, what yst?   one ower may ende us twayne
I praye, wherefore?   in heven wee mete agayne[185]

The unusual and relatively sophisticated rhetorical structure of the poem—
almost catechistic in its question-and-response formation—bears some
resemblance, at least in terms of rhetoric, to a number of poems which slightly
pre-date this one, evidence surely of her familiarity with poetic forms.[186]

Given the circumstances of the poem's composition during Elizabeth
Bourne's separation from her husband, its themes of uncertainty and longing,
and the epistolary and literary friendship she enjoyed with Conway, an autobiographical reading is highly seductive. Indeed, her correspondence of this
period, much of which was concerned with the exasperating task of trying to
secure some kind of financial provision from her husband, emphasizes her
desperate case: 'I am a wandryng woman laden wyth grefe', she described herself
in one letter; in another she lamented the loss of her daughters, 'I pray God, bless
my to daughters, hit greves me to thinke howe thaye lose thayer tyme'.[187] The
very letter in which the poem was conveyed was in fact a plea for financial help
from Conway; in it she spoke of her 'despair' at her situation. In fact the poem
acted as a preface to the request, since it was written on the reverse of the letter
after it had been folded in half, and would, therefore, be the first thing that an
addressee would read on opening the letter. While the poem's survival recovers
another Elizabethan female poet, the context of its composition argues for the
social role that poetry and indeed letters had to play in women's lives.

Poetry also features in other early modern women's letters. An epistle to Anne
Newdigate from Lady Frances Egerton ends with a verse of friendship:

then my lines comfort will appear
that I to thee am truly deare
dearer thou art then life to me
encrease my harts comfort of thee[188]

The poetic fragments that survive in Elizabeth Bourne's and Frances Egerton's
correspondence identify them as composers of original late-Elizabethan and
Jacobean verse, and argue for the relatively wider social currency of poetry during
this period. Discussions of poetry are also found in letters from the early modern
period. A defence of poetry is contained in a letter from Lady Anne Southwell
(1573–1636) to Lady Ridgeway, in which she argues for the superiority of poetry

[185] Ibid., fo. 104[v].   [186] I am grateful to Steven May for his invaluable assistance with this
poem, and allowing me to consult his *First Line Index of Elizabethan Verse*. Professor May has
suggested that Bourne's poem resembles the poem beginning 'I sigh. Why so?' in *The Paradise of
Dainties* (1576), sig. E3; and in terms of structure, if only superficially, Nicholas Breton's, 'But
whereto tends this tale?' (*STC* 3655, 1577), sig M1–1[v]; as well as Thomas Watson's 'Come gentle
death. Who calls?', in *Hekatompathia* (*STC* 25118a, 1582), sig. G4[v].
[187] BL, Addit., 23212, fo. 92: n.d.; Pollock, 'Teach Her to Live', 236.
[188] WCRO, CR136, B105: 4/05/1613.

over prose.[189] The seventeenth-century correspondence between Constance Fowler and her brother Herbert Ashton provided a poetic forum for discussion and transmission of manuscript verse.[190].

Sixteenth-century correspondence also offers further evidence of women's interest in a broader range of intellectual pursuits, including science and medicine. Peregrine Lord Willoughby de Eresby discussed with Margaret Clifford the practice of alchemy, an art in which the countess experimented: 'take of a lytle red sand', he wrote, 'to make a great deale of gold.' The letter also mentions the alchemistical studies of George Ripley, whose book *The Compound of Alchemy* (1591) Willoughby clearly assumed that Margaret Clifford was familiar with.[191] Letters were also used to exchange medical recipes: Lucy Harington, for example, included in a letter to Lord Treasurer, Burghley 'a practise for the gout'.[192] Maria Thynne sent her husband a recipe for protection against the plague.[193] Women's participation as medical practitioners within the household is also shown by their letters' requests for herbal and medical ingredients. Joan Thynne requested 'tincture of Saffron' for her daughter Dorothy.[194] The ability to write and conduct correspondence was thus connected to the household in practical ways, enabling women to perform a range of tasks: administrative, financial, legal, educational, and medical.

In that letters sometimes acted as early modern shopping lists, they offer evidence of the kinds of pursuits and activities that women were involved in: Elizabeth Bourne's request for 'ii knotes of trebell lute strings' indicates her interest in music.[195] Writing from Caus Castle, Joan Thynne likewise asked her husband to purchase for her strings for the lute and cloth for the virginals.[196] Aside from requests for musical supplies, letters mention women's musical activities, including the playing of instruments and singing. Anne Bacon described to her father Sir Thomas Gresham her recreational singing and music playing for her husband: 'My husbande causeth me to vse my singinge, & besides to learne some songes vpon ye virginalles;'[197] and Dorothy Okeover informed her father Richard Bagot that her sister Lettice played her virginals very well.[198] In addition to personal musical accomplishment, women were involved in hiring professional musicians for the household, for purposes of education and entertainment: John Hobart offered Lucy, marchioness of Winchester, the services of a musician whom he claimed could play well on all instruments.[199] Another

---

[189] Klene, *Southwell-Sibthorpe Commonplace Book*; Cavanaugh, 'Lady Southwell's Defense of Poetry', 284–85.　　[190] La Belle, 'Love's True Knot', 13–31. *Tixall Letters*, ed. Clifford, i.
[191] WD/Hoth Box 44, 23/03/n.y. Margaret Clifford's interest in alchemy is evidenced by her receipt book: (WD/Hoth/A988/5: Receipts of Lady Margaret).
[192] BL, Lansd., 18, fo. 71: 04/02/1574. See also BL, Lansd., 80, fo. 56: 29/05/1595; Bacon, 653, fo. 362.　　　　　　　　　　　　　[193] *Two Elizabethan Women*, 36 [?1607].
[194] Ibid. 19: 06/05/1601.　　　[195] BL, Addit., 23212, fo. 97, n.d.
[196] *Two Elizabethan Women*, letter 29: 18/06/1601.
[197] Folger, L.d.17: *c*.1572.　　　[198] Folger, L.a.652: 12/04/[1590].
[199] BL, Harl., 4713, fos. 278^r–278^v: n.d.

letter from the marchioness to Hobart discusses employing one of the queen's musicians to teach her son music and dancing.[200]

From the earliest development of a European-wide Republic of Letters at the start of the sixteenth century, a few exceptional classically educated women were involved in learned correspondence networks that discussed intellectual and theological ideas. Several women are numbered among the correspondents of Erasmus. Among the Dutch humanist's correspondence survive three Latin letters from women, those of Margaret of Hungary, Margaret Roper, and a letter from Margaret Welser Pautinger, which was attached to an epistle from her husband.[201] Additionally, there are twelve extant letters from Erasmus to various women, including Catherine of Aragon, Mary of Hungary, Marguerite de Valois, and Margaret Roper.[202] Several scholars working on the letters of Margaret Roper, the daughter of Thomas More, have sought to place her within a European humanist network.[203] Indeed, by writing in Latin to Erasmus she was corresponding with one of the leading continental intellectuals of the day.[204] There are also other examples of early Tudor women who engaged in epistolary exchanges with leading continental theologians: Jane Seymour wrote to Bucer and Fagius; three letters written in Greek survive from Jane Grey to Henry Bullinger; Dorothy Stafford and Elizabeth Sandys corresponded with the Italian humanist Celio Secondo Curione; and Anne Hooper (née de Tscerlas) wrote several letters to Bullinger when her husband was committed to the Fleet for objecting to the wearing of vestments.[205] These women corresponded in Latin, the international language of scholarship, they knew Greek and sometimes Hebrew, were conversant with the intellectual and theological ideas and debates of the day, and indeed discussed them in what amounted to a public forum. By the mid-seventeenth century, when the Republic of Letters was more fully established, women were at the heart of correspondence networks that sought to exchange ideas throughout Europe.[206] Female letter-writers such as Dorothy Moore and her niece Katherine Jones, Lady Ranelagh, were intimately associated with the epistolary networks of the Royal Society, which was founded during this period; they also corresponded with Samuel Hartlib, whose scriptorium aimed at facilitating the dissemination of intellectual and religious ideas in Britain and Europe.[207]

[200] BL, Harl., 4713, fo. 287: n.d.
[201] For Erasmus's correspondence see *Correspondence of Erasmus*, ed. Mynors *et al.*: 2820, 2233, 1247.   [202] O'Donnell, 'Contemporary Women in the Letters of Erasmus', 35–7.
[203] Kaufman, 'Absolute Margaret', 443–56; McCutcheon, 'Margaret More Roper', 449–80.
[204] Robinueau *et al.*, 'Correspondance entre Erasme et Margaret Roper', 29–46, 121.
[205] *Original Letters*, i. 2, 12/06/1549 (Jane Seymour); ibid. i. 4–11; BL, Addit., 46362, fos. 67^v–68^v, 69^r–70^v, 72$^{r–v}$ (Lady Jane Grey) [after 03/1551–before 05/1553]; Chavasse, 'Humanism in Exile' (Dorothy Stafford and Elizabeth Sandys).
[206] On the Republic of Letters see Ultee, 'Republic of Letters', 95–112; Hall, 'Royal Society's Role in the Diffusion of Information', 173–92.
[207] Hunter, 'Sisters of the Royal Society', 178–97; *Letters of Dorothy Moore*, ed. Hunter.

Moreover, by the mid- to late-seventeenth century the letter-writing genre had developed into a forum for literary and creative writing. Compared with the very pragmatic purposes to which medieval letters were put, the seventeenth century witnesses a proliferation in the uses and functions of letters and letter-writing. The letters of Dorothy Osborne (1627–95), for example, written during the period of her courtship with Sir William Temple (1652–4) are often praised for their *literariness*; Osborne is lauded as a 'prose stylist', her letters as attaining a 'fictional' quality.[208] Margaret Cavendish's *Sociable Letters* (1664) was in fact printed during her lifetime. The witty, practised, semi-fictional letters offered in the volume discuss wide-ranging topics including war and peace, literature, science and medicine, marriage, divorce, infidelity, and single life for women. By publishing this collection of letters, Cavendish was writing in a genre acceptable for early modern women—but she also published *Philosophical Letters* (1664), and made claim to links with the Royal Society and continental philosophers. Another famous woman of letters for whom letter-writing was a highly conscious art is Mary Wortley Montagu. Writing at the start of the eighteenth century, Lady Montagu utilized correspondence as a vehicle for lengthy description, narrative, and travel-writing. Letter-writing in this case provided a creative outlet for a woman impelled to write and 'entertain' an audience.[209] She was conscious that her own letters would record her literary achievements as a serious writer: her Turkish embassy letters were reworked from originals organized into albums and published posthumously a year after her death.[210] Given the close relationship between the letter and the epistolary novel during this period, literary scholars have often approached female letter-writing as a precursor of novels written by women.[211]

Tudor women's letters thus represent a sophisticated and layered source for the study of female education and literacy, one that provides a more nuanced and qualitative account than is possible from the study of signatures or educational treatises. Letters register parental attitudes to girls' education; document the varied nature of sixteenth-century pedagogical practices; are sites of female scribal activities; highlight female mastery of the rhetorical and stylistic conventions of Renaissance letter-writing; and shed light on a broad range of women's literary and cultural interests. The sixteenth century witnessed the diffusion of letter-writing skills to a broader range of groups of women below the ranks of court and social elites; and over the same period letter-writing became a more personal activity, increasingly disconnected from scribes and secretaries.

[208] Virginia Woolf, 'Dorothy Osborne's *Letters*', 59–66; Ottway, 'Dorothy Osborne's Love Letters', 149–59. Lerch-Davis, 'Rebellion Against Public Prose', 386–415; Fitzmaurice and Rey, 'Letters By Women in England', 149–60; Hintz, 'Desire and Renunciation'.

[209] In a letter to the countess of Mar, Lady Montagu wrote, 'It is to be hoped that my letter will entertain you': *Letters of Lady Mary Wortley Montagu*, ed. Brant, 223.

[210] Ibid., pp. xii–xiii, xvi.

[211] Perry, *Women, Letters and the Novel*; Goldsmith, *Writing the Female Voice*; Jensen, *Writing Love*; Brant, 'Eighteenth-Century Letters'.

The wider acquisition of letter-writing skills by Tudor women can be explained by a complex intersection of a multitude of 'push' and 'pull' factors influencing the spread of literacy. As levels of female writing ability rose during the period, more personal and introspective uses were made of letters, either as emotional, 'literary' or religious outlets. Moreover, the very act of writing a letter itself formed a part of the educational process. Possession of the ability to write a letter was viewed more and more as a 'functional' skill, useful to women acting as mothers, wives, and mistresses of the household, corresponding on behalf of family interests.

5

Delivery, Reception, and Reading

Thus far this book has concentrated on the ways in which sixteenth-century women's letters were composed, exploring issues of authorship and epistolary writing within the context of female literacy. This methodology approaches correspondence from the perspective of the writer or sender, rather than from that of the letter bearer, reader, or addressee: it looks at how letters were written, rather than at how they were delivered and read, each of which had an important impact on the writing of letters. By examining the delivery and reading of letters this chapter situates women's correspondence within a broader contextual framework. It outlines the various methods by which letters were delivered, and the significant roles played by bearers, figures who, although often shadowy and historically invisible, represented a corporeal extension of the letters they carried. The chapter also seeks to reconstruct the early modern reading process, identifying the variety of milieux in which letters were read and the different reading practices that recipients employed. Crucially the chapter also reassesses levels of female reading ability in order better to ascertain how far women were in fact capable of reading handwritten correspondence as opposed to printed matter. Investigations of female reading literacy raise a number of important issues that have wide implications for women's access to knowledge and information, and their ability to control legal, business, and household affairs. To what extent could women read different sorts of handwriting (distinct from women's reading of printed materials) and how did this affect their ability to read a variety of letters? What proportion of women, for example, could read script? Could women read secretary and court hands, as well as italic, or letters in Latin?

Fundamental to the chapter are issues of epistolary privacy. Writers were often apprehensive about committing confidences to paper, which in turn affected the nature of composition and the manner in which letters were dispatched. Secrets often remained unwritten, and were instead consigned for safekeeping to the memory of the letter bearer who would deliver them orally, a fact that is frustrating in its historical irretrievability. Female writers were also their own judicious self-editors, censoring the contents of their dispatches, and on occasion employing codes and symbols, euphemisms and shared language to conceal meaning. Letters were folded and sealed to shield their substance from prying eyes, and then conveyed by trustworthy bearers to the intended recipient and reader; letters also carried instructions for their burning or destruction, all of which highlights early modern concerns for privacy and security. And yet, during this period seemingly personal letters achieved wider readership: they were circulated among family and community networks for perusal; they were scribally published in manuscript; and in a number of cases even appeared in printed form. How far, therefore, can the reading of letters (as with the writing of letters) be considered a personal, private, and singular activity? Here, by way of a case study, discussion in the last section of the chapter centres on letters of petition, outlining the ways in which they were read, where, and by whom. Assessing the impact of letters of petition in this manner provides a context for studies that have approached such letters from a rhetorical perspective. Finally, while this study by its very nature focuses on women's letters, this is not to suggest that women read or interpreted letters differently from men: indeed, the reading practices identified among female correspondents apply equally well to male letter-writers.

DELIVERY OF LETTERS

In a period when the government postal service mainly carried official dispatches, the delivery of private correspondence was performed largely on an ad hoc basis.[1] Many women, especially those of the nobility and gentry, consigned letters to special messengers, such as clerks or servants. Elizabeth, countess of Shrewsbury, retained servants specifically as letter carriers: Mary Talbot writing to the countess explained, 'we haue desired your la[dyship's] leter men to bringe a letre to your la[dyship]'.[2] The precise identity of bearers, as with secretaries, is often difficult to establish. In some cases, bearers are mentioned by name in letters, but in others they are referred to more generally as 'the bearer', 'my servant', 'my man', or 'the messenger', and in the majority of letters they receive no mention at all. In addition to using servants, merchants were utilized as letter carriers.[3] Writing to his master Robert Sidney, Rowland Whyte referred to the practice of entrusting letters to ships' captains: 'Yesterday I delivered the skipper of the Unicorn a packet of letters, within yt one from Mr Secretary, and another from my lady warwick I beseache you that these skippers be well paid for they are trusty and often I can send by them.'[4] Other women used 'friends' journeying the same route, and some letter-writers entrusted correspondence to chance travellers.[5] Alternatively, women engaged the services of strangers who

---

[1] On early modern postal conditions see Robinson, *British Post Office*, 5–22; Beale, *History of the Post*; Hey, *Packmen, Carriers and Packhorse Roads*; Allen, *Post and Courier Service*; Browne, *Getting the Message*; Stone, *The Inland Posts*; LaMar, *Travel and Roads in England*; Charters, 'Road Carrying in England'; Howe, *Epistolary Spaces*.   [2] Folger, X.d.428 (114): n.d.
[3] Housden, 'Early Posts', 713–18; id., 'Merchant Strangers Posts', 739–42.
[4] HMC, *De L'Isle*, ii. 222: 28/09/1596.   [5] Robinson, *British Post Office*, 5–22.

were informally paid for delivering missives. Anne Woodhouse reported to her brother Nathaniel Bacon that 'I dyd hyer a man to cary you a letter th[a]t cam from my lord the man dwelled in iii myle of [you].'[6]

The amounts paid to bearers are occasionally recorded, either in letters themselves or in household accounts. The accounts of the Roberts family of Boarzell, Sussex, which were kept primarily by the mistress of the household Margaret, record payments of 3*d* and 12*d* to 'the carrier'.[7] Other sources indicate that the recipient paid for the cost of delivery on receipt of a letter: Elizabeth Hatton requested that Sir John Hobart 'reward the bearor acording to his paynes';[8] Anne Higginson informed Lady Ferrers that she had 'promysed' the messenger two shillings 'for the bringing of yor letter'.[9] The amount paid probably depended on how much was carried and how far the bearer travelled: accounts of the Johnson family for the period 1545–9 record the delivery of a letter by the bearer 'ned' at 1*d*, while the carrying of a basket and side of venison to London cost 8*d*.[10] Women themselves acted as bearers on occasion: Arbella Stuart thanked her uncle Gilbert Talbot for his 'short letter' which she received from 'm[istr]e[ss] Nelson'.[11] Household accounts of the second earl of Salisbury record payment of 2*s* 6*d* to 'a poore women with a lettere'.[12] Higher up the social scale, female courtiers were crucial in the delivery of letters to Elizabeth I.

Women had uneven access to letter bearers, especially those below the ranks of the landed elites. Certain women were fortunate enough to enjoy regular access to letter bearers. Indeed, during her marriage to Sir William St Loe, Bess of Hardwick was able to utilize her husband's men who acted as official carriers. St Loe explained to Francis Yaxley that he could write to him and his wife 'by Thomas Alsopp my sarvantt who ys one off the caryers from darbye to london. He or hys men cometh wekelye.'[13] However, other women commonly experienced problems dispatching letters and trustworthy bearers could not always be found or spared. Margaret, countess of Bath, apologized to her husband, writing that 'I would send letters offener unto you but I cannot gett them well conveyed'.[14] Mary Grey wrote to William Cecil attributing the infrequency of her letters to 'wantt of a conveyentt messenger'; and Anne Lady Paget reported to her son Thomas, Lord Paget that she had been unable to convey a message to one Master Connigsbie because 'I have none that is mete for the purpose nowe to spare'.[15] Of course, troped language of this nature relating to the lack or insufficiency of bearers also politely conveyed apologies for the fact that a writer

[6] Folger, L.d.626: n.d.
[7] Tittler, 'Accounts of the Roberts Family', 72–3; see also *Household Accounts and Disbursement Books of Robert Dudley*, ed. Adams, 48.   [8] Bodl., Tanner, 115, fo. 190: n.d.
[9] Folger, L.e.644: 8/05/*c.* 1600.   [10] NA, SP46/5/2, fos. 3ʳ (06/04/1545), 14ʳ (18/09/1549).
[11] *Letters of Lady Arbella Stuart*, ed. Steen, 187: 27/10/1603.
[12] Munby, *Early Stuart Household Accounts*, 178.   [13] SP12/19/47: 12/09/1561.
[14] CUL, Hengrave, 88/1, fo. 48: 15/03/n.y.
[15] SP12/42/48: 17/04/1567; Staffs RO, Paget Papers, D1734/2/5/15/M: 1583.

had not recently written, and worked in the same way as apologies for 'scribbled lines' in inscribing deference in epistolary form.

The ways in which letters were addressed (either by secretaries or women themselves) provides further information of how they were delivered. Addresses usually give the name of the recipient and or the place where the letter should be delivered. A letter from Lady Anne Lee to her brother Thomas Lord Paget was directed: 'To the ryght honorable and my very good lord and brother my lord paget of beawdesert at Burton gyve thess.'[16] Walter Bagot's letter to his wife was addressed simply 'To my louinge wiefe Mrs: Elizabeth Bagot at Blythfield'.[17] Lady Margaret Seymour's letter to John Thynne was addressed 'To the Right worshhyppfull and my uery frind Sir Jhon Thynne geue thys w[i]t[h] speade at London or ellse whear'.[18] Ordinarily letters were either placed in the hands of the addressee or deposited at their household of residence, although less formal drop-off arrangements were commonplace. In sending her husband Nathaniel a book, Dorothy Bacon arranged for it to be sent to Edmund Peckover, a Norwich draper, whose premises were used as a convenient drop-off point for letters to and from Stiffkey: 'even this morneng I wryt you a lettar and sent it to Pecafars of Norrwech to be conwayed to you, and allso the boke you wryt for I sent with it, not knoweng of Mestar Tavenars gooeng to London.'[19]

The sporadic nature of delivery imposed constraints upon women's composition of letters. Immediate or unexpected departure of bearers forced writers to hasten correspondence; letters were sometimes written hurriedly while messengers waited. Elizabeth Cecil added a postscript to a letter from her husband, the second earl of Exeter, to her kinsman Thomas Hobart apologising for the brevity of her note: 'the hast of this messenger parmits no mor[e] tim[e] but to subscribe my self your most lovinge cussen.'[20] The arrival of bearers also occasioned the writing of letters; women grasped such opportunities to send correspondence. Elizabeth Bourne informed Sir John Conway that 'I can not let yo[u]r boy pas wyth out som of my bad skrblynges'; and Mary Kitson wrote to her parents stating, 'I colde not let passe this messenger without some remembrance of my dutye unto you bothe'.[21] Expressions conveying the desire or duty to write when convenient occasion arose helped to imbue letters with a personal tone, which served to cement the bonds between letter-writer and addressee. Read literally, postal pressures of this nature may have increased letters' spontaneity and immediacy, reducing time for reflection, drafting, and refinement.

The speed of postal delivery times varied greatly according to geographical location. Using royal postmaster's records on official communications scholars have explored the efficiency of exchanges of correspondence and the speed of travel by road between London and the localities in Elizabethan and Jacobean

---

[16] Paget Papers, D603/K/1/4/6, 09/10/n.y.   [17] Folger, L.a.99: [*c*.1590?].
[18] BL, Lansd., 108, fo. 67: n.d.   [19] BL, Addit., 41140, fos. 121–2: [24/10–20/11/1597].
[20] Tanner, 285, fo. 100. See also *Letters of Lady Arbella Stuart*, 199: 02/01/1604.
[21] BL, Addit., 23212, fo. 97: 07/03/n.y.; CUL, 88/2, fo. 61: 01/04/n.y.

England, arguing for spatial variations in 'core–periphery connectivity': those located on the main arterial roads of England were better off than those in more remote locations.[22] While the dispatch of government communications from London to Reading could be completed within six hours and St Albans in three hours, letters travelling from London to Exeter could take up to 100 hours, and those from London to Plymouth almost 136 hours.[23] Letters conveyed by informal means presumably took even longer; women sometimes wrote of the difficulties of transmitting correspondence to remoter parts of the country. Margaret Hoby informed Anne Newdigate that, 'beinge neere a greter iurnie [journey] in to the northe . . . I shall almost neuer hope to heare frome you'; while Anne Clifford complained to her mother, the countess of Cumberland, that, 'I was neuer so longe without a leter from you neuer since you went into the northe as noue I have bin'.[24] Communications by letter were, therefore, more sporadic in outlying parts of the country, making it more difficult for some letter-writers to maintain social ties over a wider geographical area, and to keep abreast of current news. Similarly, women encountered problems sending letters abroad. Lady Anne Hungerford complained of the infrequency of post to Spain in 1602, two years before King James negotiated peace with Philip III.[25] Although there were regular posts to Calais during this period, Sabine Johnson's letters to her husband John met with postal complications and on several occasions were misdirected. John Johnson in one letter to his wife explained that, 'I haue now recf your l[ett]re welbeloved wife of the 23 of the last month whiche hathe bene at andwerp [Antwerp] and is come again'.[26] The passage of letters across the Atlantic during the seventeenth century was also slow and intermittent; letters conveyed by ship were sometimes lost, but more often than not delayed.[27]

   The conveying of letters was fraught with dangers and delays. Lucy, marchioness of Winchester, wrote to Sir John Hobart expressing surprise that her letter had not arrived: 'I much marvayle you receaved not my letters any soner consideringe the assured p[ro]mis of my cosin george paulet for the saffe and speadie conveiance of them.'[28] Elizabeth, dowager countess of Shrewsbury, complained to Burghley of 'the neclegence of the carryar that stayed my letters'.[29] Time-lags in delivery often resulted in letters crossing over, thus complicating the reconstruction of epistolary exchanges: in several cases, new

[22] Brayshay, Harrison, and Chalkley, 'Knowledge, Nationhood and Governance', 268–9. Archer, 'Letters to London from the South Coast Ports'; Brayshay, 'Royal Post-Horse Routes in England and Wales', 373–89; id., 'Royal Post-Horse Routes in South-West England', 79–103; id., 'Royal Post-Horse Routes of Hampshire', 121–34; Harrison and Brayshay, 'Post-Horse Routes, Royal Progresses and Government Communications', 116–33; Armstrong, 'Some Examples of the Distribution and Speed of News', 429–54.
[23] Brayshay, 'Knowledge, Nationhood and Governance', 276–7.
[24] WCRO, Newdigate Papers, CR136 B 220: 22/01/n.y.; Kendal RO, Hothfield, WD/Hoth/ Box 44: 01/05/1615.   [25] SP12/284/53: 30/06/1602.
[26] SP46/5/140: 09/11/1545.
[27] Cressy, *Coming Over*, 222–5; Steele, 'Time, Communications and Society', 1–21.
[28] Tanner, 115, fo. 3: 06/03/1599.   [29] SP12/238/116: 11/04/1591.

letters were dispatched before replies had been received, and occasionally writers corresponded with each other simultaneously without either of them having received a letter.[30] Additionally, epistles sometimes went astray and failed to reach their intended destinations, having been intercepted, lost, discarded, or carelessly mislaid. Elizabeth Graye informed her friend Anne Newdigate that 'your lines hade the miss fortune to miscary and I the unhappines to lose the benefitte of them'.[31] Fearful of subterfuge, female letter-writers sometimes employed ingenious devices to have letters carried. During her period of captivity under the keepership of George, earl of Shrewsbury, and his wife Bess of Hardwick, Mary, queen of Scots, had her correspondence regularly intercepted by Walsingham. She was, therefore, forced to employ a range of covert methods in order to ensure that her mail went undetected and was not confiscated; sources record letters that were found hidden under stones, and one letter was even secreted in the staff of a visitor.[32]

The roles performed by bearers were an integral part of the letter-writing process. Writers frequently omitted details too delicate, lengthy, or complicated to set down on paper, leaving bearers themselves to explain. In correspondence to John Conway, Elizabeth Bourne wrote, 'I wyll not trubell you wyth my longe lynes hauenyng so suffyshent a messynger that can beter tell you my mynd then I can wryte hit and wyth lesse trubel'.[33] Equally, women ordered bearers to wait for replies, which usually took the form either of letters or oral messages. Lettice, dowager countess of Essex, writing to Burghley stated that she had 'appointed this bearer M[aste]r Will[ia]ms to attende yo[u]r frendly answer'.[34] Clearly, a woman could not declare that she was waiting for an answer in this fashion unless she had the acquaintance of the addressee or was of very considerable personal standing relative to him or her. In either instance, however, bearers acted as personal representatives entrusted with women's intimate business interests and empowered to operate on their behalves in their absence. Presumably women were more likely to convey oral information to bearers whom they trusted than to those who were strangers. Absence of recipients created further complications. In such instances letters were normally left with servants with instructions to pass them on. Arbella Stuart explained to Gilbert Talbot: 'the letters to my Lord Cecill and . . . Sir Thomas Edmonds weare delivered though not so soone, as I wished, they being both absent . . . so that Sir Thomas his was delivered to the doore keeper of the Councell chamber.'[35]

In cases where bearers were unknown to recipients, writers commonly assured them of the bearer's reliability. Margaret Legh, writing to her brother Robert Penrudocke enjoined him to 'geve credit to this bearer yo[u]r seruante for he

---

[30] SP46/5/170: 21/09/1546.   [31] WCRO, CR136, B175: n.d.
[32] Durant, *Bess of Hardwick*, 75.
[33] BL, Addit., 23212, fo. 105: n.d. See also, BL, Addit., 12506, fo. 341: 08/10/1602.
[34] BL, Lansd., 24, fo. 28: 28/02/1577.   [35] *Letters of Lady Arbella Stuart*, 187: 27/10/1603.

knowes all thyngs . . . who is my frends & who is nowght'.[36] Letters thus functioned to confer authority on servants and to confirm their identity. Indeed,
servants unknown to the individuals to whom they were dispatched were
apparently expected to carry letters authorizing their activities. In general, use of
personal servants to carry letters provided an important point of contact between
sender and recipient, and the close servants of noblewomen benefited from the
reflected status of women of high standing.[37] Nevertheless, in some situations it
was considered important for senders to deliver a letter personally in order both
to ensure its safe arrival and demonstrate honour and respect to the addressee:
Robert Sidney declared to his wife Barbara, 'cause the letters of my Lo[rd] and
Lady of Sussex to be deliuered. That to my Lady is to the purpose you did devise
it and if she bee in London I would you did deliver it your self.'[38]

Bearers also often delivered to officials letters that were written on their own
behalf supporting their suits. Anne White wrote in favour of her kinsman
Mr Hilliard, who had been 'called vnto the starre chamb[e]r by suppena', a letter
which he was to present to Sir Robert Cecil. She notified Cecil that 'the cause is
longe and tedious wherefore he [Mr Hilliard] can better certyfie yo[u]r honor
then I shalbe able to write vnto you'.[39] Usually such letters were sealed, especially, one assumes, where writers were less than enthusiastic in their recommendations. In many examples bearers appear to have been present while letters
were read. Indeed, Cecil inserted the name of a bearer, one Mr Mylet, in the text
of a letter written on the man's behalf by Lucy, marchioness of Winchester.[40]
Evidently, Mylet both bore the letter and was in attendance while it was perused
by Cecil. Under these circumstances, letters formed a part of a face-to-face
social interaction of which the bearer's oral representation constituted a crucial
element. In particular, bearers had the advantage of employing verbal and extra-
verbal modes of operation that accompany business conducted in person, such as
tone of voice, a smile, a nod, or a raising of the eyebrows, gauging when to
elaborate and when to remain silent. In short, bearers were a physical extension
of what was written on the page, and by their presence were able to influence a
letter's passage and to plead their own case.

FEMALE READING ABILITY

While scholars have attended to women's reading of printed books, little consideration has been given to women's reading of handwritten documents or
manuscripts, a practice distinct from reading the printed word. This section aims
to redress this balance by considering the social practices relating both to how

---

[36] SP46/14/164: 13/04/n.y. [37] Starkey, 'Representation Through Intimacy', 187–224.
[38] CKS, De L'Isle, U1475, C81/101: 27/05/1597.
[39] Hatfield House, Cecil, 76, fo. 36: 04/02/1601. [40] Cecil, 183, fo. 140: 29/01/1603.

women read letters and to how *their* letters were read, rather than merely looking at what letters suggest about women's reading of printed materials. The extent to which women could read different types of handwriting has an obvious bearing on the types of manuscripts that could circulate among them. To what extent, for example, could women read letters, wills, deeds, promissory notes, and other legal documents written in professional secretarial and court hands, some of which were in Latin? How far were women excluded from business and legal domains because they lacked what are highly specialized literacy skills? Therefore, not only should scholars be interested in the kinds of hands that early modern women *could write*, but also further research should consider the kinds of hands that early modern women *could read*.

Most scholars judge levels of female reading ability to have been greater than levels of writing ability and have argued for women's increasing familiarity with print, evidenced by the rise in numbers of books written for female audiences.[41] Historians have argued for more complex definitions of literacy, taking into account variations in degrees of reading as well as writing ability.[42] Keith Thomas has demonstrated that an ability to read black-letter, the type used in hornbooks to teach children to read in Tudor England, did not necessarily mean that an individual was equally proficient at reading roman type, which became the dominant print form during the late sixteenth and early seventeenth centuries. Likewise, fluency in reading print does not indicate a woman's ability to decipher handwritten documents.[43] Thus, while the Elizabethan nonconformist John Penry assumed his wife Helen could read the Bible and would be able to teach their daughter to do so, he also assumed that someone else would have to read his letters to her.[44]

One of the difficulties that one confronts in assessing reading abilities during this period is that the physical activity of reading leaves very little trace. Indeed, Heidi Brayman Hackel describes reading as 'a historically invisible skill', which 'survives in the historical record only when accompanied by writing'.[45] References in women's letters to the activity of reading correspondence are usually indirect; it is, therefore, impossible to document accurately the proportion of women that could read letters. Frances Seymour wrote to her husband, the earl of Hertford, stating, 'I delyvered your letter after I had rede it to her maiesty'; and Elizabeth Bourne refused to read a letter from her estranged husband Anthony, stating: 'he should frame hym selfe to lyve of that he had and paye all his debtes and provyd for all his bastards.'[46] Other comments suggest women sometimes read letters silently and alone. Elizabeth, countess of Southampton, described to her husband reading 'a letter from London', which she maintained

---

[41] Hull, *Chaste, Silent and Obedient*; Wright, 'Reading of Renaissance English Women', 671–88.
[42] Thomas, 'Meaning of Literacy', 97–131; Cressy, *Literacy and the Social Order*; Houston, *Literacy*.   [43] Thomas, 'Meaning of Literacy', 99–100.
[44] Ibid. 100.   [45] Hackel, '"Great Variety" of Readers', 141.
[46] Longleat House, Seymour Papers, 5, fos. 168–9: *c.*08/1585; BL, Addit., 23212, fo. 86: n.d.

was 'secrit'.[47] The seventeenth-century autobiographer Lady Elizabeth Delaval recorded childhood exchanges of letters which she 'carefully kept' in her 'bosome'.[48] The solitary mode of reading that these examples describe indicates that letters were often viewed as intimate and confidential, their contents matters of secrecy to be kept from inquisitive eyes.

The ability to read manuscripts came with familiarity, a familiarity gained through contact with handwriting or being taught to read it. Lady Lisle, herself unable to write more than a scratchy signature, could nevertheless read her husband's letters.[49] It may, therefore, be that in some cases 'signing literacy', which underestimates the ability to read print, more accurately reflects women's general ability to read handwriting. Alternatively, the ability to read a particular script came with the ability to write it: those individuals who practised certain hands probably read them with the greatest ease.[50]

Unfamiliarity with a script or a person's individual rendition of that script (his or her 'hand') may mean that women found difficulty in reading correspondence, and may have limited the variety of letters that they were able to read, though this area requires further research. As an initial foray, it is perhaps useful to think in terms of a hierarchy of hands that women could read. Italic, believed by the penman Martin Billingsley to be 'the easiest hand that is written with Pen', was probably also the easiest hand to read: it was the most popular hand used by female letter-writers in the second half of the sixteenth century, and most closely resembled roman type.[51] Secretary hand, by contrast, was written by a very small number of women, though there is direct evidence of women reading it. Many women had regular contact with incoming mail written in secretary script, and others proofed secretarial letters: Anne Newdigate corrected in her own italic hand a draft of a letter to the earl of Salisbury penned by her amanuensis in secretary hand.[52] Women may have found it harder or in fact been unable to read legal hands, with which they were less well acquainted; this may have been the same for men: legal hands were separately taught by specialists, not as part of a general education. Only a small minority of well-known classically educated women could read epistles written in Latin. Greater numbers of women, however, could read letters in French.[53] For women only able to read in the vernacular, it was language rather than handwriting that prevented them from reading certain letters.

While one could be taught to read regular hands or textbook renditions of scripts, more problematic were erratic or idiosyncratic versions of these scripts, which posed greatest difficulty for those unacquainted with a writer's individual style. Anthony Bacon thought his classically educated mother Anne Bacon

---

[47] Cecil, 101, fo. 16: 08/07/1603.
[48] Cited in Wilcox, 'Private Writing and Public Function', 47.
[49] *Lisle Letters*, i. p. 32, pl. 8j; ii. p. 700; v. 1544, 1546, 1559.
[50] Thomas, 'Meaning of Literacy', 100.   [51] *The Pen's Excellencie* (1618), 37.
[52] WCRO, CR136, B307.   [53] Fleming, 'The French Garden', 19–51.

would struggle to read the earl of Essex's letters: 'I know your la[dyship] could not read my lords hande it beinge as hard as any cypher to those that are not thoroughlie acquainted therew[i]th.'[54] Where letters were written in unconventional hands, it was scribal practice to make fair copies in order that they might be more easily read. A letter from Lady Anne Dacre to Lord North written in 1592 was copied out by one of Burghley's secretaries, who endorsed it as 'the copy of Lady Dacre letter as well as I could read yt'.[55] Numerous female correspondents expressed concern that recipients would be unable to be read their handwriting: Lady Anne Townshend wrote to her son Roger, 'I wish yow might read my scriblinge', though as discussed previously expressions of this nature were often conventions of politeness.[56]

The ability to read letters appears to have been fairly widespread among women of the nobility, gentry, and merchant classes; most references to women unable to read letters occur lower down the social scale. Evidence from an early seventeenth-century courtship case records that one Robert Lowther sent a love letter to Susan Hills, in which he wrote, 'I feare you can hardly read this because you do not practise'.[57] The wife of Thomas Owldman, tanner, could not read a letter and took it to 'ould Powell of Cawston to read for her', and 'because hee could not read it' she gave it to a schoolboy, Edward Lombe.[58] In Renaissance drama too, the kinds of women represented as unable to read letters are from lower social groups: Jaquenetta, the country wench in Shakespeare's *Loves Labours Lost*, for example, asks Sir Nathaniel to read a letter for her; while Mistress Gallipot, the apothecary's wife in Middleton and Dekker's *The Roaring Girl*, has difficulty in pronouncing certain words ('Pan-da-rus', and 'Cres-sida') when reading Master Laxton's love letter.[59]

In order to understand a letter's contents, women need not have been able to read handwriting, although inability to read letters on one's own was a barrier to epistolary privacy and full personal control over correspondence. Importantly, however, many women who could read manuscript writing occasionally chose not to do so for various reasons: ill-health, social status, the nature of the letter, and their relationship with the writer or bearer. The reading of letters, as with the process of writing letters, was considered by many during the early modern period to be a task too physically taxing for women to undertake during illness or pregnancy.[60] At such times these tasks were performed by secretaries, servants, or relatives. Lady Eleanor Zouche informed her cousin Thomas Randolph: 'I haue

---

[54] LPL, Bacon, 649 (2), fo. 337: 19/10/1593.   [55] BL, Lansd., 121, fo. 80: 23/11/1592.
[56] Folger, L.d.595: 08/08/1619.   [57] Gowing, *Domestic Dangers*, 160.
[58] Adam Fox, 'Rumour, News and Popular Political Opinion', 610. Reading ability in this instance is thus also generational.
[59] Shakespeare, *Loves Labours Lost*, IV. ii. 89–91; Middleton and Dekker, *The Roaring Girl*, III. ii. 55. See also Marlowe's *Edward II* (1592), I. v. 57–68; Middleton's *The Witch* (1615–16), III. ii. 47–56.
[60] On the detrimental side effects of reading, see Porter, 'Reading Is Bad For Your Health', 11–16; Johns, 'Physiology of Reading', 138–61.

bene very sicke, & not yet so well recouered th[a]t I can in duer to wryt or to read but w[i]t[h] great payne.'[61] George Clifford, congratulating his wife on the safe delivery of their daughter Anne, apologised, 'I knowe it is troblesum now for thye to reade'.[62] Under these circumstances letters were read aloud, similar to the way in which servants in upper-class households read aloud from books.[63] Thus, when his wife was ill, George Talbot suggested that she let his son Gilbert read his letters to her, instead of using what he referred to as the 're[a]dyng m[aste]rs': 'because the re[a]dyng m[aste]rs p[er]happ trob[i]ll you lett gilbord red them to you.'[64] Given that an individual woman was physically capable of reading script, her choice of whether or not to read herself is telling of the kinds of letters she wished to keep secret, the type of information she was content to divulge, the levels of intimacy of her various relationships, and the range of people in whom she placed trust.

'PRIVATE' AND 'PUBLIC' READING PRACTICES

'New political history' has stressed the fluidity of the boundaries between the 'state' and the 'private', and the 'public' and the 'domestic'.[65] Work by feminist scholars has undermined the binary opposition of 'separate spheres'—between male political and business spheres, and restricted female domestic spheres in which the household represents the sole locus of women's lives and experiences—an opposition that works to exclude women from male definitions of power and influence.[66] Yet this reconceptualizing of traditional social categories, while essential to the better integration of women into historical narratives, often obscures meaningful distinctions between 'public' and 'private'. This section argues that an analysis of the social practices relating to reading women's letters (the ways women themselves read, as well as how women's letters were read by others) offers one way of delineating early modern social boundaries, boundaries that were in fact under constant negotiation, as individuals and groups continually expanded and contracted definitions of what constituted 'private', 'secret', and 'intimate'; 'public', 'communal', and 'shared'.

Despite the overlap between social, political and domestic spheres during this period, contemporaries readily distinguished between 'public', referring to affairs of state and office as well as to public spaces (churches, marketplaces, or law courts), and 'private', denoting matters unrelated to the state, and also implying intimate and secret.[67] In his letter-writing manual *De conscribendis epistolis*,

[61] BL, Harl., 6994, fo. 5: 28/04/1586.   [62] Kendal RO, WD/Hoth/Box 44: 06/02/1589.
[63] *Diaries of Lady Anne Clifford*, ed. Clifford 8; *Diary of Lady Margaret Hoby*, ed. Moody, 98.
[64] Folger, X.d.428 (103): 12/09/1580.   [65] Mears, 'Courts, Courtiers, and Culture', 703–22.
[66] Harris, 'Women and Politics', 259–81; Vickery, 'Golden Age to Separate Spheres?', 383–414; Goodman, 'Public Sphere and Private Life', 1–20.
[67] Willen, 'Women in the Public Sphere', 560, 575; Warnicke, 'Private and Public', 123, 126–7.

Erasmus differentiated between 'private matters' and 'public news': 'private matters would include informing an absent person of our state of health, or our progress in our studies, of how our affairs are progressing in the country, at court, in building concerns, and in the lawcourts, or of any new undertakings of ours in other spheres right down to trivial details of parties and conversations; public news concerning peace, war, kingly exploits, treaties, plagues, floods, earthquakes, storms and other such things.'[68] A study of *how* letters were read permits glimpses at what some historians perceive as an emerging (but far from fully formed) concept of privacy in sixteenth- and seventeenth-century England, observable within family and community relations.[69] Analysing not only who read the letters but also the context of their reception raises many important issues. Did addressees alone read correspondence or were letters aimed at a family or even public readership? How far was reading letters considered a personal and therefore private and solitary activity? (Was it acceptable, for instance, to open and read a letter addressed to somebody else?) What kinds of letters were intended for individuals to read and what kinds for wider circulation? When were letters read silently or aloud, alone or in company? Questions of this nature help to illuminate a peculiarly early modern social geography, in which the often collaborative nature of the letter-writing process becomes apparent, thus challenging scholarly notions of *personal* correspondence as identified with the private and the singular. Furthermore, considerations by contemporary letter-writers of the ways in which letters would be read (and indeed delivered) are intimately bound up with an understanding of epistolary forms and persuasion.

The desire for epistolary privacy among sixteenth-century correspondents manifested itself in several ways: the manner by which letters were dispatched; instructions outlining by whom letters were to be opened and read; requests for letters to be burned or returned; and use of codes and ciphers. The insecurity associated with the epistolary medium is demonstrated by Mildred Burghley's warning to Sir William Fitzwilliam to 'kepe close your frends letters; for craft and malis never raygned more'.[70] Mindful of the risk of transmitting correspondence, senders on the whole were careful to seal their folded letters, ensuring that others would not read them. Anne Hooper implored Henry Bullinger to seal letters directed to her, 'for there are certain busy bodies who are in the habit of opening and reading them'.[71] Other women expressed concern when letters arrived opened. Joan Thynne asked her husband to warn 'cousin' Halliwell that his letter 'was opened afore it came to my hand'; and Elizabeth, countess of Shrewsbury, showed annoyance when one of her husband's letters was opened

---

[68] Erasmus, *De conscribendis epistolis* [1522], 225.

[69] Houlbrooke, *English Family*, 23; Pollock, 'Living on the Stage', 79–80; Ingram, *Church Courts*, 30, 244–5; Shaw, 'Construction of the Private', 447–66.

[70] Ballard, *Memoirs of Several Ladies*, 473, addenda: 26/10/1573. Schneider, 'Politics, Deception, and the Workings of the Post', 99–127.

[71] Robinson, *Original Letters*, i. 108: 03/04/[1551]. See also SP10/10/25: 08/09/1550.

before she had a chance to read it.[72] These examples articulate a distinct anxiety among women that their letters should not fall into the wrong hands. Writers were concerned to keep secret matters of sensitivity that could harm political standing and reputation, or impair business interests. In light of this, efforts were made to ensure the use of trustworthy bearers to deliver letters.

Once in the hands of the bearer, letters were delivered straight to the addressee, who was normally expected to receive and open his or her own correspondence, although secretaries also unsealed and processed letters. Mary Markham apologized to Mr Williamson for opening his letter to her aunt, explaining that her aunt had not been 'at hom that I was bold to opin your lettar'.[73] Missives could legitimately be opened by persons trusted by or related to the addressee, where failure to do so would be a hindrance. In several cases, wives were permitted to deal with husband's correspondence when they were away from home. In her husband's absence Anne Stowghton received and answered a letter addressed to him from her cousin Nicholas Williamson that related to business affairs.[74] However, not all wives felt at ease in dealing with husbands' correspondence. Joan Thynne apologized to her husband John for opening a letter addressed to him: 'I pray you take it not ill that I opened your letter. I protest the fear of the sudden to hear that there was a messenger come from Longleat, at that time of night after my first sleep, did so amaze me, and the haste that he had to have them sent after you, was the cause that I opened Standish's (Standishis) letter, fearing all had not been well there.'[75] The very length of Joan's explanation and her obvious feeling of awkwardness at opening the letter suggests a fairly well-defined concept of private correspondence: that letters were the personal property of the addressee. Strong demands for epistolary privacy are encountered in marital correspondence, where husbands and wives expressed the desire that their letters be read solely by each other. Thomas Baskerville, in a love-letter to his wife Mary, wrote 'kepe my letter to your selfe', while his general newsletters to her he asked to be shown to his father.[76] Thus, letter-writers were concerned to control or limit the readership of letters of a more personal or romantic nature, and to keep secret matters relating to business, reputation, and honour. Privacy here was principally familial rather than individual; the solitary act of reading correspondence worked to preserve epistolary secrets transacted between family members.

The regularity with which women demanded that recipients destroy or burn their letters once they had been read further suggests fears of spying and incrimination. Elizabeth Kitson wrote frankly to her cousin John Hobart concerning the proposed marriage of a kinsman, requesting that he 'be carful of this letter & whan you hau red it. I dout no wit your good will & remembrancs

---

[72] Wall (ed.), *Two Elizabethan Women*, 11: 30/05/1595; LPL, Shrewsbury, 699, fo. 25: 13/05/1580.
[73] SP46/48/48: n.d.   [74] SP46/49/23: 13/05/1589. See also Folger, L.a.230: 10/03/1578.
[75] *Two Elizabethan Women*, 30: 05/03/1603.   [76] BL, Harl., 4762, fo. 30: n.d.

& then burn it so you shal be suer it shal not hurt', while Elizabeth Knyvett ended a letter to Sir Roger Townshend: 'I pray lett this be burnt, to tell no tales.'[77] That so many of these letters survive indicates that writer's wishes were not always granted; or it could indicate that asking someone to 'burn' a letter was a euphemism for keeping it close. Alternatively, writers asked that sensitive missives be returned once read. Jane Cartwright approached Thomas Lord Paget regarding the possibility of his marrying her sister, cautiously writing: 'I pray youre l[ordship] do me this honer if you do meane not to proceade in this matter as to send me this letter agayne.'[78]

Bearing in mind the insecurity associated with letters, many writers appear to have been reluctant to commit secrets to paper, indicating distrust of the epistolary medium. Thus, Elizabeth Bourne informed John Conway, 'I haue other causes wych toucheth me nerer wych I wyll not commyt to paper'.[79] Likewise, Elizabeth Russell reported to her nephew Robert Cecil on the libellous rumours that circulated about him, promising to apprise him fully at their next meeting: 'I heer what I am not willing to comit to paper yet as an aunt nere in blood I canot w[i]t[h] conscience but let yow know that it is brought to my eares . . . that the most vyle woords have ben openly uttered of yow.'[80] The manner in which some writers consciously left out sensitive material from their letters illustrates the often frustrating nature of correspondence for scholars. Self-censorship of this nature may well partly account for the paucity of erotic or sexual references in extant women's letters of this period. Equally, explicit letters may have been written and then destroyed or burned.

In other instances, writers overcame problems of interception by writing letters in cipher or code.[81] In her correspondence with William Cotton during her exile in 1576, Anne, countess of Northumberland, used ciphers in the form of symbols to represent names of different people.[82] Mary, queen of Scots, frequently employed ciphers in her conspiratorial correspondence during the 1580s, including in letters to Dr Lewis, Albert Fontenay, Gabriel Denis, Baron Paget, Don Bernardino de Mendoza, and Anthony Babington.[83] Anne Bacon sometimes reported sensitive matters in letters to her sons in Latin and Greek, or disguised names by transliterating them into Greek letters.[84] Codes were also used by female letter-writers during the Civil War. Jacqueline Eales has shown that Brilliana Harley used secret codes in four letters to her son Edward written in early March 1643. The technique employed by Lady Brilliana was to use a sheet of paper with cutouts in it through which a message could be written onto a

---

[77] BL, Harl., 4712, fo. 413: 03/10/1597; Folger, L.d.386: 11/12/1626. See also Folger, L.a.16: *c*.1603; 'Letters and Will of Lady Dorothy Bacon', ed. Key, 92.

[78] Paget Papers, D603, K1/5/7: 21/08/n.y.   [79] BL, Addit., 23212, fo. 119: 22/08/n.y.

[80] Cecil, 179, fo. 92: 10/1599. On the Cecil libels see Croft, 'Reputation of Robert Cecil', 43–69; ead., 'Libels, Popular Literacy and Public Opinion', 266–85.

[81] See Potter, *Secret Rites*.   [82] SP12/107, 12/108: *c*.06/1576–*c*.02/1577.

[83] Richards, *Secret Writing*, letters 11–12, 18–24, pl. II, III.

[84] Magnusson, 'Widowhood and Linguistic Capital', 23.

bottom sheet. Once the template was removed the gaps could then be filled with random words in order to create a seemingly meaningless letter, which could only be understood by placing a copy of the cutout sheet over the document. In one of her letters Brilliana explained how the sheet should be aligned: 'you must pin that end of the paper, that has the cros made in incke, vpon the littell cros on the end of this letter; when you would write to me, make vse of it, and giue the other to your sister Brill.'[85] Codes or secret language were also used during the early modern period to describe matters of a more intimate or personal nature, such as sex.[86] Though this practice was rare among sixteenth-century female letter-writers, a sexual pun in a letter from Maria Thynne to her husband, which played upon his frequently 'rising up' on his return, was written in doggerel Latin, probably to prevent it from being read by her husband's servants.[87] Women, therefore, employed codes in order both to conduct intimate, affec-tionate, and sexual relationships, and to convey confidential political and busi-ness details.

Thus far this section has stressed the private and solitary nature of reading letters; however, certain types of letters were intended to be read by people other than the addressee, which disrupts the relatively modern notion of corres-pondence as an essentially private, two-way epistolary exchange. Letters were sometimes sent open for other family members to read, seal, and then send on to the addressee. Anne Fitton wrote to her daughter Anne Newdigate: 'I would wyshe you to send to your sister this inclosed t[w]o l[ett]re[s]. I haue left them unseelled. you may reed them and seell them.'[88] In her diary, Anne Clifford recorded: 'Upon the 20th being Monday I dispatch'd Mr Marsh with letters to my Mother about the Business aforesaid [her jointure] I sent them unsealed because my Lord might see them.'[89] Other female letter-writers asked that their letters be circulated among wider family members. Anne Bacon instructed her son Anthony, 'let yo[u]r brother reade this'; Anne Fleete wrote to her kinsman Walter Bagot, 'I haue heare inclosed sent you my brother browghtons letter the which I pray you shewe unto my father wright'.[90] Abigail Steward informed her cousin Knyvett that, 'my niece did read me part of your letter', further evidence that reading letters could be an auricular activity.[91] Letter-writers distinguished also between letters intended for a single reader and those suitable for wider circulation. Katherine Philips sent two letters to Sir Charles Cotterell, 'one a private letter to him, the other for him to circulate among their friends'.[92] Correspondence containing news was often passed around close members of the immediate family. In letters to his stepmother, Bess of Hardwick, Gilbert Talbot

[85] Eales, 'Patriarchy, Puritanism and Politics', 148. *The Letters of the Lady Brilliana Hamley*, ed. T. T. Lewis, 11, 37, 40, 55, 191–9. [86] Foisil, 'Literature of Intimacy', 352.
[87] *Two Elizabethan Women*, 37–8: n.d. [88] WCRO, CR136, B122: n.d.
[89] *Diaries of Lady Anne Clifford*, 35.
[90] Bacon, 653, fo. 246: n.d.; Folger, La.491: 31/07/n.y. See also Folger, L.a.227: 17/06/[1593].
[91] BL, Addit., 27400, fo. 34: n.d. [92] Hageman, 'Making a Good Impression', 50.

was careful not to repeat news he sent to his father, since he assumed they would read each others letters: 'by wrytinge of my lords letter I becam ignorante what to wryte to yo[u]r La[dyship] unlesse I shoulde declare the same over agayne and I make none other accompte but wher I wryte to one it is to bothe.'[93] These and other examples identify a form of communal reading for sixteenth-century letters that is akin to the kinds of early modern community- or family-based reading practices documented by Naomi Tadmor during the eighteenth century, where reading was a shared, essentially sociable activity.[94] In the same way as with books, the contents of letters were often treated as communal; they were made privy to relatives, friends, and advisers, and often read aloud. Moreover, news-letters written for a broader readership were often circulated among women, providing them with access to British and continental news. Margaret Clifford forwarded to her daughter Anne letters she 'receued out of germany'.[95]

As trusted servants, secretaries in addition to handling official correspondence were often privy to the contents of seemingly more personal letters. Anne Bacon's letters to her son Anthony were commonly endorsed by secretaries, suggesting that they indeed read her correspondence, which perhaps makes understandable her over-anxious comments about epistolary privacy. One letter was labelled in French, 'de madame le 4me avril 1595'.[96] Letters to Lord Paget from family members are likewise endorsed by servants; a letter from Audrey Aleyn was secretarially endorsed, 'My Ladie Allen to my Lord'.[97] This further indicates that women's personal correspondence was not always private, in the sense that it was not solely read by the addressee.

Letters were also sometimes intended for a wider readership beyond the family and utilised for propagandist purposes. A letter of intercession from Penelope Lady Rich to Queen Elizabeth, written on behalf of her brother Robert, earl of Essex, was widely circulated both in manuscript and in printed form with Essex's *Apology*, ostensibly to round up support for Essex at the time of his fall from favour.[98] Margaret Roper's letters to her father Thomas More, urging him to conform during his imprisonment in 1534, were also apparently aimed at a wider audience, demonstrating her own acquiescence with the government in order to protect her from charges of treason.[99] Fear of interception encouraged writers to be guarded about what they wrote. Likewise, several seemingly personal letters of Margaret Pole to her son Reginald, which reproved him for his incendiary book *De unitate ecclesiae*, were written knowing that the Privy Council would deliver them to the cardinal in Italy. The countess's letters, denouncing Pole as a traitor and expressing regret that she

---

[93] Folger, X.d.428 (108): 14/05/1575.
[94] Tadmor, 'Women, Reading and Household Life', 162–74.
[95] WD/Hoth/Box 44: 27/02/1616.   [96] Bacon, 651, fo. 105.
[97] Paget Papers, D603/K/1/3/40: 25/10/1572. See also K/1/6/11, 12: n.d.
[98] Devereux, [*An apologie of the Earle of Essex*], [1600] (STC 6787.7). Margaret Hoby records having Essex's *Apology* read to her in 1600: *Diary of Lady Margaret Hoby*, 99.
[99] Kaufman, 'Absolute Margaret', 448–9.

had given birth to him, were intended as proof of loyalty to the crown of the countess and her eldest son Lord Montagu.[100] Women's letters could, therefore, work on different levels, taking into account intended and apparently 'unintended' audiences.

Model or exemplar letters by women were also read more widely. Exemplary letters, as argued previously, regularly crop up in sixteenth-century commonplace books, where they were 'scribally published'.[101] Such letters were collected, copied out, and preserved not only for their political interest, but also presumably for their rhetorical flair. Margaret Roper's letters to her father written during the 1520s were circulated in manuscript among scholars as examples of humanist eloquence and female knowledge of classical languages, and were praised for their Latinity, erudition, penmanship, and tenderness of filial affection; yet her letters were not collected and printed as with those of male scholars, which attests the 'limited opportunities for the publication of her writings'.[102] By contrast men's correspondence is likely to have been intentionally preserved for publication; published Latin letters survive for individuals including Erasmus, Guillaume Budé, Théodore Bèze, Justus Lipsius, and Roger Ascham.[103] Letters of religious male figures were frequently kept for posterity. The Puritan divine John Penry, for example, asked his wife Helen to ensure that his letters and papers were safeguarded for publication.[104] John Knox's correspondence was published as a record of the Protestant cause; though the missives from his female correspondents, including Anne Locke and Elizabeth Bowes, were not conserved in the same way: as women presumably their contributions were considered unworthy of record.[105]

Although individual women's letters were scribally published during the late 1500s, it was not until the seventeenth century in England that collections of women's letters appeared in print. In this the English experience differs from practice on the continent where numerous collections of women's letters were published during the sixteenth century. The Italian humanist Ortensio Lando produced *Lettere di molte valorose donne* (1548), and *Lettere della . . . Donna L.G. in Gazuolo con gran diligentia raccolte, & à gloria del sesso feminile nuovamente in luce poste* (1552).[106] In 1586 the Parisian printer Abel L'Angelier published *Missives de Mesdames des Roches de Poitiers, Mère et Fille*.[107] Nonetheless women continued to be detached from the mainstream of humanist letters. The thematic epistolary essays of the fifteenth-century humanist Laura Cereta, entitled *Epistolae familiares*, though circulated in manuscript by 1488–92, were not published in print until the

---

[100] *L&P*, XI 93; XIII (ii) 822: 15/07/1536.   [101] e.g. Folger, V.a.321, fos. 20ᵛ–21; X.d.178.

[102] Billingsley, 'Readers and the Dangers', 6.

[103] Jardine, *Erasmus, Man of Letters*; Bietenholz, 'Erasmus and the German Public', 61–78; Clough, 'Cult of Antiquity', 33–67; Abe, 'Boundaries of Familiarity', 1–19.

[104] BL, Addit., 48064, fos. 19–22: 1593.

[105] Collinson 'Role of Women', 258–72; Newman, 'Reformation and Elizabeth Bowes', 325–33. Cf. BL, Addit., 29546, fo. 117: 12/01/[c. 1593]: letter from Anne Stubbe, 'a notable barrowist'.

[106] Burke, *Fortunes of the Courtier*, 49.   [107] Chartier, 'Secrétaires *for the People?*', 66.

mid-seventeenth century.[108] While the publication of Renaissance humanist letter-books by men served to display their learning to would-be patrons, women's published letters, which similarly showcased cultured learning and functioned as an important means of self-representation, more commonly addressed family and friends. Women treated ranging subjects in their published letters, from private matters like the problems of familial relations (Cereta dwelt on her problematic personal relationships with her mother and husband), to more conventional humanistic themes of human greed, virtue, death, friendship, bereavement, pleasure, fate, and war.[109] The Venetian courtesan Veronica Franco, whose *Familiar Letters to Various People* were published in 1580, used the printed epistolary collection as a forum for displaying her literary achievements, philosophical thought, and social standing.[110]

Among the first English women to have her correspondence published was Katherine Philips, whose letters to Sir Charles Cotterell were published post-humously in two editions as *Letters From Orinda to Poliarchus* (1705). Examples of her letters were published earlier as 'Letters by the late Celebrated Mrs Katherine Philips' in *Familiar Letters Written by the Right Honourable John late Earl of Rochester, And Several Other Persons of Honour and Quality* (1697).[111] The purpose of the collection its preface declares was for 'entertainment'.[112] Katherine Philips's printed letters were examples of a highly literary form intended for emulation, since they avoid 'uncorrect Looseness in her stile or starch'd Affectation'.[113] Given Philips's literary repute, the publisher was keen to maintain that the letters were in fact 'the genuine Work of the matchless Orinda'.[114]

Familiar letters were established as a literary genre, and numerous examples were published of letters purportedly composed by women or aimed at a female audience. Fulwood's *Enemie of Idlenesse* (1568) and Day's *English Secretorie* (1586) both include sample letters by women, as did the first English translation of Jacques Du Bosques's *Secretary of Ladies* (1638), which is entirely correspondence between women, and Henry Care's *The Female Secretary* (1671). Towards the end of the seventeenth century other volumes of familiar letters appeared, including *Five Love Letters from a Nun to a Cavalier*, first translated from French into English in 1678. In the mid- to late-seventeenth century, Margaret Cavendish published several volumes of 'fictional' as opposed to 'real' letters. Her *Sociable Letters* (1664) was conceived as a means, 'under the cover of letters to express the humors of mankind, and the actions of man's life by the correspondence of two ladies, living at some short distance from each other'.[115] Cavendish consciously preferred the epistolary form for its brevity, rather than choosing to dramatize the 'conversations' in play form.[116] In the same year

---

[108] Cereta, *Collected Letters*, 3–4.   [109] Ibid. 4, *passim*.

[110] Franco, *Poems and Selected Letters*, 9–10. Doglio, 'Letter-Writing, 1350–1650', 13–24; Couchman and Crabb, *Women's Letters Across Europe*.

[111] *Collected Works of Katherine Philips*, ed. Thomas, ii. pp. xii–xviii.

[112] *Familiar Letters*, sig. A6^v.   [113] *Letters From Orinda to Poliarchus* (1705), sigs. A4^{r-v}.

[114] Ibid.   [115] Sigs. C2^{r-v}.   [116] Ibid., sig. C2^v.

Cavendish published her *Philosophical Letters*, which used the epistolary form to engage with 'controversies and disputations' in natural philosophy. These volumes illustrate the flexibility of the published letter medium by the end of the seventeenth century, and its utilization by women writers to display their learning and erudition. Fictive letters parading as 'genuine' correspondences between 'real' people, acted as sites of literary accomplishment, social commentary and philosophical debate, exporting epistolary conventions to a general readership strongly interested in the lives of 'private' correspondents.

READING LETTERS OF PETITION

The ways in which the content and form of letters were affected by epistolary reading practices are perhaps viewed most clearly in the case of letters of petition containing suits or requests, the sole purpose of which was persuasion. While suitor's letters have been approached from the perspective of rhetorical strategy, scholars have not considered the delivery of these letters and the contexts in which they were read, both of which informed the letter-writing process.[117] In practice numerous reading methods, with varying levels of privacy and mediation, were employed for petitionary correspondence during this period; the precise context of a letter's transmission though needs to be reconstructed where possible on an individual basis. Letters of petition were also read in various milieux, including the court, great households, and government departments, each of which contained interlocking and fleeting areas of private space—'secret cabinets', gardens, windows, and passageways—where recipients could choose to read letters in solitude. Though, as Alan Stewart has shown in his seminal work on the early modern closet, literary transactions in secret often involved the 'public withdrawal' to the private.[118] Thus, when Elizabeth I read a letter in her Privy Chamber (albeit silently), it was a public gesture of favour not only to the letter-writer, but also to the patron or intermediary delivering the letter.

The passage of letters to government officials should be viewed against the grinding task of bureaucratic administration that became an increasing feature of sixteenth-century English government.[119] Officials attended to suitors' importunities amidst a welter of other pressing concerns of state. John Clapham wrote of his master Burghley that he received between sixty and 100 suits daily.[120] Under these circumstances ornate prose and rhetorical flourishes may have been redundant. Moreover, it is unclear whether officials always read letters in full. Secretarial endorsements on the back of letters guided and assisted their reading. Robert Beale, clerk to the Privy Council, advised that when putting letters before

---

[117] Whigham, 'Elizabethan Suitors' Letters', 864–82; Smith, *Servant of the Cecils*; id., 'Secretariats of the Cecils', 481–504; Neale, 'Elizabethan Political Scene', 59–84.

[118] Stewart, 'Early Modern Closet', 81.   [119] Williams, *Tudor Regime*, 53–4.

[120] Peck, *Desiderata Curiosa*, i. 19.

the Privy Council one 'should abbreviate on the backside of the l[ett]res, or otherwise in a bie paper, the substantiall and most materiall pointes w[hi]ch are to be propounded and answered, lest the rest of the L[ord]s will not have them all redd, or shall not have leisure.'[121] Furnished with an outline of the letter's contents, an official might scan a document, focusing on important details rather than reading it in its entirety.[122]

Writers alert to the fact that their letters would be considered alongside a mass of other, sometimes competing suits, adopted strategies in order to achieve greater impact. First, the length of letters was kept to a minimum; usually no more than one side of paper. John Husee, a servant of Lord and Lady Lisle, advised that when writing to Henry VIII: 'forsee well what you write, and that the matter be shortly concluded, for else his Grace will not take pain to read it.'[123] In practice, most letters cover one side or even a half sheet of paper, only rarely continuing onto a second page. Writers unable to stem the flow of ink from their quills apologized for writing at too great a length. Margery Williams wrote deferentially to Burghley in a holograph postscript to a four-sided letter, stating 'I humbly pray yor lo[rdship] that the length of my leter may not seme tedious vnto you but that yt well please you to reade yet to the ende'.[124] Elizabeth, countess of Shrewsbury, in an epistle to Robert Cecil and John Stanhope, bemoaned the fact that her granddaughter Arbella Stuart had not 'sett downe the matter playnly as I desired she woulde in a fewe lynes'.[125] Doubtless the countess was concerned that Arbella's prolix letters would be ineffective. Secondly, women wrote frequently to reinforce suits. Thus, Lady Dorothy Perrot wrote more than once to Burghley concerning her jointure, intending to put him in mind of her 'last letters', knowing that he was 'so entertained w[i]th great publike causes'.[126] Rarely did women limit their epistolary efforts to a single 'patron', but instead bombarded a range of influential persons with their supplications.

Ensuring that letters were in fact delivered and placed in the hands of recipients at an appropriate moment was of prime importance to female correspondents. Lady Margaret Hawkins described how her letter to the queen 'was kepte iii or iiii dayes undelyuered expecting Mr Killigrewes cominge to the courte'.[127] Katherine, duchess of Suffolk, asked William Cecil for advice on how a letter might be 'speedily delivered'.[128] In order to ensure expeditious and effective dispatch, it was crucial to secure assistance from those well placed to deliver letters. Secretaries, for instance, could choose either to favour a letter,

---

[121] Beale, 'Treatise of the Office of a Councellor and Principall Secretarie to her Ma[jes]tie', 425. On Beale see Brewerton, 'Paper Trails'; Basing, 'Robert Beale and the Queen of Scots', 65–82.

[122] On secretaries and reading see Jardine and Sherman, 'Pragmatic Readers', 102–24.

[123] *Lisle Letters*, v. 1466: 30/06/1539. Cf. Erasmus, *De conscribendis epistolis*, 21.

[124] Cecil, 11, fos. 55–6: 14/08/1580.   [125] Cecil, 135, fo. 129: 02/02/1603.

[126] BL, Lansd., 39, fo. 181: 29/10/1583.   [127] Cecil, 42, fo. 81: 24/07/1596. This is probably Sir Henry Killigrew, Burghley's brother-in-law, rather than Francis Killigrew, usher of the Privy Chamber.   [128] SP10/13/6: 17/02/1551.

ensuring its priority, or hinder it, slowing its progress by burying it among other papers. Indeed, Nicholas Faunt described the private secretary of the secretary of state as 'a remembrancer of all such matters as are of most necessarie dispatch';[129] and A. G. R. Smith has claimed that secretaries were 'the "contact men" of the patronage system'.[130] Certain women therefore sought to operate informally through secretaries, requesting them to pass letters to their masters, preferably at times when they were most receptive. Lady St John, working through the mediation of Richard Frampton, approached Sir Michael Hickes to deliver a letter to Burghley thanking him for the portion assigned to her out of Sir George Treacher's ward.[131] Anne Bacon employed Henry Maynard, another of Burghley's secretaries, to forward a letter concerning the promotion of her younger son Francis Bacon.[132]

Similar postal roles to those of secretaries were performed by a range of other intermediaries who likewise enjoyed access and intimacy to leading political figures. Servants were frequently petitioned by women, requesting them to 'move' their masters. Anne Boyle wrote to Sir Gelly Merrick, steward to Robert, earl of Essex, begging him to be a means to the earl concerning a cause between her husband Henry Boyle and one William Duppa which had been put before the Council.[133] Likewise, Margaret Hocknell sent a letter to Mr Lowe, a servant of her uncle Sir Thomas Sutton, soliciting his help in persuading her uncle for a loan of money.[134] Junior-ranking officials were also entreated to act as middlemen to their superiors. Lady Mary Zouche wrote to Paul Gresham, who held a post in the auditor's office of the Court of Wards, desiring him to have 'any talke w[i]th my lord of Bur[gh]l[e]y' concerning a land transaction.[135] Equally, the circles of women surrounding leading courtiers, government officials, and regional magnates were targeted by female petitioners seeking to circumvent official channels of power. Dorothy Lady Chandos wrote to Anne Lady Bray, daughter of the earl of Shrewsbury, requesting that she would be 'a meane vnto my lord yo[u]r father to stand good lord vnto one Richard Jones now prysoner in yorke and stand vppon his tryall of lyfe and dethe'.[136] Muriel Tresham pleaded with Lady Egerton to intercede with her husband, the lord keeper, on behalf of her own husband Thomas Tresham who was imprisoned for recusancy.[137] Women worked through relatives or 'friends' as intermediaries, presumably because it was easier than approaching leading statesmen personally; the fact that letters to intermediaries often ended up among politicians' papers suggests women wrote hoping to have their letters passed on to officials.

---

[129] Hughes, 'Nicholas Faunt's Discourse', 502.
[130] Smith, *Government of Elizabethan England*, 61.
[131] BL, Lansd., 77, fo. 114: 12/05/1594.
[132] Bacon, 653, fo. 330: n.d.   [133] HMC, *Bath*, v: 06/04/1594.
[134] GLRO, ACC1876/F3/3/50: 17/12/1602.   [135] SP46/58/220: 11/03/1562.
[136] Talbot, 3205, fo. 27: 24/07/n.y.
[137] BL, Addit., 39829, fo. 35: 12/01/1599. See also Paget Papers, D603, K1/4/26: 04/03/1578.

In the case of letters intended for the monarch, to whom access was most strictly controlled, suitors regularly used courtiers 'near to the throne' to present epistles directly to the sovereign's hands. Margaret Douglas beseeched William Cecil to 'shew hir highness this my letter'; Cecil was also approached by Dorothy Stafford, herself a courtier, to deliver for her 'at his leisure' a letter to the queen.[138] Women of the Elizabethan Privy Chamber were also the focus of suitors' attentions because of their perceived intimacy with the monarch.[139] Elizabeth Bourne implored 'M[ist]r[e]s Morgan' to 'delyver me a letter to good M[ist]r[es]s Blanche parry', adding that she hoped she would 'entreat her most ernestlie to move her ma[jes]tie'.[140] Thomas Edwardes described to Elizabeth Wolley the role of 'mestrys Raclyffe', presumably Mary Radcliffe, 'Keeper of the Jewels', in forwarding her letters to the queen: 'I rec[eive]d a l[ett]re directed to mestrys Raclcyffe who impartinge theffecte thereof to the queene her Mag[es]^tie commanded to see the l[ett]res takinge greate paynes in reading.'[141] Further-more, those close to the queen were often present when letters were read and therefore well situated to support a letter by favouring a writer's cause. Bishop Thomas Bentham wrote to Katherine Ashley, an influential woman of Elizabeth's Bedchamber, informing her that 'necessitye haithe compelled me to wryte unto the Quens highnes a rud supplication whiche I beseche you helpe to deliver yf nede shall requyre or els when it is delivered to speak a good word to prosper yt'.[142] However, Elizabeth did not always tolerate intervention from her gentlewomen: Bridget Cave informed Thomas Wilkes, who had approached her to deliver his petition to the monarch, 'you shall understand that I have delyvered that w[hi]ch you sent to me unto her ma[jes]tie and at first she wished me not to meddle in it for she wold not loke upon. But then I told her ma[jes]tie that you were an old acquaintance of myne for w[hi]ch cause I did beseche her highnes to rede it.'[143] Here, these bearers (notwithstanding their elevated status and influence) represent corporeal extensions of letters: presenting, explaining, and reiterating the suits inscribed on the paper they carried in their hands. In many ways the most important factor in having a letter heard or read by a monarch was the status and influence of its bearer. Ursula Walsingham, widow of Sir Francis Walsingham, posed the question: 'what [good] is a private letter of a woman . . . without better meanes to countenance the same?'[144]

In addition to delivering and speaking in support of letters, bearers also sometimes read their petitionary despatches aloud at the moment of presenta-tion. Frances Seymour, countess of Hertford, informed her husband, 'I delyvered

[138] SP12/23/3: 12/06/1562; HMC, *Salisbury*, iii. 214: 25/01/1587.
[139] Wright, 'Change in Direction', 161; Merton, 'Women Who Served', ch. 6; Neale, 'Elizabethan Political Scene', 65; Goldsmith, 'All the Queen's Women', ch. 5.
[140] BL, Addit., 23212, fo. 187, n.d.   [141] Folger, LM/COR/9/116: 1594.
[142] O'Day and Berlatsky, 'Letter-Book of Thomas Bentham', 136: 10/09/1560. On Katherine Ashley see Mears, 'Politics in the Elizabethan Privy Chamber', 67–82.
[143] SP12/208/12: 18/01/1589.   [144] Cecil, 63, fo. 69: 23/08/1598.

your letter after I had rede it to her maiesty'.[145] Likewise, Elizabeth Russell delivered and read a letter to Burghley penned on behalf of Anthony Bacon; she described to her nephew that her brother-in-law had dealt 'verie honorably and kindlie w[i]t[h] yow in bothe readinge my l[ett]re and makinge me to reade it againe to him'.[146] Reading letters orally in this manner placed the onus on orality as much as on writing skills, allowing opportunities for embellishment, emphasis, and explanation. The emphasis on rhetoric in Renaissance humanist letter-writing manuals strongly suggests that letters were often drafted with the intention that they be read aloud.[147] Indeed, women's letters of petition, as discussed below, often closely conform to formal rhetorical models commonly found in the pages of early modern epistolographies, which points to the likelihood of oral delivery. For letters thus privileged, rhetorical content probably played a greater role than it did in everyday business letters buried in early modern packets or trunks.

Female courtiers attached high value to dealing in person, often only writing letters when forced by illness, distance, imprisonment, or failure to track down an official; such claims also helped to justify the act of writing. Mary Wingfield apologized to Robert Cecil for not attending upon him in person, stating that she would willingly 'tacke a Pilgrims staffe' but her for her 'unfitenes . . . for travell'.[148] Katherine, duchess of Suffolk, wrote to Burghley because, as she informed him, 'se[e]king you in your chamber I colde not find you'.[149] Many suitors considered it a disadvantage to solicit favour from afar. Dorothy Perrot expressed concern to Elizabeth Russell over her suit for her husband's debts: 'no doute but that ther willbe suttors inoughe, whos importunacy and presence will cause our absence to be forgotten.'[150] In a political system where individual relationships were paramount it was important to deal in person or be represented by an intermediary or patron. Mary Grey's pleas to William Cecil for assistance in regaining Elizabeth I's favour after her clandestine marriage reiterate her desire to speak personally with the monarch.[151] However, where circumstances rendered this impossible, correspondence provided an alternative way of conducting business: a letter itself acted as a form of mediation, a means by which a woman could present herself and her suit on paper.

The epistolary medium also permitted women to deal more easily with difficult matters where responses of officials were uncertain: Francis Bacon, in his essay 'Of negotiating', argued that 'letters are good . . . where it may be danger to be interrupted, or heard by pieces'.[152] Letters proved effective where women might have been intimidated or browbeaten. Frances Knyvett wrote to her cousin Sir Thomas Knyvett declaring, 'I praye you geve mee leave to wryghte my mynde seeing you are so unwilling to speeke w[i]th mee as the other daye you

---

[145] Seymour Papers, 5, fos. 168–9: *c.*08/1585.   [146] Bacon, 659, fol. 162ᵛ: 08/09/1596.
[147] Chartier, 'Secrétaries *for the People*?', 64.   [148] Cecil, 97, fo. 132a: 1602.
[149] SP12/78/42: 16/06/1571.   [150] Cecil, 168, fo. 123: 06/1592.
[151] SP12/40/66: 30/09/1566.   [152] Bacon, *Essays* (1587), ed. Hawkins (1992), 144.

showed yo[u]r selfe whan I cam to see you'.[153] Alice Norton's imprisoned husband commanded her not to sue to the queen in person for his release, fearing that the royal presence would simply overawe her, instead counselling her to petition the lord treasurer.[154] Thus, for women less well versed in court protocol, letter-writing provided a preferable *modus operandi*, enabling them to delegate responsibility and conduct business from a distance.

The ways in which sixteenth-century letters worked were complex and varied; the different reading practices and methods of delivery employed generated varying levels of privacy and mediation, which affected the manner of composition. This more sophisticated picture of reading practices moves away from a model of epistolarity that depicts the transmission of letters as representative of a simple two-way relationship between sender and recipient, towards a model that recognizes a more diverse, fluctuating, and fluid readership, both intended and unintended. It is only through an appreciation of the manner and contexts in which early modern letters were delivered and read that they achieve fuller social and cultural meaning, beyond merely concentrating on composition and material form.

---

[153] NRO, Knyvett-Wilson Papers, KNY668/372X5: 15/11/1597.
[154] BL, Addit., 48023, fos. 32b–33, 1581. Cf. ibid., 48064, fos. 19–22: John Penry to his wife Helen, 06/04/1593.

6

The Functions of Letter-Writing

On the surface, early modern letter-writing was an essentially pragmatic activity. Letters were occasioned by practical concerns, events, and crises; they were written to petition for favour, ask advice, prefer suits, seek mediation; they reflect particular states or needs, including poverty, want, grief, love, sorrow, anger, joy, thankfulness. Correspondence performed numerous important functions which expanded over the course of the sixteenth century: practical, business-related, communicative, religious, literary, intimate, personal, and introspective. As a mode of communication, letter-writing enabled women to maintain social contacts and to transmit news, instructions, and information. Court women regularly wrote to family members informing them of national and court events; wives corresponded with husbands concerning household and estate management; daughters wrote dutifully to parents assuring them of their health and progress; mothers sent letters to sons offering moral and spiritual advice. Additionally, kinswomen dispatched epistles to other kinsfolk keeping them abreast of family news and affairs, while mistresses of households penned letters to servants instructing them in their businesses.

Read for their contents and functions, women's letters help further to delineate the scope of female activity, to illuminate the important roles that elite women played within the family, locality, and at court, operating beyond the confines of the narrowly defined 'household' or 'domestic' sphere in arenas traditionally viewed as 'male'. A striking example of this is women's involvement in correspondence and manuscript news networks, as transmitters and readers of family, local, court, national, and European news; letters to and from women strongly indicate female interest in areas of news often depicted as 'masculine', such as parliamentary business, war, armed rebellions, and naval preparations. Furthermore, in a patronage society where interpersonal relationships counted for so much, women were intimately involved in building and maintaining patronage and kinship networks through various social activities, among which letter-writing was of prime importance. Indeed, letters acted as vital mechanisms through which the wheels of social relations were oiled, contacts kept up, and arrangements formed at a distance; as forms of social courtesy, letters acted as gifts, invitations, and passed on sentiments of thanks, congratulation, and consolation. In this sense, sociable letter-writing assumes a renewed 'political' importance. While on one level utilitarian, letter-writing was also, however, an autobiographical mode of writing; in addition to their outwardly functional aspects, letters had various subsidiary, more personal and introspective uses. Approaching letters as a 'technology of the self', as material sites for the self, the process of letter-writing emerges as an individualizing activity, which encouraged in women a degree of inwardness.

The early modern letter was an immensely protean and evolving form, which performed an increasing variety of uses, many of them mundane and ordinary, developed on an individual basis, and unscripted in Renaissance letter-writing manuals. In studying the functions of sixteenth-century women's letters and letter-writing, this chapter confines itself to examining four distinct uses of correspondence, each of which elucidate further the nature of women's epistolary writing: thus, letters are viewed as conveyers of news, as forms of social courtesy, as gifts, and as modes of autobiographical writing.

NEWS AND NEWSLETTERS

The treatment of news of all varieties—family, local, court, national, and European—is commonplace in women's letters of the period, indicating female involvement in correspondence and manuscript news networks. The roles played by women in the manuscript circulation of news challenges traditional depictions of news transmission and readership as an exclusively male world.[1] Ian Atherton, for example, has argued that female correspondents 'rarely included even a line of news in their letters', unlike their male counterparts, that newsletters were generally procured by men, and that women may in fact have been 'less interested in news'. To Atherton, 'the private world of the family, not the public world of politics, was seen as the sphere of women'.[2] This depiction of manuscript news and information networks as exclusively male, and confinement of women to an apolitical 'private world', rests rather uneasily with current scholarship on women's political and patronage roles within the family, locality, and on a wider national stage. In fact, women at court were at the very centre of where news was exchanged: Anne Talbot thought the court a place to 'learn' news 'worthey the wrytynge'.[3] Female courtiers were also themselves a forum for news: conduits to the monarch, courtiers, and officials, and purveyors of intelligence more generally, intelligence that found its way into the counties through correspondence and by word-of-mouth, and abroad through ambassadors' dispatches.[4] Olwen Hufton has argued that 'a court without women is like a body without a nervous system. Women are part of a vital system of communications through which messages are transmitted, channels opened up.'[5]

---

[1] On newsletters see Cust, 'News and Politics', 62–3; Levy, 'How Information Spread', 20–3; id., 'Decorum of News', 12–38; Love, *Scribal Publication*, 9–22.

[2] Atherton, 'Itch Grown a Disease', 49–50.   [3] Folger, X.d.428 (122): 29/05/1575.

[4] Wright, 'Change in Direction', 153.   [5] Hufton, 'Reflections on the Role of Women', 1.

The study of sixteenth-century women's letter-writing further demonstrates that women participated in a broad range of news-related activities. Women were indeed the recipients of newsletters: Jane Dormer, duchess of Feria, received lengthy newsletters from George Chamberberlain and Sir Francis Englefield;[6] Alice Stanley heard of 'court news' from her nephew Sir Robert Spencer;[7] Elizabeth Ralegh thanked Robert Cecil for his packet of letters which brought her news of the fire at Durham House.[8] When absent from court, Elizabeth Wingfield, herself a court lady, was apprised of events that happened there in letters from her husband Anthony.[9] In a letter sent from Windsor, he reported among other matters the various gifts presented to the queen, the health of Frances, countess of Sussex, and Lady Cobham, and the latter's retirement from the court into Kent.[10] Similarly, William Trew, one of Essex's servants, informed his wife Margaret of the rumours that the earl had been committed to the Tower in November 1599. From these letters it is evident women were kept up-to-date with events elsewhere in the country, and that their outlooks were not insular and solely focused on the household.

The letters women wrote themselves also frequently contained news of family, household and locality, and items of 'national' interest. At one level, letters described the minutiae of women's everyday lives, providing insights into their habits, pastimes, and daily routines. Dorothy Gamage wrote to her husband of the snowdrifts they were experiencing at home: 'we are here verie muche trobled w[i]th the snowe. the winde hathe so driven it that we had muche a doe to get out at some of our doors and yet worse then that it is dreven into the brooke in suche wise that it hathe choked it uppe...'[11] On a trip to London in 1538, Honor Lady Lisle described to her husband in Calais her sea-journey to England: 'This shall be to advertise you that I have had a goodly and fair passage, but it was somewhat slow, and long ere I landed, for this night, at x of the clock, I arrived. I thank God I was but once sick in all the way; and after that I was merry and well.'[12] Dorothy Gawdy explained to her husband that she had 'overslept'; Joan Herrick reported that she had lost a medical recipe through 'a hole in my poket'.[13] Other letters report news of neighbours, local feuds, and disturbances, hearings of the assize courts, and appointments of local government officials. Elizabeth Sutton informed her husband John that 'this day the constables receyved a note from the justice for the first payment of the second subsidye'.[14] Women's letters also circulated local rumour. During his legal dispute with Edward Stafford, Joan Thynne informed her husband of the latter's boasts: 'The

---

[6] NA, SP15/18/29: 05/04/1570, Louvain; SP15/18/45: 20–30/04/1570, Louvain; SP15/18/52:7–17/05/1570, Antwerp. See also SP12/14/36.

[7] BL, Addit., 25079, fo. 59: 23/09/1603.   [8] BL, Add. MS, 6177, fo. 65: 10/1600.

[9] Folger X.d.428 (127, 128): 13/10/1575, 13/12/[1575].

[10] X.d.428 (127): 13/10/1575.   [11] SP46/60/10: 09/02/1579.

[12] *Lisle Letters*, v. 1262.

[13] BL, Addit., 36989, fo. 18: 1602; Bodl., Herrick, Eng. Hist., 484, fo. 18: n.d.

[14] GLRO, F3/7/2/70: 16/05/1602.

Lord Stafford makes great brags what he will do at the next Assizes and hath given out that he means to drive and to [im]pound your cattle.'[15] Letters of this nature were written regularly, especially by wives to keep husbands informed about events at home in the provinces. In this sense women's letters provide another example of the means by which information spread from the localities to the centre.

The import of women's letters, though, was far from provincial. Margaret Hill, for example, wrote regularly from London to her cousin Richard Carnsew in the West Country, keeping him informed of events in the capital; in one of her letters she enclosed a newsbook and a copy of the earl of Essex's funeral sermon.[16] Several women wrote from the court, where they had access to news of a more national focus. The letters of Frances Seymour and Margaret Clifford to their husbands brim with news from the court and, as Elizabeth McCutcheon has recently shown, Lady Elizabeth Wolley acted as a court commentator for her father and brother when they were based in Surrey.[17] Margaret Arundell wrote to her brother Francis Willoughby of the earl of Leicester's entertainment of the court at Kenilworth.[18] These letters illustrate the ways in which women at court were able to tap into intelligence networks and participate in the wider geographical dissemination of news. Female correspondents were also central to the maintaining of patronage and kinship relations, and passing on news in letters was one of the chief ways in which these networks were strengthened. Thus, Margaret Clifford implored Julius Caesar to write to her with his news when occasion served.[19] During the seventeenth century women were also involved in sending newsletters: in the 1640s women often addressed letters containing important news because their letters were less likely to be confiscated, opened, and read; Claire Walker has highlighted the ways in which Ghent Benedictines in the 1650s put their postal services at the disposal of Charles II for delivering royalist mail.[20]

Women's involvement in manuscript news networks is further illustrated by the correspondence of Bess of Hardwick, herself the recipient of substantial numbers of letters containing news, and a woman at the centre of a dense epistolary and intelligence network.[21] When absent from London, the countess received a stream of letters from family, servants, friends, wider social contacts, and semi-professional writers of newsletters, which kept her current with court and national events and news from the capital: the monarch's health and moods, court progresses, fluctuations in royal favour, appointments to office,

[15] Wall, ed., *Two Elizabethan Women*, 24–5: 28/04/1602.
[16] SP46/71/223, 224, 226, 228: 10/05/1601, 29/03/1602, 23/10/1602, n.d.
[17] Longleat House, Seymour Papers, 5, fos. 144–5: 09/06/[1584–5]; Kendal RO, WD/Hoth Box 44, n.d.; McCutcheon, 'Playing the Waiting Game', 43–6.
[18] HMC, *Middleton*, 528–9.   [19] BL, Addit., 12506, fo. 231: 18/06/1589.
[20] Walker, 'Letter-Writing in Early Modern English Convents', 159–76.
[21] Daybell, 'News Networks of Elizabeth Talbot', 114–31.

parliamentary sessions, and aristocratic marriages. Conversely, when at court or absent from one of her residences, she received regular reports from her servants, estate stewards, and legal advisors concerning household and estate management, children and other family members, the numerous legal cases in which she was involved, the progress of her building works, and events within the locality. The countess was also regularly kept up-to-date with the latest religious and political developments in Europe by correspondents who recycled for her the contents of continental newsletters. Hugh Fitzwilliam reporting on the revolt of the Moriscos in July 1570 informed her: 'may it please [you] . . . tunderstand that by *lett*res of the xxiiiith of the last out of Spayne from a towne bordering upon the mores, sayth that the king hath driven them in to the mountaynes agayne.'[22]

For much of her news-gathering Bess of Hardwick relied on letters from immediate family, kin, household members, and other dependants. Indeed, her female correspondents at court—Mary Scudamore, Frances Cobham, Susan, countess of Kent, Elizabeth Wingfield, and Katherine, countess of Pembroke— were mostly relatives either by blood or marriage. However, she also cultivated contacts from wider social groups, such as James Montague and Dorothy Lady Stafford. Epistolary relationships were developed with these well-placed corres- pondents precisely because they were at the heart of court and political events; these were people cultivated in the main for their power, influence, and the types of news they could offer. Montagu, for example, in his position as dean of the Royal Chapel, was a man at the centre of the court and well placed to comment on events there; in his own words he was in 'continuall followinge of his Majestie in his iourneys', a polite excuse he used on at least two occasions for not writing 'so often to your honour as I would'.[23] His letters, though, do not divulge the intimate secrets of the Royal Chapel, but offer a staple diet of parliamentary affairs, conspiracies, and religious persecutions of 'preests and recusants'. In his letter of 20 February 1606 he wrote, 'I think my lord Ca[ve]ndish acquynteth you with all the parlament newes. It is a very joyfull matter to see how well the Kinge his lordes and commons doe agree together in one this parlament: and all agaynst the papists.' He continued by describing the execution of the Gun- powder Plot conspirators, and the capture and trial of the Jesuit Henry Garnet.[24] A second letter of 7 March followed similar lines: 'the newes heer is all parlament business. The matter of religion to compell every man to comunion within the space of 2 years or else they shalbe the nature of recusants.' It continued with further reports on the examinations of Garnet, that 'notorious traitor'.[25]

By contrast, news supplied by the countess of Shrewsbury's female contacts at court was privy and personalized. Their letters largely concerned the status of Bess's general standing at court, her favour with the queen, the monarch's reactions to her gifts, and the progress of suits. Several letters from the period

---

[22] Folger, X.d.428 (28): 28/07/1570.   [23] X.d.428 (59): 20/02/1606.
[24] X.d.428 (60): 07/03/1606.   [25] Ibid.

1568 to 1585 survive from her half-sister Elizabeth Wingfield, who was 'Mother of the Maids', the head of the maids of honour in the royal household. In one letter, Lady Wingfield wrote that the queen in conversation had stated, 'I assure you there ys no lady yn this land that I beter loue'; another letter told of how the queen 'toulde my lord of Lester and my lord chamberlen that you had geven her such garments thys yere as she neuer had any so well lyked her and sayd that good nobell copell they show in all things what loue they bere me'; and during Bess's turbulent separation from the earl of Shrewsbury, Elizabeth Wingfield kept her informed of efforts to move the queen on her behalf: 'your good frende my lady cheke had longe talke with her majesty latly of my lordships harde dealinge and the quene gaue many good wordes what she woulde do for your ladyship.'[26] The kind of news that court women wrote about was highly specialized; these were intimate first-hand accounts from the Privy Chamber, rather than the generalized rumour that reverberated around the corridors and halls of court, and that characterizes the letters of her male correspondents. Whereas other letters and other forms of news may have circulated more widely, the news conveyed by court women was highly privileged and in some cases confidential. Dorothy Lady Stafford was concerned that the details of her discussion with the queen regarding potential husbands for Arbella Stuart, an account of which she imparted in a letter to Bess, should go no further: 'I beseeche you good Maddam seing it pleased her Ma[jes]tie to saie so muche unto mee touching her care of my La[dy] Arbella that yo[u]r La[dyshi]p will vouchesafe mee so muche favo[u]r as to kepe it to yo[u]r selfe not making anie other acquainted w[i]th it but rather repose the truste in mee for to take my opportunitie for the puttinge her Ma[jes]tie in mynde thereof w[hic]h I will doe as carefullie as I can.'[27] While Montagu did not divulge secrets of this nature in his letters, the close familial and social bonds that Bess had with her female court contacts perhaps explain their willingness to commit intimate and privy news to paper.

Furthermore, the kind of news conveyed in women's correspondence illustrates female interest in areas of news traditionally viewed as 'masculine': parliamentary business, war, armed rebellions, and naval preparations. Viewed from the perspective of women's reading, it suggests a broader, less restricted range than might hitherto have been assumed. The assassination of the French king, Henri III, by Jacques Clément in 1589, for example, was reported to the countess of Shrewsbury in all its macabre details: the letter describes the 'cruel varlet' priest who, when delivering a letter to the monarch, drew a 'sharpe poynted knyfe' from his sleeve and stabbed the king several times in the side.[28] James Hudson's letters to Elinor Bowes contained news of 'the daylie tidinges of new murders hardshipps & slaughters on ye borders', which put her in 'melanchollie moode'.[29] Although tempting to read news as gendered according

---

[26] X.d.428 (129, 130, 131), 21/10/1568, 02/01/1576, 08/12/1585.
[27] X.d.428 (120): 13/01/1601.   [28] X.d.428 (115): 01/07/1589.
[29] LPL, Shrewsbury, 658, fo. 60: 07/1596.

to environment, women writing about household, family, and locality, men about affairs in London, the court, or abroad, this public–private split is too schematic and oversimplified. Through conversation, social interaction, and correspondence aristocratic women had access to a range of news from beyond their immediate locale.

LETTERS OF SOCIAL COURTESY

In addition to news-related functions, letters of social courtesy became increasingly common during the sixteenth century, demanded for a growing number of occasions and events in order to thank, congratulate, invite, or console. Elizabeth Chudlygh wrote appreciatively to her kinsman Nicholas Herrick offering 'contenuall thankes' for his 'kind entertaynment'; Elizabeth Bourne thanked Sir John Conway for his hospitality, having merrily passed Christmas at his house.[30] Alice, countess of Derby, wrote to thank the earl of Shrewsbury for attending her husband's funeral, declaring herself 'much blame woorthy that I sent not to you before'.[31] Elizabeth, countess of Shrewsbury, congratulated Sir Robert Cecil on his appointment to principal secretary.[32] Furthermore, women dispatched letters of gratitude, often accompanying tokens and gifts, to government officials for favours granted. Elizabeth Hoby corresponded with William Cecil, stating that, 'althoughe wordes be verie small recompens for yowr so manie benefitts and cortesies toward my husband and me by writing I thought it my parte to shew some litle part of gratefullnes this waie till occasion serve otherwaies'.[33] Julius Caesar similarly received numerous letters of thanks from various women including Lady Elizabeth Drury, Lady Katherine Howard, and Elizabeth, countess of Bath.[34] The last mentioned thanked Caesar for his 'late curtousy' in granting her request, assuring him that she was beholden, and asked that he retain his good disposition towards her.[35]

Letters were also utilized by women to offer formal invitations for weddings, christenings, and funerals. Barbarie Hart invited Framlingham Gawdy and his wife Dorothy to the wedding of her daughter.[36] Writing to her kinsmen Anthony and Francis Bacon, Anne Bacon (née Butts) implored them to repair to Redgrave to attend her daughter's marriage ceremony, saying that the feast would be 'greatlie honored' by their presence.[37] Margaret Stanhope and her husband wrote to request the company of Elizabeth, countess of Rutland, and

---

[30] Bodl., Herrick, Eng. Hist., 474, fo. 139, 12/09/[before 1592]; BL, Addit., 23212, fos. 88, 110, n.d.   [31] LPL, Talbot, 3203, fo. 14: 17/06/1594.

[32] Hatfield House, Cecil, 32, fo. 48: endorsed, 20/05/1595. The countess's congratulations were somewhat pre-emptive, since although Cecil was the acting secretary from 1590, he was not formally appointed to the post until 5 July 1596.   [33] SP15/13/10: 07/04/1566.

[34] BL, Addit., 12507, fo. 123: 23/05/1588; BL, Addit., 12506, fo. 389: 1598; BL, Addit., 12506, fo. 101: 11/02/1593.   [35] BL, Addit., 12506, fo. 101.

[36] HMC, *Gawdy*, 60.   [37] LPL, Bacon, 648, fo. 18: 16/03/1592.

her son the earl of Rutland at the wedding of their daughter Anne to John Holles in May 1591.[38] Lady Elizabeth Russell issued a similar invitation to her nephew Robert Cecil and his wife for the wedding of her son Thomas Hoby and Margaret Dakins, stating that she had also invited Sir Robert Sidney and Sir William Brooke. An invitation to a second daughter's wedding indicated that he would be master of the house, a great honour as head of the family, and presented detailed plans of the wedding supper, guests at which would include the earls and countesses of Worcester, Cumberland, and Bedford, and Lady Warwick.[39] Lucy, marchioness of Winchester, invited her uncle Robert Cecil to attend the christening of her son, desiring also that he stand as godfather to the child.[40] In replying to a letter from Julius Caesar inviting her to stand as godmother to his daughter, Elizabeth Clinton, countess of Lincoln, informed him that she had asked her cousin Coot to act as her deputy at the christening, and would send with her a gift of plate.[41] Letters were also utilized to issue offers of hospitality. After the death of their mother, Abigail Willoughby invited her sister Bridget by letter to visit her at Wollaton Hall.[42] Mary Fulwood wrote to John Coke that she hoped some 'happy occasion would send you amongst us', 'lest long absence breed too much forgetfulness amongst us'.[43] Hearing rumours of Queen Elizabeth's royal progress into her county, Elizabeth Russell extended the offer to Robert Cecil to lie at Donnington Castle when the progress came that way, along with the lords Worcester and Shrewsbury and their ladies.[44] These activities, which were socially significant in their strengthening of social and political networks, were in no sense a purely feminine preserve in the way that social correspondence in the eighteenth and nineteenth centuries developed into a female domain. Tudor women wrote on these occasions because they had the position and influence so to do.

Condolence letters were also written during times of grief and bereavement to provide solace and relief, often closely following epistolary formulae of consolation.[45] Queen Elizabeth's oft scribally published letter 'to the Lady Norris vpon the death of her sonne' acts as a model of stoical consolation in its prescription, 'let that christian discretion stay the flouds of yor immoderate greivinge'.[46] In its emphasis on reason and self-control, the queen's epistle is reminiscent of Thomas Wilson's letter to the duchess of Suffolk on the death of her two sons, which he published in his *Arte of Rhetorique* (1553).[47] Elizabeth Russell wrote several

[38] HMC, *Rutland*, i. 290: 25/04/1591. See also Cecil, 43, fo. 34: 01/08/1596; Cecil, 186, fo.134: 06/1600.   [39] Cecil, 43, fo. 34: 01/08/1596; Cecil, 186, fo. 134: 06/1600.
[40] Cecil, 178, fos. 125, 127: 23/02/1601.   [41] BL, Addit., 12506, fo. 55: 17/09/1584.
[42] HMC, *Middleton*, 604: 12/06/1595.
[43] HMC, *Cowper*, i. 29: 15/06/1601. See also HMC, *Middleton*, 604: 12/06/1595.
[44] Cecil, 106, fo. 39: 03/08/1602.
[45] Houlbrooke, *Death, Religion and the Family*, 221, 223; Pigman, *Grief and English Renaissance Elegy*, ch. 1.
[46] Folger, X.d.178: 22/09/1597. For other copies see Folger, V.b.214, fo. 68ʳ; SP12/264/118, 119; BL, Addit., 38137, fo. 160; May, *Queen Elizabeth I*, 227.   [47] Fos. 36ᵛ–47ʳ.

consolatory epistles to her nephew Robert Cecil during 1597, after the death of his wife Elizabeth.[48] On one occasion Lady Russell dispatched a letter stating:

... if yow be so w[i]t[h]owt comfort of worldly delight as yow seme, it is most ill to the helth of yow both of body and sowle. I speake by experience and know to well th[a]t to be trew w[hi]ch I say and therfore both am I sory to here it and besech the god of all consolation and comfort to remedy it w[i]t[h] giveng yow a contrary mynde, else will yow fynd this *Daemonius meridianus*[49] to crepe so farr into yo[u]r hart w[i]t[h] his variety of vertues seeming goode to be yelded to (melancoly I meane) as in [the] end will shorten lyfe by combrouse conceyts and sickness when it is rooted so as with pevish perswasions of good therby and solytary eiaculations it will bring foorth the fruet of stupidytie. forgetfulnes of your natural disposition of swete and apt speches fit for yowr place and in stede therof breede and make yow sullen sharpe sowre plumme, no better then in trewth a very melancoly moyle and a misenthropos hateful to god and man.[50]

Lady Russell's epistle, rich in both classical and biblical references, was conventional in its advocacy of a strategy of diversion or recreation. However, the repetition of such sentiments in other letters to Cecil suggests Elizabeth Russell's apparent concern for her nephew and the genuine sympathy that lay behind her elegant and ritual language. Indeed, another letter reminded Cecil 'not to offend God w[i]t[h] sorow w[i]t[h]owt cawse and to no end to overwhelme y[ou]r self w[i]t[h] discontent for what is gods will'.[51] Letters by many other women exhibit more simple and unaffected, although equally commonplace, expressions of compassion and understanding. In 1602 Margerie Lawson wrote comfortingly to Sir Thomas Sutton on the death of his wife: 'hearing of the sad and heavie news of the death of... your wife... I do make my self partaker of yo[u]r sorrowes and do much lamente hir deathe yet nothinge doubtinge but she is at reste w[i]th god.'[52] Anne Corbet wrote comfortingly to Sir Roger Townshend, hoping that he was not too overcome with sorrow and that God would send him wisdom to mitigate his grief.[53] Over the course of the sixteenth century, with the rise of literacy and spread of letter-writing skills, one witnesses an expanding repertoire of uses for English vernacular correspondence; letters performed on paper an increasing range of functions of social courtesy that previously would have been dispensed face-to-face or through the auspices of a bearer.

LETTERS AS GIFTS

Closely related to functions of social courtesy, letters importantly acted as 'gifts' both figuratively and literally: as the textual bearers of commendations, thanks,

[48] Cecil, 52, fo. 52: 24/06/1597; 53, fo. 26: 11/07/1597; 175, fo. 92: 06/1597.
[49] 'The noonday demon', which echoes Psalms 91: 6, 'the destruction that wasteth at noonday': Farber, 'Letters of Lady Elizabeth Russell', 193.   [50] Ibid. 175, fo. 92.
[51] Cecil, 53, fo. 26: 11/07/1597.   [52] GLRO, ACC1876/F/5/3/2: 11/07/1597.
[53] Folger, L.d.235: n.d.

prayers, news, poetry, love, affection, and emotion, and conveyers of social duty and obligation; they were also used to convey material goods, gifts, medical recipes, tokens, and literary texts; and letters represented material gifts in their own right, much in the same manner as did early modern presentation books and manuscripts, 'tokens' of affectionate or memorials of the sender. Scholars interested in the dynamics of early modern social relations have often looked at the practice of giving gifts, and at gift-giving theory as a way of modelling, explaining, and describing the nature of human interaction and behaviour. Perhaps the most influential study of the non-market exchange of gifts and service is Marcel Mauss's classic anthropological account of gift-giving, in which parties to a relationship of gift-exchange are obligated to give gifts, to receive them, and to repay them in appropriate ways.[54] It is implicit here that the value of the gift or object lies in the social relations created between giver and receiver, rather than its exchange value. Literary texts functioning as gifts have also been the locus of recent critical inquiry, as a way of elucidating client–patron relations.[55] The textual remains (letters, poems, epistles, dedications, and other writings) produced by patronage relations are imbued with a language of mutual benefits, classically derived from Seneca's *De beneficiis* and Cicero's *De officiis*.[56] In the political system of early modern England preferment and favour rested on personal relations with the monarch, government officials, family and wider kin, dependants, neighbours, and 'friends', all of which entailed coded gift-exchanges, differentiated by social status, power, and position. Moreover, the very nature of early modern correspondence or 'epistolarity' made it a form of ritual gift-giving: the process of composing and sending a letter was in itself an act of gift-giving, the gift of a missive delivered from letter-writer to addressee.[57] Such an epistolary transaction demanded reciprocation—a mutual exchange—a reply to the signatory penned, or at least dictated, by the letter's recipient. The nature of replying by letter was fraught with coded social implications: failure to write could issue a slight; epistolary silence could be viewed as a snub; delay or irregularity in writing could be interpreted as a lack of respect.

The act of writing letters to family and other social acquaintances was customary during the early modern period, regarded as a duty or obligation. In an epistle to her stepmother Lady Anne Gresham, Anne Bacon wrote of the 'dutie [that] bindeth me to writ'; on another occasion she wrote, 'Madame, I thought it good for me to writ somthinge to yo[u]r La[dyship] though I wrot ye lesse, least

---

[54] Mauss, *The Gift*. Cf. Malinowski, *Argonauts of the Western Pacific*. For recent studies on early modern gift-giving see Davis, *The Gift in Sixteenth-Century France*; Ben-Amos, 'Gifts and Favors', 295–338.

[55] Scott-Warren, *Sir John Harrington*; Montrose, 'Gifts and Reasons', 433–61; Scott, 'Marketing the Gift', 135–59; Fumerton, 'Exchanging of Gifts', 57–97.

[56] Peck, 'Benefits, Brokers and Beneficiaries', 109–27; Scott-Warren, *Harrington*, 16. See also Salmon, 'Seneca and Tacitus', 169–88. On the relationship between gift-giving and patronage see Kettering, 'Gift-Giving and Patronage', 131–51. Cf. Eisenstadt and Ringer, 'Patron–Client Relations', 42–77.   [57] Altman, *Epistolarity*.

by not writinge I sholde seame to forget yt dutie, w[hi]ch I iustly owe vnto yo[u]r La[dyship]'.[58] Similarly, Elizabeth Smith writing to Elizabeth, countess of Shrewsbury, averred, 'I thought it my duty to sende to geue your honor humbel thanckes'; Anne Lee explained to her brother Thomas Lord Paget that 'if I shuld let this messenger passe withe out a letter I feare youe wold thinke me very slowghfull'.[59] Correspondents also conventionally apologized for not having written sooner or more often, anxious not to cause offence by a 'lack of duty'; the apologetics associated with the dispatch of letters, as with excuses for poor handwriting (whether real or feigned), were part of the humility topoi employed by letter-writers corresponding with social superiors. Margaret Ligon expressed great regret to her sister Olive Talbot for not corresponding with her at an earlier date: 'i prey you thinke not ani discortesi in me in that i haue not written vnto you before this time. it hathe not benne wante of good will, but occasions of busines hate letted me.'[60] Katherine, countess of Pembroke, wrote to her father, the earl of Shrewsbury, blaming the vagaries of the post for her lack of communication: 'I coulde not fynde meanes since my arryuall from beyond the seas till now to send according to my most earnest desier to enquier of your health.'[61] Lettice Kinnersley took great pains to explain to her brother Walter Bagot the length of time since her last letter: 'Good brother you may think me very forgetfull that I haue not wryt vnto you neuer since I came hether but I had thought be fore now to haue seene you and now heareing by this bearerer [*sic*] that my fatherinlaw is gon to london I donot know when wee shall com into staffordshere.'[62] In each case, the letter was conveyed up the social hierarchy; the duty of letter-writing here was one owed from a social inferior or dependant to a superior.

The reciprocal nature or obligation of letter-writing is further highlighted by maternal expectations for regular correspondence with children, indicative of a merging of duty and affection. Lady Bacon, for example, chided her sons Anthony and Francis Bacon for not writing in reply to her letters: 'I may think much lacke of kindnes & duty in yow & yo[u]r brother [Francis Bacon] that nev[e]r write to me'; and Gertrude, marchioness of Exeter, complained to her son the earl of Devonshire that he had been 'slack' in his duty in not sending her a letter or 'token'.[63] Other letter-writers textualized the reciprocal ideal of communicating by letter by expressing unease or embarrassment at being in somebody's 'debt' by 'owing' them a letter. Indeed, Elizabeth Cecil in an epistle to her cousin Sir Thomas Hobart, acknowledged that lately she had not written: 'I confes you have ressoun to haue sum suspicion of us . . . hauinge not all this while tell now saluted you with any linnes and yett resayud from you iii

---

[58] Folger, L.d.16: *c*.1572; L.d.18: 02/1573.
[59] Talbot, 3205, fo. 34: 10/12/1578; Staffs RO, Paget Papers, D603/K/1/10/23: 12/07/n.y.
[60] SP15/26/2: 22/01/1580.
[61] Talbot, 3205, fo. 32: 03/10/1575. See also Folger, L.a.595 (1, 2): 02/02/1602.
[62] Folger, Bagot, L.a.595 (1, 2): 02/02/1602.
[63] Bacon, 656, fo. 47: 18/03/1597; SP11/6/25: 12/10/1555.

leatters.'[64] The merchant John Johnson, responding to his wife's complaints that she had received none of his letters despite the fact that she had sent him two or three of her own, jokingly wrote, 'I thincke by this tyme I owe you not a l[ett]re but I thincke I have by this tyme payd you l[ett]re for l[ett]re and yet suppose I you be ii or iii l[ett]res in my debt'.[65]

The conducting of correspondence was thus a way of fostering and maintaining social relations between two people separated by distance: between mother and child, husband and wife, brother and sister, master or mistress and servant, patron and client, and between kinsfolk as well as friends. This is given eloquent expression by the diarist, Margaret Hoby in a letter to her friend and social equal Anne Newdigate, in which she describes the reinforcement of friendship and social bonds generated by their letters: 'I doe now desire not only to perswaide you that my loue is in the hieste degree of trewe frindshepe, but that you will so far nurrishe it as when you haue conuenient messhingeres I may somtimes heare from you and so shall you giue me best proffe of your acceptinge my affectione, make my selfe more ingagede by your kindnes, and us both maintaine the better aprobatione of whatt we haue alredie conceiued one of another.'[66] Among the upper classes, the writing of letters, as with other exchanges of sociability, such as visits, gifts, favours, and tokens, worked to cement family and social ties; the value of the letter lay not in its intrinsic monetary worth, but in what it conveyed. Here the letter functioned as a carrier of 'love' and 'affection', a 'paper visitation' by a writer not present in person.

Letters were also the conveyers of material gifts. Anne Clifford's letter to her mother of December 1615 was accompanied by a New Year's gift: 'Maddam', she wrote, 'I intended to haue wroght a peece of worke with my on handes for a nuers gifte for your La[dyship], but this hathe bine so trubellsom a yere with mee as I had nether lesuer to worke or doe aney thing ellce but weepe and greefe therfore I beeciche your La[dyship] bee plesed to receue thes pillabers [pillow-cases] as a nuers gifte and poore remembrance of my duty and affection.'[67] Elizabeth, countess of Desmond, sent Robert Cecil a harp as a gift accompanying a letter.[68] The circulation and exchange of gifts by letter is best glimpsed in the Lisle letters of the 1530s, which show the immense array of commodities, items, and objects which often accompanied letters, including foodstuffs, clothing, cloth, jewellery, birds and animals, books, rosaries, holy water from Avignon, and more exotically, the tip of a unicorn's horn.[69] Mary Basset informed her sister Philippa: 'I send you a purse of green velvet, and a little pot for my sister Frances: also, a gospel to my sister Katherine, and a parroquet to my lord my father, because he maketh much of a bird.'[70] Gifts conveyed by letter helped to

---

[64] Bodl., Tanner, 283, fo. 138: 16/12/n.y.   [65] *L&P*, XX (ii) 820: 19/11/1545.
[66] WCRO, Newdigate Papers, CR136/B221: 28/12/1596.   [67] WD/Hoth/Box 44: 1615.
[68] Cecil, 55, fo. 16: 04/1597.
[69] *Lisle Letters*, passim. Newman, 'Sundry Letters, Worldly Goods', 139–52; Hanawalt, 'Lady Honor Lisle's Networks of Influence', 188–212.   [70] *Lisle Letters*, iii. 588: 13/03/1536.

lubricate family, kin, and other social relationships, and sweeten requests. In a letter to Honor Lisle asking her to intercede with her husband, Ralph Broke sought to curry favour by sending her two cheeses; Sir Brian Tuke offered her 'venison' when it was again in season, in response to the gifts from Lady Lisle he received.[71] Frances Grey and Abigail Digby were likewise keen to source supplies of venison to give as gifts to well-placed politicians.[72] Exchanges of gifts which sustained kin and patronage networks had important 'political' implications as secondary patronage functions in which women were intimately involved.[73]

The importance of gift-giving and the reciprocation that this demanded is demonstrated in a letter to the countess of Bath from Katherine Ashley, thanking her for the tokens she sent:

My most bounden duty remebred w[i]t[h] my most humble thankes my very good lady for your tokyns, beyng sory to take any thynge of yow seyng I am not able to do you any pleasuer but acordyng my pore you shal comande me duryng my lyfe. I caryed your tokyns yn my hande yn to ye quines preui chamber & hyr hines demanded off me where I had yt & I declred yt your ladyshyp dyd send yt me most desyrus to hyr off your hines helthe & how you haue your helthe. hyr maigeste answered yt now very kyndly donne off yow wellyng me to geue you hyr harty thankes & leke comendacyons both to my lord & you other wayes yff I coude pleasuer you my very good lady I wold be bothe gladde & redy.[74]

The act of writing and sending a token of remembrance, as represented in this reply, obligated Katherine to reciprocate the gesture in some manner, something she perhaps over-modestly claimed was not in her power. Yet as a gentlewoman of the Queen's Bedchamber, Katherine Ashley was a well-placed court contact close to the queen. The semi-public occasion of her receiving the token was recognized by the queen, and presented an opportunity for Lady Ashley to pass on the Baths' enquiries about Elizabeth's health, a gesture which the queen herself reciprocated with commendations. Another letter from Lady Ashley acknowledges receipt of tokens from Lord and Lady Bath, regretting that she had been unable herself to present them to the queen, but instead had them conveyed by her husband, Sir John Ashley.[75] Tokens were thus commonly dispatched by women for presentation to the monarch: Elizabeth, countess of Rutland, asked her cousin Mary Radcliff to convey a token to Queen Elizabeth.[76] Nowhere is the symbolism of gifts more explicit than in the giving of New Year's gifts to the monarch, a ceremony at which gift-giving between the king or queen and members of the court was rigidly hierarchal, and signified status, current standing, and court favour.[77] The issue of what gifts to present to the queen at

---

[71] Ibid. ii. 331; v. 1323.
[72] Talbot, 3206, fo. 189: 15/06/n.y.; BL, Addit., 12506, fo. 440: 21/08/1593.
[73] Harris, 'Women and Politics', 265–7. Donawerth, 'Women's Poetry', 3–18.
[74] CUL, Hengrave, 88/1, fo. 123: n.d.   [75] Ibid. 88/1, fo.143: 02/01/1560.
[76] HMC, *Rutland*, i. 318.
[77] Starkey, 'The Presence Chamber', 126–30; Glanville, 'Plate and Gift-Giving at Court', 131–5.

New Year is discussed at length in letters between Elizabeth, countess of Shrewsbury, and her half-sister Elizabeth Wingfield:

... presently after I rec[eived] yow ladships letter I went to my lady cobham and we longe confarde of the matter. I see by her she was much against yow honour givinge money. Mr w[ingfield] and I founde her so muche agannst the same that we ment if we coulde have founde any fine rare thinge to have bestowed thurty or fortye pounde of some suche thinge, but howe she would like the best coulde be hade beinge not her owne doinge we muche douted, now we have concluded she shall provide the same which she sayth she wyl do to her maty liking truly if yow honour had geven money I feare yt woulde have bene ell liked.[78]

In a society preoccupied with rank, status, reputation, power, and influence, giving a gift that would best please the monarch was important political capital.

Highly wrought calligraphic letters, like presentation manuscripts of poems or books, or embroidered samplers, were often presented as gifts. Anne Clifford and Alathea Talbot both bestowed on family members beautifully penned letters written on paper with decorative borders.[79] The young princess Elizabeth's letters were equally exquisite examples of penmanship; and Lady Arbella Stuart used an ornate italic hand for formal presentation court letters, distinct from the informal hand used for other letters. More generally, letters acted as 'tokens' of remembrance. Thus, Elizabeth Bourne begged Sir John Conway to accept her letter as 'a tokene of remembrance'; Elizabeth Cornwallis asked Margaret Bourchier to 'pardon my boldnes in scryblyng of this rud letter hauyng no other token worthy to send unto your ladyshyp'.[80] The sending of a letter as a token represents an expression of affection; thus a love token, while sometimes material (for example, a handkerchief or ring) could also be textual, a letter or note. It also acted as a memorial or remembering of the sender to the recipient; in the same way Anne Newdigate and Mildred Marey sought to keep themselves in each others' memory by exchanging portraits.[81] As with a portrait, the absent person is made figuratively present by the letter. Thus, the countess of Pembroke informed Elizabeth, countess of Shrewsbury, that she was 'loth to let pass any messenger without visiting your la[dyship] with my letters'.[82] The trope of correspondence as a form of 'visiting'—'a paper visitation'—renders letter-writing an act of physical sociability; the letter form is represented as a textual embodiment of the writer visiting the addressee.[83]

By far the most common commodity exchanged in letters was news. In many ways news acted as a kind of gift (solicited or otherwise), which helped to cement the relationship between sender and addressee. Sixteenth-century news-letters represent a distinct stage in the development of the genre, before the increasing professionalization of newsletters during the seventeenth century.[84] The newsletters that women received were not purchased with money; for the

---

[78] Folger, X.d.428 (132): 03/12/1585.   [79] *Proud Northern Lady*, 43.
[80] BL, Addit., 23212, fo. 94: 12/01/n.y.; Hengrave, 88/3, fo. 81: 25/10/1560.
[81] WCRO, CR136 B272, 273.   [82] Hunter, *History of Hallamshire*, 113.
[83] Whyman, 'Paper Visits', 15–36.   [84] Powell, *John Pory*, 55.

most part those who wrote to women about news were family and servants, people who by ties of blood, kinship, or service were duty-bound or obligated to write. In reporting news to his stepmother and mother-in-law Elizabeth, countess of Shrewsbury, Gilbert Talbot was 'fulfilling' her 'commandement' and 'discharging' his 'duty by wryting'; after their return to Dunstable, he and his wife Mary felt called upon to deliver 'Suche newes as on the Quenes hye wayes we have mett'.[85] The transmission of news in letters flows from social inferior to superior: from son or daughter to mother, from kinsman or kinswoman to aristocratic relative, from servant or agent to mistress, and from client to patroness. Rarely did news travel down the social hierarchy, although occasionally it was passed between equals. As is customary, news in letters from social subordinates is presented couched in a language of deference, familial obedience, and service, which allowed the writer and addressee to uphold social decorum. While 'humbly craving' her mother's 'moste honorab[le] and continuall bo[u]nty', Frances Pierrepont conveyed news of an insurrection heard from 'on[e] of the kinges chamber'.[86] William Kniveton, the son of Bess of Hardwick's half-sister Jane, closed a detailed report on enclosure riots in Lincolnshire, the current parliamentary session, and King James's progress to the Isle of Wight with the phrase: 'Thus being bould to troble yor ho[nour] with these small matters w[hi]ch are the certaynest newes that I can att this tyme write to yo[u]r ho[nour].'[87] Concern about the 'certainty' or credibility of news is a recurrent theme of newsletters. An unnamed correspondent prefaced a three-sided letter to the countess of Shrewsbury on national and international news with the disclaimer: 'Yf it were not for my bounden duetie sake, I wolde be lothe to write, bycause there is so smale certaynetie in occurrences but seing I am bounde to write it is but smale that I see w[i]t[h] my owne eyes, that is worthe writing; and therefore I am forced to supplye by that I do heare; w[hi]ch I write as I do heare by credeble reporte; other wyse I sholde not write at all; and therefore, if I do erre, it is p[ar]donable.'[88] This self-deprecating downplaying of the importance of news, indicative of an awareness of the unreliability of information, is again symptomatic of the deferential nature of the relationship between newsletter-writer and recipient. Because of the unequal balance of power within the relationship, the letter-writer distances herself or himself from the news in case it is inaccurate, absolving herself or himself from blame in advance so as not to lose favour for supplying incorrect information.

LETTERS, AUTOBIOGRAPHY AND THE 'SELF'

Sixteenth-century women's letters also performed a range of 'autobiographical' functions. Indeed, letters have traditionally been viewed by both literary critics and historians, as autobiographical documents that are uniquely self-reflective.

---

[85] Folger, X.d.428 (107, 114): 28/06/1574 [1589]. [86] X.d.428 (68): [1603].
[87] X.d.428 (41): 22/06/1607. [88] Talbot, 3196, fo. 221: 24/01/1569.

For feminist critics women's letters in particular are 'private' texts expressive of 'women's voices'; for historians they offer a uniquely female point of view on social affairs, and an entrée into women's self-perception.[89] Letters are indeed characterized by strongly autobiographical elements, and often convey a rich flavour of a writer's 'personality'. Written in the first person, with a firm sense of authorial identity, they describe the dealings, events and experiences of writers' everyday lives; they establish relationships between writers and the recipients of their letters; as the conveyors of sentiments and feelings they express various emotional states; and they display women's opinions, attitudes, and judgements on a range of matters. Letters are, therefore, seen as outward exhibitions of self-expression, representations of the outer self; letter-writers possess the language to describe personal thoughts and feelings: 'I', 'my', 'mine', and 'my self'. Writing to William Cecil regarding the wardship of her son, the dowager countess of Oxford wrote 'I [would] rather bend my selfe for my p[ar]te'.[90] And yet what of 'interiority' and the inner self? Some scholars have argued that the process of letter-writing itself encouraged a degree of inwardness, an interior self-consciousness; that outward expressions of love or grief were reflective of an inner life, of inward feelings or emotions. As Roger Smith has argued, 'the letter significantly enhanced a person's capacity to become self-absorbed and self-aware, that is, to become individual'; letters were 'the material medium of private thought'.[91]

Modern-day historians, theorists, and literary scholars, however, have argued that 'the self'—an inner personal identity, an authenticity or individuality, or in a Burckhardtian sense a self-conscious 'spiritual individual' who 'recognized himself as such'[92]—is in fact a linguistic, cultural, or social construct and not a transparent historical entity.[93] Indeed, post-structuralists would argue that subjectivity itself, the quality or condition of viewing things through the medium of one's own mind, and the expression of personality, individuality, or consciousness in literature, is not autonomous.[94] Instead, subjectivity is produced within and by discourse and language; it is contingent and unstable, historically and culturally relative; construction of the subject is discursive.[95] Outward

---

[89] Wilcox, 'Private Writing and Public Function', 47–62; Walker, *Women Writers*, ch. 2; Daybell, *Early Modern Women's Letter Writing*; Laurence, *Women in England*, 172; Fletcher, *Gender, Sex and Subordination*, ch. 8; Houlbrooke, *English Family*, 4, 101.

[90] BL, Lansd., 6, fos. 69[r-v]: 30/04/1563.   [91] Smith, 'Self-Reflection and the Self', 55.

[92] Burckhardt, *Civilization of the Renaissance*, 81. Recently, however, Burckhardt's central argument that the Renaissance witnessed the birth of the concept of 'self' for mankind has received strong rebuttal by various scholars: his mankind was Italian, literate, elite, and above all, male. Burke, 'Representations of the Self', 17–18; Duby, *History of Private Life*; Oppenheimer, *Birth of the Modern Mind*; Burrow, 'Autobiographical Poetry', 389–412.

[93] Burke and Porter, *Language, Self, and Society*; Porter, 'Introduction', and Sawday, 'Self and Selfhood' in Porter, *Rewriting the Self*, 1–14, 29–48; Dragstra *et al.*, *Betraying Our Selves*; Mousley, 'Renaissance Selves and Life Writing', 222–30.

[94] Seigel, 'Problematizing the Self', 281–314. Cf. Shell, 'Often to my Self', 259–78.

[95] Heale, *Autobiography and Authorship*, 4.

expressions of the self are seen to be strategic and conventional, termed variously as 'self-fashioning', 'self-presentation', 'self-stylization'; individuals constructed 'personas' or adopted masks in public for various social situations, though this in itself often presupposes the notion of a fixed self behind the façade. Turning to the inward self, scholars have pointed out the inability of language to adequately reflect 'inner states'—emotions, feelings, motives, moods, intentions—an emotional world that lies in the realm of psychology.[96] Stephen Greenblatt argues that literary and fictional selves, from More to Shakespeare, were shaped in response to social anxiety or conflict: 'self-fashioning', he asserted, 'involves some experience of threat.'[97] In recent years, New Historicist approaches have increasingly come under attack. Elizabeth Heale, for example, questions the ability of first-person narrated poems to express the inner self, arguing that such texts were harnessed for self-promotional means by writers seeking social advancement; these outer self-constructions, she argues, reveal conflicts and contradictions in available models of the self. Powerful challenges have also been put forward by historians who likewise argue for a greater need for historical specificity. Tom Webster locates the rise of the spiritual journal in seventeenth-century England in 'a response to the specific demands of a particular religiosity', and explores more fully the meanings and functions of this form of 'self-writing' in a Protestant context.[98]

Historical inquiry that is truly interdisciplinary has altered the ways in which historians approach historical texts. As a result of valuable conversations with other disciplines (conversations to which the discipline of history has much to contribute), historians are now increasingly versed at treating historical documents as complex texts which conform to 'literary' conventions; they are alert to strategies, discourses, and rhetorical tropes, and talk of 'personas' and constructions or the production of the self. The self, according to Roy Porter, is bound up with historical understanding of the nature and functioning of language: 'In so far as self-consciousness depends upon possessing the appropriate language, the words to say "I", we should think of the emergence of modern subjectivity not just as the creation of an intensely private realm, but as rendered possible by certain sorts of public discourse.'[99] In the study of Renaissance letters too, several scholars have questioned the ability of letters to convey an inner self, instead concentrating on the outward public manifestations of epistolary selves.[100]

One way of examining women's letters and 'the self' in a historical context is by approaching letter-writing as a 'technology of the self', a vehicle through

---

[96] Bound, 'Writing the Self?', 1–19; Rousseau, 'Towards a Semiotics of the Nerve', and Porter, 'Expressing Yourself Ill' in *Language, Self, and Society*, 213–75, 276–99.
[97] Greenblatt, *Renaissance Self-Fashioning*, 9. See also Maus, *Inwardness and the Theatre*. Cf. Webber, *The Eloquent 'I'*.
[98] Webster, 'Writing to Redundancy', 40–1. Baldwin, 'Individual and the Self', 341–64; Aers, 'Whisper in the Ear', 177–202. Cf. Todd, 'Puritan Self-Fashioning', 236–64.
[99] Porter, *Language, Self, and Society*, 12.   [100] e.g. Jardine, *Erasmus, Man of Letters*.

which female letter-writers composed a self through writing—indeed a 'material site' for the self.[101] In the broadest sense, increasing female literacy over the course of the sixteenth century meant that the reading and writing of correspondence became a more private affair, separated from secretarial gaze and communal facilitation. Scholars have long recognized that the spread of literacy skills and contact with the written word encouraged more autonomous introspection: an interaction between the writer and the printed or manuscript page.[102] Cultural and artistic genres including 'ego-documents' such as letters, diaries, biographies, autobiographies, accounts, almanacs, dramatic soliloquies, and verse (not to mention visual genres such as portraits and self-portraits) have also been viewed as capable of expressing heightened perceptions of individuality.[103] For many the 'private' act of writing, connected with seclusion and withdrawal into a separate, private space, is associated with the 'self': women's closets are often figured as a refuge in which women could express their inner thoughts freely.[104]

In its simplest mechanical form, the writing of a letter prompted women to view themselves externally and in relation to others, and to categorize themselves by more identifiable traits, including temperament, health, age, looks, education, skills, and aspirations, in addition to factors such as gender, the body, social status, nationality, and religion. Thus, in a hierarchical society which encouraged in correspondence apologies for 'rude' writing, deferential language, and modes of address appropriate to rank, signatories were constantly forced to define themselves in comparison with recipients. While many of the constituent elements that made up an individual's identity were shared with others, what made one unique is the precise mixture of these elements. It is, therefore, not as simple as thinking in terms of a woman writing to a man, a mother writing to her son, or a wife writing to her husband; equally important, for example, might be that a given letter-writer was a countess, a widow, highly educated, and of a fiery or determined disposition. This process of self-classification is clearly more fully developed in letters than in other media. A single woman might assume several selves, and present herself in different ways dependent upon with whom she was corresponding, and the circumstances in which the letter was sent. In the same way Elizabeth Heale has argued that short verses gave the opportunity for poets to present themselves in various first-person voices.[105] Thus, Bess of Hardwick wrote letters as a mother, wife, kinswoman, grandmother, mistress of the household, countess, patroness, suitor, friend, and confidante. As Alan Stewart

---

   [101] Foucault, 'Technologies of the Self', 16–49. In this essay Foucault demonstrates the letter form (classical in his example, Marcus Aurelius' letter of AD 144–5 to Fronto) as a vehicle for introspection: 'the examination of conscience begins with this letter writing' (pp. 28–30). Webster, 'Writing to Redundancy', 40.
   [102] Ong, 'Writing is a Technology that Restructures Thought', 23–50.
   [103] Porter, *Rewriting the Self*, 3; Decker, 'Ego-documents', 61–72.
   [104] Orlin, 'Gertrude's Closet', 44–67; Ziegler, 'My Lady's Chamber', 73–90.
   [105] Heale, *Autobiography and Authorship*, 9. Greene, 'Flexibility of the Self', 241–64.

has shown in his study of Anne Bacon, women could write with multiple 'voices', in the case of Lady Bacon those of daughter, wife, widow, and godly matron, through the media of translations, verse, and correspondence.[106]

While composing their letters women could select from a wide variety of available social or cultural scripts, adopting the voices of maternal complaint, wifely obedience, filial respect, authority, and command. Model letters, one could argue, are central to this kind of multiple voicing or self-construction precisely because they specify the social roles of writer and recipient (and therefore their relationship), and often the occasion on which the letter is written. Although scholars need to be alert to generic conventions and standard forms, historians have been at pains to stress the divergence between prescriptive or social models and practice. Some women did indeed style themselves as good mothers, dutiful wives, obedient daughters, and devout or submissive women, perhaps internalizing behavioural precepts in constructing their selves; other writers, however, manipulated such conventions, exposing the fissures between behavioural models and actual behaviour. Linda Pollock, for example, has noted the tension inherent within upper-class educational practices for girls, which taught them to be submissive and obedient, and to curb or crush wilful personalities, while simultaneously preparing women for authority, to command and instruct as mistresses of large households.[107] This discrepancy between precept and practice, the interaction of models with reality, is explored further in Chapter 8, which examines marital correspondence as seen against accepted ideals of the dutiful wife.

Female letter-writers commonly wrote about themselves or constructed an identity in relation to family, religion, and gender. Notions of self, however, were by no means uniform during this period, but rather were in a continual state of flux created by religious and political upheavals. Natalie Zemon Davis has argued that during this sixteenth-century turmoil the family provided women with a 'firm' basis for personal identity.[108] Letters indicate the central importance of family for most women; aristocratic women thought in terms of lineage, posterity, and honour, their lives and existence inextricably intertwined with ancestry, birth, and blood, though such preoccupations were not wholly irreconcilable with selfhood.[109] Women often wrote as family representatives in defence of family interests—as widowed mothers petitioning for their sons' wardships, as wives securing the release of husbands, as kinswomen seeking advice about matters of inheritance and family estates, writing as 'weak' and 'feeble' women petitioning for male assistance. Identity is, therefore, intrinsically bound up with the nature, purpose, and form of letter-writing.

[106] Stewart, 'Voices of Anne Cooke', 88–102.   [107] Pollock, 'Teach Her to Live', 231–58.
[108] On women's self-definition in relation to the family see Davis, 'Boundaries and the Sense of Self', 53–63.
[109] On the centrality of family to early modern women's lives see Harris, *English Aristocratic Women*; Larminie, 'Fighting for Family', 94–108; Heal, 'Reputation and Honour', 161–78.

Religious identity also formed an important part of the foundation for the exterior make-up with which many early women presented themselves to the outside world.[110] Susan Doran, for example, has examined the rhetoric of religious self-representation in Elizabeth I's correspondence, arguing that in her religious conservatism she resembled 'an old sort of Protestant'; and Brilliana Harley's Civil War letters, as Jacqueline Eales has shown, present her as a woman of firm Puritan conviction.[111] Elizabethan Catholic women, on the other hand, found it was often necessary (publicly at least) to hide their confessional identities for fear of prosecution. Thus, Margaret Neville, writing to Queen Elizabeth to extricate herself from accusations of recusancy, resolutely maintained her innocence and 'simplicity', claiming that she had been 'allured' from her 'obedience and loyalty' by the 'subtilty' of papists.[112] For Puritan women, though, their religion functioned as a badge of identity, an image of deep personal piety which was inscribed in correspondence, carved and enshrined in stone, and memorialized in print in the form of funeral sermons. In the correspondence of Anne Bacon there is something almost ostentatious in the way she styled herself as a godly Puritan. Her letters to her son Anthony display an intense concern for his soul as well as her own, and the importance of living a godly life. A letter to Burghley written in February 1585, after she had witnessed Archbishop Whitgift's response to the Commons concerning nonconformity in the aftermath of the Lambeth Conference, displays her Puritan persona, wearing her conscience very much upon her sleeve. Arguing that preachers should be heard in person by the queen, Lady Bacon petitioned her brother-in-law to intervene. She charged that: 'the report of the late conference at Lambath hath ben so handled to the discrediting of those learned that labor for right reformation in the ministery of the gospell that it is no small greff of mynde to the faythfull prechers, because the matt[e]r is thus by the oth[e]r syde caried away as thowgh their cawse cowld not sufficiently be warra[n]ted by the Worde of God.', 'I confess', she went on to argue, 'as one that hath fownde mercy that I have profyted more in the inward feeling knowledge of God his holy wyll thowgh but in a small measure by such syncere & sownd opening of the scrypture by ordinary preching.'[113] The dividing line here between the outward self and the inner self (or more precisely how this was represented) in actual fact becomes blurred: Lady Bacon describes her relationship with God in interior terms, as an 'inward feeling', and the letter itself in many ways represents a manifestation of religious conscience, a motivation that impelled her to action, to write, as it did other religious female patrons.

The writing of letters for early modern women appears to have performed a range of personal and introspective functions, which it is helpful to consider in

---

[110] e.g. Heal and Holmes, '*Prudentia ultra sexum*', 100–24, 314–17.

[111] Doran, 'Elizabeth's Religion', 699–720; Eales, 'Patriarchy, Puritanism and Politics', 143–58.

[112] *Correspondence of Dr Mathew Hutton*, ed. Raine, 313.

[113] BL, Lansd., 43, fos. 119–20: 26/02/1585. *Letters and Life of Francis Bacon*, ed. Spedding, i. 40–2; Jardine and Stewart, *Hostage to Fortune*, 96–7.

thinking about 'interiority' and women's inner selves. In particular, the sixteenth-century letter could act as a medium for spiritual self-examination by pious women (or at least provides material evidence of this devotional practice) similar to the way that in the next century the spiritual diary or journal developed as a mechanism for Puritan soul-searching. Women conducted religious correspondence with leading theologians, preachers, and chaplains which provided a source of spiritual sustenance and solace during a period of doctrinal upheaval. In particular, Patrick Collinson has shown the range of Protestant women, predominantly upper class, who corresponded with preachers including John Knox, Edward Dering, Thomas Cartwright, and Thomas Wilcox.[114] While it is mainly the men's side of the correspondence that survives, kept and published for posterity, it is possible to infer from the replies of male respondents that clearly women also wrote letters, in which they articulated their own theological and devotional concerns. Indeed, Margaret Hoby recorded in her diary writing letters to her chaplain, Mr Rhodes.[115] This 'confessional' mode of correspondence also appears to have been practised among Catholics: Jane Dormer received letters of spiritual counsel from popes Gregory XIII, Sixtus V, and Clement VIII in which they commended themselves to her prayers.[116] Religion, despite its emphasis on sin, guilt, and submission to God, could be a powerfully individualizing force, promoting deep introspection.

One extant example of this kind of religiously inward-looking correspondence is an autobiographical letter from Margaret Clifford to her chaplain Dr Leyfield, in which she represented her life as organized into seven decades.[117] In many ways the letter acted as a vehicle for self-analysis, facilitating understanding of her experiences. The opening phrases illustrate the epistle's purpose and offer insight into Margaret Clifford's relationship with her chaplain: 'for your comforts given to me in all my sorrows, there is much more due to you, than thanks from me . . . I can yield no other fruit than that my toil of sorrow will give, hear my complaint.'[118] The letter continues by outlining the main events of the countess's life, from birth and childhood to marriage and middle age, interpreting them within a religious framework. For example, describing the early stages of her marriage to George Clifford, she depicted her isolation from family and friends and the problems that she faced:

in a country [county] contrary to my religion, his [her husband] mother and friends all separate in that opinion, himself not settled but carried away with young men's opinions, Oh God where was I then. Not one to comfort me, but the favour of the time, that might

[114] Collinson, 'Role of Women', 258–72; id., 'Mirror of Elizabethan Puritanism'. Newman, 'Reformation and Elizabeth Bowes', 325–33; Felch, 'Letters of John Knox to Anne Vaughan Lok', 47–68; Frankforter, 'Correspondence with Women', 159–72.
[115] *Diary of Lady Margaret Hoby*, ed. Moody, 118, 119, 121, 125, 126, 127, 128, 136, 139, 162.
[116] Stevenson, *Life of Jane Dormer*, 161. See also Rahner, *Ignatius' Letters to Women*.
[117] Williamson, *George Third Earl of Cumberland*, 285–8. Only the first five decades of the countess's life are dealt with in the letter.   [118] Ibid. 285.

come in the ways of a religious course placed with me, more than by ways what con-
trarietys, must needs arise from hence, time made me haste, and with thought grew
almost continually sick, looking as a ghost that wanted the soul of comfort, and at last
without hope of Life's often recovering, being forc'd to change the air.[119]

The degree of inward examination and personal detail exhibited in such correspondence indicates the intimacy that often existed between women and
chaplains or preachers; indeed, Professor Collinson has argued that women 'leant
on the preachers as a Catholic would lean on his confessor'.[120]

Furthermore, epistles more generally acted as an outlet for women's piety and
religious introspection. Indeed, several of Lady Jane Grey's familiar epistles can be
viewed within a devotional framework. In a letter to her father the duke of Suffolk,
dispatched from the Tower a few weeks before her execution Lady Jane wrote:

And thus, good father, I have opened unto you the state wherein I presently stand, my
death at hand, although to you perhaps it may seem woful, yet to me there is nothing that
can be more welcome than from this vale of misery to aspire to that heavenly throne of all
joy and pleasure, with Christ my Saviour: in whose steadfast faith (if it may be lawful for
the daughter so to write to the father) the Lord that hath hitherto strengthened you, so
continue to keep you, that at the last we may meet in heaven with the Father, Son and
Holy Ghost.[121]

Jane Grey's letters in which she presented herself as an innocent and pious
woman were almost certainly intended for a wider audience and written with an
eye to future generations. However, they also contain unmistakably personal
elements, in that they were seemingly composed as a spiritual exercise to
strengthen her in the face of adversity and to make sense of her own experience.

In the same way, periods of illness prompted inward contemplation: health,
fitness, and welfare are frequently discussed in correspondence; symptoms and
diseases were self-diagnosed, pain and 'affliction' described; herbal remedies or
informal treatments were conveyed by epistolary exchange. This was a time when
to be ill or sick—as with states of madness, passion, and overt sorrow or grief—
was not to be one's 'proper' self.[122] Thus, the countess of Derby, describing the
grave illness of her sister, regretted that she was not yet herself.[123] Anne Bacon's
letters to her son Anthony contain lengthy descriptions of the state of her health,
and register her stoic acceptance of pain, suffering, and ultimately her own death
as God's will. Writing on one occasion she stated, 'my fitts encrease & I weker
tyll the tyme god hath appointed'.[124] Life-threatening illnesses and the fear or
acceptance of impending death similarly encouraged inward self-reflection and
spiritual preparation; the prospect of death was an occasion for repentance.[125]

---

[119] Ibid. 286.   [120] Collinson, 'Role of Women', 260.
[121] Nicolas, *Literary Remains of Lady Jane Grey*, 48.
[122] Porter, 'Expressing Yourself Ill', 276–99; id., 'The Patient's View', 175–98; Wear, 'Puritan
Perceptions of Illness', 55–99.   [123] WD/Hoth/Box 44: 27/09/1578.
[124] Bacon, 653, fo. 201: n.d.   [125] Houlbrooke, *Death, Religion and the Family*, 69–77.

A letter to Elizabeth, countess of Bath, from Jane Baker, a nurse formerly in the countess's employ, reveals something of her attitudes towards death: 'praye for me lying at dethes doore and . . . I praye you also haue me recomendyd unto my pore chylde willing her to praye unto almightie god . . . to rydd me quyckely out of this untollerable afflyccone.'[126] The inward self-scrutinizing process of preparing oneself for death is eloquently expressed in a letter from Margaret Clifford to her daughter Anne. Having made her will and sorted out matters of inheritance, the countess wrote, '[I]now trouble not my self any further w[i]th care of any earthlie thinges but my daly prayers to god, for his mercie and goodness to yourself and my litle sweet daughter'.[127] Reassuring her daughter of the inevitability of death for all, she wrote: 'remember good daughter ye certaintie of death to all and the uncerteyntie when and how, yet in respect of deathe it is no death but a chaunging to those yt liue in god in christ jesus.'

It is in the secular domain, however, that one locates the most potent expressions of the self—here defined in opposition to the family, neighbours, or wider community—arising out of situations of conflict. In numerous cases friction arose during legal, marital, or family disputes, occasions when women defended themselves using a conventional discourse of rights and social expectations to voice their demands and prerogatives, and to claim equity before the law.[128] The language of equity, in the sense of fairness or impartiality, is pervasive in women's correspondence.[129] The letters of Elizabeth Bourne written during her separation from her husband Anthony, for example, explicitly demonstrate her recognition of her own person as an individual with social and legal rights (albeit ill-defined). A sense of her independence, self-reliance, and the personal injustice and self-pity that she felt, however calculated, is clearly articulated in her writing. In a letter to her mother she declared, 'I haue chowesed wyth sylence to kepe my grefes to my selfe'; writing to John Conway, Elizabeth Bourne informed him that she had been badly wronged and hoped for equitable treatment; elsewhere she stated, 'kepe as much gould as you may by cause hit is easier caryeng and I am a wandryng woman laden wyth grefe and therfore had ned of lyt caryge and coumfortable'; and in another epistle to Conway she wrote, 'I must nedes speke my mynd . . . never promyse me any thinge but p[er]forme hit or else tell me som cause whye you may breke promyse . . . or else I canot be contented. yf I speke reason saye so and mend your fawtes.'[130] Her letters, charged with indignation, determination, and defiance, present a woman often isolated from family help and support who deeply felt that she had been wronged and badly mistreated. Denied the stable, self-defining centre of a husband and family, Elizabeth Bourne was

[126] Hengrave, 88/I, fo. 86: n.d.   [127] WD/Hoth/Box 44: 16/05/1616.
[128] Graham, 'Women's Writing and the Self', 215; Hutson, ' "Double Voice" of Renaissance Equity', 142–63.
[129] On Tudor theory of equity see Guy, 'Law, Equity and Conscience', 179–98. Cioni, 'Elizabethan Chancery and Women's Rights', 159–82.
[130] BL, Addit., 23212, fos. 182, 132, 92, 177.

forced to think in terms of herself. Correspondence also afforded an opportunity for female self-defence, a chance for women to defend themselves and their actions, and to maintain honour and reputation. Accused of financial misdealing, Elizabeth Wingfield asserted her innocence to Mary, countess of Shrewsbury, writing that 'I am not a leytl greuede your la[dyship] hath no more care of my want and credet . . . I never reseued a peney for any suche thinge for althow I be neuer so poore god wilinge I wyl use a good concience'.[131]

Thus, while on the surface the purposes of writing letters were essentially pragmatic, there was a range of ancillary, more personal and introspective uses to which letters were put by women during this period. Letters appear to have performed a cathartic or purgative function, enabling some women to unburden themselves of anxieties, fears, and worries, and to take the sting out of feelings of disappointment, failure, or hardship, given the need in some cases of presenting oneself as an object of pity or distress. In a letter to her brother Sir Henry Neville, Dorothy Seymour informed him that 'I would not haue been so silent . . . when I haue so much increaste in needful matters against my will'.[132] An insomniac Elizabeth Bourne also wrote to John Conway unburdening herself of her troubles: 'after the wrytyng of my lette[r] and I gon to bed I fynde my selfe som thinge trubled so as I can take no reste tyll I haue imparted hit to you I had thought to haue kept hit tyll I dyd speke w[i]t[h] you but I p[er]seve that shalbe god knowes when.'[133] Frances Willoughby, partly out of desperation, wrote to her sisters fearing for her life and described how she had been 'turned . . . out of doors' and 'beaten' by her husband.[134] In this instance letter-writing enabled an abused woman to unload her emotional distress, while simultaneously urging more practical support from her family.

The sixteenth century is thus marked by women's growing familiarity and inventiveness with letters and letter-writing practices, and by the developing flexibility of the genre as it was appropriated for an increasing range of purposes, formal and informal, pragmatic and personal. On the one hand, correspondence acted simply as a method of communication, allowing women to conduct business concerns; muster practical, financial and emotional support; keep in touch with immediate family members; and undertake important roles in maintaining kinship and patronage networks. Letters also performed a confessional function, acting as an outlet for piety and religious zeal, and by the mid-seventeenth century letters were being utilized by women as literary outlets, as vehicles for storytelling and travel narratives. Furthermore, the very practice of letter-writing was an individualizing technology, promoting inwardness and introspection; letters were the material sites of the self, central in the construction of early modern subjectivity.

---

131 Shrewsbury, 702, fo. 59: 06/03/n.y.
132 Berks RO, Neville Family Papers, D/EN/F/6/2/7: 18/01/n.y.
133 BL, Addit., 23212, fo. 157: n.d.   134 HMC, *Middleton*, 607: n.d.

7

Social Relations Inscribed in Correspondence

Letters have long been plundered by social historians for what they reveal about the quality of family and social relationships. Paying particular attention to modes of address, deferential and authoritative language, and tone, scholars belonging to the 'sentiments school' of family history have examined relations between husbands and wives, parents and children, and kinsfolk, looking at the strength of familial bonds (whether positive or negative), the emotional nature of family life, the incidence of authority and discipline, love and affection.[1] While Lawrence Stone and his acolytes characterized the sixteenth-century family as cold and uncaring, more recently historians such as Ralph Houlbrooke, Keith Wrightson, and Alan Macfarlane have argued for the more widespread existence of positive bonds within family life than previously was acknowledged.[2] Related to this historiographical debate is the issue of women's status and place within the family and wider society. What do letters tell us about the status of women within family, household, and other social hierarchies? Central here is the question of how far the manner of women's writing was affected by the gender of recipients. In light of prescriptive exhortations for female obedience and submissiveness—wifely obedience to husbands, and daughterly respect for parents—how far in practice were women subservient in their writing to men other than their husbands and fathers? Did women regard themselves as socially inferior to men, and to what extent is this registered in correspondence? Are women's letters characterized by a deferential language symptomatic of inherent male superiority? Did letters to male correspondents differ significantly from those to female correspondents?

In postal interactions with relatives and wider social contacts, levels of female confidence, assurance and authority, deference, respect, and reverence were closely related to women's roles and positions within the family and society: factors such as rank, social status, local and wider influence, as well as the nature

---

[1] Anderson, *Approaches to the History of the Western Family*, 39–64; Houlbrooke, *English Family*, 5.
[2] Stone, *Family, Sex and Marriage*; id., *Past and the Present Revisited*, chs. 17, 18; Slater, *Family Life*, 25–31. Cf. Houlbrooke, *English Family*, 14–16, 18–26; Wrightson, *English Society*, ch. 4; Macfarlane, *Marriage and Love*, 190–8.

of the correspondence, had as much impact as gender, if not more, on the tone of a letter. Early modern gender codes, as Margaret Sommerville has persuasively argued, were relatively elastic, allowing women to operate within overlapping areas of female influence and authority. Thus, in theory, while women in their capacities as daughters and wives owed dutiful respect to fathers and husbands, as mothers they commanded filial obedience from sons, and acting as mistresses of households they were empowered to instruct male servants.[3] The essential differences between precept and actual female behaviour have also been stressed by numerous scholars, who have argued that women were not uniformly constrained by restrictive patriarchal ideologies.[4] In practice, female experience was richly nuanced as spheres of female authority expanded and contracted: women could and did achieve command within the family and household, as mothers, kinswomen, and housewives; the balance of power in individual relationships was also dynamic and fluctuating, influence was contested and negotiated on an individual basis.

Letters written by women touch on their everyday lives, shedding light on the nature of family and other social relationships, and the complex position of women within a socially and gendered hierarchical society, where codes of female obedience and authority were set in constant tension to one another. By analysing how women wrote to a range of individuals, to superiors, subordinates, and social equals, and to men as well as other women, it is possible to investigate the balance of power within a range of relationships. This chapter analyses a broad range of letters produced in different contexts, paying attention to style, language, form, and mode of address as a way of focusing on the status, position, influence, and power of women within society, which was continually under negotiation, forever expanding and contracting. Examination of letters in this manner has an important bearing on issues relating to the scope of female authority; the prevalence of restrictive, authoritarian behavioural codes, and the degree to which they were internalized by women; the affective or emotional content of family relationships viewed from the perspective of epistolary evidence; and the extent to which letter-writing was a matter of duty and social courtesy.

DAUGHTERS TO FATHERS

Daughters' letters to fathers illustrate the range of relations possible within this dynamic in sixteenth-century England, from seemingly authoritarian relationships at one extreme to relatively more open and relaxed at the other extreme. Numerous examples exist of overtly deferential letters to fathers, especially from young girls. Lucy St John's holograph letter to Burghley, signed as 'your

---

[3] Sommerville, *Sex and Subjection*, 66–70.
[4] Wall, 'Elizabethan Precept', 23–38; Pollock, 'Teach Her to Live', 231–58; Houlbrooke, *English Family*, 101; Fletcher, *Gender, Sex and Subordination*, ch. 8.

lo[rdship's] humble and moste obedyent doughter', is exemplary of this kind of reverential epistle. Addressing Burghley as 'right honorable and my very good lorde', Lucy 'humbly' remembered herself in her letter, apologized for her 'bade writynge', offered 'humble thanks' for his 'great care', acknowledged herself most 'bounde for the most parte of my chief hapines', and ended 'humbly craving' his blessing and with prayers for his 'longe life and much happiness'.[5] Similar expressions of filial respect can be viewed in correspondence between Lady Anne Drury and her father Sir Nicholas Bacon II of Redgrave Hall. Having informed her father, whom she addressed as 'Sir', that she had sent him a letter from her uncle, Parker, Lady Anne hoped 'itt shall not be any way prejudiciall unto you to satisfy his desyre'. The letter continues, excusing her causing him trouble: 'I am very loth to be thus troblesome unto you but that I assu[re] my selfe, this sprite waches all occasions to doo no good betweene your selfe and my husband which I am still driven to cross and pray for prevention.'[6] The reiteration of deferential tropes of humility and thanksgiving in both letters served to convey daughterly respect and obedience. As argued in the previous chapter, letters to senior male family members, especially where a favour was being sought, often employed a vocabulary of petition or supplication and a subordinate demeanour.

The very act of composing letters to parents was viewed as a mark of filial respect; written humbly, one of the main purposes of corresponding to fathers was to offer commendations and remembrances. In 1575 Katherine, countess of Pembroke, wrote a short letter to her father George, earl of Shrewsbury, to enquire after his health, and to inform him that the queen daily asked after his well-being; in the same letter she conveyed her husband's heartiest commendations.[7] Letters of this nature, which at least overtly contained no request, were a performance of daughterly duty. On the eve of her ninth birthday Anne Clifford dutifully wrote to her father:

> I humbly intreate your blessing and
> euer comend my duety and saruice
> to your lo[rdship] praying I maybe made
> happy by your loue I comend my
> seruice and leaue my trobling of
> your lo[rdship] being your
>
> > Daughter in all
> > obedient duety
>
> > Anne Clifford
>
> Jan xxxi
> 1598.[8]

---

[5] BL, Lansd., 104, fo. 175: 09/1588.

[6] Joseph P. Regenstein Library, University of Chicago, Bacon Papers of Redgrave Hall, [4169]: [c.1600].   [7] LPL, Talbot, 3205, fo. 32: 03/10/1575.

[8] *Proud Northern Lady*, 43.

Doubtless Anne Clifford's letter was written partially for handwriting practice; however, the epistle's elegance, surrounded by a decorative border, suggests that it may have been composed as a presentation for her father, a sign of her desire to please. Thus, from an early age letter-writing reinforced children's subservience to parents, as codes of deference and obedience were inscribed in text.

A letter from Mary Kitson to her father Sir Thomas Kitson begins in similarly respectful vein, humbly remembering her duty, beseeching him for his blessing, and enquiring after his good health. However, beneath this rhetoric of politeness there is an underlying tone of complaint, which erodes prescriptions of silent and unquestioning daughterly compliance. After the conventional epistolary platitudes, the letter becomes more critical as Mary Kitson bemoans to her father the poor quality of the horse which was sent to convey her to her parental home: 'in deede father he was a very colde horse and went soe smothly that I was afrayde he would haue layd me in the myre.'[9] Letters from daughters of the gentry more commonly eschew the honorific language and overly courteous opening conventions and commonplaces displayed in the letters from daughters of noble birth. Writing to her father Sir Thomas Gresham, Lady Anne Bacon addressed him simply as 'my very good father', before registering her concern that he had been 'ill handled' by the 'sorenesse' of his leg and expressing her desire that she might see him soon in Norfolk. The letter, however, ends conventionally enough, asking for her father's blessing and sending her prayers for his health and long life.[10]

Letters that performed more practical functions than simply signifying filial duty also adhered less closely to epistolary conventions and were less respectful of codes of politeness. Anne Broughton's correspondence to her father Richard Bagot acted simultaneously as inventories of goods and items accompanying the bearer, as shopping lists, and as repositories for news. A letter to her 'good father' from the 1580s listed the provisions (sugar-loaves, pepper, cloves, and salad oil) which she was sending by the carrier; promised that her mother would have her gown as soon as she could have it made; reported that her partner was attending to Bagot's accounts, and that her brother Anthony was at Croydon 'where the quene lieth' and that he had delivered his letter to Mr Greville. The letter continues expressing Anne's sorrow that her uncle John 'continueth in his old disordered life', and informing her father that she is having coats made up out of buffin for sons Lil and Wat.[11] Although she signed herself as an 'obedient' daughter, Anne Broughton's open, matter-of-fact style, and the way in which she mixed details of household provisioning, family news, and business arrangements with the minutia of everyday life, indicates a positive relationship between a father and his married daughter, one that was perhaps less unequal in social

[9] CUL, Hengrave, 88/2, fo. 62: 20/03/n.y.   [10] Folger, L.d.23: 09/1573.
[11] Folger, L.a.223: 11/05/[1587]. See also L.a.222, 225–9: 24/11/1580, 02/04/[1593], 31/05/[1593], 17/06/[1593], 18/01/[1595], 24/04/1596.

terms than in cases where daughters were younger or unmarried. Marriage in this sense could improve upon a woman's social standing.

MOTHERS TO SONS

As mothers, women could also attain a high degree of status, and the 'voice' of maternal authority is one that echoes strongly from the early modern archive in letters from mothers to sons. Commonly, mothers wrote plainly and unrestrainedly to sons, exhibiting obvious concerns for material and spiritual welfare. The most extensive series of letters between mother and son for the sixteenth century are those of the Puritan Anne Lady Bacon and her elder son Anthony, which number several hundred items. In addition to offering insight into her own life, experiences, and religious beliefs, Lady Bacon's writings are crowded with moral advice relating to her son's health, diet, businesses, and lifestyle; a mixture of maternal rebuke and censure, advice and command, the letters ultimately betray her pious interest in the future of Anthony's soul. In May 1595, for example, Anne Bacon wrote, 'god bless yow & make yow able to heare wholsome publick doctrine for yo[u]r bett[e]r understanding every way'.[12] She frequently chided her son for the company that he kept: writing in August, she berated him for his acquaintance with Catholics, warning that he would 'verely' be 'cownted a practiser', and asking God to keep him from 'spanish subteltyes & popery'.[13] A letter dated April 1595 admonished Anthony to take more exercise, fearing that he would lose the use of his legs 'by disuse'.[14] Another letter warned against debt: 'owe nothing to eny sayth the lorde in his worde, but to love one another.'[15] Lady Bacon's letter to her other son Francis (or Frank, as she referred to him) was full of motherly concern for his diet and daily regimen: 'looke verie well to your healthe. supp not nor sit vp late suerlie I thinke your drinkinge to bedwardes hinderethe yowr and your brothers digestion verie muche.'[16]

The matriarchal 'voice' of authority and complaint evident in Lady Bacon's correspondence with her sons was also utilized to berate the earl of Essex for his rumoured sexual profligacy and bed-swerving. In a letter of December 1596 she chastised the earl for 'carnall dalyance' and 'infaminge a noble manes wyfee and so nere aboute her Ma[jes]tie', advising him to 'abstaine from fornication' and not be in thrall to 'the luste of concupiscence'.[17] By contrast, Anne Bacon's tone

---

[12] LPL, Bacon, 651, fo. 156: 12/05/1595.   [13] Ibid., fo. 326: 08/1595.
[14] Ibid., fo. 89: 08/04/1595.   [15] Ibid., fo. 328: 05/08/1595.
[16] Ibid., 650, fo. 255: 20/08/1594. For Francis Bacon's letters to his mother see 648, fo. 8 (18/02/1592); 649, fos. 60 (14/02/1593), 433 (04/10/1593); 650 fo. 217 (06/06/1594). An unsigned copy of a letter to Lady Bacon also survives, which was either by Anthony or Francis: 650, fo. 101 (25/02/1594).
[17] Ibid., 660, fos. 149^{r-v}: 01/12/1596. Hammer, *Polarisation of Elizabethan Politics*, 320–1, n. 24.

in writing to her stepson Nicholas Bacon is more detached. A letter of March 1600 lacks the maternal censure of her other correspondence—presumably unsuited for this particular occasion of writing—but instead exudes a cordial firmness as she pushes Nicholas for payment of her annuity: 'I thincke myselfe beholdinge to yow for havinge care of payenge me myne anuytie in good tyme for I have neede of yt always before yt commeth to my handes. At this tyme yow have written to one Mr Cooke to paye me a hundered poundes at the Ladye daye next, of whome I shalbe verye well content to receave yt yf he paye yt to me then, but if he dothe fayle me and yow then, at the daye, I hope yow will have care of me, to see me payed.'[18] The relative formality of this letter might be read against an earlier correspondence with Nicholas, a postscript scrawled on one of his father's letters, asking her stepson to help the 'ould mother' about whom the letter was written, and informing him of his father's gout.[19]

The recusant Agnes Throckmorton wrote similar letters of motherly rebuke to her own son Robert. One such epistle warned him to desist from horse-racing in order to maintain a low profile in the county: 'I . . . see', she wrote, 'you begin now agayne to kepe runninge horsis . . . this mater hath bin . . . very carfully kept from me till all the contrye tallketh of it that papist hath so much monie that thay run it a waye'.[20] Incensed by her son Lord Beauchamp's behaviour, Frances, countess of Hertford, snappily reminded him, 'I am sure you know from whence you descended. Let not a base mind possess so honorable a person: make your choice like unto yourself. Remember the care your lord father has had for your upbringing.'[21] As a widow, Joan Thynne wrote with a certain strictness to her son Thomas, concerning money owed to her daughter Dorothy after her father John Thynne's death. A letter from Joan dated 25 August 1611, requesting the payment of the money to Dorothy as agreed when she was of 'full age', was apparently ignored by Thomas. His silence on this matter was met coldly: 'methinks you might have sent some messenger with answer unto them as I would have done to you if you had writ to me touching matters of like importance', Joan wrote on 24 September. When in fact Thomas did attempt to deal with his sister's financial affairs his mother wrote, 'your letter was expected long before I heard from you', and ordered him to 'have the whole sum all together for three weeks or a month longer if you please'.[22] In these instances the purpose of writing was censure, often occasioned by friction or dispute; such letters, therefore, highlight the authoritarian aspects of sixteenth-century motherhood, which could easily exist alongside more affectionate modes of behaviour.

Scholars have emphasized the complexity of relationships between mothers and sons, inflected as they were by the peculiarities of inheritance, age,

---

[18] Bacon Papers of Redgrave, [4167]: 03/03/1600.   [19] Ibid., [4123A]: 16/11/1572.
[20] WCRO, Throckmorton Papers, CR1998/Box 60, folder 1/6.
[21] Longleat House, Seymour Papers, 5, fos. 130: 18/03/1582.
[22] Wall (ed.), *Two Elizabethan Women*, letters 66, 67, 68.

circumstance, and individual character, which generated positive as well as negative bonds; relationships between male heirs and widowed mothers could be problematic, and mothers often related differently to infant, adolescent, and adult children, as well as to the eldest son and younger sons.[23] Widowed mothers often relied on eldest sons for material assistance: Anne Lady Paget asked her son Thomas to advise her on the 'assurance' of her house, writing that she had 'little judgement' in 'these matters'.[24] Mothers' epistles to sons highlight the potential strength of maternal bonds and the degree of intimacy within the mother–son relationship. Several women took a keen interest in their sons' educations: Katherine Paston and Brilliana Harley corresponded with sons while they were away at university, and frequently discussed their studies with the sons' tutors.[25] A letter from Lady Gower to her son Thomas, an undergraduate at Wadham College, Oxford, in 1618, betrays her concern for his material and spiritual welfare: 'Tom: I am so fearefull of you now being so fur from me that your younge yeares should forgett your maker, which hath beene so beneficiall vnto you, I charge you to continue w[i]th your daly prayers vnto him.' The letter continues by complaining of his failure to write to his grandmother, warning him against the 'sin' of duelling, and demanding repayment of a loan that she made to his cousin.[26] Schoolboys were likewise the recipients of letters from anxious mothers. Lady Lisle wrote to her 10-year-old son James Basset during his schooling in Paris, where he was educated under the personal care of the merchant Sir William le Gras; and she clearly expected regular reports from the youngest of her offspring on how he was progressing.[27]

High degrees of epistolary intimacy are also evident in the letters of Lettice Dudley, countess of Leicester, and Gertrude Courtenay, marchioness of Exeter, to their grown-up sons.[28] Lettice Dudley's correspondence with her son the earl of Essex (her 'sweete' or 'dearest' Robert) mixed maternal affection and cordiality with political guidance: 'you gaue us an alarme swet Ro[bert] to make us beleue we shuld se you', she wrote in December 1597, adding that the company at Drayton would have been 'proud' of his presence. The letter also warns of the 'cross workings' of his 'suttell enemys', and advises him to seek the council of the countess of Warwick and Lady Leighton.[29] In a letter to her son Edward Courtenay, the disgraced and exiled earl of Devon, the marchioness of Exeter offered to use her influence as a gentlewoman of Mary's Privy Chamber to his advantage: 'If my waiting can do you good, if I may get a chamber I will wait,

---

[23] Harris, 'Property, Power and Personal Relations', 606–32; Pollock, 'Younger Sons', 23–9.

[24] Staffs RO, Paget Papers, D1734/2/5/15/M: 1583.

[25] *Correspondence of Lady Katherine Paston*, ed. Hughey; Lewis, *Letters of the Lady Brilliana Harley*.

[26] Davies and Garnett, *Wadham College*, 21, 145. *Catalogue of the Muniments of Wadham College*, 4/27.

[27] *Lisle Letters*, iv., ch. 10. The only side of this epistolary exchange that survives is the letters of James Bassett, although he refers to letters received from his mother and father.

[28] WCRO, 'Essex Letter Book, *c*.1595–1600', MI 229; NA, SP11/5/15, SP11/5/16, SP11/5/34, SP11/6/25, SP11/6/47.   [29] 'Essex Letter Book': 12/1597.

although my years require rest.'[30] Mothers also corresponded with sons as intermediaries for suitors: Jane Cecil's letters with her son William Lord Burghley are almost exclusively concerned with patronage suits. A letter of 22 April 1587 requested that he award the bailiff of Lutterworth to his kinsman and her friend Stephen Pecke; another recommended Anthony Atkinson for a searcher's place at Hull; and a third sought the wardship of William Croftes for his uncle John Croftes.[31] Less high-powered correspondences than those of these well-connected aristocratic women reveal something of the day-to-day interactions of family life, and the easy familiarity possible between mothers and sons. The Leicestershire mercantile wife Mary Herrick wrote simply to her son William, thanking him and his wife for gifts of pomegranate, marmalade, and red herring, and informing him that she had sent him a pair of knitted hose and gloves; if the gloves were too small, she added, he was to give them to his brother-in-law's children, and she would send him another pair.[32]

LETTERS TO MALE KIN

Similar close relationships between women and other male family members can be glimpsed through correspondence. Audrey Aleyn frequently corresponded with her brother Thomas Lord Paget, with whom she appears to have enjoyed a positive relationship. One of her news-filled letters claimed that she had been moved to write to see how he did with his company rather than from any other motive, before reporting that William Aleyn had measles; Lord and Lady Cobham had come into Kent; her husband, having kissed the queen's hands at court, was in one of the Cinque Ports preparing for her majesty's arrival; Mistress Cartwright was now in the country; fifteen of the queen's ships had gone to sea; Christopher Hatton's health was amended; the duke of Modena is at Spain, and the Lord Windsor's going there is stayed. The letter ended with news of 'mres holcrofts marriag to earl of rutland and mrs stafford to a gentleman in norfolk'.[33] Likewise, Lettice Kinnersley, who frequently wrote to her brother Walter Bagot, turned to him for support during a dispute with her husband, with whom she had fallen out because he blamed her that the household had run out of provision of beer. Claiming that she had been abused with 'maney bitter corsses', had the 'charge of the house' taken from her, was commanded to keep to her chamber, and that her mother-in-law's maid stood by her door to report what she said, Lettice Kinnersley asked him to write or let her brother Anthony intercede on her behalf. In the event of her leaving her husband, which is openly

---

[30] SP11/5/34: 08/06/1555.
[31] BL, Lansd., 104, fos. 170, 172; SP12/67/41: 03/04/1570. BL, Lansd., 104, fos. 160, 162, 174.
[32] Bodl., Herrick, Eng. Hist., 474, fo. 68: 1578.
[33] Paget Papers, D603/K/1/5/9: 08/07/[1573]

suggested in the letter, she argued for the necessity of keeping her children: 'if I may but haue the rule of my children and some what to mentayne them and my selfe I wold desier nomore.' The letter ends with a sisterly plea: 'good brother wryte unto me what weare my best corse in this my distreses as you loue me let not my mother know.'[34] In this letter, emotional and practical aspects are intertwined; letter-writing offers Lettice a way of unburdening herself of her troubles to her brother, and enabling her to call upon his services as head of the family. Her plea in itself appeals to fraternal affection which resides hand-in-hand with more practical considerations of brotherly responsibility.

In the absence of fathers and husbands, brothers could provide an invaluable resource of advice, protection, and material support. In more 'patriarchal' families the dependency of female relatives on senior male kin appears to be accentuated in correspondence, with differences in social standing being more rigidly maintained. In her study of the 'singlewomen' of the infamously authoritarian Verney family, Susan Whyman argues that without fathers and brothers to support them such women were reliant upon 'patriarchal patronage', a dependency articulated through epistolary deference.[35] Similar deferential rhetoric was employed by other women to male kin, especially in letters containing requests. Anne Newdigate, for example, 'beseeched' her uncle Sir Francis Fitton to have one of his men deliver a letter;[36] Mabel Fortescue informed her 'governor' Francis Yaxley that she would behave in a manner acceptable to him and his friends, signing herself in another letter 'your obedient charge'.[37] Olive Talbot wrote a series of letters to her kinsman Gilbert Lord Talbot in July and August 1583 seeking his assistance in obtaining the wardship of her son. Socially his inferior, Olive carefully delivered her meaning in supplicatory terms to the future earl of Shrewsbury. Addressing Talbot as 'Myne espesiall good lord', the first letter rejoices at the birth of his son before 'craving' his favour in her suit for her own son; a later letter apologizes for her 'bouldnes' in reminding him of her suit for her 'boy'; a third, written upon hearing from Talbot, lavishes him with thanks for 'his many other favours', for which Olive Talbot claims she is 'bound' to him, and will commit him to God in her prayers.[38] The rich language of entreaty and rhetoric of deference which runs through this and other family correspondence, while it may betoken social differentiation and the unease of request-making, cannot hide the determination with which women forwarded and indeed reiterated their claims. Deference to seniority could also register itself materially in the use of significant space in the layout of the letter's text: thus, Ann Hobart, writing to her uncle Sir John Hobart, left a one-centimetre gap between the mode of address ('Good Sy') and the start of her letter; at the

---

[34] Folger, L.a.598: 14/09/[1608].   [35] Whyman, 'Gentle Companions', 177–93.
[36] WCRO, Newdigate Papers, CR136/B304a: 04/03/1602.
[37] SP12/12/4: 10/04/1560; SP12/14/51: 30/11/1560.
[38] Talbot, 3203, fos. 366, 364, 368: 07/071583, 21/07/1583, 24/08/1583.

end, she left space of four centimetres before signing herself 'your assured louing nece'.[39]

Numerous examples, however, also survive of Tudor women who were far from submissive and subservient in writing to male family members. Alison Wall's fine study of the Thynne correspondence ably demonstrates that the women of the Thynne family of Longleat often wrote with confidence and authority to husbands and other male relatives, and this trait of female boldness can be seen in the letters of women from many other families.[40] Lady Susan Bourchier, for example, was particularly vitriolic in a letter to Sir Thomas Kitson, whom it appears had taken great offence at his sister-in-law's behaviour, 'misliking' her departure at 'Christmas tyme', which led him to 'conceive' the 'opinion' that she esteemed neither his 'friendship' nor his 'goodwill'. Writing in reply to these accusations, Lady Bourchier justified her absence, 'protesting' that he had 'without any iuste cause' condemned her as guilty; her 'meaninge', she maintained, was 'honeste and voyde of any synister dealinge', and she did not deserve to be 'condemned amonge those unthanckfull ons that neyther deserve feythe nor frendly favor'. The letter ends with a curt request: '. . . wherefore brother I praye yow to lette me understande by your letter as sone as yow maye convenientlye whether yow will be contented ageyne to receyve me and whether I maye be welcome unto yow or no w[hi]ch yf I shall I will for all this unkynd dealinge be glade to come unto yow yf not I must be dryven to seke further to place my selfe not dowtinge but the reste of my frendes will se me unprovyded.'[41] As a woman of aristocratic, Lady Susan was socially superior to her brother-in-law, which may partly explain her outraged tone. Similar assurance is displayed in a letter from Lady Poole to her brother Nicholas Williamson concerning a lawsuit, in which she explained her willingness to protect her position and standing: 'howe soeuer I shalbe unkindly delte w[i]th all I will mainteine my creditt sufficiently in any greater matter againste anye th[a]t shall maliciouslye . . . impugne it.'[42]

LETTERS OF COMMAND AND INVECTIVE

In examining the issue of female subservience in letters addressed to men, a useful comparison with family correspondence is letters from noblewomen and gentlewomen to male servants, usually sent to deliver written instruction. The modes of address employed by mistresses in letters to men in their employ are typically curt and formal: Lady Mary Sidney addressed Edmund Molyneux, a servant of the Sidney family, simply as 'Molineux'; Elizabeth, countess of Shrewsbury, wrote to her servants James Crompe and Thomas Baldwin as

---

[39] BL, Eg., 2715, fo. 94: 10/06/[1608].   [40] Wall, 'Deference and Defiance', 77–93.
[41] Hengrave, 88/2, fo. 10: 30/12/1567.   [42] SP46/49/191: 06/07/n.y.

'Crompe' and 'Baldwyn'.[43] Occasionally, softer forms were adopted: Katherine, countess of Hertford, addressed her servant Anthony Penne as 'Good Pene'; Margaret Clifford termed her servant Ralph Coniston 'my most trosty sarvant'.[44] Unlike letters of petition, requests in these letters take the form of orders; commands were often issued abruptly and directly. In a letter to her servant John Cockram, Mary Sidney 'willed' him to send her a sum of £3, 'the money for the household', urging that she must have it by nightfall, and that if her husband made any question of it to let him know that no money shall be abated; the letter ended, 'fayle not hear of as you will answer my commandment'.[45] Similar directness is found in a letter to Cockram's wife, commanding her in her husband's absence to deliver Mary Sidney's household money to her page. Towards the end of the missive Lady Sidney affirms her authority, announcing that her 'letter or warrant' is sufficient for Mrs Cockram to discharge her orders.[46] Meanwhile, a letter from Lady Sara Hastings to Robert Herrick reads as little more than a provisioning order: 'Good Mr Herricke I pray you send me by this bearer six dozen of the best trenchers you have and halfe a dozen of your beste vennis glasses wth covers, for drinkinge glasses lyke wyse yf you have any more of the same bole glasses w[hi]ch I had of I praye you sende them & lett them be safely packte up for breakinge.'[47] An early letter from Cecilia, marchioness dowager of Dorset, to Thomas Cromwell, dating from his time as servant of her son Thomas Grey, marquess of Dorset, bears none of the courteous deference that marks the letters of aristocratic ladies writing to him when he attained high office and entered the peerage. Instead the dowager marchioness's letter is formal and to the point, issuing Cromwell with a set of instructions: 'Cromwell I woll that yow send to me in hast the trussyng bed of cloth of tyssewe and the fether bed wyth the fustyans and a materas longyng to the same wyth the cownt[er]poynt.'[48]

While social position could provide women with authority, sanctioning them to command men within their employment, other letters reveal women challenging men. Affronts to male authority are particularly marked in letters provoked by some kind of conflict, where women utilized the letter form as a way of discharging anger, outrage, and frustrations, either by corresponding with family and friends recounting the injuries, hurt, and dishonour received at the hands of wrongdoers, or by writing to confront offending parties with their offences, to get even, issue insults, and vent bile and spleen. In numerous instances the recipients of these poisoned-pen letters were men. Elizabeth, countess of Shrewsbury, sent a malicious message to Sir Thomas Stanhope hoping that he

[43] CKS, De L'Isle, U1475/C7/6: 01/09/1574; Folger, X.d.428 (83): 08/03/[1560]; Talbot, 3206, fo. 1017: 17/01/1580.
[44] BL, Lansd., 819, fos. 108, 109: 16/10/n.y., n.d.; Kendal RO, WD/Hoth Box 44: 17/04/1616.
[45] De L'Isle, U1475/C1/1: 02/06/1573.
[46] Ibid., U1475/C1/4: 29/01/1574. Cf. Magnusson, *Shakespeare and Social Dialogue*, 44–9.
[47] Bodl., Herrick, Eng Hist, 477, fo. 72: 21/08/1582.
[48] BL, Cott., Vespasian, F.XIII. Art. 123, fo. 174: n.d.

would be 'damned p[er]petuallie in hell fyre' and describing him as 'more wretched vyle and myserable than any creature lyveinge, and . . . more uglie in shape then the vylest toade in the worlde, and one to whome none of reputacon would vouchsafe to send any messadge'.[49] Margaret, countess of Bath, dispatched a scornful epistle to one Mr Savage who had both cursed and wished upon her 'plage' and 'pestilence'. While maintaining a morally superior tone, the countess's letter delivered a skilful and effective rebuke, playing on the man's name and questioning his conduct and gentlemanly honour:

> . . . when I remember your name Savage I find it not moch dissenting from your natural disposition for indede if I might so grossly terme it. this beastly blessing of yours declare you to be more savage or brutish than discrete or reasonable in so cruelly cursing me . . . then seemed you more ruffyanlyke than gentlemanlyke . . . thus leave I you, praying god in the stead of your plage and pestilence wished me to send you instead of a malycious mind an honest one whereof ye have nede as it appereth.[50]

Likewise, Bridget Willoughby, the daughter of Sir Francis Willoughby, wrote to one Mr Fisher a letter 'full of outrage and incivility'.[51] She blamed Fisher for trying to cause dissension between herself, her father, and her husband, writing: '. . . malicious knave thou art that canst not spare poor gentlewomen and infants with thy tongue and practices; gentleman thou knowst thyself to be none and tho at this instant I have no better means of revenge then a little ink and paper let thy soul and carkes be assured to hear and tast of these injuries in other sort and terms then from and by the hands of a woman.'[52] Women, therefore, clearly utilized letters to 'heap contumely', wreaking revenge on enemies with countersnubs and attacks.

Such onslaughts, however, were not solely confined to women writing to men of lower social status. Anne Dudley berated her brother-in-law William Bourchier, earl of Bath, for his ill-treatment of his wife, her sister Elizabeth. In a powerfully worded missive written in 1594, she threatened to harm Bourchier's standing with the queen unless he amended his behaviour:

> . . . it seemeth yow have altogether forgotten both your selfe and frendes, soe as now the world shall take knowledge of your weaknes. And seinge you are become soe voyd of judgment and discretion to offer such abuses still unto her [your wife] who beinge borne and brought up as she hath byn, and who by reporte of all hath soe dutifullie demeaned herself towards yow yow shall well knowe that she hath frends who will not suffer her anie longer to be thus abused without cause and therfore of that which I heare be true I purpose to acquainte her Majestie therwith, and doe not doubte but it shall be redressed, and indeed unless yow had [*sic*] more governement of your selfe I will seeke that my sister may have her portion and go lyve from yow, seeing yow esteme nothinge of her, neither respect your owne posterity.[53]

[49] BL, Lansd., 99, fo. 274: 15/02/1593. [50] Hengrave, 88/1, fo. 75: n.d.
[51] HMC, *Middleton*, 577. See also 568. [52] Ibid., 577.
[53] HMC, *Portland*, ii. 19: 16/04/1594.

In this example the countess not only sought to chastise her brother-in-law, criticising his judgement, discretion, and care for his lineage, but also aimed to protect her sister by forcing the earl to curb his ill-treatment of her. Alternatively, such vehement indignation and rancour could be expressed to third parties. Thus, Frances Withipole wrote to Sir John Hobart complaining of her father's financial neglect of her and his other children:

...if all dutys of a father be ^included^ in begetting what doth he less (as a resonable soule) that spitts or begetts a childe, you may say, he may gett a good man or woman. I say ther is no more to be atributed to him then to the carpenders tooles for his worke, nay what greater wrong then only to begett a child who is lest able of all other creaturs to healp it self but the contience of mayntayning the hows is alegd that erthly imaginary eternyty (never brought forth by God nor nature) but say it is it lawful to take from the most wicked to bilde an hospitale more unlawful must it be because more unaturale to take from ones owne children when he is concluded a infidell that provides not for his family.[54]

Though women's letters could be vituperative, they do not contain the threats of physical violence that marked the missives of certain male letter-writers, including Philip Sidney, who wrote to his father's secretary Edmund Molyneux warning him, 'I assure yow before God, that if ever I know yow do so muche as reede any lettre I wryte to my Father [Sir Henry Sidney], without his commandement, or my consente, I will thruste my Dagger into yow'.[55]

On a more sophisticated level, women also used epistles to lampoon men, illustrating the ways that female humour could be directed against the opposite sex. Penelope Lady Rich, for example, appropriated and altered a letter written from her husband, Lord Rich, to her brother Robert Devereux, earl of Essex. Her purpose in doing this seems to have been for the amusement of herself and her brother—suggestive of their close relationship—and at the expense of her husband. Lord Rich had been offered the services of a French secretary by Essex, and the letter was written to decline the offer. In Lord Rich's version the letter read: 'as yo[u]r lo[rdship] wel knoweth [I] am a pore man of no language only in the french havenge therin but a littell sight.' However, after Lady Rich's alterations to the text Lord Rich seemed to be admitting that he had the pox. The altered version reads: 'as yo[u]r lo[rdship] wel knoweth [I] am a pore man of no language only in the french ^desease^ havenge but a littell ^under^ sight ^with coming over^.' The humour of the letter also works materially through the subverting of manuscript conventions. In the letter, Penelope Rich hijacked her husband's use of deferential space. Where Rich had left an honorific gap between the last line of his letter and his signature, Lady Rich inserted a postscript, appropriating the manuscript space for her own purpose: to playfully remark to her brother, 'you may imagin my lo[rd] Riche hath no imploiment for a langusist secretary exsept he hath gotten a mistris in France.'[56] Lady Rich's mockery of her husband is pronounced, distancing her from the ideal of wifely obedience. Yet while Lady Rich and a handful of other female letter-writers are perhaps marked out from other women by the verve and inventiveness with which they indited their epistles, she is, as has been witnessed, far from exceptional in her willingness to question and flex the boundaries of male authority. Indeed, this and other letters indicate greater levels of female confidence, tenacity, and forcefulness in writing to men than might previously have been suspected.

Epistolary diatribe could equally be levelled against women, both relations and non-family members. Lady Anne Jermyn expressed her malice directly to Anne Spring, daughter of Margaret, countess of Bath, for publicly disdaining herself and her husband: 'troble yo[u]r self no more in wrytinge unto me of yo[u]r doings for you shall be well assured I will never speak nor do in yo[u]r behalf yf I may speak or do to the contrary.'[57] In response to this missive, the countess of Bath corresponded with Lady Jermyn on her daughter's behalf, denying allegations that either of them had abused Lady Jermyn's husband. The countess rather sarcastically informed Anne Jermyn that: '. . . you needed not to have written of your husbands poverty for his wealth is knowne to all the contrye [county] and for byting and eating of you I think nobody mindeth the same, for you are too old and tough to be eaten or bitten. I shall find better meate. your tauntes be too much and if you wiste how littel they are estemed you wold not waste penne and ink about them.'[58] Caustic writing of this nature directed towards other women is by no means exceptional for sixteenth-century women's letters. Elite women through letter-writing appear to have engaged in the type of vituperative personal battles characteristic of oral street culture so vividly described by Laura Gowing, though without the emphasis on female sexual honour, and importantly not in the street.[59]

MOTHERS AND DAUGHTERS

In studying female interaction—a subject increasingly preoccupying scholars of gender—analysis of modes of address and the tone of letters permits an examination of women's relations with other women, both older and younger and of differing social status.[60] Letters from daughters to mothers, as with those from sons, can sometimes read as rather restrained, as writers outwardly displayed filial obedience. A letter from Jane Long to her mother the countess of Bath was very formally written: in it she 'humbly' remembered her duty, 'beseeched' her mother for her 'daily blessing', 'advertised' her of her sister's health and that of all

---

[56] 'Essex Letter Book': 23/12/1596.   [57] Hengrave, 88/I, fo. 116: 07/08/1558.
[58] Ibid., fo. 117: 07/08/1558.   [59] Gowing, *Domestic Dangers*.
[60] Harris, 'Sisterhood, Friendship', 21–50; Frye and Robertson, *Maids and Mistresses*.

the family, apologized that she sent no token ('the wante thereof is poverty'), and signed herself 'your moste obedient dowghter'.[61] Anne Bacon (née Gresham), apologizing to her stepmother Lady Anne that she had not written as often as duty bound her, hoped that she would not take this as ill-meant.[62] Likewise, Elizabeth Cavendish wrote in deferential terms to her mother Bess of Hardwick: 'Good madame hauinge no betar menes to manifast mi thanckefolnes to youer onar bot bi thes lines i umbli pra your ladiship to axsept them and ine theme mi reuerant thanckes for youer onares mani ande gret fauoueres.'[63] The formality of Anne Basset's adolescent letters sent to her mother Lady Lisle from the de Riou household in France where she was boarded, similarly reflects the social differentiation between an early Tudor daughter and her mother. This is well illustrated by a letter penned for Anne by one of the de Riou family scribes in March 1536:

Madame, As humbly as I may have me always recommended to your good grace. Madame, I have received the letter it hath pleased you to write me, by the which I am very glad to hear good news of you. ... Madame, I humbly thank you for all your kindness shewed unto me, which is more than my deserving is. Madame, I would beseech you to send me some linen to make me smocks, which shall not be so thin as that which you last sent me, with some pairs of hosen, and a little money for my devotions. Madame, you write me to know if my lady have a mind to anything, I have made enquiry but can nothing discover that she would have save a little needlecase, which is a thing wherein one putteth needles.[64]

While the scribal process may well have accentuated social hierarchies, the reiteration of 'Madame' throughout the letter, and the deferential way in which requests are made, also serve to reinforce the strict boundaries of the mother–daughter relationship. The obedient tone of these early letters might be contrasted with a letter that Anne sent her mother a couple of years later, during her appointment as a maid-of-honour, in which she wrote with much greater assurance and confidence: 'I perceive that you think that I am at the Court, and that your pleasure is that I shall sue to the King's Highness for the pardon of John Harris. It is not possible that I should speak for his pardon, for Mistress Mewtas and I are now at Guildford, going to London; and I think we shall not see the King again till his Grace come to Grafton . . .'[65]

[61] Hengrave, 88/2, fo. 129: 29/10/n.y.   [62] Folger, L.d.16: *c*.1572.

[63] Folger, X.d.428 (50): [1574]. Elizabeth Cavendish was Bess's daughter by her husband Sir William Cavendish. See also X.d.428 (51). The countess also received deferential letters from her daughters Frances Pierepont (née Cavendish) and Mary (née Cavendish) as well as from her stepdaughters, Grace (née Talbot) and Katherine (née Talbot), and Anne Talbot (née Herbert), wife of her stepson Francis: X.d.428 (67, 68, 118, 119, 78); Hunter, *History of Hallamshire* (1869), 113; X.d.428 (121, 122).

[64] *Lisle Letters*, iii. 592: 24/03/1536. See also iii. 573, 578, 584. A similar deferential style is evident in letters from Mary Basset (1522/5–98), Honor Lisle's youngest daughter: iii. 575, 587, 590, 597a, 615, 617, 619, 620, 622a, 623a, 624.

[65] Ibid., v. 1513: 08/08/1539. See also v. 1126: 15/03/1538.

Attempts by daughters to recover maternal favour also accentuated social differences, as a means of fostering reconciliation. Thus, Anne Radcliffe, countess of Sussex, in a rambling letter to her mother Lady Calthorp wrote in grovelling terms, craving her mother's natural love, and seeking to defend herself against accusations of adultery.[66] Margaret Kitson too wrote in an overly respectful manner to her mother Lady Elizabeth Kitson asking for forgiveness. Margaret's missive presented herself in a manner that conformed to conventional precepts of filial obedience. Humbly submitting to her mother's will, and asking for her forgiveness on bended knee, Margaret argued that in future she would play the model daughter in accordance with Lady Kitson's commandments, 'specially', she claimed '. . . haveinge nowe of late redde the very same (your commandmentes) a mongeste the preceptes and rules of the wyse Cato expressed in these words *deo supplica, ama parentes, Magistrum metue*,[67] the which in efecte are the very three preceptes wherof you did chefly admonish me at Hengrave. I trust they are nowe so setled in my breaste that I hope never hearafter to be forgetfull of them.'[68] This letter illustrates what Alison Wall has noted for the Thynnes, that women were fully aware of the behavioural codes that sought to regulate their conduct—in this instance, daughterly respect rather than wifely obedience—and that they gave them expression in their correspondence. While a 'voice' of filial obedience was a useful cultural script for certain social situations or interactions, itself suggestive of the prevalence of authoritarian social attitudes in Tudor England, the extent to which these codes were internalized ('settled in' women's 'breasts') is, however, harder to discern.

Behind the conventions of daughterly reverence, women's letters to their mothers could in fact be open and intimate, much more so than letters to fathers. Daughters discussed with their mothers personal matters of some delicacy. While at court Elizabeth Talbot, the future wife of Henry Grey, earl of Kent, wrote a small note home in which she confidentially described to her mother Mary, countess of Shrewsbury, the health-related problems that she was suffering: 'I had yesterday a lettel payne in my lefte brest there was a letel harde knot that was red.'[69] Conventional mentions of one's good or ill health are commonplace in women's letters, yet the detail with which Elizabeth mentioned her condition is unusual in its intimacy, suggestive perhaps of her closeness with her mother. Elizabeth Wetherton, for her part, sent to her mother Elizabeth Wynnenton a letter written on a fragment of a printed breviary with plainsong notation; use of this improvised writing material conceivably indicates limited access to paper and the secretive nature of the epistle. Unhappy in the household in which she was currently placed, Elizabeth Wetherton discussed with her mother the

---

[66] BL, Cott., Vespasian, F.IX, fo. 115^r–117^v: 03/09/1549.

[67] This is a version of the opening lines of Cato, the standard schoolboy text for teaching Latin phrases: '*Itaque deo supplica*. So, pray to God. | *Parentes ama*. Love your parents. | *Cognatos cole*. Respect your kindred. | *Magistrum metue*. Fear (respect) your teacher.'

[68] Hengrave, 88/2, fo. 60, n.d.   [69] LPL, Shrewsbury, 708, fo. 169: 14/03/n.y.

prospect of her entering Lady Corbet's service, a matter that she had already mentioned to William Cecil. Her writing exhibits a fine balance of deference and forcefulness, dependence and self-reliance, as in her closing remarks: 'for god sake neuer will me to tare here no longer for you know not thynges so well as I do mother I desayre you not to fayle but sende me worde by this berer what youre will is.'[70]

Equally, Anne Clifford's correspondence to her mother Margaret, countess of Cumberland, although sometimes formal and respectful, reveals an attachment to and reliance upon her.[71] Her earliest surviving letter to her mother, written in late August 1605 at the age of 15, exhibits a mixture of filial reverence and conspiratorial address. Addressing her mother as 'Madone' and signing herself 'your La[dyship's] moost obedient and dutyfull daughter', Anne Clifford informed her that she would not be residing with Arbella Stuart in her chamber at court in Oxford as her mother had desired, relating to her that 'I haue had a gret dell, of talke, with my lord about that matter you knoe of, for that mache, and my lord hath promesed mee, that ther sholld nothing pase, for any marage, what so euer, but that your consent sholld bee asked'.[72] Most of her correspondence with her mother, however, survives from 1614 to 1616. The regularity with which the two women wrote to each other and the very length of their letters documents a strong, mutually supportive relationship. Anne's letters to her mother are packed with news of daily life: an account of her daughter's illness in one letter is followed by news of 'my Lord of Somerset and his Lady', which she claims is the wonder of the world.[73] Another letter described recent Christmas festivities at Bollbroke House, dealings between her husband and uncle, and ended announcing the birth of 'two fine pups'.[74] It is in her later letters, written during the protracted disputes with her uncle Francis, fourth earl of Cumberland, over her lands of inheritance that the procedure of writing to her mother appears to have facilitated for Anne Clifford the sorting out, ordering, and articulating of her thoughts and problems on paper. The relationship with her mother glimpsed in these letters is a close one; they were penned at a time when she was under enormous pressure from her husband, the earl of Dorset, to come to what for her would have been an unfavourable arrangement with her uncle. In a letter of 6 December 1615 she reported her husband's continued efforts to take money and force a settlement with her 'uncle of Cumberland'; she 'beseeched' her mother not to trouble herself, for 'so long as you live and are there, there is still hope for me'.[75] Anne seems to have utilized her letters to her mother as a way of exploring her relationship with her husband and the

---

[70] SP46/24/91: 02/11/[temp. Mary/Eliz].

[71] WD/Hoth/Box 44. Hodgkin, 'Diary of Lady Anne Clifford', 148–61.

[72] WD/Hoth/Box 44: 08/1605. Williamson, *Lady Anne Clifford*, pl. 8. The 'match' here probably refers to her first husband Richard Sackville, Lord Buckhurst, whom she later married in 1610.   [73] WD/Hoth/Box 44: 10/11/1615.

[74] Ibid., 01/1615.   [75] Ibid., 06/12/1615.

possibility of marital separation. In one letter she explained to her mother that her husband had threatened to leave her and to go and live in France if she did not drop her claims for the Clifford lands and accept a financial settlement. Forced to decide between her husband and her rightful inheritance, Anne wrote to her mother seeking counsel and laying out her various options for manoeuvre:

I am noue in a naroe strate and knoe not which way to turne mysellfe. my Coussen Russell wolld haue mee doe it, and uses all the parswasions hee can to that ende hee hathe sente you a leter to that purpos . . . I beecich you sende mee an aunser with as much speede as you can for I shall bee ernestley prest to doe it, or ellse absolutley to denie it, which will make cich [such] a breche beetwene my Lorde and mee as will not eseley bee mended. I will doe nothing with out your La[dyship's] knolledge therfor I beecich you let mee knoe your resolucion as son as possable you may.[76]

In some senses then, letters provided women with a sounding-board for ideas and arguments; read carefully, with attention to rhetoric and purpose, such documents can offer insights into women's thought and planning.

Margaret Clifford's own side of the correspondence reveals her role in supporting her daughter throughout the difficulties with her husband over the disputed inheritance. In a letter that ran to six sides, the countess of Cumberland attempted to strengthen her daughter's resolve in the matter. She pressed Anne not to pass away her inheritance, stating in confessional terms that once it is done, 'your soro can not recalle you and yours shall ever repent'. Later in the letter the countess addresses head-on her daughter's concern and misery that as a wife she is being unfaithful in crossing her husband in this manner: 'for in wat estate so evry yo bein', she wrote, 'ther ar and will be som discontiments with land and without land, with a howsbant, and without, on tille we injoy that most bliset howsbant Jesus Christ.'[77] In the years after her husband's death the countess of Cumberland devoted much of her energy to working towards the restitution of her daughter's estates.[78] She wrote on 30 July 1615, 'I most lok forder, bouth for you and my selfe and as on writes ther is som resulucion in the femallys'.[79] Close to death, Margaret Clifford wrote to her 'der dauter' telling her of her illness, and even to the end strove to galvanize Anne's resolution, committing her to God who would give her the strength to endure and overcome; the letter is touchingly endorsed in Anne Clifford's own handwriting, 'the last leter which I reseved from my dear mother of her own hand writinge, it beeing towards the later end of Aprell 1616', a conscious textual monument to their affectionate relationship.[80]

---

[76] Ibid., 20/01/1616.   [77] Ibid., 14/01/1616.

[78] George Clifford (d. 1605): Clifford, *Collectanea Cliffordiana*, 28.

[79] WD/Hoth/Box 44: 30/07/1615.

[80] Ibid., 16/04/1616. Margaret Clifford died 24 May 1616, and was buried in Appleby Church on 11 July: Williamson, *George Third Earl of Cumberland*, 303–4.

Other Tudor mothers wrote to their daughters offering emotional and material support during times of particular need, adversity, and uncertainty. Alice Marvin wrote to encourage her daughter Elizabeth Bourne during a period of marital difficulty with her husband Anthony Bourne, promising to 'wryte to make suche frends as I can for the favo[u]r of yo[u]r cause'. Despite Anthony's attempts to win Lady Marvin to his side in the dispute, she assured her daughter of her backing: 'his despytes cannot more move me, then the vomyting of a dronken man, or the raving of a madde man.'[81] Mothers' letters to daughters could also be relaxed and affectionate: Anne Fitton wrote to her daughter Anne Newdigate ('My owne dere nan'), sending the bearer to hear news of 'howe you and your cheekynes [chickens] doo'; and in a postscript to a letter from her husband Edward, she informed her daughter 'this letter must do from us both', writing that she hoped to hear from her soon, promising herself to send any good news.[82] Amidst discussions of provisioning and household servants, a letter from Isabella Foxe to her married daughter Margaret Herbert informed her that her sister Martha was delivered of a daughter, and discussed details of who were to stand as godparents at the christening.[83]

Expressions of maternal longing are also common in correspondences between mothers and daughters, displaying the affective or positive emotional bonds present in these relationships, often obscured by social custom and familial obligation. Indeed, epistolary exchanges frequently developed from desires to maintain contact with family. Elizabeth Talbot wrote to her daughter Mary Lady Talbot asking to hear of her situation: 'I pray you let me heare this nighte how you and your good lorde dothe else shall I not slepe quiatly.'[84] Likewise, Agnes Mordant, anxious to obtain news of her daughter, sent a letter to her son-in-law Nicholas Williamson, writing, 'I wold be very glad to here howe you doe for I wold desire you to send me word by this messenger for I haue sent unto your wyfe to knowe how she dothe but the messenger is not retorned'.[85] These letters further indicate that conducting domestic correspondence fulfilled women's emotional needs to receive news of the health, life, and progress of relatives and other social contacts.

MOTHERS- AND DAUGHTERS-IN-LAW

The openness and intimacy possible in correspondence between mothers and daughters often contrasts with the reserve and relative formality of women's letters to mothers-in-law. Lucy, marchioness of Winchester's invitation to her mother-in-law, the dowager marchioness, to her child's christening was formal

[81] BL, Addit., 23212, fo. 195: n.d.   [82] WCRO, CR136/B120a: n.d.
[83] *Herbert Correspondence*, ed. Smith, 65–6 [*c*.1600–10].   [84] Talbot, 3205, fo. 64: n.d.
[85] SP46/48/51: n.d.

and cordial: 'madam my l[ord] and my selfe should thinke our selues very happy amongest other our good frindes to inioye y[ou]r ladiships presence being the worthiest of all the rest at the christening of our child vppon thursday next.' Beyond the formulaic invitation that it imparted, the letter carefully broached the question of whether or not the dowager would in fact be able to attend, without causing offence: 'Madam notwthstanding the comfort wee should receiue if yt shall please you to vouchsaue the paines to doe vs the favor and honor to be heere at that time, yet doe we not forgett the care wee ought to haue of y[ou]r la[dyshi]ps health and weake estate of body at this time of yeere especially. And therefore wee leaue the consideracon and disposicon of this our desire to y[ou]r la[dyshi]ps good pleasure.'[86] Likewise, Anne Lady Bray's letter to Jane, Dowager Lady Bray was courteous; requests were cloaked in a vocabulary of polite entreaty. At one point in her letter Lady Bray 'beseeched' her mother-in-law to send her servant William Gaylor when convenient.[87] In both cases, the daughters-in-law had inherited the family title along with their husbands upon the death of their fathers-in-law, which elevated their social standing; nevertheless, their letters to their widowed mothers-in-law indicate the respect and deference that these senior women commanded.

Friction between mothers-in-law and daughters-in-law, however, was also common, particularly where both women resided under the same roof; this was a fairly widespread occurrence during the sixteenth century, as newly wedded wives often spent the first part of their married lives living with their husbands' family. Joan Thynne, for example, complained to her husband John early on in their marriage of the way in which she was treated by her mother-in-law.[88] Perhaps the most striking rift between a mother- and daughter-in-law is that between Joan and her own daughter-in-law, Maria Thynne (née Audley), a relationship which Alison Wall has so carefully documented and analysed.[89] Their fraught relationship, which was at best strained and at worst abusive, can be studied through a series of correspondences over several years, written in the wake of Maria's clandestine marriage to Joan's son Thomas Thynne, a hasty match that greatly angered the Elizabethan matriarch.[90] Aware of her mother-in-law's great displeasure and the need to placate her, Maria wrote several apologetic letters to Joan in which she sought reconciliation, and at the same time maintained her innocence. 'If I did know that my thoughts had ever entertained any unreverent conceit of you (my good mother)', she wrote in September 1601, 'I should be much ashamed so impudently to importune your good opinion as I have done by many entreating lines, but having been ever embouldened with the knowledge of my unspotted innocence.' The letter itself

[86] BL, Harl., 4713, fo. 277: 01/03/1600. See also 4713, fo. 266: 1600.
[87] Talbot, 3205, fo. 26: 17/07/1553.　　　[88] *Two Elizabethan Women*, 2: 07/12/1576.
[89] Wall, 'Elizabethan Precept', 23–38; ead., 'Deference and Defiance', 77–93.
[90] Wall, 'For Love, Money or Politics?', 511–33.

contains a lock of Maria's red hair under the seal, material testimony of the writer's desire for conciliation.[91]

The situation changed, however, on the death of Joan's husband in 1604, when Maria and her husband Thomas inherited the family lands; Maria, not Joan, was now mistress of Longleat, a shift in social position that altered the balance of power between the two women. The only surviving correspondence between them that survives from this time is a rather striking letter from Maria, which is bereft of the deference and subservience of her earlier missives. Written in response to Joan's complaints about the way in which Maria was neglecting the gardens of Longleat, the letter openly and brutally insults her mother-in-law, describing her as an 'odious' and 'corpulent' grandmother who she suspected 'soiled' her land with her own 'manure':

Indeed, if you or your heirs have an expectation in reversion of Longleat house or garden, there were reason your speak should pass currant without offence or exception. But being as it is, methinks you should not unkindly intermeddle, more than Mr Thynne doth with all your lands of inheritance. I confess (without shame) it is true my garden is too ruinous, and yet to make you more merrier you shall be of my counsel, that my intent is, before it be better, to make it worse. For, finding that great expense can never alter it from being like a porridge pot, nor never by report was like other, I intend to plough it up and sow all variety of fruit at a fit season. I beseech you laugh, and so will I at your captiousness. Now, whereas you write your ground put to basest uses, is better manured than my garden, surely if it were a grandmother of my own and equal to myself by birth, I should answer that odious comparison with telling you I believe so corpulent a Lady cannot but do much yourself towards the soiling of land, and I think that hath been, and will be all the good you intend to leave behind you at Corsley.[92]

While Maria's superior social position enabled her to unleash such invective, having no need to play the sycophantic daughter-in-law anymore, the letter itself viewed within the context of her other correspondence reveals her as one of the most erudite, flamboyant, and menacingly acerbic of early modern female letter-writers.

FEMALE CORRESPONDENCE NETWORKS: KIN AND FRIENDS

Despite the relative ease with which scholars might catalogue disputes between female relations, many women corresponded freely and unreservedly with other female family members and circles of female friends, women to whom they were emotionally attached, and from whom they derived support. Anne Newdigate had several female correspondents, including her mother, her sister Mary, Arbella

---

[91] *Two Elizabethan Women*, 21: 15/09/1601. See also letters 33, 39, 41, 43, 46: 24/02/1602–14/05/1603.　　　　　　　　　　　　　　　　　　　[92] Ibid. 34: 24/02/1602.

Stuart, the diarist Lady Margaret Hoby, and Lady Elizabeth Grey. The last-named was a frequent correspondent; her epistles to Lady Newdigate resonate with sentiments of friendship. Thanking Anne for her letters, Elizabeth Grey wrote, 'I holde it the greatest happines I can in ioy to see your thoughts and so faithfully exspresed to mee'.[93] As further witness of her friendship she informed her in another letter that 'I finde it much comfort to my thoughts to see you in my letters for never can my ies [eyes] ore hart see ore thinke ore [*sic*] any liuinge that can be more deere to me'.[94] A letter from Mildred Marey complained about the fact that now that she was going into the country she would be unable to hear from her so often, hoping that there would be 'som mene or other that we both may write one to the other'.[95]

A series of lengthy, intimate, almost chatty letters survive from Meryell Littleton, the widow of John Littleton of Frankley, Worcestershire, to her aunt Lady Muriel Knyvett, in which she openly discussed topics ranging from legal affairs, health, religion, and household matters to family events, such as births, marriages, and deaths.[96] The relaxed informality of the epistolary relationship between aunt and niece is disclosed by the prolixity of the letters, which often run to two or three sides of paper: one letter was brought to a conclusion with the lines, 'I dare not wandar any further lest I know not how to end beinge unwillinge to bid my good aunt adwe'; the purpose of another, she claimed, was to 'present my loue by thes lines of paper'.[97] Another thanked Lady Muriel for her own 'louinge l[ett]re' which she informed her 'gaue me more content then all the obieckts w[hi]ch I haue met w[i]t[h] in this sittye for that the[y] ar the pledges of your Lastinge Affection w[hi]ch hath evar bin to me a dear juell'.[98] Heightened though this stylized language of family affection may be, the emotional hyperbole of Meryell Littleton's letters should not shroud the relative freedom and openness with which she corresponded with her aunt. Complaining of the expense of her sons' education she wrote: 'I haue this springe sent my eldest sonn to Oxenford my other two sonns to a free skooll God Allmighty send yt may be for ther good and my comfort. more charge I haue found yt then happily others will beleeue or truly I did my self expeckt. yt is a deare time good Auntt to trayn vppe youth in. techars aske much and thes times aparill requir to to much.'[99] Her letters to her aunt, in addition to acting as repositories of family news, performed a more personal, cathartic or purgative function, enabling her to unburden herself of anxieties, fears, and worries. Writing after the death of her husband, Meryell Littleton discussed in great detail with her aunt the legal disputes arising from her husband's will: 'I can not be silent vnto my good Aunte of my own trobles. I am put in hope my tender busines shall shortly com to an

---

[93] WCRO, CR136/B169.
[94] Ibid., CR136/B174: n.d. See also B177.   [95] Ibid., CR136/B272.
[96] BL, Eg., 2714, fos. 194, 300–1; Eg., 2715, fos. 93, 96, 101, 114, 129: 1602–12.
[97] Ibid., fos. 300–1: 16/06/1603; Eg., 2715, fo. 114: 29/06/1610.
[98] BL, Eg., 2715, fo. 129: 12/02/1612.   [99] Ibid., fo. 114: 29/06/1610.

end. and then farewell london for it hath wel near begared me. mucha doe I haue had with your old frend Mr Attorny and as hard mesure offered me as euar was to any in my vnfortunate estate. comessions vpon comessions . . .'[100] Her purpose in writing was not material—it was not her aunt's influence or assistance she sought—but rather to share with her the tergiversations of her life. She 'imparted' news of 'owr good kinges graciousnes vnto me' in order that her aunt might 'reioyce and prays Aulmighty God for my better fortunes';[101] in the same way she wrote, 'I partake w[i]th you in the joy for the great belly my cozin Paston hath'.[102]

Further evidence of the closeness of female relationships is abundant: Margaret Lady Verney implored Mary Lady Talbot for a portrait by which to remember her: 'I haue no hope to see you in the coentery and therfore must stile continew my shut [suit] for your picture w[hi]ch is won of the chieffest things that I shall beholde w[i]th delite in your absens.'[103] Jane Bolde wrote to her sister Anne Williamson, stating that 'I was greatlie trobeled w[i]th dreaminge of yow w[hi]ch caused me to feare greatlye yow were not well'.[104] The evident ease and directness of those letters dispatched to female correspondents illustrates the possible warmth of female friendships, suggesting that women were sometimes more comfortable writing to women than to men, and perhaps less inhibited in laying bare their feelings and dealing with confidential subjects.

The uncovering of early modern women's alliances offers a plausible alternative to the narrative of women 'identified with and serving men and male interests', yet female networks did not exist in isolation but, as Barbara Harris has shown, 'coexisted' and were compatible with primary loyalties to the patrilineages of women's marital families.[105] Female alliances, while not exclusive, were useful to women in numerous ways, and many women assiduously maintained links, sustaining these 'horizontal' ties through letters, visits, and the exchange of favours and gifts. Female contacts were useful in placing girls either at court or in aristocratic households, and in arranging marriages; they also provided material and emotional support during legal disputes, and offered emotional and material support during pregnancy and childbirth.

Anne Lady Hungerford appears to have gained much comfort from writing to her sister Jane, duchess of Feria, and her lady-in-waiting, Dorothy Essex, at a time when she was engaged in a protracted lawsuit with her estranged husband Sir Walter Hungerford, who in 1568 sued for divorce on the grounds that she had committed adultery with William Darrell; Hungerford also claimed that she had attempted to poison him in 1564.[106] In a lengthy letter to Dorothy Essex,

---

[100] BL, Eg., 2714, fo. 194: 03/05/1602. [101] Ibid., fo. 300: 16/06/1603.
[102] BL, Eg., 2715, fo. 114: 29/06/1610. [103] Talbot, 3205, fo. 42: 04/08/n.y.
[104] SP46/49/26: 02/07/1589. [105] Harris, 'Sisterhood, Friendship', 21–50.
[106] Letters between Anne Hungerford and Darrell, her 'good will', survive, which may lend some credence to Walter Hungerford's accusations: SP46/44 (Darrell Papers), fos. 186, 188, 190–1, 194–4d, 196–7. Hall, *Society in the Elizabethan Age*, 260–3; Bindoff, *Commons*, ii. 413–14.

she lamented her desperate situation, that Hungerford had charged her with murder, adultery, and attempted poisoning and refused to pay her charges, that she had not heard of her children for a year, and that her daughter Susan had forgotten how to read: 'Oh my deare Doll what endelles messeres I live in. O what frendes had I that this most wrechedly hathe utterly caste me and all mine away. I am not abell to write ye one quarter of my troubles whiche I have indured.'[107] A shorter missive to her sister Jane complained that her husband refused to pay her any living expenses, for which he was imprisoned in the Fleet, and that she was cut off from her children.[108]

Furthermore, female family members and friends commonly corresponded with women during periods of pregnancy, and those unable to assist in person at the time of childbirth regularly wrote offering comfort and reassurance. Lady Elizabeth Grey, hearing of the ill-health of the expectant Anne Newdigate, sent a soothing letter to her relation, writing, 'I hope noue to heere of your safe delyure [delivery]'.[109] Lady Sidney whilst pregnant on the continent received a letter from her sister, Mary, countess of Pembroke, wishing that 'god send you a goodly boy'. Lady Herbert also attempted to dispel her sister's worries concerning the use of a foreign wetnurse, offering her instead the services of a 'most quiet and careful' English nurse who, she stated, could be shipped over from England.[110] Lady Anne Bacon, the acknowledged illegitimate daughter of Sir Thomas Gresham, discussed with her stepmother Anne Gresham the possibility that she might be pregnant: 'I myself am somwhat sickly Some p[er]swade me, yt it is to a good end. My owne experience as yo[u]r La[dyship] knoweth is small to iudg. Suer I am ther is yet no certaeintie of yt.'[111] With her pregnancy confirmed, Anne Bacon later wrote to her natural mother Mistress Dutton thanking her for 'linnen cloth', and informing her: 'it is more, than was hetherto bestowed vpon me by any towardes my lyinge downe.'[112]

Although letter-writing could reinforce social distinctions between female correspondents and recipients through polite conventions of address, deferential language, use of manuscript space, and self-deprecating apologies for 'scribbled lines', what emerges from studying a broad range of women's correspondences is the complexity of women's emotional lives and the range in quality of relationships they experienced: distant and familiar, hostile and passionate. As indicators of the differing intensities of individual relationships, letters yield confident, deferential, personal, privy, and powerful forms of expression, and display an array of feelings and emotions. Positions of social and familial authority conferred status and authority on women, bequeathing them a voice of command, counsel, and censure that was directed towards men as well as

---

[107] SP15/18/19: 25/03/1570.   [108] SP15/18/14: 20/03/1570
[109] WCRO, CR136/B170: n.d.   [110] BL, Addit., 15232, fo. 1: 09/09/1590.
[111] Folger, L.d.18: 03/02/1573. Jardine and Stewart, *Hostage to Fortune*, 30, 33, 38; *Papers of Nathaniel Bacon*, ed. Hassell Smith *et al.*, i. *passim*.   [112] Folger, L.d.20: 06/1573.

women, and both within and outside of the family. Indeed, sixteenth-century women's correspondence reveals in practice a striking degree of female independence, confidence, and forcefulness; women operated within the confines of male authority, and simultaneously transgressed restrictive codes of female submission, testing and flexing the parameters of their subordination. Above all, what marks early modern women's letters is their variety and idiosyncrasy; penned by a vast range of women of different personalities, propensities, and backgrounds, such letters register the richness of individual experience.

8

Marital Correspondence

Letters written by married women offer a useful corrective to prescriptive texts, such as conduct books and sermons, which expound the values of wifely obedience and subordination. Although it is difficult to capture how sixteenth-century couples actually conversed with each other, letters offer some indication of the ways in which they communicated, albeit on paper, and the kinds of topics they discussed; wives' correspondence affords further insights into women's thoughts, attitudes, and opinions, and the nature of their responsibilities and interests during this period. Study of epistolary exchanges between couples permits comparison of women's and men's writing, in terms of modes of address, language, style, level of openness, and content. A primary concern here is the nature of correspondence, the manner in which couples expressed themselves to each other, whether mannered, customary, individualized, open, or intimate. Husbands, it will be argued, more frequently articulated emotion and affection in their correspondence than did wives, though equivalent expressions of warmth and endearment are evident in some women's letters. Furthermore, women's use of deferential language expressing wifely submissiveness could easily coexist with displays of affection, self-confidence and determination. Used as an indicator of the quality of early modern marriage, husbands' and wives' letters reveal the widespread existence of emotional as well as social, economic, and political bonds within marriage, and indicate mutual favourable expectations of conjugal relationships. This chapter highlights the variety and complexity of individual marital experience during the sixteenth century, the degrees of conjugal affection, love, and cooperation within relationships, and the development of particular relationships over time. The chapter also assesses the extent to which restrictive ideals of female behaviour were enforced in practice, mapping the location of power within marital relationships.

Moreover, the chapter argues for the complexity of marital correspondence as a source: seemingly spontaneous and personal, marital letters were sometimes collaborative and even sometimes scribally published; they are also often highly formulaic, following epistolary and rhetorical models, and register meaning both textually and by material forms. Letters between husbands and wives should, therefore, not be viewed merely as receptacles of unadorned historical fact or as social documents capable of reflecting individual subjectivity and unmediated emotion. Letter-writing within sixteenth-century marriages functioned as a pragmatic way of conducting business and conveying information; and yet increasingly over the course of the period letters between husbands and wives simultaneously performed more personal functions and assumed an emotional significance.

LETTERS AND LETTER-WRITERS: WIVES AND HUSBANDS

Women's marital correspondence represents one of the largest categories of familial epistles surviving for the sixteenth century: there are well over 200 extant letters dispatched by forty-six women during the period 1540 to 1603, making possible a re-evaluation of marital relations among the landed elite and mercantile groups. On the whole, the number of women corresponding with husbands increases over the period, with the 1570s marking a dramatic rise in numbers of wives writing.[1] However, a significant proportion of letters and several important collections of correspondence also survive for the earlier half of the period. These include for the mid-Tudor period the extensive Johnson correspondence, and the letters between Margaret, countess of Bath, and her husband John Bourchier, second earl of Bath, and the correspondence of Lord and Lady Lisle written during the 1530s.[2]

For many women only one or two letters to their husbands remain, which provide a mere snapshot of a specific moment within a relationship. Elizabeth Anthony's single letter to her husband, written during her last stages of pregnancy, is interesting for the fear and foreboding that it expresses at her impending child-labour: 'husband your long absence at this time hate [hath] bread shuch discontent in my mind that I canot be reed of it. You knowe that my time of payne and sorowe is nere and and I am unprovid of loging and other thinges nedfull.'[3] What a single letter cannot convey, though, is a picture of a particular relationship over time. However, various other writers left greater numbers of letters. Furthermore, several women's correspondence spans a number of years. Dorothy Gamage wrote a series of letters to her husband John between 1572 and 1582, and Frances Devereux's letters to Robert, earl of Essex, date from the period 1594 to 1599.[4] The correspondence of Margaret Clifford to her husband spans the 1580s and 1590s, while letters from Elizabeth Willoughby and Joan Thynne to their spouses cover most of their married lives.[5] The survival of extensive correspondences facilitates study of the development

---

[1] Over 80% of the surviving letters were written after 1570: 8% were written 1540–9; 6% 1550–59; 2% 1560–9; 17% 1570–9; 24% 1580–9; 26% 1590–9; 17% 1600–3.

[2] *L&P*, XX (i, ii), NA, SP46/5–7; CUL, Hengrave, 88/1; *Lisle Letters*, v.

[3] SP46/126/38: [temp Eliz].   [4] SP46/60; Hatfield House, Cecil, 4, 9; 'Essex Letter Book', MI 229.

[5] Kendal RO, WD/Hoth/Box 44; BL, Lansd., 46; HMC, *Middleton, passim*; Wall (ed.), *Two Elizabethan Women*.

and complexity of relationships over longer periods of time. Analysis thus moves away from marriage viewed schematically as a static institution, in terms of good or bad, loving or hostile matches, towards an approach which places greater emphasis upon fluctuations and shifts in spousal feelings and attachments. This more nuanced analysis highlights the pressures imposed on relationships by changes of fortune in business and husbands' careers, and the ways in which couples dealt with the main domestic events and upheavals in their lives: births, deaths, and separation.

A more balanced picture of particular marriages is possible where husbands' correspondence survives in addition to that of wives. In all almost a quarter of the cases of wives dispatching letters to husbands, the spouse's correspondence survives as well, enabling a comparison of female and male epistolary styles, conventions, and modes of address. For the period as whole, letters survive from over fifty different men writing to their wives, often with some regularity. Robert Sidney dispatched several hundred letters to his wife Barbara during the course of their married life.[6] Commonly, however, collections of marital correspondence tend to be one-sided. For example, whereas some twenty-seven of Dorothy Gamage's letters to her husband John survive, only one of his replies is extant. Nevertheless, for several couples the material is more evenly proportioned, such as the correspondence between Lord and Lady Lisle, John and Sabine Johnson, and the earl and countess of Bath, with large numbers of letters surviving for both parties. It is possible in these cases to re-create epistolary exchanges, and to view how both partners negotiated married life.

The social composition of the group of women for whom marital corres-pondence survives is diverse, comprising aristocratic women such as Margaret, countess of Cumberland, and Frances, countess of Essex, at one extreme, and merchants' wives, including Joan Herrick, wife of the London goldsmith William Herrick, and Katherine Mucklowe, wife of Richard Mucklowe, a Midlands cloth merchant, at the other. Not unsurprisingly, few if any examples of letters survive from plebeian women from the sixteenth century; although from church court records one can glimpse women lower down the social scale receiving love-letters during periods of courtship.[7] The majority of wives were of either noble or gentle status, and almost a quarter were women from middling groups.[8] As a source for looking at marriage, letters therefore privilege landed and urban elites. However, one can achieve a sense of the roles played by wives from divergent social groups.

Correspondence also displays women participating in marriage at different stages of their lives, including first marriages and remarriages. The importance of looking at the development of familial relationships over time, as individuals

---

[6] CKS, De L'Isle, U1475 C/81.

[7] O'Hara, 'Language of Tokens', 16; ead., *Courtship and Constraint*, 70–1.

[8] Overall, 41% of wives for whom examples of marital correspondence survives were members of the nobility; 35% were gentlewomen; 24% merchants' wives.

pass through different stages of the life-cycle, has been emphasized by several historians of the family.[9] Barbara Harris has argued for the importance of paying attention to the 'uxorial lifecycle' as a useful paradigm for studying the shifting power relations within early modern marriages between husbands and wives. Thus, the experience of newly married women, who often lived with their parents-in-law for the first few years of married life, was very different from that of women who had been married for a considerable length of time, or women who married two or three times; maturity, experience, gained confidence, and indeed wealth all worked to affect the social dynamics of women's self-perception and how they negotiated individual relationships.[10] Conversely, women entering first marriages tended to be younger and less experienced, and were therefore in a weaker position to exert power and influence; later in life, as mothers of male heirs, wives gained in maternal and social status.[11]

The personal development that individual women underwent as they journeyed through different stages of the life-cycle is well illustrated by the example of Joan Thynne, whose letters to her husband John cover the period from their initial courtship in 1575 to his death in 1604. Her early letters before and immediately after the arranged marriage to John Thynne are on the whole, short, perfunctory, and formal; aged 18, a merchant's daughter who had married into a leading Wiltshire gentry family, she wrote complaining to John about the way she was treated by his mother: 'almost daily my Lady keeps her accustomed courtesy towards me which I may count a hell to heavenly joys or such a lady's love that will force me to leave this country.'[12] The letters from the 1590s and early 1600s, at which point Joan had been married for nearly two or three decades, register a woman far removed from the inexperienced teenager of the early correspondence; instead we are confronted by a strident Elizabethan gentlewoman acting in the capacities of wife, mother, landowner, and mistress of Longleat and Caus Castle. A letter dating from 1602 written from Caus Castle, the ownership of which had been ferociously disputed by Lord Stafford, reveals Joan's managerial and advisory roles and confidence: 'This day divers of the jury were here for the view of the castle ... whose indifference you need not fear if there be any truth in men.'[13]

In addition, levels of affection, expectation, and outlook within marriage may also have varied with age. One might compare the sober counsel and business advice of the mature Elizabeth Sutton to her second husband Sir Thomas Sutton, founder of Charterhouse Hospital, with the youthful, innocent pleadings of Anne, countess of Oxford, to her errant husband Edward de Vere, a former ward of

---

[9] Hareven, 'Impact of the History of the Family', 317–44; Beer, 'Private Correspondence', 947–8.

[10] Harris, 'Space, Time', 245–64.

[11] Early marriage was far commoner at the top of society; first-time brides of the nobility, gentry, and urban elites were two to ten years younger than their counterparts among plebeian women: Houlbrooke, *English Family*, 65; Hollingsworth, 'Demography of the British Peerage'; O'Hara, *Courtship and Constraint*, 175, 178; Wrigley, 'Age at Marriage', 219–34.

[12] *Two Elizabethan Women*, 2: 07/12/1576.   [13] Ibid., 27: 21/06/1602.

her father Lord Burghley.[14] In both cases the epistolary voice of the wife is also shaped by circumstance, and by a range of variables such as personality, character, social status, and religion, which points to the importance of analysing correspondences and the individual relationships they document within a historical and biographical context.

MODES OF ADDRESS

Historians of the 'sentiments school' of family history have in the past studied opening and closing epistolary modes of address in an attempt to look at the nature of early modern relationships, and the degrees of detachment and rigidity, intimacy and affection that characterized early modern spousal relations.[15] The degree of formality or informality with which husbands and wives wrote to one another has thus been taken as an index of the 'quality' of marriage; it also registers the extent to which restrictive patriarchal gender codes enforcing wifely subservience and subordination could be gently eroded within a marital context. The starting-point for many historians looking at the meaning of marriage as an institution is contemporary prescriptive writings, which instructed wives to address husbands with humility and respect; familiarity and use of pet names were deemed to be inappropriate for women. Indeed, early seventeenth-century Puritan writers warned wives against orally employing first names, contractions of Christian names, such as 'Jack', 'Tom', 'Will', and 'Hal', or affectionate terms such as 'Sweet', 'Sweeting', 'Sweet-Heart', 'Heart', 'Love', 'Joy', 'Dear', 'Duck', 'Chick', and 'Pigsnie'.[16] William Whately, in *A Bride-Bush* (1617), wrote that 'the wife must expresse reuerence towards her husband in her speeches and gestures before him'.[17] Influenced largely by his reading of this conduct literature, Lawrence Stone asserted a high degree of formality in modes of address between husbands and wives during the sixteenth and seventeenth centuries, which supported his model of emotional detachment within marriage in this period.[18] He further argued for widespread use of deferential modes by wives, which he interpreted as 'concrete symbols of patriarchy in the family', material representations of wifely subordination within the household.[19] More recently, Ralph Houlbrooke has convincingly shown that more personal and informal salutations were in fact utilized, especially by men, from the sixteenth century onwards.[20] Several issues, however, remain unexplored: the extent to which wives

---

[14] GLRO, 1876/F/3/7/1–3, 5–6, F/3/7/2/68, 70: 1600–2; BL, Lansd., 104, fo. 164: 07/12/1581.

[15] Stone, *Family, Sex and Marriage*, 198, 329–30, 413–15, 668; Houlbrooke, *English Family*, 100–1, 104, 170.

[16] Gouge, *Of Domestical Dvties* (1622), 283. Houlbrooke, *English Family*, 100–1; Wall, 'Deference and Defiance', 77–93. Puritan discouragement of terms of endearment may been a reaction to what went on in actual practice.   [17] p. 39.

[18] Stone, *Family, Sex and Marriage*, 329–30.   [19] Ibid., 198–9.

[20] Houlbrooke, *English Family*, 100–1, 104.

adopted informal modes of address; how far phraseology was merely conventional; and thus, whether opening and closing epistolary forms represent an appropriate indicator of the quality of marital relationships. There has also been little attempt to explain why husbandly salutations became increasingly individualized over the period.

A study of sixteenth-century marital correspondence further indicates greater informality and affection in modes of address employed by wives as well as husbands than has been previously assumed. Only 26 per cent of women addressed their husbands formally in writing: using surnames, for example 'Mr Bacon', 'Mr Sutton', and 'Mr Gresham'; referring to their spouses as 'worshipful bedfellow'; or merely opening with 'my hearty commendations'. By far the dominant mode of address employed by wives during the sixteenth century, however, was an impersonal form, such as 'husband' and 'lord', softened by the use of more intimate, endearing terms: 'my loving husband', 'my sweet lord', and 'my own dere lord'.[21] Salutations of this nature, which account for over 50 per cent of letters surveyed, illustrate the widespread use of warmer modes of address by wives. Furthermore, significant numbers of women, some 17 per cent, utilised terms of endearment or more egalitarian forms of Christian names, such as 'mine own', 'dere heart', and 'sweet Bas'. Joan Herrick wrote to her husband William as 'Sweet Hart'; Frances Devereux named her husband 'dere life'; and Frances, countess of Hertford, teasingly called her husband 'sweet slouen'.[22] Wives often varied the form of address employed: on different occasions Lady Lisle wrote to her husband as 'Mine own sweet heart', 'Good mine own', 'Mine own sweet heart root', and 'Good sweet heart', spontaneously using variations of the same phrase, in spite of the fact that her letters were penned by a secretary.[23] Such examples display a variety and individuality that clearly deviated from the cold formulae of conduct books. Letter-writers chose nuanced phrases specifically to convey an express sense of the closeness or warmth within a relationship.

The increasing usage of relaxed and intimate modes of address becomes more pronounced in contrast to late medieval epistolary forms, which, influenced by the *ars dictaminis*, were generally more formal and impersonal, and narrow in vocabulary, thereby accentuating the apparent distance between husband and wife. For example, in 1484 Margaret Cely wrote to her husband as 'Ryght [re]uer[en]d and worchupfull Ser'; Jane Stonor, corresponding slightly earlier, addressed her husband Thomas merely as 'Syr'.[24] While medieval epistolary modes of address were almost always formal, impersonal forms are evident

---

[21] The term 'bedfellow' was neither endearing nor romantic, but rather descriptive; it merely referred to the fact that two people slept in the same bed. Indeed, male servants who shared the same bed could also be described as bedfellows: Folger, X.d.428 (9): n.d.

[22] Bodl., Herrick, Eng Hist., 484, fo. 18: n.d.; Cecil, 21, fo. 1: 1591; Longleat House, Seymour Papers, 5, fos. 144–5: 09/06/*c.*1584. [23] *Lisle Letters*, v. 1262, 1264, 1294, 1544.

[24] *Cely Letters*, ed. Hanham, 222: [*c.*14/09/1484]; *Stonor Letters*, ed. Kingsford, i. 62–3, 109–10: 02/08/1463, [*c.*1470].

during the late fifteenth century—Elizabeth Stonor wrote to her husband as 'Ryght entirely and beste belovyd husbonde', and Margery Paston called her husband 'Myne owyn swete hert'—yet such examples are exceptional.[25] By the first half of the seventeenth century informal modes of address and endearing terms were employed more widely, and the shortened forms of Christian names that emerged during the sixteenth century were used with greater regularity: Elizabeth Bagot wrote to 'My good Walt', and Lady Unton Dering signed herself to her husband, the Kentish politician Sir Edward Dering, with the pet-name 'numps'.[26]

On one level, it seems likely that this relaxation in modes of address reflects changes in epistolary conventions, rather than any significant shift in the emotional quality of marriage or rise in the social status of women. While it is tempting to argue for an increased intimacy between husbands and wives, there is a sense in which there was something of a formality in being informal, 'a studied carelessness' to letter-writing.[27] Humanist epistolary manuals drawing on simpler classical forms encouraged an easy, personal style and tone in correspondence: Erasmus admired Pliny's letter-writing for what he described as its 'controlled extemporaneity'.[28] The opening phrases common among the greater number of sixteenth-century wives' letters undoubtedly owe much to the forms of address adopted in letter-writing manuals of the period, such as 'good husband', or 'entirely beloved husband'.[29] What is noticeable, though, is the degree to which female letter-writers adapted and personalized the standard inaugural formulae provided by exemplar letters. Elizabeth Wriothesley, for example, addressed her husband as 'my deare lo[rd] and only joye of my life'.[30] Far from being uniform and conventional, wives' opening modes of address rather display an unexpected richness and variety. The choice of form, therefore, becomes telling, particularly where one is able to study a woman's correspondence over a period of time. In her letters before she separated from him, Elizabeth, countess of Shrewsbury, wrote to her husband as 'my deare harte' and 'my none [own]', whereas after their separation she addressed him more formally as 'my lord'.[31] Nuances in terms of address consequently may reflect developments and changing circumstances within relationships as they mature or encounter difficulties.

The range of closing phraseology used by wives, on the other hand, is less extensive. Most common were the phrases, 'your wife' and 'your loving wife' which were employed by some 67 per cent of letter-writers. These closural forms, current in epistolary manuals, are entirely conventional, which presents problems of interpretation. That they were employed customarily possibly conceals

---

[25] *Stonor Letters*, ii. 18–19: 11/12/1476; Houlbrooke, *English Family*, 104.

[26] Folger, L.a.48: 7/07/1614; *Dering Love Letters*, ed. Cresswell, 49.

[27] Erasmus, *Conficiendarum epistolarum formula* (1521), 258.

[28] Ibid., 258. Gerlo, 'Opus de conscribendis epistolis', 103–14.

[29] Day, *English Secretorie* (1595), ii. 67; Fulwood, *Enemie of Idlenesse* (1568), sigs. 110–11[v].

[30] Cecil, 100, fo. 61: 30/05/1603.

[31] LPL, Talbot, 3198, fo. 331: 09/06/1586; 3205, fos. 66–7, 68, 70: 1577, 1582.

warmer sentiments, in the same way that current usage of phrases such as 'yours sincerely', 'yours faithfully', and 'best wishes' are merely formulaic. It is only where endings deviate from standard forms, that one can ascribe greater levels of meaning. A degree of intimacy, for example, is perhaps discernible in Sabine Johnson's signing a letter to her husband John, 'By your loving wife that was never thus weary with writing'.[32] Likewise, Maria Thynne registered her frustration with her position as a new wife by styling herself 'Your loving wife, howsoever', at the end of a letter in which she explained to her husband Thomas her displeasure at the fact that she was not trusted to discharge business affairs in his absence.[33]

In addition, analysis of closing modes of address conclusively proves that women employed deferential forms much less frequently than Stone suggested. Endearing or affectionate concluding expressions were adopted by 13 per cent of wives: 'ever thine', 'thine and no one else's', and 'your everloving wife'. Moreover, Stone's claim that wives habitually signed letters to their husbands with 'your faithful and obedient wife' is overstated.[34] In fact, of the forty-six women investigated only eight ended letters with this submissive form, and the majority of those were either separated or estranged from husbands. Furthermore, two of the women using the 'obedient' adjective concluded other letters with alternative and less deferential phrases. In her first year of marriage Joan Thynne signed herself 'your obedient wife' in letters to her husband John. Conceivably, as a merchant's daughter entering into an arranged marriage with the heir of an established gentry family, Joan's use of deferential endings was both natural and customary. However, after a year's acculturation within her new environment she regularly styled herself 'your ever loving wife', or by variation 'Your loving wife for ever'.[35] The use of exaggerated deference, as argued elsewhere in the book, was also sometimes deliberate and purposeful. Those women seeking reconciliation with husbands often strove to display obedience and submissiveness. Elizabeth Willoughby, for example, calculatedly assured her husband of her determination, 'to conforme all my wordes as I may best content & please yo^w, as also to performe all good duties that do become a loving & obedient wife towardes her husband'.[36] Finally, deferential modes are more apparent within socially conservative groups, especially among Puritan women, who were more likely to internalize the behavioural codes outlined in conduct books. In the seventeenth century Brilliana Harley consistently addressed her husband as 'Sir' or 'Deare Sir'. Jacqueline Eales has argued that this manner of respectful address reflects Lady Harley's broad acceptance of 'patriarchal relationships' within the family, an outlook conditioned by her Puritan beliefs.[37] However, deferential modes of address are not always consistent with a conservative confessional identity: the Puritan diarist Margaret Hoby addressed her third husband, Sir

[32] *L&P*, XX (ii) 754: 08/11/1545.　[33] *Two Elizabethan Women*, 32: [c.1604–6].
[34] Stone, *Family, Sex and Marriage*, 198.　[35] *Two Elizabethan Women*, 1–3.
[36] BL, Lansd., 46, fo. 61^v: 1585.　[37] Eales, 'Patriarchy, Puritanism and Politics', 143–58.

Thomas Posthumous Hoby, as 'Deare harte', signing herself 'Your assured and Lovinge wiffe'.[38]

Turning to consider husbands' letters to wives, one can find examples of formal, more distant modes of address: writing in 1549, Henry, earl of Sussex, addressed his wife merely as 'madam', although it is perhaps important here to note that the letter was penned in response to his wife's letters berating him for lack of good-will, and lecturing him on how to be a loving husband; the couple were later divorced.[39] On the whole, however, husbands' letters reveal greater freedom, informality, and intimacy in opening and closing forms than letters written by wives. The phrases employed by sixteenth-century husbands are highly personalized, in marked contrast to those found in Renaissance epistolary models and late medieval correspondence. Some 70 per cent of husbands used either pet names, terms of endearment, or wives' forenames, compared with only 17 per cent of women. The actor Edward Alleyn addressed his wife as 'my good sweett harte and loving mouse'; Thomas Baskerville wrote to his wife as 'sweet mall'; Robert Sidney playfully nicknamed his wife 'sweete wenche'; William St Loe, wearied by his overlong stay at court, fondly addressed Bess of Hardwick as 'my honest swete chatesworth' as a way of poking fun at her obsession with the building works; and John Thynne, perhaps unflatteringly, called his wife Joan 'My good Pug'.[40] While pet names may indicate intimacy, jocularity at a wife's expense, however good-humoured, does much to indicate the balance of power within a particular relationship. Men also used abbreviations or acronyms: William Trew wrote to his wife Margaret as 'My G S M', which possibly stands for 'M[y] G[ood] S[weet] M[all]', a shortened form of Margaret.[41] Irrespective of whether or not Trew intended to keep his salutation from prying eyes, his use of abbreviations suggests a kind of code or secret language shared with his wife. The remaining letters employed standard and rigid phrases: three men opened letters merely expressing commendations; eight others employed the term 'wife', but in most cases this was softened by the prefix of either 'dear', 'good', or 'beloved'. The use of over-formal modes of address was to some a source of amusement. Sabine Johnson teased her merchant husband John for addressing her as Mistress Johnson: 'After my hartie comaendacions welbeloved husbond my hart I comend me to you good Mr johnson for so it doyth [be]com me mytche better to call you than you to call me mystres.'[42]

In terms of endings, approximately half the men studied employed customary closing phraseology, signing letters to wives as 'loving', or 'beloved' husbands; three men also interestingly styled themselves as 'faithful' or 'assured' husbands.

---

[38] *Diary of Lady Margaret Hoby*, ed. Moody, p. xl.

[39] BL, Cott., Titus, B.II, fo. 51. Wood, *Letters of Royal and Illustrious Ladies*, iii. 236.

[40] *Catalogue of the Manuscripts and Muniments of Alleyn's College*, 5–6: 02/05/1593; BL, Harl., 4762; De L'Isle, U1475, C81/11: 16/09/1588; Folger, X.d.428 (77): 24/10/[1560]; *Two Elizabeth Women*, 17, 20: 13/02/1601, 26/07/[1601].   [41] Folger, L.a.912: 29/11/1599.

[42] SP46/5/159: 15/05/1546.

As with opening modes of address, men's epistles more commonly display individualized, affectionate closing forms than wives' letters. 38 per cent of men closed letters with endearing salutations: 'my love and life is only thine', 'all yours as you know', and 'your loving husband with aching hart until we meet'. Baskerville signed his letters to his wife 'thy dearest frend'.[43] The increased incidence of affectionate terms utilized in sixteenth-century husbands' correspondence compared with earlier periods may reflect what Stanley Chojnacki, in his study of marital relationships in patrician society in Renaissance Venice, terms a 'new language of husbandly love'.[44] What we discern is a new effectiveness among men in expressing marital affection, though again whether this represents a change in emotional bonds between husbands and wives—that is, new feelings that were stimulating a new articulacy—is unclear. Indeed, the prevalence of an affectionate language, as Professor Chojnacki argues, could indicate that it had become conventional, which further questions how far words function as an accurate index of feelings. Nevertheless, he concludes that even the adoption of the language of love 'as a cultural convention would suggest that affection between spouses was becoming normative'.[45] How far this would have contributed to a change in marital, even romantic, expectations is uncertain. Yet, as argued below, analysis of the letters themselves indicates increased expectations in terms of the emotional quality of marriage: wives encouraged husbands to write when they were absent; letters performed more personal functions within marriage; and couples provided each other with mutual support. An alternative cause of this apparent rise in husbandly affection might be the increased social status of wives. Although few upper-class wives in sixteenth-century England enjoyed the kind of economic power and independence of Chojnacki's well-born Venetian wives, Barbara Harris has demonstrated overwhelmingly the relative importance of marriage for women, arguing that aristocratic women as they remarried accrued 'support and retained resources from each of their families as they moved from one to another'; 'they occupied central places . . . as mothers of the next generation and as widows responsible for the transmission of much of their husbands' property'.[46] The experience of elite Englishwomen thus differs in its historical and cultural specificity from Christiane Klapisch-Zuber's model of female relations in Renaissance Florence, where she argues that women were merely 'passing guests' in their husbands' houses in terms of lineage and physical buildings.[47]

[43] BL, Harl, 4762, fo. 6: 05/11/n.y. Several cases exist of couples referring to each other as 'friends': 'Essex Letter Book'; *Dering Love Letters*, 22; *Lettres de Henri VIII à Anne Boleyn*, 103.

[44] Chojnacki, *Women and Men in Renaissance Venice*, 161–3. See also Harris, *English Aristocratic Women*, 74–5.   [45] Chojnacki, *Women and Men in Renaissance Venice*, 163.

[46] Harris, *English Aristocratic Women*, 10; Chojnacki, *Women and Men in Renaissance Venice*, 157. Chojnacki relates the rise in social status of Venetian patrician wives to a growth over the period in dowry size. Cf. Houlbrooke, *English Family*, 100.

[47] Klapisch-Zuber, *Women, Family, and Ritual*, 117–18.

More broadly, a gendered comparison of sixteenth-century modes of address employed in marital correspondence suggests that men were in general more emotionally articulate than women, or at least more confident in showing easy affection, unencumbered by the rules of decorum governing wifely behaviour. Furthermore, higher levels of male literacy and greater linguistic facility among men may also explain why husbands were more likely than wives to express warmth of feeling. Conversely, greater formality in wives' letters may indicate that women were less used to or more uncomfortable with expressing themselves in writing. The difference in levels of affection textualized in husbands' and wives' modes of address may also be explained, as Keith Wrightson has suggested, by the age differential between young wives and often substantially older husbands among the aristocracy and upper gentry; the making of marriages at this level was also subject to greater parental influence than for the rest of the population at large.[48] Of course generalizations of this nature break down in individual cases, where variants such as age, social status, religion, character, and personality affect the propensity of wives to display tenderness. Here the case of the effusive Maria Thynne is a good example of a woman married to man who was below her in social status: she was of aristocratic birth and served as a maid-of-honour at Elizabeth I's court, but her husband was from a local gentry family. The self-assurance of her letters to her husband ('Mine own sweet Thomken') may also be explained by the fact that the relationship was a possible love match.[49]

DEFERENCE, INTIMACY, LOVE, AND AFFECTION

Correspondence between wives and husbands reflects the varying experience and quality of sixteenth-century marriages, supporting Edward Shorter's argument that 'many constellations of sentiment are . . . possible within any given structure'.[50] The letters surveyed obviously include examples of marital discord and deep-seated hatred. However, the survey also indicates the companionate nature of many conjugal relationships, based upon shared social, economic, and political concerns; the mutual affection and love possible within marriage; and the compatibility of such warmth of feeling with more authoritarian attitudes. The differences that existed between 'practice' and 'precept' in early modern marriage have been strongly asserted by several social historians, who have laid bare the inadequacy of approaches that rely too heavily upon prescriptive conduct literature.[51] Among much of sixteenth-century English society marital

[48] Wrightson, *English Society*, 95.
[49] *Two Elizabethan Women*, p. xxvi. Wall, 'For Love, Money or Politics?', 511–33.
[50] Shorter, *Making of the Modern Family*, 9.
[51] e.g. Wall, 'Elizabethan Precept', 23–38; ead., *Power and Protest*, ch. 5; Houlbrooke, *English Family*, 101; Wrightson, *English Society*, 92.

companionship mutually coexisted with harsher behavioural codes that sought to enforce wifely subservience. This point has been eloquently made by Wrightson, who has argued for 'the *private* existence of a strong complementary and companionate ethos, side by side with, and often overshadowing, theoretical adherence to the doctrine of male authority and *public* female subordination'.[52] Above all, marital correspondence illustrates the complexity of and development within individual relationships that over time display a range of feelings and emotions as couples negotiate everyday life.

Analysis of the style and tone of marital correspondence as an index of the quality of relationships is complicated by social and linguistic conventions. Barbara Harris has argued that 'social convention' during the first half of the sixteenth century 'encouraged close relatives to use the language of economic advantage and favour in their dealings with one another', which 'may well have masked a great deal of emotion that is consequently invisible to historians'.[53] Indeed, wives' letters to husbands are generally civil and polite. Instructions were regularly couched in respectful terms: wives 'beseeched' or 'entreated' husbands to perform requests. Elizabeth Sutton, in a letter to her second husband, Sir Thomas, wrote: 'I pray you good mr sutton let me intreat you to remember my humble dutie unto my lady of warwicke'; Joan Thynne urged her husband, 'I beseech you not to care for anything to hurt yourself, but to make much of yourself for my good and your children's comfort'.[54] The use of such phrases, which appear reserved, rigid, or businesslike to modern readers, is more likely to reflect the formality of language utilized during this period rather than the coolness of marital relations. Moreover, rigidity of style may also indicate a letter-writer's unfamiliarity with the epistolary medium, which led to their resorting to conventional assumptions and vocabulary.

The formality with which couples wrote is related to the fact that sixteenth-century marital correspondence was essentially pragmatic, a means by which couples communicated instructions and concerns, and kept up-to-date with matters relating to the running of households and estates. While some employed letters for more personal functions, including the expressing of affection, these were ancillary to the main utilitarian purpose of letter-writing. Letters were often used simply for the task of issuing instructions or directions. There is little emotive content, for example, in Dorothy Gamage's frequent epistles to her husband John, as revealed in the following example:

> M[r] Gamage after my most hartyst com[m]endac[i]ons I haue
> me com[m]endid vnto yow. I send yow by the carryer
> the flytche[55] w[i]th bawn[56] twentye Eggs v puddings

---

[52] Wrightson, *English Society*, 92.
[53] Harris, 'Marriage Sixteenth-Century Style', 371–2. See also Head, 'Plurilingual Family', 577–93.
[54] GLRO, ACC1876/F/3/7/2/68: 30/05/1602; *Two Elizabethan Women*, 11: 30/05/1595.
[55] *OED*, 'a side of bacon'.   [56] *OED*, 'ready or prepared'.

one pounde of butter and two mow swarthes[57]
other thangs I haue not to send this weke
Thus prayenge god to kepe yow in healthe
from kyngsey this xxvth of January
         your lovinge wyf
         dorothe Gamage
I praye yow send worde what order shalbe
taken or what order yow haue
taken for the weyinge of your wooll[58]

The rudimentary opening commendations are followed by an inventory of the parcels of food that accompanied the letter; it was common practice for letters to accompany deliveries of goods and money in order to ensure their safety. The postscript is also utilitarian, prompting her husband for instructions concerning the weighing of wool. Dorothy's Gamage's letter is representative of the twenty or so other letters that she wrote to her husband from their home in Kingsey, Oxfordshire, during his visits to London in 1579 and 1580.[59] Written roughly on a weekly basis, the letters discuss the progress of business and estate matters, often doubling as shopping lists with detailed requests for household provisions. The letters indicate that Dorothy possessed a working knowledge of farming and the economic realities of the agricultural market-place: she knew when to purchase seeds at the best price and when to sell for the greatest profits. Her role within the relationship also extended to giving advice, and she was clearly a hard-headed businesswoman. In one letter she wrote of her distrust of a customer's oral agreement to pay for the wool he had bought, stating that 'yet he is a man substanciall for so much, but men ar[e] mortall'.[60] Nowhere in these letters, however, does Dorothy write of missing her husband or urge him to return home, phrases that, although sometimes empty, frequently occur in marital correspondence of this period. Nevertheless, the frequency with which she wrote is in itself suggestive of the existence of close bonds within this working partnership.

Some historians have viewed the tendency of wives' letters to convey at least outward signs of respect and demeanour as evidence of wifely subservience and compliance with restrictive conduct codes. Margaret Rowghane, for example, reverently assured her husband Sir Dennis Rowghane that 'I will be Readie to accomplishe yo[u]r will as my duetie is'; and Dorothy Bacon, corresponding with her husband over the lease of Gorleston parsonage, wrote, 'I will dooe notheng nowe but as you shall appont me'.[61] Other female writers, however,

[57] *OED*, 'skin, rind … any covering, as in the rind of bacon'.
[58] SP46/60/7: 25/01/[1580].
[59] For Dorothy Gamage's remaining correspondence to her husband see: SP46/60/1, 8–8d, 10, 12, 13–14, 15, 17, 19–19d, 21–21d, 23–23d, 25, 27, 29, 30, 31, 32, 34, 36, 38, 40, 42–42d. A letter also survives from John Gamage to his wife: SP46/60/2.
[60] SP46/60/8–8d: 01/02/1580.
[61] SP12/239/158/1: 05/08/1591; BL, Addit., 63109, fo. 10: 20/11/[1597]. See also Key, 'Letters and Will of Lady Dorothy Bacon', 106, n. 48.

were less submissive in their letters, displaying greater precision and vigour in directions and demands to husbands. Dorothy Gamage wrote to her husband John cordially but firmly asking to be sent a bottle of salad oil: 'I praye yow let it be good and cleare for that whiche I had before was full of drosse and baggage at the bottom.'[62] Likewise, Anne Williamson sought to persuade her husband to offer her sister business advice: 'my Syster Bolde doth verye earnestlye requeste you to doe so muche for her as to come downe to her for she woolde gladlye speake w[i]th you for dyuers cawses whereof you knowe some yo[u]r selfe alreadye. she sayth yo[u]r comminge might pleasure her muche at this presente yf yo[u]r busynes be suche as you can nott come, then I pray you sende me worde by this bearer. butt I woulde verye fayne yf you coulde haue you to come.' In a postscript Anne reiterated her demands, a clear sign of her resolution: 'I beseeche you yf you can convenientlye shewe my syster so muche pleasure as to come to her'.[63] In numerous cases, the actual working of sixteenth-century marriage, far from evincing unquestioning female obedience to husbands, is identified with high levels of conjugal negotiation and compromise, as well as occasional friction.

Furthermore, many women, usually those enduring cruelty or separation from husbands, were more forceful and defiant in their demands and language. Mary Windebank pleaded with her husband Thomas, clerk of the Signet and Privy Seal, to permit her absence from the wedding of his daughter Mildred. She argued that the bridegroom's father had attacked and insulted her on other occasions, and that she could not bear to see him again. She wrote: 'if youe wil note yeald to this reasnoab [reasonable] request but ourg [urge] me ther unto of purpose I protest on my soule th[a]t shale be the laste breach betwen ous in this world for my pacyence hath bin so mutch tried as ey find my self not abel to induer it no longer.'[64] Nazareth Paget corresponded with her estranged second husband, Thomas Lord Paget, to force him to perform his promise to pay her £50, warning: 'let me not be druin [driven] to make much adow for that i must have.'[65] In these examples wives were driven to assert themselves by adverse circumstances, ill-treatment, and financial necessity.

In contrast to the open defiance and self-assertion evident here, female obedience and submissiveness could be employed to positive effect. Tropes of wifely subservience are well rehearsed in letters from women to husbands from whom they were estranged or separated. A letter from Elizabeth, countess of Shrewsbury, to George Talbot well illustrates the skill with which a wife could present herself as dutiful, while simultaneously criticizing her husband's conduct and behaviour. The countess's letter, one of several sent to her husband after their separation in 1583, was written in June 1586 during a period of apparent attempted reconciliation.[66] In the aftermath of the separation, a commission of

[62] SP46/60/29: 16/03/1580.   [63] SP46/49/50: 28/10/1590.
[64] SP12/275/3: 02/06/1600.
[65] Staffs RO, Paget Papers, D603, K/1/6/12: n.d. The couple formally separated in March 1582. Strype, *Annals of the Reformation*, iii. I, 88.   [66] Durant, *Bess of Hardwick*, 117–50.

inquiry was appointed to investigate the marital dispute, which ordered the earl of Shrewsbury to settle his differences with his wife. With the backing of the commissioners, 'friends' at court, and the queen, the countess wished to be seen as trying to forge a reunion. Yet though she claimed to be writing in 'all bounden duty', her letter was also almost certainly intentionally barbed. Throughout she contrasts her own innocence and obedience with her husband's 'wrath' and 'heavy displeasure': 'I will in all duty & hu[m]bleness subiecte my selfe to any other mann[er] of correction ether by dispossession of any erthly benefytes in p[re]sent or future or any other way of losse or punishm[en]t whatsoever, so as it myghte ples yo[u]r l[ordship] to forbeare to chastyse me w[i]th the extreme rygoure of words w[hi]ch wolde depryve me of all ioy or comforte of lyffe or worldly thyngs...'[67] Her letters evidently angered the earl; a response to earlier correspondence complained of the emptiness of his wife's 'earnest' letters, which contradicted the 'insatiable greed' of her 'devices and desires': 'your faire words are nought but forme. They have the showe and tast they have had, though they appeare butifull yet they are mixed with a hidden poison.'[68]

Concomitantly, numerous women appear to have paid lip-service to ideals of dutiful wifehood. Alison Wall has argued that both Joan and Maria Thynne 'subverted' the rhetoric of female submissiveness, asserting opposition and defiance.[69] In the early years of her marriage Maria, frustrated by the limited role in estate management allowed her by her husband, expressed herself in a letter to him to be both sorry and ashamed 'that any creature should see that you hold such a contempt of my poor wits, that being your wife, you should not think me of discretion to order (according to your appointment) your affairs in your absence'.[70] In other letters she openly mocked female behavioural codes. On one occasion, bemoaning the fact that she was not in London with her sisters, but at home 'talking of foxes and ruder beasts', Maria wrote:

Mine own sweet Thomken, I have no longer ago than the very last night written such a large volume in praise of thy kindness to me, thy dogs, thy hawks, the hare and the foxes, and also in commendation of thy great care of thy businesses in the country, that I think I need not amplify any more on that text, for I have crowned thee for an admirable good husband with poetical laurel, and admired the inexpressible singularity of thy love in the cogitations of *piamater*, I can say no more but that in way of gratuity, the dogs shall without interruption expel their excremental corruption in the best room (which is thy bed) whensoever full feeding makes their bellies ache...[71]

In a later letter she pays lip-service to precepts enjoining female silence, while consciously mocking them: 'My best Thomken I know thou wilt say (receiving two letters in a day from me) that I have tried the virtue of aspen leaves under my tongue, which makes me prattle so much, but consider that all is business, for of

[67] Talbot, 3198, fo. 331: 09/06/1586.   [68] HMC, *Bath*, v. 62: 23/10/1585.
[69] Wall, 'Elizabethan Precept'; ead., 'Deference and Defiance'.
[70] *Two Elizabethan Women*, 32: [*c*.1604–6].   [71] Ibid. 32: [after 08/1604].

my own natural disposition I assure thee there is not a more silent woman living than myself.'[72]

In each of these letters humour appears to function as a means for early modern women to test or flex the parameters of female subordination and the balance of marital power.[73] In addition to the subversive elements of Maria's writing, which plays with the ideal of the obedient, dutiful, and loving wife, the sarcasm evident in the letters suggests an alternative reading to female opposition, the diametrical opposite of female subordination. Thus, the humour evident in Maria's letters, while critiquing public codes of wifely behaviour, also exposes a private playfulness and compatibility with her husband. Such a reading is one of companionship, rather than opposition. Of course each of these positions (and a multitude of positions in between) was possible within an individual marriage, as husbands and wives engaged in a conjugal tug-of-war involving power and personality: for many, sixteenth-century marriage was a process of continual negotiation; it functioned as a crucible of patriarchy in which early modern gender codes could be enforced or mitigated.

Not all upper- and mercantile-class women conformed to deferential models; many wives manipulated archetypal and antitypical female conventions, images, and behavioural traits in a light-hearted manner. Elizabeth, countess of Southampton, during pregnancy wrote tenderly to her 'sweet lord', playing on the stereotyped image of the scolding wife. Asking her husband to send her a portrait of himself, the countess admonished: 'look that your pickter be uery finely done and brot hether as son as may be or else I will do nothing but chide with you when you come to me.'[74] Similarly, in a letter to her 'none [own] sweet lord', Frances, countess of Hertford, second wife of Edward Seymour, repeatedly expressed her desire to be reunited with her husband. 'I can not liue longe wyth out your company', she wrote, promising that, 'you shall finde me a wycht [witch] for I will be reuenged of you for all the engeres [injuries] you haue done me'.[75] Husbands also poked fun at female gender stereotypes. The Staple merchant John Johnson gently teased his wife Sabine for her melancholy disposition, referring to her as 'good wyf (but sometime a shrewe)'.[76] On another occasion Johnson wrote: 'fare well and good nyght wif. I had almost sayd good wyf but that it were synne to lye, as ye knowe, nevertheles my hope is that old fachons wilbe lefte and then if I wilnot saie good wyf I shalbe wourthie to be called a lyar.'[77] The playfulness of John's three letters is entirely characteristic of the shared sense of humour and mutual understanding displayed in the couple's extensive correspondence with one another. The fact that the Johnson marriage was a love match may also explain John's easy familiarity in letters to his wife.[78]

[72] Ibid., 48: [early 1610]. [73] See also Brown, *Better a Shrew*.
[74] Cecil, 109, fo. 31: n.d. [75] Seymour Papers, 5, fo. 144: 09/06/*c*.1584.
[76] *L&P*, XX (i) 629: 01/05/1545. [77] SP46/5/141: 15/11/1545.
[78] Sabine was the niece of John's master Anthony Cave, in whose household they were both brought up: Winchester, *Tudor Family Portrait*, 62–6.

Clearly within companionate marriages husbandly sensitivity, fondness, joviality, and kindness could mitigate the harsher effects of early modern gender restrictions relating to women.

Other letters illustrate further the possibility of humour and laughter within conjugal relationships. Dorothy Bacon, taking the opportunity of a carrier to send her husband Nathaniel a second letter in one day, self-deprecatingly joked that 'you will thinke me but dooll witted yf I coold not frame somwhat to wryt of at this tyme all so'.[79] Alternatively, Elizabeth, countess of Southampton, included a humorous tale in a letter to her husband for his own amusement: 'all nues I can send you that I thinke will, make you mery is that I reade in a letter from London that Sir John Falstaf is by his M[ist]r[e]s dame Pintpot made father of a goodly milers thumb, a boye thats all heade and veri litel body, but this is a secirt.'[80] These examples indicate the mutual sense of humour that could exist between husband and wife, and the high degree of spousal compatibility and like-mindedness attainable during the sixteenth century.

For many couples marriage was a partnership based upon mutual interest and economic and social practicalities, though this was not necessarily incompatible with affectionate bonds. The practical aspect of marital relationships is much evident in the letters between Margaret Bourchier and her husband John, second earl of Bath. The couple, each of whom had been widowed twice, married in 1548 in middle age with ten years separating them.[81] They both, therefore, entered into matrimony with experience and maturity gained in previous relationships.[82] Indeed, Margaret appears to have accepted Bath's suit only after a period of sober reflection: her steward recommended the earl as a potential future husband on the basis that his lordship was 'a man of much honer and gentleness'.[83] Furthermore, as part of the negotiations a further marriage was arranged between Margaret's 13-year-old daughter Frances Kitson and the earl's eldest son Lord Fitzwarine, aged 19.[84] Though the marriage of the earl and countess was not a love match, neither was it merely a marriage of convenience: the correspondence indicates their mutual respect, fondness, and affection for each other.

In particular, the countess's letters articulate a clear sense of marriage as a shared enterprise in which both partners assumed responsibility for, and ultimately benefited from, maintenance of family honour and reputation. Her care for the future standing of the family is evident in the countess's discussion with her husband over clearing his debts, in order, she wrote, that 'we myght after ward lyve the more nerely to gether and contynew our famylye as we have begoone'.[85] The concern for financial probity, allied with a desire to preserve the

[79] BL, Addit., 41140, fos. 121–2: *c.*1597.   [80] Cecil, 101, fo. 16: 08/07/1603.
[81] The countess was ten years younger than her husband.
[82] GEC, ii. 16–17; Gage, *History and Antiquities of Hengrave* (1822), 121–3.
[83] Hengrave, 88/1, fo. 10: 27/12/1547.   [84] Gage, *History and Antiquities of Hengrave*, 121.
[85] Hengrave, 88/1, fo. 54: 21/02/n.y.

family land and estates, are continual motifs in the countess's letters; elsewhere she complains of the expenses incurred by court attendance and the problems of maintaining vast households.[86] Another letter complains of having insufficient money for the upkeep of the household at Hengrave, but again her overriding concern was with posterity: she was adamant that the earl should sell no more land, since this would reduce his 'inheritance'.[87] Likewise, the earl of Bath was anxious not to diminish his land-holdings. In May 1557, faced with the costs of military service and impending subsidy payments, he confided in his wife that he knew not how to pay: 'For an I should sell any more land, I should undo my posteritie that shall cum after me. I had nev[e]r land, offyce, nor fee given to me in all my life, save only that, the which it pleased the Quenys Ma[jest]^{ie} to give me.'[88] He further urged her while she was at court to speak to William Lord Paget concerning his suit for money.[89] As with the countess's letters, the fact that the earl discussed these matters with his wife, and encouraged her to operate at court in his absence, indicates intimacy, trust, shared interest, and cooperation within the marriage, impulses or elements that could engender strong emotional attachment.[90]

The correspondence surveyed indicates extensive cooperation between couples in managing family interests and women's importance in decision-making processes. Analysis of the contents of wives' letters reveals the high proportion of wives charged with running households, estate administration, and business matters during periods spent by husbands either abroad on military and diplomatic service, elsewhere in the country engaged in litigation, politics, and local administration, or in prison.[91] Letters discuss various matters, including farming, tenants, building maintenance, household provisions, medical recipes, accounts, and servants. Topics of this nature occur more frequently than mention of family matters, which indicates that the prime function of correspondence for married couples was to facilitate the smooth running of household affairs during husbands' absences. In many cases husbands instructed wives how to proceed, and wives typically deferred to husbands' advice. Margaret Gresham asked her husband to 'come home as shonllie [soon] as maye be that I m[ay] have youre councell'; Elizabeth Ognell wrote to her husband asking him to send his 'determination' regarding the sale of a mill; and Katherine Mucklowe sought her husband's advice in suing a tenant for non-payment of rent.[92] Other women, as with Dorothy Gamage, ostensibly acted in more of an advisory capacity, offering suggestions and counsel. Unsurprisingly, the women who participated in

---

[86] Ibid., fos. 22, 23, 24, 63, 65.   [87] Ibid., fo. 22: 8/08/n.y.
[88] Gage, *History and Antiquities of Hengrave*, 164.   [89] Ibid., 164.
[90] Chojnacki, *Women and Men in Renaissance Venice*, 160.
[91] On wifely roles in the absence of husbands see Eales, 'Patriarchy, Puritanism and Politics', 143–58; Harris, *English Aristocratic Women*, ch. 4; Cliffe, *World of the Country House*, ch. 4; Larminie, 'Marriage and the Family', 1–22.
[92] SP46/58/262, n.d.; SP46/20/67, 16/05/1595; Birmingham Central Library, Z Lloyd, 53/4, *c.*1570.

administrative tasks had views on how best to act. Elizabeth Sutton, certain that her husband had been overcharged in a tailor's bill, wrote, 'it maketh me amased it cometh to so muche . . . the bill . . . is to large and therefor you must mittigat it when you pay'.[93] However, the extent of wives' engagement in business interests when husbands were present is less clear, since correspondence was on the whole produced during periods of separation.[94] While women often deferred to male judgement, husbands clearly appreciated and respected wives' opinions: the earl of Bath thanked his wife for her advice, writing, 'I will followe the contents of your sayed letter wiche I marke very well and . . . your good advyse'.[95] Likewise, Robert Sidney entrusted his wife to oversee building work at Penshurst, writing, 'I need not send to know how my buildings goe forward for I ame sure yow are so good a huswyfe as you may be put in trust with them'.[96] Wives participated fully in a range of areas within marriage and were expected to do so.

The kinds of advice proffered by wives extended beyond the household to include counselling husbands on their public and political careers. Jane Neville advised and acted as an intermediary at court for her husband Charles, earl of Westmoreland, during his exile from England for his involvement in the abortive Northern Rising. In 1575, after he had been further implicated in the Ridolfi Plot, the countess urged Westmoreland, who had continuously tried to negotiate his return from the continent, to 'write to her ma[jes]ty' and to 'give manifest proof of dutiful demeanor keeping yourself free from practices of forrein prin- ces . . . the soner you send these l[ett]res the better grounds you give me to speak on and the more caus to her ma[jes]ty willingly to hear me'.[97] Jane Neville, who enjoyed close proximity to the monarch, was obviously well placed to know how to proceed in the political arena. Joan Thynne, on the other hand, although herself distant from court and unable to intercede directly, was still able to offer her husband encouragement in his suits, though her guidance was not always couched in the kindest of terms. In one letter she reported the recent knighting of her husband's cousin, Henry Townshend, at the same time registering her regret that John Thynne had not been awarded the same honour, and suggesting how he might curry favour at court: 'if all your courtly friends can not procure you that title I think they will do very little for you; if men can not procure it, yet methinks some of your great Ladies might do so much for you.'[98] In light of the fact that a title for her husband would mean a rise in her own social status, Joan's disappointment at his lack of success is understandable. Wives' fortunes were in this sense bound up with those of their husbands, which naturally could foster

---

[93] GLRO, ACC1876, F3/7/1/2: 29/01/1600.

[94] An interesting exception is Margaret Hoby, who recorded writing to her husband while he was still in the house: *Diary of Lady Margaret Hoby*, 99, n. 176.

[95] Hengrave, 88/I, fo. 136: 09/11/1559.   [96] De L'Isle, U1475/C81/40: 05/1594.

[97] BL, Addit., 46367, fos. 35ᵛ–36ᵛ: 22/09/1575.

[98] *Two Elizabethan Women*, 19–20: 18/06/1601.

tighter bonds within a marriage. In other letters Joan was more sympathetic and consoling in her support of her husband:

My love to yourself is not to be broken by knives or anything else whiles I live, yet much to be increased by your unfeigned performances which I have good hope of. And I trust your troubles will turn all for the best and to both our comforts, although the strain be great for the present, yet I hope our meeting shall be joyful to us both. And therefore my good husband I beseech you not to care for anything to hurt yourself, but to make much of yourself for my good and your children's comfort.[99]

The 'troubles' referred to here are not explained, which points to shared references or understandings between Joan and her husband lost to modern readers. Presumably 'troubles' relates again to John's dealings at court, which he may well have either discussed with his wife in person or written about to her in non-extant letters. Indeed, from his surviving correspondence to his wife it is clear that Thynne informed her about aspects of court life: in one letter he described the part he played in resisting the Essex Revolt.[100]

Other letters record wives acting as political confidantes for their husbands. George Clifford reported to his wife of the 'fickle memories of the people who I deal with'.[101] Robert Sidney was equally frank in correspondence with his own wife Barbara, informing her of his weariness of the court.[102] William St Loe informed his wife of the queen's displeasure at his long absence from London: 'the quene hath fownde greatt fawt wyth my long absens sayenge she wolde talck wyth me farder and that she wolde w[e]ll chyde me.'[103] The manner in which these husbands used letters as a means of unburdening worries and frustrations, and to complain of enemies, often with great candour, attests to the emotional support that men expected from their wives. Furthermore, it indicates that husbands openly discussed and shared with wives details of their careers and business affairs. The occasional almost chatty informality exhibited by sixteenth-century wives' letters further documents the levels of familiarity possible between married partners, giving a sense of the kinds of topics that couples must have talked about when they were together. Yet while letters may approximate conversations, significant differences exist between oral and written media. During this period letters were not used for over-lengthy description or discussion: husbands frequently mentioned that they would speak in greater detail and more openly on their return, further suggesting the insecurity attached to the epistolary medium.

In the same way that men used wives as confidantes, so too women shared with husbands their thoughts, opinions, and feelings about the matters that impacted upon their lives. A remarkable level of openness appears to mark the correspondence of numerous wives. Dorothy Gawdy, for example, expressed to

[99] Ibid., 11: 30/05/1595.
[100] For John's letters see ibid., 17–18, 20; Wall, 'Account of the Essex Revolt', 131–3.
[101] WD/Hoth/Box 44: n.d.   [102] De L'Isle, U1475/C81/141: n.d. See also C81/1: 1587.
[103] Folger, X.d.428 (77): 24/10/1560.

her husband, the Norfolk gentleman Sir Bassingbourne Gawdy, the freedom with which she felt able to write: 'sweet bas pardon my brevity, I am able to wright as I desire.'[104] Writing to her husband Nathaniel, Dorothy Bacon urged him to intervene in a wardship case on behalf of her sister, explaining that without his assistance 'a strangar shall obtayn it [the wardship] and so show that extremyty to her as was showed to me'.[105] Wives also used letters to convey concerns regarding health, informing husbands of illness and ailments. Usually references to ill-health are only made in passing, though occasionally they read more urgently. Frances Devereux informed her husband the earl of Essex that 'entolerabell pane' in her 'hed and fes [i.e. face]' had rendered her 'allmost blind'.[106] Perhaps the most striking example, though, is a letter from Eleanor, countess of Cumberland, written in 1543, in which she described in great detail to her husband the symptoms of her illness, asking him to send for 'Doctor Stephyns': 'sens yo[u]r departure frome me I haue ben very seke & att thys present my watter ys very Redd wherby I suppos I haue the iaun[d]es & the aygew bothe, for I have none abytyde [appetite] to meate & I haue suche payns in my syde & towards my bake as I had att Brauham, wher ytt be gane with me furst.'[107]

During pregnancy wives expressed fears concerning the event of childbirth, a time when they were forced to consider the possibility of their own death.[108] Sabine Johnson implored her husband to 'make all sped hom' from Calais in order that he might be with her at the birth, adding: 'good husbond what a great comfort it shalbe to me to have [you] here at that tyme, trustyng in the lord that he woll send you a son, but what so ever it be praye we to the ˆsamê lord that maye be borne to his honor and goodly well.'[109] Worried that the practical arrangements had not been made for her lying-in, Elizabeth Anthony wrote to her husband requesting his presence and support during what she described as her 'time of payne and sorowe'.[110] Whether or not these husbands were actually present at childbed at the time of the birth is unknown—supervision of the birth generally lay within the female sphere; nevertheless the letters indicate that husbands were close at hand as a source of comfort and solace.[111] Furthermore, in the absence of physical presence letters offered an important form of emotional support.

Letters also record wives' discussions with husbands of the upbringing of infants and children. Several letters mention the choice of wetnurses and godparents; others report on the health and progress of young children. Sabine Johnson, whose daughter Charity had been put out to wetnurse, informed her husband in May 1545 that the infant was now 'wayned [weaned]' and 'is com

---

[104] BL, Addit., 36959, fo. 14: 1601.   [105] Ibid. 41140, fo. 123: c.1597.
[106] Cecil, 21, fo.1: 1591.   [107] WD/Hoth/Box 44: 14/02/1543.
[108] On women's fear of dying during childbirth see Pollock, 'Embarking on a Rough Passage', 39–67.   [109] SP46/5/160: 17/05/1546.
[110] SP46/126/38: [temp. Eliz.]   [111] Pollock, 'Childbearing and Female Bonding', 286–306.

home'; Joan Thynne asked her husband on his stay in London to 'entreat' her sister 'to provide me of a good midwife'.[112] On the whole, wives, in their role as mothers, appear to have enjoyed greater influence over the upbringing and instruction of daughters. However, some women were interested in the education and careers of sons. Margaret, countess of Bath, expressed strong opinions concerning the training and suitable careers of her husband's sons. She advised the earl that his son John should be 'bestowed in soome noble mans servyce',[113] and recommended his son George be sent to one of the Inns of Chancery, having already talked with the principal of Furnivals Inn.[114] Solicitous mothers also involved themselves in the selection of tutors for boys: Joan Thynne suggested to her husband that they might engage the services of a scholar from Oxford to teach their two sons.[115]

The confidential nature of these functional and emotional aspects of marital correspondence bred a demand for epistolary privacy and a desire to communicate during periods of separation, which are clearly articulated in both husbands' and wives' correspondence. Spouses frequently asked to receive letters from each other, desiring to hear of health, children, and other news. In the first year of her marriage, Joan Thynne chided her husband for his lack of letters during his absence in London: 'Mr Thynne, I may not impute it unto you for not writing to me, for either the messenger[s] are very slack in bring[ing], or you slothful for not writing to me, for I either think that your health is not so perfect as I would swear, or that your business falleth otherwise than you looked for.'[116] Joan Thynne's catalogue of possible explanations for the lack of letters indicates an expectation that her husband would write that is perhaps more widespread. The duty of letter-writing was a reciprocal act: receipt of a letter occasioned the dispatch of a reply. Certain couples kept an informal tally of the number of letters sent and received: Sabine Johnson informed her husband that she had written two letters to him since last he wrote.[117] Communication by letter between marital partners was motivated by a mixture of duty, concern, and affection. On his frequent sojourns in London Thomas Posthumous Hoby frequently corresponded with his wife to let her know of his well-being. His diligence is recorded in his wife's diary: the entry for 17 January 1602 records her husband's 'Iournie towardes London', while the next entry, for 19 January, states 'I receiued a letter from him that he was in helth', indicating that Hoby immediately dispatched of news of his safe arrival to his wife at his journey's end.[118] Letters of this nature exhibiting anxieties about the health, welfare, and safety of a spouse are more pronounced during plague years. On hearing that he was unwell, Dorothy Gawdy asked her husband to send 'a line or two' informing her of his health, and further 'entreated' him to 'shake of all heavy

[112] *L&P*, XX (i) 778: 20/05/1545; *Two Elizabethan Women*, 6: 10/03/1590.
[113] Hengrave, 88/1, fo. 37: 03/03/n.y. [114] Gage, *History and Antiquities of Hengrave*, 156.
[115] *Two Elizabethan Women*, 11–12: 30/05/1595. [116] Ibid., 2: 1576.
[117] SP46/5/170: 21/09/1546. [118] *Diary of Lady Margaret Hoby*, 176.

melancholy'.[119] At other times wives openly expressed the joy felt on delivery of husbands' letters. Elizabeth, countess of Shrewsbury, begged her husband to write: 'I longed greatly to here frome you and thanke you moste hartely for your letter whyche wos a great coumfort to me, nexte to your selfe ther ys not any thynge coulde be more welcome.'[120]

Husbands, by comparison, were usually more overtly affectionate in requesting wives' letters. Thomas Baskerville asked his wife to 'wryght to me often for in thy absents I make love to thy letters'.[121] George Clifford expressed the heartfelt pleasure with which he read letters from his 'Good Mege': 'thye abcense hathe brede suche store of corseeis [curses] in my discontented harte, as whyle I wait thye company maye no waye be cured, although sumwhat lestened by thye louynge lynes.'[122] George, earl of Shrewsbury, wrote to Bess of Hardwick of the despondency with which he greeted the lack of letters from her: 'I harde nott from you offe all this tyme tyll now, whyche drove me in dumpes, but now [I am] relyved agen by yo[u]r wrytinge unto me.' The earl further explained that writing to her placed her in his thoughts: 'as the pene wrytes so the hart thynks that offe all erthly joys that hath happenyd unto me I thanke god chefest for you for w[hi]ch . . . I have all joye & cotentenasyon of mynde & w[i]thout you dethe is more plesante to me than lyfe if I thought I shulde be long from you . . . '[123] Although separation may have led to exaggerated sentiment in letters unrepresentative of the experiences of daily married life spent within the household, these examples indicate the emotional support and comfort that couples derived from each other, as well as the importance of correspondence during periods of absence. In some senses then, the very process of letter-writing—the need for writers to visualise the addressees and to think of them in relation to themselves—may have provided couples with a feeling of connection with each other. Indeed, Elizabeth, countess of Southampton, informed her husband that she would not let the messenger carrying her letter depart 'w[i]th owet som lines to you that may be a mean to place me into your minde wher I wolde euer reman'.[124]

Many couples experienced high levels of conjugal affection and romantic attachment, which is exemplified by the fond, loving, sometimes passionate nature of the language utilized by spouses. In particular, husbands' letters often reveal an unrestrained tenderness of emotion. An evident playfulness or eroticism is evident in John Johnson's letters to his wife, 'in hast going to bed at x of the clocke at nyght and wold ye were in my bed to tary me. I byd you good nyght good wyf some tymes.'[125] Thomas Baskerville's letters to his 'sweete Malle' are filled with expressions of fondness and declarations of love. He assured her in one letter 'that the self sam humor and desirs posses me, thatt yow have, and my

[119] BL, Addit., 36989, fo. 17: 1602.
[120] Talbot, 3205, fo. 73: n.d. See also *Two Elizabethan Women*, 25: 30/04/1602; *L&P*, XX (ii) 781: 12/11/1545.   [121] BL, Harl., 4762, fo. 19: 26/05/n.y.
[122] WD/Hoth/Box 44: n.d.   [123] Folger, X.d.428 (86): n.d.
[124] Cecil, 100, fo. 61: 30/05/1603.   [125] SP46/5/139: 08/11/1545.

love I protest is Infynittly stirred'.[126] Similarly, Percival Willoughby's remarkable love-letters exhibit passionate devotion to his wife: one of the epistles from the early stages of the marriage contains a love poem; another features a sketch of a heart transfixed with darts.[127] Usage of the language and imagery of 'love' in this manner in husbands' letters is more pronounced towards the end of the sixteenth century, with the notable exception of Henry VIII's love-letters to Anne Boleyn.[128] The more personal endearments that one discerns in epistolary exchanges between married couples from the 1500s onwards were added to letters that traditionally dealt with business concerns; expressions of fondness or longing, therefore, appear next to instructions, requests, and details of commercial transactions. The evident functionality of the epistolary genre may explain why there are so few examples of actual love-letters dating from this period, that is, letters the sole purpose of which was the declaration of love. The seventeenth century, by contrast, yields many instances of letters that were written, especially by men, for purely romantic reasons. In 1632 Edward Dering, for example, sent a couple of lines to his 'Deare Jewell' simply to declare his love: 'though the messenger do call in hast, yett thou must have a line. My true love to thee and my blessing to my children, wishing my selfe a hundred times with thee, I rest, Thy ever faythfull and affectionate EdwarDering [*sic*].'[129]

Conversely, sixteenth-century wives' letters rarely display the intensity of expression of romantic love found in men's letters. Conceivably, women who were educated to be chaste and to suppress sensuality were unwilling to commit such loving sentiments to paper. Indeed, William Alison in a letter to his wife, his 'owne deare Cate', asked her to write to him more openly of her feelings: 'be no more so strange nor dayntie of your writing. let love vanquishe feare.'[130] Various women, however, did write to husbands with some degree of tenderness. Margaret, countess of Bath, wrote with as much feeling as decorum to her husband, explaining, 'I doo perceve thowgh your selfe beyng absent your harte ys present the w[hi]ch of my parte shalnot be for gottone'; and Sabine Johnson looked forward to the 'cold nyghtes' on her husband's return and their being in bed together.[131] Elizabeth, countess of Southampton's correspondence to her husband is likewise filled with declarations of love and affection. She wrote to him as 'you whom I loue as my sole', declaring elsewhere 'I do already more than long to hear from you whom I every hour wish myselfe with and can never live contented till I do enjoy that happiness'.[132] Such expressions of warmth and compassion are far more numerous in sixteenth-century wives' letters than they are in correspondence from the late medieval period.

[126] BL, Harl., 4762, fo. 21: n.d.; fo. 109: 24/09/n.y. See also Folger, X.d.428 (87): 13/12/1568.
[127] HMC, *Middleton*, 558–9, n.d.
[128] *Lettres de Henri VIII à Anne Boleyn*, 138–40; Ives, *Anne Boleyn*, 102–8; Stemmler, 'Songs and Love-Letters of Henry VIII', 97–111; Lerer, *Courtly Letters*, 88.
[129] *Dering Love Letters*, 22.   [130] SP12/155/100: 20/11/1582.
[131] Hengrave, 88/1, fo. 23, n.d.; *L&P*, XX (ii) 855: 23/11/1545.
[132] Cecil, 100, fos. 61, 91: 30/05/1603, 11/06/1603.

In a more overtly amorous manner, Dorothy Gawdy wrote to her 'Dear Bass', pleading 'come to me tonight, your company will be more pleasing than you think possible', also explaining that she desired his 'love more ernestly then any thing under heaven'.[133] Elsewhere in Dorothy Gawdy's correspondence expressions of love for her husband are mixed with gestures of wifely respect: 'I beseech you hold this opinion ever of me that I do and will ever endeavour myself withall my heart and soul to deserve your love and in that will remain to my last houre of life your most lovinge and faithful wife.'[134] Dorothy's letters suggest a closeness with her husband, despite the fact that theirs was an arranged marriage.[135] In the case of arranged marriage, love and affection could clearly develop over time and coexist with more authoritarian attitudes. Affection was also compatible with female domestic roles. Indeed, Margaret Gayton's affection for her husband was mingled with wifely concern, and expressed itself in an anxiety that he should have enough shirts for his journey abroad: 'I know not how you will doe for shirtes when you shall goe abroad unles you can bie you some. if you can they will haue some time to make them and to haue them washed and dride.'[136] The conjugal love exhibited in these letters was entirely compatible with sixteenth-century Protestant thinking on marriage, which highly valued marital love as a basis for a workable, enduring, and companionate relationship; such love was far removed from romantic or erotic love, which was uncontrollable and sinful, and akin to irrationality.[137]

Beyond registering feelings of companionate love, sixteenth-century wives' letters also demonstrate romantic passion, and occasionally carnal appetites and erotic desires. Although much correspondence of an explicit sexual nature may have been destroyed, Maria Thynne, writing around 1607 (at which point she would have been in her late twenties) in reply to her husband's 'wanton letters', is unmistakably sexually forward or aggressive. In her letter she reminded her 'best beloved Thomken' and 'best little Sirrah' of 'how you made my modest blood flush up into my bashful cheek', adding 'thou threatened sound payment, and I sound repayment, so as when we meet, there will be pay, and repay which will pass and repass'. This is followed by reference to her husband's frequent sexual arousal on his return.[138] The letter continues, 'thou knowest my mind, though thou dost not understand me. Well now laying on side my high colour, know in sober sadness that I am at Longleat, ready and unready to receive thee, and here will attend thy coming.'

---

[133] BL, Addit., 36989, fo. 18: 1602.   [134] Ibid., fo. 15: 1602.

[135] Smith, *County and Court*, 178; Hasler, *Commons*, ii. 176–7.   [136] SP46/19/39: 1591.

[137] Houlbrooke, *English Family*, 102–5; Cressy, *Birth, Marriage, and Death*, 260–3; Harris, *English Aristocratic Women*, 73–5. E.g. Smith, *De Republica Anglorum* (1583), 13; Smith, *A Preparatiue to Mariage* . . . (1591), 50–1, 53, 54; Gouge, *Of Domesticall Dvties* (1622), 197; Gataker, *A Good Wife Gods Gift* . . . (1623), 11.

[138] *Two Elizabethan Women*, 37, 38, n. 3: n.d. On the survival of archival material of a sexual nature see Hall, 'Sex in the Archives', 1–12.

Ritual exchanges of letters were also part of early modern courtship practices.[139] Margery Brews's 'voluntyne' letters to her future husband John Paston III, written in February 1477, the year of their marriage, while respectful and formal nevertheless manage to convey significant amorous feelings: 'I am not in good heele [health] of body ner of herte, nor schall be tyll I here from yowe.'[140] Two of Joan Thynne's (née Hayward) letters survive from before her marriage to John Thynne. The letters, despite their formal brevity, intimate an obvious attraction or 'mutual liking'; the second of the letters ends: 'But as fire can not be separated from heat nor heat from fire, so is the heart of faithful friends which share one desire.'[141] Griffin Markham wrote a series of love letters to his cousin Margaret Willoughby from university in which he complained that his tutor prevented him from leaving Cambridge; he signed himself in one: 'Yours whilst life doth rule his vital breath.'[142] Additionally, there is evidence of unmarried women writing love-letters. In his diary the musician Thomas Wythorne described how a young girl within the household where he then served placed a love-letter in the strings of his lute.[143] Love-letters and valentines of this nature, as Diana O'Hara has noted, 'illustrate the communication of love by literate means'.[144] There is also evidence, however, that love notes were used as tokens of affection between lovers lower down the social scale; indeed, O'Hara has suggested that the practice of sending love-letters, while 'associated more with higher status, literacy and education' and with 'marriages formed over distance', may as the form developed have replaced 'the need for ritual gift exchanges and symbolic modes of communication'.[145] Love notes, usually penned by men, come to light in disputed courtship cases, where they were introduced as evidence of matrimonial intent.[146] In 1626 Robert Lowther was accused of having written to Susan Hills while away at sea as a remembrance of his love.[147] While courtship letters by elite women survive, especially from the seventeenth century, it is harder to measure the extent to which plebeian women actually exchanged love-letters with male suitors.[148] However, occasional examples survive of women sending notes or letters. It was alleged in 1565 that one Thomasyn Lee sent Thomas Sething of Sandwich a letter which contained within it a handkerchief 'wrought with black works'.[149] For the seventeenth-century, scriveners' notebooks record women who paid to have letters penned to

[139] On love-letters see Macfarlane, *Marriage and Love*, 190–8, 301–3; Bell, *Elizabethan Women*, 68; White, 'Rise and Fall', 35–47, Moody, 'Courtship Letters and Poems of Philip Wodehouse', 44–53. [140] *Paston Letters*, ed. Davis, i. 415: 02/1477.
[141] *Two Elizabethan Women*, 1: [after 10/10/1575].
[142] HMC, *Middleton*, 592–4: [before 1587].
[143] *Autobiography of Thomas Whythorne*, ed. Osborn, 30–1.
[144] O'Hara, 'Language of Tokens', 16. [145] O'Hara, *Courtship and Constraint*, 11, 70–1.
[146] Gowing, *Domestic Dangers*, 70–1. [147] Ibid., 160.
[148] e.g. *Dorothy Osborne: Letters to William Temple*, ed. Parker; Folger, X.d.493, fos. 3–6 (Mary Hatton to Randolph Helsby, 1653–5); Folger, X.d.477, fos. 2–33 (Lydia Dugard to Samuel Dugard, [c.1665]–c.1672). [149] O'Hara, *Courtship and Constraint*, 84.

lovers. An entry in the diary of Robert Lowe states, 'Ann Barrow came to towne and moved me to write a letter for her in answer to a love letter from Richard Naylor'.[150] Conversely, letters were employed by women to spurn the advances of unwonted suitors. The British Library contains a transcript in the hand of Michael Hickes of an answer of refusal from 'a woman unnamed' to a letter of courtship sent to her by one Mr Hocknell.[151] It is unclear, however, whether this example represents a letter that was actually dispatched and then transcribed for documentary purposes, or whether it was an epistolary model copied out for practice or amusement.

Model love-letters are widespread in early modern letter-writing manuals; such exemplars offered guidelines (usually for male letter-writers) for how to write to lovers; how women should respond to unwonted amorous advances; and how the spurned male lover should frame his reply. Castiglione encouraged his ideal courtier to disclose his love for a lady by letter.[152] Erasmus's *De conscribendis* deals with amorous epistles under the heading 'the letter of Friendship', while both Fulwood and Day include exemplary love-letters.[153] The amatory epistle form also received serious treatment in Elizabethan literature, as for example in George Gascoigne's *Adventures of Master F.J.* (1573), John Lyly's *Euphues* (1579), and John Grange's *The Golden Aphroditis* (1577), and from the 1580s the form was parodied by future generations of writers.[154]

While social historians have traditionally viewed marital correspondences as historical documents capable of reflecting early modern emotion, literary scholars have been more sanguine about the ability of letters to express any kind of subjective emotional experience.[155] Viewing letters as 'texts' rather than as repositories of 'fact', and from the perspective of genre, epistolary models, and conventions, literary critics have stressed the highly conventional and ritualized characteristics of Renaissance letter-writing. In her study of the love-letter Fay Bound proffers a more complex understanding of the epistolary form, which attains meaning through literary tropes and material forms. Letters, like gifts, were replete with symbolic currency; they functioned not merely as reflectors of emotion, but as ways of exploring and representing it.[156] The overall thrust of humanist epistolary theory was to render letters consciously more intimate— Erasmus's 'conversation between friends'. Lisa Jardine has argued for the controlled production of feeling in Renaissance letters, interpreting Erasmus's

---

[150] *Diary of Robert Lowe*, ed. Sachse, 24, 28, 53.   [151] BL, Lansd., 107, fo. 45.

[152] Castiglione, *The Booke of the Courtier* (1528; 1561), ed. Cox (1994), 276.

[153] *De conscribendis epistolis*, 203–4. *Enemie of Idlenesse* (1571), 131–5; *English Secretorie* (1586; 1595), ch. 19. See also Breton, *Poste With a Madde Packet of Letters* (1602), sig. B4ʳ. Robertson, *Art of Letter Writing*, 19.

[154] White, 'The Rise and Fall'. E.g. Shakespeare, *Twelfe Night or What You Will* (1602), II. v. 136–72.

[155] For traditional approaches to love-letters see Stone, *Family Sex and Marriage*, 226, 227; Sharpe, *Early Modern England*, 66; Houlbrooke, *English Family*, 103–4; MacFarlane, *Marriage and Love*, 189, 190–8, 301–3.   [156] Bound, 'Writing the Self?', 1–19.

letters as crucially 'affective', and 'a major contribution to the Renaissance's construction of letter-writing and reading as emotionally charged events'.[157] Likewise, Gary Schneider argues that Renaissance letter-writers, influenced by epistolographies and tropes of orality and physical presence, inscribed a 'specialized epistolary rhetoric in order to textualize emotions such as love'.[158] Such approaches work to erode (though not delete) simple notions of male or female subjectivity, and unfettered emotion. Thus, affection and intimacy, as has been observed with wifely obedience, could be scripted; and language can conceal and construct feelings and emotions, as much as it can reflect them.

In light of the fact that marital letters are influenced by generic conventions, the interpretation of 'emotion' can be subjected to rhetorical analysis. Peter Mack has argued that in contrast to oratory where 'the grand style is the source of the strongest emotional effects', emotion in letters 'is often expressed most strongly through simple expressions'.[159] In seeking to assess the effectiveness or force of emotional rhetoric used by early modern husbands, Mack contrasts the letters of John Donne to his wife Ann, which elaborately express his desire to write, with what he regards as the more 'moving' letters of Thomas Knyvett that elicit consistent affection through greetings to his wife.[160] Likewise, Roger Ascham's letter to his wife upon the death of their child, an exemplar that circulated in manuscript, elaborately counsels that they place their trust in the 'wisdom' and 'goodness' of God; yet the tenderness of the letter is achieved through his simple evocation of companionship and mutual support in seeking to endure the tragedy: 'god and good will hath so joined you and me together as we must not only the one be comforte to the other in sorrow, but also full partakers together in any joye.'[161] Having said this, the fact that Ascham's letters to his wife were scribally published further impedes an understanding of them as private missives of marital intimacy. Nevertheless, the rhetorical art of writing love-letters, however artificial and conventional, is not incompatible with marital affection; the choice and selection of phrases and tropes, albeit conscious, registers a desire or willingness to express amorous feelings.

Overall, comparison of men's and women's marital correspondence for the sixteenth century shows that husbands' letters, in terms of endearing modes of address, affectionate language, and freedom and intimacy of expression, are more frequently open, confident, and warm than wives' letters, though wives sometimes conveyed equal tenderness in their correspondence. This discovery that sixteenth-century husbands were more emotionally expressive than wives is counter-intuitive, and contrasts with the findings of Felicity Heal and Clive

---

[157] Jardine, 'Reading and the Technology of Textual Affect', 78–97.
[158] Schneider, 'Affecting Correspondences', 31–62.   [159] Mack, *Elizabethan Rhetoric*, 123.
[160] Ibid. 123–4. Bell, 'John Donne's Love Letters', 25–52; *John Donne's Marriage Letters*, ed. Hester *et al.*
[161] BL, Add, 33271, fo. 39b: n.d. Cf. Folger, V.a.321, fo. 16: 'A l[ett]re written by Chidiock Tichborne to his wyfe the night before he suffred.'

Holmes, whose study of gentry marital correspondence between the 1580s and the Civil War period led them to conclude that 'women were perhaps more commonly expressive of emotion than men'.[162] While their study does not make clear the criteria used to judge letters, it is not necessarily incompatible with the present study, since their analysis extends much later into the seventeenth century, during which period levels of female literacy and letter-writing activity were higher, which may have allowed women to develop a greater articulacy. Taken together, the conclusions of both studies indicate a rise in women's emotional articulacy during the early modern period, a rise that became marked in the sixteenth century.

What remains unanswered, however, is why women became more emotionally articulate in the second half of the Tudor period, and why letters in particular were utilized as a means of expressing personal feelings or sentiments. Several factors may help to account for this. First, higher female literacy rates, better education, and greater familiarity with epistolary media contributed to making women better able to express themselves in written form. By penning their own correspondence, female letter-writers achieved more control over the language they used, had a greater say in how they presented themselves, and in the kinds of feelings and close bonds they wished to convey. Furthermore, as increasing numbers of women wrote for themselves, letters became more personal. In other words, privacy in the act of writing letters encouraged women to correspond more freely and openly; this may have been more so in the case of letters to husbands. There is also, however, a definite sense that sixteenth-century couples wanted to correspond more intimately, that they wished their letters to convey emotion. Related to this, the expressing of affection by women also appears to have become more acceptable during the period: gender codes which increasingly defined wives' domestic roles accepted that loving companionship was an important part of marriage.[163] Finally, the immediacy and generic flexibility of letters made them well suited to emotional self-expression; letters were appropriated for various functions beyond that of communication, the expression of affection and emotion for many couples playing a significant part.

---

[162] Heal and Holmes, *Gentry in England and Wales*, 71, argues that while expressions of male emotion are less common than for women, 'equal warmth from husbands is not difficult to find'.
[163] Sommerville, *Sex and Subjection*, 129–31.

9

Letters of Petition

Letters of petition, suitors' letters, or letters of request (that is, requests for favour), account for almost one-third of women's letters written during the sixteenth century. Female petitioners made a broad range of patronage suits, both for themselves and on behalf of family, dependants, and other groups outside of the household, intervening in areas of crown, ecclesiastical, and more local forms of patronage usually seen as the preserve of men. Viewed as historical documents, letters of petition delineate the peculiarities of the early modern patronage system, and facilitate an examination of female involvement in patronage and politics. Indeed, correspondence represents the dominant written form by which women exerted power and influence: petitionary letters directly evidence female petitioning and networking during the Tudor period, while suitors' letters reveal women themselves as a focus for requests for favour. An important aim of this chapter is to map the nature and scope of women's petitioning activities. Allied to this, the chapter also explores the nature of letters of petition as an epistolary sub-genre. In comparison with 'familiar' correspondence, which permits letter-writers greater freedom in terms of content and structure, letters of petition conform more rigorously to epistolary conventions and models relating to structure, rhetoric, language, and manuscript layout.[1] Read as texts in this manner, paying close attention to genre, letters of petition highlight female mastery of the literary, rhetorical, and formal conventions of the epistolary form, and shed light on the skills, albeit textual and rhetorical, associated with courtiership and the pursuit of patronage.

By approaching patronage from the viewpoint of women's letters of petition this chapter adopts a different perspective from that of scholarship concentrating on patrons and clientage networks, instead viewing patronage from the bottom upwards: from the perspective of suitors. Its main purpose is to analyse forms of approach and persuasion: the ways in which requests were presented to patrons or officials; the strategies and techniques utilized; the rules and conventions that governed such entreaties; and the impact of gender on petitioning strategies—the ways in which women in particular sued for favour as distinct from men. Such an approach concentrates on the products rather than the rewards of

---

[1] Mack, *Elizabethan Rhetoric*, 115–16.

patronage, and methodologically is perhaps more characteristic of literary scholars, who study texts addressed to patrons as a way of probing the dynamics and tensions of client–patron relationships.[2] The chapter is, therefore, to some degree a response to the methodological blinkeredness that has often stymied fruitful exchange between literary and historical disciplines. In the words of Frank Whigham, 'those who study stylistic manipulations do not read historical documents and those who read historical documents do not study style', a situation that, despite the advent of new historicism and cultural materialism (and even 'new new historicism'), still holds to some extent today.[3]

While letters represent important documentary and textual evidence of women's petitioning activities, and usefully help to reconstruct the early modern patronage process, they are necessarily one-sided; only in a few cases is it possible to establish through correspondence whether a particular suit was successful. The fulfilment of requests is recorded elsewhere by various sources: bishops' registers indicate preferment to benefices; Signet Office books detail grants of offices, land, and pensions; Court of Wards records show bestowal of wardships; household and estate papers identify recipients of widows' grants of offices and appointments of feoffees, sureties, secretaries, executors, household servants, and chaplains. Furthermore, individual women's letters of petition and recommendation competed with those of other rival claimants. Supplicants rarely worked through one channel, but approached several 'intermediaries' or patrons to exert influence on their behalf, operating in various ways by letter, bestowal of gifts, and payment of perquisites or bribes.[4]

The nature of 'petitioning' itself as an activity has been looked at by social and legal historians working on female litigants and the law courts.[5] However, as these scholars fully acknowledge, the material used displays considerable legal influence; indeed, the relationship between women's oral testimonies and the production of such legal documents remains unclear, presenting problems of methodology and interpretation. Likewise, the authorship of women's petitions to parliament during the Civil War is far from clear.[6] Letters of petition, on the other hand, which are more closely associated with actual female composition, are better suited to an analysis of women's rhetorical, literary, and presentation skills. Nevertheless, distinct similarities in language, style, and strategies emerge when comparing these different forms of petition. Indeed, the degree of linguistic facility among literate women is matched by the ordinary female

---

[2] See Brown, *Patronage, Politics*; Brown and Marotti, *Texts and Cultural Change*.

[3] Whigham, 'Elizabethan Suitors' Letters', 864; Fumerton and Hunt, *Renaissance Culture and the Everyday*, 1–17.

[4] On patronage see e.g. MacCaffrey, 'Patronage and Politics', 21–35; id., 'Place and Patronage', 95–127; Peck, *Court Patronage and Corruption*; Adams, 'Patronage of the Crown', 20–45; Hammer, 'Patronage at Court', 65–86.

[5] Davis, *Fiction in the Archives*; Stretton, *Women Waging Law*, ch. 8; Gowing, *Domestic Dangers*; Walker, 'Expanding the Boundaries', 235–45.

[6] Higgins, 'Reactions of Women', 177–222; McArthur, 'Women Petitioners', 698–709.

deponents who manipulated language and narratives for political ends.[7] Furthermore, the deferential tropes and language of female submission exhibited in female suitors' letters is mirrored in the petitions of women to parliament during the Civil War, and finds residual echoes in classical and medieval models.[8] In this sense, women's letters of petition from the sixteenth century should be regarded in the context of a long-standing tradition of female petitioning activity.[9]

Lastly, suitors' letters have long been recognized by literary scholars for their artistry and rhetorical qualities, and for the light they shed on early modern patronage relations, though such studies tend to focus on men's rather than women's letters.[10] In his seminal article on 'The Rhetoric of Elizabethan Suitors' Letters', Frank Whigham observed the 'enacted courtesy' displayed in the letters of male suitors writing to Sir Christopher Hatton; such 'texts', he argued, produced within a 'class-stratified patronage system' represented acts of 'self-conscious artistry'.[11] Jonathan Gibson has argued in relation to male clients' letters that the tensions in dictaminal theory are 'strikingly homologous to those at the centre of Renaissance patronage relations'.[12] The characteristics of female suitors' letters in particular have been explored by Lynne Magnusson, who identifies two different recurring linguistic strategies or 'social scripts' that were used in female suitors' letters, those of 'humility and entreaty' and 'supposal and assurance', and argues that there was a correlation between a woman's language and her self-perception of her power.[13] In this analysis, women suitors' letters differ very little from those of male writers, which followed similar social hierarchies based on rank and social position. The importance of this reading lies in the confidence and self-assurance that it attributes to women dealing with patronage matters; indeed, as this chapter argues, many women demonstrated in their letters an easy familiarity in using a language of patronage, favour, and 'political friendship'—a language viewed as predominantly male. Where this chapter extends upon Magnusson's work is in its examination of the kinds of rhetorical strategies employed by women in their letters of petition that are distinct from men's letters: tropes of female weakness and fragility for strategic effect; emphasis on the plight of widows; the duty of wives, mothers, and kinswomen to intervene on behalf of family and friends. Moreover, it posits a distinctly 'feminine' mode of petitioning, a 'scripted' *female voice* that could be appropriated by both men and women.

---

[7] Gowing, *Domestic Danger*, 201, 235–9.

[8] Higgins, 'Reactions of Women'; Margolis, 'Cry of the Chameleon', 37–70.

[9] Houlbrooke, 'Women's Social Life', 171–89.

[10] Whigham, 'Elizabethan Suitors' Letters'; Gibson, 'Arthur Gorges', ch. 2; Tyacke, 'Edwin Sandys and the Cecils', 87–91; Carter and Condick, 'Study in Patronage', 137–58; Ilardi, 'Crosses and Carets', 1127–49.

[11] Whigham, 'Elizabethan Suitors' Letters', 864, 866.

[12] Gibson, 'Elizabethan Clients' Letters'. See also, Lyall, 'Construction of a Rhetorical Voice', 127–35.

[13] Magnusson, 'Rhetoric of Requests', 55, 63. Cf. Bowden, 'Women as Intermediaries', 215–23.

DEFINITIONS

Letters of petition are clearly defined as a sub-genre of letters in sixteenth-century letter-writing manuals. Writing of 'epistles petitorie' in his *The English Secretorie* (1586), Angel Day stated that 'inasmuch as these Epistles are so named, for the earnest *Petition* or request in euery of them conteined'.[14] In practice such letters were employed in forwarding suits and applying for favour; their intention was to persuade and convince the recipient of the writer's cause. Erasmus adopted a classical rhetorical scheme of categorization for epistles, grouping petitionary letters in the deliberative or persuasive class, distinct from demonstrative, judicial, and familiar letters.[15] Other writers, including Day, adopted this Erasmian method of classification.[16] Distinctions between types of letter are, however, often blurred. The definition can be used more broadly to embrace all requests. Letters of 'recommendation', according to Erasmus, are 'closely related' to the petitionary form, 'for when we recommend someone, we are really making a request in another's name'.[17] Thus, letters of recommendation or introduction, written preferring suitors, and letters of intercession or supplication seeking intervention on behalf of third parties are examined in this chapter; as requests strictly made on behalf of others they are essentially petitionary.

Importantly, these epistles are different from legal petitions (a formal application made in writing to a court), parliamentary petitions (the form by which the Houses of Parliament formerly presented a measure for the monarch's granting, or by which parliament was itself approached), and petitions or 'bills', which are formulaic documents, written in the third person, that were presented to the monarch for signing only when a provisional promise of royal favour had been secured. Letters of petition represent informal requests for favour that could be employed flexibly at different stages of the patronage process. They might aim to secure the monarch's provisional favour, or to seek assistance from government officials in procuring the royal signature and finalizing details. Lady Ellen McCarthy wrote to Robert Cecil concerned that her petition 'cannott have so speedy recourse or hearinge ... at the Counsell table'.[18] In other cases, letters supported the petition itself. Lady Stafford forwarded to Burghley a petition to the queen for a fee farm, accompanied by a letter urging him to deliver the petition to the monarch at his 'leisure'.[19] Letters from women also supported petitions of others. In 1604 Alice Stanley, countess of Derby, wrote to Julius Caesar supporting the petition of Richard Leake and the inhabitants of the

---

[14] p. 169.
[15] Erasmus, *De conscribendis epistolis*, 71; id., *Conficiendarum epistolarum formula*, 264.
[16] *English Secretorie*, 41–2.   [17] Erasmus, *De conscribendis epistolis*, 181, 71–72, 108.
[18] Hatfield House, Cecil, 102, fo. 144: 21/06/1603. See also BL, Addit., 12506, fo. 381: 02/02/ 1604.   [19] Cecil, 14, fos. 43, 44: 25/01/1587.

parish of Dent in Yorkshire for the erecting of 'a free schoole'.[20] Women's letters of petition, therefore, represent a part of a much larger process; at the same time, they help document the layers of social transactions involved in the quest for patronage and favour.

More fundamentally, elements of the letter of petition are found in almost every kind of Renaissance letter. Indeed, Day maintains that 'epistles petitorie' are: 'the moste ordinarye of any sortes of Letters that are indited, for the greatest nomber of directions are commonly concluded in this matter, the requestes whereof doe either specially concerne the wryter, or are otherwise to be respected in the behalfe of some other.'[21] In practice, suits or requests were often contained in correspondence where the petition was apparently not the sole purpose of the letter. This works further to erode distinctions between 'domestic' or 'familiar' letters and letters of petition or 'practical' letters; letters to family members could in many cases adopt a strategy of petitioning; petitioning could also include a language of affection or friendship.[22] In a lengthy letter to her brother, Thomas Lord Paget, Audrey Aleyn discussed various matters, including his wife's pregnancy, her own successful childbirth, provision of a wetnurse, and the choice of Lady Cobham as godmother to her child, before requesting that he 'cause' money to be delivered.[23] The pragmatic nature of much early modern women's correspondence occasioned the making of requests, usually to family patriarchs, men upon whose patronage women relied.

The petitionary mode was commonly used in letters from daughters (and sons) to parents, from nieces to uncles and aunts, sometimes in letters from wives to husbands, as well as in other letters where the addressee was socially superior to the writer. Writing to her father Sir John Littleton for forgiveness, Elizabeth Willoughby appropriated the language of petition, 'beseeching' him 'for the love of god' to take pity on her as his 'naturall childe', and to have 'compassion' on her as 'a distressed woman'. The letter ends by presenting the image of her in the abject position of humble petitioner submitting herself before him upon her knees.[24] More typical of the ways in which requests were framed in letters to family members is a letter from Anne Broughton to her father Richard Bagot, in which she asked for his assistance in placing one Roger with the dean of Lichfield, a request couched in a language of supplication: 'I wolde crave of you to be soe good if you cold possiblie to help Roger by mr deanes meanes to be placed at Lichfield yf the place be the meane he might staye untill a better fall unto him.'[25] Requests were thus often at the heart of relationships documented by letters, inflecting them with a vocabulary of petition or deference. For social historians interested in studying early modern correspondence as literary evidence of the nature and quality of family, social, and gender relations, this has important

---

[20] BL, Addit., 12506, fo. 185: 07/02/1604. See also ibid., fo. 89: 26/07/1599.
[21] *English Secretorie* (1595), 184.   [22] Schneider, 'Affecting Correspondences', 31–62.
[23] Staffs. RO, Paget Papers, D603, K/1/3/40: 25/10/1572.
[24] BL, Lansd., 46, fo. 60: 1585.   [25] Folger, L.a.229: 24/04/1596.

implications, rendering it hard to discern how far letters of this nature reflect traditional social hierarchies rather than the difficulties, awkwardness, or epistolary conventions of request-making.

THE SCOPE OF PETITIONING ACTIVITY

Tudor women's surviving correspondence includes a significant body of letters of petition: approximately 1,000 epistles, composed by some 350 women. These documents, however, represent only a small fraction of the women's letters of request written during the sixteenth century. Levels of female petitioning, therefore, whilst lower than levels of male petitioning, are likely to have been higher than is suggested by numbers of surviving letters. Nevertheless, the surviving evidence documents significant female activity in this sphere. Letters were addressed to a range of political figures: monarchs, government officials, regional magnates, and intermediaries surrounding such personages, including secretaries, servants, and family members. Analysis of the relationships between letter-writers and recipients indicates the channels through which women operated. In 81 per cent of cases women were not related to the recipient of the letter; the remaining 19 per cent of letters, however, were written to those with whom female signatories enjoyed family connections. There is, therefore, a degree of overlap between petitionary and family correspondence which erodes distinctions between the categories of the domestic and the political. While women related to officials and patrons could invoke family obligations, their letters exhibit many of the characteristics of other letters of request, in terms of style, tone, and favours sought. More striking, however, is the degree to which female petitioners were not restricted to working through the family, but could approach government officials. This observation offers an alternative interpretation of women's political involvement that is complementary to several important recent studies of women and patronage which have argued that women worked through male family members.[26] A study of letters of petition in general reveals the variety of individuals through whom women worked, and the fluidity of patronage connections. In their correspondence women seldom wrote to a single person, but rather solicited the favours of a range of well-placed individuals. Thus, Mary Grey wrote to both William Cecil and Robert Dudley to secure her release from the Tower; and when Essex fell from favour it was to his 'factional' enemies the Cecils that the women of his family wrote seeking his political rehabilitation, and it was Robert Cecil whom Penelope Rich

---

[26] e.g. Payne, 'Aristocratic Women, Power, Patronage', 164–81; ead., 'Cecil Women at Court', 265–81; Croft, 'Introduction', and 'Mildred, Lady Burghley', in *Patronage, Culture and Power*, pp. ix–xxi, 283–300.

approached in her brother's absence on patronage matters.[27] Examining the patronage system from the perspective of suitors (in this case female supplicants) exposes a system that is fluid, overlapping, and driven by suitors' demands.

The letters themselves fall into two main types: letters written by women for themselves (letters of request or petition) and those on behalf of another party (letters of recommendation or intercession). Well over 300 individual letters contain women's personal suits for themselves, concerning issues including, grants of land and wardship, awards of pensions and annuities, disputes over jointure and inheritance, seeking favour and advice, influencing local officials, and securing justice and release from imprisonment. Elizabeth Collinwood wrote to Sir Thomas Sutton for charitable support, 'vouchsafing' him to let her 'taste of comfort' from him.[28] Faced with charges of recusancy Elizabeth Beaumont wrote to the Justices of the Peace to absent herself from appearing before them, claiming 'by reason of sicknes, age and debiliting of bodye I have not bene able to ryde no abide ayre abroade of longge tyme'.[29] These examples, typical of the kinds of requests in women's own letters of petition, differ from the competitive personal demands for office that marked the letters of male suitors.

Although they could not normally hold government office—with the exception of formal court positions—female letter-writers did, however, join in the scramble for the lease or sale of confiscated crown lands for personal gain.[30] Jane Neville, countess of Westmoreland, asked Lord Burghley to procure from the queen the lease of the parks at Branspeche.[31] Ursula Lady Walsingham wrote to Robert Cecil 'praying' for his help to 'obtain' the reversion of the lease for the Priory of Carisbrooke on the Isle of Wight.[32] Wardship was another area in which women were active as petitioners, not only as mothers concerned to secure the wards of their children, but also as individuals eager to profit from the lucrative sale of this crown prerogative. On the death of her husband, Mary Grey wrote to the earl of Leicester for help in securing the wardship of her son Henry Grey.[33] Lady Margery Williams moved Burghley as master of the Court of Wards for the 'reserving of the wardship of Withipoole of Ipswiche for me and myne'.[34] In more macabre fashion, Katherine Lady Newton, on hearing that 'one Mr roberte Chamberlen of Oxfordsher' lay 'dangorosly seake', wrote to Robert Cecil for first refusal on the wardship of his son in the case that the father

[27] NA, SP12/42/48, 12/41/37, 12/40/66, 12/40/61, 12/39/65, 12/38/15, 12/36/65; HMC, *Pepys*, 95; Cecil, 75, fo. 83; 68, fo. 10; 178, fos. 115, 117; 32, fos. 87, 95; 33, fo. 67; 30, fo. 90; 40, fo. 42; 43, fo. 40; 55, fo. 56.   [28] GLRO, ACC 1876/F/3/1/6: 26/11/1610.

[29] SP12/189/17/2: 06/04/1586. See also LPL, Talbot, 3205, fo. 52: 24/09/1594.

[30] An exception to the rule that women were not awarded crown offices is Lady Elizabeth Russell, who in 1589 was appointed keeper of the Queen's Castle of Donnington and bailiff of the Honor, Lordship, and Manor of Donnington: Cecil, 178, fo. 132; 106, fo. 39: 05/03/1600, 03/08/1602.   [31] BL, Lansd., 18, fo. 200: 10/10/1574. See also Cecil, 14, fos. 43, 44: 25/01/1587.

[32] Cecil, 93, fo. 38: 10/05/1602. Cf. SP46/28/172: 03/07/1569.

[33] BL, Addit., 34079, fo. 7: 25/11/1564.

[34] Cecil, 11, fos. 55–6: 14/08/1580. See also BL, Lansd., 57, fo. 118: 10/09/1588.

died.[35] Jane Jobson, the daughter of Anne White, wrote to Robert Cecil more generally, pressing him to 'remember' her 'for any wardshippe or any lease of a wards landes'.[36]

In addition to writing for themselves, large numbers of women petitioned on behalf of family members: husbands, children, and kindred.[37] The suits pressed in letters for family were similar to those that women pursued for themselves, suits concerning land, inheritance, judicial trials, and imprisonment. Mary, dowager countess of Southampton, put before Robert Cecil the suit of her niece who was saddled with her husband's debts.[38] Frances, countess of Essex, 'entreated' Robert Cecil to 'favour' her 'very freind and neere kinsman' Henry Sidney of Norfolk, who was called before the council to answer certain questions regarding 'engrossing corn'.[39] A high proportion of women's petitionary correspondence concerned the securing of children's marriages and careers. Anne Lady Cobham sought Robert Cecil's advice about the proposed match between her daughter Philippa and one Mr Coverley of Coverley, the ward of Lady Gargrave of Yorkshire.[40] Lady Stafford presented her son to Burghley to be 'proferred' in marriage to 'any of' his 'bloode'.[41] Elizabeth Longstone commended her son Thomas to William Davidson, secretary to the Queen, 'beseeching' him 'to vouchsaffe to take him into' his 'service'.[42] Lady Harington of Exton implored the earl of Essex to receive her son into his 'protectyon', claiming that 'from hys cradell' she had 'dedycatyd' his 'sarvyce' to him.[43] Maternal letter-writers were also active in trying to place their daughters in positions at court. In protracted attempts at promoting two daughters from her first marriage, Anne and Katherine Bassett, for service in Jane Seymour's household, Honor Lady Lisle sent a constant flow of letters, in addition to tokens and gifts, to various people she deemed capable of wielding influence on her behalf.[44] Here, women rather than men were seen as influential in distributing positions. Thus, John Hussee counselled his mistress Lady Lisle to refrain from writing to Cromwell or Francis Bryan: 'for it is thought by my Lady Sussex and other your Ladyship's very friends that it is no meet suit for any man to move such matters, but for such ladies and woman as be your friends.'[45] Likewise, Elizabeth, countess of Rutland, herself 'inexperienced in the fashions of the court', looked to further the career and marriage prospects of her daughter

---

[35] Cecil, 78, fo. 79: 20/04/1600.   [36] Cecil, 86, fo. 122: 25/06/1601.

[37] Over 350 of the letters of petition surviving for the period 1540–1603 were penned on behalf of family members. In most cases, though not in all, identifying on whose behalf a letter was written is straightforward: usually the name of the beneficiary and their relationship to the signatory are specified. Certain letters, however, simply refer to 'bearers', who remain otherwise anonymous.

[38] Cecil, 181, fo. 82: 1600.   [39] Cecil, 56, fo. 46: 24/10/1597.

[40] Cecil, 70, fo. 66: 30/05/1599.   [41] Cecil, 14, fo. 44: 25/01/1587.

[42] SP12/194/36: 12/10/1586. See also BL, Lansd., 28, fo. 150: 27/12/1579.

[43] Cecil, 178, fo. 21: 03/12/1598.

[44] *Lisle Letters*, iii. pp. 175–6, 717, 718, 729, 742a, iv. pp. 104–6, 863, 850(ii), 880, 884, 887, 891–3, 894, 902, 1101a; Harris, *English Aristocratic Women*, 219–21.

[45] *Lisle Letters*, iv. 896. Harris, 'Women and Politics', 276.

Bridget Manners by placing her with the countess of Bedford, who introduced her to court circles, finding her a position as one of the queen's maids of honour.[46] In this sense, the category of the 'political' should not only be extended to include women, but also redefined to incorporate a gendered dynamic of power and influence.

Perhaps more significantly, over a quarter of women's letters of petition were penned on behalf of groups outside of the immediate and extended family: servants (technically within the 'household'), tenants, neighbours, 'friends', and clients. The range and nature of requests made by women acting as intermediaries or patrons elucidates female intervention in the dispensing of crown, ecclesiastical, and more local forms of patronage. Women wrote concerning the preferment of suitors to offices, both ecclesiastical and secular, and the bestowing of titles and honours, thus performing many of the same patronage functions as men. Mary, countess of Pembroke, preferred a 'poore' servant to Sir Julius Caesar in his capacity as master of the Court of Requests; Alice, countess of Derby, sponsored one John Owen for a military post to be in charge of troops levied in Northamptonshire for dispatch to Ireland.[47] Muriel Knyvett wrote to her cousin Sir Bassingbourne Gawdy on behalf of one William Chartery for a benefice that was in his power to present.[48] Lady Bacon, preferring one Mr Holmes to Burghley, wrote that the advancement of the former would be for 'the great benefit of o[u]r land & specially of the adva[n]cem[en]t of the gospell herin'.[49]

The obligations that noblewomen had towards neighbours, 'friends' or clients who sought their advocacy in patronage matters are clearly visible in their letters. Dorothy, countess of Northumberland, preferring a gentleman to her brother the earl of Essex, wrote that 'I can not deny him my letter to intreat you'; Mary Wriothesley, dowager countess of Southampton, wrote to her son the earl that 'I am desyred by my La[dy] Cutts (whom you knowe I may not deny) to commend a kynsman of hers . . . to your favo[u]r'.[50] It was also incumbent upon upper-class women as mistresses of the household to further the interests of servants and retainers, to mediate in their affairs and to forward their suits. Such duties are expressed in many noblewomen's letters. Penelope Lady Rich, writing to her brother the earl of Essex, declared with barely disguised lack of enthusiasm her obligation to forward the suit of a male servant: 'my sarvant Geralde make[s] me troble you with an other letter.'[51] Furthermore, bound by duty to further the interests of servants, a noblewoman did not even need to know the precise details of a suit in order to promote it. This is well illustrated in a letter from Katherine

---

[46] HMC, *Rutland*, i. 250, 273–4.

[47] BL, Addit., 12506, fo. 235: 01/06/1596; BL, Addit., 25079, fo. 53: [1600].

[48] NRO, Knyvett/Wilson Papers, KNY932/372/X6: 1602. See also BL, Eg., 2713, fo. 319: 09/12/1593.   [49] BL, Lansd., 79, fo. 79: 22/05/1595.

[50] WCRO, 'Essex Letter Book *c.*1595–1600', MI 229: n.d.; Cecil, 70, fo. 35: 18/05/1599. See also SP12/44/37: 08/11/1567.   [51] 'Essex Letter Book': 06/1596.

Bertie, duchess of Suffolk, to William Cecil, written on behalf of her gardener, whose brother was involved in a dispute in Jersey:

I most dessere you good master Cyssell to showe yo[u]r frendship to thys poor berar in a sortten suite that won off jarrsey hathe agenst his brother. His reqwyst is but that it wely plyese my lorde of Somersett ether to derycte hys letter or eles to commande his undercapeten in Jarrsey to cal the matter befor hym & to make some honest ende of it, for otherwyes the poor soly [soul] is lyke to be undon, but watt this matter is I am nott ably to tell you & I pray god the poor soly him selfe be ably to do it but if he can I pray you than to helpe him, even for charytes sake & w[i]th the more spyde [speed] that he may the soner retorne to his gardyn at hom[e] for I can have no saleds tel he retorne nyther shal the[re] be of swytt erbes [herbs] if you helpe him not w[i]t[h] his suit. & so I commytt him w[i]t[h] al his elve [evil] englyshe to you & you to god.[52]

As a man of Jersey the gardener almost certainly spoke Norman French, which may account for his 'evil' attempt to convey to the duchess the matter of his suit.

In terms of social status, it was mainly upper-class women who composed letters of petition, and a significant percentage of these were court ladies. Thus, the majority of female writers of letters of petition were well connected and of high birth, operating within a relatively wide social ambit, though a small proportion of letters derived from women of the professional and middling classes, the wives and widows of lawyers and merchants. It is, therefore, highly likely that many women were acquainted with the officials to whom they corresponded and in a position to exert influence.[53] Petitionary correspondence containing personal suits from women lower down the social scale does, however, survive in small numbers among institutional archives: Sir Thomas Sutton, as the founder of Charterhouse Hospital, recieved several letters from more ordinary women complaining of hardship.[54]

Analysis of letter-writers by marital status reveals that married women account for a high proportion of letters of petition dispatched. Indeed, married women sent over 60 per cent of letters written for family members and other groups. Numerous women took charge of patronage interests during the absence of husbands. Elizabeth Bourchier, countess of Bath, at her husband's 'desyer' 'moved' Sir Julius Caesar on behalf of 'a very honest nabour' for a case before him as judge of the Admiralty.[55] Lady Anne Dacre wrote to Caesar concerning Christopher Bowier, one of her husband's tenants, against whom Lord Dacre had exhibited a bill in the Court of Requests for attempting to repossess land previously sold to him. Her use of the collective term 'we' to refer to herself and her husband indicates a strong degree of marital partnership: 'I am to intreate yow that we maie have yo[u]^r lawfull favo[u]^r & furtherance in this suite, to mytigate that extremytie w[hi]^{ch} lawe might happely enforce vs to.'[56] Frances Devereux was also involved in her husband's patronage, often writing letters

[52] SP10/10/39: 02/10/1550.   [53] MacCaffrey, 'Place and Patronage', 99.
[54] GLRO, ACC 1876/F.   [55] BL, Addit., 12506, fo. 217: n.d.
[56] Ibid., fo. 411: 09/02/1592. See also BL, Harl., 4712, fo. 275: 07/08/n.y.

of recommendation on Essex's behalf in his absence.[57] In October 1597 the countess wrote supporting Anthony Doughty in order that he might retain his customership of the port of Boston in Lincolnshire: 'I am bold in the absence of my lord to become an earnest sutor unto you lordship that yow wilbee pleased to restore him againe unto his office.'[58] Orders were issued to displace Doughty from the Customs Office on account of his alleged 'lewd behaviour', which led to several suitors clamouring to fill the post, including one Henry Aldis who petitioned Burghley directly, and Edwarde Ashe who was supported by William Dynley, the mayor of Boston, and Anthony Irby.[59] The countess of Essex's effort for Doughty was thus in the face of other opposing claimants. Other women were in second or third marriages, which often conferred upon them greater wealth, latitude, and confidence. Commonly, women who remarried conducted business for offspring produced by previous relationships. As a whole these letters indicate the various roles and responsibilities assumed by women within the marital sphere.

Widows were also active correspondents, responsible for over 50 per cent of letters containing personal suits and over 35 per cent of letters written on behalf of third parties. Such women often enjoyed greater freedom of manoeuvre than either married or single women, the latter generally presenting personal suits for themselves. However, widows were more active as suitors for themselves than as intermediaries for others; the opposite is true of married women. Conceivably the latter, operating in association with husbands, had greater opportunity for utilizing influence than widows. Nonetheless, in the absence of men women took charge of family patronage undertakings. From the last two decades of Elizabeth's reign, in the cases of the Russell and Manners families, women assumed the mantle of the family's patronage responsibilities during the minority of a young earl. Lady Elizabeth Russell, in a letter to Sir Robert Cecil on behalf of Henry Grey, earl of Kent, who sought appointment to a lord-lieutenancy, wrote that 'but being intreated therto I could not but do thus much in respect of my Duty to my de[a]d'.[60] Despite the coolness with which she recommended the earl's candidacy, it was evidently an issue of family obligation to Lady Russell that she write to her nephew once she had been approached to solicit Sir Robert's favour: an obligation either to her 'dead' ancestors or to her late husband John Russell, who served on the bench with the earl of Kent in Bedfordshire.[61] In this manner, upper-class women were essential to protect, promote, and continue family interests and honour.

Furthermore, some women received payment for their services as intermediaries and letter-writers.[62] There is evidence that Anne Lady Glemham received money from clients to approach her father the lord treasurer. In 1603 Robert Cecil wrote to Michael Hickes, his secretary, directing him to give Lady Glemham

[57] e.g. BL, Harl., 6996, fo. 164: 05/06/1594; 'Essex Letter Book': 03/04/1596.
[58] SP12/264/155: 28/10/1597.
[59] SP12/264/154: 28/10/1597; SP12/266/46: 06/02/1598.
[60] Cecil, 30, fo. 26: 27/01/1596.   [61] Farber, 'Letters of Lady Elizabeth Russell', 159, n. 7.
[62] Wright, 'Change in Direction', 161–2.

'a purse' of £100 to deal directly with her father, the lord treasurer.[63] Thomas
Lichfield 'delivered' to Lady Gerrard two 'silver saltes' for Mrs Julian Penn to
intercede with Hickes, her son, to obtain a grant; in his letter he requested that
these be 'redeliver[ed]' since his suit was not granted.[64] Elizabeth Bourne
implored Mrs Morgan to be 'earnest' with Blanche Parry, a gentlewomen of
Elizabeth I's Bedchamber, concerning repayment of a £1,000 debt to the queen.
In the event that Blanche Parry could persuade the queen to allow repayment of
the debt at £100 per annum, Elizabeth Bourne promised to pay Mistress Morgan
200 marks; if, however, the amount of repayment had to be increased to £1,200 in
order to be able to repay at £100 a year, then she would pay only £100.[65]

Finally, women were also patrons in their own right. Through ownership and
control of property women were placed in positions of authority with their own
patronage to dispense in the form of offices, benefices, and other types of local
patronage that were in their gift. Powerful women were thus the focus of suitors'
letters.[66] Protector Somerset sent letters favouring his servant Sir John Thynne to
Elizabeth, countess of Shrewsbury, for the stewardship of the manor of Bamp-
ton, a post that she had intended for a member of her own council.[67] As lords of
the manor of Stanford-in-the-Vale, Berkshire, Elizabeth and Lettice Knollys
were the focus of tenants' suits and complaints.[68] A petition from one Alice
Gardiner, widow, addressed 'To the right worshippfull Mrs Elizabeth and M^rs
Lettuce Knowles Ladies of the manner of Stanforde and hir vey good landladies',
sought licence to surrender the right and title of land to the use of one Thomas
Davis and his son.[69] Another undated petition addressed to Elizabeth Knollys
and her mother Margaret by the tenants of Stanford made request for a 'pound'
in which to keep strays.[70] Letters of petition thus document a broad spectrum of
patronage-related activities: women wrote as humble suitors for themselves, they
acted as influential and well-connected intermediaries, and dispensed local forms
of patronage that were in their gifts.

RHETORICAL MODELS

Moving away from what letters of petition tell us about female social and political
roles, an examination of the structure of letters sheds light on women's control
over language, their mastery of rhetorical form, and the extent to which textbooks
might have scripted social relations.[71] The structure of letters of petition,

[63] BL, Lansd., 88, fo. 105.
[64] Ibid., 107, fo. 205: 20/09/n.y.　　[65] BL, Addit., 23212, fo. 187: n.d.
[66] e.g. Blaisdell, 'Calvin's Letters to Women', 67–84.
[67] Longleat House, Seymour Papers, 4, fo. 119: 22/12/1547.
[68] Howse, *Stanford-in-the-Vale*, iv. 133, 142–3, 145; Maine, *Berkshire Village*, 58–60.
[69] BL, Addit., 36901, fo. 64: 1598.　　[70] Ibid., fo. 109: n.d.
[71] Tudor women's familiarity with classical rhetorical and epistolary models is explored more
fully in James Daybell, 'Scripting a Female Voice', 3–20; id., 'Rhetoric and Friendship in Sixteenth-
Century Women's Letters of Intercession'.

influenced in different measure by the classical letter form of the medieval *ars dictaminis*, early modern rhetorical theory, and revived theory of the 'familiar' letter, consisted of five main rhetorical parts which were commonly employed in Renaissance epistles: *exordium* (introduction), *narratio* or *propositio* (declaration of the substance of the letter, which often included a request or *petitio*), *confirmatio* (amplification), *confutatio* (refutation of objections), and *peroratio* (conclusion). Not all of these rhetorical parts were relevant for use in all situations.[72] In general, good letters, framed by a salutation and subscription, were those that combined 'aptness' and 'brevity' with 'comeliness' and 'persuasiveness', and were 'skilfully' written with 'invention', 'disposition', and 'elocution'.[73] For Erasmus the 'best' letters of persuasion were 'effective and pithy'.[74] Ultimately, Erasmus proposed a flexible approach, distinguishing between both direct and indirect approaches, and honourable and dishonourable requests: 'since the nature of the things we ask for varies, and since there is a great variety of persons who make and receive the requests, the method of asking should vary too.'[75] Angel Day also emphasized the flexibility of the petitionary letter, and epistolary manuals such as William Fulwood's *The Enemie of Idlenesse* (1568), John Browne's *The Merchants' Avizo* (1589), Nicholas Breton's *A Poste With a Madde Packet of Letters* (1602), and Abraham Fleming's *A Panoplie of Epistles* (1576) provided exemplary models ostensibly for letter-writers to follow or to adapt. Vernacular manuals of this sort, apparently aimed at a wider, more popular audience, suggest that women below the ranks of the nobility and gentry had access to models and instructions explaining how to pen letters of request.[76] In most cases, however, the examples given of letters of petition were not specifically of women writing, though an exception is Angel Day's 'A Letter remuneratory from a Gentlewoman of good sort to a noble man her kinsman', printed in the 1607 edition of his *English Secretorie*.[77] Indeed, there was little difference in the nature and style of letters recommended for emulation by men and women of equivalent social status.[78]

The direct evidence of the letters themselves strongly indicates women's conversance with the formal rhetorical structure of Renaissance letters, whether from the pages of Erasmus and Angel Day, through formal tuition, or perhaps more commonly from regular practical contact with the form. By way of example, a letter to Queen Elizabeth from Margaret Hawkins (d. 1619), widow of the Admiralty official Sir John Hawkins (1532–95), closely follows the conventional form of a letter of petition.[79] Transcribed in full below—with

---

[72] Day, *English Secretorie* (1586), 22. On the rhetorical structure of letters see Gibson, 'Letters', 615–19; Henderson, 'Reading the Rhetoric', 143–61; ead., 'Defining the Genre', 89–105.
[73] Day, *English Secretorie*, 19–21.   [74] *De conscribendis epistolis*, 19.
[75] Ibid., 172.   [76] Robertson, *Art of Letter-Writing*; Hornbeak, *Complete Letter-Writer*.
[77] Day, *English Secretorie* (1607), ii. 64.
[78] Suitors' letters to noblewomen were also included in printed collections of male correspondents. Roger Ascham's letters for example include a Latin epistle addressed to Anne, countess of Pembroke: *Disertissimi viri Rogeri*, 149–51.   [79] Hasler, *Commons*, ii. 280–1.

marginal annotations to indicate the different rhetorical parts of the epistle—the letter begins with a highly formal salutation, 'Maye it please your moste excellent majestie', followed by an *exordium* currying favour with the monarch. The letter then provides a background narration (*narratio*) of her suit: in short, that on the death of her late husband, among other debts, she is left owing the crown £2,000 from his 'late vnfortunate voiage'. Amplifying upon this (*propositio*), Margaret Hawkins humbles herself to accept the queen's 'pleasure', stating that if the charges are imposed on her she will 'sell all' she possesses, leave herself 'a beggar', 'putt awaye' her servants and 'sojourne' with her 'frendes'. It is then that the request or *petitio* is delivered, asking the queen to 'deale the more graciouslye w[i]th me', before exonerating (*confutatio*) John Hawkin's character as a man who lost his life in her majesty's 'service' and received 'former losses in his lyfe tyme' while in royal service. Before a final standard closing salutation, the letter concludes (*peroratio*) by stressing Lady Hawkin's 'dutyfull obedience', her willingness to raise the required sum by selling 'plate' among 'other stuffe', and her desire to 'vnderstand' her majesty's 'pleasure':

Maye it please yo[u]^r moste excellent ma[jes]^{tie} to be aduertysed, that the gracious message I receaued from you highenes by diuers, but especiallye the first by Mr Killigrew makes mee presume when eny harde measure is offred mee to flye to yo[u]r ma[jes]^{tie} for relyefe in whom onelye it resteth to deale most graciouslye with mee.	*Exordium*

Yt pleased your highenes to geue Mr hawkins leave to aduenture 5000^{li} in this late vnfortunate voiage, w[hi]^{ch} I canne verye well proue he hathe dysbursed, and aboue 5000^{li} more for the benefite of that jeorney, All this beinge vtterlye loste, besides the losse of his lyfe w[hi]^{ch} I accompt the greateste onely for verye gryef and sorrowe that he colde not effecte that w[hi]^{ch} he had vndertaken for your ma[j-es]$^{t[ie]s}$ benefite; is not by some thought sufficiente, but they come to me nowe in your highenes name for 2000^{li} more, towardes the satysfaction of suche as are yet vnpaide, Insomuche as in this worlde I see there is nothinge but one affliction and myserye heaped vppon another, so as nexte vnder god I receaue no worldlye comforte in eny thinge; but onelye in the continewaunce of yo[u]r ma[jes]$^{t[ie]s}$ most gracious & mercyfull inclynacion towardes mee:	*Narratio*

Yf it shalbe your highenes pleasure to impose this charge vppon mee, I muste and will sell all that euer I possesse, leaue my selfe a beggar, putt awaye my servaunts and soiourne w[i]th my frendes, rather then leaue it vnperformed and haue yo[u]^r dyspleasure. But yet I doubt not but yo[u]^r ma[jes]^{tie} w[i]th [*sic*] deale the more graciouslye w[i]th me for Mr hawkins sake; who besides the losse of his lyfe and the greatest parte of his substaunce therewith in yo[u]^r service, receaued many forme^r losses in his lyfe tyme; As 7000^{li} in S[i]^r Fr[ancis] Drakes voiage about the worlde; all men having receaued their onely excepted,	*Propositio*

Petitio

portions himself And at the least 10000^{li} in the late carracque [carrack *Confutatio*
or galleon] where his portion was kepte from him and geauen to others,
very well knowen to the Lo[rd] Thr[easu]er and Lo[rd] Admyrall,
Besides that he euer serued yo[u]^r ma[jes]^{tie} in a moste painefull and
chargeable office, where in I doubte not but yo[u]^r highenes doth
conceaue he hath done very acceptable service. All w[hi]^{ch} being considered I submytt in all dutyfull obedience to yo[u]^r highenes most
gracious pleasure, And am ready to performe assoone as possiblye I
maye make money of suche plate and other stuffe that is lefte mee,
eny thing that yo[u]r ma[jes]tie shall determine yf I maye vnderstand *Peroratio*
yo[u]^r pleasure by Mr Killigrewe or eny other. And so beseechinge
the Allmightye to blesse and preserue your highenes in all health and
happines, longe to raigne ouer vs. depforde this xvith julye 1596.

your ma[jes]t[ie]s most humble and obedient s[er]vant
Margaret Hawkins[80]

The rigid structure of this letter is more pronounced than that of most other
letters because of its official, almost ceremonial nature. Letters to the monarch in
particular represent the most formal epistles that one could be expected to write,
and they followed strict conventions. Indeed, Peter Mack argues that highly
pragmatic letters followed 'well established norms' of Renaissance rhetoric:
'where renaissance letters of friendship are characterised by considerable freedom
in structure and content, as the letter-writing manuals observe, practical letters
devoted to the conduct of business tend to convey expected content in a standard
form.'[81] In practice, the degree to which other letters of petition followed
structural conventions depended, as Alison Truelove has remarked in relation to
the Stonor letters, on the formality of the letter: 'structurally, the more formal
the subject, the more adherent to convention the letter seems to have been'.[82]
Additionally, the extent to which women's letters of petition deviate from
conventional forms reflects both the nature of the suit and the social status of the
letter-writer in relation to the recipient. In this sense, women's letters can be
viewed as coded according to early modern social hierarchies.

Women's letters of recommendation similarly reflect the rhetorical structures,
arguments, and instructions outlined in Renaissance epistolary manuals.[83] A
letter to Sir Julius Caesar from Frances, countess of Kildare, begins by entreating
his 'fauor' on behalf of two Irish merchants who had a suit before him in the
Court of Admiralty. The countess explained that the men were her neighbours,
and that she would be glad to procure them what friendship she might in their

[80] Cecil, 42, fo. 48: 16/07/1596.
[81] Mack, *Elizabethan Rhetoric*, 115–16. He argues in the case of letters of recommendation and
consolation that, 'by following well established norms they conveyed a sense of order and reassurance. Originality in letters of this type would be a sign of anxiety, of uncertain or inappropriate
sentiments on the part of the writer' (p. 116).
[82] Truelove, 'Commanding Communications', 50.   [83] Mack, *Elizabethan Rhetoric*, 114–16.

'just and honest cause'. She then offered thanks, expressing her readyness to 'requite' the favour 'by any good meane', before leaving the men and their cause to Caesar's 'goode and fauorable consideration'.[84] Following a similar format Joyce Wrotesley wrote to her cousin Walter Bagot preferring suits for two men— the letter-bearer and her neighbour John Smyth—both of whom wished to keep their posts under Bagot as high sherriff of Staffordshire. In both instances the suit of each man is recommended, his honesty and ability to 'discharge' the post praised. The letter ends with the writer's commendations, with no mention of requittal of favours rendered. The absence of an offer to repay the favour might explain the postscript to the letter penned by Walter Wrotesley, in which he endorses his wife's support for the bearer, and promises reciprocation in kind should the favour be granted.[85]

A final example, of a letter written by Katherine, duchess of Suffolk, in 1550 to William Cecil, illustrates the flexibility possible in letters of recommendation. An accomplished letter-writer herself, the duchess was fully aware of the structural conventions of the letter form; the Cecil letter betrays a playful, even artful self-consciousness of the act of letter-writing and of the function of letters. 'This letter must serve you for many purposes', she informed the newly appointed secretary Cecil. 'First, you shall hereby find you be not forgotten, but amongst the biggest remembered, and farther, you shall hereby take occasion not to be idle, but to be occupied by me.' With remembrances delivered, the letter then expands upon the business of the suit that would 'occupy' Cecil, in short, that he intercede in '[William] Naunton's cause', a matter about which she had written to him on a previous occasion. Where next there should be a promise of favour reciprocated, the letter moves rather to a discussion of friendship, arguing that benefits should be given gracefully and quickly. The letter then reiterates the suit, 'I pray you save them innocent from being condemned', before knowingly closing with a more formulaic salutation: 'And thus, two parts being played, the third is to bid you farewell with my hearty commendations to mistress Mildred and yourself.'[86] The originality of the letter and the duchess's deliberate deviation from epistolary norms exhibit her practiced dexterity as a letter-writer, and are also symptomatic of her high social standing and close relationship with Cecil.

While many letters of petition are indeed formulaic, both structurally and linguistically, choice and adaptation of or deviation from conventional forms indicate more personal elements of women's petitions. In a letter to the master of wards concerning the wardship of her eldest son, Anne Newdigate consciously adapted the rather commonplace promise of prayers for the recipient to great effect, writing: 'although it be an ordinarie phrase to say I will pray for your honoure, yet I beseeche yow favoure me so much as to beleeve that w[i]th all constant heartes sinceritie I will not faile daylie to solicite the Almightie in your

<hr>

[84] BL, Addit., 12506, fo. 258: 06/02/1592.   [85] Folger, L.a.1000: 15/05/1599.
[86] SP10/10/32: 18/09/1550. On the duchess's patronage of William Naunton, her husband's second cousin, see Harris, *English Aristocratic Women*, 199–200.

most earnest devotiones to graunt unto yow the blessed happines of your owne desires.'[87] Other letter-writers, too, demonstrate an inventiveness of expression and phrasing: Ursula Walsingham, in a letter to Thomas Windebank, likened herself in her importuning to 'the beggar that hauntes most where hee findes best relief'.[88] Furthermore, letters occasionally exhibit signs of tension between convention and an outward display of deference on the one hand, and a writer's personality and temperament and the import of an epistle on the other. In a letter of petition to Sir Francis Windebank, Lady Falkland adapted the traditional part of the letter, offering to remunerate the recipient for a favour granted, registering in an almost sarcastic tone to the secretary of state her dislike of his describing her as a 'collapsed lady': 'if the service of a collapsed lady; as you called hir, may bee of use to you, you shall euer command Sir.'[89]

The process by which women narrated their suits also gave opportunity for more individualized or idiosyncratic elements to their letter-writing. This part of the letter, used to impart circumstantial, personal and explanatory details, allowed greater freedom for originality. A long letter to Sir Julius Caesar from Elizabeth Bourne describes in detail her estrangement from and ill-treatment by her violent and wayward husband Anthony Bourne. The letter, written at a time when Caesar was investigating the possibility of a divorce for the Bournes, chronicles Anthony Bourne's faults: his taking away of another man's wife, by whom he had four 'bastards'; his refusal of his own wife's company; the fact that he has 'wasted' his own substance and her 'ancient inheritance'; that he had 'sworne' her 'death and dystruction', attempted to 'blowe upp' her, her house, and her children with gunpowder, and to poison her; and that he had sent a man from France, 'burnt in the hand', to stab her 'with a dagger'.[90] In recounting her husband's numerous 'women' she is particularly waspish about one Anne Vaughan, a women, according to Elizabeth Bourne, 'most famous for her ill life', 'as common a harlot, as anie in bridewell', and who was apparently so syphilitic that she needed to be wheeled around in a cart: 'shee was', Bourne informed Caesar, 'not able to bee removed, but in a cart; the pocks had so consumed her.'[91]

For women involved in both family and business disputes letters provided an opportunity to represent and defend themselves, and to relate circumstantial details. In her letters to Cromwell begging him to intervene in her disastrous marriage, Elizabeth, duchess of Norfolk, catalogued the many occasions of violence that she had received at the hands of her husband and his mistress, Elizabeth Holland. In one letter she denounced the 'bawd' and 'harlots' that her husband kept in his house, describing how 'they bound me, and pinnacled me,

---

[87] WCRO, Newdigate Papers, CR136/B308: n.d.   [88] SP12/284/8: 10/05/1602.
[89] *Elizabeth Cary, Lady Falkland: Life and Letters*, ed. Wolfe, 379: [22–30]/06/1632.
[90] BL, Addit., 12507, fo. 204: 11/08/1582. Ibid 38170, fos. 17–27: 'The case of Elizabeth Bourne for a divorce (a mensa et toro) from her husband, with notes from the canon law on the subject of divorce, and "briefe answeres" to questions on her behalf, by Sir J Caesar; December, 1582.'
[91] BL, Addit., 38170: fo. 17^v.

and sat on my breast till I spit blood'.[92] Letter-writing was possibly the only avenue that the duchess of Norfolk had for securing redress: she was well-nigh ostracized by her brother, Henry Stafford, and her family, who sought reconciliation between her and the duke of Norfolk and blamed the duchess's violent conduct and language for the rift between the couple.[93] By writing these letters to Cromwell the duchess attempted to secure help, and make her appalling situation more widely known. 'I pray you shew my lord my husband this letter', she wrote to Cromwell.[94] This is not to suggest that one must accept these letters at face value. As in persecution narratives, emphasis is on exaggerating the cruelty of the persecutors, and providing forceful and compelling testimony to buttress the suitor's claims to secure redress. The effectiveness of Elizabeth Howard's epistolary pleas (as with Elizabeth Bourne's documenting of her husband's misdemeanours) lies not in the accuracies or inaccuracies of the reports of violence committed against her, but the persuasiveness with which she described the brutal acts. Above all, letters of this sort are an exercise in the art of persuasive argument, a matter central to Renaissance letter-writing manuals.

MODES OF ADDRESS AND DEFERENCE

In addition to their general adherence to rules of rhetorical structure, women's letters of petition closely adhere to epistolary conventions in their use of opening and closing modes of address and salutations, further proof of female familiarity with letter-writing forms.[95] The formulations chosen—modulated by a highly tuned sense of differences in social status—directly resemble those found in the pages of Renaissance epistolary manuals.[96] What marks letters of petition in particular is the level of deferential language employed in presenting suits. On the surface, the demeanour exhibited by these letters is partly a product of the nature of making requests, inasmuch as petitioners were dependent on the good-will of patrons and officials, sometimes for suits of a delicate nature, and frequently against competition from other suitors. In addition, certain solicitations—for money or release from imprisonment—were awkward to make and are generally more humble and beseeching than other requests requiring less commitment from a patron to fulfil. Thus, in some senses the letters mirror patron–client relations, reflecting not only the writer's obligation and gratitude to a potential benefactor, but also the problems of how to approach a patron.

---

[92] Wood, *Letters of Royal and Illustrious Ladies*, ii. 361: 24/10/1537; ii. 371: 26/06/[1536]. Harris, 'Marriage Sixteenth-Century Style', 371–82, offers an account of this marriage.

[93] *Letters of Royal and Illustrious Ladies*, ii. 218.   [94] Ibid. ii. 225: 30/12/1536.

[95] Dianne Watt has noted a similar adherence to the convention of the medieval *ars dictaminis* in the salutations of women's letters of the Paston family: 'No Writing For Writing's Sake', 122–38.

[96] Fulwood, *Enemie of Idlenesse* (1568), sigs. C7$^{r–v}$, M5$^{r–v}$; Magnusson, *Shakespeare and Social Dialogue*, 80–8.

The utilization of often elaborate and exaggerated language of deference, humility, and service, advocated by courtly conduct manuals and letter-writing guides, was entirely conventional for patronage relations in the early modern period. Frank Whigham, for example, has noted in men's letters the use of 'a conventional vocabulary of begging'.[97] Marked deference, however, does not necessarily reflect differences in standing. Linda Levy Peck, in analysing the demeanour of male suitors in early Stuart England, has argued that 'the distance in status between patron and client, often both members of the political elite, was frequently exaggerated by rhetorical gesture'.[98] Likewise, some noblewomen employed a subordinate manner when writing to officials of inferior rank. It is, therefore, often difficult to assess whether the abasement displayed in women's letters simply mirrors conventions and codes regulating letter-writing; whether it reflects a writer's genuine sense of inferiority as a woman, or is rather a canny strategy employed for rhetorical effect.

In practice, women's petitionary letters exhibit distinct variations in levels of deference, generated by the social status of both sender and recipient, the degree of familiarity between them, and the nature of the suit forwarded, as well as other factors which are more difficult to pin down, including the age, character, and self-confidence of individual letter-writers, and the success-rate of suits granted. These differing levels of deference and demeanour and methods of forwarding requests are well illustrated by the papers of Sir Julius Caesar and William Lord Burghley, two officials of unequal social status: the former was knighted only in 1603; the latter rose to the peerage in 1571. In particular, deferential modes of address adopted display an awareness of rank and reflect the differences in the career stages of the two men. As master of the Court of Requests, Caesar commanded respect, but the titles used to write to him—'Good m[aste]r Caesar', 'Good m[aste]r doctor Caesar', and 'Good Sir Julius Caesar' or simply 'Sir', after his knighthood in May 1603—although courteous, are descriptive, not elaborate. By contrast, those used in letters to Burghley—'my very good lord', 'my singular good lord', 'right honourable my very good lord'—signify greater deference, occasioned by his noble status and political position as lord treasurer, master of wards, and a privy councillor. Closing salutations also vary, reflecting again the rigidly hierarchical social distinctions in Tudor England. Letters to Caesar commonly conclude with declarations of friendship—'your assured frend', 'your assured good frend', 'your loving frend'—while correspondence to Burghley evokes the language of service: 'your lordships assured and most bounde', 'your lordships as I am bounde', 'your lordships humbly to command'. The closural phrases used in writing to Caesar, whilst assuring a woman's loyalty, articulate a greater equality in relationship between sender and recipient than is implied in Burghley's correspondence. The language of friendship is generally only used

---

[97] Whigham, 'Elizabethan Suitors' Letters', 866.
[98] Peck, *Court Patronage and Corruption*, 48.

among equals, which suggests the degree of confidence with which women dealt with government officials.[99] A heightened awareness of rank and the correct forms of address is displayed in a letter from Katherine, duchess of Suffolk, to William Cecil on his appointment as secretary of state. Addressing the letter to 'my good cecil', the duchess good-naturedly jests: 'but shall I call you so still now you be master secretary choose you if you will not have it so for till you deny it I will call you so'.[100] In this sense it is social rank rather than gender which underwrites the language of 'supposal and assurance' utilized by female letter-writers and is the main determinant of stylistic register.

On the whole, the language and phrasing of letters of petition to both officials is courteous and respectful. Petitioners routinely extended commendations and humbly remembered their duty in line with epistolary custom, but again different levels of deference were adopted. Letters to Burghley typically contain a rich vocabulary of entreaty. Lettice Devereux, corresponding with Burghley over her son's wardship, beseeched him to have 'favourable consideracion' of her 'state and great charge w[hi]ch cannot be maynteyned w[i]th slender allowance'; and Frances Cooke, moving Burghley on behalf of her brother, described herself as 'most humbly intreatinge your lo[rdships] honorabell fauoure, withe my moste humbell dewty'.[101] Letters to Thomas Cromwell similarly contain a vocabulary of earnest entreaty: Catherine Fitzalan wrote, 'I mekely beseche your good lordship to be my good lord and contynew your goodnes towards me as my especiall trust is in you'.[102] Female petitioners also presented themselves as 'humble' suitors. Mary Windebank styled herself 'an humbel suter' in a letter to Sir Robert Cecil, and Lady Hungerford wrote to Cecil 'as ane humble suter requesting yowr fauor'.[103]

In addition to the humility topos of the 'humble suitor', a range of other deferential modes were utilized by female petitioners. In the early Tudor period it was common for a woman to describe herself simply as an 'oratrix', a female petitioner or plaintiff. Elizabeth, countess of Kildare, signed herself to Cromwell, 'by your oratrice'; Margery Calthorpe, abbess of Brosyard, 'promised' Cromwell by her 'faith', 'you shall be sure of a true oratrice as long as my poor life endures'.[104] Alternatively, women styled themselves as beadswomen, promising prayers for the addressee. Katherine, duchess of Northumberland, signed herself to Cromwell as 'yo[u]r powre bedewoman', as did Elizabeth Lady Wheathill, Anne Lady Russell, and Lettice Lady Lee.[105] This form appears to have declined after the Reformation, but was used in 1582 in a letter by Elizabeth Dudley to the earl of Leicester, in which she beseeched him as his 'beadswoman'.[106] More

---

[99] James, 'English Politics', 330–2.   [100] SP10/10/32: 18/09/1550.

[101] BL, Lansd., 24, fo. 28: 28/02/1577; 69, fo. 79: 03/02/1592. See also 67, fo. 108: 11/1591.

[102] BL, Cott., Vespasian F.XIII, Art. 107, fo. 158: 08/10/n.y.

[103] Cecil, 45, fo. 11: 26/09/1596; 52, fo. 41: 22/06/1597.

[104] *Letters of Royal and Illustrious Ladies*, ii. 318: 16/07/[1537]; ii. 51: [1529].

[105] BL, Cott., Vespasian, F.XIII, Art. 109, fo. 160: 10/10/n.y.; *Letters of Royal and Illustrious Ladies*, iii. 6, 8, 11, 158.   [106] SP12/148/2: 12/03/1582.

common by the end of the sixteenth century is the term 'handmaid', which occurs in numerous letters of petition. Jane Yetsweirt described herself to Sir John Puckering as his 'servant and handmayden',[107] and Arbella Stuart styled herself in a letter to John Stanhope and Robert Cecil as 'Hir Majesties most humble and dutifull handmaide'.[108]

This heightened language of supplication and humility, which aggrandizes the position of the official or patron, however, is absent from those letters written to Caesar. In general, letters to Caesar display greater levels of female self-confidence and authority than those written to Burghley: devoid of elaborate supplications, business is often dealt with very directly, reminiscent of gentlewomen's authoritarian letters to male servants. Mary Scudamore, writing to Caesar concerning a case before him in Requests, omitted both greeting and commendation, opening by stating the concern of her letter: 'Sonne Ceasar wheras I did write vnto yo^u the laste terme in the behalfe of my good frend m^r John Pettus concerning a suite depending before yo^u in your courte of Requestes...'[109] Such confidence is more commonly detected in letters to men of inferior rank or standing. A letter from Elizabeth, marchioness of Northampton, requesting money from William More is exemplary of the kind of terse confidence with which an aristocratic woman might write to a functionary: 'My nedfull stayt causythe me at thys tyme to desyar of you to plesuer me so muche as to lend me x L pond, as spedely as you can, and you shallbe rapayed at ester at the furdest, deny me not thys my request as you frynd me, and I shall not only trewly pay you but be muche thankefull ^to you^ for dooyng me so good and great plesur. scrybell hastly by your frynd E Northampton.'[110] In this sense, social status was for aristocratic women often more important than gender in dictating how they perceived themselves hierarchically, and affecting the ways in which they addressed men.

Letters of petition addressed to noblewomen from male letter-writers of lesser social standing utilize similar kinds of deferential tropes as those exhibited by women petitioners. A letter from the priest John Rugge to Honor Lady Lisle provides a good example of a 'humble' male suitor writing to a noblewoman. The mode of address adopted is formal and respectful: Lady Lisle is exalted as 'Lady most of honour', 'your goodness' and 'your highness', in contrast to Rugge's own 'humble obeisance' as her 'pouer and true bedman'.[111] The male deference of Rugge's letter is also characteristic of the incoming correspondence of Margaret Knollys (1549?–1606), a woman who received a stream of letters relating to property in Warwickshire and elsewhere, which she inherited as the sole heiress of Sir Ambrose Cave (d. 1568) and widow of Henry Knollys (d. 1582).[112]

[107] BL, Harl., 6997, fo. 20: 1595; cf. BL, Harl., 6997, fo. 18: 07/05/1595.
[108] *Letters of Lady Arbella Stuart*, ed. Steeen, 138: 06/02/1603.
[109] BL, Addit., 12506, fo. 481: 26/01/1599.   [110] Folger, L.b.559: [*c.*1550].
[111] *Lisle Letters*, i. 56.
[112] BL, Addit., 36908: court-books of the manors of Nuneaton (1571–1600), and Grymeshill (1584–96) in Warwickshire belonging to Margaret Knollys and her husband Henry. Hasler, *Commons*, ii. 415–16; Fetherston (ed.), *Visitation of the County of Warwick in the Year 1619*, 19.

Representative of the petitions that flowed from the pens of male letter-writers is a letter from Henry DuPort dated 1597. DuPort, who had himself been a supplicant for Margaret Knollys's favour, wrote on behalf of one William Olney, a man who owed her money: 'Although I p[er]ceue my credit w[i]th you is alsmost worne out, yet at the ernest request of one of my frends I make bold to move you in the behalf of M^r W[illia]^m Olney of Tachebrok who is shortly to paye you a some of money: That it would pleese yow (yf conveniently you maye) to forbere him xx^{li} or xv^{li} of yo[u]r money for vij monethes . . . yo[u]^r favo[u]^r toward him herein I shall deserve as I maye . . . '[113] Repeatedly male letter-writers' requests for 'favour' employ a beseeching vocabulary, asking Lady Knollys to judge them worthy of the suit, promising her their service in return.[114]

PETITIONING STRATEGIES

Women's letters of petition exhibit several strategies that were commonly adopted by women in their framing of suits, in order to exhort or persuade. The most frequent trope is the depiction of themselves and other women as objects of pity, victims of poverty and suffering. Great effort was made by women to emphasize their distress, their unfortunate, miserable condition, and often their desperation and lack of comfort elsewhere. Thus, Mary Holcroft, writing to contest the will of her mistress Lady Mary Hastings, portrayed herself to Burghley as a 'poore distressed gentlewoman'; and Frances de Burgh, widow of the earl of Essex, petitioned Julius Caesar describing herself as 'the most vnfortunate creture leueng'.[115] This kind of imagery was also used in soliciting help for other women: Lady Dorothy Walsingham wrote to Sir Walter Mildmay to solicit his help on behalf of a 'pore distresed gentelwoman & her pore small children who is now w[i]t[h] me in wo[e]full plyt beinge pr[e]sently (w[i]t[h]out yo[u]r pytttifull helpe) to be destytut bothe of house goodes & fod'.[116] In representing themselves as pitiable, women drew on conventional petitioning strategies as advocated in epistolary manuals. Indeed, Erasmus recommended the mobilization of images that evoked a reader's pity as a means of enhancing an argument: through 'the invocation of pity . . . the deepest emotions will be stirred if one gives a vivid picture of the consequences'.[117] This is not to doubt the plight of many importunate or unfortunate individuals, but to recognize women's rhetorical skill in wringing out the maximum empathy for their situation.

A commonplace trope of self-abasement employed by female letter-writers was the remarkably vivid image of a subject prostrated on her knees begging for mercy. Mary Everard wrote to Bassingbourne Gawdy, 'I will kneele on my knees

---

[113] BL, Addit., 36901, fo. 62: 26/09/1597.   [114] Ibid., fo. 113: n.d.; fo. 93: 14/12/1602.
[115] BL, Harl., 6996, fo. 95: 08/04/1594; BL, Addit., 12506, fo. 381: 02/02/1604. See also BL, Harl., 6997, fo. 18: 07/05/1595.   [116] SP46/31/22: 23/02/1577.
[117] Erasmus, *De conscribendis epistolis*, 81.

vnto you to crave your favour'.[118] Muriel Tresham, writing to secure leniency for her recusant husband, described herself as 'a looly wife on my knees with importunacy'.[119] By writing in this manner, women were presenting on paper an act of obeisance usually performed in person. This in itself indicates the flexibility of epistles, which increasingly performed functions that women previously would have discharged face-to-face.

Letters of intercession penned by women on behalf of husbands and other relatives imprisoned or otherwise out of favour similarly attempted to evoke pity in the addressee. Assuming the role of the importuning wife, Lady Elizabeth Gorges wrote to Robert Cecil concerning the release of her husband, whom she described as 'a trewe and faythfull subiect (and ever hathe byne) for whome I [would] pawne my lyfe and all myne'.[120] A central strategy in such cases was to stress the plight of the imprisoned men, emphasizing their distress and anguish, the need for merciful pardon, and their loyalty to the crown. In a letter to Henry VIII, Lady More petitioned for the release of her husband Thomas More from the Tower, describing him as the king's 'true, poor, heavy subject and beadsman', and begging Henry 'to have tender pity and compassion upon his long distress and great heaviness, and for the tender mercy of God to deliver him out of prison and suffer him quietly to live the remnant of his life with your said poor beadswoman his wife and other of your poor suppliants his children'.[121] Many wives were at pains to accentuate the physical and mental symptoms of their own distress at their husbands' imprisonments. A particularly graphic description of emotional turmoil is contained in a letter from Jane Dudley pleading for the life of her husband, the duke of Northumberland, during his commital to the Tower for his abandoned attempt to place Jane Grey on the throne. The letter, written to Anne Lady Paget, wife of William Lord Paget, one of Edward VI's leading councillors, contains a moving plea; the duchess—literally sick with worry—urges Lady Paget to move her husband to do 'as he may':

... good madame desyre yo[u]ʳ lord as he may doe: in spekynge for my husbondes lyff: in way of cheryte I crave hyme to doe ^ytt^ madame I have held upe my hed fore my grett hevynes of hartt that all the world knowes canott be lyttyll: tyll nowe that inded I doe begyne to growe in ~~to~~ weke seknes: & also seche a ryssyng in the nyghte frome my stomake upe to ward that in my jugmentt my brethe ys lyke clene to goe away as my ^wemen^ ~~well~~ cane full saye ytt as they knowe ytt to be trewe by there owene payne they take w[i]ᵗ[ʰ] me[122]

An equally emotive postscript begs favour for her 'powere v sones': 'nayture cane noe othere wyss doe butt sue fore theme althoughe I doe nott so meche care for

---

[118] BL, Eg., 2722, fo. 34: n.d.   [119] BL, Addit., 39828, fo. 84: 27/05/1583.
[120] Cecil, 102, fo. 103a: 1603.
[121] *Last Letters of Thomas More*, ed. de Silva, 109: *c*.Christmas 1534.
[122] Keele U. Library, Paget Letters, Miscellaneous, Box C: [1553]. See Gunn, 'Letter of Jane, Duchess of Northumberland', 1267–71.

them as fore there fathere who was to me & to my mynd the moste beste gentylmane that evere levynge womane was mached w[i]^t[h]all.'^123

A rhetorical model for female petitioners may have been provided by the complaints of abandoned women found in Ovid's *Heroides*, which was available in English translation by 1567.^124 Indeed, Sheila Ottway has noted the 'Ovidian' aspects of Dorothy Osborne's letters, reading Osborne as a woman in a 'state of tension, between the assertive, optimistic, and extrovert side of her character, on the one hand, and the melancholy, despondent side of her character on the other'.^125 Many sixteenth-century women letter-writers, who emphasize their pitiful state, employed in their letters the kind of overtly melancholic rhetoric—a rhetoric distinctly gendered female—utilized by Ovid's classical heroines. This is clearly observable in a letter from Mary Grey to William Cecil in which she complained of her imprisonment. The letter states that she recieved 'no lytell comfort' but 'greatte greffe' that Cecil's 'earnest' suit with the queen was unable to obtain her majesty's 'favour'. Lamenting the loss of the queen's favour, Mary Grey confessed that although she deserved the 'conterary', having found her majesty 'marcyfull' she 'trusted' to have 'obtayned' her favour 'befor thyes tyme' and never to have lost it again. The letter continues describing herself as an 'unhappy cretur': 'but nowe I perceue that I am so unhappy a cretur as I must yett be witheout that greatte and longe desiered iuell. will it plesse god to put in her maiestes harte to forgeue and pardonn me my greatt and haynusse cryme allthoughe with as sorrowfull a hartte as euer any pour subiectte did.'^126

The missives Arbella Stuart wrote during her imprisonment exhibit similar tropes of melancholia, which on occasion appear to approach madness. Writing to Henry Brounker on 9 March 1603, the day before her attempted escape, Stuart wrote of her 'malincholy thoughts': 'I thinck the time best spent in tiring you with the idle conceits of my travelling minde till it make you ashamed to see into what a scribling melancholy (which is a kinde of madnesse and theare are severall kindes of it) you have brought me and leave me, if you leave me till I be my owne woman and then your trouble and mine too will cease.' Arbella continues, accentuating her 'sorrow', 'distress', and 'malincholy innocence'; the letter even issues an apparent threat of suicide as her only form of relief: 'with speed because my weake body and travelling mind must be disburdned soone or I shall offend my God.'^127

The 'male-scripted' textual voice of female complaint or lament found among Ovid's heroines was, as Danielle Clarke has argued, eminently appropriable by men as well as women.^128 Indeed, this Ovidian text was recommended by

---

^123 Paget Letters, Miscellaneous, Box C: [1553].
^124 *Heroycall Epistles of the Learned Poet Publius Ouidius Naso* (1567).
^125 Ottway, 'Dorothy Osborne's Love Letters', 150.   ^126 SP12/38/15: 16/12/1565.
^127 *Letters of Lady Arbella Stuart*, 16.
^128 Danielle Clarke, 'Women, Rhetoric and the Ovidian Tradition', 61–87. See also LeBlanc, 'Rewriting the *Heroides*', 71–87.

Erasmus for emulation by schoolboys learning Latin letter-writing.[129] Furthermore, Jonathan Gibson notes Ovidian echoes in some of the letters written during the 1590s by Essex and Ralegh. Such letters written during periods of intense disfavour, emphasized the client's pitiful state, with use of what he describes as an 'excessively melancholic' rhetoric.[130] This is much evident in Sir Walter Ralegh's letters of November 1603 written to King James pleading for his life: 'I do therefore on the knees of my hart beseich your Majesty'; a second letter written under sentence of death refers to his miserable and broken state: 'If I write now what doth not now becum mee most mighty kinge vouchsaufe to ascribe it to the councell of a dead hart and to a minde which sorrow hath broken.'[131] The letters of other men accused of treason or suffering disfavour employed similar strategies of submission, often in the most grovelling terms. Frances Howard advised her husband, the earl of Hertford, that having fallen into disfavour, 'I thynke it beste you wrytt a letter to the quene in deschargnge your sylfe'; and Henry Lord Morley reported to his wife that he had written 'humble letters to the quenes mageste'.[132] This essentially 'female' rhetoric was also utilized by women writing on behalf of men, as is evident in Penelope Rich's 1601 letter of intercession to Elizabeth I on behalf of her brother Essex. The letter, infused with classical tropes and images ('charriots', 'divine oracles', 'giants'), opens by acknowledging Elizabeth's diplesasure and lamenting the miseries of Essex's fall from favour:

Early did I hope this morning to have had myne eyes blessed w[i]th your ma[jes]ties Beuties but seeing the sunne departed into a cloude and meeting w[i]th spirits that did presage by the wheels of theire charriots some thunder in the ayre I complained and expressed my feares to that heigh *Maistie* and divine Oracle from whence I receiued but a doubtfull answere vnto whose powre neuertheles I sacrificed againe the teares and prayers of the afflicted w[hi]ch must needs despaire if they should not importune heauen when they feele the miseries of hell or find that words directed to yo[u]r Sacred wisdome are delliuered out of season . . .

Lady Rich's missive insists on Essex's 'dejected' state and harshness of his misfortune: 'my un fortunate brother whome all men have liberty to defame as if his were capitall and hee so base and deiected a creature that his love his life his service to yo[u]r beuties and the state could deserve noe absolucon after so hard punishment nor so much grace as to answere in yo[u]r faire presence . . . .' She continues by criticizing what are described as his 'combining enemyes', who 'labour upon false grounds to build ruyne urging his faults as criminall to yo[u]r divine honor', and who by 'mallice' and 'councells' seek to 'glutt themseleues in theire priuate revenge', and for their own 'ambicous ends to rise by his

---

[129] *De conscribendis epistolis*, 24.
[130] Gibson, 'Elizabethan Clients' Letters'.
[131] Cecil, 102/67/1, 102/111. See also BL, Addit., 6177, fo. 155: Lady Ralegh to Cecil, 17/11/1603.   [132] Seymour Papers, 5, fo. 168[v]: 12/08/1585; SP12/71/7: 08/06/1570.

ouerthrowe'. Fearful that by 'evill instruments' his enemies intended to take 'his last breath', Lady Rich warned of the 'poyson in theire harts to infect ye seruice'. The letter then makes an extended and impassioned plea for royal mercy to preserve his life and reputation. Written on her brother's behalf, Lady Rich's letter utilizes a consciously 'female' voice of lament to plead for his life: the letter simultaneously stresses the disgraced earl's plight and suffering, while implicitly criticizing the queen by holding up to her a mirror of just queenship, and imploring her not to let her power be 'eclipsed' by those of Essex's enemies who would 'abuse' it.[133]

Working in a similar way to strategies that evoked pity, the position of widowhood, with its religious, emotional, and moral significance, was also exploited to some effect by female letter-writers. Indeed, many widows' requests for favour and annuities appear to have accentuated the extent of their poverty, stressing their vulnerability and isolation from the support of family and friends, and emphasizing the number of orphans for whom they were responsible. Lady Mary Denny moved Robert Cecil for a pension, styling herself as a 'fatherles and frindless widowe destitute of all means' and charged with the task of 'bring[ing] up 9 children'.[134] A widow's plight achieved greater moral strength in the case of pregnancy. Thus, the recently widowed Lady Mary Clifford begged the favour of Cecil, writing: 'I am the more importunate to your honour to hasten this by your fauour, by reason of my weaknes and being w[i]th child, and that I would be certayn of my estate to keepe my sonn from the mesery of the world.'[135] Images of widowhood and family responsibility were again used to bolster men's suits; specifically, letters of intercession seeking reprieve from execution stressed the widow and orphans that would be left upon the prisoner's death.

The representation of women in their own letters as objects of pity evoked the duties and social responsibilities incumbent on governors and magistrates to assist and defend them. Susan, countess of Kent, beseeching Cecil to forward her petition to the queen, called upon him for charity, stating, 'I must confes that for my owne part I haue not disarued so great a fauor from you except of your owne honorabel mynd in petying a poore widow and fatherless child it would haue pleased you to do it'.[136] Widows were traditionally regarded as the responsibility of good governors.[137] Frances, countess of Essex, who after the execution of her husband sought Cecil's assistance, wrote that she had presented to his view 'the image of the importunate widow mentioned in the scriptur[e]'.[138] Furthermore, many letters by way of praise and flattery reminded officials or patrons of their wider public obligation to provide equitable and virtuous government. In this manner Lady Hungerford implored Cecil to follow the example set by his father,

---

[133] Folger, V.a.164, fos. 121–3.
[134] Cecil, 100, fo. 64: 30/05/1603. See also SP12/148/2: 12/03/1582.
[135] Cecil, 179, fo. 109: 1600.   [136] Cecil, 52, fo. 30: 18/06/1597.
[137] Bush, 'Protector Somerset and Requests', 460–1. See also Sommerville, *Sex and Subjection*, 228–9.   [138] BL, Lansd., 88, fo. 28: 1601.

indicating that she was encouraged to write because of his 'piti towards the distressed'.[139] The countess of Essex requested Cecil to further a petition, writing that 'I heard by other deere frends of mine beesides how christianly and religiously you pittied the case'.[140] As well as invoking the religious duty of magistrates to defend widows, numerous female petitioners called upon men to take upon them the paternal role of a father or husband. Fearful that her husband would be taken from her by sickness, Bridget Eayre 'begged' Sir Humfrey Ferrers in the event of her husband's death to take his place, 'to become a father vnto my sonne & a head vnto me'.[141]

What emerges as perhaps most distinct to women suitors' letters as opposed to men's, however, is the use of negative female gender assumptions by women in letters of deference: female 'weakness', 'frailty', 'vulnerability', and women's intellectual and physical 'inferiority' to men were standard deferential tropes, 'cultural scripts' that could be employed to their own advantage to manipulate male assumptions.[142] Lady Julyane Holcroft, seeking to avoid paying a crown loan, appealed to Sir William Cecil as 'a lone woman [who] shall suffer . . . for lack of experience in matters that wemen use not to dealle wyth'; and in approaching Burghley to oversee the executorship of her late husband's will, Elizabeth, countess of Rutland, wrote that 'I who am a weak and sickly woman am unable to manage an affair of that importance'.[143] In 1533 Gertrude, marchioness of Exeter, wrote to Henry VIII explaining that her association with Elizabeth Barton, the 'Nun of Kent', whose 'prophesies' had attacked the king, was due to female irrationality and gullibility: 'I am a woman whose fragylitee and brittelnes ys suche as moost facillie easelie and lightlie ys seduced and brought into abusion'.[144] Evidently some women utilized their gender more self-consciously and in a more calculated manner than others. Mary Throckmorton described to her father a letter that she had written in reply to Sir Thomas Jerningham: 'I haue answered his letter like a woman very submissively if that will serve for I perceive that they do not indure to be tolde of theyr faults nether can I abide any wronge but I must make it knowne to them.'[145] Images of female weakness, therefore, were not only employed by men writing about women (usually in a negative sense) but also by women about themselves as a trope or strategy to elicit a favourable response to their suits: it was often useful and effective for women to convey a sense of their own fragility.

Alternatively, women acting on behalf of immediate family members drew on a range of domestic roles and ideal types of female behaviour, styling themselves as 'natural' mothers, and 'faithful' and 'dutiful' wives. Acting in these capacities,

---

[139] Cecil, 52, fo. 41: 22/06/1597.   [140] Cecil, 90, fo. 81: 1601.

[141] Folger, L.e.502: 14/02/[temp. Eliz.]. See also SP12/163/16: 23/10/1583.

[142] Stretton, *Women Waging Law*, ch. 8; Pollock, 'Teach Her to Live', 234, 251; Fletcher, *Gender, Sex and Subordination*, 123–4.

[143] SP12/71/73: 07/1570; HMC, *Rutland*, i. 245: 03/04/1588.

[144] BL, Cott., Cleo.E.IV., fo. 82. *Letters of Royal and Illustrious Ladies*, ii. 98–101.

[145] WCRO, Throckmorton Papers, CR1998/Box 60/Folder 3/11: 25/12/n.y.

elite women claimed to be performing specific domestic duties which they were expected to fulfil: wives upheld that they were bound to honour and obey their husbands and to assume sundry household functions; mothers that they were obliged to raise and guide their children, to provide for their future material welfare by means of education, marriage, and career.[146] In an epistle on behalf of her husband, Sir William Musgrave, who was seemingly out of favour despite his role in the suppression of the Pilgrimage of Grace, Elizabeth Musgrave in 1537 wrote to Thomas Cromwell claiming that her husband's 'heuynes must nedys be myne by gods law that hathe joynyd us to gether in maryage'.[147] Anne, duchess of Somerset, requested that William Cecil give 'fryndly consell' to her son, arguing it was her 'motherly passyons' that influenced her writing: 'I as a mother do wysh the best to my child.'[148] The positions of mother and wife constituted a significant element in women's conceptions of self-identity, motivating them to operate on behalf of husbands and children.

In many cases familial responsibility provided a firm moral justification for women's intervention in business matters beyond the strictly defined domain of the 'household'. Erasmus was fully aware of the potency of such associations; in particular, he considered the term 'mother' to be both 'respectful' and 'charged with emotion'.[149] Numerous women employed maternal imagery as a petitioning strategy, capitalizing on the moral aspects of motherhood. Frances Cooke, in an epistle concerning the financial provision made by her eldest son for herself and her children, wrote that: 'I shoulde thinke my sonne very vnnaturall, if he should geue that away frome me who hathe breade, and braughte him vp withe great care and payne, and geue it to those that neuer toke one carfull thoughte for him.'[150] The letter emphasizes not only the effort taken by the writer as a mother in nurturing her son and trying to arrange for him 'a very good match', but also the duty to her that her son owed. Katherine, duchess of Suffolk, expressed to William Cecil her 'natural desire' that her children should succeed to her title and lands when she died.[151]

In the absence of other parents, grandmothers could assume prominent roles in writing on behalf of grandchildren. The letters of these senior female family figures again stress that in acting for the interests of their grandchildren they were merely abiding by the laws of nature. Lady Yonge petitioned the lord treasurer as a 'naturall' grandmother on behalf of her granddaughter's 'poore distressed orphans', who she claimed were detained from their whole portions by Sir Edward Newton.[152] Elizabeth, countess of Shrewsbury's attempts to secure an annuity for her granddaughter Arbella Stuart are couched in a language of natural grandmotherly affection. On one occasion she wrote to Burghley that

[146] Houlbrooke, *English Family*, 19, 97, 106; Sommerville, *Sex and Subjection*, 67.
[147] *L&P*, XII (i) 244: 26/01/1538.   [148] SP12/16/52: 19/04/1561.
[149] *De conscribendis epistolis*, 51.   [150] BL, Lansd., 74, fos. 200ʳ⁻ᵛ: 19/07/1593.
[151] Cecil, 157, fos. 52–3: 05/08/1570.   [152] Cecil, 177, fo. 41: 18/06/1598.

her 'specyall care' for Arbella was 'not only such as a naturall mother hath of her best beloued chyld, but much more greatter in respecte howe she ys in bloude to her ma[jes]ty'.[153] In writing in this manner, women were enforcing traditional social hierarchies and behavioural codes, and powerfully articulating not only what they considered to be their family responsibilities, but also a strong sense of how they felt they should be treated by other family members. Letters by women concerning family disputes, like Frances Cooke's to Burghley, frequently assert that their 'unfair' treatment was a dereliction of family duty.

The deliberate and emotive utilization of the mother figure is nowhere more prominent than in widows' letters suing for the wardships of their children.[154] In petitioning for wardship, widows above all sought to demonstrate the existence of natural and loving bonds between a mother and child, and to argue, therefore, that it was more appropriate for wards to be placed with mothers than with 'strangers', who would take less of an interest in the child's welfare. Such strategies pre-empted the 1611 procedural changes that gave mothers and kin prior claim in cases of wardship.[155] A striking example of the overt use of maternal imagery is a letter from Lady Anne Newdigate seeking custody of her eldest son, in which she described herself as 'the unfortunate mother of five young children all nurssed upon myne owne breastes'.[156] Unconventional though the practice of breast-feeding one's own children was for upper-class women during this period, Lady Newdigate clearly sought to convey her own deep sense of maternal attachment to her children.[157]

Widows' suits for wardship that centred on the strength of mother–child bonds, when directed to other women, tended to emphasize the mutual connections between them both as mothers. Thus, corresponding with Mildred Lady Cecil concerning the wardship of her son, Dorothy Tamworth appealed to her to influence her husband, the master of the wards, Lord Burghley:

graunte vnto mee yo[u]r honorable favor and promise for the havinge of the wardshippe of my sonne for the w[hi]ch I moste humble thanke yo[u]r la[dyshi]p for the same by reason of the greate sutes troubles and charges. I meane godwillinge to attende your la[dyshi]p about the same, referringe unto your la[dyshi]ps wise consideracion (in regarde yow are a mother of children) what discomfort it woulde be to a naturall mother to depart from her owne childe and to leave him to the custodie and curtesie of strangers.[158]

In appealing on the basis of shared female experiences of motherhood—a line of persuasion that is distinctly female—Dorothy Tamworth assumed that Lady Cecil as a mother would understand how it felt to have a child taken from her

[153] BL, Lansd., 34, fo. 143: 06/05/1582.
[154] On wardship see Bell, *Introduction to the History and Records of the Court of Wards and Liveries*.
[155] Hurstfield, *Queen's Wards*, 92. The 1611 reforms only came into effect if applications for wardship were made within a month of the father's death.
[156] WCRO, CR136/B307, n.d.
[157] Fildes, 'Historical Changes in Patterns of Breastfeeding', 118–29.
[158] Cecil, 26, fo. 48: 01/05/1594.

care. Conceivably she wrote directly to Mildred Burghley in this case expecting greater sympathy from her as a woman, suggesting that the framing of the petition was influenced by the addressee's gender.

Finally, women mobilized obligations of kinship in their own petitions, though these were more fluid than obligations to immediate family.[159] Elizabeth Lady Ormond, seeking favour from her cousin Lord Robert Dudley, appealed to him to 'answer . . . as a frende and kinsman in all my rightful causes'.[160] Similar familial obligations and bonds sanctioned activity on behalf of kinsfolk; women were prevailed upon themselves by relatives to act as intermediaries to secure places and favour. Lady Katherine Berkeley asked the earl of Leicester to prefer the bearer of her letter, writing that, 'being somewhat akin to my Lord, I am desirous to advance him, that he may be preferred to the queen's service'.[161] Anne, duchess of Somerset, commended her nephew Edward Stanhope to Burghley for the office of master of Requests, explaining that 'by nature, & name, I muste be earneste w[i]th yo[u]r lo[rdship] on his behalfe: The rather for that not onelie I, and all myne, but all that name'.[162] For a noblewomen to forward a kinsman she aligned him or her with her own interests; granting the petition was thus in some sense a personal favour to her.

LANGUAGE OF 'FRIENDSHIP'

In addition to the utilization of strategies of deference, pity, and familial duty, letters of recommendation and intercession also illustrate women's easy familiarity in using a language of patronage, favour, and 'political friendship'—a language of equality typically seen as exclusively male—which is suggestive of the high degree of confidence and authority with which many women wrote. The basis upon which women laid claim to this language was founded in large part on material power, social status, and influence. Although excluded from official, formal, and direct forms of power—in most cases, for example, they could not hold office—women exerted significant influence through unofficial and indirect channels, such as family and court networks, playing key roles in the sustaining vital kinship and patronage networks. Court posts and landownership likewise bequeathed status and influence. Furthermore, the fact that women were approached to write in the first place in support of suitors indicates underlying assumptions about their abilities to intercede effectively. Women's choice of language is thus reflective of social standing and position. And yet language constructs as well as reflects reality. There is a sense, therefore, that women's selection of a language of political friendship, and the dexterity with which they deployed this rhetoric, are in themselves instrumental in constructing an image

---

[159] Houlbrooke, *English Family*, 49.   [160] HMC, *Bath*, v. 153: 01/1560.
[161] HMC, *Pepys*, i. 181: 21/02/[before 1590].   [162] BL, Lansd., 33, fo. 6: 07/05/1581.

of their authority and equality with the addressee.[163] Female letter-writers frequently invoked the friendship of the addressee: Agnes Stubbings asked Julius Ferrers to continue her 'friend'.[164] Philadelphia Lady Scrope asked Julius Caesar to show his 'friendly favour' to the letter-bearer, her cousin Morgan, who was to come before Caesar concerning a farm lease.[165] Letters also evidence female involvement in 'friendship' networks: women are represented as situated within groups of friends, and establishing useful political contacts. Writing to his wife from London, Thomas Lord Paget informed her that several of her 'friends at court' had asked after her.[166] Joan Bradborne informed her brother-in-law Sir Humphrey Ferrers that she would take advice from her 'frendes' about her jointure.[167]

The meaning of the term 'friend' is slippery for this period, and was used to refer to family (even between husbands and wives) as well as more broadly to cover persons unrelated by blood or marriage, where 'friendship' assumes political connotations. In relation to early modern marriage, Diana O'Hara shows how the term 'friends' referred to family and kinship groups, both 'biological' and 'fictive'; groups that were simultaneously advantageous (as sources of counsel, advice, and support) and constraining for the individual (in that their 'goodwill' often needed to be sought).[168] Furthermore, the meaning of friendship as a concept, as Lorna Hutson has argued, itself changed over the course of the sixteenth century with the impact of humanism, 'from that of a code of "faithfulness" assured by acts of hospitality and the circulation of gifts through the family and its allies, to that of an instrumental and affective relationship which might be generated, even between strangers, through emotionally persuasive communication'. This model of friendship derives from a form of exchange between humanistically educated men. The extent to which it achieved more widespread epistolary currency is uneven—late medieval social and cultural modes survived well into the Tudor period—but in general terms late Elizabethan business letters (specifically, letters of recommendation and intercession), in contrast to early Tudor examples such as the Lisle letters, follow more closely humanistic models that rely on a greater degree of rhetorical persuasion. Furthermore, at the heart of this humanistic conceptualization of friendship lies the suggestion that rhetorical skill is in fact capable of engendering friendships, not merely mobilizing existing networks, a conceptualization that needs to be extended to include women. Women's conducting of correspondence was central to oiling the wheels of kinship and patronage networks, and in cultivating useful contacts that could be called upon for future assistance.[169]

---

[163] James, 'English Politics', 330–2; Bray, 'Homosexuality', 3–8; id., *The Friend*; Hutson, *Usurer's Daughter*; Tadmor, *Family and Friends*.   [164] SP46/18/164: 06/05/1598.
[165] BL, Lansd., 158, fo. 30: 21/11/1596.   [166] Paget Papers, D603, K1/3/23: 02/05/1572.
[167] Folger, L.e.474: 04/11/1600.   [168] O'Hara, 'Ruled by my friends', 9–41.
[169] Hutson, *Usurer's Daughter*, 2–3.

In its simplest practical form, friends merely meant allies, supporters, or well-wishers. Such was the meaning of Alice Marvin when she informed her daughter Elizabeth Bourne, after her split from her husband, 'I will wryte to make suche frends as I can for the fauor of yo[u]r cause'.[170] In a reply, Elizabeth asked her mother to thank Lady Conway for her efforts on her behalf, and in particular for writing to the countesses of Warwick and Sussex to garner their support. Friends here are defined in opposition to 'enemies', groups of people who sought to cause one 'harm'.[171] While friends could be called upon by women for advice and support, friendship worked both ways, and women frequently promoted the suits of persons described as 'friends'. Interventions on behalf of 'friends' outside of family and household groups were common: Lady Southwell preferred Dr Some to the bishopric of Exeter 'at the request of a friend'; Magdalen Montagu petitioned her godson Julius Caesar 'on the behalfe of a speciall friende'.[172] Frances Lady Cobham informed Lady Paget that she had been approached by her 'verie friends' 'to intreate' her ladyship to commend to her husband the cause of one Mr Paramore, who was at Westminster over a land dispute.[173]

The language of friendship was ultimately one of reciprocity, a Senecan language of mutual benefits that pervaded early modern patronage relations.[174] In their letters women commonly extended offers of 'friendship', either their own friendship or, in the case of married women generally, their husbands' as well. Joan Wincombe, writing to Essex, excused her husband's absence because of illness and assured him of both their friendships.[175] For the early Tudor period Barbara Harris has noted the 'regularity' with which wives 'offered to return favours "with a like pleasure"', which she argues 'suggests that they had some voice in how their husbands distributed their patronage'.[176] In other instances women offered their own friendship: Mary, countess of Shrewsbury, assured Cecil that she and all her friends would 'w[i]t[h]out all ceremony remen your most thankeful and constant frendes for euer'.[177] Jane, countess of Westmoreland, asked Burghley 'to accept' her 'thankefull minde and the offre of' her 'poore freendship.'[178]

In general, suits on behalf of others were often couched in personal terms. Anne Glemham petitioned Julius Caesar for a 'speciall frend', expressing her desire 'that you doe vouchsafe to consider [the suit] for my sake'.[179] Lady Frances Wilkes asked William Wallop, mayor of Southampton, to show special favour to her poore kinsman 'rather of myne instance'.[180] Anne, countess of Warwick, approaching Caesar on behalf of a former servant embroiled in a land dispute,

---

[170] BL, Addit., 23212, fo. 195: n.d. [171] Ibid., fo. 180: n.d.
[172] Cecil, 58, fo. 57: 08/1597; BL, Addit., 12506, fo. 115: 20/03/1603. See also Cecil, 59 fo. 84: 20/02/1599. [173] Paget Papers, D603, K1/4/26: 04/03/1578.
[174] Salmon, 'Seneca and Tacitus', 169–88, 321–6. [175] Cecil, 81, fo. 85: 09/1600.
[176] Harris, 'Women and Politics', 270. [177] Cecil, 86, fo. 32: 06/05/1601.
[178] BL, Addit., 46367, fo. 35ᵛ: 22/09/1575. [179] BL, Lansd., 158, fo. 78: 06/10/1599.
[180] *Letters of the Fifteenth and Sixteenth Centuries*, ed. Anderson, 209–10: 04/12/1596. See also SP46/24/35: n.d.; Paget Papers, D603, K1/10/32: n.d.

wrote: 'I doe therefore praie yo^w acordinge to the uprightnes and equitie of the cause, to afford him [her servant] all the lawfull favour yo^w maie, and the rather for my sake for w[hi]ch you shall finde him verie thankfull, and beinge a good cause I hope yo^w will helpe him to a more speedie ende for w[hi]ch I shall allso (doinge it at my request) thinke my selfe more behouldinge vnto yo^w.'[181] In these examples, the suitability or merits of the beneficiaries of letters of commendation were typically not described except in broad terms, assuring that, in the case of male suitors, they were 'honourable', 'worthy', or of 'good repute'. Instead, the performance of a request for a suitor was normally presented as a favour for the noblewoman herself; a favour that, it was promised, would be returned in kind. Frances Lady Chandos assured Sir Julius Caesar that she would be 'ever ready to requite' him 'in a greater matter when occasion shalbe offered'.[182]

The practice of reciprocal exchange evident in these letters was at the heart of sixteenth-century patronage relations, whether it be the exchange of favours in kind, or the exchange of money (as in the example of clients' fees) or material gifts. In a letter to Thomas Fanshawe, rembrancer of the Exchequer, Lady Abigail Digby wrote on behalf of a servant, John Cowp, and a neighbour, one Butler, against whom a process had been issued. The letter made clear that she undertook to pay the debt that two men owed, asking Fanshawe to 'frend the poor' men, and to 'pleasure' her 'so much as you may effect my request therein, which I am assured resteth much in you to perform. In requittal thereof I will do you or any friend of yours any curtesie I may either by my self or any frend I have. Here or where as occasion shall serve.' The letter then moves to literal exchange, as Lady Digby acknowledges her debt of a brace of bucks which Fanshawe 'deserved' for his 'former frendlyness', promising to perform the same this season if he let her know 'when or where they may pleasure you'.[183] This language of exchange permeated the political scene, and is implied in a letter from Katherine Ashley to the countess of Bath, thanking her for her token, but 'beyng sory to take any thynge of yow seyng I am not able to do you any pleasuer'.[184] There is a strong sense that the act of receiving, albeit a token, formed an obligation to requite a favour. Letters in themselves were part of this form of exchange.

In adopting this vocabulary of 'friendship', mutual exchange, and reciprocity, women were borrowing conventional forms available in letter-writing manuals of the period. Yet these were not empty rhetorical gestures. What is significant here, however, is that women chose to employ these epistolary forms for the purposes for which they were writing. In so doing, women asserted their own influence and capabilities, conscious that they were indeed able to repay political favours in kind, operating through family and kinship connections, through court and country contacts, and in their own right as landowners and patrons. It also further demonstrates the legitimacy with which women involved

---

[181] BL, Addit., 12506, fo. 219: 22/01/1596.   [182] BL, Addit., 12507, fo. 9: 10/03/1604.
[183] SP46/35/87: 01/07/1588.   [184] CUL, Hengrave, 88/1, fo. 123: n.d.

themselves in patronage activities. Thus, in this sense, there is a correlation between a woman's language and her self-perception of her power; the authority invoked by women in their letters might be interpreted as much as an act of rhetorical self-presentation as a reflection of actual status. In contrast to the images of female weakness, many women adopted the persona of a patron. Acting in her capacity as patroness of the benefice of Horton in Buckingham-shire, Abigail Digby wrote to her cousin John Fortescue at the Exchequer on behalf of the incumbent of the benefice, Mr Wickham, chaplain to the bishop of Lincoln. In her letter she asked Fortescue to support Wickham's promise to compound the first-fruits and tenths subsidies to the crown for payment of his debts, 'the rather because I am patronesse of the benefice in question & knowe the promises to be true'.[185]

Women who wrote letters of petition on behalf of family members, servants, neighbours, 'friends', and clients were conforming to the unwritten rules that governed the pursuit of patronage. Whilst both men and women did petition for favour themselves, it was generally regarded as more acceptable to get someone else to sue on one's behalf; to refuse a supplicant directly was difficult or awkward for a patron. Thus, Castiglione advised in *Il Cortegiano* that 'very sildome or (in maner) never shall he [the courtier] crave any thinge of his Lorde for himselfe, least the lorde having respect to denie it him for him selfe should happen to graunte it him with dyspleasure, which is farr worse'.[186] In addition, a person could express certain matters more easily in a letter on somebody else's behalf than for themselves. Bacon's essay 'Of Friendship' discusses the way that one friend might pursue a suit for another, writing: 'How many things are there which a man cannot, with any face or comeliness, say or do himself! A man can scarce allege his own merits or modesty, much less extol them; a man cannot sometimes brook to supplicate or beg; and a number of the like. But all these things are graceful in a friend's mouth, which are blushing in a man's own.'[187] In practice, some suitors preferred indirect modes of approach, considering it unseemly themselves to write. Thus, Elizabeth Nunne wrote to her nephew Sir Bassingbourne Gawdy on behalf of her nephew Cressmor because, as she explained, 'he [her nephew] fearethe youe should thinke hime ouer boulde he hathe desirede me to breake the mattere vnto you'.[188]

The responsibility owed to dependants, social inferiors, and acquaintances explains why noblewomen petitioned on their behalf; it also explains why they were first approached. The strong expectation of the exercise of beneficence generated by client–patron and servant–master relationships clearly extended to include noblewomen and mistresses of households.[189] Francis Bacon, in his essay

---

[185] SP46/38/76: 11/06/1591.
[186] Castiglione, *The Book of the Courtier* (1561), ed. Cox (1994), 121.
[187] Bacon, *The Essays* (1575), ed. Hawkins (1992), 86.
[188] BL, Egerton MS, 2722, fo. 156: 04/08/n.y.
[189] On the expectations that patrons would be beneficent see MacCaffrey, 'Patronage and Politics', 21–35 (21); Sacks, 'The Countervailing of Benefits', 272–91.

'Of Suitors', stated that 'nothing is thought so easy a request to a great person as his letter'.[190] To write on behalf of a suitor was to fulfil one's obligation, and with less exertion of effort than through dispensing more material forms of patronage. By acting in this capacity women were concerned with personal and family reputation within a wider community of honour. For many, the commending of suitors formed a significant and powerful part of their sense of social responsibility. Elizabeth Bourne valued her role as intermediary, promising her future son-in-law Edward Conway that: 'yf the travel of my pen wyth the reste of my body could brynge you the fauour of the hyer powers or the welth of an emproure [emperor] then you showld se I would make no spare of them.'[191] Writing to her son Anthony, Anne Lady Bacon expressed the importance she attached to commending one of her servants for an office in her own person: 'he is my man & therfore have I written.'[192] Lady Bacon appears to have considered the act a matter of personal dignity; she therefore cautioned her son not to interfere on the man's behalf. This illustrates the dual sense of obligation and self-worth felt by women, and the degree to which they internalized honour codes relating to nobility, rank, and duty towards suitors usually associated with male patrons and nobles.

Moreover, the fact that elite women appropriated these 'powerful' rhetorical forms, especially in employing a Senecan language of favour and political 'friendship', with its attendant promise of reciprocal benefits in kind, asserts the high degree of confidence and authority with which many operated within the realm of patronage and politics, an arena often depicted as exclusively male. As such, the study of women's epistolary rhetoric as manifested in letters of recommendation contributes towards an increasing recognition among scholars that any attempt to reconfigure what constituted the category of 'political' during the early modern period should necessarily include women's discursive activities.

On one level, the examination of sixteenth-century women's letters of petition reveals the broad scope (as well as the boundaries) of female petitioning activities, which extends to an involvement in appointments to office, grants of titles and land, and influencing government officials in numerous other matters of patronage. Acting in their capacity as mothers, wives, kinswomen, and mistresses of households, women's familial and other social functions and duties necessitated and indeed justified their operation in areas that extended beyond what might traditionally be viewed as the domestic or household sphere. Their activities in these areas both extend as well as blur what constituted the public and business sphere, which supports Barbara Harris's insightful argument that the family constituted 'the most basic political unit' within sixteenth-century English society.[193] Furthermore, analysis of these letters offers direct evidence that women were by no means excluded from classical rhetorical traditions.

[190] Bacon, *Essays*, 149. [191] BL, Addit. MS, 23212, fo. 184: 24/02/n.y.
[192] LPL, Bacon MS, 653, fo. 248: n.d. [193] Harris, 'Women and Politics', 260, 281.

Viewed as texts, the letters of petition indicate the sophistication, flexibility and, range of women's epistolary and rhetorical skills. They demonstrate the extent of women's knowledge—either through readership of Renaissance letter-writing manuals, formal tuition, or contact with the form—of conventional epistolary forms relating to structure, opening and closing modes of address, salutations, and use of manuscript space; and the ways in which they used letters in their trade of courtiership. In many ways women operated in a manner typical of male petitioners, deploying deferential language and a vocabulary of favour and patronage, also bolstering suits with claims of familial and social obligation and responsibility. Conversely, the language of abject petition—a 'scripted' female voice of melancholic lamentation—was appropriated by men as well as by women, further attesting to the interchangeable nature of gendered tropes of petitioning. Yet where women's letters of petition emerge as distinct from those of their male counterparts is in their strategic deployment of the powerful and emotive imagery of motherhood, wifehood, widowhood, and female frailty. That it was culturally understood that women were able to manipulate male assumptions of women's social roles as 'good' wives and 'good' mothers, and of female incapacity, exposes the ways in which women could work within the limitations and constraints imposed by early modern society.

10

Conclusion

Letters are unrivalled as immediate records of Tudor women's lives and experiences, and represent by far the largest corpus of sixteenth-century women's writing that is both privy and powerful. As indicators of literacy, they permit an important re-examination of levels of female education and literacy, indicating the widespread social dissemination of letter-writing among women, and strongly suggesting that by the end of Elizabeth's reign most women from elite and mercantile groups could achieve functional reading and writing literacy. Read as documents that inscribe social and gender relations, letters shed light on the complex range of women's personal relationships, as female power and authority fluctuated, negotiated on an individual basis. Concomitantly, correspondence highlights the important political roles played by early modern women. Female letter-writers were integral in cultivating and maintaining patronage and kinship networks, which could be mobilized in times of need; they were also active as suitors for crown favour, and operated as political intermediaries and patrons in their own right, using letters to elicit influence. As readers and writers of newsletters, women were also involved in manuscript news networks that circulated intelligence at court, locally, and abroad.

As a source, early modern letters are immensely complex documents, and should not be treated simply as repositories of historical fact or transparent carriers of feeling and emotion. Indeed, to differing degrees letters conformed to epistolary conventions which themselves shifted and altered over time. Linguistically, letters were socially and culturally coded, and in some cases markedly rhetorical and strategic; they also generate meaning not only as texts, but also as material forms, through the symbolic use of manuscript space and other epistolary matter. Letters further acted as gifts, which need to be understood as a part of a ritual exchange of correspondence; individual letters merely record a single snapshot at a particular moment—in this sense they are static and unrepresentative of historical change over time. On the whole, women's letters were not the products of abundant leisure time; the unpolished immediacy that characterizes familiar correspondence resulted partly from constraints on letter-writing imposed by the exigencies of women's daily routines and responsibilities, engulfed by business and legal affairs. The sporadic nature of delivery also affected composition: unexpected or imminent departure of bearers often forced letter-writers to hurry correspondence. Equally, the generic flexibility of Renaissance epistolary forms, able to accommodate diverse subjects and styles, accorded women's correspondence an almost protean quality. Moreover, viewed from the perspective of the mechanics of composition, our understanding of letters as private and singular is challenged. Letters were often written collaboratively, distanced from personal writing technologies, which offers a broader, nuanced interpretation of early modern subjectivity. Attention to modes of dispatch and reading further complicates interpretations of letters as privy and intimate: bearers functioned as corporeal extensions of letters, as the carriers of oral report; and missives were commonly intended for wider readership within and outside of the family.

The overriding purpose of letter-writing was pragmatic, which further impacts upon the nature of early modern correspondence. Letters were reactive, written largely for practical reasons, and reflective of particular events, crises, and emotional states which occasioned the writing of a letter. Communication and social courtesy aside, letters performed a range of other ancillary functions. While the main reason for correspondence between married couples, for instance, was practical, to discuss the day-to-day running of household and business matters in the husband's absence, such letters also commonly acted as sites for conveying conjugal affection. Letter-writing was also associated with other seemingly personal functions: formulaic letters of petition often doubled as a form of redress; letters to confidantes sometimes worked as sounding-boards for ideas; and letter-writing could also provide cathartic release. In many ways letter-writing was intimately connected with the self: as an individualizing technology that constructed women's epistolary selves, and as a process that stimulated self-awareness and inwardness. The very act of writing a letter forced women to represent themselves in relation to others and to create a textual self inflected by social position and circumstance as well as by gender. Meanwhile, the experience of illness and dying encouraged self-reflection in letters; and women's spiritual correspondence to ecclesiastics prompted confessional inward self-examination.

In many ways women's correspondence differs very little from that of their male counterparts. The vast range of correspondence examined resists an oversimplified distinction between women's and men's letters based on content. Indeed, female letter-writers shared many of the same concerns as male letter-writers, dealing with patronage and business issues, imparting news of state, court, and national events, and discussing matters such as health, education, and children. Similarities also exist in terms of methods of delivery, composition, and reading, and the materiality of letters. This book is thus in many ways as much a study of the manuscript letter as it is of women's letters per se. Nevertheless, viewed broadly, several factors distinguish women's letters from those of men. First, men's letters survive in far greater numbers than women's, indicating that men had more occasions to write letters as well as higher levels of literacy. Male letter-writers were also less likely to use the more eccentric spellings exhibited in some women's correspondence, although this was also a function of social status, generation, education, and region. Although most female and a large majority of male letter-writers conducted correspondence in the vernacular, only a handful of women wrote letters in Latin in comparison with the number of male correspondents who dominated the Republic of Letters. In addition, a female writer's gender also restricted the range of individuals to whom she could write, in a way that a man's social status did not. In relation to marital correspondence, husbands more frequently articulated emotion and affection in their letters than wives, though equivalent expressions of warmth and endearment are evident in some women's letters. Female letter-writers also brought a different perspective from men to social affairs, such as gift-giving and childbirth. Lastly, women's letters of petition differ from men's in the strategic use of female gender codes, a practice denied to male petitioners by their own gender. This is not, however, to suggest universality in the lives of early modern women, whose experiences were differentiated by social status among other factors. The letters surveyed, for example, reveal broad variations in levels of women's scribal ability over the period, discernible within social groups and related to generational differences, as well as individuals' aptitudes and educational backgrounds.

Overall, the sixteenth century witnessed the diffusion of letter-writing skills to a broader range of groups of women below the ranks of royalty, and court and social elites; and over the same period letter-writing became a more personal activity, increasingly disconnected from scribes and secretaries. Indeed, the proportion of women who wrote letters with their own hands rises from 50 per cent in the 1540s to approximately 70 per cent by the 1590s, which partly reflects growing female literacy and the wider acquisition of letter-writing skills by Tudor women, as such skills percolated down the social hierarchy. Concomitantly, greater epistolary familiarity is attested by the broadening range of uses for which women employed letters. The conducting of correspondence increasingly formed a part of the educational process for girls, utilized as a form of socialization, and viewed as a 'functional' skill useful for women in their daily lives. However, for those women capable of writing, use of personal literacy for epistolary composition was also determined by social convention and shifts in letter-writing practices. Although during this period it became increasingly desirable for women to write familial correspondence with their own hands, certain types of writing, particularly those relating to business, were deemed by some members of the aristocracy to be degrading, laborious, and best delegated to a secretary. A fundamental distinction, therefore, existed in the nature and purpose of writing between business correspondence on the one hand, which was considered menial, standard, and technical, and private and personal writing on the other, which was spontaneous, intimate, and creative.

The emancipating effect of literacy on women must not be exaggerated, especially when viewed from late medieval and early Tudor perspectives. Indeed, women whose apparent illiteracy prevented them from writing could employ an amanuensis for various scribal functions. Letters produced cooperatively, especially those that were dictated, often exhibit strong signs of female authorial autonomy and high degrees of control exerted by women over the final text. This argues for acceptance of a broad definition of *women's* writing to encompass letters of a collaborative, mediated, or secretarial nature, which demonstrate female mastery of a range of skills associated with textual production, including invention, legal or technical knowledge, and attention to detail. In the final analysis, however, acquisition of full literacy—the ability to read and write—imparted distinct benefits. These include conducting personalized correspondence in sustaining social and business relationships, closer supervision of household and estate management, confidentiality in business, keeping secret matters of a politically sensitive nature, the conducting of more private and intimate family relationships, as well as greater personal control over language and expression. Thus, while access to a scrivener or scribe enabled women of all social groups to conduct correspondence, the advantages connoted by full personal literacy were denied to women who were themselves unable to write.

Viewed as an index of the nature and quality of social relationships, letters betray the complex diversity of women's emotional lives. While writing to relatives was regarded in many ways as a duty, correspondence provided an important means of communication, allowing women to keep in touch with family and close acquaintances separated by distance from whom they derived both emotional and material support. Letters between mothers and sons, female relatives, and wives and husbands indicate the high incidence of intimate and positive familial bonds during the sixteenth century. Such warmth of feeling, however, coexisted with colder and more impersonal forms of attachment, and was not wholly incompatible with more authoritarian attitudes towards family relationships. In addition, marital correspondence displays the varying quality of sixteenth-century marriage, allowing scholars to observe within specific relationships fluctuations of spousal feelings and attachments over time, as well as the frequency of marital cooperation, mutual compatibility, and affection. Examined over a longer duration, apparent shifts in sentiments and opinions are more likely to reflect the changing character and nature of source material, influenced by the introduction of less rigid forms of address and increasing levels of female literacy and epistolary privacy, than for example alterations in women's position within society and a rise in familial affection.

Female influence and authority were contingent on factors such as social and marital status, and position. Women of the nobility and gentry customarily demanded respect from subordinates, both female and male; sons owed filial respect to mothers, while widows often attained greater levels of freedom and autonomy than married women, and female relatives of officials were approached by suitors to act as intermediaries or as informal channels of influence to husbands, fathers, and kinsmen. Female courtiers close to the monarch were also deemed by many to be well placed to expedite the passage of suits. Women letter-writers utilized gender as a rhetorical tool, manipulating to their own advantage stereotypes of female incapacity, wifely submissiveness, and pitiable widowhood; other women playfully subverted positive and negative female conventions and images. Within individual marital relationships, husbandly affection and sensitivity and a shared sense of humour could mitigate many of the harsher effects of female behavioural codes that demanded wifely obedience. These aspects of the study indicate the relative flexibility of sixteenth-century patriarchy, with individual relationships acting as the crucibles in which the parameters of female subordination were tested.

Women's letters thus usefully complement early modern prescriptive literature, which widely considered women to be both intellectually inferior to men and governed more by emotions, and also sought to restrict female involvement in areas beyond the domestic sphere. In highlighting the extensive range of women's activities, letters elucidate the degree to which they operated outside the narrow confines of the 'household', traversing the fluid boundaries between the 'public' and the 'private', the 'political' and the 'domestic'. Familial and other wider social obligations incumbent on women in roles as wives, mothers, kinswomen, and mistresses of households necessitated female intervention in matters traditionally regarded as solely the preserve of men, including appointments to office and bestowing of titles. The habitual and easy manner with which women employed a vocabulary of patronage, political friendship, and favour in letters of intercession further attests to the legitimacy of their operations within such arenas. As such, letters reveal female facility with language, and the social role that letters had to play in women's lives; they thus help to locate differing forms of female power within the family, locality, and occasionally on the wider political stage, and offer invaluable primary evidence from which to reconstruct the lives of early modern women.

Selected Bibliography

PRIMARY SOURCES

Manuscripts

Berkshire Record Office, Reading
D/EN, Neville Family Papers

Birmingham Central Library
Z. Lloyd 53, Mucklowe Family Papers

Bodleian Library, Oxford
MSS. Add. D. 109–112, four volumes of English State Papers of the time of Elizabeth I and James I
Ashmole MSS
Herrick Family Papers, MS Eng. Hist. b.216, c.474, 475, 477, 484
MSS North, family and estate papers of the North family of Wroxton, Oxfordshire
Rawlinson MSS
Tanner MSS. 114, 115, 125, 241, 283, 285, 286

Bristol Record Office
AC/C, Papers of the Smyth Family of Ashton Court, Correspondence

British Library, London
Additional MSS: 79, 104, 1136, 6177, 6668, 6704, 11308, 12503, 12506, 12507, 12529, 15232, 15552, 15914, 23212, 23213, 24783, 25079, 25707, 27400, 27401, 27447, 27959, 27960, 29546, 29550, 32091, 32092, 33271, 33410, 33597, 34079, 34175, 34195, 34218, 35830, 36901, 36908, 36989, 38170, 39828, 39829, 40629, 40630, 40746, 40838, 41140, 41306, 46188, 46362, 46367, 48023, 48064, 48150, 48064, 63109
Cottonian MSS: Caligula B. II, B. VII, C. IX; Cleopatra E. IV; Julius F. VI; Titus B. II; Vespasian F. IX, F. XII
Egerton MSS: 2148, 2410, 2598, 2713, 2714, 2722, 2804, 2812
Harleian MSS: 1B, 416, 422, 523, 787, 2194, 4712, 4713, 4762, 6986, 6994, 6995, 6996, 6997, 7001, 7002
Lansdowne MSS: 2, 3, 6, 7, 8, 9, 10, 12, 13, 14, 17, 18, 22, 23, 24, 25, 27, 28, 30, 31, 33, 34, 36, 39, 43, 46, 57, 63, 65, 67, 68, 69, 71, 74, 76, 80, 82, 84, 87, 88, 99, 104, 108, 109, 115, 158, 162, 819, 1238
Royal MSS: 12 A.I; 13 B.I; 15 A; 17 B.I; 20 B. XVII, letter-writing Treatise dedicated to Anne Boleyn 1530 by Loye de brun
Stowe MS: 150

Cambridge University Library
E.e.5.23 (C), Commonplace Book c.1620
MSS 88/1–3, Hengrave Hall MS
MS Lett.9, Original letters, temp. Elizabeth

Centre For Kentish Studies, Maidstone
De L'Isle MSS: U1475, U1500
Dering MSS

Chethams Library, Manchester
Farmer-Chetham MS

City of Coventry Archives
BA/H/Q/A79, Letters to the Coventry Corporation

Corpus Christi College, Cambridge
MS 119

Derbyshire Record Office, Matlock
D258, Gell Family of Hopton Hall

Doncaster Archives
DZ, Mucklowe Family, Correspondence
DZ, FL Miscellaneous

Dulwich College Archive, London
Henslowe and Alleyn Papers

Flintshire Record Office, Hawarden
D/E/2398, 2401, Erdigg MSS

Folger Shakespeare Library, Washington, DC
L.a., Bagot Papers
L.b., Loseley MSS
L.d., Bacon/Townshend MSS
L.e., Tamworth MSS
V.a.321, A Seventeenth-Century Letter-Book
V.b.36, 8, fo.1^r, 'Greetinges Subscritpions & farewelles of letters' [*c.*1610]
V.b.198, Southwell-Sibthorpe Commonplace Book
V.b.296, 'Dering Family Remembrance Book *c.*1580–1644'
X.d.30, Privy Council Letters, 1545–1621
X.d.428, Cavendish/Talbot MSS
X.d.477, Letters from Lydia Dugard to Samuel Dugard, [*c.*1665]–*c.*1672
X.d.486, 'Account Book of Sir William and Lady Cavendish, 1548–1550'
X.d.493, Letters from Mary Hatton to Randolph Helsby, 1653–1655

Greater London Record Office
ACC 1876/F, Sir Thomas Sutton Charterhouse Hospital Archives, Correspondence

Hatfield House, Hatfield, Hertfordshire
Cecil Papers:
Manuscripts: 8, 9, 10, 11, 12, 16, 17, 21, 22, 23, 24, 25, 26, 27, 28, 29, 30, 31, 32, 33, 34, 35, 36, 37, 38, 39, 40, 41, 42, 43, 44, 45, 46, 47, 48, 49, 50, 51, 52, 53, 54, 55, 56, 57, 58, 61, 62, 63, 64, 65, 66, 67, 68, 69, 70, 71, 72, 73, 74, 75, 76, 77, 78, 79, 80, 81, 82, 83, 84, 85, 86, 87, 88, 89, 90, 91, 92, 93, 94, 95, 96, 97, 98,

99, 100, 101, 102, 103, 106, 112, 113, 114, 115, 128, 132, 133, 134, 135, 136, 145, 146, 147, 150, 151, 152, 154, 157, 159, 160, 161, 164, 168, 170, 172, 175, 176, 177, 178, 179, 180, 181, 182, 183, 184, 186, 187, 188, 194, 202, 203, 204, 205, 206, 232, 250, 251
Petitions: 104, 291, 396, 643, 764, 798, 853, 980, 1013, 1012, 1610, 1661, 1772, 1776, 1793, 1906, 1940, 1941, 1947, 2178, 2189, 2320, 2329, 2329a, 2352, 2362, 2389, 2421, 2469, 2470, 2477

Huntington Library, San Marino, California
Ellesmere MSS
Hastings MSS

Keele University Library
Paget Letters, Miscellaneous, Box C

John Rylands University Library, University of Manchester
Legh of Lyme Correspondence

Joseph P. Regenstein Library, University of Chicago
Bacon Papers of Redgrave Hall

Kendal Record Office
WD/HOTH Box 44, Hothfield MSS, Correspondence, unfoliated
WD/Hoth A 988/5, Hothfield MSS, Receipts of Margaret Clifford (*c*.1598)

Lambeth Palace Library
MSS. 647–662, The Papers of Anthony Bacon
MSS. 596–638, The Carew MSS
MSS. 3470–3533, Fairhurst Paper
MSS. 929–942, Gibson MSS
MSS. 694–710, Shrewsbury MSS
MSS. 3192–3206, Talbot MSS

Lincolnshire Archives, Lincoln
Ancaster MSS

Leeds District Archives
Ingram Correspondence

Leeds University Library
North Family Papers

Longleat House, Wiltshire
Devereux Papers: MSS 1
Dudley Papers: MSS 1, 2
Seymour MSS: MSS 4, 5
Talbot MSS: MSS 1, 2
Thynne MSS: MSS 5, 6, 7, 8

National Archives, Kew
REQ Court of Requests Records
SP1–7, Letters and Papers of Henry VIII
SP10, State Papers Domestic, Edward VI
SP11, State Papers Domestic, Mary I
SP12, State Papers Domestic, Elizabeth
SP15, State Papers Domestic, Addenda
SP46/-, State Papers Domestic, Supplementary
    5–7 Johnson Papers
    9 Papers of Thomas Sexton
    13 General Correspondence, 1559–1565
    14 General Correspondence, 1556–1570
    15 General Correspondence, 1571–1575
    16 General Correspondence, 1576–1580
    18 General Correspondence, 1587–1591
    19 General Correspondence, 1591–1600
    20 General Correspondence, 1594–1597
    21 General Correspondence, 1597–1598
    23 General Correspondence, 1601–1603
    24 General Correspondence, Temp. Elizabeth
    27–42 Exchequer Papers
    44 Darrell Papers
    47–49 Williamson Papers
    51–53 Daniel Papers
    57 Catesby Papers
    58 Reskymer Papers and Gresham Papers 1553–1576, Correspondence of Paul Gresham, of the Auditors Office, Court of Wards
    60 Papers of John Gamage
    71 Carnsew Papers, 1535–1603
    124 General Correspondence, 1547–1558
    125 General Correspondence, 1559–1601
    126 General Correspondence, Temp. Elizabeth
    162 General Correspondence, 1523-Temp. Elizabeth
WARD, Court of Wards Records

National Library of Wales, Aberystwyth
Brogyntyn MSS
Clenennau MSS
Papers of the Wynn Family of Gwydir

Norfolk Record Office, Norwich
Aylsham MS 16
Jerningham MSS
KNY 668 Knyvett/Wilson Papers

Northampton Record Office
Isham Correspondence
Westmoreland and Apethorpe MSS

Nottingham University Library
Clifton Collection
Middleton Collection

Pepys Library, Magdalen College, Cambridge
PL 2002–2004, State Papers

Shakespeare Birthplace Trust, Stratford-upon-Avon
DR 10, DR 37, Correspondence

Sheffield Archives
Bacon Frank Muniments
Wentworth Woodhouse Muniments

Staffordshire Record Office, Strafford
D603, D1734, Paget Papers

Suffolk Record Office, Ipswich
Adair MSS

Surrey History Centre, Woking
Loseley MSS

Warwick Record Office
CR 136/B, Newdigate Family of Arbury Papers
CR 1998/Box 60, Throckmorton Family Papers
MI 229, 'Essex Letter Book *c.*1595–1600', unfoliated

West Sussex Record Office, Chichester
Kytson of Hengrave Hall MSS

Yorkshire Archaeological Society Library, Leeds
DD149, Slingsby of Scriven MSS
MD59/13, Middleton of Stockheld MSS

Printed Primary Sources

Place of publication London unless otherwise shown; no place of publication for books published before 1900.
Anon., *A Very Proper Treatise, Wherein is Briefly Sett Forthe the Arte of Limming* (1573).
Anon., *Cupids Messenger or, A Trusty Friend Stored with Sundry Sorts of Serious, Wittie, Pleasant, Amorous, and Delightful Letters* (1629).
Anon., *The Prompters Packet of Private and Familiar Letters* (1612).
ASCHAM, ROGER, *Disertissimi viri Rogeri Ascami angli, regiæ olim maiestati à latinis epistolis, familiariuni epistolarum . . .* (1576; 1590).
BACON, DOROTHY, 'The Letters and Will of Lady Dorothy Bacon, 1597–1629', ed. Jane Key, *Norfolk Record Society*, 56 (1993), 77–112.
BACON, FRANCIS, *The Essays* (1575), Everyman edn., ed. Michael J. Hawkins (1992).
—— *The Letters and Life of Francis Bacon, Including all his Occasional Works*, ed. J. Spedding, 7 vols. (1861–74).

BALLARD, GEORGE, *Memoirs of Several Ladies of Great Britain* (1752).

Barrington Family Letters, 1628–1632, ed. Arthur Searle, Camden Society, 4th ser., 28 (1983).

BEALE, ROBERT, 'A Treatise of the Office of a Councellor and Principall Secretarie to her Ma[jes]tie', in C. Read, *Mr Secretary Walsingham and the Policy of Queen Elizabeth*, 3 vols. (Oxford, 1925), i. 423–43.

BILLINGSLEY, MARTIN, *The Pen's Excellencie or The Secretaries Delighte* (1618).

BIRCH, THOMAS, *Memoirs of the Reign of Queen Elizabeth*, 2 vols. (1754).

BRADOLINO, AURELIO LIPPO, *De ratione scribendi libri tres* (1498).

BRAUNMULLER, A. R. (ed.), *A Seventeenth-Century Letter-Book: A Facsimilie Edition Folger MS V.a. 321* (Cranbury, NJ, 1983).

BRETON, NICHOLAS, *A Poste With a Madde Packet of Letters* (1602).

BROWNE, JOHN, *The Merchants' Avizo, Verie Necessarie For Their Sons and Seruants When They First Send Them beyond the Seas* (1589).

BRUTO, GIOVANNI MICHELE, *The Necessarie, Fit, and Convenient Education of a Yong Gentlewoman . . .* (1598).

Calendar of the Carew MS. Preserved in the Archiepiscopal Library at Lambeth, ed. J. S. Brewer and William Bullen, 6 vols. (1867–73).

Calendar of the Correspondence of the Smyth Family of Ashton, ed. J. H. Bettey, Bristol Record Society, 35 (1982).

Calendar of the Herrick Family Papers, ed. P. M. Pugh (1972).

A Calendar of the Shrewsbury and Talbot Papers in the Lambeth Palace Library and the College of Arms. Volume 1: Shrewsbury MSS in Lambeth Palace Library (MSS 694–710), ed. C. Jamison, rev. E. G. W. Bill (1966).

A Calendar of the Shrewsbury and Talbot Papers in the Lambeth Palace Library and the College of Arms. Volume II: Talbot Papers in the College of Arms, ed. G. R. Batho (1971).

Calendar of State Papers Domestic, Edward VI, 1547–1553, ed. C. S. Knighton (1992).

Calendar of State Papers: Domestic Series of the Reign of Mary I, 1553–1558, ed. C. S. Knighton (1998).

Calendar of State Papers: Domestic Series of the Reign of Elizabeth I, ed. R. Lemon and M. A. E. Lemon (1865–70).

Calendar of State Papers: Foreign Series of the Reign of Elizabeth I, ed. S. C. Lomas, A. B. Hinds, and R. B. Wernham (1914–50).

Calendar of the State Papers Relating to Ireland in the Reigns of Henry VIII, Edward VI, Mary, and Elizabeth, 1509–1603, ed. H. C. Hamilton, E. G. Atkinson, and R. P. Mahaffy, 11 vols. (1860–1912).

Calendar of State Papers Relating to Scotland and Mary, Queen of Scots, 1547–1603, ed. W. K. Boyd, J. D. Mackie, H. W. Meikle, A. I. Cameron, and M. S. Giuseppi, 13 vols. (Edinburgh and Glasgow, 1910–69).

Calendar of the Wynn (of Gwydir) Papers, 1515–1690, in the National Library of Wales and Elsewhere (Aberystwyth, Cardiff, and London, 1926).

CARE HENRY, *The Female Secretary, or, Choice New Letters Wherein Each Degrees of Women May Be Accommodated with Variety of Presidents [Precedents] for the Expressing Themselves Apply and Handsomly On Any Occasion Proper to Their Sex: With Plain, Yet More Exact and Pertinent Rules and Instructions for the inditing and Directing Letters in General, Than Any Extract* (1671).

CARY, ELIZABETH, *Elizabeth Cary, Lady Falkland: Life and Letters*, ed. Heather Wolfe (Tempe, Ariz., and Cambridge, 2001).

CASTIGLIONE, BALDASSARE, *The Booke of the Courtier* (1528); trans. Sir Thomas Hoby (1561), ed. Virginia Cox (1994).

Catalogue of the Manuscripts and Muniments of Alleyn's College of God's Gift at Dulwich, ed. George F. Warner (1881).

A Catalogue of the Muniments of Wadham College, Oxford (1962).

CAVENDISH, MARGARET, DUCHESS OF NEWCASTLE, *Sociable Letters* (1664), ed. James Fitzmaurice (New York and London, 1997).

CAWDREY, ROBERT, *A Table Alphabetical* (1604).

CELTIS, KONRAD, *Methodus Conficiendarum Epistolarum* (1537).

The Cely Letters, 1472–1488, ed. Alison Hanham, EETS 273 (1975).

CERETA, LAURA, *Collected Letters of a Renaissance Feminist*, ed. and trans. Diana Robin (Chicago, 1997).

CHAMBERLAIN, JOHN, *The Letters of John Chamberlain*, ed. N. E. McClure, 2 vols. (Philadelphia, 1939).

CICERO, MARCUS TULLIUS, *De officiis*, trans. Walter Miller (1913).

CLEMENT, FRANCIS, *The Petie Schole* (1587).

CLIFFORD, ANNE, *The Diaries of Lady Anne Clifford*, ed. D. J. H. Clifford (Stroud, 1990; repr. 1994).

Clifford Letters of the Sixteenth Century, ed. A. G. Dickens, Surtees Society, 172 (1962).

Collectanea Cliffordiana, ed. Arthur Clifford (Paris, 1817; repr. 1980).

COLLINS, ARTHUR, *Letters and Memorials of State in the Reign of Queen Mary, Queen Elizabeth, King James, King Charles the First, Part of the Reign of King Charles the Second and Oliver's Usurpation . . .* (1746).

[CONWAY, SIR JOHN], *Meditations and Praiers Gathered out of the Sacred Letters and Vertuous Writers* (1569) (*STC* 5651).

COOK, G. H., *Letters to Cromwell and Others on the Suppression of the Monasteries* (1965).

COOTE, EDMUND, *The English Schoole Maister* (1596).

CORNWALLIS, LADY JANE, *The Private Correspondence of Jane Lady Cornwallis 1613–1644*, ed. Lord Braybrooke (1842).

CROMWELL, THOMAS, *Life and Letters of Thomas Cromwell*, ed. R. B. Merriman, 2 vols. (1902).

CURIONE, LODOVICO, *LaNotomia delle Cancellaresche corsiue* (Rome, 1588).

DAY, ANGEL, *The English Secretorie or Plaine and Direct Method for the Enditing of all Manner of Epistles or Letters Aswell Familiar as Others etc.* (1586).

—— *The English Secretorie . . .* (1595).

DEBEAU CHESNE, JOHN, *La Clef de L'Escriture* (1593).

—— and BAILDON, JOHN, *A Booke Containing Divers Sortes of Hands, as Well the English as French Secretarie With the Italian, Roman, Chancelry & Court Hands* (1569; 1585).

DE COURTIN, ANTOINE, [*Nouveau Traité de la Civilité*] *The Rules of Civility, or Certain Ways of Deportment Observed Amongst all Persons of Quality upon Several Occasions* (1671; 1685).

DERING, Sir EDWARD, *The Dering Love Letters: A Collection of Seventeenth-Century Love Letters Sent by Sir Edward Dering to his Wife Unton*, ed. Helen Cresswell (Maidstone, 1994).

[DEVEREUX, ROBERT, 2nd Earl of Essex], [*An apologie of the Earle of Essex*] [1600], (*STC* 6787.7).

DEVEREUX, W. B., *Lives and Letters of the Devereux, Earls of Essex in the Reign of Elizabeth I, James I and Charles I, 1540–1646*, 2 vols. (1853).

DONNE, JOHN, *John Donne's Marriage Letters in The Folger Shakespeare Library*, ed. Thomas M. Hester, Robert Parker Sorlien, and Dennis Flynn (Washington, DC, 2005).

DOWLING, MARIA and SHAKESPEARE, JOY, 'Religion and Politics in Mid Tudor England Through the Eyes of an English Protestant Woman: The Recollections of Rose Hickman', *BIHR* 55 (1982), 94–102.

DU BOSQUE, JACQUES, *The Secretary of Ladies or, A New Collection of Letters and Answers, Composed by Moderne Ladies and Gentlewomen* (1638).

DUGARD, LYDIA, *Cousins in Love: The Letters of Lydia DuGard, 1665–1672*, ed. Nancy Taylor (Tempe, Ariz., 2003).

The Egerton Papers, ed. J. Payne Collier, Camden Society, 12 (1840).

ELLIS, H., *Original Letters Illustrative of English History*, 11 vols. (1824–46).

ELLIS, R.H., *Catalogue of Seals in the Public Record Office, Personal Seals*, 2 vols. (1978–81).

ELYOT, SIR THOMAS, *The Boke Named The Governor* (1531), ed. S. E. Lehmberg (1962).

ERASMUS, D., *Collected Works of Erasmus: The Correspondence of Erasmus*, ed. R. A. B. Mynors *et al.*, 11 vols. (Toronto, 1974–98).

—— *De conscribendis epistolis* (1522) and *Conficiendarum epistolarum formula* (1521), in *Collected Works of Erasmus*, 25, ed. J. K. Sowards (Toronto, 1985).

—— *Opus Epistolarum Des. Erasmi Roterdami*, ed. P. S. Allen, 12 vols. (1906–58).

EVANS, JOHN, 'Extracts from the Private Account Book of Sir William More of Loseley, in Surrey, in the Time of Queen Mary and of Queen Elizabeth', *Archaeologia*, 36: 2 (1855), 284–93.

FETHERSTON, JOHN, (ed.), *The Visitation of the County of Warwick in the Year 1619*, Publications of the Harleian Society, 12 (1877).

FLEMING, ABRAHAM, *A Panoplie of Epistles, or a Looking Glasse For the Vnlearned, Conteyning a Perfecte Plattforme of Inditing Letters of all Sorts, etc.* (1576).

The Fortescue Papers, ed. S. R. Gardiner, Camden Society (1871).

FRANCO, VERONICA, *Poems and Selected Letters*, ed. and trans. Ann Rosalind Jones and Margaret F. Rosenthal (Chicago, 1998).

FULWOOD, WILLIAM, *The Enemie of Idlenesse: Teaching the Maner and Stile How to Endite, Compose, and Write All Sorts of Epistles and Letters: as Well by Answer, as Otherwise* (1568).

GAGE, JOHN, *The History and Antiquities of Hengrave in Suffolk* (1822).

GASCOIGNE, GEORGE, *A Hundreth sundrie Flowres bounde vp in one small Poesie* (1573).

GATAKER, THOMAS, *A Good Wife Gods Gift and, A Wife Indeed. Two Mariage Sermons* ... (1623).

GAWDY, PHILIP, *Letters of Philip Gawdy of West Harling, Norfolk, and of London to Various Members of his Family, 1579–1616*, ed. I. H. Jeayes (Edinburgh, 1906).

GENT, I. W., *A Speedie Post With Certaine New Letters* (1625).

GOUGE, WILLIAM, *Of Domestical Dvties, Eight Treatises* (1622).

GRAHAM, ELSPETH, HINDS, HILARY, HOBBY, ELAINE, and WILCOX, HELEN (eds.), *Her Own Life: Autobiographical Writings by Seventeenth-Century Englishwomen* (1989).

The Hardwick Inventories of 1601, ed. Lindsay Boynton (1971).

HARLEY, BRILLIANA, *The Letters of the Lady Brilliana Harley, Wife of Sir Robert Harley*, ed. T. T. Lewis, Camden Society, 58 (1854).

HARRISON, G. B., *The Letters of Queen Elizabeth* (1935).

HASTINGS, SIR FRANCIS, *The Letters of Sir Francis Hastings, 1574–1609*, ed. Claire Cross, Somerset Record Society, 69 (1969).

HAYNES, SAMUEL (ed.), *A Collection of State Papers Relating to Affairs in the Reigns of King Henry VIII, King Edward VI, Queen Mary and Queen Elizabeth From the Year 1542–1570* (1740).

HEGENDORPH, CHRISTOPH, *Methodus epistolis conscribendi* (1526).

Herbert Correspondence: The Sixteenth and Seventeenth Century Letters of the Herberts of Chirbury, Powis Castle and Dolguog, Formerly at Powis Castle in Montgomeryshire, ed. W. J. Smith (Cardiff, 1963).

The Heroycall Epistles of the Learned Poet Publius Ouidius Naso, In Englishe Verse set out and Translated by George Turberuile (1567).

HMC, *Third Report, Appendix* (1872).

—— *Report on the Manuscripts of the Earl of Ancaster, Preserved at Grimsthorpe* (1907).

—— *Calendar of the Manuscripts of the Marquis of Bath, Preserved at Longleat, Wiltshire*, 5 vols. (1907–80), vols. ii, iv, v.

—— *Report on the Manuscripts of his Grace the Duke of Buccleuch and Queensbury, Preserved at Drumlanrig Castle*, 2 vols. (1897–1903), vol. i.

—— *Report on the Manuscripts of the Earl Cowper, Preserved at Melbourne Hall, Derbyshire*, 2 vols. (1888), vol. i.

—— *Report on the Manuscripts of Lord De L'Isle & Dudley, Preserved at Penshurst Place*, 6 vols. (1935–66), vols. i–iii.

—— *Report on the Manuscripts of Allan George Finch, Esq. Of Burley-On-The-Hill, Rutland*, 4 vols. (1913–65), vol. i.

—— *Report on the Manuscripts of the Family of Gawdy Formerly of Norfolk* (1885).

—— *Report on the Manuscripts of the Late Reginald Rawdon Hastings, Esq. of the Manor House, Ashby-De-La-Zouche*, 3 vols. (1928–34), vol. ii.

—— *Report on the Manuscripts of Lord Kenyon* (1894).

—— *Report on the Laing Manuscripts, Preserved in the University of Edinburgh*, 2 vols. (1914–25), vol. i.

—— *Report on the Manuscripts of Lord Middleton, Preserved at Wollaton Hall, Nottinghamshire* (1911).

—— *Report on the Manuscripts of Lord Montagu of Beaulieu* (1900).

—— *Report on the Manuscripts of the Marquis of Ormonde, Preserved at The Castle, Kilkenny*, 8 vols. (1895–1920), vol. i.

—— *Report on the Pepys Manuscripts, Preserved at Magdalene College, Cambridge* (1911).

—— *Report on the Manuscripts of his Grace the Duke of Portland, Preserved at Welbeck Abbey*, 10 vols. (1891–1931), vol. ii.

—— *Report on the Manuscripts of his Grace the Duke of Rutland, Preserved at Belvoir Castle*, 3 vols. (1888), vol. i.

—— *Calendar of the Manuscripts of Major-General Lord Sackville, Preserved at Knole, Sevenoaks, Kent*, 2 vols. (1942–66), vol. i.

—— *Calendar of the Manuscripts of the Most Honourable The Marquess of Salisbury, Preserved at Hatfield House Hertfordshire*, 24 vols. (1883–1973), vols. i–xv, xxiii.

—— *Report on Manuscripts in Various Collections*, 7 vols. (1901–14), vols. ii, vii.

HOBY, MARGARET, *The Private Life of an Elizabethan Lady: The Diary of Lady Margaret Hoby, 1599–1605*, ed. Joanna Moody (Stroud, 1998).

HOLLES, JOHN, *Letters of John Holles, 1587–1637*, ed. P. R. Seddon, 3 vols., Thoroton Society, 31, 35, 36 (1975–86).

HONDIUS, JODOCUS, *Theatrum artis scribendi* (1594).

HOTMAN, F., *Correspondance de François Hotman*, ed. P. J. Blok, Archives du Musée Teyler, 12/2 (Haarlem, 1911).

HOULBROOKE, RALPH A., *English Family Life, 1576–1716: An Anthology of Diaries* (Oxford, 1988).

Household Accounts and Disbursement Books of Robert Dudley, Earl of Leicester, 1558–1561, 1584–86, ed. Simon Adams, Camden Society, 5th ser., 6 (1995).

HUGHES, CHARLES, 'Nicholas Faunt's Discourse Touching the Office of the Principal Secretary of Estate, & c. 1592', *EHR*, 20 (1905), 499–508.

HUTTON, MATTHEW, *The Correspondence of Dr Mathew Hutton, Archbishop of York*, ed. James Raine, Surtees Society, 17 (1843).

Index to the Papers of Anthony Bacon (1558–1601) in Lambeth Palace Library (MSS. 647–662) (1974).

JOSSELIN, RALPH, *The Family Life of Ralph Josselin, a Seventeenth-Century Clergyman: An Essay in Historical Anthropology*, ed. Alan Macfarlane (Cambridge, 1970).

Kingsford's Stonor Letters and Papers 1290–1483, ed. Christine Carpenter (Cambridge, 1996).

KLENE, JEAN, *The Southwell-Sibthorpe Commonplace Book, Folger MS. V.b. 198* (Tempe, Ariz., 1997).

LABANOFF, ALEXANDRE, *Lettres, instructions et mémoires de Marie Stuart*, 7 vols. (1844).

LANDO, ORTENSIO, *Lettere della . . . Donna L.G. in Gazuolo con gran diligentia raccolte, & à gloria del sesso feminile nuovamente in luce poste* (Venice, 1552).

—— *Lettere di molte valorose donne* (Venice, 1548).

LEEDHAM-GREEN, E. S., *Books in Cambridge Inventories: Book-Lists From Vice-Chancellor's Court Probate Inventories in the Tudor and Stuart Periods, i: The Inventories* (Cambridge, 1986).

[LE MOYNE, J.], *Le stile de manière de composer, dicter, et escrire toute sorte d'espistres* (1566).

Letters and Papers, Foreign and Domestic, of the Reign of Henry VIII, ed. J. S. Brewer, J. Gairdner, R. H Rodie, *et al.*, 21 vols. and Addenda (1862–1932).

The Letters of Henry VIII: A Selection With a Few Other Documents, ed. Muriel St Clare Byrne (1936; 2nd edn. 1968).

Letters of the Fifteenth and Sixteenth Centuries From the Archives of Southampton, ed. R. C. Anderson, Publications of the Southampton Record Society, 22 (1921).

Lettres de Henri VIII à Anne Boleyn: Avec la Traduction; Prècèdèes d'une Notice Historique sur Anne Boleyn (1826).

LIPSIUS, JUSTUS, *Epistolica institutio* (1591).

The Lisle Letters, ed. Muriel St Clare Byrne, 6 vols. (Chicago, 1981).

LODGE, EDMUND, *Illustrations of British History, Biography and Manners in the Reigns of Edward VI, Mary, Elizabeth and James I*, 3 vols. (1791; 2nd edn., 1838).

The Loseley Manuscripts, ed. A. J. Kempe (1835).

LOWE, ROBERT, *The Diary of Robert Lowe of Ashton-in-Makerfield, Lancashire, 1663–74*, ed. William L. Sachse (New Haven, 1938).

LUPTON, THOMAS, *A Thousand Notable Things of Sundrie Sorts* (1579).

MACROPEDIUS, GEORGIUS, *Methodus de conscribendis epistolis* (1543).

MARCUS, LEAH S., and MUELLER, JANEL (eds.), *Elizabeth I: Autograph Compositions and Foreign Language Originals* (Chicago and London, 2003).

——, —— and ROSE, MARY BETH (eds.), *Elizabeth I: Collected Works* (Chicago and London, 2000).

MARLOWE, CHRISTOPHER, *Edward II* (1592).

MAY, STEVEN W., *Queen Elizabeth: Selected Works* (Washington, DC, 2003).

MIDDLETON, THOMAS, *The Witch* (1615–16).

—— and DEKKER, THOMAS, *The Roaring Girl* (1611).

MONTAGUE, LADY MARY WORTLEY, *The Letters of Lady Mary Wortley Montagu*, ed. Clare Brant (1992).

MOODY, JOANNA, 'The Courtship Letters and Poems of Philip Wodehouse (1633)', *Seventeenth Century*, 18/1 (2003), 44–53.

—— (ed.), *The Private Correspondence of Jane Lady Cornwallis Bacon, 1613–1644* (2003).

MOORE, DOROTHY, *The Letters of Dorothy Moore, 1612–64: The Friendships, Marriage, and Intellectual Life of a Seventeenth-Century Woman*, ed. Lynette Hunter (Aldershot, 2004).

MORE, THOMAS, *The Correspondence of Sir Thomas More*, ed. Elizabeth Rogers (1947).

—— *The Last Letters of Thomas More*, ed. Alvaro de Silva (Grand Rapids, Mich., 2000).

MULCASTER, RICHARD, *Positions Wherin Those Primitive Circvmstances Be Examined, Which Are Necessarie For The Training Vp Of Children* ... (1581).

MUNBY, LIONEL M. (ed.), *Early Stuart Household Accounts*, Hertfordshire Record Society (1986).

MURDIN, WILLIAM (ed.), *A Collection of State Papers Relating to Affairs in the Reign of Queen Elizabeth From the Year 1571–1596* (1759).

NEWDIGATE-NEWDEGATE, LADY (ed.), *Gossip From the Muniment Room, Being Passages in the Lives of Anne and Mary Fytton, 1574 to 1618* (1897).

NICOLAS, NICHOLAS HARRIS, *The Literary Remains of Lady Jane Grey: With a Memoir of Her Life* (1825).

NICOLSON, M. H., *The Conway Letters: The Correspondence of Anne, Viscountess Conway, Henry More and Their Friends, 1642–1648* (1930), rev. Sarah Hutton (Oxford, 1992).

O'DAY, ROSEMARY and BERLATSKY, JOEL (eds.), 'The Letter-Book of Thomas Bentham, Bishop of Coventry and Lichfield 1560–1561', *Camden Miscellany*, 27 (1979), 113–238.

The Official Papers of Sir Nathaniel Bacon of Stiffkey, Norfolk, as Justice of the Peace, 1580–1620, Camden Society (1915).

OSBORNE, DOROTHY, *Dorothy Osborne: Letters to William Temple 1652–54: Observations on Love, Literature, Politics and Religion*, ed. Kenneth Parker (Aldershot, 2002).

OSLEY, A. S., *Scribes and Sources: Handbook of the Chancery Hand in the Sixteenth Century: Texts From The Writing Masters* (1980).

The Oxinden Letters, 1607–1642: Being the Correspondence of Henry Oxinden of Barham and His Circle, ed. Dorothy Gardiner (1933).

The Oxinden and Peyton Letters, 1642–1670: Being the Correspondence of Henry Oxinden of Barham, Sir Thomas Peyton of Knowlton and Their Circle, ed. Dorothy Gardiner (1937).

The Papers of Nathaniel Bacon of Stiffkey, 1556–1602, ed. A. Hassell Smith *et al.*, 4 vols., Norfolk Record Society, 46, 49, 53, 64 (1978–2000).

Papers of Sir Nicholas Bacon in the University of Chicago Library, List and Index Society, 25 (1989).

PARKER, MATTHEW, *Correspondence of Matthew Parker, Archbishop of Canterbury*, ed. John Bruce, Parker Society (1853).

PARKHURST, JOHN, *The Letter Book of John Parkhurst, Bishop of Norwich Compiled During the Years 1571–1575*, ed. Ralph A. Houlbrooke, Norfolk Record Society, 43 (1974, 1975).

PARTRIDGE, JOHN, *The Treasurie of Commodious Conceits, and Hidden Secrets Commonlie Called The Good Huswives Closet of Prouision, for the Health of her Houshold. Meete and Necessarie for the Profitable Vse of all Estates* (1591).

PASTON, LADY KATHERINE, *The Correspondence of Lady Katherine Paston, 1603–1627*, ed. R. Hughey, Norfolk Record Society, 14 (1941).

Paston Letters and Papers of the Fifteenth Century, ed. Norman Davis, 2 vols. (Oxford, 1971–6).

PAYNE, PADDY and BARRON, CAROLINE M., 'The Letters and Life of Elizabeth Despenser, Lady Zouche (d. 1408)', *Nottingham Medieval Studies*, 41 (1997), 126–56.

PECK, F., *Desiderata Curiosa*, 2 vols. (1732).

PHILIPS, KATHERINE, *The Collected Works of Katherine Philips, the Matchless Orinda, Vol. 2: The Letters*, ed. Patrick Thomas (Stump Cross, 1992).

PHILLIP, WILLIAM, *A Booke of Secrets: Shewing Diuers Waies to Make and Prepare All Sorts of Inke, and Colours . . .* (1596).

PISAN, CHRISTINE DE, *The Treasure of the City of Ladies* (1405), trans. Sarah Lawson (1985).

Plumpton Correspondence: A Series of letters, Chiefly Domestic, Written in the Reigns of Edward IV, Richard III, Henry VII and Henry VIII, ed. Thomas Stapleton, Camden Society, 4 (1839).

The Plumpton Letters and Papers, ed. Joan Kirby, Camden Society, 5th ser., 8 (1996).

POLE, REGINALD, *The Correspondence of Reginald Pole: Volume 1. A Calendar, 1518–1546: Beginnings to Legate of Viterbo*, ed. Thomas F. Mayer (Aldershot, 2002).

POLLOCK, LINDA, *With Faith and Physic: The Life of a Tudor Gentlewoman, Lady Grace Mildmay, 1552–1620* (1993).

PRYOR, FELIX (ed.), *The Faber Book of Letters: Letters Written in the English Language, 1578–1939* (1988).

RAHNER, HUGO, *Saint Ignatius Loyola: Letters to Women* (1960).

RIPLEY, GEORGE, *The Compound of Alchemy* (1591).

ROBINSON, HASTINGS (ed.), *Original Letters Relative to the English Reformation Written During the Reigns of Henry VIII, King Edward VI and Queen Mary: Chiefly From the Archives of Zurich*, 2 vols., Parker Society, 52, 53 (1846–7).

ROUTLEDGE, F. J., 'Six Letters of Cardinal Pole to the Countess of Huntingdon', *EHR*, 28/111 (1913), 527–31.

SADLER, RALPH, *The State Papers and Letters of Sir Ralph Sadler, Knight-Banneret*, ed. Arthur Clifford, 2 vols. (Edinburgh, 1809).

A Select Collection of Interesting Autograph Letters of Celebrated Persons, English and Foreign, From the Sixteenth Century to the Present (Stuttgart, 1849).

SENECA, LUCIUS ANNAEUS, *Moral Essays*, iii, trans. John W. Basore (Cambridge, Mass. and London, 1935).

SHAKESPEARE, WILLIAM, *The Complete Works*, ed. Stanley Wells and Gary Taylor (Oxford, 1988).

A Short-Title Catalogue of Books Printed in England, Scotland and Ireland, and of English Books printed Abroad, 1475–1640, ed. A. W. Pollard and G. R. Redgrave, 3 vols., 2nd edn. (1976–91).

SIDNEY, MARY, *The Collected Works of Mary Sidney Herbert, Countess of Pembroke*, ed. Margaret P. Hannay, Noel J. Kinnamon, and Michael G. Brennan, 2 vols. (Oxford, 1998).

SIDNEY, ROBERT, *Domestic Politics and Family Absence: The Correspondence (1588–1621) of Robert Sidney, First Earl of Leicester, and Barbara Gamage Sidney*, ed. Margaret P. Hannay, Noel J. Kinnamon, and Michael G. Brennan (Aldershot, 2005).

SLINGSBY, SIR HENRY, *The Diary of Sir Henry Slingsby*, ed. Daniel Parsons (1836).

SMITH, HENRY, *A Preparatiue to Mariage . . .* (1591).

SMITH, SIR THOMAS, *De Republica Anglorum. The Maner of Gouernement or Policie of the Realme of England . . .* (1583).

Stemmata Shirliana: or the Annals of the Shirley Family (1873).

STEVENSON, JOSEPH (ed.), *The Life of Jane Dormer, Duchess of Feria . . .* (1887).

STOCKWELL, THOMAS, *The Miscellaneous Papers of Captain Thomas Stockwell 1590–1611*, ed. J. Rutherford, 2 vols., Publications of the Southampton Record Society, 32, 33 (1932–3).

The Stonor Letters and Papers, 1290–1483, ed. C. L. Kingsford, 2 vols., Camden Society, 3rd ser., 29–30 (1919).

Stradling Correspondence: A Series of Letters Written in the Reign of Queen Elizabeth, ed. John M. Traherne (1840).

STRICKLAND, AGNES, *Letters of Mary Queen of Scots and Documents Connected with Her Personal History*, 2 vols. (1842).

STRYPE, JOHN, *Annals of the Reformation and the Establishment of Religion . . .*, 4 vols. (1824).

STUART, LADY ARBELLA, *The Letters of Lady Arbella Stuart*, ed. Sara Jayne Steen (Oxford, 1994).

'Supplementary Stonor Letters and Papers (1314–1482)', ed. C. L. Kingsford, *Camden Miscellany*, 13, Camden Society, 3rd ser., 34 (1924), pp. i–viii, 1–26.

TITLER, ROBERT, 'Accounts of the Roberts Family of Boarzell, Sussex, *c.*1568–1582', Sussex Record Society, 71 (1977–9).

Tixall Letters, ed. Arthur Clifford, 2 vols. (1815).

TREVELYAN, Sir WALTER CALVERLY and TREVELYAN, SIR CHARLES EDWARD, *Trevlyan Papers Volume III*, Camden Society (1872).

TYTLER, P. F., *England Under the Reigns of Edward VI and Mary Illustrated in a Series of Original Letters Never Before Printed With Historical Introduction and Biographical Notes* (1839).

UNGERER, GUSTAV, *A Spaniard in Elizabethan England: The Correspondence of Antonio Perez's Exile*, 2 vols. (1974).

VERNEY, F. P. (ed.), *Memoirs of the Verney Family During the Civil War*, 4 vols. (1970).

VIVES, JUAN LUIS, *De conscribendis epsitolis* (1534), ed. Charles Fantazzi (Leiden, 1989).

—— *A Very Frutefull and Pleasant Boke Called the Instructio[n] of a Christen Woma[n]* (1529).

WADHAM, DOROTHY, *The Letters of Dorothy Wadham, 1609–1618*, ed. R. B. Gardiner (1904).

WALL, ALISON D. (ed.), *Two Elizabethan Women: Correspondence of Joan and Maria Thynne, 1575–1611*, Wiltshire Record Society, 38 (1982).

WATSON, FOSTER (ed.), *Vives and the Renascence Education of Women* (1912).

WELCH, MARY A., 'Willoughby Letters of the First Half of the Sixteenth Century', Thoroton Society, 24 (1967), 13–74.

WHATELEY, WILLIAM, *A Bride-Bush, or a Wedding Sermon Compendiously Describing the Duties of Married Persons: By Performing Whereof, Marriage shall be to them a Great Helpe, which Now Finde It a Little Hell* (1617).

WHYTHORNE, THOMAS, *The Autobiography of Thomas Whythorne*, ed. J. M. Osborn (Oxford, 1961).

WILMOT, JOHN, EARL OF ROCHESTER, *Familiar Letters Written by the Right Honourable John late Earl of Rochester, And Several Other Persons of Honour and Quality. With Letters Written by the Most Ingenious Mr. Thomas Otway, and Mrs. K. Philips. Published in their Original Copies* (1697).

WILSON, THOMAS, *The Arte of Rhetorique* (1553).

WOLLEY, HANNAH, *The Gentlewoman's Companion Or, A Guide to the Female Sex* (1675), ed. Caterina Albano (Totnes, 2001).

WOOD, M. A. E., *Letters of Royal and Illustrious Ladies from the Twelfth Century to the Close of Mary's Reign*, 3 vols. (1846).

WRIGHT, THOMAS (ed.), *Queen Elizabeth and Her Times: A Series of Original Letters Selected From the Unedited Private Correspondence of the Lord Treasurer Burghley, The Earl of Leicester, the Secretaries Walsingham and Smith, Sir Christopher Hatton and Most of the Distinguished Persons of the Period*, 2 vols. (1838).

—— *Three Chapters of Letters Relating to the Suppression of Monasteries*, Camden Society (1843).

SELECT SECONDARY SOURCES

ABE, YOKO, 'Boundaries of Familiarity: Epistolary Theory and the Publication of Private Correspondence in Seventeenth-Century England', *Studies in English Literature/ Eibungaku Kenkyu* (2001), 1–19.

ADAMS, SIMON, 'The Patronage of the Crown in Elizabethan Politics: The 1590s in Perspective', in John Guy (ed.), *The Reign of Elizabeth I: Court and Culture in the Last Decade* (Cambridge, 1995), 20–45.

ADAMSON, J. W., 'The Extent of Literacy in England in the Fifteenth and Sixteenth Centuries: Notes and Conjectures', *The Library*, 4th ser, 10 (1929), 163–93.

AERS, DAVID, 'A Whisper in the Ear of Early Modernists; or Reflections on Literary Critics Writing the "History of the Subject" ', in David Aers (ed.), *Culture and History, 1350–1600: Essays on English Communities, Identities and Writing* (New York and London, 1992), 177–202.

AGO, RENATE, 'Marie Spada Veralli, la buona mogli', in G. Calvi (ed.), *Barocca al Femminile* (Rome, 1992).

ALBERTI, JOHANNA, *Gender and the Historian* (2002).

ALCOCK, N. W., 'The Ferrers of Tamworth Collection: Sorting and Listing', *Archives*, 19/86 (1991), 358–63.

ALFORD, STEPHEN, *Kingship and Politics in the Reign of Edward VI* (Cambridge, 2002).

ALLEN, E. J. B., *Post and Courier Service in the Diplomacy of Early Modern Europe* (The Hague, 1973).

ALTMAN, JANET GURKIN, *Epistolarity: Approaches to a Form* (Columbus, Oh., 1982).

—— 'Political Ideology in the Letter Manual: France, England, New England', in John W. Yolton and Leslie Allen Brown (eds.), *Studies in Eighteenth-Century Culture*, 18 (1988), 105–22.

ANDERSON, MICHAEL, *Approaches to the History of the Western Family, 1500–1914* (Basingstoke, 1980).

ARCHER, M. S., 'Letters to London from the South Coast Ports 1573–1601', *The Philatelist*, 7 (1987).

ARMSTRONG, C. A. J., 'Some Examples of the Distribution and Speed of News in England at the Time of the Wars of the Roses', in R. W. Hunt, W. A. Pantin, and R. W. Southern (eds.), *Studies in Medieval History Presented to Frederick Maurice Powicke* (Oxford, 1948), 429–54.

ATHERTON, IAN, 'The Itch Grown a Disease: Manuscript Transmission of News in the Seventeenth Century', in Joad Raymond (ed.), *News, Newspapers, and Society in Early Modern Britain* (1999), 39–65.

BACKSCHEIDER, PAULA R. and DYKSTAL, TIMOTHY (eds.), *The Intersections of the Public and Private Spheres in Early Modern England* (London and Portland, 1996).

BALDWIN, GEOFF, 'Individual and Self in the Late Renaissance', *HJ*, 44/2 (2001), 341–64.

BARON, HELEN, 'Mary Fitzroy's Hand in the Devonshire Manuscript', *RES*, 45/179 (1994), 314–35.

BARON, SABRINA A., 'The Guises of Dissemination in Early Seventeenth-Century England: News in Manuscript and Print', in Brendan Dooley and Sabrina A. Baron (eds.), *The Politics of Information in Early Modern Europe* (London and New York, 2001), 41–56.

BARRY, JONATHAN and BROOKS, CHRISTOPHER WILSON (eds.), *The Middling Sort of People: Culture, Society and Politics in England, 1550–1800* (Basingstoke and London, 1994).

BASING, PATRICIA, 'Robert Beale and the Queen of Scots', *BLJ*, 20 (1994), 65–82.

BEAL, PETER, *In Praise of Scribes: Manuscripts and Their Makers in Seventeenth-Century England* (Oxford, 1998).

—— and EZELL, MARGARET J. M. (eds.), *English Manuscript Studies. Volume 9: Writing by Early Modern Women* (2000).

BEALE, P. O., *A History of the Post in England from the Romans to the Stuarts* (Aldershot, 1998).

BEDDARD, R. A., 'Six Unpublished Letters of Queen Henrietta Maria', *BLJ*, 25/2 (1999), 129–43.

BEER, MATHIAS, 'Private Correspondence in Germany in the Reformation Era: A Forgotten Source for the History of the Burgher Family', *SCJ*, 32/4 (2001), 931–51.

BELL, H. E., *An Introduction to the History and Records of the Court of Wards and Liveries* (Cambridge, 1953).

BELL, IlONA, *Elizabethan Women and the Poetry of Courtship* (Cambridge, 1998).

—— ' "Under ye Rage of a Hott Sonn & Yr Eyes": John Donne's Love Letters to Ann More', in Claude J. Summers and Ted-Larry Pebworth (eds.), *The Eagle and the Dove: Reassessing John Donne* (Columbia, 1986), 25–52.

BELL, MAUREEN, PARFITT, GEORGE, and SHEPHERD, SIMON (eds.), *A Biographical Dictionary of English Women Writers, 1580–1720* (Boston, 1990).

BEN-AMOS, ILANA, 'Gifts and Favors: Informal Support in Early Modern England', *Journal of Modern History*, 72/2 (2000), 295–338.

BENNETT, H. S., *The Pastons and Their England* (Cambridge, 1922; epr. 1991).

BENNETT, R. E., 'Donne's Letters from the Continent in 1611–12', *Philological Quarterly*, 19 (1940), 66–78.

BERGERON, DAVID M., *King James and Letters of Homoerotic Desire* (1999).

BIETENHOLZ, P. G., 'Erasmus and the German Public, 1518–1520: The Authorized and Unauthorized Circulation of this Correspondence', *SCJ*, 8, Supplement (1977), 61–78.

BILLINGSLEY, DALE B., 'Readers and the Dangers of Reading in More's Works', *Moreana*, 115/116 (1993), 5–18.

BINDOFF, S. T., (ed.), *The House of Commons, 1509–1558*, 3 vols. (1982).

BLAISDELL, CHARMARIE JENKINS, 'Calvin's Letters to Women: The Courting of Ladies in High Places', *SCJ*, 13/3 (1982), 67–84.

BOCK, GISELA, 'Women's History and Gender History: Aspects of an International Debate', *Gender and History*, 1/1 (1989), 7–30.

BOFFEY, JULIA, 'Women Authors and Women's Literacy in Fourteenth- and Fifteenth-Century England', in Carol M. Meale (ed.), *Women and Literature in Britain, 1150–1500* (Cambridge, 1993), 159–82.

BOLGAR, R. R., 'The Teaching of Letter-Writing in the Sixteenth Century', *History of Education*, 12/4 (1983), 245–53.

BOTONAKI, EFFIE, 'Seventeenth-Century Englishwomen's Spiritual Diaries: Self-Examination, Covenanting, and Account Keeping', *SCJ*, 30 (1999), 3–21.

BOUND, FAY, 'Writing the Self? Love and the Letter in England, *c.*1660–*c.*1760', *Literature and History*, 11/1 (2002), 1–19.

BOWDEN, CAROLINE, 'Women as Intermediaries: An Example of the Use of Literacy in the Late Sixteenth and early Seventeenth Centuries', *History of Education*, 22/3 (1993), 215–23.

BRACHER, TRICIA, 'Esther Inglis and the English Succession Crisis of 1599', in James Daybell (ed.), *Women and Politics in Early Modern England, 1450–1700* (Aldershot, 2004), 132–46.

BRADFORD, C. A., *Hugh Morgan, Queen Elizabeth's Apothecary* (1939).

BRANT, CLARE, and PURKISS, DIANE (eds.), *Women, Texts, and Histories, 1575–1760* (1992).

BRAUNMULLER, A. R., 'Accounting for Absence: The Transcription of Space', in W. Speed Hill (ed.), *New Ways of Looking at Old Texts: Papers of the Renaissance English Text Society, 1985–1991* (Binghamton, NY, 1993), 47–56.

—— 'Editing Elizabethan Letters', *Text*, 1 (1981), 185–99.

BRAY, ALAN, *The Friend* (Chicago, 2003).

—— 'Homosexuality and the Signs of Male Friendship in Elizabethan England', *HWJ*, 29 (1990), 1–19.

BRAYSHAY, MARK, HARRISON, PHILIP, and CHALKLEY, BRIAN, 'Knowledge, Nationhood and Governance: The Speed of the Royal Post in Early-Modern England', *Journal of Historical Geography*, 24/3 (1998), 265–88.

BRAYSHAY, MARK, 'Royal Post-Horse Routes in England and Wales: The Evolution of the Network in the Late Sixteenth and Early Seventeenth Century,' *Journal of Historical Geography*, 17 (1991), 373–89.

—— 'Royal Post-Horse Routes in South-West England in the Reigns of Elizabeth I and James I', *Devonshire Association Report and Transactions*, 123 (1991), 79–103.

—— 'The Royal Post-Horse Routes of Hampshire in the Reign of Elizabeth I', *Proceedings of the Hampshire Field Club and Archeological Society*, 48 (1992), 121–34.

BREISACH, ERNST, *Historiography: Ancient, Medieval and Modern* (Chicago, 1983).

BRIQUET, CHARLES MOÏSE, *Les Filigranes. Dictionnaire Historique des Marques du Papier dès Leur Apparition vers 1282 Jusqu'en 1600* . . . , 4 vols. (Paris, 1907).

BROADWAY, JAN, 'John Smyth of Nibley: A Jacobean Man-Of-Business and his Service to the Berkeley Family', *Midland History*, 24 (1999), 79–97.

BROWN, CEDRIC C. (ed.), *Patronage, Politics and Literary Traditions in England, 1558–1658* (Detroit, 1993).

—— and MAROTTI, ARTHUR (eds.), *Texts and Cultural Change in Early Modern England* (Basingstoke, 1997).

BROWN, PAMELA ALLEN, *Better a Shrew Than a Sheep: Women, Drama and the Culture of Jest in Early Modern England* (Ithaca, NY, 2003).

BURCKHARDT, JACOB, *The Civilization of the Renaissance* (1859; repr. Oxford, 1944).

BURKE, PETER, *Fortunes of the Courtier: The European Reception of Castiglione's 'Cortegiano'* (Cambridge, 1995).

—— 'Representations of the Self From Petrarch to Descartes', in Roy Porter (ed.), *Rewriting the Self: Histories from the Renaissance to the Present* (1997), 17–28.

—— and ROY PORTER (eds.), *Language, Self, and Society: A Social History* (Cambridge, 1991).

BURKE, VICTORIA E. and GIBSON, JONATHAN (eds.), *Early Modern Women's Manuscript Writing: Selected Papers from the Trinity/Trent Colloquium* (Aldershot, 2004).

BURROW, J. A., 'Autobiographical Poetry in the Middle Ages: The Case of Thomas Hoccleve', *Proceedings of the British Academy*, 68 (1982), 389–412.

BUSH, M. L., 'Protector Somerset and Requests', *HJ*, 17/3 (1974), 451–64.

BYRNE, MURIEL ST CLARE, 'Elizabethan Handwriting for Beginners', *RES*, 1/2 (1925), 198–209.

CAVANAUGH, JEAN 'Lady Southwell's Defense of Poetry', *ELR*, 14 (1984), 284–85.

CERASANO, S. P. and DAVIES, MARION WYNNE (eds.), *Gloriana's Face: Women, Public and Private in the English Renaissance* (Hemel Hempstead, 1992).

CHARLTON, KENNETH, *Education in Renaissance England* (1965).

—— 'Mothers as Educative Agents in Pre-Industrial England', *History of Education*, 23 (1994), 129–56.

—— ' "Not publike only but also private and domesticall": Mothers and Familial Education in Pre-Industrial England', *History of Education*, 17/1 (1988), 1–20.

—— 'Women and Education', in Anita Pacheco (ed.), *A Companion to Early Modern Women's Writing* (Oxford, 2002), 3–21.

—— *Women, Religion and Education in Early Modern England* (1999).

CHARTERS, J. A., 'Road Carrying in England in the Seventeenth Century: Myth and Reality', *Economic History Review*, 30/1 (1977), 73–94.

CHARTIER, ROGER, 'Secrétaires *for the People?* Model Letters of the Ancien Régime: Between Court Literature and Popular Chapbooks', in Roger Chartier (ed.), *Correspondence: Models of Letter-Writing From the Middle Ages to the Nineteenth Century* (Cambridge, 1997), 59–111.

CHAVASSE, R. A., 'Humanism in Exile: Celio Secondo Curione's Learned Women Friends and *Exempla* for Elizabeth I', in S. M. Jack and B. A. Masters (eds.), *Protestants, Property and Puritans: Godly People Revisited: A Festschrift in Honour of Patrick Collinson on the Occasion of His Retirement* (Sydney, 1996), 165–85.

CHERAWATUK, KAREN and WIETHAUS, ULRIKE (eds.), *Dear Sister: Medieval Women and the Epistolary Genre* (Philadelphia, 1993).

CHOJNACKI, STANLEY, *Women and Men in Renaissance Venice Twelve Essays on Patrician Society* (Baltimore, 2000).

CIONI, MARIA L., 'The Elizabethan Chancery and Women's Rights', in D. J. Guth and J. W. McKenna (eds.), *Tudor Rule and Revolution: Essays for G. R. Elton from His American Friends* (Cambridge, 1982), 159–82.

CLARKE, DANIELLE, ' "Formd into words by your divided lips": Women, Rhetoric and the Ovidian Tradition', in Danielle Clarke and Elizabeth Clarke (eds.), *'This Double Voice': Gendered Writing in Early Modern England* (Basingstoke, 2000), 61–87.

—— *The Politics of Early Modern Women's Writing* (Harlow, 2001).

CLARKE, ELIZABETH, 'Elizabeth Jekyll's Spiritual Diary: Private Manuscript or Political Document?', *EMS*, 9 (2000), 218–37.

CLASSEN, ALBRECHT, 'Female Epistolary Literature From Antiquity to the Present: An Introduction', *Studia Neophilologica*, 60 (1988), 3–13.

CLIFFE, J. T., *The World of the Country House in Seventeenth-Century England* (New Haven and London, 1999).

CLOUGH, CECIL H., 'The Cult of Antiquity: Letters and Letter Collections', in Cecil H. Clough (ed.), *Cultural Aspects of the Italian Renaissance: Essays in Honour of Paul Oskar Kristeller* (Manchester, 1976), 33–67.

COLLINSON, PATRICK, *The Birthpangs of Protestant England: Religious and Cultural Change in the Sixteenth and Seventeenth Centuries* (Basingstoke, 1988).

—— 'A Mirror of Elizabethan Puritanism: The Life and Letters of "Godly Master Dering" ', in *Godly People: Essays on English Protestantism and Puritanism* (1983), 273–324.

COLLINSON, PATRICK, 'The Role of Women in the English Reformation Illustrated by the Life and Friendships of Anne Locke', in G. J. Cuming (ed.), *Studies in Church History*, 2 (1965), 258–72.

CONSTABLE, GILES, *Letters and Letter Collections*, Typologie des Sources du Moyen Âge Occidental, 17 (1976).

CORMICAN, JOHN D., 'The Letter as a Genre in Early Modern English', *The USF Language Quarterly*, 16 (1978), 23–5.

COUCHMAN, JANE and CRABB, ANN (eds.), *Women's Letters Across Europe, 1400–1700* (Ashgate, 2005).

CRAIG, JOHN, 'Notes and Queries: Margaret Spitlehouse, Female Scrivener', *Local Population Studies*, 46 (1991), 54–7.

CRAWFORD, ANNE, *Letters of the Queens of England* (Stroud, 1994).

CRAWFORD, PATRICIA, *Bodies, Blood and Families in Early Modern England* (Harlow, 2004).

—— 'Public Duty, Conscience, and Women in Early Modern England', in John Morrill, Paul Slack, and Daniel Woolf (eds.), *Public Duty and Private Conscience in Seventeenth-Century England: Essays Presented to G. E Aylmer* (Oxford, 1993), 57–76.

—— 'Women's Published Writings 1600–1700', in Mary Prior (ed.), *Women in English Society 1500–1800* (1985; repr. 1996), 211–82.

CRESSY, DAVID, *Birth, Marriage, and Death: Ritual, Religion, and the Life-Cycle in Tudor and Stuart England* (Oxford, 1997).

—— *Coming Over: Migration and Communication Between England and New England in the Seventeenth Century* (New York, 1987).

—— 'Describing the Social Order in Early Modern England', *Literature and History*, 3 (1976), 29–44.

—— 'Kinship and Kin Interaction in Early Modern England', *P&P*, 113 (1986), 38–69.

—— *Literacy and the Social Order: Reading and Writing in Tudor and Stuart England* (Cambridge, 1980).

—— 'Social Status and Literacy in North East England 1560–1630', *Local Population Studies*, 21 (1978), 19–23.

CROFT, PAULINE, 'Libels, Popular Literacy and Public Opinion in Early Modern England', *Historical Research*, 68 (1995), 266–85.

—— 'The Reputation of Robert Cecil: Libels, Political Opinion and Popular Awareness in the Early Seventeenth Century', *TRHS*, 1 (1991), 43–69.

—— (ed.), *Patronage, Culture and Power: The Early Cecils 1558–1612* (New Haven and London, 2002).

CUST, RICHARD, 'News and Politics in Early Seventeenth-Century England', *P&P*, 112 (1986), 60–90.

DALRYMPLE, ROGER, 'Reaction, Consolation and Redress in the Letters of the Paston Women', in James Daybell (ed.), *Early Modern Women's Letter-Writing in England, 1450–1700* (Basingstoke, 2001), 16–28.

DAVIDS, ROY, 'The Handwriting of Robert Devereux, Second Earl of Essex', *Book Collector*, 37 (1988), 351–65.

DAVIES, C. S. L. and GARNETT, JANE (eds.), *Wadham College* (Oxford, 1994).

DAVIS, NATALIE ZEMON, 'Boundaries and the Sense of Self in Sixteenth-Century France', in Thomas C. Heller *et al.* (eds.), *Reconstructing Individualism: Autonomy, Individuality, and the Self In Western Thought* (Stanford, 1986), 53–63.

—— *Fiction in the Archives: Pardon Tales and Their Tellers in Sixteenth-Century France* (Stanford, 1987).

—— *The Gift in Sixteenth-Century France* (Oxford, 2000).

—— '"Women's History" in Transition: The European Case', *Feminist Studies*, 3 (1976), 83–103.

DAVIS, NORMAN, 'The *Litera Troili* and English Letters', *RES*, 16/63 (1965), 233–44.

—— 'A Paston Hand', *RES*, 3 (1952), 209–21.

—— 'A Scribal Problem in the Paston Letters', *English and Germanic Studies*, 4 (1951), 31–64.

DAVIS, TOM, 'The Analysis of Handwriting: An Introductory Survey', in Peter Davison (ed.), *The Book Encompassed: Studies in Twentieth-Century Bibliography* (Cambridge, 1992), 57–68.

DAWSON, GILES E. and KENNEDY-SKIPTON, LAETITIA, *Elizabethan Handwriting, 1500–1650: A Guide to the Reading of Documents and Manuscripts* (1966).

DAYBELL, JAMES, 'Interpreting Letters and Reading Script: Evidence for Female Education and Literacy in Tudor England', *History of Education*, 34/6 (2005), 695–715.

—— '"Ples acsep thes my skrybled lynes": The Construction and Conventions of Women's Letters in England, 1540–1603', *Quidditas*, 20 (1999), 207–23.

—— 'Recent Studies in Seventeenth-Century Letters', *ELR*, (2006), 135–70.

—— 'Recent Studies in Sixteenth-Century Letters', *ELR*, (2005), 331–62.

—— 'Rhetoric and Friendship in Sixteenth-Century Women's Letters of Intercession', in Judith Richards and Alison Thorne (eds.), *Rhetoric, Gender and Politics: Representing Early Modern Women's Speech* (2006).

—— 'Scripting a Female Voice: Women's Epistolary Rhetoric in Sixteenth-Century Letters of Petition', *Women's Writing*, 13/1 (2006), 3–20.

—— 'The Social Conventions of Women's Letter-Writing in England, 1540–1603', in James Daybell (ed.), *Early Modern Women's Letter-Writing in England, 1450–1700* (Basingstoke, 2001), 59–76.

—— '"Suche newes as on the Quenes hye wayes we have mett": The News Networks of Elizabeth Talbot, countess of Shrewsbury (*c.*1527–1608)', in James Daybell (ed.), *Women and Politics in Early Modern England* (Aldershot, 2004), 114–31.

—— 'Women's Letters and Letter-Writing in England, 1540–1603: An Introduction to the Issues of Authorship and Construction', *Shakespeare Studies*, 27 (1999), 161–86.

—— (ed.), *Early Modern Women's Letter Writing, 1450–1700* (Basingstoke, 2001).

—— (ed.), *Women and Politics in Early Modern England, 1450–1700* (Aldershot, 2004).

DECKER, RUDOLF M., 'Ego-documents in the Netherlands, 1500–1814', *Dutch Crossing: A Journal of Low Countries Studies*, 39 (1989), 61–72.

DENHOLM-YOUNG, N., *Handwriting in England and Wales* (Cardiff, 1954).

DICKSON, DONALD R., 'Humanistic Influences on the Art of the Familiar Epistle in the Renaissance', in George Douglas (ed.), *Studies in The History of Business Writing* (Urbana, Ill., 1985), 11–22.

DIERKS, KONSTANTIN, 'Letter Manuals, Literary Innovation, and the Problem of Defining Genre in Anglo-American Epistolary Instruction, 1568–1800', *Papers of the Bibliographical Society of America*, 94 (2000), 541–5.

DOGLIO, MARIA LUISA, 'Letter-Writing, 1350–1650', in Letizia Panizza and Sharon Wood (eds.), *A History Of Women's Writing in Italy* (Cambridge, 2000), 13–24.

DONAWERTH, JANE, 'Women's Poetry and the Tudor-Stuart System of Gift Exchange', in Mary E. Burke *et al.* (eds.), *Women, Writing and the Reproduction of Culture in Tudor and Stuart Britain* (Syracuse, NY, 2000), 3–18.

DORAN, SUSAN, 'Elizabeth's Religion: Clues from Her Letters', *Journal of Ecclesiastical History*, 51 (2000), 699–720.

DOWLING, MARIA, *Humanism in the Age of Henry VIII* (1986).

DRAGSTRA, HENK, OTTWAY, SHEILA, and WILCOX, HELEN (eds.), *Betraying Our Selves: Forms of Representation in Early Modern English Texts* (Basingstoke, 2000).

DUBY, GEORGES (ed.), *A History of Private Life*, Vol. 2. *Revelations of the Medieval World*, trans. Arthur Goldhammer (Cambridge, Mass., 1988).

DURANT, DAVID N., *Bess of Hardwick: Portrait of a Dynast* (1977; rev. edn. 1999).

EALES, JACQUELINE, 'Patriarchy, Puritanism and Politics: The Letters of Lady Brilliana Harley (1598–1643)', in James Daybell (ed.), *Early Modern Women's Letter Writing, 1450–1700* (Basingstoke, 2001), 143–58.

—— *Puritans and Roundheads: The Harleys of Brampton Bryan and the Outbreak of the English Civil War* (Cambridge, 1990).

—— *Women In Early Modern England, 1500–1700* (1998).

EARLE, REBECCA (ed.), *Epistolary Selves: Letters and Letter-Writers, 1600–1945* (Aldershot, 1999).

EISENSTADT, S. N. and RINGER, LOUIS, 'Patron–Client Relations as a Model of Structuring Social Change', *Comparative Studies in Society and History*, 22/1 (1980), 42–77.

—— and LEMARCHAND, RENÉ (eds.), *Political Clientelism, Patronage and Development* (Beverly Hills and London, 1981).

ELTON, G. R., *The Tudor Constitution: Documents and Commentary* (Cambridge, 1960; 2nd edn. 1982).

—— 'Tudor Government: The Points of Contact; iii: The Court', *TRHS*, 5th ser., 26 (1976), 211–28.

—— *The Tudor Revolution in Government: Administrative Changes in the Reign of Henry VIII* (Cambridge, 1953).

ERICKSON, AMY LOUISE, *Women and Property in Early Modern England* (1993).

ERLER, MARY and KOWALESKI, MARYANNE (eds.), *Women and Power in the Middle Ages* (Athens, Ga., 1988).

EZELL, MARGARET J. M., 'The Myth of Judith Shakespeare: Creating the Canon of Women's Literature', *New Literary History*, 21 (1990), 579–92.

—— *The Patriarch's Wife: Literary Evidence and the History of the Family* (Chapel Hill, NC, 1987).

—— *Social Authorship and the Advent of Print* (Baltimore, 1999).

—— *Writing Women's Literary History* (Baltimore and London, 1993).

FAIRBANK, ALFRED and DICKINS, BRUCE, *The Italic Hand in Tudor Cambridge* (1962).

—— and WOLPE, BERTHOLD, *Renaissance Handwriting: An Anthology of Italic Scripts* (1960).

FELCH, SUSAN M., ' "Deir Sinter": The Letter of John Knoz to Anne Vaughan Lok', *Renaissance and Reformation*, 19(1995), 47–68.

FERGUSON, MARGARET W., 'Renaissance Concepts of the "Woman Writer" ', in Helen Wilcox (ed.), *Women and Literature in Britain 1500–1700* (Cambridge, 1996), 143–68.

FETHERSTON, JOHN (ed.), *The Visitation of the County of Warwick in the Year 1619*, Publications of the Harleian Society, 12 (1877).

FILDES, V. A., 'Historical Changes in Patterns of Breastfeeding', in S. Teper, P. Diggory, and D. M. Potts (eds.), *Natural Human Fertility: Social and Biological Determinants* (Basingstoke and London, 1988), 118–29.

FINLAY, MICHAEL, *Western Writing Implements in the Age of the Quill Pen* (Carlisle, 1990).

FITZMAURICE, JAMES and REY, MARTINE, 'Letters By Women in England, the French Romance, and Dorothy Osborne', *The Politics of Gender in Early Modern Europe: Sixteenth Century Essays and Studies*, 12 (1987), 149–60.

FITZMAURICE, SUSAN, *The Familiar Letter in Early Modern English* (2002).

FLEMING, JULIET, 'Dictionary English and the Female Tongue', in Jean R. Brink (ed.), *Privileging Gender in Early Modern England* (Kirksville, 1993), 175–204.

—— '*The French Garden*: An Introduction to Women's French', *ELH*, 56/1 (1989), 19–51.

—— *Graffiti and the Writing Arts of Early Modern England* (Philadelphia, 2001).

FLETCHER, ANTHONY J., *Gender, Sex and Subordination in England, 1500–1800* (1995).

FOISIL, MADELEINE, 'The Literature of Intimacy', in Roger Chartier (ed.), *History of Private Life, vol. 3. Passions of the Renaissance* (Cambridge, Mass., 1989), 327–61.

FORD, W.P., 'The Problem of Literacy in Early Modern England', *History*, 78 (1993), 22–37.

FOUCAULT, MICHEL, 'Technologies of the Self', in L. H. Martin, H. Gutman and W. W. Paden (eds.), *Technologies of the Self: A Seminar With Michel Foucault* (Amherst, Mass., 1988), 16–49.

FOX, ADAM, *Oral and Literate Culture in England 1500–1700* (Oxford, 2000).

—— 'Rumour, News and Popular Political Opinion in Elizabethan and Early Stuart England', *HJ*, 40/3 (1997), 597–620.

FRANKFORTER, A. DANIEL, 'Correspondence with Women: The Case of John Knox', *Journal of the Rocky Mountains Medieval and Renaissance Association*, 6 (1985), 159–72.

FREEMAN, THOMAS S., ' "The Good Ministrye of Godlye and Vertuouse Women": The Elizabethan Martyrologists and the Female Supporters of the Marian Martyrs', *JBS*, 39/1 (2000), 8–33.

FRIEDMAN, ALICE T., *House and Household in Elizabethan England: Wollaton Hall and the Willoughby Family* (Chicago, 1989).

—— 'The Influence of Humanism on the Education of Girls and Boys in Tudor England', *History of Education Quarterly*, 39 (1985), 57–70.

—— ' "Portrait of a Marriage": The Willoughby Letters of 1585–1586', *Signs*, 11/3 (1986), 542–55.

FROIDE, AMY M., *Never Married: Singlewomen in Early Modern England* (Oxford, 2005).

FRYE, SUSAN, 'Sewing Connections: Elizabeth Tudor, Mary Stuart, Elizabeth Talbot, and Seventeenth-Century Anonymous Needleworkers', in Susan Frye and Karen Robertson (eds.), *Maids and Mistress, Cousins and Queens: Women's Alliances in Early Modern England* (New York and Oxford, 1999), 165–82.

—— and ROBERTSON, KAREN (eds.), *Maids and Mistress, Cousins and Queens: Women's Alliances in Early Modern England* (New York and Oxford, 1999).

FUMERTON, PATRICIA, 'The Exchanging of Gifts: The Elizabethan Currency of Children and Poetry', *ELH*, 15 (1986), 57–97.

—— and HUNT, SIMON (eds.), *Renaissance Culture and the Everyday* (Philadelphia, 1999).

GAGE, JOHN, *The History and Antiquities of Hengrave in Suffolk* (1822).

GARDINER, DOROTHY, *English Girlhood at School: A Study of Women's Education Through Twelve Centuries* (Oxford, 1929).

GARRARD, RACHEL P., 'English Probate Inventories and their Use in Studying the Significance of the Domestic Interior, 1570–1700', in Ad Van Der Woude and Anton Schuurman (eds.), *Probate Inventories: A New Source for the Historical Studies of Wealth, Material Culture and Agricultural Development* (Utrecht, 1980), 55–82.

GERLO, ALOÏS, 'The *Opus de conscribendis epistolis* of Erasmus and the Tradition of the *Ars Epistolica*', in R. R. Bolgar (ed.), *Classical Influences on European Culture A.D. 500–1500* (Cambridge, 1971), 103–14.

GIBSON, JONATHAN, 'Letters', in Michael Hattaway (ed.), *A Companion to English Renaissance Literature and Culture* (Oxford, 2000), 615–19.

—— 'Significant Space in Manuscript Letters', *The Seventeenth Century*, 12/1 (1997), 1–9.

GILROY, AMANDA and VERHOEVEN, W. M. (eds.), *Prose Studies: Correspondences: A Special Issue on Letters*, 19/2 (1996).

GIROUARD, MARK, *Life in the English Country House: A Social and Architectural History* (1978).

GIRY-DELOISON, CHARLES, and METTAM, ROGER (eds.), *Patronages et Clientelismes, 1550–1750, France, Angleterre, Espagne, Italie* (Lille, 1995).

GLANVILLE, PHILIPPA, 'Plate and Gift-Giving at Court', in David Starkey (ed.), *Henry VIII: A European Court in England* (1991), 131–5.

GOLDBERG, JONATHAN, *Desiring Women Writing: English Renaissance Examples* (Stanford, 1997).

—— *Writing Matter: From the Hands of the English Renaissance* (Stanford, 1990).

GOLDSMITH, ELIZABETH V. (ed.), *Writing the Female Voice: Essays on Epistolary Literature* (1989).

GOODMAN, DENA, 'Public Sphere and Private Life: Toward a Synthesis of Current Historiographical Approaches to the Old Regime', *History and Theory*, 31 (1992), 1–20.

GOWING, LAURA, *Domestic Dangers: Women, Words and Sex in Early Modern London* (Oxford, 1996).

GRAFTON, ANTONY and JARDINE, LISA, *From Humanism to the Humanities: Education and the Liberal Arts in Fifteenth- and Sixteenth-Century Europe* (1986).

GRAHAM, ELSPETH, 'Women's Writing and the Self', in Helen Wilcox (ed.), *Women and Literature in Britain 1500–1700* (Cambridge, 1996), 209–33.

GRAZIA, MARGRETA DE, 'What Is A Work? What Is A Document?', in W. Speed Hill (ed.), *New Ways of Looking at Old Texts: Papers of the Renaissance English Text Society, 1985–1991* (Binghamton, NY, 1993), 199–207.

GREENBLATT, STEPHEN, *Renaissance Self-Fashioning: From More to Shakespeare* (Chicago and London, 1980; repr. 1984).

GREENE, THOMAS, 'The Flexibility of the Self in Renaissance Literature', in P. Demetz (ed.), *The Disciplines of Criticism* (New Haven, 1968), 241–64.

GRIFFITHS, R. A., 'Public and Private Bureaucracies in England and Wales in the Fifteenth Century', *TRHS*, 5th ser., 30 (1980), 109–30.

GRUND, GARY R., 'From Formulary to Fiction: The Epistle and the English Anti-Ciceronian Movement', *Texas Studies in Literature and Language*, 17/2 (1975), 379–95.

GUILLÉN, CLAUDIO, 'Notes Toward the Study of the Renaissance Letter', in Barbara Kiefer Lewalski (ed.), *Renaissance Genres: Essays on Theory, History and Interpretation* (Cambridge, Mass., 1986), 70–101.

GUNN, S. J., 'A Letter of Jane, Duchess of Northumberland in 1553', *EHR*, 114/459 (1999), 1267–71.

—— 'The Structures of Politics in Early Tudor England', *TRHS* 6th ser., 5 (1995), 59–90.

GUY, JOHN, 'Law, Equity and Conscience in Henrician Jurist Thought', in John Guy and Alistair Fox (eds.), *Reassessing the Henrician Age: Humanism, Politics and Reform, 1500–1550* (Oxford, 1986), 179–98.

HABERMAS, JÜRGEN, *The Structural Transformation of the Public Sphere*, trans. Thomas Burger (Cambridge, Mass., 1989).

HACKEL, HEIDI BRAYMEN, 'The Countess of Bridgewater's London Library', in Jennifer Anderson and Elizabeth Sauer (eds.), *Books and Their Readers in Early Modern England: Material Studies* (Philadelphia, 2002), 138–59.

—— 'The "Great Variety" of Readers and Early Modern Reading Practices', in David Scott Kastau (ed.), *A Companion to Shakespeare* (Oxford, 1999), 139–57.

HACKETT, HELEN, 'Courtly Writing by Women', in Helen Wilcox (ed.), *Women and Literature in Britain 1500–1700* (Cambridge, 1996), 169–89.

HAGEMAN, ELIZABETH H., 'Did Shakespeare Have Any Sisters?: Editing Women Writers of the Renaissance and Reformation', in W. Speed Hill (ed.), *New Ways of Looking at Old Texts: Papers of the Renaissance English Text Society, 1985–1991* (Binghamton, NY, 1993), 103–9.

—— 'Making a Good Impression: Early Texts of Poems and Letters by Katherine Philips, the "Matchless Orinda"', *South Central Review*, 11 (1994), 39–65.

—— 'Recent Studies in Women Writers of the English Renaissance', in Elizabeth H. Hageman (ed.), *Women in the Renaissance: Selections From English Literary Review* (Amherst, Mass., 1990), 228–75.

HALASZ, ALEXANDRA, *The Marketplace of Print: Pamphlets and the Public Sphere in Early Modern England* (Cambridge, 1997).

HALL, H., *Society in the Elizabethan Age* (1888).

HALL, LESLEY A., 'Sex in the Archives', *Archives*, 93/22 (1995), 1–12.

HALL, MARIE BOAS, 'The Royal Society's Role in the Diffusion of Information in the Seventeenth Century', *Notes and Records of the Royal Society*, 29 (1975), 173–92.

HAMMER, PAUL E. J., 'Patronage at Court, Faction and the Earl of Essex', in John Guy, (ed.), *The Reign of Elizabeth I: Court and Culture in the Last Decade* (Cambridge, 1995), 65–86.

—— *The Polarisation of Elizabethan Politics: The Political Career of Robert Devereux, 2nd Earl of Essex, 1585–1597* (Cambridge, 1999).

—— 'The Uses of Scholarship: The Secretariat of Robert Devereux, Second Earl of Essex, c.1581–1601', *EHR*, 109/430 (1994), 26–51.

HANAWALT, BARBARA A., 'Lady Honor Lisle's Networks of Influence', in Mary Erler and Maryanne Kowaleski (eds.), *Women and Power in the Middle Ages* (Athens, Ga., 1988), 188–212.

HANNAY, MARGARET P., 'Unpublished Letters by Mary Sidney: A Preliminary Report', *Sidney Newsletter*, 4/2 (1984), 13.

—— 'Unpublished Letters by Mary Sidney, Countess of Pembroke', *Spenser Studies*, 6 (1986), 165–90.

—— (ed.), *Silent But For the Word: Tudor Women as Patrons, Translators and Writers of Religious Works* (Kent, Oh., 1985).

HAREVEN, TAMARA K., 'The Impact of the History of the Family and the Life Course on Social History', *Social Science History*, 20 (1996), 317–44.

HARRIS, BARBARA J., *English Aristocratic Women, 1450–1550: Marriage and Family, Property and Careers* (New York and Oxford, 2002).

—— 'Marriage Sixteenth-Century Style: Elizabeth Stafford and the Third Duke of Norfolk', *Journal of Social History*, 15 (1981–2), 371–82.

—— 'Property, Power and Personal Relations: Elite Mothers and Sons in Yorkist and Early Tudor England', *Signs*, 15/3 (1990), 606–32.

—— 'Sisterhood, Friendship and the Power of English Aristocratic Women, 1450–1550', in James Daybell (ed.), *Women and Politics in Early Modern England, 1450–1700* (Aldershot, 2004), 21–50.

—— 'Space, Time, and the Power of Aristocratic Wives in Yorkist and Early Tudor England, 1450–1550', in Ray Mentzer (ed.), *Sixteenth-Century Essays and Studies* (2001), 245–64.

—— 'The View From My Lady's Chamber: New Perspectives on the Early Tudor Monarchy', *HLQ*, 60/3 (1999), 215–47.

—— 'Women and Politics in Early Tudor England', *HJ*, 33 (1990), 259–81.

HARRIS, BOB, 'Historians, Public Opinion, and the "Public Sphere" ', *Journal of Early Modern History*, 1/4 (1997), 369–77.

HARRIS, FRANCES, 'The Letterbooks of Mary Evelyn', *EMS*, 7 (1998), 202–15.

HARRISON, BRIAN and McMILLAN, JAMES, 'Some Feminist Betrayals of Women's History', *HJ*, 26/2 (1983), 375–89.

HARRISON P. and BRAYSHAY, M., 'Post-Horse Routes, Royal Progresses and Government Communications in the Reign of James I', *Journal of Transport History*, 18 (1997), 116–33.

HARVEY, ELIZABETH, *Ventriloquized Voices: Feminist Theory and English Renaissance Texts* (1992).

HASLER, P. W. (ed.), *The House of Commons 1558–1603*, 3 vols. (1981).

HEAD, RANDOLPH C., 'A Plurilingual Family in the Sixteenth Century: Language Use and Linguistic Consciousness in the Salis Family Correspondence, 1580–1610', *SCJ*, 26 (1995), 577–93.

HEAL, AMBROSE, *The English Writing-Masters and Their Copy-Books, 1570–1800: A Biographical Dictionary and Bibliography* (Hildesheim, 1962).

HEAL, FELICITY, 'Reputation and Honour in Court and Country: Lady Elizabeth Russell and Sir Thomas Hoby', *TRHS* (1996), 161–78.

—— and HOLMES, CLIVE *The Gentry in England and Wales 1500–1700* (Basingstoke, 1994).

—— and HOLMES, CLIVE, ' "*Prudentia ultra sexum*": Lady Jane Bacon and the Management of her Families', in Muriel C McClendon *et al.* (eds.), *Protestant Identities: Religion Society and Self-Fashioning in Post-Reformation England* (Stanford, 1999), 100–24.

HEALE, ELIZABETH, *Autobiography and Authorship in Renaissance Verse: Chronicle of the Self* (Basingstoke, 2003).

—— 'Women and the Courtly Love Lyric: The Devonshire Manuscript (BL Additional 17492)', *Modern Language Review*, 90/2 (1995), 296–313.

—— *Wyatt, Surrey and Early Tudor Poetry* (1998).

HEAWOOD, EDWARD, *Watermarks: Mainly of the Seventeenth and Eighteenth Centuries* (Hilversum, 1950).

HECTOR, L. C., *The Handwriting of English Documents* (1958).

HENDERSON, JUDITH RICE, 'Defining the Genre of the Letter: Juan Luis Vives' *De conscribendis epistolis, Renaissance and Reformation*, 7/19 (1983), 89–105.

—— 'Erasmus on the Art of Letter-Writing', in James J. Murphy (ed.), *Renaissance Eloquence: Studies in the Theory and Practice of Renaissance Rhetoric* (Berkeley, 1983), 331–55.

—— 'On Reading the Rhetoric of the Renaissance Letter', in Heinrich F. Plett (ed.), *Renaissance-Rhetorik Renaissance Rhetoric* (Berlin and New York, 1993), 143–62.

HEY, DAVID, *Packmen, Carriers and Packhorse Roads: Trade and Communications in North Derbyshire and South Yorkshire* (1980).

HICKS, M. A. 'The Piety of Margaret, Lady Hungerford (d. 1478)', *Journal of Ecclesiastical History*, 38 (1987), 19–38.

HIGGINS, PATRICIA, 'The Reactions of Women, With Special Reference to Women Petitioners', in B. Manning, (ed.), *Politics, Religion and the English Civil War* (1973), 177–222.

HIRSH, JOHN C., 'Author and Scribe in *The Book of Margery Kempe*', *Medium Aevum*, 44 (1075), 145–50.

HIRSHFIELD, HEATHER, 'Early Modern Collaboration and Theories of Authorship', *PMLA*, 116/3 (2001), 609–22.

HOBBS, MARY, *Early Seventeenth-Century Verse Miscellany Manuscripts* (Aldershot, 1992).

HOBBY, ELAINE, *Virtue of Necessity: English Women's Writing, 1649–88* (1988).

HODGKIN, K., 'The Diary of Lady Anne Clifford: A Study of Class and Gender in the Seventeenth-Century', *HWJ*, 19 (1985), 148–61.

HOLLINGSWORTH, T., 'The Demography of the British Peerage', supplement to *Population Studies*, 18 (1964).

HOLMES, CLIVE, 'Drainers and Fenmen: The Problem of Popular Political Consciousness in the Seventeenth Century', in Anthony Fletcher and John Stevenson (eds.), *Order and Disorder in Early Modern England* (Cambridge, 1985), 166–95.

HÖLTGEN, KARL JOSEF, 'Sir Robert Dallington (1561–1637): Author, Traveller, and Pioneer of Taste', *HLQ*, 47 (1984), 147–77.

HORNBEAK, KATHERINE GEE, *The Complete Letter-Writer in English 1568–1800* (Northampton, Mass., 1934).

HOULBROOKE, RALPH, A., *Death, Religion and the Family in England, 1480–1750* (Oxford, 1998).

—— *The English Family, 1450–1700* (Harlow, 1984).

—— 'Women's Social Life and Common Actions in England From the Fifteenth Century to the Eve of the Civil War', *Continuity and Change*, 1/2 (1986), 171–89.

HOUSDEN, J. A. J., 'Early Posts in England', *EHR*, 18 (1903), 713–18.

—— 'The Merchant Strangers Posts in the Sixteenth Century', *EHR*, 21 (1906), 739–42.

HOUSTON, R. A., *Literacy in Early Modern Europe: Culture and Education, 1500–1800* (1988; 2002).

HOWE, JAMES, *Epistolary Spaces: English Letter Writing from the Foundation of the Post Office to Richardson's 'Clarissa'* (Aldershot, 2003).

HOWSE, VIOLET M., *Stanford-in-the-Vale, A Parish Record*, 5 vols. (Oxford, 1962).

HUEBERT, RONALD, 'The Gendering of Privacy', *The Seventeenth Century*, 16 (2001), 37–67.

HUFTON, OLWEN, 'Reflections on the Role of Women in the Early Modern Court', *The Court Historian*, 5/1 (May 2000), 1–13.

—— 'Women in History: Early Modern Europe', *P&P*, 101 (1983), 125–41.

HULL, SUZANNE W., *Chaste, Silent and Obedient: English Books for Women, 1475–1640* (San Marino, Calif., 1982).

HUMILIATA, SISTER MARY, 'Standards of Taste Advocated for Feminine Letter Writing, 1640–1797', *HLQ*, 13 (1949–50), 261–77.

HUNTER, DARD, *Papermaking: The History and Technique of an Ancient Craft* (New York, 1947).

HUNTER, J., *History of Hallamshire* (1869).

HUNTER, LYNETTE, 'Sisters of the Royal Society: The Circle of Katherine Jones, Lady Ranelagh', in Lynette Hunter and Sarah Hutton (eds.), *Women, Science and Medicine, 1500–1700* (Thrupp, 1997), 178–97.

HUNTER, MICHAEL, 'How to Edit a Seventeenth-Century Manuscript: Principles and Practice', *The Seventeenth Century*, 10 (1995), 277–310.

HURSTFIELD, JOEL, *The Queen's Wards: Wardship and Marriage Under Elizabeth I* (1958).

HUTSON, LORNA, 'The "Double Voice" of Renaissance Equity and the Literary Voices of Women', in Danielle Clarke and Elizabeth Clarke (eds.), *This Double Voice: Gendered Writing in Early Modern England* (Basingstoke, 2000), 142–63.

—— *The Usurer's Daughter: Male Friendship and Fictions of Women in Sixteenth-Century England* (1994).

ILARDI, VINCENT, 'Crosses and Carets: Renaissance Patronage and Coded Letters of Recommendation', *American Historical Review*, 92/5 (1987), 1127–49.

INGRAM, MARTIN, *Church Courts, Sex and Marriage in England 1570–1640* (Cambridge, 1987).

IVES, ERIC W., *Faction in Tudor England* (1979).

JAMES, MERVYN, 'English Politics and the Concept of Honour, 1485–1642', in *Society, Politics and Culture: Studies in Early Modern England* (Cambridge, 1986), 308–415.

JARDINE, LISA, *Erasmus, Man of Letters: The Construction of Charisma in Print* (Princeton, 1993).

—— 'Isotta Nogarola: Woman Humanists: Education for What?', *History of Education*, 12 (1983), 231–44.

—— 'Reading and the Technology of Textual Affect: Erasmus's Familiar Letters and Shakespeare's *King Lear*', in *Reading Shakespeare Historically* (London and New York, 1996), 78–97.

—— 'Unpicking the Tapestry: The Scholar of Women's History as Penelope Among her Suitors', in *Reading Shakespeare Historically* (London and New York, 1996), 132–47.

JENKINSON, HILARY, 'Elizabethan Handwriting: A Preliminary Sketch', *The Library*, 4th ser., 3 (1922), 1–35.

—— *The Later Court Hands* (New York, 1927).

—— 'Notes on the Study of English Punctuation of the Sixteenth Century', *RES*, 2/6 (1926), 152–8.

JENSON, KATHERINE A., 'Male Models of Feminine Epistolarity: Or, How to Write Like a Woman in Seventeenth-Century France', in Elizabeth V. Goldsmith (ed.), *Writing the Female Voice: Essays on Epistolary Literature* (Boston, 1989), 25–45.

—— *Writing Love: Letters, Women, and the Novel in France, 1605–1776* (1995).

JEWELL, HELEN M., *Education in Early Modern England* (Basingstoke, 1998).

JOHNS, ADRIAN, 'The Physiology of Reading in Restoration England', in James Raven, Helen Small, and Naomi Tadmor (eds.), *The Practice and Representation of Reading in England* (Cambridge, 1996), 138–61.

JOHNSON, LYNN STANLEY, 'The Trope of the Scribe and the Question of Literary Authority in the Works of Julian of Norwich and Margery Kempe', *Speculum*, 66 (1991), 820–38.

JOHNSON, PAUL, *Elizabeth I: A Study in Power and Intellect* (1974).

JONES, ANN ROSALIND and STALLYBRASS, PETER, *Renaissance Clothing and the Materials of Memory* (Cambridge, 2000).

JUSTICE, GEORGE L. and TINKER, NATHAN, *Women's Writing and the Circulation of Ideas: Manuscript Publication in England, 1550–1800* (Cambridge, 2002).

KAUFFMAN, LINDA S., *Discourses of Desire: Gender, Genre and Epistolary Fictions* (Ithaca and London, 1986).

KAUFMAN, G., 'Juan Luis Vives on the Education of Women', *Signs*, 3/4 (1978), 891–96.

KAUFMAN, PETER IVER, 'Absolute Margaret: Margaret More Roper and "Well Learned" Men', *SCJ*, 20/3 (1989), 443–56.

KELLY, JOAN, 'Did Women Have a Renaissance?', in *Women, History and Theory* (Chicago, 1984), 19–50.

KELSO, RUTH, *Doctrine for the Lady of the Renaissance* (Urbana, Chicago, and London, 1956).

Kendal Record Office, *Proud Northern Lady: Lady Anne Clifford 1590–1676* (Kendal, 1990).

KERMODE, JENNY and WALKER, GARTHINE (eds.), *Women, Crime and the Courts in Early Modern England* (1994).

KETTERING, SHARON, 'Gift-Giving and Patronage in Early Modern France', *French History*, 2/2 (1988), 131–51.

—— 'The Patronage Power of Early Modern French Noblewomen', *HJ*, 32/4 (1989), 817–41.

KLAPISCH-ZUBER, CHRISTIANE, *Women, Family, and Ritual in Renaissance Italy*, trans. Lydia Cochrane (Chicago, 1985).

KLENE, JEAN, 'Recreating the Letters of Lady Anne Southwell', in W. Speed Hill (ed.), *New Ways of Looking at Old Texts: Papers of the Renaissance English Text Society, 1985–1991* (Binghamton, NY., 1993), 239–52.

KNOWLES, JAMES, ' "Infinite Riches in a Little Room": Marlowe and the Aesthetics of the Closet', in Gordon McMullan, (ed.), *Renaissance Configurations: Voices/Bodies/ Spaces, 1580–1690* (Basingstoke, 1998), 3–29.

LA BELLE, JENIJOY, 'A Love's True Knot: The Letters of Constance Fowler and the Poems of Herbert Aston', *Journal of English and Germanic Philology*, 79 (1980), 13–31.

LAMAR, VIRGINIA A., *Travel and Roads in England* (Charlottesville, 1960).

LAMB, MARY ELLEN, 'The Cooke Sisters: Attitudes Towards Learned Women in the Renaissance', in Margaret P. Hannay (ed.), *Silent But For the Word: Tudor Women as Patrons, Translators and Writers of Religious Works* (Kent, Oh., 1985), 107–25.

LARMINIE, VIVIENNE, 'Fighting for Family in a Patronage Society: The Epistolary Armoury of Anne Newdigate (1574–1618)', in James Daybell (ed.), *Early Modern Women's Letter Writing, 1450–1700* (Basingstoke, 2001), 94–108.

—— 'Marriage and the Family: The Example of the Seventeenth-Century Newdigates', *Midland History*, 9 (1984), 1–22.

—— *Wealth, Kinship and Culture: the Seventeenth-Century Newdigates of Arbury and Their World* (Woodbridge, 1995).

LASLETT, BARBARA, 'The Family as a Public and Private Institution: An Historical Perspective', *Journal of Marriage and the Family*, 35 (1973), 480–92.

LAURENCE, ANNE, ' "Begging Pardon for all mistakes and errors in this writing I being a woman and doing it myself": Family Narratives in Some Early Eighteenth-Century Letters', in James Daybell (ed.), *Early Modern Women's Letter Writing, 1450–1700* (Basingstoke, 2001), 194–206.

—— *Women in England, 1500–1760: A Social History* (1994).

LASLETT, P, *The World We Have Lost Further Explored* (1965; 3rd edn., repr. 1994).

LEBLANC, YVONNE, 'Queen Anne in the Lonely, Tear Soaked Bed of Penelope: Rewriting the *Heroides* in Sixteenth-Century France', *Disputatio*, 1 (1996), 71–87.

LERCH-DAVIS, GENIE S., 'Rebellion Against Public Prose: The Letters of Dorothy Osborne to William Temple (1652–4)', *Texas Studies in Language and Literature*, 20 (1978), 386–415.

LERER, SETH, *Courtly Letters in the Age of Henry VIII: Literary Culture and the Arts of Deceit* (Cambridge, 1997).

LEVY, F. J., 'The Decorum of News', in Joad Raymond (ed.), *News, Newspapers, and Society in Early Modern Britain* (1999), 12–38.

—— 'How Information Spread Among the Gentry, 1550–1640', *JBS*, 21/2 (1982), 11–34.

LEWALSKI, BARBARA KIEFER, *Writing Women in Jacobean England* (Harvard, 1993).

LOVE, HAROLD, *Scribal Publication in Seventeenth-Century England* (Oxford, 1993).

LYALL, RODERICK, 'The Construction of a Rhetorical Voice in Sixteenth-Century Scottish Letters', *Prose Studies*, 19/2 (1996), 127–35.

MACCAFFREY, WALLACE T., 'Patronage and Politics Under the Tudors', in Linda Levy Peck (ed.), *The Mental World of the Jacobean Court* (Cambridge, 1991), 21–35.

—— 'Place and Patronage in Elizabethan Politics', in S. T. Bindoff *et al.* (eds.), *Elizabethan Government and Society* (1961), 95–127.

MCARTHUR, ELLEN A., 'Women Petitioners and the Long Parliament', *EHR*, 24 (1909), 698–709.

MCCUTCHEON, ELIZABETH, 'Margaret More Roper: The Learned Woman in Tudor England', in Katherina M. Wilson (ed.), *Women Writers of the Renaissance and Reformation* (Athens, Ga., 1987), 449–80.

—— 'Playing the Waiting Game: The Life and Letters of Elizabeth Wolley', *Quidditas*, 20 (1999), 31–53.

MACEK, ELLEN, 'The Emergence of a Feminine Spirituality in *The Book of Martyrs*', *SCJ*, 19/1 (1988), 63–80.

MACFARLANE, ALAN, *Marriage and Love in England: Modes of Reproduction, 1300–1840* (Oxford, 1986).

MACK, PETER, *Elizabethan Rhetoric: Theory and Practice* (Cambridge, 2002).

MACLEAN, I., *The Renaissance Notion of Woman: A Study in the Fortunes of Scholasticism and Medical Science in European Intellectual Life* (Cambridge, 1980).

MCKITTERICK, DAVID, 'Women and their Books in Seventeenth-Century England: The Case of Elizabeth Puckering', *The Library*, 7th ser., 1/4 (2000), 359–80.

MCMULLEN, NORMA, 'The Education of English Gentlewomen 1540–1640', *History of Education*, 6/2 (1977), 87–101.

MAGNUSSON, LYNNE, 'A Rhetoric of Requests: Genre and Linguistic Scripts in Elizabethan Women's Suitors', in James Daybell, (ed.), *Women and Politics in Early Modern England, 1450–1700* (Aldershot, 2004), 51–66.

—— *Shakespeare and Social Dialogue: Dramatic Language and Elizabethan Letters* (Cambridge, 1999).

—— 'Widowhood and Linguistic Capital: The Rhetoric and Reception of Anne Bacon's Epistolary Advice', *ELR*, 31/1 (2001), 3–33.

MAINE, Revd. LEWIN G., *A Berkshire Village, Its History and Antiquities* (Oxford and London, 1866).

MALINOWSKI, BRONISLAW, *Argonauts of the Western Pacific: An Account of Native Enterprise and Adventure in the Archipelagoes of Melanesian New Guinea* (1922; repr. New York, 1961).

MARGOLIS, NADIA, ' "The Cry of the Chameleon": Evolving Voices in the Epistles of Christine de Pisan', *Disputatio*, 1 (1996), 37–70.

MAROTTI, ARTHUR F., *Manuscript, Print and the English Renaissance Lyric* (Ithaca and London, 1995).

MASTEN, JEFFREY, *Textual Intercourse: Collaboration, Authorship, and Sexualities in Renaissance Drama* (Cambridge, 1997).

MAUS, KATHERINE EISAMAN, *Inwardness and the Theatre in the English Renaissance* (Chicago, 1995).

MAUSS, MARCEL, *The Gift: Form and Reason for Exchange in Archaic Societies* (1950), trans. W. D. Halls (1990).

MAY, STEVEN W., 'Two Unpublished Letters by Mary Herbert, Countess of Pembroke', *EMS*, 9 (2000), 88–97.

MEALE, CAROL M. and BOFFEY, JULIA, 'Gentlewomen's Reading', in Lotte Hellinga and J. B. Trapp (eds.), *The Cambridge History of the Book in Britain, Vol. 3. 1400–1557* (Cambridge, 1999), 526–40.

MEARS, NATALIE, 'Courts, Courtiers, and Culture in Tudor England', *HJ*, 46/3 (2003), 703–22.

—— 'Politics in the Elizabethan Privy Chamber: Lady Mary Sidney and Kat Ashley', in James Daybell (ed.), *Women and Politics in Early Modern England, 1450–1700* (Aldershot, 2004), 67–82.

—— *Queenship and Political Discourse in The Elizabethan Realms* (Cambridge, 2005).

MENDELSON, SARA, 'Debate: The Weightiest Business: Marriage in an Upper-Class Gentry Family in Seventeenth-Century England', *P&P*, 85 (1979), 126–35.

—— 'Stuart Women's Diaries and Occasional Memoirs', in Mary Prior (ed.), *Women in English Society 1500–1800* (1985; repr. 1996), 181–210.

—— and CRAWFORD, PATRICIA, *Women in Early Modern England, 1550–1720* (Oxford, 1998).

MITCHELL, LINDA C., 'Entertainment and Instruction: Women's Roles in the English Epistolary Tradition', *HLQ*, 66/3, 4 (2003), 331–47.

——, and POSTER, CAROL (eds.), Letter-Writing Manual, From Antiquity to the Present (Forthcoming; Columbia, SC, 2006).

MONTROSE, LOUIS, 'Gifts and Reasons: The Contexts of Peele's *Arraynement of Paris*', *ELH* 47 (1980), 433–61.

MORAN, JO ANN HOEPPNER, *The Growth of English Schooling, 1340–1548: Learning, Literacy, and Laicization in Pre-Reformation York Diocese* (Princeton, 1985).

MORGAN, PAUL, 'Frances Wolfreston and "Her Bouks": A Seventeenth-Century Woman Book Collector', *The Library*, 6th ser., 11/3 (1989), 197–219.

MOUSLEY, ANDREW, 'Renaissance Selves and Life Writing: The *Autobiography* of Thomas Whythorne', *Forum for Modern Language Studies*, 26/3 (1990), 222–30.

MOUSNIER, ROLAND, *Les Institutions de la France sous la monarchie absolue, 1598–1789* (Paris, 1974).

MUELLER, JANEL, ' "To My Very Good Brother the King of Scots": Elizabeth I's Correspondence with James VI and the Question of Succession', *PMLA*, 115 (2000), 1063–71.

MUNNS, JESSICA and RICHARDS, PENNY (eds.), *Gender, Power and Privilege in Early Modern Europe* (2003).

NAJEMY, JOHN M., *Between Friends: Discourses of Power and Desire in the Machiavelli-Vettori Letters of 1513–1515* (Princeton, 1993).

NEALE, J. E., 'The Elizabethan Political Scene', in *Essays in Elizabethan History* (1958), 59–84.

NEVITT, MARCUS, 'Women in the Business of Revolutionary News: Elizabeth Alkin, "Parliament Joan", and the Commonwealth Newsbook', in Joad Raymond (ed.), *News, Newspapers, and Society in Early Modern Britain* (1999), 84–108.

NEWMAN, CHRISTINE M., 'The Reformation and Elizabeth Bowes: A Study of a Sixteenth-Century Northern Gentlewoman', in *Studies in Church History 27: Women in the Church*, ed. W. J. Sheils and Diana Wood (Oxford, 1990), 325–33.

NEWMAN, KAREN, 'Sundry Letters, Wordly Goods: The Lisle Letters and Renaissance Studies', *Journal of Medieval and Renaissance Studies*, 26 (1996), 139–52.

O'DAY, R., *Education and Society 1500–1800: The Social Foundations of Education in Early Modern Britain* (1982).

—— 'Tudor and Stuart Women: Their Family Lives Through Their Letters', in James Daybell (ed.), *Early Modern Women's Letter Writing, 1450–1700* (Basingstoke, 2001), 127–42.

O'DONNELL, ANNE M., 'Sixth Annual Bainton Lecture: Contemporary Women in the Letters of Erasmus', *Erasmus of Rotterdam Society Yearbook*, 9 (1989), 34–72.

O'DOWD, MARY, *A History of Women in Ireland, 1500–1800* (Harlow, 2005).

O'HARA, DIANA, *Courtship and Constraint: Rethinking the Making of Marriage in Tudor England* (Manchester, 2000).

—— 'The Language of Tokens and the Making of Marriage', *Rural History*, 3 (1992), 1–40.

—— '"Ruled by my friends": Aspects of Marriage in the Diocese of Canterbury, c.1540–1570', *Continuity and Change*, 6/1 (1991), 9–41.

O'MARA, V. M., 'Female Scribal Ability and Scribal Activity in Late Medieval England: the Evidence?', *Leeds Studies in English*, 27 (1996), 87–130.

ONG, WALTER J., 'Latin Language Study as a Renaissance Puberty Rite', *Studies in Philology*, 56/2 (1959), 103–24.

—— *Orality and Literacy: The Technologizing of the Word* (1982).

—— 'Writing is a Technology that Restructures Thought', in Gerd Baumann (ed.), *The Written Word: Literacy in Transition, Wolfson College Lectures 1985* (Oxford, 1986), 23–50.

OPPENHEIMER, PAUL, *The Birth of the Modern Mind: Self Consciousness and the Invention of the Sonnet* (Oxford, 1989).

ORLIN, LENA COWEN, *Elizabethan Household: An Anthology* (Washington, DC, 1995).

—— 'Gertrude's Closet', *Shakespeare Jahrbuch*, 134 (1998), 44–67.

ORME, NICHOLAS, *Education and Society in Medieval and Renaissance England* (1989).

OTTWAY, SHEILA, 'Dorothy Osborne's Love Letters: Novelistic Glimmerings and the Ovidian Self', *Prose Studies*, 19 (1996), 149–59.

OWEN, A. E. B., 'A Scrivener's Notebook from Bury St. Edmunds', *Archives*, 14/61 (1979), 16–22.

—— 'Sir John Wolley's Letter-Book as Latin Secretary to Elizabeth I', *Archives*, 11 (1973), 16–18.

PAGET, HUGH, 'The Youth of Anne Boleyn', *BIHR*, 54 (1981), 163–64.

PANTIN, W. A., 'A Medieval Treatise on Letter Writing with Examples', *Bulletin of the John Rylands Library*, 12 (1929), 326–82.

PARKES, M. B., 'The Literacy of the Laity', in *Scribes, Scripts and Readers* (1991), 275–97.

PARR, JOY, 'Gender History and Historical Practice', *Canadian Historical Review*, 76 (1995), 354–76.

PATTERSON, ANNABEL, 'Letters to Friends: The Self in Familiar Form', in *Censorship and Interpretation: The Conditions of Writing and Reading in Early Modern England* (Madison, Wisc., 1984), 203–32.

PAYNE, HELEN, 'Aristocratic Women, Power, Patronage and Family Networks at the Jacobean Court, 1603–1625', in James Daybell, (ed.), *Women and Politics in Early Modern England, 1450–1700* (Aldershot, 2004), 164–81.

PAYNE, HELEN, 'The Cecil Women at Court', in Pauline Croft (ed.), *Patronage, Culture and Power: The Early Cecils 1558–1612* (New Haven and London, 2002), 265–81.

PEARSON, JACQUELINE, 'Women Reading, Reading Women', in Helen Wilcox (ed.), *Women and Literature in Britain 1500–1700* (Cambridge, 1996), 80–99.

PECK, LINDA LEVY, 'Benefits, Brokers and Beneficiaries: The Culture of Exchange in Seventeenth Century England', in Bonnelyn Young Kubze and Dwight D. Brautigam (eds.), *Court, Country, and Culture: Essays on Early Modern British History in Honor of Perez Zagorin* (Rochester, NY, 1992), 109–27.

—— *Court Patronage and Corruption in Early Stuart England* (Boston, 1990; London, 1993).

PENNELL, SARA, 'Perfecting Practice? Women, Manuscript Recipes and Knowledge in Early Modern England', in Victoria E. Burke and Jonathan Gibson (eds.), *Early Modern Women's Manuscript Writing: Selected Papers from the Trinity/Colloquium* (Aldershot, 2004), 237–58.

PENNY, D. ANDREW, 'Family Matters and Foxe's *Acts and Monuments*', *HJ*, 39/3 (1996), 599–618.

PERRY, RUTH, *Women, Letters and the Novel* (New York, 1980).

PETERS, CHRISTINE, *Women in Early Modern Britain, 1450–1640* (Basingstoke, 2004).

PIGMAN III, G. W., *Grief and English Renaissance Elegy* (Cambridge, 1985).

POLLOCK, LINDA A., 'Childbearing and Female Bonding in Early Modern England', *Social History*, 22 (1997), 286–306.

—— 'Embarking on a Rough Passage: The Experience of Pregnancy in Early Modern Society', in Valerie Fildes (ed.), *Women as Mothers in Pre-Industrial England: Essays in Memory of Dorothy McLaren* (1990), 39–67.

—— 'Living on the Stage of the World: The Concept of Privacy Among the Elite of Early Modern England', in Adrian Wilson (ed.), *Rethinking Social History: English Society 1570–1920 and Its Interpretation* (Manchester, 1993), 78–96.

—— ' "Teach Her to Live Under Obedience": The Making of Women in the Upper Ranks of Early Modern England', *Continuity and Change*, 4/2 (1989), 231–58.

—— 'Younger Sons in Tudor and Stuart England', *HT*, 39/6 (June 1989), 23–9.

PORTER, ROY, ' "Expressing Yourself Ill": The Language of Sickness in Georgian England', in Peter Burke and Roy Porter (eds.), *Language, Self, and Society: A Social History* (Cambridge, 1991), 276–99.

—— 'The Patient's View: Doing Medical History From Below', *Theory and History*, 14 (1985), 175–98.

—— 'Reading Is Bad For Your Health', *HT*, 48/3 (Mar. 1998), 11–16.

—— (ed.), *Rewriting the Self: Histories from the Renaissance to the Present* (1997).

POTTER, LOIS, *Secret Rites and Secret Writing: Royalist Literature, 1641–1660* (Cambridge, 1989).

POWELL, WILLIAM S., *John Pory, 1572–1636: The Life and Letters of a Man of Many Parts* (Chapel Hill, NC, 1977).

PRESTON, JEAN F. and LAETITIA YEANDLE, *English Handwriting, 1400–1650* (Binghamton, NY, 1992).

RAMBUSS, RICHARD, *Spenser's Secret Career* (Cambridge, 1993).

RANUM, OREST, 'The Refuges of Intimacy', in Roger Chartier (ed.), *A History of Private Life, Vol. 3. Passions of the Renaissance* (Cambridge, Mass., 1989), 207–63.

RAWLINS, RAY, *Four Hundred Years of British Autographs: A Collector's Guide* (1970).

RAWSON, M. S., *Bess of Hardwick and Her Circle* (1910).

RAYMOND, JOAD, *The Invention of the Newspaper: English Newsbooks, 1641–1649* (Oxford, 1996).

—— 'The Newspaper, Public Opinion, and the Public Sphere in the Seventeenth Century', *Prose Studies*, 21/2 (1998), 109–40.

—— (ed.), *News, Newspapers, and Society in Early Modern Britain* (1999).

READ, CONYERS, *Mr Secretary Cecil and Queen Elizabeth* (1955).

RICHARDS, SHEILA R., *Secret Writing in the Public Records: Henry VIII–George II* (1974).

RICHARDSON, MALCOLM, 'The Fading Influence of the Medieval *Ars Dictaminis* in England after 1400', *Rhetorica*, 19 (2001), 225–47.

ROBERTS, SASHA, 'Shakespeare "creepes into the womens closets about bedtime": Women Reading in a Room of Their Own', in Gordon McMullan, (ed.), *Renaissance Configurations: Voices/Bodies/Spaces, 1580–1690* (Basingstoke, 1998), 30–63.

ROBERTSON, JEAN, *The Art of Letter-Writing: An Essay on the Handbooks Published in England During the Sixteenth and Seventeenth Centuries* (1942).

ROBERTSON, KAREN, 'Negotiating Favour: The Letters of Lady Ralegh', in James Daybell (ed.), *Women and Politics in Early Modern England 1450–1700* (Aldershot, 2004), 99–113.

—— 'A Revenging Feminine Hand in *Twelfth Night*', in David M. Bergeron and Robert S. Knapp (eds.), *Reading and Writing in Shakespeare* (Newark and London, 1996), 116–30.

—— 'Tracing Women's Connections From a Letter of Elizabeth Lady Ralegh', in Karen Robertson and Susan Frye (eds.), *Maids and Mistresses, Cousins and Queens: Women's Alliances in Early Modern England* (New York and Oxford, 1999), 149–64.

ROBINSON, HOWARDS, *The British Post Office: A History* (Princeton, 1948).

ROBINUEAU, SOEUR MARIE-CLAIRE, DONNELLY, SISTER GERTRUDE-JOSEPH, REYNOLDS, E. E. and BIERLAIRE, F., 'Correspondance entre Erasme et Margaret Roper', *Moreana*, 12 (1966), 29–46, 121.

ROSE, MARY BETH, *Women in the Middle Ages and the Renaissance: Literary and Historical Perspectives* (Syracuse, NY, 1988).

ROUSSEAU, G. S., 'Towards a Semiotics of the Nerve: The Social History of Language in a New Key', in Peter Burke and Roy Porter (eds.), *Language, Self, and Society: A Social History* (Cambridge, 1991), 213–75.

RYLANDS, PAUL J., 'Merchants' Marks and Other Mediaeval Personal Marks', *Transactions of the Historic Society of Lancashire and Cheshire*, 62 (1911), 1–34.

SACKS, DAVID HARRIS, 'The Counterveiling of Benefits: Monopoly, Liberty and Benevolence in Elizabethan England', in Dale Hoak (ed.), *Tudor Political Culture* (Cambridge, 1995), 272–91.

SALMON, J. H. M., 'Seneca and Tacitus in Jacobean England', in Linda Levy Peck (ed.), *The Mental World of the Jacobean Court* (Cambridge, 1991), 169–88.

SÁNCHEZ, MAGDALENA S., *The Empress, The Queen and the Nun: Women and Power at the Court of Philip III of Spain* (Baltimore, 1998).

SAUER, ELIZABETH, 'Maternity, Prophecy and the Cultivation of the Private Sphere in Seventeenth-Century England', *Explorations in Renaissance Culture*, 25 (1998), 119–48.

SAWDAY, JONATHAN, 'Self and Selfhood in the Seventeenth Century', in Roy Porter (ed.), *Rewriting the Self: Histories from the Renaissance to the Present* (1997), 29–48.

SCHOFIELD, R. S, 'The Measurement of Literacy in Pre-Industrial England', in Jack Goody (ed.), *Literacy in Traditional Societies* (Cambridge, 1968), 311–25.

SCHLEINER, LOUISE, *Tudor and Stuart Women Writers* (Bloomington and Indianapolis, 1994).

SCHNEIDER, GARY, 'Affecting Correspondences: Body, Behavior, and the Textualization of Emotion in Early Modern English Letters', *Prose Studies*, 23 (2000), 31–62.

—— 'Politics, Deception, and the Workings of the Post: Some Features of Epistolarity in Early Modern England', *Explorations in Renaissance Culture*, 28/1 (2002), 99–127.

—— *The Culture of Epistolarity: Vernacular Letters and Letter Writing in Early Modern England, 1500–1700* (Delaware, 2005).

SCHULZ, HERBERT C., 'The Teaching of Handwriting in Tudor and Stuart Times', *HLQ*, 6 (1942–3), 381–425.

SCOTT, ALISON V., 'Marketing the Gift: Jonson, Multiple Patronage, and Strategic Exchange', *Parergon*, 20/2 (2003), 135–59.

——, *Gender and the Politics of History* (New York, 1988).

SCOTT, JOAN, 'Gender: A Useful Category of Historical Analysis', *American History Review*, 91 (1986), 1053–75.

—— 'The Problem of Invisibility', in S. Jay Kleinberg (ed.), *Retrieving Women's History: Changing Perceptions of the Role of Women in Politics and Society* (Providence and Oxford, 1988; 1992), 5–29.

SCOTT-ELLIOT, A. H. and YEO, E., 'Calligraphic Manuscripts of Esther Inglis (1571–1624): A Catalogue', *The Papers of the Bibliographic Society of America*, 84 (1990), 11–63.

SCOTT-WARREN, JASON, 'Reconstructing Manuscript Networks: the Textual Transactions of Sir Stephen Powle', in Alexandra Shephard and Phil Withington (eds.), *Communities in Early Modern England* (Manchester, 2000), 18–37.

—— *Sir John Harington and the Book as Gift* (Oxford, 2001).

SCRAGG, D. G., *A History of English Spelling* (Manchester, 1974).

SEIGEL, JERROLD, 'Problematizing the Self', in Victoria E. Bonnell and Lynn Hunt (eds.), *Beyond the Cultural Turn: New Directions in the Study of Culture and Society* (Berkeley, 1999), 281–314.

SHARPE, J. A., *Early Modern England: A Social History 1550–1760* (1987).

SHARPE, KEVIN M. and LAKE, PETER (eds.), *Culture and Politics in Early Stuart England* (1994).

—— and ZWICKER, STEVEN (eds.), *The Politics of Discourse* (Berkeley and Los Angeles, 1987).

SHAW, DIANE, 'The Construction of the Private in Medieval London', *Journal of Medieval and Early Modern Studies*, 26/3 (1996), 447–66.

SHELL, ALISON, ' "Often to my Self I make my mone": Early Modern Women's Poetry from the Fielding Family', in Victoria E. Burke and Jonathan Gibson (eds.), *Early Modern Women's Manuscript Writing: Selected Papers from the Trinity/Trent Colloquium* (Aldershot, 2004), 259–78.

SHOEMAKER, ROBERT and VINCENT, MARY (eds.), *Gender and History in Western Europe* (1998).

SHORTER, EDWARD, *The Making of the Modern Family* (1976).

SIMON, J., *Education and Society in Tudor England* (Cambridge, 1966).

SISSON, CHARLES, 'Marks as Signatures', *The Library*, 4th ser., 91 (1928), 1–34.

SLATER, MIRIAM, 'Debate: The Weightiest Business: Marriage in an Upper-Class Gentry Family in Seventeenth-Century England', *P&P*, 85 (1979), 135–40.

——*Family Life in the Seventeenth Century: The Verneys of Claydon House* (1984).

——'The Weightiest Business: Marriage in an Upper-Class Gentry Family in Seventeenth-Century England', *P&P*, 72 (1976), 25–54.

SMITH, A. G. R., *The Government of Elizabethan England* (1967).

——'The Secretariats of the Cecils, circa 1580–1612', *EHR*, 83 (1968), 481–504.

——*Servant of the Cecils: The Life of Sir Michael Hickes* (1977).

SMITH, ROGER, 'Self-Reflection and the Self', in Roy Porter (ed.), *Rewriting the Self: Histories from the Renaissance to the Present* (1997), 49–57.

SOMMERVILLE, MARGARET R., *Sex and Subjection: Attitudes to Women in Early-Modern Society* (1995).

SOWARDS, J. K., 'Erasmus and the Education of Women', *SCJ*, 13 (1982), 77–89.

SPUFFORD, MARGARET, 'First Steps in Literacy: The Reading and Writing Experiences of the Humblest Seventeenth-Century Spiritual Autobiographers', *Social History*, 4/3 (1979), 407–35.

——'The Limitations of Probate Inventory', in John Chartres and David Hey (eds.), *English Rural Society, 1500–1800: Essays in Honour of Joan Thirsk* (Cambridge, 1990), 139–74.

STARKEY, DAVID, 'The Presence Chamber: New Year, 1538', in David Starkey (ed.), *Henry VIII: A European Court in England* (1991), 126–30.

——'Representation Through Intimacy: A Study in the Symbolism of Monarchy and Court Office in Early-Modern England', in I. Lewis (ed.), *Symbols and Sentiments: Cross Cultural Studies in Symbolism* (1977), 187–224.

STEELE, Ian K., 'Time, Communications and Society: The Atlantic, 1702', *Journal of American Studies*, 8 (1974), 1–21.

STEEN, SARA JAYNE, 'Behind the Arras: English Renaissance Women's Letters', in W. Speed Hill (ed.), *New Ways of Looking at Old Texts: Papers of the Renaissance English Text Society, 1985–1991* (Binghamton, NY, 1993), 229–38.

——'Fashioning an Acceptable Self: Arbella Stuart', *ELR*, 18 (1988), 78–95.

——' "How Subject to Interpretation": Lady Arbella Stuart and the Reading of Illness', in James Daybell (ed.), *Early Modern Women's Letter Writing, 1450–1700* (Basingstoke, 2001), 109–26.

——'Manuscript Matters: Reading the Letters of Lady Arbella Stuart', *South Central Review*, 11/2 (1994), 24–38.

——'Reading Beyond the Words: Material Letters and the Process of Interpretation', *Quidditas*, 22 (2001), 55–69.

——'Recent Studies of Women Writers of the Seventeenth Century, 1604–1674 (1990–mid-1993)', *ELR*, 24/1 (1994), 243–74.

STEMMLER, THEO, 'The Songs and Love-Letters of Henry VIII: On the Flexibility of Literary Genres', in Uwe Baumann (ed.), *Henry VIII In History, Historiography and Literature* (1992), 97–111.

STEPHENS, W. B., 'Male and Female Adult Illiteracy in Seventeenth-Century Cornwall', *Journal of Educational Administration and History*, 9/2 (1977), 1–7.

STEUART, A. FRANCIS, (ed.), *The Trial of Mary Queen of* Scots (London, Edinburgh, and Glasgow, 1923; 2nd edn. 1951).

STEVENS, FORREST TYLER, ' "Erasmus's 'Tigress' ": The Language of Friendship, Pleasure, and the Renaissance Letter', in Jonathan Goldberg (ed.), *Queering the Renaissance* (1994), 124–40.

STEWART, ALAN, *Close Readers: Humanism and Sodomy in Early Modern England* (Princeton, 1997).

—— 'The Early Modern Closet Discovered', *Representations*, 50 (1995), 76–100.

—— 'Gelding Gascoigne', in Constance C. Relihan and Goran V. Stanivukovic (eds.), *Prose Fiction and Early Modern Sexualities* (Basingstoke, 2001), 147–69.

—— 'The Voices of Anne Cooke, Lady Anne and Lady Bacon', in Danielle Clarke and Elizabeth Clarke (eds.), *This Double Voice: Gendered Writing in Early Modern England* (Basingstoke, 2000), 88–102.

—— and JARDINE, LISA, *Hostage to Fortune: The Troubled Life of Francis Bacon* (1998).

—— and WOLFE, HEATHER *Letterwriting in Renaissance England* (Washington, DC , 2004).

STOIANOVICH, TRAIAN, *French Historical Method: The Annales Paradigm* (Ithaca and London, 1976).

STONE, J. M. W., *The Inland Posts, 1392–1672* (1987).

STONE, LAWRENCE, *The Family, Sex and Marriage in England, 1500–1800* (1977).

—— *The Past and the Present Revisited* (1987).

STRETTON, TIMOTHY, *Women Waging Law in Elizabethan England* (Cambridge, 1998).

STRICKLAND, AGNES, *Lives of the Queens of England from the Norman Conquest*, 12 vols. (1840–48).

STUCHEN, JOHNYE C., 'The Letters of Lydia Dugard: A Seventeenth-Century Rural English Gentlewoman', *Papers of the Missouri Philological Association*, 3 (1978), 32–8.

SUTTON, PETER C. *et al.*, *Love Letters: Dutch Genre Paintings in the Age of Vermeer* (Greenwich, Conn., and Dublin, 2003).

TADMOR, NAOMI, *Family and Friends in Eighteenth-Century England: Household, Kinship, and Patronage* (Cambridge, 2001).

—— ' "In the even my wife read to me": Women Reading and Household life in the Eighteenth Century', in James Raven, Helen Small, and Naomi Tadmor (eds.), *The Practice and Representation of Reading in England* (Cambridge, 1996), 162–74.

TANSKANEN, KAISA SANNA, ' "No Lesse Plesaunt than Profitable": Early Modern Letter-Writing Manuals Revisited', in Marita Gustafsson (ed.), *Essays and Explorations: A 'Freundschrift' for Liisa Dahl* (1996).

TAYLOR, J., 'Letters and Letter Collections in England, 1300–1420', *Nottingham Medieval Studies*, 24 (1980), 57–70.

THOMAS, KEITH, *History and Literature* (Swansea, 1988).

—— 'The Meaning of Literacy in Early Modern England', in Gerd Baumann (ed.), *The Written Word: Literacy in Transition, Wolfson College Lectures 1985* (Oxford, 1986), 97–131.

THOMAS, MAX W., 'Reading and Writing the Renaissance Commonplace Book: A Question of Authorship', in Martha Woodmansee and Peter Jaszi (eds.), *The Construction of Authorship: Textual Appropriation in Law and Literature* (Durham and London, 1994), 402–15.

THOMPSON, ELBERT N. S., 'Familiar Letters', in *Literary Bypaths of the Renaissance* (1924), 91–126.

THORNTON, PETER, 'A Short Commentary on the Hardwick Inventory of 1601', in Lindsay Boynton (ed.), *The Hardwick Inventories of 1601* (1971), 15–20.

TODD, MARGO, 'Puritan Self-Fashioning: The Diary of Samuel Ward', *JBS*, 31 (1992), 236–64.

TRILL, SUZANNE, 'Early Modern Women's Writing in the Edinburgh Archives, *c.*1550–1740: A Preliminary Checklist', in Sarah M. Dunnigan, C. Marie Harker, and Evelyn S. Newlyn (eds.), *Woman and the Feminine in Medieval and Early Modern Scottish Writing* (Basingstoke: 2004), 201–25.

—— 'Religion and the Construction of Femininity', in Helen Wilcox (ed.), *Women and Literature in Britain 1500–1700* (Cambridge, 1996), 30–55.

TRIMPI, WESLEY, 'The Epistolary Tradition', in *Ben Jonson's Poems: A Study in Plain Style* (Stanford, 1962), 60–75.

ULTEE, MAARTEN, 'The Republic of Letters: Learned Correspondence, 1680–1720', *The Seventeenth Century*, 2 (1987), 95–112.

VAN HOUDT, T. *et al.* (eds.), *Self-Presentation and Social Identification: The Rhetoric and Pragmatics of Letter Writing in Early Modern Times* (Leuven, 2002).

VAN UCHELEN, ANTHONY R. CROISET, 'Dutch Writing-Masters and the 'Prix de la Plume Couronnée', *Quaerendo*, 6 (1976), 319–46.

VELZ, JOHN W., 'Giving Voices to the Silent: Editing the Private Writings of Women', in W. Speed Hill (ed.), *New Ways of Looking at Old Texts: Papers of the Renaissance English Text Society, 1985–1991* (Binghamton, NY, 1993), 263–72.

VICKERY, AMANDA, 'Golden Age to Separate Spheres', *HJ*, 36 (1993), 383–414.

VINCENT, DAVID, *Literacy and Popular Culture, England 1750–1914* (Cambridge, 1989).

—— *The Rise of Mass Literacy: Reading and Writing in Modern Europe* (Cambridge and Oxford, 2000).

WALKER, CLAIRE, ' "Doe not supose me a well mortifyed Nun dead to the world": Letter-Writing in Early Modern English Convents', in James Daybell (ed.), *Early Modern Women's Letter Writing, 1450–1700* (Basingstoke, 2001), 159–76.

WALKER, GARTHINE, 'Expanding the Boundaries of Female Honour in Early Modern England', *TRHS*, 6th ser., 6 (1996), 235–45.

WALKER, KIM, *Women Writers of the English Renaissance* (New York, 1996).

WALKER, SUE, 'The Manners on the Page: Prescription and Practice in the Visual Organisation of Correspondence', *HLQ*, 66/3, 4 (2003), 307–29.

WALL, ALISON D., 'An Account of the Essex Revolt, February 1601', *BIHR*, 54 (1981), 131–3.

—— 'Deference and Defiance in Women's Letters of the Thynne Family: The Rhetoric of Relationships', in James Daybell (ed.), *Women's Letters and Letter-Writing in England, 1450–1700* (Basingstoke, 2001), 77–93.

—— 'Elizabethan Precept and Feminine Practice: The Thynne Family of Longleat', *History*, 75 (1990), 23–38.

—— 'For Love, Money or Politics? A Clandestine Marriage and the Elizabethan Court of Arches', *HJ*, 38/3 (1995), 511–33.

—— *Power and Protest in England, 1525–1640* (2000).

WARD, JENNIFER, *English Noblewomen in the Later Middle Ages* (Harlow, 1992).

—— 'Letter-Writing by English Noblewomen in the Early Fifteenth Century', in James Daybell (ed.), *Early Modern Women's Letter-Writing in England 1450–1700* (Basingstoke, 2001), 29–41.

WARDROP, JAMES, *The Script of Humanism* (Oxford, 1963).

WARNICKE, RETHA, 'Private and Public: The Boundaries of Women's Lives in Early Modern England', in Jean R. Brink (ed.), *Privileging Gender in Early Modern England* (Kirksville, 1993), 123–40.

WATT, DIANE, ' "No Writing For Writing's Sake": The Language of Service and Household Rhetoric in the Letters of the Paston Women', in Karen Cherawatuk and Ulrike Wiethaus (eds.), *Dear Sister: Medieval Women and the Epistolary Genre* (Philadelphia, 1993), 122–38.

WEAR, ANDREW, 'Puritan Perceptions of Illness in Seventeenth Century England', in Roy Porter (ed.), *Patients and Practitioners* (Cambridge, 1985), 55–99.

WEBBER, JOAN, *The Eloquent 'I': Style and Self in Seventeenth-Century Prose* (Madison, Wisc., 1968).

WEBSTER, TOM, 'Writing to Redundancy: Approaches to Spiritual Journals and Early Modern Spirituality', *HJ*, 39/1 (1996), 33–56.

WHIGHAM, FRANK, 'The Rhetoric of Elizabethan Suitors' Letters', *PMLA*, 96, 5 (1981), 864–82.

WHITE, MICHELINE, 'Recent Studies in Women Writers of Tudor England, 1485–1603', *ELR*, 30 (2000), 457–93.

WHITE, ROBERT S., 'The Rise and Fall of an Elizabethan Fashion: Love Letters in Romance and Comedy', *Cahiers Élisabéthains*, 30 (1986), 35–47.

WHITEHEAD, BARBARA J. (ed.), *Women's Education in Early Modern Europe: A History, 1500–1800* (New York and London, 1999).

WHYMAN, SUSAN E., 'Gentle Companions: Single Women and Their Letters in Late-Stuart England', in James Daybell (ed.), *Early Modern Women's Letter Writing in England, 1450–1700* (Basingstoke, 2001), 177–93.

—— ' "Paper, Visits": The Post-Restoration Letter as Seen Through the Verney Family Archive', in Rebecca Earle (ed.), *Epistolary Selves: Letters and Letter-Writers, 1600–1945* (Aldershot, 1999), 15–36.

—— *Sociability and Power in Late-Stuart England: The Cultural Worlds of the Verneys 1660–1720* (Oxford, 1999).

WILCOX, HELEN, 'Private Writing and Public Function: Autobiographical Texts by Renaissance Englishwomen', in S. P. Cerasano and Marion Wynne Davies (eds.), *Gloriana's Face: Women, Public and Private in the English Renaissance* (Hemel Hempstead, 1992), 47–62.

WILLEN, D., 'Women in the Public Sphere in Early Modern England: The Case of the Urban Working Poor', *SCJ*, 19/4 (1988), 559–75.

WILLIAMS, EDITH CARLETON, *Bess of Hardwick* (1959).

WILLIAM, PENRY, *The Tudor Regine* (Oxford, 1979).

WILLIAMS, ROBERT, 'A Moon to their Sun: Writing Mistresses of the Sixteenth and Seventeenth Centuries', *Fine Print*, 11/2 (1985), 88–98.

WILLIAMSON, GEORGE C., *Lady Anne Clifford, Countess of Dorset, Pembroke and Montgomery 1590–1676: Her Life, Letters and Work* (Kendal, 1922).

——*George Third Earl of Cumberland (1558–1605): His Life and His Voyages* (Cambridge, 1920).

WINCHESTER, BARBARA, *Tudor Family Portrait* (1955).

WINKELMANN, CAROL L., 'A Case Study of Women's Literacy in the Early Seventeenth Century: The Oxinden Family Letters', *Women and Language*, 19/2 (1996), 14–20.

WITT, RONALD G., 'Medieval "Ars Dictaminis" and the Beginnings of Humanism: A New Construction of the Problem', *RQ*, 35 (1982), 1–35.

WOLFE, HEATHER, 'The Scribal Hands and Dating of *Lady Falkland: Her Life*', *EMS*, 9 (2000), 187–217.

WOLPE, BERTHOLDE, 'John de Beauchesne and the First English Writing Books', *Journal for the Society of Italic Handwriting*, 82 (1975), 2–11.

WOOD, M. A. E., *Lives of the Princesses of England*, 6 vols. (1849–55).

WOOLF, DANIEL, ' "The Common Voice" ', History, Folklore and Oral Tradition in Early Modern England', *P&P*, 120 (1988), 26–52.

WOOLF, VIRGINIA, 'Dorothy Osborne's *Letters*', in *The Common Reader, Second Series* (1932), 59–66.

——*A Room of One's Own* (1928; Penguin edn., 1945).

WOUDHUYSEN, H. R., *Sir Philip Sidney and the Circulation of Manuscripts, 1558–1640* (Oxford, 1996).

WRIGHT, LOUIS B., 'The Reading of Renaissance English Women', *Studies in Philology*, 28 (1931), 671–88.

WRIGHT, NANCY E., 'The Name and the Signature of the Author of Margaret Roper's Letter to Alice Alington', in David Quint *et al.* (eds.), *Creative Imitation: New Essays on Renaissance Literature in Honor of Thomas M. Greene* (Binghamton, NY, 1992), 239–57.

WRIGHT, PAM, 'A Change in Direction: The Ramifications of a Female Household, 1558–1603', in David Starkey (ed.), *The English Court From the Wars of the Roses to the Civil War* (Harlow, 1987), 147–72.

WRIGHTSON, KEITH, *English Society, 1580–1680* (1982).

WRIGLEY, E. A., 'Age at Marriage in Early Modern England', *Family History*, 12 (1982), 219–34.

YEANDLE, LAETITIA, 'The Loseley Collection of Manuscripts at the Folger Shakespeare Library, Washington, D.C.', *SQ*, 38 (1987), 201–7.

ZIEGLER, GEORGIANNA, 'My Lady's Chamber: Female Space, Female Chastity in Shakespeare', *Textual Practice*, 4/1 (1990), 73–90.

——'Recent Studies in Women Writers of Tudor England, 1485–1603 (1990–mid-1993)', *ELR*, 24/1 (1994), 229–42.

Unpublished Theses and Papers

BOWDEN, CAROLINE M. K., 'Female Education in the Late Sixteenth and Early Seventeenth Centuries in England and Wales: A Study of Attitudes and Practice', Ph.D. thesis, London University (1996).

BRACHER, TRICIA AMANDA, 'Representations of Intimacy and the Historiography of Early Modern Private Life', Ph.D. thesis, University of London (2000).

BRANT, CLARE, 'Eighteenth-Century Letters: Aspects of the Genre with Reference to the Epistolary Novel and the Familiar Letter of Personal Correspondence', D.Phil. thesis, Oxford University (1988).

BREWERTON, PATRICIA, 'Paper Trails: Re-reading Robert Beale as Clerk to the Elizabethan Privy Council', Ph.D. thesis, University of London (1998).

CLARKE, CATHERINE M., 'Patronage and Literature: The Women of the Russell Family 1520–1617', Ph.D. thesis, University of Reading (1992).

DAYBELL, JAMES, 'The Political Role of Upper-Class Women in Early Tudor England as Evidenced by Their Correspondence', MA diss., University of Reading (1996).

—— 'Women's Letters and Letter-Writing in England, 1540–1603', Ph.D. thesis, University of Reading (2000).

FARBER, ELIZABETH, 'The Letters of Lady Elizabeth Russell (1540–1609)', Ph.D. diss. Columbia University (1977).

GIBSON, JONATHAN, 'Elizabethan Clients' Letters' paper delivered at the University of Reading Early Modern Research Seminar, Feb. 2003.

—— 'Sir Arthur Gorges (1557–1625), and the Patronage System', Ph.D. thesis, University of London (1998).

GOLDSMITH, J. B. GREENBAUM, 'All the Queen's Women: The Changing Place and Perception of Aristocratic Women in Elizabethan England, 1558–1620', Ph.D. diss., Northwestern University (1987).

HINTZ, CARRIE, 'Desire and Renunciation: The Letters of Dorothy Osborne', Ph.D. diss., University of Toronto (1998).

McDONOUGH, MICHELLE 'The Life and Letters of Lady Anne Glemham', MA diss., University of London (2003).

MERTON, CHARLOTTE, 'The Women Who Served Queen Mary and Queen Elizabeth: Ladies, Gentlewomen and Maids of the Privy Chamber 1553–1603', Ph.D. thesis, Cambridge University, (1992).

PAYNE, HELEN MARGARET, 'Aristocratic Women and the Jacobean Court, 1603–1625', Ph.D. thesis, University of London (2001).

SCHNEIDER, GARY, 'The Culture of Epistolarity: Letters and Letter Writing in Early Modern England, 1500–1700', Ph.D. diss. Wayne State University (2001).

STRETTON, TIM, 'Women and Litigation in the Elizabethan Court of Requests', Ph.D. thesis, Cambridge University (1993).

TRUELOVE, ALISON, 'An Edition of the Stonor Letters and Papers', Ph.D. thesis, University of London (2000).

Index

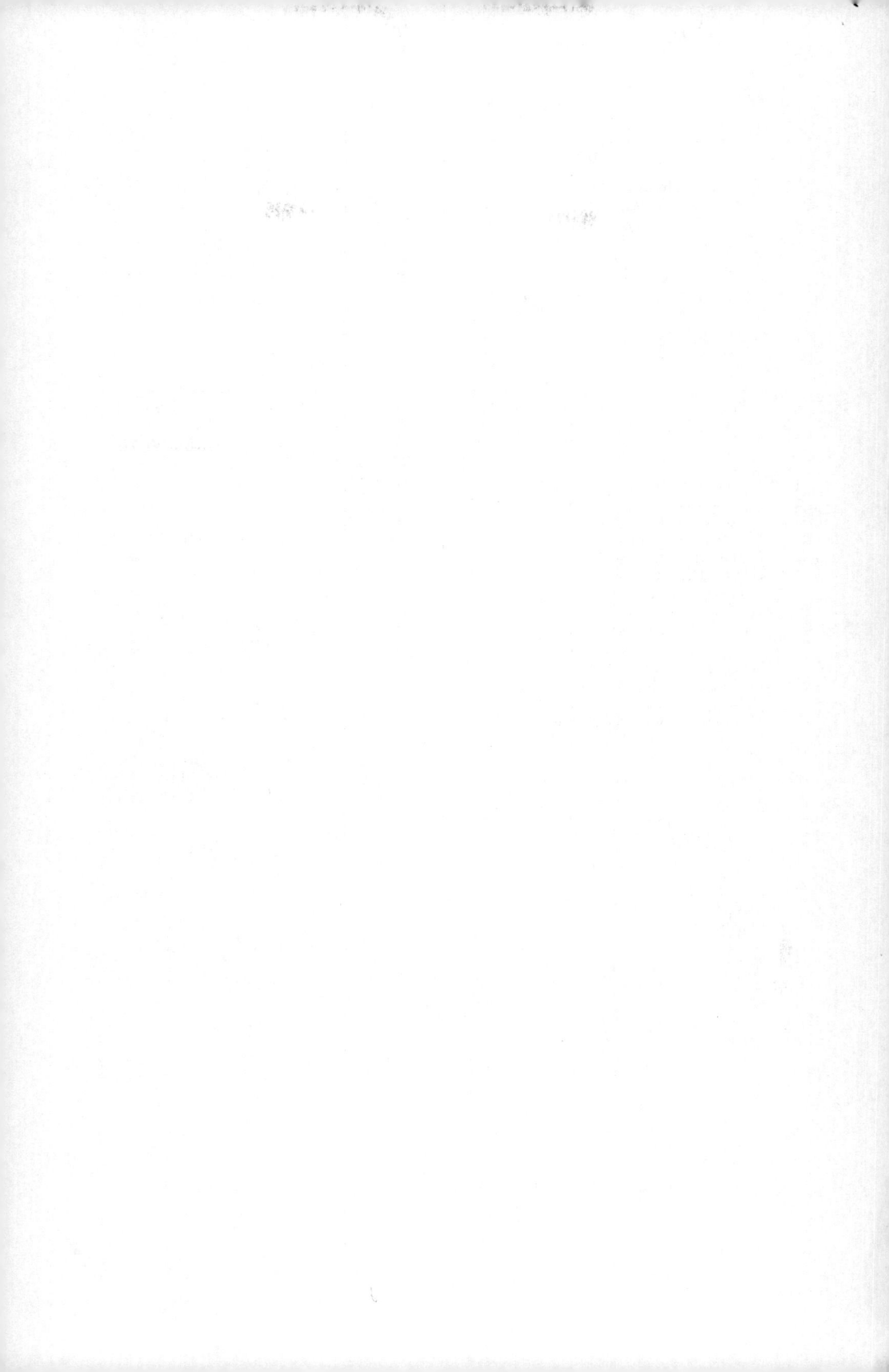

Printed and bound by CPI Group (UK) Ltd, Croydon, CR0 4YY